Modern Computational Models of Semantic Discovery in Natural Language

Jan Žižka
Mendel University in Brno, Czech Republic

František Dařena
Mendel University in Brno, Czech Republic

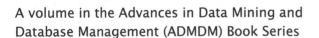
A volume in the Advances in Data Mining and Database Management (ADMDM) Book Series

Managing Director:	Lindsay Johnston
Managing Editor:	Austin DeMarco
Director of Intellectual Property & Contracts:	Jan Travers
Acquisitions Editor:	Kayla Wolfe
Production Editor:	Christina Henning
Development Editor:	Austin DeMarco
Cover Design:	Jason Mull

Published in the United States of America by
Information Science Reference (an imprint of IGI Global)
701 E. Chocolate Avenue
Hershey PA, USA 17033
Tel: 717-533-8845
Fax: 717-533-8661
E-mail: cust@igi-global.com
Web site: http://www.igi-global.com

Library of Congress Cataloging-in-Publication Data

Modern computational models of semantic discovery in natural languages / Jan Zizka and Frantisek Darena, editors.
    pages cm
 Includes bibliographical references and index.
 ISBN 978-1-4666-8690-8 (hardcover) -- ISBN 978-1-4666-8691-5 (ebook) 1. Semantics--Data processing. 2. Natural language processing. 3. Computational linguistics. I. Zizka, Jan, editor. II. Darena, Frantisek, 1979- editor.
 P325.5.D38M63 2015
 401'.430285--dc23
                    2015015532

This book is published in the IGI Global book series Advances in Data Mining and Database Management (ADMDM) (ISSN: 2327-1981; eISSN: 2327-199X)

British Cataloguing in Publication Data
A Cataloguing in Publication record for this book is available from the British Library.

All work contributed to this book is new, previously-unpublished material. The views expressed in this book are those of the authors, but not necessarily of the publisher.

For electronic access to this publication, please contact: eresources@igi-global.com.

Advances in Data Mining and Database Management (ADMDM) Book Series

David Taniar
Monash University, Australia

ISSN: 2327-1981
EISSN: 2327-199X

ISSN: 2327-1981
EISSN: 2327-199X

MISSION

With the large amounts of information available to organizations in today's digital world, there is a need for continual research surrounding emerging methods and tools for collecting, analyzing, and storing data.

The **Advances in Data Mining & Database Management (ADMDM)** series aims to bring together research in information retrieval, data analysis, data warehousing, and related areas in order to become an ideal resource for those working and studying in these fields. IT professionals, software engineers, academicians and upper-level students will find titles within the ADMDM book series particularly useful for staying up-to-date on emerging research, theories, and applications in the fields of data mining and database management.

COVERAGE

- Quantitative Structure–Activity Relationship
- Information Extraction
- Factor Analysis
- Neural Networks
- Heterogeneous and Distributed Databases
- Data Analysis
- Educational Data Mining
- Database Security
- Web-based information systems
- Web mining

IGI Global is currently accepting manuscripts for publication within this series. To submit a proposal for a volume in this series, please contact our Acquisition Editors at Acquisitions@igi-global.com or visit: http://www.igi-global.com/publish/.

Titles in this Series

For a list of additional titles in this series, please visit: www.igi-global.com

Mobile Technologies for Activity-Travel Data Collection and Analysis
Soora Rasouli (Eindhoven University of Technology, The Netherlands) and Harry Timmermans (Eindhoven University of Technology, The Netherlands)
Information Science Reference • copyright 2014 • 325pp • H/C (ISBN: 9781466661707) • US $225.00 (our price)

Biologically-Inspired Techniques for Knowledge Discovery and Data Mining
Shafiq Alam (University of Auckland, New Zealand) Gillian Dobbie (University of Auckland, New Zealand) Yun Sing Koh (University of Auckland, New Zealand) and Saeed ur Rehman (Unitec Institute of Technology, New Zealand)
Information Science Reference • copyright 2014 • 375pp • H/C (ISBN: 9781466660786) • US $265.00 (our price)

Data Mining and Analysis in the Engineering Field
Vishal Bhatnagar (Ambedkar Institute of Advanced Communication Technologies and Research, India)
Information Science Reference • copyright 2014 • 405pp • H/C (ISBN: 9781466660861) • US $225.00 (our price)

Handbook of Research on Cloud Infrastructures for Big Data Analytics
Pethuru Raj (IBM India Pvt Ltd, India) and Ganesh Chandra Deka (Ministry of Labour and Employment, India)
Information Science Reference • copyright 2014 • 570pp • H/C (ISBN: 9781466658646) • US $345.00 (our price)

Innovative Techniques and Applications of Entity Resolution
Hongzhi Wang (Harbin Institute of Technology, China)
Information Science Reference • copyright 2014 • 398pp • H/C (ISBN: 9781466651982) • US $205.00 (our price)

Innovative Document Summarization Techniques Revolutionizing Knowledge Understanding
Alessandro Fiori (IRCC, Institute for Cancer Research and Treatment, Italy)
Information Science Reference • copyright 2014 • 363pp • H/C (ISBN: 9781466650190) • US $175.00 (our price)

Emerging Methods in Predictive Analytics Risk Management and Decision-Making
William H. Hsu (Kansas State University, USA)
Information Science Reference • copyright 2014 • 425pp • H/C (ISBN: 9781466650633) • US $225.00 (our price)

Data Science and Simulation in Transportation Research
Davy Janssens (Hasselt University, Belgium) Ansar-Ul-Haque Yasar (Hasselt University, Belgium) and Luk Knapen (Hasselt University, Belgium)
Information Science Reference • copyright 2014 • 350pp • H/C (ISBN: 9781466649200) • US $175.00 (our price)

DISSEMINATOR OF KNOWLEDGE

www.igi-global.com

701 E. Chocolate Ave., Hershey, PA 17033
Order online at www.igi-global.com or call 717-533-8845 x100
To place a standing order for titles released in this series, contact: cust@igi-global.com
Mon-Fri 8:00 am - 5:00 pm (est) or fax 24 hours a day 717-533-8661

Editorial Advisory Board

Table of Contents

Detailed Table of Contents

Chapter 1
Jalel Akaichi, University of Tunis, Tunisia

In this work, we focus on the application of text mining and sentiment analysis techniques for analyzing Tunisian users' statuses updates on Facebook. We aim to extract useful information, about their sentiment and behavior, especially during the "Arabic spring" era. To achieve this task, we describe a method for sentiment analysis using Support Vector Machine and Naïve Bayes algorithms, and applying a combination of more than two features. The output of this work consists, on one hand, on the construction of a sentiment lexicon based on the Emoticons and Acronyms' lexicons that we developed based on the extracted statuses updates; and on the other hand, it consists on the realization of detailed comparative experiments between the above algorithms by creating a training model for sentiment classification.

Chapter 2
*Pavel Makagonov, Russian Presidential Academy of National Economy and Public
    Administration, Russia*

The measure of perfection of the contents and semantic value of an integrated text is connected with the indicators of perfection in the distribution of content words. This criterion is the coordination of their "frequency-rank" distribution with the Zipf or Zipf-Mandelbrot law. In this chapter the hypothesis verified is that a perfect system should have not only perfect distribution of its elements - objects, but also perfect connections between them. A model is suggested in which the degree of the text perfection from the point of view of the quality of connections between significative words is determined by the quality of distribution of syntactic and link words in the "rank - frequency" representation. As a simplified criterion the ratio of the significant and syntactic words used in the analyzed text and the degree of the closeness of this ratio to the "golden section" is considered.

Chapter 3
*Olga Acosta, Pontificia Universidad Católica de Chile, Chile
Gerardo Sierra, UNAM, México
César Aguilar, Pontificia Universidad Católica de Chile, Chile*

The automatic extraction of hyponymy-hypernymy relations in text corpus is one important task in Natural Language Processing. This chapter proposes a method for automatically extracting a set of hyponym-hyperonym pairs from a medical corpus in Spanish, expressed in analytical definitions. This kind of definition is composed by a term (the hyponym), a genus term (the hyperonym), and one or more differentiae, that is, a set of particular features proper to the defined term, e.g.: conjunctivitis is an infection of the conjunctiva of the eye. Definitions are obtained from definitional contexts, and then sequences of term and genus term. Then, the most frequent hyperonyms are used in order to filter relevant definitions. Additionally, using a bootstrapping technique, new hyponym candidates are extracted from the corpus, based on the previous set of hyponyms/hyperonyms detected.

Chapter 4

František Dařena, Mendel University in Brno, Czech Republic
Jan Žižka, Mendel University in Brno, Czech Republic

The chapter introduces clustering as a family of algorithms that can be successfully used to organize text documents into groups without prior knowledge of these groups. The chapter also demonstrates using unsupervised clustering to group large amount of unlabeled textual data (customer reviews written informally in five natural languages) so it can be used later for further analysis. The attention is paid to the process of selecting clustering algorithms, their parameters, methods of data preprocessing, and to the methods of evaluating the results by a human expert with an assistance of computers, too. The feasibility has been demonstrated by a number of experiments with external evaluation using known labels and expert validation with an assistance of a computer. It has been found that it is possible to apply the same procedures, including clustering, cluster validation, and detection of topics and significant words for different natural languages with satisfactory results.

Chapter 5

Jan Žižka, Mendel University in Brno, Czech Republic
František Dařena, Mendel University in Brno, Czech Republic

The automated categorization of unstructured textual documents according to their semantic contents plays important role particularly linked with the ever growing volume of such data originating from the Internet. Having a sufficient number of labeled examples, a suitable supervised machine learning-based classifier can be trained. When no labeling is available, an unsupervised learning method can be applied, however, the missing label information often leads to worse classification results. This chapter demonstrates a method based on semi-supervised learning when a smallish set of manually labeled examples improves the categorization process in comparison with clustering, and the results are comparable with the supervised learning output. For the illustration, a real-world dataset coming from the Internet is used as the input of the supervised, unsupervised, and semi-supervised learning. The results are shown for different number of the starting labeled samples used as "seeds" to automatically label the remaining volume of unlabeled items.

Chapter 6

Goran Klepac, Raiffeisen Bank Austria d.d., Croatia
Marko Velić, University of Zagreb, Croatia

This chapter covers natural language processing techniques and their application in predicitve models development. Two case studies are presented. First case describes a project where textual descriptions of various situations in call center of one telecommunication company were processed in order to predict churn. Second case describes sentiment analysis of business news and describes practical and testing issues in text mining projects. Both case studies depict different approaches and are implemented in different tools. Language of the texts processed in these projects is Croatian which belongs to the Slavic group of languages with more complex morphologies and grammar rules than English. Chapter concludes with several points on the future research possible in this domain.

Chapter 7

Abel Browarnik, Tel Aviv University, Israel
Oded Maimon, Tel Aviv University, Israel

In this chapter we analyze Ontology Learning and its goals, as well as the input expected when learning ontologies - peer-reviewed scientific papers in English. After reviewing the Ontology Learning Layer Cake model's shortcomings we suggest an alternative model based on linguistic knowledge. The suggested model would find the meaning of simple components of text – statements. From them it is easy to derive cases and roles that map the reality as a set of entities and relationships or RDF triples, somehow equivalent to Entity-relationship diagrams. Time complexity for the suggested ontology learning framework is constant ($O(1)$) for a sentence, and $O(n)$ for an ontology with n sentences. We conclude that the Ontology Learning Layer Cake is not adequate for Ontology Learning from text.

Chapter 8

Sergey Maruev, Russian Presidential Academy of National Economy and Public
Administration, Russia
Dmitry Stefanovskyi, Russian Presidential Academy of National Economy and Public
Administration, Russia
Alexander Troussov, Russian Presidential Academy of National Economy and Public
Administration, Russia

Nowadays, most of the digital content is generated within techno-social systems like Facebook or Twitter where people are connected to other people and to artefacts such as documents and concepts. These networks provide rich context for understanding the role of particular nodes. It is widely agreed that one of the most important principles in the philosophy of language is Frege's context principle, which states that words have meaning only in the context of a sentence. This chapter puts forward the hypothesis that semantics of the content of techno-social systems should be also analysed in the context of the whole system. The hypothesis is substantiated by the introduction of a method for formal modelling and mining of techno-social systems and is corroborated by a discussion on the nature of meaning in philosophy. In addition we provide an overview of recent trends in knowledge production and management within the context of our hypothesis.

Chapter 9

Jasmina Milićević, Dalhousie University, Canada
Àngels Catena, Universitat Autònoma de Barcelona, Spain

Translation of sentences featuring clitics often poses a problem to machine translation systems. In this chapter, we illustrate, on the material from a Serbian ~ Catalan parallel corpus, a rule-based approach to solving translational structural mismatches between linguistic representations that underlie source- and target language sentences containing clitics. Unlike most studies in this field, which make use of phrase structure formalisms, ours has been conducted within the dependency framework of the Meaning-Text linguistic theory. We start by providing a brief description of Catalan and Serbian clitic systems, then introduce the basics of our framework to finally illustrate Serbian ~ Catalan translational mismatches involving the operations of clitic doubling, clitic climbing, and clitic possessor raising.

This chapter gives a short introduction to machine translation (MT) and its use within commercial companies with special focus on the localization industry. Although MT is not a new field, many scientists and researchers are still interested in this field and are frequently coming up with challenges, discoveries and novel approaches. Commercial companies need to keep track with them and their R&D departments are making good progress with the integration of MT within their complicated workflows as well as minor improvements in core MT in order to gain a competitive advantage. The chapter describes differences in research within university and commercial environments. Furthermore, there will be given the main obstacles in the deployment of new technologies and typical way in which a new technology can be deployed in corporate environment.

This research focuses on the corpus stylistic analysis of the treatises of Great Athanasius. In this interdisciplinary study classical texts are approached through linguistic tools and the main purpose is to describe the style of Great Athanasius in these treatises, after having extracted all these quantitative data utilizing computational tools. The language Great Athanasius uses is a language that expresses intensely his speculations on the achievement of religious change and restructuration. His language expresses his religious ideology. His speeches are persuasive, ideological and represent the rhetorician's opinion. They are based on the speaker's intentionality; it directs him to the specific rhetorical framework, since he aims at one and unique inspirational result, that is, persuasion.

Preface

Advanced natural languages are one of several predominant conveniences that support our successful being and significantly distinguish us from animals and plants, not speaking of machines. We can communicate, exchange knowledge, acquire or transmit new information, cooperate, manage, govern, and without such a tool known as language, all those matters would be considerably more difficult, if possible at all. Informally said, our languages – and there are several thousands current ones – have a certain syntax given by sets of rules – grammar –, unfortunately including many exceptions, as well as the contents called *semantics*. Respecting the grammar rules, the contents can be expressed in various forms like speech or written text. Nowadays, tremendous amount of textual documents, created in natural languages, exists and ceaselessly grows because modern electronic tools like various types of databases enable effortlessly storing, retrieving, and transmitting textual data. Provided that the data contains meaningful contents that may be useful, its processing from the semantic point of view is important but how to cope with such big data volumes? Machines – computers – can (and must) help us even if their "thinking" principles are far from ours.

The idea to process natural languages by machines had been born a very long time before the first really working computer – as we commonly use it today – was constructed and put into operation. Probably one of the first scientists, who considered the idea, was a famous German philosopher and mathematician Gottfried Wilhelm Leibniz in the seventeenth century (Hutchins, 1986). He was perhaps inspired by his invention of a mechanical pinwheel calculator along with his deep interest in linguistics and a possibility to create a universal language, including machine translation. From that time, Leibniz's thoughts have not lost their significance, which has come alive in 1950 by Alan Turing (and later by Noam Chomsky) plus many others based on the introduction of modern powerful computers.

In addition to the traditional analytic tools like statistics, contemporary natural language processing and computational linguistics research (Clark, et al., 2012) focuses strongly on supervised, unsupervised, and semi-supervised learning algorithms in the area of machine learning (Mitchell, 1997), which is part of artificial intelligence (Rusell & Norvig, 2009). Such algorithms are able to learn from data that was (supervised learning) or was not (unsupervised learning) hand-annotated with the desired answers, or using a combination of annotated and non-annotated data (semi-supervised learning). The need to intelligently process data has led to the rise of new informatics areas like data mining (Gaber, 2010) and, from the natural language point of view, text mining (Weiss et al., 2005). The text mining discipline is the intention of this book.

THE BOOK INTENTION

This book, *Modern Computational Models of Semantic Discovery in Natural Language*, addresses some problems related to automated semantic processing of electronic textual data written in natural languages, including instances of possible solutions demonstrated by carefully selected typical and applicable examples. Providing reliable results of semantic analysis that discovers meaning of textual documents – or their relevant parts – is what we expect from machines as a consequence of increasingly growing very large text-data volumes. Today, the problem solution utilizes combinations of modern computer algorithms including artificial intelligence, machine learning, statistics, and text mining together with linguistic approaches. Natural language processing is now one of the most topical areas both from the research and application point of view because there are – for example, via the Internet – various textual documents available for a common computer-user in many very different professional areas. Using real demonstration examples and representative problem solutions, a reader can learn some of the current possibilities of one of modern computer applications. Natural language processing using common computers (PC's, laptops) is a very present task with many possible applications because there exist data resources like the Internet that can provide – for example, as a result of browsing – almost unlimited volumes of data as answers. Many areas enable people to freely write their opinions, meaning, sentiment, or reports simply as plain text using any natural language. After collecting a lot of textual documents, the data may contain valuable information that is waiting for its discovery. Because computers and humans use different methods of reasoning, and due to the extremely large volumes of data, new methods supporting semantic analysis have been developed. This publication aims at presenting the contemporary and applicable research results because the progress in this area is very fast, and hopefully may further inspire the next required progress. Natural language processing and text mining are today standard courses at many advanced universities, thus this book can hopefully also serve as a point of departure.

The target audience of the book includes students, teachers, and researchers from schools and universities as well as professionals from companies or organizations that must deal with data having the form of text written in natural languages. The book aims at problems when due to the very large textual-data volumes humans cannot process them manually from the semantic point of view. In practice, companies and interested persons can use this book as an inspiration or startpoint for developing their own particular semantic-analysis tools, for example, applied to business intelligence, filtering and categorizing e-mail messages, analyzing meaning of service/goods customers, revealing significant cores or topics in blogs and discussion groups, and so like, or for considering which software tools could be applied according to their needs in the processing of the big accumulated text-data.

Knowing that English is today the most widely used language, the book editors wished also to demonstrate the computational modeling of semantic discovery in other languages because – as a reader certainly knows well – there are many languages coming from different origins that underwent various progress and development.

ORGANIZATION OF THE BOOK

The book is organized into eleven chapters. A brief description of each of the chapters follows:

In the first chapter, *Sentiment Classification: Facebook Statuses Mining in the "Arabic Spring" Era*, its author, Jalel Akaichi from Tunis, deals with reverberations sent through social networks by the notable political event known as Arabic Spring. The echoes left their tracks also on popular Facebook. The huge number of informal messages was posted every instant of the day. Feelings seem to be frequently important in these texts for expressing friendship, showing social support, or as part of online arguments. However, existing sentiment analysis studies tend to be commercially-oriented, designed to identify opinions about products rather than user behaviors and state of minds. In his analysis, the author focuses on the application of text mining and sentiment analysis techniques to analyzing Tunisian users' statuses updates on Facebook. The chapter describes how to extract useful information about the Facebook users' sentiment and behavior, especially during the Arabic Spring era. To achieve this task, the study describes a method of performing the sentiment analysis by employing the Support Vector Machine and Naïve Bayes data/text mining tools, as well as applying a combination of more than two features. The output of this work consists, on one hand, on the construction of a sentiment lexicon based on the Emoticons and Acronyms' lexicons that was developed based on the extracted statuses updates; on the other hand, it consists of the realization of detailed comparative experiments between two mentioned machine learning algorithms, Support Vector Machine and Naïve Bayes, by creating a training model for sentiment classification.

The second chapter named *Model of the Empirical Distribution Law for Syntactic and Link Words in "perfect" Texts* by its author Pavel Makagonov applies mathematically directed modeling to measuring the perfection of the contents and semantic value of an integrated text using connections with the indicators of perfection in the distribution of content words. The criterion for the content of semantically significant words is the coordination of their "frequency-rank" distribution with the Zipf law for short texts and Zipf-Mandelbrot law for long texts. The verified hypothesis is that a perfect system should have not only perfect distribution of its elements – objects, but also perfect connections between them. A model is suggested in which the degree of the text perfection from the point of view of the quality of connections between significative words is determined by the quality of distribution of syntactic and link words in the "rank-frequency" representation. The search for a mathematical representation of this model was conducted proceeding from the assumption that such a model should be a common one not only for the integrated textual document, but also for any system which is considered harmonious, or "perfect", that is, a system for the objects of which the Zipf law of distribution holds. As a simplified criterion the ratio of the significant and syntactic words used in the analyzed text and the degree of the closeness of this ratio to the "golden section" is considered.

The third chapter, *Extracting Definitional Contexts in Spanish through the Identification of Hyponymy-Hyperonymy Relations*, from Olga Acosta, Gerardo Sierra, and César Aguilar, makes a reader familiar with the automatic extraction of hyponymy-hypernymy relations in text corpus, which is an important task in Natural Language Processing. This chapter proposes a method for automatically extracting a set of hyponym-hyperonym pairs from a medical corpus in Spanish, expressed in analytical definitions. This kind of definition is composed by a term (the hyponym), a genus term (the hyperonym), and one or more differentiae, that is, a set of particular features proper to the defined term, for example: conjunctivitis is an infection of the conjunctiva of the eye. Definitions are obtained from definitional contexts, and then sequences of term and genus term. Then, the most frequent hyperonyms are used in order to filter relevant definitions. Additionally, using a bootstrapping technique, new hyponym candidates are extracted from the corpus, based on the previous set of hyponyms/hyperonyms detected.

The fourth chapter, *Revealing Groups of Semantically Close Textual Documents by Clustering: Problems and Possibilities,* written by František Dařena and Jan Žižka, introduces clustering as a family of algorithms that can be successfully used to organize text documents into groups without prior knowledge of them. The chapter also demonstrates using unsupervised clustering to group large amount of unlabeled textual data (customer reviews written informally in five natural languages) so it can be used later for further analysis. The attention is paid to the process of selecting clustering algorithms, their parameters, methods of data preprocessing, as well as to the methods of evaluating the results by a human expert with an assistance of computers. The feasibility is demonstrated by a number of experiments with external evaluation using known labels and expert validation with the assistance of a computer. It was found that it was possible to apply the same procedures, including clustering, cluster validation, and detection of topics and significant words to different natural languages with satisfactory results.

Similarly, the following fifth chapter, *Semantics-based Document Categorization Employing Semi-supervised Learning,* from the same authors, Jan Žižka and František Dařena, presents possibilities of another machine-learning based procedure known as semi-supervised learning. The automated categorization of unstructured textual documents according to their semantic contents plays more and more important role particularly linked with the ever growing volume of such data originating from the Internet. Having a sufficient number of labeled examples, a suitable supervised machine-learning based classifier can be trained. When no labeling is available, an unsupervised learning method (clustering) can be applied, however, the missing label information often leads to worse classification results. This chapter demonstrates an alternative method based on semi-supervised learning when a smallish set of manually labeled examples significantly improves the categorization process in comparison with clustering, and the results approach the supervised learning output. For the illustration, a real-world dataset coming from the Internet is used as the input of the supervised learning (Naïve Bayes, Nearest Neighbor, Support Vector Machines), unsupervised one (special k-Means), and semi-supervised one (self-training, co-training). The results are shown for different number of the starting labeled samples used as initial "seeds" to automatically label the large remaining volume of unlabeled items.

The sixth chapter with the title *Natural Language Processing as Feature Extraction Method for Building Better Predictive Models* comes from the authors Goran Klepač and Marko Velić. This chapter covers natural language processing techniques and their application to predictive model development. Two case studies are presented. First case describes a project where textual descriptions of various situations in a call center of one telecommunication company were processed in order to predict churn. Second case describes sentiment analysis of business news and describes practical and testing issues in text mining projects. Both case studies depict different approaches and are implemented in different tools. Language of the texts processed in these projects is Croatian which belongs to the Slavic group of languages with more complex morphologies and grammar rules than English. Chapter concludes with several points on the future research possible in this domain.

Chapter seven, *Departing the Ontology Layer Cake*, has two authors: Abel Browarnik and Oded Maimon. Most Ontology Learning approaches follow a model called the Ontology Learning Layer Cake and share many features such as statistical based information retrieval, machine learning, and data and text mining, making resort to linguistics based techniques for certain tasks. The chapter analyzes ontology learning and its goals, as well as the input one would expect when learning ontologies – peer-reviewed scientific papers in English, papers that undergo quality control. After reviewing the model's shortcomings, the authors suggest an alternative model based on linguistic knowledge. The suggested model would find the meaning of simple components of text – statements. From these statements it should be easy to derive cases and roles that map the reality as a set of entities and relationships or RDF triples, much in the same way as Entity-relationship diagrams do. An analysis of the time complexity of the suggested ontology learning framework shows that this complexity is constant ($O(1)$) for a sentence, and O(n) for an ontology based on n sentences. The conclusion is that the Ontology Learning Layer Cake is not adequate for Ontology Learning from text.

In the eighth chapter, *Semantics of Techno-Social Spaces*, the authors Sergey Maruev, Dmitry Stefanovskyi, and Alexander Troussov present a solution related to the so-called techno-social space. Nowadays, most of the digital content is generated within techno-social systems like Facebook or Twitter, where people are connected to other people and to artefacts such as documents and concepts. These networks provide rich context for understanding the role of particular nodes. It is widely agreed that one of the most important principles in the philosophy of language is Frege's context principle, which states that words have meaning only in the context of a sentence. This chapter puts forward the hypothesis that semantics of the content of techno-social systems should be also analyzed in the context of the whole system. The hypothesis is substantiated by the introduction of a method for formal modeling and mining of techno-social systems and is corroborated by a discussion on the nature of meaning in philosophy. In addition, the authors provide an overview of recent trends in knowledge production and management within the context of our hypothesis.

The ninth chapter, named *Translational Mismatches Involving Clitics (Illustrated from Serbian ~ Catalan Language Pair)* and written by Jasmina Milićević and Àngels Catena, shows that translation of sentences featuring clitics often poses a problem to machine translation systems. The goal of this chapter is to illustrate, on the material from a Serbian ~ Catalan parallel corpus, a rule-based approach to solving translational structural mismatches between linguistic representations that underlie source- and target language sentences containing clitics. Unlike most studies in this field, which make use of phrase structure formalisms, this one was conducted within a dependency framework, that of the Meaning-Text linguistic theory. The authors start by providing a brief description of Catalan and Serbian clitic systems, then introduce the basics of their framework to finally illustrate Serbian ~ Catalan translational mismatches involving the operations of clitic doubling, clitic climbing, and clitic possessor raising.

Chapter ten, *Machine Translation Within Commercial Companies*, deals with what its name suggests: machine translation from the very practical point of view. The chapter author, Tomáš Hudík, gives a short introduction to machine translation and its use within commercial companies with a special focus on the localization industry. Although machine translation is not a new field, many scientists and researchers are still interested in this area and are frequently coming up with challenges, discoveries, and novel approaches. Commercial companies need to keep track with them, and their research & development departments are making good progress with the integration of machine translation within their complicated workflows as well as minor improvements in the core machine-translation in order to gain a competitive advantage. The chapter describes differences in research within university and commercial environments. Furthermore, there are given the main obstacles in the deployment of new technologies and typical ways in which a new technology can be deployed in a corporate environment.

The concluding chapter number eleven, *A corpus-stylistic approach of the Treatises of Great Athanasius about Idolatry,* brings one more excellent demonstration of the natural language processing possibility, this time directed at a historical textual document from the fourth century. The chapter author, Georgios Alexandropoulos, describes the style of the treatises (Contra Gentes and De incarnatione verbi) using corpus analysis tools. This research focuses on certain elements as the most frequently used words, the use of adjectives, pronouns, verbs, lexical bundles, and the most frequently intertextualistic sources. In this interdisciplinary study, classical texts are approached through linguistic tools and the main purpose is to describe the style of a historical person, Great Athanasius, or Saint Athanasius of Alexandria, Egypt – the twentieth bishop in the Coptic Orthodox Church, in these treatises, after having extracted all these quantitative data utilizing computational tools. The extraction of the certain data provides us with secure results and leads us to understand that these speeches have certain ideological orientation which is reflected on their linguistic choices. In this way, it is confirmed that the language and style are strictly connected with the ideological intentionality of Great Athanasius, who tries to persuade his audience about the rotten background of idolatry promoting and emphasizing positive things about his religious ideology.

SUMMARY

The presented book demonstrates selected recent attempts to use modern computers as well as advanced scientific tools from the areas like informatics, mathematics, linguistics, machine learning, and artificial intelligence, for mining information and knowledge hidden in real-world textual data-sets that visibly overflow our lives. The intention was to show various applications of modern computational tools to natural language processing without being limited to only one language. Authors from ten countries (Canada, Chile, Croatia, Czech Republic, Greece, Israel, Mexico, Russia, Spain, Tunisia) in eleven chapters presented topical and current points of view to several recent problems and their possible solutions, often as case studies. This book hopes to contribute to the area of the computer-based natural language processing by demonstrating how theory can be used in practice. Also, the editors hope that the book contents can attract new researchers and users of recent, constantly developing area connecting humans and machines.

Jan Žižka
Mendel University in Brno, Czech Republic

František Dařena
Mendel University in Brno, Czech Republic

REFERENCES

Clark, A., Fox, C., & Lappin, S. (Eds.). (2012). The Handbook of Computational Linguistics and Natural Language Processing. New York, Wiley-Blackwell.

Gaber, M. M. (Ed.). (2010). *Scientific Data Mining and Knowledge Discovery*. Berlin, Heidelberg: Springer. doi:10.1007/978-3-642-02788-8

Hutchins, J. (1986). *Machine translation: past, present, future. (Ellis Horwood Series in Computers and their Applications.)*. Chichester: Ellis Horwood.

Mitchell, M. T. (1997). *Machine Learning*. New York: McGraw-Hill.

Russell, S., & Norvig, P. (2009). *Artificial Intelligence: A Modern Approach* (3rd ed.). New York: Prentice Hall/Pearson.

Weiss, S. M., Indurkhya, N., & Zhang, T. (2005). *Text Mining: Predictive Methods for Analyzing Unstructured Information*. Berlin, Heidelberg: Springer. doi:10.1007/978-0-387-34555-0

Acknowledgment

First and foremost, the editors would like to thank very much to all the chapter authors for their contributions that took – from the start to the successful ending – more than a year of their maximum efforts dedicated to this book. Without their enthusiasm and expertise, this book would never have become a reality.

At the same time, the editors are pleased to express their recognition for the valuable support of the editorial board and reviewers regarding the improvement of quality, coherence, and content presentation of the chapters. It was not always an easy task to opt for a contribution or choose the right point of view within the defined frame of this book. We owe them a great deal for their demanding work!

And the least the editors can also do is to express their appreciation for the cooperation and patience of people in the IGI Global Publisher, who were involved in creating of this book from the very beginning.

Jan Žižka
Mendel University in Brno, Czech Republic

František Dařena
Mendel University in Brno, Czech Republic

Chapter 1
Sentiment Classification:
Facebook' Statuses Mining in the "Arabic Spring" Era

Jalel Akaichi
University of Tunis, Tunisia

ABSTRACT

In this work, we focus on the application of text mining and sentiment analysis techniques for analyzing Tunisian users' statuses updates on Facebook. We aim to extract useful information, about their sentiment and behavior, especially during the "Arabic spring" era. To achieve this task, we describe a method for sentiment analysis using Support Vector Machine and Naïve Bayes algorithms, and applying a combination of more than two features. The output of this work consists, on one hand, on the construction of a sentiment lexicon based on the Emoticons and Acronyms' lexicons that we developed based on the extracted statuses updates; and on the other hand, it consists on the realization of detailed comparative experiments between the above algorithms by creating a training model for sentiment classification.

INTRODUCTION

Recently, social networks, such as Facebook, Twitter, etc., have taken a significant part of people's lives and activities. Billions of internet users are using social networks not only to stay in touch with their friends, discover new acquaintances and share user-created contents, but also to share their points of views related to variety of subjects through a variety of manners such as wall posting, comments, videos, pictures, etc.

Arab countries count among countries having a huge number of social network users. Social networks become a magic tool for Arab people to promote freedom of speech, human rights and democracy. In 2011, social networks were the spark that makes unexpected revolutions that took place in the Arab countries. At the beginning, it was Tunisia that performed its revolution that lay the country into the "delightful" road of democracy. Tunisia was then the trigger that pushes other countries such as Egypt, Yemen, Syria, etc., to taste the path of "freedom".

DOI: 10.4018/978-1-4666-8690-8.ch001

On social networks interfaces, people had the opportunities to call for the change, by expressing their sentiments through a multiplicity of posts. Commented images, videos, pictures, articles, etc., were shared on social networks to show dictators' crimes, inequalities between regions, etc.

During the Tunisian revolution, and the rough conditions that they have been enduring, especially during the curfews, Facebook has become the common source of information and one of the most important tools of communication for the Tunisians. From the first of July 2011 until the beginning of December 2012, Facebook gains hundreds of thousands new Tunisian users. At that time, Tunisian Facebook users had tendency to share their feelings, their thoughts and to inform their friends about conditions of their cities or neighborhoods by sharing videos and pictures and especially posting short posts on their walls which was the preferred way to interact with others.

However, there is no previous research that dealt with a novel collection of textual data, which consists of Tunisian Facebook users' statuses, and applied machine learning techniques in order to evaluate their performances on such a dataset.

This work explores the potential applications of text and sentiment mining on statuses updates in order to analyze the Tunisian's behavior during the revolution. For this purpose, we choose a random population having Facebook accounts. It includes males and females, students, workers, housewives, etc. The age of targeted population is varying between 21 and 54 years old.

Through the application of text mining, sentiment analysis techniques and especially machine learning algorithms, we aim to identify the nature of the statuses updates, and to link them to behaviors and sentiments characteristics. This, obviously, will be useful, not only for people that want to know themselves, but also for political decision makers that want to know better their potential electorate.

This chapter is organized as follows. The state of the art and the background of social networks text mining are described in section 2. In section 3, we discuss the methodology of our work and describe the proposed architecture. In section 4, the process of our experiments is described and the results are discussed and evaluated. Finally, section 5 concludes and proposes possible directions for future research.

The expected output of this work consists of the following items:

1. A dataset: There are not any existing data sets of Tunisian Facebook users. Therefore, we create our own dataset which consists of a list of Facebook users (50) and their statuses update (approximately 13 statuses per user).
2. The development of sentiment lexicons: The informal language used on online social networks is a main point to consider before performing any text mining techniques. This is why, we built our special lexicons: Emoticons' lexicon, an Acronyms' lexicon and an Interjections' lexicon.
3. The study of the impact of n-grams ($1 < n < 3$) on analyzing sentiments from Facebook statuses updates. Compared to previous published work, we show that the highest accuracy is reached when we use a combination of unigrams and bigrams as features. We used other features such as part of speech tags and stemming. We do not discuss them in detail due to the lack of significant improvements.
4. The experiments: We study two different machine learning classifiers; Support Vector Machine and Naïve Bayes, which consist on a probabilistic model on the preprocessed data. For experiments, a training model for text polarity was created. Our aim is then to examine which feature set can achieve the highest performance in sentiment classification and which classifiers performs better than the other one.

BACKGROUND

This section reviews, on one hand the history of the social networks and their analysis, in particular Facebook, and on the other hand the research literature in the field of text mining and sentiment analysis. It discusses the challenges of mining Facebook data and the motivations for performing text mining techniques.

Next, the field of opinion mining (or sentiment analysis) applied on text documents is discussed. Opinion mining is a relatively new and challenging field dedicated to detecting subjective content in text documents, with a variety of uses in real world applications.

Overview of Social Networks

The origins of social networks analysis is more than hundred years old. It is rooted in the field of sociology in 1934 with the publication of Jacob Moreno's introduction "Who Shall Survive?" Then, in the early of the 1970s, Harrison White produced an amazing number of important contributions related to social network theory and research. During this era, the studies of social networks analysis brought attention to small social networks and groups. However, with the recent produced huge data and the complex networks populating the Web, it became difficult to analyze and/or mine. The computing sciences were attracted by this field and invent many successful tools for social networks analysis. For example, the algorithmic aspects of the social networks were studied in (Kleinberg, 2000) and their range of applicability was analyzed as well in (Staab et al., 2005).

In the nineteenth, numerous social networks appeared. Classemates.com is often considered as the first social networking site which aims to bring together past peers. Other social networking sites quickly followed; such as SixDegrees.com that focuses on helping people to connect with and to send messages to former school friends. The next wave of social networking sites embarks on when Adrian Scott, an entrepreneur, launched the business social networking site Ryze. Later on, one of the most popular and successful business social networking sites, Friendster, was launched in 2002. A year after, another business social networking site, LinkedIn, was triggered. The aim of business social networking sites is not only destined to professionals in order to maintain a list of connections and to seek out partnership opportunities for their business, but also for job seekers to find out more about potential employers and for human resource positions to find out the potential employees to fill job vacancies.

MySpace, Facebook, Bebo and Twitter were the next and performant generations of social networking sites. They are, actually, the most popular sites in the world. The number of social networks' users is rising every day all over the world, to the point that social networks become an important part of our everyday lives. In this work, we focused on Facebook which we consider as the most popular.

Facebook and Data Mining

Facebook was founded on February 4, 2004 by Mark Zuckerberg at the University of Harvard as a site for college student. Quickly, it has grown to a popular social networking site that its main mission becomes to make the world more open and connected. People use Facebook to stay connected with friends and family, to discover what's going on in the world, and to share and express what matters to them.

Since its creation, Facebook has become omnipresent with more than billion active users worldwide, of whom 50% log in on a daily basis. This huge number of users generates rich information and various new sources of knowledge such as text, images, videos, etc. However, it has become harder to analyze such huge and complex contents. These huge volumes of information create many new research issues such as social web storage, search and mining social networks, etc. These research issues have been receiving growing attentions in data mining in the recent years. Data mining techniques provide researchers the tools needed to analyze and to mine large and complex social networks data.

There is a variety of challenges for mining Facebook data that attracted many researchers and companies. Actually, Facebook users have tendency to describe themselves like products. Pempek et al. (2009) and Zhao et al. (2008) found also that self-presentation was one of the most popular reasons that users were attracted to. The reason why, Facebook is considered as an eMarketing tool that enables business firms to access markets, learn about customer attitudes, behaviors and trends, and get in touch with them (Holzner, 2009) in order to enlarge their market share and increase their revenues (Albee, 2010). Facebook did even publish a document titled "Best Practice Guide Marketing on Facebook" which serves as an official resource on how to take advantage of Facebook's advertising products, social plug-ins, analytics and other tools to grow one's business.

Another challenge for mining Facebook data is to reveal Facebook usage time and Facebook access frequency via various predictive data mining techniques in order to identify users' patterns in Facebook (Bozkir et al., 2011). One other challenge for analyzing Facebook is the use of it as an educational tool. This challenge was explored in several papers. Most of them concluded that Facebook had very little educational use (Ismail et al., 2010; Pempek et al. 2009).

Detecting users' happiness and humor is one other challenge for researchers to mine into Facebook users' comments and statuses updates. Such study was conducted by the Facebook data team by creating an index called Gross National Happiness in order to measure the feelings of the users and their state of minds. This was achieved by analyzing statuses updates and categorizing them, whether they were positive or negative. As a result, the analysts are able to track users' state of minds at any instant. However, this study focused solely on English words and statuses of American users.

If one of the benefits of Facebook is to provide means to users to express their points of views, then political activities are one of the fields that people give their opinions about. Therefore, political activities on Facebook are considered as one of the challenges for mining its content. Indeed, Barak Obama's election campaign for Presidency of the United States made use of social networks and especially Facebook to get his message out to the public, donors and volunteers, arrange campaign volunteers and get people to vote.

Due to the impact of Facebook on politics and election campaigns, Facebook has announced on the 12th of January 2012 a partnership with the American website of Information and Politics Analytics. This partnership consists on the application of sentiment analysis of the users' political messages, comments and statuses. The aim of this study is to predict the coming presidential election of the United States. Therefore, text mining and sentiment analysis are the suitable and the most performing techniques in studying human behaviors and opinions, and discovering useful information in particular purposes.

Text Mining

Text mining is known as text data mining, knowledge discovery from textual databases (Feldman and Sanger, 2007), an extension of data mining or knowledge discovery from structured databases (Fayyad, 1996). In general, it refers to the process of extracting useful information by identifying and exploring interesting and non-trivial patterns from unstructured text documents. Feldman and Sanger (2007) mentioned that text mining uses techniques from the following aspects:

- Information retrieval which is the search for information based on a given query. Common information retrieval systems include popular search engines such as Google.
- Information extraction which is the fact of pinpointing relevant information and transforming them from unstructured textual data into a structured format, typically in a tabular format that it can be used for data mining purposes based on machine learning language.
- Natural language processing which refers to the process that computers use to convert human language (written or spoken) into useful knowledge that a computer can understand and use while interacting with other computers. Natural language processing involves processing text using lexical, syntactic and semantic knowledge (Binali et al., 2010)

Text mining also connects with the algorithms and methods of the following techniques:

- Knowledge discovery from databases which is a non-trivial process of identifying valid, novel, potentially useful, and ultimately understandable patterns in data (Fayyad et al., 1996).
- Data mining which is the analysis of (often large) observational data sets to find unsuspected relationships and to summarize the data in novel ways that are both understandable and useful to the data owner (Hand et al., 2001).
- Machine learning which was defined by Mitchell (1997) as the ability of a machine to improve its performance based on previous results and experiences. A perfect example is today's Facebook news feed which is programmed to display user friend content. If a user frequently tags or writes on the wall of a particular friend, the news feed changes its behavior to display more content from that friend.
- Statistics which is a branch of mathematics of the collection, the organization, the analysis and the interpretation of numerical data.

The text mining techniques were performed in the same fields of knowledge discovery from databases, but they focused on the textual data. For instance, in the field of marketing, the text mining has been used in analytical customer relationship management in order to improve predictive analytics models for customers churn (Coussement et al., 2008). Text mining was also applied in the field of biomedical such in the online text mining application GoPubMed (Doms et al., 2005). One other field of text mining applications is helping text search and custom publishing electronic documents. Moreover, the text mining is performed in detecting and identifying problems and frauds, and tracking terrorism activities. Understanding the opinions of customers or other kinds of users is one of the fields that text mining also interested in it.

Sentiment Analysis

Sentiment analysis refers to the extraction of subjective information from raw data (text, images, videos, etc.). The sentiment can refer to the opinions or emotions which are considered as related concepts; however they are not the same. When the sentiment analysis is based on opinions, a distinction is made, for example, between positive and negative ones. Nevertheless, when the sentiment analysis is based on emotions, it is about the distinction between different kinds of emotions like sadness, fear, joy, love, etc. The sentiment analysis, considered in the research, is based on opinions.

An Overview of Sentiment Analysis

With the growing availability of opinion-rich resources such as social networks sites, blogs and forums, new challenges arise as people actively use information technologies to seek out and understand the opinions of others in many domains such as asking about a particular product, politics, etc. (Pang & Lee, 2008). Instead of conducting costly market studies, customer satisfaction analysis or traditional surveys techniques, sentiment analysis provides companies offering products or services with means to analyze published reviews, to estimate the extent of product acceptance and to determine strategies to improve product or service quality. Sentiment analysis also facilitates policy makers or politicians to analyze public sentiments with respect to policies, public services or political issues.

Therefore, text mining has been used to perform sentiment analysis in public forums, blogs and especially social network sites. In fact, textual information is categorized into two types: Facts which are objective expressions about entities, events and their proprieties, and opinions which are subjective expressions that describe people's sentiment toward entities, events and their properties (Liu, 2010). Sentiment analysis, known as opinion mining as well, takes the written text and translates it into different context, such as positives, negatives or neutral. Several subtasks can be identified within sentiment analysis:

- Determining document subjectivity which is often called subjectivity classification. This subtask defines whether a given text is objective (expressing a fact) or subjective (expressing an opinion or emotion) (Pang & Lee, 2004; Yu & Hatzivassiloglou, 2003).
- Determining document orientation which is often called sentiment classification or document-level sentiment classification. This subtask defines the polarity of a given subjective text. In other word, it determines whether this text expresses, for example, a positive or a negative sentiment on its subject matter (Pang et al., 2004; Turney, 2002).
- Determining the strength of document orientation which decides, for example, whether the positive sentiment expressed by a text on its subject matter is weakly, mildly or strongly positive (Wilson et al., 2004; Popescu & Etzioni, 2005).

Earlier studies on sentiment analysis have concentrated on the classification of product reviews (Denecke, 2008; Liu and Hu, 2004; Pang et al., 2002). Their aim was the extraction of positive or negative sentiments from user opinions of a product.

Sentiment Analysis' Techniques

The sentiment analysis is a challenging field which has attracted a lot of researchers during the few last years. Therefore, we can find in the literature a variety of techniques related to sentiment analysis. The two main ones are the machine learning and the dictionary-based approaches.

The machine learning techniques are frequently used for text classification. There exist two main types of machine learning methods: Supervised and unsupervised learning. For the supervised learning, the class labels are known before the learning process; however for the unsupervised learning, the classes are unknown from the beginning.

For the sentiment classification problem, the machine learning methods treat the sentiment classification as a topic-based text classification problem where topic words, such as "sport", "politics", "science", etc., are important. Any text classification algorithm can be employed, such as Naïve Bayes, Support Vector Machine or Maximum Entropy, etc. (Liu, 2010); however, in sentiment classification opinionated words such as "awesome", "good", "best", "perfect", etc., are more important.

Turney (2002) developed an unsupervised learning algorithm, known as Point wise Mutual Information and Information Retrieval, in order to classify texts as recommended or not recommended.

Pang et al. (2002) used three machine learning techniques (Naïve Bayes, classification maximum entropy, and Support Vector Machine) to classify movie reviews as positive or negative. They tested different feature combinations including unigrams, unigrams and bigrams, and unigrams and part-of speech tags, etc. Those techniques outperformed the human-generated baseline, and the Support Vector Machine was the technique that gave the best results. Other examples of machine learning approaches in the sentiment analysis area were proposed such as regression models to predict a review's usefulness (Zhang and Zhu, 2006) and a semi-supervised method of performing a binary classification of texts as positive or negative (Esuli & Sebastiani, 2005). Durant and Smith (2006) investigated the utility of Naïve Bayes and Support Vector Machine on political web logs and they showed that a Naïve Bayes classifier significantly outperforms a Support Vector Machine one.

Hurst and Nigam (2004) applied the simple online classifier Winnow to determine the polarity of documents. They showed that human agreement can merely achieve 75% to 80% of precision and recall on polarity prediction. The recall obtained by Winnow is very poor, achieving only 43% for positive reviews and 16% for negative reviews.

Hang et al. (2006) conducted a comparative experiment on sentiment classification for online products reviews using the following classifiers: Passive-aggressive algorithm based classifier (Shalev-Shwartz et al., 2004), language modeling based classifier (Manning & Schütze, 1999), and also Winnow Classifier. The results of their experiments showed that the passive-aggressive algorithm reached the higher accuracy (90.07%) compared to the others.

Kang et al. (2012) conducted a sentiment analysis related to restaurant reviews by building a senti-lexicon, and proposed two improved versions of the Naïve Bayes algorithm. Then, they evaluated their performances by comparing them to the original Naïve Bayes and Support Vector Machine algorithms. Results showed that the improved versions of Naïve Bayes proved its effectiveness.

The dictionary-based approaches extract the polarity of each sentence in a document. Afterwards, the sense of the opinion words in a sentence is analyzed in order to classify the sentiment in the text. Generally speaking, the techniques that follow this approach are based on lexicons, and use a dictionary of words mapped to their semantic value (Denecke, 2008).

The lexicon of a language forms its vocabulary. The first version and the most well-known one is WordNet (Fellbaum, 1998) which is a semantic lexicon where words are grouped into sets of synonyms called Synsets.

Another famous example of lexicon is SentiWordNet (Esuli & Sebastiani, 2006b). This one is a sentiment lexicon that represents an index of sentiment words, and it has the polarity information of the relevant word irrespective of whether it carries a positive sentiment or a negative one. The SentiWordNet is considered as an extension of WordNet. It assigns WordNet Synsets a graded measure with respect to two scales: A positive/ negative scale and a subjective/ objective scale. It is important to notice that the classification is based on Synsets, not on words, because a word can have different meanings (Esuli and Sebastiani, 2006a).

The core application areas of sentiment analysis and opinion mining are Finance (Devitt & Ahmad, 2007), reviews (Dave et al., 2003; Pang et al., 2002; Turney, 2002), politics (Kim & Hovy, 2006), and news (Godbole et al., 2007).

There has been a large amount of research in the field of sentiment analysis, and in particular sentiment classification. Most of them have focused on classifying large texts, like reviews (Pang et al., 2002). Others have been interested in short informal texts, such as Tweets (Go et al., 2009), SMS texts (Leong et al., 2012), Myspace (Thelwall et al., 2010), etc. Therefore, in this chapter, we perform text mining and sentiment analysis on a novel collection which represents Facebook's statuses updates related to Tunisian users in order to analyze sentiments and behaviors during the revolution of January 2011. Recent research on sentiment analysis (Liu, 2010) has focused on the mining of massive volume of texts with opinions and sentiments. Unlike most text, wall posts are comparatively short and they are considered, probably, as the most popular Facebook feature.

METHODOLOGY

This section presents our methodology. Firstly, the general architecture is presented. Secondly, the extraction and the collection of the raw data are explained. Then, the construction of the lexicons is discussed, and the resulting data is pre-processed. Finally, our training model polarity classification is described using two different machine learning algorithms: Naïve Bayes and Support Vector Machine.

Proposed Architecture

In this sub section, we propose the main 6 steps performed by our system:

- Step 1 consists on raw data collection. This step lies on the extraction of users' statuses update. This is done through a web application called "I Told You", and stores them into a custom database.
- Step 2 consists on the Lexicon development. This step focuses on the informal language of online social networks. For this reason, three types of Lexicons were created: A Lexicon for social acronyms, A Lexicon for emoticons and a Lexicon for interjections.
- Step 3 consists on the data preprocessing. The data preprocessing involves the cleaning of the raw data and the removal of the useless words that would not carry any relevant meaning for the classification task.
- Step 4 consists on the features' extraction. The features' extraction is the first step to perform on the extracted statuses updates; accordingly we can achieve computations and apply appropriate statistical methods.
- Step 5 consists on the creation of a training model for text polarity determination. This step generates a model using two different classifiers; Naïve Bayes and Support Vector Machine destined to classify text into two polarity levels: Positive and Negative.
- Step 6 consists on performing classification using machine learning methods. Based on the created training model, this step comprises the classification of the unlabeled statuses using the Support Vector Machines and the Naïve Bayes algorithms. Once we conduct the classification step, we discuss its associated results in details.

In what follows, we present the main features of our Facebook statuses updates' data. We describe the way we handle those features and we explain in details the steps, presented above, of the proposed architecture.

Raw Data Collection

One of the duties of Facebook is to ensure protection of its users' data; mostly for privacy reasons. That's why; collecting and extracting, automatically, data from this social network is a tough and sometimes impossible task. The Facebook developer team provided during the last few months of 2010 some web services such as Graph API Explorer. By signing up for an access token, we can access to information about users and their activities, experiment with Graph API commands and see and explore the results. However, there are some limitations of using Graph API to extract users' data. Among them, the amount of information accessible depends on our relationship to that targeted user. One other constraint to consider in this step is that with Graph API we cannot go back in time to a specific period. In other words, the number of extracted comments is limited; and as we mentioned above, the main focus of this chapter is on the period of the Tunisian revolution.

One other tool used for extracting Facebook's statuses is located in StatusHistory.com. The role of this application is to retrieve old statuses of Facebook, sort them by date, by number of comments or by number of likes on each status. This application allows also having a general view and statistics about the user's profile; however, it is not able to retrieve statuses written in Arabic language.

To cope with all those constraints, we used "I Told You" application whose role is to retrieve old statuses of Facebook and export them either to a PDF, text file or document file. Thus, we have collected our own Facebook corpus in order to accomplish the targeted experiments.

The language of the given text plays a primordial role in the preprocessing task and the classification one. The Tunisian Facebook user speaks at least two languages; Arabic, which is his mother tongue, and French or English or both of them. Therefore, the extracted statuses were often written using a combination of several languages. This produces a multitude of structures, grammars and dictionaries for the considered words. Besides, the tools of text mining and sentiment analysis usually use only one language at the same time, and not too many. Therefore, focusing solely on one language is necessary to be able to preprocess efficiently the data, extract its features and create the classification model. Subsequently, a translation to English was applied to all the extracted statuses.

Once we have a raw translated data, we perform data pre-processing in order to ensure the cleaning of them, the removal of stop words and the extraction of the relevant features necessary for our analysis. Those steps are explained in the next sub-sections.

Lexicon Development

Facebook statuses updates have many unique attributes, which differentiates our research from previous research:

- Length: From our training set, we suppose that the average length of a Facebook status update is limited to 8 words. This is very different from the previous sentiment analysis research that focused on longer textual documents such as movie reviews.

- Language model: Facebook users post statuses from many different media devices, including their cell phones. The frequency of misspelling and slang in messages is much higher than in any other domain. One other thing to notice, that the language usually used is informal.
- Emoticons: They are descriptive representations of a facial expression using punctuation marks and letters. Emoticons are usually used to express a person's sentiment or state of mind.
- Social acronyms: Acronyms are popular expressions used in online social networks and online chatting systems. For example, the acronym "LOL" denotes the expression "Laughing out loud".
- Intentional misspelling: It is denoted by, especially, by the successive repetition of a letters in the same word, for example "Yeaaaaaaah".
- Interjections: They are words used to express a sentiment on the part of the speaker, for example "Wow".

For this purpose, we developed three types of lexicons: Emoticons, acronyms and interjections. The lexicons are not exhaustive and we did not cover all possible emoticons, acronyms and interjections. We only cover the most used ones on Facebook in general and on our extracted data set.

Emoticons' Lexicon

Emoticons have an important role in stressing on the sentiment conveyed in a sentence; they can therefore give a direct access to the writers' own sentiment (Yuasa et al., 2006). We collected a lexicon of the most used emoticons on Facebook and annotate them manually whether they express a positive or a negative sentiment (Table 1).

Acronyms' Lexicon

This lexicon denotes the most used acronyms by Tunisian Facebook users (Table 2).

Interjections' Lexicon

The interjection lexicon contains the main interjections used in our data set and in Facebook in general (Table 3)

We notice that we eliminated the objective (Neutral) expressions because they don't provide, at our point of view, useful information in our sentiment analysis process.

Data Preprocessing

The process of sentiment text preprocessing is similar with the traditional text preprocessing performed for text classification. The goal behind preprocessing is to clean the considered dataset by removing words and punctuations that don't have an influence on sentiment classification. This increases the performance of the classification task. Therefore, the preprocessing is a primordial task which involves two main tasks: Stop words removal and Stemming.

Table 1. Emoticons' Lexicon

Emoticon	Sentiment
:) or:-)	Positive
:p or:-p	Positive
:(or:-(	Negative
:/	Negative
:'(	Negative
;)	Positive
:>	Positive
:* or:-*	Positive
:<	Negative
:-x	Positive
<3	Positive

Table 2. Acronyms' Lexicon

Acronym	Sentiment
LOL	Positive
GR8	Positive

Table 3. Interjections' Lexicon

Interjection	Sentiment
Wow, waw	Positive
Haha, hihi, hehe	Positive
Oh dear	Negative
Thank you	Positive
Help	Positive
No way	Negative
Oy	Positive

Removing Stop Words

The stop words are words that do not add meaningful content to the data set; for example pronouns, prepositions, conjunctions, etc. Therefore, removing them reduces the space of the items significantly in the training and testing sets and decreases the diversity of used words in posted statuses. Examples of such words include 'the', 'a', 'of', 'and', 'to', etc. Accordingly, the first step in preprocessing is removing these stop words (Table 4).

Table 4. Example of removing stopwords

Input	Output
The Tunisian women accept the polygamy!!! Tunisia after 14/01 from bad to worse: ((	The Tunisian women accept the polygamy!!! Tunisia after 14/01 from bad to worse: ((

Stemming

Stemming is the process of removing prefixes and suffixes leaving the stem or the root of the considered word. For example, the words love, loved, loving and loves would be reduced to the root word love. This reduces the diversity of conjugations in which a word can occur, and as a consequence reduces the amount of data. The Porter stemmer (Porter, 1980) is a well-known algorithm destined for this task.

Feature Extraction

The features' extraction is the process of extracting the main characteristics of the considered text. For a machine learning algorithm to perform well, it is essential to have features that are descriptive of the text. In our context, we need to be able to identify the words that express sentiment. Previous researches experimented with different features in the sentiment analysis and compare which features worked well and gave the best performance of the classification. The following features are discussed: the text representation, the n-gram and the part of speech tagging.

Text Representation

A text cannot be directly interpreted by a classifier. Hence, a representation process is necessary to map the text into a compact representation to provide to the machine learning algorithms. Each document is typically represented by a feature vector.

The two main approaches of document representation are the Bag of Words Model (BOW) (Sebastiani, 2002) and the Vector Space Model (VSM) (Salton et al., 1975).

In the BOW model, the text is represented by a feature vector containing all the words appearing in it (Table 5). Thus, the dimension of the feature space is equal to the number of different words in all the text. Each word is associated to a giving weight. There is a multitude of methods to calculate the weights, such as the frequency. The simplest is the binary in which the feature weight is either one, if the corresponding word is present in the text, or zero otherwise. In this work, we adopted the binary one to assign weights to our posted statuses.

Despite the simplicity and efficiency of the BOW method in text classification, a great deal of the information from the original text is useless; word order is neglected, and the syntactic structures are broken. Hence, using other feature extraction methods for sentiment classification tasks is required; such as part of speech tagger, higher order n-grams, etc.

In the vector space model, documents are represented as a vector where each component is associated with a particular word in the text collection vocabulary. Generally, each vector component is assigned a weight such as frequency, binary measure, etc. More complex weighting schemes are possible that take into account the frequencies of the word in the document, in the category, and in the whole collection.

Table 5. Example of the BOW model

Input	Bag of word model
Stop saying Ok, it looks like you don't care.	Ok Saying Like You It Stop Care Don't Looks

Vector space model is now recognized as the best document representation model. Its basic idea is to consider the document as a vector in which feature term weight is present as a component. The most popular weighting schema is term frequency inverse document frequency of tfidf (Sebastiani, 2002):

$$tfidf\left(w\right) = TermFreq\left(w,d\right) * \log\left(\frac{N}{df\left(w\right)}\right)$$

Where:

- tf(w) is the term frequency or the number of word occurrences in a document.
- df(w) is the document frequency or the number of documents containing the word.
- N is the number of all documents.
- tfidf(w) is the relative importance of the word in the document.

The tfidf measure is composed of the term frequency and the inverse of the document frequency. The inverse document frequency is used to measure the rareness of a word across all the documents. When the value of the inverse document frequency is high, the word across the set of documents is rare.

However, Pang et al. (2002) obtained better performance using presence rather than frequency. A binary-valued feature vectors in which the entries merely indicate whether a term is present (value 1) or not (value 0) formed a more effective basis for review polarity classification than did real-valued feature vectors in which entry values increase with the occurrence frequency of the corresponding term. We chose the presence representation because it yielded a higher accuracy representation than the standard frequency feature representation in previous related research.

N-Gram

One of the main steps of feature extraction is the application of the n-gram model (Carpenter, 2005). The n-gram is a contiguous sequence of n words (Table 6). The n-gram model consists of extracting a bag-of words representation of the text's field. Each feature corresponds to an n word, with the value of true if that feature is present and false otherwise. In this work, we explore the usage of unigrams, bigrams, trigrams, unigrams and bigrams and parts of speech as features.

Table 6. Example of the N-gram model

Input	Output
I have tears in my eyes	**Unigrams:** I / have / tears / in / my / eyes **Bigrams:** I have / have tears / tears in / in my / my eyes **Trigrams:** I have tears / have tears in / tears in my / in my eyes

A unigram is a single word, and a bigram is a pair of words that appear next to one another, etc. Unigrams are the most typical type of text feature; however bigrams and trigrams may carry more information. In this work, we extracted those features in order to evaluate their effectiveness in the context of sentiment analysis.

Go et al. (2009) achieved better results with the combination of unigrams and bigrams than just unigrams or just bigrams respectively. However, Pak and Paroubek (2010) achieved better accuracies with the unigrams than with the bigrams.

Part-Of-Speech Tagging

Part-of-speech is similar to the word bigrams discussed above except that instead of pairs of words, they are pairs of grammatical categories. The part of speech tagging consists on marking up a word in a text to a particular part of speech based on its context and its definition. We use part of speech as feature because the same word may have many different meanings depending on its usage. For instance, "like" as a verb may have a positive connotation. "Like" may also be used as a preposition to cite an example, this does not carry a positive or negative connotation. In English, we have 9 parts of speech: Noun, verb, article, adjective, preposition, pronoun, adverb, conjunction and interjection.

Creating Training Model for Text Polarity

The classification process is learning a function that maps or classifies a data item into one of the several predefined classes (Weiss et al., 1991). Every classification task consists splitting the dataset into three sets:

- A Training set: Supervised learning algorithms usually require hand-labeled training data with a classes (for example, Positive or Negative). The training set is used to train the data and generate the classification model. Therefore, the training dataset should be rich and varied, providing the algorithm with a healthy cross section of the types of texts records for which classification may be needed in the future and more specifically in the testing process.
- A testing set: The testing set is an unlabeled dataset. It is used to measure the performance of the generated classification model.
- A validation set: Proper procedure uses three sets which are the training, validation and testing sets. The validation set is used to tune the model and minimize the classification error on the test dataset. It is not used to test the data; however it is some portion of the training set that is not used for creating the model.

As for what percentage of the data should be used for training and what percentage for testing, it depends on the data set size. Typically 60% to 90% of instances are used for training and the remainder for testing. The more data there is the more that can be used for training and still get statistically significant test predictions. In our context, we split our preprocessed data into two sets: 60% of our preprocessed data is used for the training set and 40% for the testing set. We labeled our training set with part of speech if the status expresses a positive sentiment or NEG otherwise. Then, the task is to generate a classification model that is able to assign the correct class to a new status update. To measure the performance of the classification model, we classify the testing set with the training model and compare the classified results, consisting of predicted labels by the model, with the associated true labels.

Classification Using Machine Learning Methods

Our aim is to gauge the effectiveness of well-known sentiment classification algorithms on our novel corpus of Facebook statuses. We focus on two different machine learning techniques: Naïve Bayes and Support Vector Machine to determine their applicability in our context and compare their accuracies.

Naïve Bayes

A Naïve Bayes classifier (Mitchell, 1997) is a probabilistic classifier based on probability models that incorporate strong independence assumptions among the extracted features. It models the distribution of the documents in each class using a probabilistic model with independence assumptions about the distributions of different terms. Two classes of models are commonly used for Naive Bayes classification. Both models essentially compute the posterior probability of a class, based on the distribution of the words in the document (Aggarwal et al., 2012). The two classes of models are described in the following:

- Multivariate Bernoulli Model: In this model, the presence or absence of words in a text document is used as features to represent a document. Thus, the frequencies of the words are not used for the modeling of a document, and the word features in the text are assumed to be binary, with the two values indicating presence or absence of a word in text. Since the features to be modeled are binary, the model for documents in each class is qualified as Multivariate Bernoulli Model.
- Multinomial Model: In this model, the frequencies of terms in a document are captured by representing a document with a bag of words. The documents in each class can then be modeled as samples drawn from a multinomial word distribution. As a result, the conditional probability of a document given a class is simply a product of the probability of each observed word in the corresponding class.

As we mentioned before, we choose to represent our text based on the presence representation. Therefore, in our classification process, we chose to use the Multivariate Bernoulli Model.

Given a collection of N statuses, where each status is represented as a vector $t = (x_1, x_2 \ldots x_{|v|})$ of words and where |v| is the vocabulary which represents the number of distinct words in training set. Note that, x_i is equal to 1 for the presence of the word w_i; xi is equal to 0 otherwise. Since we choose to use the multivariate Bernoulli model, we focus on the presence or the absence of a word in the status t. We derive the Naïve Bayes classifier by first observing that by Bayes' rule. The probability of a status t occurring in class C_i is given as:

$$P\left(C_i|t\right) = \frac{P\left(C_i\right)P\left(t|C_i\right)}{P\left(t\right)}$$

Our Naïve Bayes classifier assigns a given statuses t to the most likely class c*. This prediction is called a Maximum A Posteriori (MAP) class. The probability P(t) is the prior probability of a document occurring in class C_i and it plays no role in assigning c* because it is constant for all categories. Therefore, it can be dropped. The probability P(c|t) represents the posterior probability of C_i.

$$c* = Argmax_c P\left(c|t\right) = Argmax_c P\left(t|c\right)P\left(c\right), c \in \left\{POS, NEG\right\}$$

The model parameters includes P(w_i|c), which is the conditional probability of a word w_i occurring in a status t of class C and it is estimated from the training set, class prior probability P(c_i), and assuming an independence of the words, and thus {P(w_i = 1|C) ; P(w_i = 0|C)}, P(w_i = 1|C) + P(w_i = 0|C) = 1, and

$$P\left(t = \left(x_1, \ldots, x_{|v|}\right)|C\right) = \prod_{i=1}^{|v|} P(w_i = x|C) = \prod_{i=1; x=1}^{|v|} P(w_i = 1|C) * \prod_{i=1; x=0}^{|v|} P(w_i = 0|C)$$

If we only need a decision on the most probable class for a new status (or test set) t = ($x_1 \ldots x_{|v|}$); x = {0, 1}, we compute, using the following formula, to decide the most probable class for the test case:

$$c* = Argmax_c P\left(c|t\right) = Argmax_c P\left(t|c\right)P\left(c\right) =$$

$$Argmax \prod_{i=1}^{|v|} P(w_i = x|C) = Argmax Log P\left(c\right) + \sum_{i=1}^{|v|} Log P(w_i = x|C)$$

Therefore, we choose to use a Naïve Bayes classifier because of its simplicity and its performance in previous studies (Pang et al., 2002; Durant & Smith, 2006) on our chosen feature set representation.

Support Vector Machine

Support Vector Machine classification (Joachims, 1998) method is a very effective way for classification, and its results are better than other classification algorithms in general such Naïve Bayes and decision trees, etc. The aim of the Support Vector Machine classifier is to identify a hyper plane that separates two classes of data. The chosen hyper plane creates the largest margin between the two classes to make the points belonging to different classes and also to make those points away from the hyper plane as far as possible. Therefore, the Support Vector Machine algorithm seeks to maximize the distance to the closest training point from either class in order to achieve better classification performance on the test set. In other word, using Support Vector Machine classification method is equivalent to solving a constrained optimization problem.

A binary setting of the classification problem can be described as follows. Given a set of training data $\{x_1, x_2 . . . x_i\}$ and their labels $\{y_1, y_2, . . ., y_i\}$, where $y_i \in \{-1, 1\}$, the goal is to estimate a prediction function f such that it can be able to classify an unlabeled status.

As mentioned above, Support Vector Machines are hyper planes that separate the training data by a maximal margin. All vectors lying on one side of the hyper plane are labeled as -1, and all vectors lying on the other side are labeled as 1. The training instances that lie closest to the hyper plane are called support vectors. The Support Vector Machine learning algorithm aims to find a linear function of the form:

$$f(x) = w * x_i + b$$

Such that data point x is assigned to a label $+1$ if f(x) > 0, and a label -1 otherwise. Then, the linear Support Vector Machine classifier can be obtained by solving the following optimization problem:

$$\begin{cases} \min \frac{1}{2}\|w\|^2 \\ \forall i\, y_i \left(w * x_i + b\right) \geq 1 \end{cases}$$

Where the margin between the support vectors is $\frac{2}{\|w\|}$.

We choose Support Vector Machine as the classifier because of its often reported best performance and its adoption by many previous text classification studies (Pang et al., 2002; Durant & Smith, 2006; Zheng et al., 2006; Go et al., 2009). In the next section, we are going to follow the steps of our methodology as described above, discuss the classification process using machine learning algorithms and compare their results.

EXPERIMENTS AND DISCUSSION

This section presents the experimental evaluation of our methodology. First, the data of our experiments is collected and analyzed and the manual method of classifying the positive and the negative is explained. Then the experiments using the Support Vector Machine and the Naïve Bayes classifiers are exposed. Finally, the results of each classifier are discussed and then compared using the performance measures.

Facebook Statuses Updates

To build our lexicon, we choose a random population from Facebook users. This population contains Tunisian males and females having different ages and different occupations. This step consists of extracting statuses updates of each user during the Tunisian revolution happening from January 1st, 2011 to June 1st, 2011. As explained in section 3, we used "I Told You" application to extract Facebook statuses updates turning around approximately 260 statuses.

The used supervised learning algorithms require the training data to be already classified into positive and negative. This classification must be manually labeled and before the sentiment analysis is performed. Therefore, we randomly annotate 157 statuses of 260. The output of this step is a labeled training set with part of speech if the status expresses a positive sentiment or with NEG if it expresses a negative one. The objective statuses are eliminated from our data set.

Experimental Setting

Our experiments are divided into two phases which are the training and the classification phases.

The training phase consists on the building a training model. Based on this model, unlabeled statuses updates are classified in the classification phase. The preprocessing step eliminates the stop words and other unnecessary characters. The stemming process is performed as well. After that, a part of speech for each word from the training set is tagged. In the feature extraction step, the n-gram pattern made up of n word, as explained in section 3, is extracted. We extracted 7 n-gram patterns:

- A unigram pattern which is made up of one word for extracting a sentimental pattern.
- A bigram pattern which is made up of two words.
- A trigram pattern which is made up of three words.
- A unigram + bigram pattern which is a combination of a unigram and bigram pattern.
- A unigram + trigram pattern which is a combination of a unigram and trigram pattern.
- A unigram + bigram + trigram pattern which is a combination of a unigram, a bigram and trigram pattern.

Once we have extracted the features in the training step, a training model is generated according to each algorithm. For the Naïve Bayes algorithm, a model is built by calculating the probability value based on the frequency of the extracted pattern. And for the Support Vector Machine algorithm, a model is built for finding the optimal hyper plane in order to divide the two classes.

We have experimented with unigrams, bigrams, and trigrams. Pang et al. (Pang et al., 2002) found out that unigrams outperform bigrams when performing the sentiment classification of movie reviews, and Dave et al. (Dave et al., 2003) have obtained contrary results stating that bigrams and trigrams worked better for the product-review polarity classification. We tried to determine the best settings for our Facebook's statuses updates. Our set of experiments compares the two machine learning techniques by making different combinations of the extracted features.

To perform our experiments, we use the WEKA machine learning toolkit, version 3.6.8. We use the Naïve Bayes' implementation and we choose Naïve Bayes' Multivariate Bernoulli Model. For the Support Vector Machine, we use the Sequential Minimal Optimization (SMO) kernel implementation. SMO breaks the large quadratic optimization problem into smallest quadratic optimization problems which can be solved analytically (Pang et al., 2002).

For the validation, we choose to use the validation technique that was used for all classifiers stratified 10-fold cross validation. In stratified 10-fold cross validation, the training set is randomly divided into 10 sets with approximately equal size with additional constraint that the fold distribution are similar to the original distribution of the classes. For each fold, the classification process is applied 10 times with one of the folds as test and the remaining (10 - 1= 9) folds as training set. This procedure is repeated for each of the 10 groups. The cross-validation score is the average performance across each of the 10 training runs (Durant & Smith, 2006).

Performance Measures

To evaluate the performance of the performed sentiment classification, we use the standard classification performance metrics used in previous information retrieval and text classification studies: accuracy, precision, recall, and F-measure.

Accuracy

The accuracy is the most intuitive measure. It represents the overall correctness of the model and it is calculated, as follows, by dividing the sum of correct classifications by the total number of classifications:
   Where:

- a is the number of statuses updates correctly assigned to this class.
- b is the number of statuses updates incorrectly assigned to this class.
- c is the number of statuses updates incorrectly rejected to this class.
- d is the number of statuses updates correctly rejected to this class.

Precision

The precision measures the exactness of a classifier by calculating, as follows, the accuracy of a specific class that has been predicted:

$$Precision = \frac{a}{a+b}$$

Recall

The recall is commonly called sensitivity and it is a measure of the ability of a prediction model to select instances of a certain class from a data set. It represents the number of correct classifications penalized by the number of missed items:

$$Recall = \frac{a}{a+c}$$

F-measure

The F- measure is a derived effectiveness measurement. It is a weighted average of the precision and recall. The best value is 1 and the worst is 0. It is calculated as follows:

Table 7. Classifier accuracy

Features	# of features	Accuracy (%)	
		Naïve Bayes	**Support Vector Machine**
Unigrams	610	72.15	**74.68**
Unigrams + Bigrams	1629	**74.05**	**75.31**
Unigrams + Trigrams	1655	71.33	71.97
Unigrams + Bigrams + Trigrams	2688	72.61	71.97

$$F - measure = \frac{2 * Precision * Recall}{Precision + Recall}$$

Results and Discussions

We compared the performances of different feature sets using Naïve Bayes and Support Vector Machine classifiers. We choose 60% of our dataset as training data and the remaining 40% as testing data. We used 10-fold cross validation to conduct the evaluation. Table 7 summarizes the accuracy for all seven feature sets. We highlighted in bold font the best accuracies.

Compared to unigram features, when we use unigrams and bigrams as features, the accuracy is improved for Naïve Bayes (from 72.15% to 74.05%); there was, also, an increase of accuracy as regards to Support Vector Machine (from 74.68% to 75.31%). Note that, for Pang et al. (2002), there was a decline for both Naïve Bayes and Support Vector Machine methods.

When, we used unigrams and trigrams as features, and compared to unigrams and bigrams, there was a decrease of the accuracy for Naïve Bayes (from 74.05% to 71.33%) and Support Vector Machine (from 75.31% to 71.97%).

Moreover, when we compare the unigrams features to the combination of the three n-gram as features, there is a slight improvement for Naïve Bayes' accuracy (from 72.15% to 72.61%), but a decrease of Support Vector Machine's accuracy (from 74.68% to 71.97%).

The two classifiers reached their highest accuracies when a combination of unigrams and bigrams is used as features. However the lowest accuracies were reached when we use a combination of unigrams and trigrams. Therefore, using the combination n-gram (unigram + bigram) as a feature tends to be the best in terms of accuracy for Naïve Bayes and Support Vector Machine.

In addition to, we found out that the Support Vector Machine's algorithm outperformed the Naïve Bayes one in all cases. This confirms the previous published researches in (Pang et al., 2002; Go et al., 2009). The Support Vector Machine method reached its highest accuracy (75.31%) in the case of using the combination of unigrams and bigrams as features.

In table 8, we zoomed into the performance of Naïve Bayes and Support Vector Machine in the case of using the combination of unigrams and bigrams as features by calculating the precision, the recall and the F-measure.

Using Naïve Bayes, a Facebook status update that has a positive sentiment is correctly identified as such with 74.1% of recall. However, for Support Vector Machine, the recall is less than the Naïve Bayes's

Table 8. Results for Unigrams + Bigrams using Naïve Bayes and Support Vector Machine

	Naïve Bayes			Support Vector Machine		
Sentiment	**Precision (%)**	**Recall (%)**	**F-measure (%)**	**Precision (%)**	**Recall (%)**	**F-measure (%)**
Positive	75	74.1	75	89.2	71.2	89.2
Negative	73.1	74	73.1	60	83.3	60

one, which means that a Facebook status update having a positive sentiment is correctly identified as such with 71.2% of recall.

For Support Vector Machine, a Facebook status update given a positive classification is 89.2% likely to be correct. But a Facebook status given a negative classification is only 60% likely to be correct.

Although, the accuracy of Support Vector Machine seems good (75.31%), the precision and recall indicate that the numbers are confusing. This is clearly visible in the F-measure rates (89.2% for Positive and 60% for Negative). One possible explanation for these results is that the model in this case study was built with many more positive statuses than negative ones, and the test data contains mostly positive statuses. Therefore, we can conclude that most of the published statuses on Facebook during the revolution have a positive sentiment. This would be surprising due to the rough conditions that the users have been enduring.

FUTURE RESEARCH DIRECTIONS

During our research, some limitations were observed. First, the most frequent language used by Tunisian Facebook users is Tunisian Arabic. Therefore, we think that it is necessary to focus mostly on just this language to perform more significant analysis. In this work, we opted for the translation of our data into English, in order to be in phase with available tools. Classifying directly Arabic statuses would be very interesting to deal with in future work. Second, the demographic data are neglected; Additional user information, such as age, gender, racial group, region, education, etc., might be very useful and can even improve the evaluation of the classifiers' output.

Finally, the overall performance of the proposed methodology is satisfactory, however, we would like to further improve our research by tracking changes within people's sentiment on a particular topic, explore the time dependency of our data and analyze their trendy topics dynamically. It would be very interesting to involve the temporal feature on this kind of analysis and not to focus solely on previous posts or discussions. In other word, we should take advantages of the dynamics of status updates streams. Thus, we can apply stream classification algorithms such as Naïve Bays, Ensemble (Wang et al., 2003), etc. and compare their effectiveness in streaming texts.

Taking into account the evolution and history aspects related to status updates is also considered as a future challenge. We think that historizing data and results in a trajectory data warehouse will be a good solution to overcome this challenge. In fact, it will permit more deep spatio-temporal analysis and/or mining.

CONCLUSION

In this work, we have investigated the utility of sentiment classification on a novel collection of dataset which is Tunisian Facebook users. The originality of this collection in inherent in not only on the nationality of the users, but also on the period of posting their statuses updates which is related to the Tunisian revolution. This period was very special and unique for them, therefore their wall posts are with no doubt unique and encouraging to analyze.

Using the most well-known machine learning algorithms, we conducted a comparative experimental procedure between the Naïve Bayes and the Support Vector Machine algorithms by combining different extracted features. Those algorithms can achieve high accuracy for classifying sentiment when combining different features. Although Facebook statuses have unique characteristics compared to other corpuses such as reviews, news, etc.); machine learning algorithms are shown to classify statuses with similar performance. Moreover, we have confirmed previous works findings to be correct in their conclusion that using a combination of unigrams and bigrams as feature give better results that unigrams or trigrams

REFERENCES

Aggarwal, C. C., & Cheng, X. Z. (2012). *Mining Text Data*. New York, USA: Springer. doi:10.1007/978-1-4614-3223-4

Albee, A. (2010). eMarketing Strategies for the Complex Sale Marketing Interactions. New York, USA: Mv Graw Hill.

Binali, H., Wu, C., & Potdar, V. (2010). Computational approaches for emotion detection in text. In *Proceeding of the 4th IEEE International Conference of Digital Ecosystems and Technologies (DEST)*. Dubai, United Arab Emirates. doi:10.1109/DEST.2010.5610650

Bozkir, A. S., Mazman, S. G., & Sezer, E. A. (2011). Identification of User Patterns in Social Networks by Data Mining Techniques: Facebook Case. In *Proceedings of the Technological Convergence and Social Networks in Information Management Conference (IMCW) 2010*. Ankara, Turkey.

Carpenter, B. (2005). Scaling high-order character language models to gigabytes. In *Proceedings of the association for computational linguistics software workshop*. Ann Arbor, Michigan, USA. doi:10.3115/1626315.1626322

Coussement, K., & Poel, D. V. (2008). Integrating the voice of customers through call center emails into a decision support system for churn prediction. *Journal of International Management, 45*(3), 164–174.

Dave, K., Lawrence, E., & Pennock, D. M. (2003). Mining the peanut gallery: opinion extraction and semantic classification of product reviews. In *Proceedings of the 12th international conference on World Wide Web*. New York, USA. doi:10.1145/775152.775226

Denecke, K. (2008). Using SentiWordNet for Multilingual Sentiment Analysis. In *Proceeding of the IEEE 24th International Conference Data Eng. Workshop (ICDEW 2008)*. Cancun, Mexico: IEEE Press. doi:10.1109/ICDEW.2008.4498370

Devitt, A., & Ahmad, K. (2007). Sentiment Polarity Identification in Financial News: A cohesion-based Approach. In *Proceeding of the 45th Ann. Meeting Assoc. Computational Linguistics*. Prague, Czech Republic: ACL Press.

Doms, A., & Schroeder, M. (2005). *GoPubMed: exploring PubMed with the Gene Ontology*. Retrieved from http://nar.oxfordjournals.org/content/33/suppl_2/W783.long

Durant, K. T., & Smith, M. D. (2006). Mining Sentiment Classification from Political Web Logs. In Proceedings of Knowledge Discovery on the Web (WEBKDD'06). Philadelphia, Pennsylvania.

Esuli, A., & Sebastiani, F. (2005). Determining the semantic orientation of terms through gloss analysis. In *Proceedings of the 14th ACM International Conference on Information and Knowledge Management (CIKM'05)*. Bremen, Germany.

Esuli, A., & Sebastiani, F. (2006a). Determining term subjectivity and term orientation for opinion mining. In *Proceedings of the 11rd Conference of the European Chapter of the Association for Computational Linguistics (EACL'06)*. Trento, Italy.

Esuli, A., & Sebastiani, F. (2006b). SentiWordNet: A publicly available lexical resource for opinion mining. In *Proceedings of the 5th International Conference on Language Resources and Evaluation*. Genoa, Italy.

Fayyad, U., Piatetsky-Shapiro, G., & Smyth, P. (Eds.). (1996). *Advances in Knowledge Discovery and Data Mining*. Cambridge, USA: MIT Press.

Feldman, R., & Sanger, J. (2007). *The Text Mining Handbook: Advanced Approaches in Analyzing Unstructured Data*. New York, USA: Cambridge University Press.

Fellbaum, C. (Ed.). (1998). *Wordnet: An Electronic Lexical Database*. Cambridge, MA: MIT Press.

Go, A., Huang, L., & Bhayani, R. (2009). Twitter sentiment classification using distant supervision. In CS224N Project Report, Stanford, USA.

Godbole, N., Srinivasaiah, M., & Skiena, S. (Eds.). (2007). *Large-scale sentiment analysis for news and blogs*. International conference on weblogs and social media (ICWSM'2007). Boulder, Colorado, USA.

Hand, D., Mannila, H., & Smyth, P. (2001). *Principles of Data Mining*. Cambridge, MA, USA: MIT Press.

Hang, C., Vibhu, M., & Mayur, D. (2006). Comparative Experiments on Sentiment Classification for Online Product Reviews. In *Proceeding of the 21st national conference on Artificial intelligence (AAAI'06)*. AAAI Press.

Holzner, S. (2009). *Facebook Marketing: Leverage Social Media to Grow Your Business*. Indianapolis, Illinois, USA: Que Publishing.

Hurst, M., & Nigam, K. (2004). Retrieving topical sentiments from online document collections. In *Document Recognition and Retrieval XI Conference*.

Ismail, L., Chang, E., & Karduck, A. P. (2010). In *Proceedings of the IEEE international conference on digital ecosystems and technologies (DEST 2010)*. Dubai, United Arab Emirates: IEEE Press.

Joachims, T. (1998). Text categorization with support vector machines: Learning with many relevant features. In *Proceedings of the Tenth European Conference on Machine Learning*. Berlin, Germany: Springer. doi:10.1007/BFb0026683

Kang, H., Yoo, S. J., & Han, D. (2012). Senti-lexicon and improved Naive Bayes algorithms for sentiment analysis of restaurant reviews. *Expert Systems with Applications*, 39(5), 6000–6010. doi:10.1016/j.eswa.2011.11.107

Kim, S. M., & Hovy, E. (2006). Identifying and analyzing judgment opinions. In *Proceedings of the Joint Human Language Technology/North American Chapter of the ACL Conference (HLT-NAACL)*. Stroudsburg, PA, USA: ACL. doi:10.3115/1220835.1220861

Kleinberg, J. (2000). The small-world phenomenon: An algorithmic perspective. In *Proceedings of the 32nd ACM Symposium on Theory of Computing*. Portland, OR, USA: ACM.

Leong, C. K., Lee, H. Y., & Mak, W. K. (2012). Mining sentiments in SMS texts for teaching evaluation. [Elsevier.]. *Expert Systems with Applications*, 39(3), 2584–2589. doi:10.1016/j.eswa.2011.08.113

Liu, B. (2010). Sentiment Analysis and Subjectivity. In N. Indurkhya & F. J. Damerau (Eds.), *Handbook of Natural Language* (2nd Ed.). Dublin, Ireland: CRC Press.

Liu, B., & Hu, M. (2004). Mining and Summarizing Customer Reviews. In *Proceeding of ACM SIGKDD International Conference on Knowledge Discovery and Data Mining*. New York: ACM Press.

Manning, C. D., & Schütze, H. (1999). *Foundations of Statistical Natural Language Processing*. Cambridge, MA, USA: MIT Press.

Mitchell, T. (1997). *Machine Learning*. Cambridge, MA, USA: McGraw Hill.

Pak, A., & Paroubek, P. (2010). Twitter as a corpus for sentiment analysis and opinion mining. In *Proceedings of Seventh International Conference on Language Resources and Evaluation (LREC)*. Valletta, Malta.

Pang, B., & Lee, L. (2004). A Sentimental Education: Sentiment Analysis using Subjectivity Summarization based on Minimum Cuts. In *Proceedings of the 42nd Meeting of the association for Computational Linguistics (ACL'04)*. Barcelona, Spain. doi:10.3115/1218955.1218990

Pang, B., & Lee, L. (2008). Opinion Mining and sentiment analysis. In D. W. Oard & M. Sanderson (Eds.), *Foundations and Trends in Information Retrieval*. doi:10.1561/1500000011

Pang, B., Lee, L., & Vaithyanathan, S. (2002). Thumbs up? Sentiment classification using machine learning techniques. In *Proceeding of the International conference on empirical methods in natural language*. Philadelphia, USA: Association for Computational Linguistics.

Pempek, T. A., Yermolayeva, Y. A., & Calvert, S. L. (2009). College students' social networking experiences on Facebook. *Journal of Applied Developmental Psychology*, 30(3), 227–238. doi:10.1016/j.appdev.2008.12.010

Popescu, A. M., & Etzioni, O. (2005). Extracting product features and opinion from reviews. In *Proceedings of Human Language Technology Conference and Conference on Empirical Methods in Natural Language Processing*. Vancouver, British Columbia, Canada: Association for Computational Linguistics. doi:10.3115/1220575.1220618

Porter, M. F. (1980). An algorithm for Suffix Stripping. *Program*, *14*(3), 130–137. doi:10.1108/eb046814

Sebastiani, F. (2002). Machine Learning in automated text categorization. *ACM Computing Surveys*, *34*(1), 1–47. doi:10.1145/505282.505283

Shalev-Shwartz, S., Singer, Y., & Ng, A. (2004). Online and batch learning of pseudo-metrics. In *Proceedings of the Twenty-First International Conference on Machine Learning*. Banff, Alberta, Canada. doi:10.1145/1015330.1015376

Staab, S., Domingos, P., Mike, P., Golbeck, J., Li, D., & Finin, T. et al. (2005). Social Networks Applied. *IEEE Intelligent Systems*, *20*(1), 80–93. doi:10.1109/MIS.2005.16

Thelwall, M., Wilkinson, D., & Uppal, S. (2010). Data mining emotion in social network communication: Gender differences in MySpace. *Journal of the American Society for Information Science and Technology*, *61*(1), 190–199. doi:10.1002/asi.21180

Turney, P. D. (2002). Thumbs up or thumbs down? Semantic orientation applied to unsupervised classification of reviews. In *Proceedings of the 40th annual meeting on association for computational linguistics*. Philadelphia, Pennsylvania.

Wang, W., Fan, P., Yu, S., & Han, J. (2003). Mining concept-drifting data streams using ensemble classifiers. In *Proceedings of the Ninth ACM SIGKDD International Conference on Knowledge. Discovery and Data Mining*. New York, USA: ACM Press. doi:10.1145/956750.956778

Weiss, S. I., & Kulikowski, C. (1991). *Computer Systems That Learn: Classification and Prediction Methods from Statistics*. San Francisco, California, USA: Neural Networks, Machine Learning, and Expert Systems.

Wilson, T., Wiebe, J., & Hwa, R. (2004). Just how mad are you? Finding strong and weak opinion clauses. In *Proceedings of the 21st Conference of the American Association for Artificial Intelligence (AAAI'04)*. San Jose, USA.

Yu, H., & Hatzivassiloglou, V. (2003). Towards answering opinion questions: Separating facts from opinions and identifying the polarity of opinion sentences. In *Proceedings of the Conference on Empirical Methods in Natural Language Processing (EMNLP)*. doi:10.3115/1119355.1119372

Yuasa, M., Saito, K., & Mukawa, N. (2006). Emoticons convey emotions without cognition of faces: an FMRI study. In *Proceeding of Extended Abstracts on Human Factors in Computing Systems (CHI EA '06)*. ACM. doi:10.1145/1125451.1125737

Zhang, X., & Zhu, F. (2006). The influence of Online consumer reviews on the demand for experience goods: The case of video games. In *Proceedings of the 27th international conference on information systems (ICIS)*, Milwaukee, USA: AISPress.

Zhao, S., Grasmuck, S., & Martin, J. (2008). Identity construction on Facebook: Digital empowerment in anchored relationships. *Computers in Human Behavior*, *24*(5), 1816–1836. doi:10.1016/j.chb.2008.02.012

Zheng, R., Li, J., Chen, H., & Huang, Z. (2006). A Framework for Authorship Identification of Online Messages: Writing-Style Features and Classification Techniques. *Journal of the American Society for Information Science and Technology*, *57*(3), 378–393. doi:10.1002/asi.20316

KEY TERMS AND DEFINITIONS

Classification: Could refer to categorization which is the method in which concepts and objects are accepted, distinguished, and assumed.

Features: In machine learning, a feature is a separate quantifiable heuristic property of a phenomenon being observed.

Lexicon: In linguistics, a lexicon is a language's catalog of lexemes.

Machine Learning: Machine learning is the creation and study of algorithms that can learn from data. Such algorithms work by constructing a model based on inputs which is used to make predictions or decisions.

Naïve Bayes: In machine learning, Naïve Bayes algorithms are a set of simple probabilistic classifiers based on Bayes' theorem with strong or naive independence assumptions between the features.

Sentiment Analysis: In written texts, sentiment analysis determines the decision or estimation, sentimental state, or the envisioned emotional communication of a writer with respect to some subject or the general background polarity of a document.

Support Vector Machine: In machine learning, support vector machines are supervised learning representations with related learning algorithms which analyze data and identify patterns, employed for classification and regression analysis.

Text Mining: Text mining is the practice of arising first-class information from texts. First-class information is characteristically resulting from concocting patterns and tendencies thanks to various computing.

Chapter 2
Model of the Empirical Distribution Law for Syntactic and Link Words in "Perfect" Texts

Pavel Makagonov
Russian Presidential Academy of National Economy and Public Administration, Russia

ABSTRACT

The measure of perfection of the contents and semantic value of an integrated text is connected with the indicators of perfection in the distribution of content words. This criterion is the coordination of their "frequency-rank" distribution with the Zipf or Zipf-Mandelbrot law. In this chapter the hypothesis verified is that a perfect system should have not only perfect distribution of its elements - objects, but also perfect connections between them. A model is suggested in which the degree of the text perfection from the point of view of the quality of connections between significative words is determined by the quality of distribution of syntactic and link words in the "rank - frequency" representation. As a simplified criterion the ratio of the significant and syntactic words used in the analyzed text and the degree of the closeness of this ratio to the "golden section" is considered.

INTRODUCTION

In this study we shall consider an integrated text, a complete document or a work of art as a system the degree of perfection of which is estimated by the end user (reader, consumer of the information contained in the document). Treating a text as a semantic structure raises the problem of the text content segmentation, with various units suggested to isolate the quantum of the text information. As shown in a number of studies, there is a hierarchy of semantic addend found in the text, the latter "exists as a hierarchical unity breaking down into more and more fractional components" (Babenko and Kazarin, 2004). In this aspect, it is possible to consider not only the semantic importance of significant words, but also the influence of syntactic words on the meaning and content of the text. A model is suggested

DOI: 10.4018/978-1-4666-8690-8.ch002

in which the degree of the text perfection from the point of view of the quality of connections between significative words is determined by the quality of distribution of syntactic and link words in the "rank - frequency" representation. The hypothesis verified is that a perfect integrated text should have not only perfect frequencies distribution of significative words, but also perfect connections between them.

There is a common opinion that in mathematical text models the semantically significant part of the text – content words have an unlimited tendency to enrichment and development, and the set of syntactic words is conservative. That is why it is important as well to study ratio of content significative) and syntactic words in "perfect" texts.

GOLDEN SECTION IN THE RATIO OF CONTENT AND SYNTACTIC WORDS IN "PERFECT" TEXTS

Let's analyze now several integrated complete texts recognized "ideal" in the world literature. These are internationally acclaimed written masterpieces, oral folklore products written down, for example, fairy tales.

Basically, here there can also be collections of scientific texts on narrow subjects, exhaustively reflecting the subject of study.

Thirteen most well-known and popular texts which can be regarded as "systems close to perfection" have been analyzed:

- Homestead Act of 1862 (U.S. Congress, 1862).
- Carroll, L. (1991). Alice's adventures in wonderland. The millennium fulcrum edition. Duncan Research.
- Кэрролл, Л. Приключения Алисы в стране чудес (Russian text Carroll, L. Alice's adventures in wonderland, in translation N. M. Demurova, 1991).
- Carroll, L. Alicia en el país de las maravillas (Caroll, 2003).
- The Valiant Little Tailor – a fairytale (Grimm & Grimm, n.d.).
- Храбрый портняжка – Russian version of The Valiant Little Tailor Grimms' Fairy Tales (Grimm & Grimm, n.d.).
- El sastrecillo valiente (Siete de un golpe) – a short story (Grimm & Grimm, n.d.).
- Das tapfere Schneiderlein – a fairytale (Grimm & Grimm, n.d.).
- The Three Little Pigs (Steel, n.d.).
- Сказка про трёх поросят (The Three Little Pigs Russian version) (Talebook.com, n.d.).
- Stevenson, R. L. Heather Ale: A Galloway Legend (Stevenson, 2001).
- Вересковый мёд (Heather Ale Russian – a ballad by R. L. Stevenson (Marshak, n.d.).
- Pushkin, A. C. A Tale about a Fisherman and a Fish (Russian text), (Pushkin, 1960).

The collection of texts includes four fairy tales and one ballad in English, Russian, German and Spanish, and additionally one old globally world known legal act. This minimum multilingual corpus was specially formed for detailed comparison and statistical analysis of the text of similar content and, consequently, similar in the semantic content of the texts, the corpus so formed to be used to check the hypotheses concerning the model of distribution of syntactic and link words and their role in the enhancement of the text as a semantic system.

Table 1. Texts containing more than 1800 words and more than 180 words in the SLW frequency list

		Alice's Adventures in Wonderland			Das tapfere Schneiderlein (The Valiant Little Tailor)			
		English version	Spanish version	Russian version	German version	English 1 version	English 2 version	Russian version
Signifi-cative words	Word List	2197	3584	4148	727	559	559	871
	Number of Words Usage "*b*"	9676	10580	8811	b=1262	b= 1213	b= 1156	1205
	%	**38.56**	42.04	45.46	42.42	**38.01%**	36.23%	45.01
Syntactic and link words (SLW)	Word List	279	304	498	229	180	180	280
	Number of Words Usage "*a*"	15415	14584	9531	a=1713	a=1978	a=2035	1472
	%	**61.44**	57.96	54.54	57.58	**61.99**	63.77	54.99
Total quan-tity	Word List	2474	3887	4646	956	739	739	1151
	Number of Words Usage a+b	25091	25164	18342	2975	3191	3191	2677
	%	100%	100%	100%	100%	100%	100%	100%
Golden section for text	c=(a+b)/a	**1.6277**	1.725	1.924	1.7367	**1.6132**	1.5681	1.8186
	d=a/b	**1.5931**	1.378	1.082	1.3574	**1.6307**	1.7601	1.2216
	(c+d)/2	**1.6104**	1.552	1.503	1.54705	**1.62195**	1.6641	1.5201

The percentage ratio of various link words (SLW) and significative words (rows "word list") is considerably changed in favor of significative words with the growth of words quantity (rows "Total"), and the percentage of link words used in the text remains close to 61.8%, which corresponds to the asymptotic value of the ratio of the Fibonacci numbers or the reverse value 100/61.8 =1.618 known as the *golden section* (Dunlap, 1997).

Let's consider the statistics of syntactic and link words (SLW) and significant words in these texts (Tables 1 and 2)

For values ***a*** and ***b*** the golden ratio (or golden section) is

$$\frac{a+b}{a} = \frac{a}{b} \overset{def}{=} \varphi,$$ (1)

Its' value is:

$$\varphi = \frac{1+\sqrt{5}}{2} \approx 1.6180339887...$$ (2)

The golden section can also serve as an indirect criterion of perfection of the text if one precisely follows the understanding what words should be referred to link ones.

Short texts contain fewer than 180 words in the SLW frequency list; therefore, the nature of their distribution in the ideal case practically does not differ from the distribution of significant words. However, as is seen from the analysis of Table 1, with increase of the number of words in the text the number of SLW increases, but reaches the saturation level, and it is for this reason that the ratio of the number

Table 2. Golden Section for Short Texts

		The Three Little Pigs	The Three Little Pigs (Russian version)	Heater Ale	Heater Ale (Russian version)	Fisherman & Fish (Russian original text)
Significa-tive words (SW)	Word list	227	219	165	189	296
	Words usage; "b"	622	387	234	217	582
	%	42.34	50.79	45.44	64.39	62.72
Syntactic and Link Words (SLW	SLW list	110	111	56	52	90
	SLW Usage; "a"	847	375	281	120	346
	%	57.66	49.21	54.56	35.61	37.28
Total Quantity c=(a+b)	Total Words List	337	330	221	241	386
	Total Words Usage;	1469	762	515	337	928
	%	100%	100%	100%	100%	100%
Golden Section for Text	c=(a+b)/a	1.734	2.032	1.833	2.808	2.682
	d=a/b	1.362	0.969	1.201	0.553	0.595
	(c+d)/2	**1.548**	1.500	1.517	1.68	1.638

of SLW and SW (significative words) used for "perfect" texts becomes stabilized. As it will be shown below, these test systems differ from the systems of "ideal" network nodes in which N nodes correspond to about $O(N^2)$ non-oriented arcs.

The number of SLW for one and the same work in different languages can be different because of differences in the grammars of the languages.

For texts with more than 180 elements in the SLW list the "golden section" parameter value can be used for fast preliminary estimate of the text perfection. One can see that this criterion does not work for short texts though they can be contensively "ideal".

However, the golden section ratios for longer texts show that dividing the words of the text into syntactic and significant corresponds to the objective reality of their essentially different role. Therefore, they should be studied separately as different characteristics.

MODELS OF RANK DISTRIBUTIONS OF SYNTACTIC WORDS IN AN INTEGRATED TEXT

Thus, the object of our research is a fixed, integrated text, completed from the point of view of the author, its semantic integrity consisting in the unity of its topic, subject domain, so that we will consider this text further as a system. From this aspect, we can surmise that significant words are the objects of this system constituting the dictionary of the subject domain of the text topic. The semantic value of all elements of a subject-oriented dictionary is fixed in the language, if one does not look for any deep change in the meaning of the word within the limits of a context, and remains, at least, within the whole isolated text subjected to analysis.

Let us mention that within one integrated text there are usually no problems of homonymy and interpreting of the semantic meaning of the word. Thus, in this aspect we can consider that significant words are objects of this system. However, any system is characterized not only by its objects, but also by the connections between them. It is logical to accept that significant words of a textual document are objects, and syntactic words are connections between them. Syntactic words function, first of all, as connections between significant words. Syntactic words have a vague semantic meaning. It is determined first of all from the context of the phrase or paragraph in which the syntactic word is found.

A sign of perfection of a system is usually seen in good coordination of the distribution of any main quantitative characteristic of the system objects with the Zipf distribution (Auerbach F., 1913; Axtell, 2001; Adamic & Huberman, 2002; Gabaix, 1999; Van der Galien, 2003; Hill, 1970; Kali, 2003; Li, 1992; Neumann, 2011; Orlov, 1980; Zipf, 1935; Zipf, 1949).

In case of the Zipf law, the coordination of ranked distribution of the objects with the law is determined through the deviation from the straight line (on a bilogarythm form) of the points of actual distribution of the object characteristics:

$$Y = A - K\,X, \tag{3}$$

Where $Y = \log(F)$; $X = \log(i)$, "i" – rank of a system element at arrangement by the decrease of attribute F; A – numerical constant close to F_1; K – numerical constant close to one.

On the one hand, attribute Fi should be an essential feature of the system objects, and, on the other hand, the objects should clearly differ by this parameter. Mandelbrot suggested a mathematical generalization of this law, stating it in the form of the Zipf-Mandelbrot law, based on the solution of the problem of the information coding "cost" minimization:

$$F = F_1 / (i+B)^K \tag{4}$$

or $Y = A - K{\times}\log(i+B)$ (5),

where a new element in comparison with the previous formula (3) is only constant B.

George K. Zipf himself proposed that neither speakers nor hearers using a given language want to work any harder than necessary to reach understanding, and the process that results in approximately equal distribution of effort leads to the observed Zipf distribution (Zipf, 1935; Zipf, 1949).

The same argument can evidently be applied at forming a model of distribution of syntactic words characteristics:

$$Z = Y^G = -K*X+A \text{ (6),}$$

similar to that obtained for model 1, see formula (11).

Parabola (6) can be also presented as

$Y^G = -K * (X-B)$ (7),

where $B = -A/K$ is the point of intersection of the curve with axis X. This point is poorly traced on a straight line corresponding to the distribution of significant words, but is well visible on the distributions connected with syntactic words.

In similar situations the criterion used in MS Excel is the Coefficient of determination **(R^2)**, also designated as R^2, and defining how well the distribution points correspond to the given line.

In according to our research practice we will apply (and follow) **the preliminary rule of concordance with Zipf law evaluation** or (in case of a linguistic system) with Zipf-Mandelbrot law **or evaluation of "perfectness" of some distribution**:

- The R^2 or **R^2** values in the notation form accepted in MS Excel sufficiently close to one are considered satisfactory if **R^2≥ 0.97**.
- The values close to 0.96 - 0.94 speak about a weak correspondence of the distribution to Zipf law,
- Lower values of about 0.93 – 0.91(or less) testify to a practical non-correspondence of the distribution to Zipf law.

If perfection of the significant words distribution is a sign of perfection of the text content, should not the distribution of the connections between semantically significant words be perfect, too? That is, the hypothesis suggests that a perfect text system (as well as other perfect systems) should have not only a perfect distribution of its objects-elements, but also perfect connections between them.

We have already made attempts to look for approaches to check this hypothesis (Makagonov, 2001; Makagonov, Sanchez, & Sboychakov, 2009; Makagonov & Sanchez, 2004; Makagonov, Reyes, & Sidorov, 2012; Makagonov, Sánchez & Reyes, 2013). However, there the problem was stated somewhat differently and consequently the systems investigated were not close enough to the ideal ones.

Therefore to begin with we chose for the analysis of distribution of significant and syntactic words the above texts that are perfect in public consciousness, with their impact not limited by place or the epoch, their topicality unchanged for many centuries, though at various times being interpreted and perceived differently.

Let us show what models and characteristics can be considered on the example of a system of point masses distributed in integer points of a numerical axis and having an ideal distribution of masses corresponding to the Zipf law.

Characteristics of Connections between the Objects the Weights of Which Are Distributed According to the Zipf Law

Let us consider *model 1* of a system consisting of 81 elements (objects), the weight attributes of which (V) are given by the formulas: $V = 100/N$ or $V = 100 / (82-N)$. This distribution of V is the perfect Zipf distribution: $\log V = \log 100 - \log N$.

Let these elements be arranged along the horizontal axis, and their coordinates "i" will vary sequentially according to the element number and consequently coincide with their numbers N (from 1 to 81).

We assume here that D_m is the distance between the objects (network nodes) with numbers "i" and "j"; m is the index of the distance between the objects with numbers "i" (i=1, 2, … 81) and "j" (81 ≥ j> i); and $m_{max} = \frac{1}{2} N_{max} (N_{max}-1)$.

Figure 1. Distribution (X, Y) of distances between the objects of model 1 (left), and transformation of this distribution U=X^4, W=Y^4 (right) with the straight line approximating it

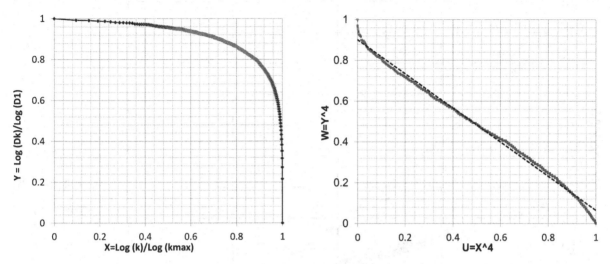

This distribution can be approximated as

$$X^4 + Y^4 = 1 \tag{8}$$

In Figure 1 we accept X=Log (k)/Log (k_{max}); Y = Log (D_k)/Log (D_1). In this notation the distribution of distances between the elements is represented as it is shown in Figure 1 (the left diagram).

Introducing new variables U=X^4, W=Y^4 we obtain a line which is approximated by a straight line (Figure 1, the right diagram).

$$W = -1,0029\ U + 0,9742 \tag{9}$$

at the value of the determination factor criterion R^2 equaling 0,9981.

Power 4 in formula (1) corresponds to the maximum value of the coefficient of determination R^2 which determines reliability of the approximation of distribution (W, U) in under the formula (9)

The coefficient of determination (R^2) also determines the best approximation by the straight line of any other characteristics of the connections between the system objects.

In fig. 2 distribution of the strength of connections between the elements F (i, j) is presented.

The strength of connections is defined by the formula

$$F\ (i, j) = V_i\ V_j / (N_i - N_j)^2 \tag{10}$$

Let us set number m (i, j) as the rank of the connection between elements i and j, in the decreasing order of values F (i, j). Then F_m = F (i, j); and in the designations: X_m =log (m); Y_m = log (F_m); A - numerical coefficient close to log (F_1), we have

$$Z_m = Y^G_m = -K * X_m + A; \tag{11}$$

Figure 2. Distribution of the strength of connections between the elements F (i, j) for model 1

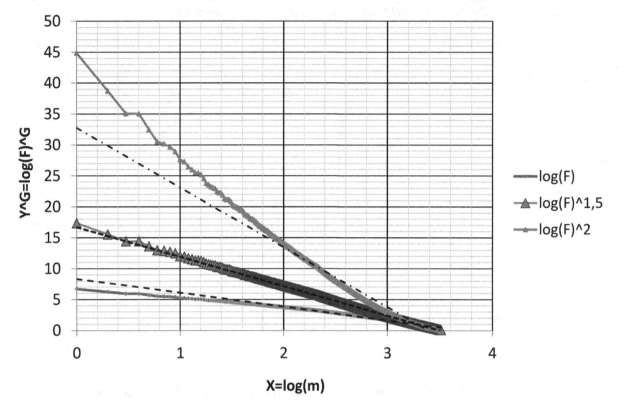

Table 3. Linear (straight line's) approximation

G	Linear (straight line's) approximation	R^2
1	$Y^1 = Z= -2.2354\ X +8.3309$	0.9806
1,5	$Y^{1.5} = Z = -4.7702\ X + 16.706$	0.9981 (max)
2	$Y^2 = Z = -9.6627\ X + 32.791$	0.9629

The best representation of the straight line corresponds to the sesquialteral degree of initial distribution (G=1.5), with the determination factor $R^2=0.9981$. (See also table 3)

Empirical Models of Distribution of Syntactic Words

Let us return to textual documents. If significative words (objects) are characterized by the frequency of occurrence in the system (in the text), syntactic (and links) words can be characterized both by the frequency of occurrence, and by the "strength of the connection" with significant words. We shall calculate the strength of the connection as the sum of all uses of the given syntactic word with the number of the significant words directly connected to the given syntactic word. Some of the syntactic words is so doing have to be considered separately, as the differences in the semantic meaning of the link word demand separate accounting of the syntactic words despite their being written in the same way.

The English word "to" can serve as an example. It is considered in the connection strength distribution twice: as a particle of the infinitive and as a preposition. In Russian these are called grammatical homonyms.

TEXT DOCUMENT AS A SYSTEM OF OBJECTS AND CONNECTIONS BETWEEN THEM

To make it possible to use the further narration as a method to estimate the quality of the document, it is necessary that the researcher should be able to compile a frequency list of the words of the text document. For this purpose we used the DDL program (Makagonov, Reyes, & Sidorov, 2012) which defines the boundaries of words by non-letter (non-alphabetic) symbols. The rules of dividing the text into semantically significant units are not used.

A finished artistic or scientific work presentable in the form of a text document may be considered as a social system. Such a system is usually recognized to be perfect if the common opinion of a representative social group recognizes it as such.

As well as in other cases, this system (the text document) should consist of objects and connections between them. As objects, it is natural to consider all significative words (SW). The frequency list of the system objects – list of significative words can be composed by removing from the general frequency list of the words of the text document those which are not significative (content words). The residual part of the general frequency list should be the frequency list of syntactic and link words (SLW) - links between the system objects. It is possible to conclude that all the words not included in the list of syntactic or link words are significative, and vice versa.

For further study, it is necessary to manually divide the general frequency list of the analyzed text into a list of significant words and a list of link and syntactic words. The results of such division can have a subjective nature in some details, but as a whole the most part of the lists should remain stable, as it is determined by objective rules.

FORMATION AND ANALYSIS OF THE FREQUENCY LIST OF SYNTACTIC AND LINK WORDS (SLW)

We consider the words to be link or syntactic if they are non-derivative, or if derivative, contain parts of significative words which have practically lost their meaning within the context of the text document that we investigate.

Examples of non-derivative words in English are, for example, *prepositions, postpositions, conjunctions, particles, articles, pronouns, prepositions, and auxiliary verbs,* such *as verb ligament (have to be), the allied words. Academic grammar of the entrenched view in Vinogradov* (2011) *according to which the official words include "speech" particles: particles, prepositions and conjunctions unions.* In European linguistics significative word is generally not opposed to syntactic words and significant parts of speech.

If significative words or their parts contained in derivative link words have not lost their original meaning, they are not included in the SLW list.

The principle of identifying these words is synthetic, combining the logical semantic and grammatical approaches.

Table 4. Items included in list of SLW, or partly included in list of SLW.

Items included in list of SLW	Items partly included in list of SLW by syntactic words and linkers.
Lastly, Also, Further, Since	Firstly, secondly, finally
Because, Because of	The first point is
As, So, Hence, Therefore, Thus	The following
The, a, an	owing to the fact that
For, of, off, above, in, to	due to the fact that
While	Consequently
Whereas	This means that
He, she, We, they …	As a result, as a rule, In addition
What, whatever, somewhere, whose, …….	In spite of the fact
These, *us, them, our*	For example, For instance
Themselves	it is said, as I see it
And, or	As well as that

Table 5. The SLW frequency lists

Alice Engl	G	K	A	R^2
Y=LogSLW X=logN Y^G=-K×X+A	2.5	7.5362	17.487	0.9939
	2.25	5.9343	13.951	0.9954
	2	4.6612	11.132	0.9901
	1.75	3.6459	8.8779	0.9763

The examples mentioned below show the words and word combinations included in the SLW frequency list and the words not included in this list as they can be encountered in the text as significant words, as well.

For example, we have included in the list of linking ones such words as COULD, MIGHT, BEING, PERHAPS, THROUGH, FEW, MOST, HADN['t], EXCEPT, LESS, NEITHER, OTHERWISE, AROUND, BELOW, NEEDN['t] AFTERWARDS; out of the list of link words "designating generalization (summarizing)": In short, In brief, In summary, In conclusion, In a nutshell – we have left only "IN"; out of the linkers: To summarize, To conclude –we keep only "TO".

Table 5 represents the SLW frequency lists for English text: Alice's Adventures in Wonderland by Lewis Carroll.

Distribution of significant words in the text of "Alice", shown in Figure 3, visually has satisfactory conformity to the Zipf-Mandelbrot distribution. Only 3 first words "SAID", "ALICE" and "LITTLE" stand aside from the distribution. Applying approximation of the distribution by Zipf-Mandelbrot function {logW =-K×log (N+B) +A} for the curve in Figure 3, we shall obtain: log (W) = - 1.0683× log (N+25.5) +3.4663 with **R^2 = 0.9693.**

Figure 3. "Alice" significative words frequencies (in bilogarithmic scale)

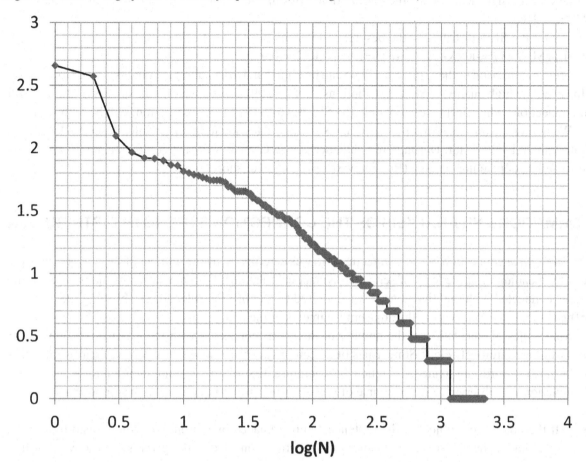

Here W - frequency of the significant word having rank N. It is seen that R^2 is only slightly less than the value corresponding to the criterion of a "perfect text" suggested above for the Zipf-Mandelbrot distribution. Whereas for the SLW distribution the best result is

$$Y^{2.25} = -5.9343 \log (N) + 13.951 \quad R^2 = 0.9954$$

For the Spanish version of "Alice" the approximation of the significant words distribution by the Zipf Mandelbrot function is presented by a slanting line:

$$\log (W) = - 0.8423 \times \log (N+15) + 2.8799 \text{ at } R^2 = 0.9527.$$

Whereas for the SLW distribution the best result is:

$$\text{LogSLW}^G = -K \times X + A \text{ where } G=2 \text{ at the greatest } R^2 = 0.9912.$$

For the Russian version of "Alice" the approximation of distribution of all words by the Zipf function we obtain

$$\log (W) = - 0.8466 \times \log (N) + 2.998 \text{ with } R^2 = 0.9402,$$

and for the significant words the distribution looks like log (W) = - 0.6258× log (N) +2.1504 with R^2 = 0.9165.

But for the SLW distribution the best result looks like

(LogSLW)^G =-K×X+A where G=1.5 and R^2 = 0.9932.

From comparison of these three results it can be seen that in translation the quality of the work is lost. However, the high quality of SLW distributions (R^2 ≥ 0.99) gives hope that the quality of the strength of connections which influences not only the SW, but also the SLW distribution, will be high enough.

We will verify this assumption on several texts – fairy tales about the Little tailor in several languages (The Valiant Little Tailor, Das tapfere Schneiderlein (in German), El sastrecillo valiente (Spanish version) and Храбрый портняжка (Russian version)) and other short texts.

FORMATION AND ANALYSIS OF THE CONNECTION STRENGTH DISTRIBUTION

The strength of connection of each syntactic word was determined by the number of the words connected to it by meaning or at the level of semantic-syntactical relations. For calculation of the number of the words connected with the given one it was required to identify the rules for establishing the zones of influence of link words within the adjacent fragments of the text.

Some rules of calculation of the number of the words connected with the given syntactic word or link word are intuitively clear. Some rules of detecting various relations between the significant words and syntactic words are treated ambiguously. Therefore, first of all, we paid attention to their accurate formulation and observance in the course of text analysis. We will quote those most important:

- If the noun – the subject of the sentence can be replaced by a pronoun without distortion of the meaning of the phrase, at calculation of the words connected to the given syntactic word or link word the noun was disregarded.
- If the adverb serves only to intensify, and not to modify the meaning, it was not taken into account at calculation. At night he lay down as usual **in** bed. Here when considering the preposition the only words considered were: lay down **in** bed.
- The search for connections is limited only to the words in one phrase, everything outside it is disregarded.
- Connection is traced only to the place in the text where other words can be substituted with no distortion of the meaning.
- Idiomatic expressions are included completely into a fragment adjacent to the link word.

Examples:

- from the text *so he put his head **out** of the window, and called out* at calculation of the words connected with the underlined one only the following abstract of six connected words was considered: *put his head **out** of the window;*
- from the text *The woman, **who** had expected to find a good customer, gave him what he asked for, but went off angry* at calculation of the words connected with the underlined one only the following abstract of four connected words was considered: ***who** had expected to find;*

- from the text *He looked at every one of them, **and** lifting all the lids, applied his nose to each ...* at calculation of the words connected with the underlined one only the following abstract of seven connected words was considered: *looked at every one of them, **and** ... applied*;
- Following are fragments in which all words were considered at calculation of the words connected with the underlined one: *For **a** long time; After **a** while; set apart for **him;** both his pockets; his only daughter.*

After that, proceeding from these rules a frequency list of the "connection strengths" (CS) was drawn.

Distribution of the significant words in the English version of "Tailor" better satisfies the Zipf law, than the Zipf-Mandelbrot law. And even in this case it is seen that log (SW Frequency) = - 0.6372 ×log N +1.6639 and has the reliability criterion R^2 value of only 0.9282. Such value of R^2 allows to conclude that the quality of the text is not too high.

Approximation of the SLW distribution for "Tailor" (English version) is shown in table. 6, and CS (connection strength) distribution is given in table. 7.

The best approximation for CS is obtained in this text at the G degree equaling 2.75. At the same time it is necessary to pay attention to that parameter R^2 changes slightly (from 0.9941 to 0.9961) in a wide range of changes of G (from 2.5 to 3). Thus, at a poor quality of distribution of the significant words and high quality of SLW distribution in the aggregation, being the "connection strength" attribute, we obtain high quality for the CS distribution according to indicator R^2 and poor quality according to indicator G in comparison with G=1.75 for the SLW distribution. Considerable values of indicator G testify to decrease of the CS distribution quality. On the whole it turns out that the high quality of SLW can somewhat improve, but not completely compensate the quality loss related to significant words.

Good Zipf distribution for objects (significative words) essentially improves the parameters of the CS model. High level of non-linearity of SLW distribution and its exponential transformation is basically an indicator of the system imperfection.

Good distribution of connections between the objects also improves the SLW distribution characteristics, but to a lesser degree than the high-quality Zipf distribution for the objects.

Table 6. SLW distribution for "Tailor" (English version)

Tailor Engl	G	K	A	R^2
Y=LogSLW	2	2.4184	5.0637	0.9868
X=logN	**1.75**	2.0685	4.4118	**0.9960**
Y^G= -K×X+A	1.5	1.7629	3.8482	0.9924

Table 7. Connection strength (CS) distribution for "Tailor" (English version)

Tailor Engl	G	K	A	R^2
Y=LogCS	3.25	11.103	23.165	0.9891
X=logN	3	8.9381	18.883	0.9941
	2.75	7.1786	15.389	**0.9961**
Y^G= -K×X+A	2.5	5.7471	12.535	0.9944

Let us show that a heterogeneous system even from two "perfect" texts close in the subject and genre can appear imperfect.

For this purpose, we will consider a consolidated frequency list of the texts of "Alice" and "Tailor".

The consolidated list contains 258 SLW. 99 from them are absent in the SLW list for "Tailor", 4 are absent in the SLW list for "Alice" and 155 are present in both lists.

Nevertheless, for the consolidated list the maximum R^2 =0.9943 is less (that is, worse), and the degree of G = 2.5 is more (that is, also worse) than for the separate distributions for each text.

Both texts belong to one genre, but differ in the list of significant words. Syntactic words "decorate" the text, fill it with accents and shades, significant words fill the text with content, but good style can improve the text as a whole, though good semantic content should be shown even in case of poor style. The last statement is especially important and true for a technical text or an official document.

Let us show it on an example of the analysis of the Homestead Act of 1862. "The Homestead Act of 1862 brought about significant changes to the United States by giving government land to individuals in 30 states this law allowed nearly any man or woman a chance to live the American Dream".

It is one of the most well known historical documents of the USA, issued the same year when Charles Dodgson, an Oxford mathematician (whose penname of Lewis Carroll) wrote his fairy tale "Alice's Adventures Underground."

The Homestead Act of 1862 contains 300 different significant words used 604 times, 100 various SLWs used 871 times, with a total of 1,475 words. Thus, it is rather a short text.

The golden section for this text, calculated by the same technique as in section 2, is c = (a+b)/a =1.693456; or d=a/b=1.442053 or (c+d)/2=1.567754 at a=871, b=604 and a+b=1475. These values are close enough to the ideal:

The results of calculation of SW, SLW and CS distributions are shown in table. 9.

According to the standard practice we should have taken for the SW distribution model the Zipf or Zipf-Mandelbrot distribution. However, from table 9 it follows that the approximation with G=1.25 yields the best result which corresponds to the transition to the second model (formula (6)). Nevertheless, even

Table 8. Characteristics of the consolidated list of SLW frequencies in the texts of "Alice" and "Tailor".

Text document	R^2 max	G for SLW
"Alice &"Tailor"	0.9943	2.5
"Alice"	0.9954	2.25
"Tailor"	0.996	1.75

Table 9. Results of approximation of SW, SLW and CS distribution

Homestead Act of 1862 (Engl) Y^G=-K×X+A; Y=LogF; X=logN.				
Analyzed objects	**G**	**K**	**A**	**R^2**
	1	0.6365	1.483	0.9293
Significative words distribution (SW)	1.25	0.6011	1.3858	0.9316
SLW distribution	1.5	1.5922	3.0834	0.9899
Distribution of Strength of connections between words in text (CS)	1.75	2.6464	5.2921	0.9852

this best result hardly satisfies the lower acceptable level of the perfection criterion. At the same time two other distributions (SLW and CS) deliver a positive result, namely R^2 is quite close to one, and the degree of G is rather small for both approximations. This proves a high level of "perfection" of the text of the document subjected to analysis.

Let us return again to the analysis of the collection of texts of the fairy tale about a brave tailor in different languages.

For the German fairy tale "Das tapfere Schneiderlein" and its Russian, English and Spanish versions we obtained the results presented in table 10 in the designations accepted herein:

From Table 10 it is seen that distribution of significant words is poorly approximated by the Zipf law, and its coordination with the Zipf-Mandelbrot law is even worse. Apparently it is a feature of any short texts connected with the limited SW vocabulary. Nevertheless, the number of syntactic words is still enough for satisfactory SLW distribution, and this distribution brings a positive contribution to CS distribution. The CS distribution for the German and Spanish variants was not calculated, but for the Russian and English variants participation of significant words in forming CS does not materially worsen this distribution.

LIMITATIONS FOR THE APPLICATION OF MODELS FOR VERY SHORT TEXTS

The results obtained for five very short texts are presented in table 11. In the CS results for the Russian version of the "Three little pigs" we have left two G exponent values for which very close values of criterion R^2 were obtained, but, as it has been shown above, transition to a higher G exponent corresponds to a considerably greater loss of quality of the text in comparison with an insignificant reduction of the R^2 value.

Let us return to table 2 where the results of calculation of the golden section parameters for the same texts are presented. Three of them are original texts, the two others - translations into another language. Comparison of the distributions quality characteristics for all short texts in tables 2 and 11 shows that

Table 10. Results for "Das tapfere Schneiderlein" in different languages.

Name of the fairy tale	Distribution parameters and models				
	Distribution parameters	**G optimal**	**K**	**A**	**R^2**
Das tapfere Schneiderlein	SW	1	0.5435	1.4542	0.8995
	SLW	1.5	1.6386	3.521	0.9767
Храбрый портняжка (Russian version)	SW	1	0.3917	1.069	0.8072
	SLW	1.25	1.1442	2.6706	0.9786
	CS	1.5	1.6821	4.1046	0.9898
The Valiant Little Tailor	SW	1	0.6372	1.6639	0.9282
	SLW	1.75	2.0685	4.4118	0.9960
	CS	2.75	7.1786	15.389	0.9961
El sastrecillo valiente (Spanish version)	SW	1.5	0.4438	1.1803	0.8493
	SLW	1.5	1.7864	3.6579	0.9769

Table 11. Results of the analysis of very short texts

Name of the fairy tale	Distribution parameters and models				
	Distribution parameters	**G optimal**	**K**	**A**	**R^2**
The Three Little Pigs – original text	SW	1	0.7557	1.7051	0.9451
	SLW	1.5	1.4644	2.9337	0.9896
	CS	1.75	2.5178	4.9713	0.9875
The Three Little Pigs – Russian version	SW	1.75	0.5507	1.1817	0.8741
	SLW	1.25	1.1442	2.6706	0.9786
	CS	1.25	1.1589	2.4315	0.9786
	CS	1.5	1.3114	2.6590	0.9797
Heather Ale – English original	SW	1	0.4282	0.8591	0.8269
	SLW	1.25	1.2188	2.0137	0.9708
Heather Ale – Russian version	SLW	1.25	0.762	1.1836	0.9079
A Tale about a Fisherman and a Fish (Russian text)	SW	1	0.6416	1.4748	0.8946
	SLW	1.25	0.9664	1.8022	0.9580
	CS	1.5	1.0063	1.8973	0.9706

in most cases the originals have better indicators, than their translations. As the original texts are recognized masterpieces in their genre, it is suggested to take the numerical estimations of SW, SLW and CS distributions obtained here as acceptable values for estimation of the perfection of very short texts.

Thus, for perfect texts with a length of more than 2000 words the following values of the G, R^2 and Golden section (c and d) parameters should be considered admissible:

R^2 $\geq$ 0.92 for the SW distribution according to the Zipf or Zipf-Mandelbrot law

R^2 $\geq$ 0.97 at G $\leq$ 2 for the SLW distribution

R^2 $\geq$ 0.97 at G $\leq$ 2 for the CS distribution

Golden section $\varphi_1 = c \geq 1.37$; $\varphi_2 = d \leq 1.87$.

For perfect texts with a length of less than 2000 words the following values of the G, R^2 and Golden section (c and d) parameters should be considered admissible:

R^2 $\geq$ 0.89 for the SW distribution according to the Zipf or Zipf-Mandelbrot law

R^2 $\geq$ 0.95 at G $\leq$ 2 for the SLW distribution;

R^2 $\geq$ 0.97 at G $\leq$ 2 for the CS distribution.

CONCLUSION AND FUTURE RESEARCH DIRECTIONS

Criteria of satisfactory distribution of syntactic and link words in the texts the significative words of which follow the Zipf-Mandelbrot have been proposed and substantiated.

Distribution of a population of link words and syntactic words in some integral text is given by a parabola $y^G = A - KX$ with a rational exponent G. Taking $Z = y^G$, it is possible to present the parabola graph in a bilogarithmic form (diagram with Logarithmic scales on both axe) by a straight line. *The coefficient of determination* of the approximation reliability (R^2) *indicates how well data points fit a line or curve.*

The quality of approximation is defined by the value of the determination factor and the parameter G value at which R^2 reaches the maximum. The smaller the G value for this maximum, the more perfect the joint distribution of syntactic and link words. The best works have the G value of about 1.5 to 2.0. However, the quality of the list of syntactic words and link words can be considered satisfactory at the R^2 values of about $0.98 - 0.99$.

Satisfactory distribution of syntactic and link words leads to a better text image, making the poor opinion of the text quality a rare, but admissible event. For more confident inference of the high quality of the text another formal criterion is suggested – the strength of connections between significative words which is provided by syntactic and link words.

The strength of connections in this case is represented by the frequency of occurrence in the text of each linking word increased by the number of the words of any nature linked by it. The G and R^2 parameters serve as a criterion of perfection of texts at linear approximation of the connections strength dependence in a bilogarithmic form.

Identical approaches for estimation of the quality of connections in the systems presented by abstract graphic objects and specific populations of words yielded almost identical results. This allows to conclude that the suggested model of distribution of the strength of connections between the objects has a system-wide character.

For accelerated estimation of the degree of perfection of the text of a complete product it is possible to be limited to the estimation of the determination factor for the Zipf distribution performed for significative words and for distribution of the population of syntactic and link words. Good characteristics of both these distributions make poor quality of the complete text hardly probable.

Deviations of the frequency of separate syntactic words' distribution from the approximating straight line specify their anomalous use in the text and allow making recommendations about the text correction by the frequency of usage of these syntactic units.

The statistical criteria of "perfection" of the text should to a certain extent specify perfection of its semantics. Hence, the earlier known criteria (for example, the Zipf law) and criteria suggested in this study (connected with the R^2 and G parameters) can be used for selection (filtration) of more "perfect" texts to form a collection or corpus of texts belonging to a narrow subject domain. In turn, from the texts so selected it is possible to form ontologies of the subject domain and identify semantic characteristics of the text clusters belonging to the collected body of texts. In our previous works a toolkit - set of algorithms and programs – named "System for the electronic library development" (DDL system) was presented (Makagonov, Reyes, & Sidorov, 2012).

This toolkit includes algorithms specially focused at the use of a search image of the textual document (TDSI). At the beginning of processing a dictionary aimed for a specific subject domain should be developed (DOD = domain oriented dictionary). DOD contains only significant words which in the texts of a narrow subject domain have relative frequencies three times higher than in the common lexicon. Each TDSI contains only words belonging to DOD (Makagonov, Reyes, & Sidorov, 2012).

Therefore implementation of lexicographic analysis by means of TDSI makes it possible to pass directly to the semantic analysis, laying aside the sentence analysis problems (morphological and syntactical analysis). The toolkit mentioned here can be used for the construction and analysis of an ontology of texts of some subject domain or sphere of knowledge.

Our toolkit – Visual heuristic cluster analysis (VHCA) was used for construction of hierarchically classified text corpora (Makagonov et al., 2005; Makagonov, Ruis Figueroa, & Gelbukh, 2006). Using this approach, we have an opportunity of semantic structuring of the documents collected for their subsequent "semantic analysis". This approach is somewhat similar to the "uncontrollable and knowledge free approach" of Florian Holz (2008).

Within the limits of one integrated text the number of syntactic words with the text volume exceeding 1800 words reaches the asymptote around the first two-three hundreds of words, and their frequency of use in the text tends towards 62%, while the number of the significant words in the dictionary of the integrated text grows, but the word usage number falls to 38 percent. These percent values correspond to the golden section characteristic of perfect biological and social systems. With the text quality deviating from the "perfect" one, the ratio of the number of syntactic and significant words can deviate from that of the golden section, falling to 30% and, probably, even lower.

The golden section parameters $c = (a+b)/a$, and $d=a/b$ where "a" and "b" are SLW and SW frequencies may be used as some palliative estimates replacing the analysis of the models of distribution of these text elements. For example, the golden section can be used for the analysis of some special texts - dialogue between people with a different status, such as a service system operator and a client of the same system. The key property of the emotional dominant in the speech of the client should be reflected in a greater variety of the SLW list, while the domination of logic in the speech of the operator should be shown by its containing a greater amount of specific significant words.

The measurement of the SLW and SW ratio for the participants of a telephone conversation will show us the role of each of them in this dialogue.

Our future work is connected with the development of the weight of the texts corresponding to the degree of their perfection, and accounting of these weights at forming a text corpus for constructing an ontology of a narrow subject domain. The same approach can be used by other researchers solving similar tasks.

It also seems useful to consider the variant of the strength of connections between significant words in the form of a gravitational law in which instead of the number of the words connected by a syntactic word the frequencies of the words connected would be used as weights. In this case it would be inevitable to automate a part of the work to calculate the connection strength distribution.

REFERENCES

Adamic, L. A., & Huberman, B. A. (2002). Zipf's law and the Internet. *Glottometrics*, *3*, 143–150.

Auerbach, F. (1913). Das Gesetz der Bevolkerungskonzentration. *Petermanns Geographische Mitteilungen*, *LIX*, 73–76.

Axtell, R. L. (2001). Zipf distribution of US firm sizes. *Science*, *293*(5536), 1818–1820. doi:10.1126/science.1062081 PMID:11546870

Babenko, L. G., & Kazarin, Y. V. (2004). The Linguistic Analysis of the Literary Text. Theory and Practice Manual. Moscow: Flinta: Nauka.

Caroll, L. (2003). Alicia En El País De Las Maravillas. Ediciones del Sur. Retrieved from http://www. ucm.es/data/cont/docs/119-2014-02-19-Carroll.AliciaEnElPaisDeLasMaravillas.pdf

Demurova, N. M. (1991). Кэрролл, Л. Приключения Алисы в стране чудес. Moscow: Наука. Retrieved from http://lib.ru/CARROLL/carrol1_1.txt

Dunlap, R. A. (1997). *The Golden Ratio and Fibonacci Numbers*. World Scientific Publishing.

Gabaix, X. (1999). Zipf's Law for Cities: An Explanation. *The Quarterly Journal of Economics*, *114*(3), 739–767. doi:10.1162/003355399556133

Grimm, J., & Grimm, W. (n. d.). *Das tapfere Schneiderlein*. Retrieved from http://www.grimmstories. com/de/grimm_maerchen/das_tapfere_schneiderlein

Grimm, J., & Grimm, W. (n. d.). *The Valiant Little Tailor*. Retrieved from http://www.grimmstories. com/en/grimm_fairy-tales/the_gallant_tailor

Grimm, J., & Grimm, W. (n. d.). *Храбрый портняжка*. Retrieved from http://www.grimmstories.com/ ru/grimm_skazki/hrabryj_portnjazka

Grimm, J., & Grimm, W. (n. d.). *El sastrecillo valiente (Siete de un golpe)*. Retrieved from http://www. grimmstories.com/es/grimm_cuentos/el_sastrecillo_valiente

Hill, B. M. (1970). Zipf's law and prior distributions for the composition of a population. *Journal of the American Statistical Association*, *65*(331), 1220–1232. doi:10.1080/01621459.1970.10481157

Holz, F. (2008). Semantic Structuring of Document Collections and Building of Term Hierarchies – An Unsupervised and Knowledge-free Approach. In *Proceeding of the 8th International Conference on Terminology and Knowledge Engineering (TKE)*.

Kali, R. (2003). The city as a giant component: A random graph approach to Zipf's law. *Applied Economics Letters*, *10*(11), 717–720. doi:10.1080/1350485032000139006

Li, W. (1992). Random Texts Exhibit Zipf's-Law-Like Word Frequency Distribution. *IEEE Transactions on Information Theory*, *38*(6), 1842–1845. doi:10.1109/18.165464

Makagonov, P., Reyes, C. B., & Sidorov, G. (2011). Document Search Images in Text Collections for Restricted Domains on Websites. In R. F. Brena & A. Guzman-Arenas (Eds.), *Quantitative semantics and soft computing methods for the Web: perspectives and applications*. (pp. 183–203). Hershey: IGI Global.

Makagonov, P., Ruiz Figueroa, A., Sboychakov, K., & Gelbukh, A. (2005). Learning a Domain Ontology from Hierarchically Structured Texts. In *Proceedings of Workshop Learning and Extending Lexical Ontologies by using Machine Learning Methods at 22nd International Conference on Machine Learning, ICML 2005. Bonn, Germany*.

Makagonov, P., Sánchez, L. E., & Reyes, C. B. (2013). Based on measuring the human sense of harmony methods and tools for improving the urban image. *моделирование и анализ данных (Modelling and data analysis, 2013*(1), 97-109.

Makagonov, P., Sánchez, L. E., & Sboychakov, K. (2009). Criterio de armonia como habilidad inherente del ser humano, aplicada en proyectos arquitectonicos. In E. Köppen (Ed.), *Imagenes en la ciencia. Ciencia en las imagines.* (pp. 83–101).

Marshak, S. (n. d.). Р. Л. Стивенсон. Вересковый мед. Retrieved from http://www.poetry.kostyor.ru/marshak/?n=101

Homestead Act of 1862. (2014). National Park Service. Retrieved from http://www.nps.gov/home/index.htm

Neumann, P. G. (2011). *Statistical metalinguistics and Zipf-Pareto-Mandelbrot.* SRI International Computer Science Laboratory.

Orlov, Y. K. (1980). Invisible Harmony. *Mysl´ i chislo (Thought and Number), 3*, 70-106.

Pushkin, A. C. (1960). *Собрание сочинений в 10 томах.* Moscow: Государственное издательство художественной литературы. Retrieved from http://rvb.ru/pushkin/01text/03fables/01fables/0799.htm

Steel, F. A. (n. d.). *Three little pigs.* Retrieved from http://classiclit.about.com/od/threelittlepigs

Stevenson, R. L. (2001) Heather Ale: A Galloway Legend. In Edmund Clarence Stedman, ed. (1833–1908). *A Victorian Anthology, 1837–1895.* New York: Bartleby.Com. Retrieved from http://www.bartleby.com/246/961.html

Talebook.com. (n. d.) *Сказка про трёх поросят.* Retrieved from http://www.talebook.ru/eng/01/index.htm

U.S. Congress. (1862). *Homestead Act of 1862.* Retrieved from http://www.nathankramer.com/settle/article/homestead.htm

Van der Galien, J. G. (2003). *Factorial randomness: the Laws of Benford and Zipf with respect to the first digit distribution of the factor sequence from the natural numbers.* Retrieved from http://home.zonnet.nl/galien8/factor/factor.html

Vinogradov, V. V. (2011). *The Russian language. Grammatical doctrine of word. Edition Russky yazyk (Russian language)* (G. A. Zolotova, Ed.). Moscow.

Zipf, G. K. (1935). *The Psychobiology of Language.* Houghton-Mifflin.

Zipf, G. K. (1949). *Human Behavior and the Principle of Least Effort.* Cambridge, Massachusetts: Addison-Wesley.

ADDITIONAL READING

Adamic, L. *Zipf, Power-laws, and Pareto – a ranking tutorial.* From http://www.hpl.hp.com/research/idl/papers/ranking/ranking.html

Eftekhari, A. (2006). Fractal geometry of texts: An initial application to the works of Shakespeare. *Journal of Quantitative Linguistics, 13*(2-3), 177–193. doi:10.1080/09296170600850106

Makagnov, P., & Sánchez, L. E. (2004). Implementación de la Ley de Zipf para el análisis visual de patrones del ambiente urbano. *Temas de Ciencia y Tecnología, 8*(24), 3–8.

Makagonov, P. (2001). *Management of the urban territory development. Academic book*. Moscow: Russian Institute of State Service.

Makagonov, P., Ruiz Figueroa, A., & Gelbukh, A. (2006). Studying Evolution of a Branch of Knowledge by Constructing and Analyzing its Ontology. In *Natural Language Processing and Information Systems – 11th International Conference on Applications of Natural Language to Information Systems, NLDB 2006*. Klagenfurt, Austria, May/June 2006 (pp. 37-45). Berlin Heidelberg: Springer. doi:10.1007/11765448_4

Miller, G. A., & Newman, E. B. (1958). Tests of a statistical explanation of the rank-frequency relation for words in written English. *The American Journal of Psychology, 71*(1), 209–218. doi:10.2307/1419208 PMID:13521031

Shuper, V. A. (1995). *Self-organizing of an urban population. (Russian)*. Moscow: Russian Open University.

KEY TERMS AND DEFINITIONS

Coefficient of Determination: *(*of the approximation reliability), R^2, also designated as R^2, and, indicates how well data points fit a line or curve.

DOD: The list of words of the domain oriented dictionary DOD formed from word frequency list of the whole by elimination link or syntactic words. DOD represents domain knowledge, contains new words, concept-words, and a lot of them (near half of the list) are *hapax legomena. (A hapax legomenon* is a word which occurs only once in a text collection).

Link or Syntactic Word: We consider the words to be link or syntactic if they are non-derivative, or if derivative, contain parts of significative words which have practically lost their meaning within the context of the text document that we investigate.

Text as a Perfect Social System: A finished artistic or scientific work presentable in the form of a text document, written art product, written down verbal work of art may be considered as a perfect textual and social system, if the common opinion of a representative social group of the world literature, culture or science recognizes it as such.

The Golden Section: Also known as the divine proportion, golden mean, or golden ratio, is one of numbers $\varphi = (\sqrt{5} - 1)/2$ or $\Phi = (\sqrt{5} + 1)/2$, so that $\Phi - \varphi = 1$. The golden section appears when we divide any quantity into two parts "a" & "b" so that whole quantity divided by larger part is equal to Φ and larger part divided by smaller part is the same. A lot of people recognize the Golden Section as a constant for harmony.

The System Harmony: Should be defined by two criteria: minimum deviation of the main attribute of the objects from Zipf law, and minimum deviation of connections between the objects and the distribution law of connections between the system elements.

Zipf's Law: Is known as a phenomenological model of the "object rank – frequency of occurrence" or "rank – dimension" type with a very low probability of deviation for perfect systems. That is why the deviation of the practical distribution from the Zipf distribution can be taken as the criterion of the system "ideality".

Chapter 3

Extracting Definitional Contexts in Spanish Through the Identification of Hyponymy– Hyperonymy Relations

Olga Acosta
Pontificia Universidad Católica de Chile, Chile

Gerardo Sierra
UNAM, México

César Aguilar
Pontificia Universidad Católica de Chile, Chile

ABSTRACT

The automatic extraction of hyponymy-hypernymy relations in text corpus is one important task in Natural Language Processing. This chapter proposes a method for automatically extracting a set of hyponym-hyperonym pairs from a medical corpus in Spanish, expressed in analytical definitions. This kind of definition is composed by a term (the hyponym), a genus term (the hyperonym), and one or more differentiae, that is, a set of particular features proper to the defined term, e.g.: conjunctivitis is an infection of the conjunctiva of the eye. Definitions are obtained from definitional contexts, and then sequences of term and genus term. Then, the most frequent hyperonyms are used in order to filter relevant definitions. Additionally, using a bootstrapping technique, new hyponym candidates are extracted from the corpus, based on the previous set of hyponyms/hyperonyms detected.

INTRODUCTION

The automatic extraction of lexical relations in text corpora is one of the current interests in artificial intelligence (AI), particularly for area of natural language processing (NLP). One of the most exploited lexical relations is hyponymy-hypernymy. According to Murphy (2003), in artificial intelligence, hypo-

DOI: 10.4018/978-1-4666-8690-8.ch003

nymy-hypernymy enables inference mechanisms in terms of entailments such that a statement entails another statement that includes one of the word's hyperonyms (*A cat stole my food-An animal stole my food*). On the other hand, this relation is implicit in analytical definitions where a term (hyponym) is defined by means of a *genus* (hypernym) plus one or more *differentiae* (*Conjunctivitis is an infection of the conjunctiva of the eye*). Finally, in grammatical terms, selectional restrictions, for example, on the object of a verb can be phrased in terms of a hyperonym, and hyponyms of that word can then also selected as potential objects: *I need a beverage* (*beverage* can be coffee, tea, juice, and so on).

There are several reasons for automatically extracting lexical relations. On the one hand, current technologies have enabled the accumulation of huge amounts of text information. Consequently, this situation has also increased the need to obtain useful information from these text sources saving time and effort. On the other hand, applications focused on NLP such as text summarization, information retrieval and information extraction can be benefited with new approaches of automatic extraction of useful information in order to improve performance.

To reach this goal, we propose a method that takes advantage of hyponym-hyperonym pairs extracted from candidate analytical definitions found in specialized corpus, considering the association established between the term defined and its *genus*. We obtain these analytical definitions from definitional contexts (DCs) in Spanish, based on the methodology developed by (Sierra *et al.* 2008). Once identified these DCs, we extracted term and *genus*. Then, we use the most frequent hyperonym subset in a *bootstrapping* step for finding candidate hyponyms in the same specialized corpus (Acosta *et al.* 2011). In this phase, relational adjectives are used as relevant features linked with a hyperonym.

STATE OF ART

There are some significant efforts in order to accomplish conceptual extraction task. For instance, based on the use of machine readable dictionaries (MRDs), Calzolari (1984), Alshawhi (1987), and Dolan *et al.* (1993) made experiments for finding hyponyms inserted in definitions. Given the regularity found in definitions of dictionaries, precision of these approaches is relatively high. For example, Alshawi reports a precision of 77%, Dolan *et al.* (1993) 87% and Calzolari (1984) more than 90%. On the other hand, an important advance in this kind of experiments is the work of Wilks *et al.* (1995), where these authors proposed the IS-A operator as a way to extract and categorize lexical items (concretely, terms and *genus*) linked in a relation of hyponymy-hypernymy.

Following these works, the experiment made by Hearst (1992) offers a significant method for identifying lexical-syntactic patterns associated to hyponyms in large-corpora. However, although Hearst's patterns have high precision, Cimiano *et al.* (2004) and Ryu and Choy (2005) have observed they are rarely used, even when a big corpus is analyzed. So, there are other alternative approaches based on the method developed by Hearst:

- Clustering: this approach emphasizes the distribution of context in corpus. According to this approach, words are characterized by its context and grouped by its similarity between contexts. More representative works about this approach are Pereira *et al.* (1993) and Faure and Nedellec (1998).
- Finding patterns using the Web: in this approach new characteristic patterns and instances of the lexical relation of interest are extracted taking into account the Web as a huge source of textual information. This approach was proposed by Pantel and Pennacchiotti (2006). In Spanish, Montes

et al. (2007) carried out an experiment to find new patterns and instances of the hyponymy-hypernymy relation in open text collections as the Web.

- Machine learning: Finally, an approach for finding hyponymy-hypernymy relations was developed by Snow *et al.* (2006), considering the application of machine learning methods, oriented to recognize useful patterns employing dependency paths.

Works mentioned above have been principally done for English language with exception to Montes *et al.* (2007). All of them consider a *seed set* in order to learn new patterns and instances of the target relation. This set generally is obtained from external sources (e.g., lexicons, dictionaries) or directly provided by a human. In this work, we propose a method in order to automatically extract this set of hyponym-hyperonym pairs from specialized texts and use them to filter candidate conceptual information. Thus, these instances of the relation can be useful for extracting new patterns and instances from the same corpus. Additionally, we extract hyponyms derived from a hyperonym plus an adjective because of they can represent relevant terms or subordinate categories of the hyperonym (e.g. *mitochondrial disease*).

CONCEPTS AND CATEGORIES

Definition of concepts is a theme of intense debate between areas involved such as philosophy and psychology. According to Smith (2003) concepts allow us to divide the world into classes or categories. Our knowledge is impregnated of concepts and relations among them. Without concepts we would have to remember all objects or entities like unique, so that communication and reasoning processes would be practically impossible.

It is recognized concepts form the subject-matter of taxonomies and ontologies, however, a very common problem is the concept of concepts is rarely defined (Smith, 2003; Buitelaar *et al.* 2005). In this work, we intended on the automatic extraction of a subset of hyponymy-hypernymy relations from candidate analytical definitions, so that we consider a view of concepts must be assumed. Here, we take into account a cognitive view of concepts for three reasons:

- Cognitive science is an interdisciplinary science concerned with the kinds of knowledge that underlie human cognition, the details of human cognitive processes, and the computational modeling of these processes (Cohen & Lefebvre, 2005).
- Works giving rise to the interest of the Artificial Intelligence (AI) community in categories, a very important function of concepts, started from a cognitive perspective (Collins & Quillian, 1969; Minsky, 1975).
- There is an important wealth of results explaining behavior in categorization tasks in humans and how this can be caught from language (Croft & Cruse, 2004).

The Classical Theory of Concepts

The traditional view of concepts is philosophical one and it is commonly called classical theory. Classical theory holds that most concepts, especially lexical concepts, have a definitional structure. What this means is that most concepts encode necessary and sufficient conditions. Necessary conditions must be met by something to be a member of a category, and anything that satisfies all conditions must be a member.

One of the most recognized advantages of classical approach consists in its formalization capacity. As Sowa (2005) claims, in a classical approach it is possible to reason with respect to types and subtypes. The inheritance, important mechanism of this approach, enables a kind of *cognitive economy* allowing to link features of the *differentiae* following a specific path. For instance, Collins and Quillian (1969) applied this principle in their proposal of a hierarchical model for storing semantic information in a computer. From this hierarchical view, common facts to the instances of a category are stored with the node for that category, rather than being redundantly stored at the nodes for each of the instances. For example, the property *sweet* is stored only with category *fruit* and *round* only with category *apple*. As *apples* are *fruits*, property *sweet* can be inherited to *apples*:

IS-A(apple, fruit)

ROUND(apple)

SWEET(fruit)

IS-A(apple, fruit) $\Rightarrow$ SWEET(apple)

From a philosophical perspective, Aristotle's classical view was questioned by Wittgenstein (1953), and practically collapsed by Rosch's groundbreaking work in cognitive psychology. This latter focused on two implications of the classical theory:

i.   Typicality: if categories are defined only by properties that all members share, then no member should be a better example of the category than any other member. If so, a *canary* should not be a better example of *bird* than a *penguin*.

ii. Unclear membership: if categories are defined only by properties inherent in the members, then categories should be independent of the peculiarities of any beings doing the categorizing. In this sense, biology is one of the better fields giving several examples. For instance, Smith and Medin (1981) mention disagreements among biologists respect to *Euglena* concept about whether should be classified as an animal or a plant.

Rosch's conclusions demonstrated that categories have best examples and that all of the specifically human capacities do play a role in categorization. Such theory was called Prototype Theory. This theory has changed our idea about categorization and it will be described later. Additionally, there are other theories of concepts such as exemplar theory and knowledge theory. According to Murphy (2002), both prototype and exemplar theories are unclassical theories designed to account for the problematic cases from the classical view, but knowledge theory arose as a reaction to the latter two approaches, and it is in some sense built upon them. The latter two theories are relevant topics, but they go beyond the scope of this chapter.

The Prototype Theory

The prototype theory was formulated by Rosch in the 70s. This theory holds that instances of a concept vary in the degree to which they share certain properties, and consequently vary in the degree to which they represent the concept (typicality). For example, according to Smith and Medin (1981), if we try of formulating a unitary description of the concept *cup*, we might consider five relevant properties: (1) concrete object, (2) concave, (3) can hold liquids, (4) has a handle, and (5) can be used to drink hot liquid out of. An important question is: are all the properties true of all the cups? We might think properties 1-3 are the most important properties, but not everyone would agree that 4 and 5 are true for all cups. Therefore, if we remove properties 4 and 5 from the unitary description some non-cups are included, for example, *bowls*. This kind of analysis led to argue that there are a great deal of concepts where is difficult to posit a unitary description according to the classical view, so that it was necessary a new view where a unitary description of concepts remains, but the properties are true of most though not all members. From this perspective, some instances are going to have more of the critical properties than others, and these will be the most representative of the concept.

Principles of Categorization

Studies about the human conceptual system emerged from works carried out by Rosch and colleagues in the 70s. Rosch (1978), in her article *Principles of Categorization*, proposed two basic and general principles in order to the formation of categories. These principles together give rise to the human categorical system.

The first principle refers to the function of categorical systems and holds that the task of these systems is to provide of maximum information with the least cognitive effort. On the other hand, a second principle focuses on the structure of the information and states that the perceived world (no metaphysical) is not an unpredictable and uncorrelated set of attributes, but rather it has structure. Thus, maximum information with least cognitive effort is achieved if categories mirror structure of the perceived world as better as possible.

According to Rosch, the *cognitive economy* principle combined with the structure of perceived world have important implications in the abstraction level of categories formed by a culture and in the intern structure of those categories once formed. Rosch proposed to view the conceptual system from two perspectives: vertical and horizontal. Vertical dimension refers to the category's level of inclusiveness, that is, the subsumption relation between different categories, for example:

Poodle ⊂ dog ⊂ mammal ⊂ animal

Implications of the two principles of categorization mentioned above in the vertical dimension consist on that not all the levels of categorization are equally useful levels, that is, there is a basic level, that is the most inclusive where categories can mirror the structure of attributes perceived in the world. This inclusiveness level is the mid-part between the most inclusive and least inclusive levels, in the case of figure 1, levels associated with categories such as *dog* and *whale*. Categories higher up the vertical axis, which provide less detail, are called superordinate categories, in this case, *mammal*. Those lower down the vertical axis, which provide more detail are called subordinate categories, for the case of *dog* category, *collie*.

On the other hand, horizontal dimension focuses on segmentation of categories in the same level of inclusiveness, that is, the dimension in which *dog* and *whale* vary. The implications of the two principles of categorization for horizontal dimension consist on that increasing the level of differentiation and flexibility of the categories, these tend to be defined in terms of prototypes. These prototypes have

Figure 1. The human categorization system.

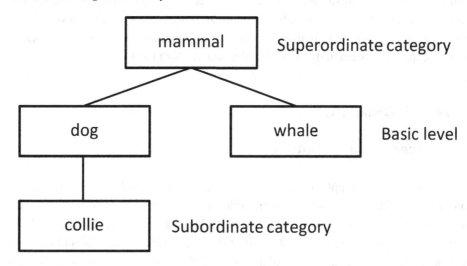

the most representative attributes of the instances within a category, and less representative attributes of elements of other categories. This horizontal dimension is related to the principle of structure of the perceived world.

Basic Level Categories

Experiments in cognitive psychology have shown language itself reveals a preponderance of the basic level in several ways. Firstly, in a linguistic level, basic level terms tend to be monolexemic: *dog, car, chair,* and subordinate terms have at leat two lexemes: *rocking chair,* and often include basic level names (Berlin, 1992; Rosch *et al.* 1976). Secondly, the basic level is the most inclusive and thus the least specific level at which it is possible to form a mental image. For instance, for natural categories (The term natural categories refers to categories that people naturally and normally use in everyday life –not to categories of nature. So, furniture and guns would be considered natural categories, because these are categories people use in every life (Murphy, 2002)) or artifactuals, categorisation arises from perceptual stimuli, that is, in order to categorise objects, we take into account several types of sensory-perceptual input: shape, size, colour, and texture. On the other hand, if we considered the superordinate level, it is difficult to form an image of the category, for example, *furniture,* without imagining a specific item like a *chair* or a *table.* Finally, Rosch *et al.* (1976) found that basic level categories emerge in children's vocabulary before superordinate terms.

Despite preponderance of the basic level, superordinate and subordinate levels also have very relevant functions. According to Ungerer and Schmid (1996), superordinate level emphasizes functional attributes of the category, while also performing a collecting function. Meanwhile, subordinate categories fulfill a specificity function.

Expertise Influences Categorization

Knowledge in a specific domain influences basic level categories. As Rosch *et al.* (1976) suggested the specificity and nature of the basic level might depend on expertise. Specifically, experts would have much more knowledge respect to subordinate categories. If so, although superordinate categories such as *tree* might be salient for *tree* experts, subordinates categories like *maples* and *oaks* would be more salient, because experts would know many features that are distinctive to these categories. This latter was supported by experiments carried out by Tanaka and Taylor (1991).

CONCEPTUAL INFORMATION

Sources of Conceptual Information

If we assume words denote concepts, then a good source to find them is text information. Nowadays, computational lexicography and terminology are able to recognize concepts in large-text corpora. To focus on this recognition, it is important to establish what the best source for obtaining relevant concepts is. In this sense, Sager (1990) and Smith (2003) point out the value of scientific and technical literature as a source to obtain such concepts. In particular, Sager (1990) considers definitions as a linguistic representation of concepts, because definitions synthesize all the conceptual information linked to terms circumscribed to a domain-specific knowledge. This conception is close to the observation of Pinker (1999), because the definitions (in our case, specialized definitions) transcend the particular level of our everyday experiences.

On the other hand, Buitelaar and Cimiano (2008), in the context of the ontology learning, point out that one of the questions still unanswered is the kind of textual evidence to take into account to support processes of construction of ontologies. In this respect, if we take into account the Gruber's ontology perspective, ontologies represent consensual knowledge by members of a community, so that we consider an adequate source are specialized domains because the probability of finding consensual concepts is more high than in contexts of general language.

In this research, we consider as conceptual information that information expressed by specialized definitions, particularly in analytical definitions constituted by *genus* and *Differentia*, according to Smith (2003) and Wilks *et al.* (1995). These authors have used this kind of definition for searching hyponymy-hypernymy relations established between terms and *genus*.

Finally, according to what we mentioned earlier, we can argue that if we analyze specialized domains, then it is much more likely to find basic level or subordinate categories in position of the *genus* within an analytical definition, so that these can be exploited in order to search more relevant information.

Automatic Extraction of Conceptual Information

Sierra *et al.* (2008) developed a based-pattern method for extracting terms and definitions in Spanish, which are expressed in textual fragments inserted in specialized documents. These fragments are called definitional contexts (or DCs) and are constituted by a term, a definition, and linguistic or metalinguistic forms, such as verbal phrases, typographical markers and/or pragmatic patterns, for example:

La energía primaria, *en términos generales, se define como aquel recurso energético que no ha sufrido transformación alguna, con excepción de su extracción. (Eng. The* **primary energy**, *in general terms, is defined as a resource that has not been affected for any transformation, with the exception of its extraction.)*

Table 1. Verb predications and link elements

Infinitive verb	Link element
To be	
To characterize, to conceive, to consider, to describe, to define, to understand, to know, to refer	As
To denominate, to call, to name	ε, as

We can see here a DC sequence formed by the term *energía primaria* (Eng. Primary energy), the definition *aquel recurso...* (Eng. That resource that...) and the verbal pattern *se define como* (Engl. is defined as), as well as other characteristic units such as the pragmatic pattern *en términos generales* (Eng. in general terms) and the typographical marker (bold font) that in this case emphasizes the presence of the term.

For achieving this extraction, Sierra *et al.* (2008), as well Aguilar (2009) and Alarcón (2009) employ verbal patterns that operate as connectors between terms and definitions. Such patterns syntactically are predicative phrases (or PrP), configured around a verb that operates as a head of this PrP. Among verbs that work as heads of PrPs, the verb *ser* (Eng. to be) is the most frequent, mainly because it allows to structure operators such as IS-A. Nevertheless, other verbs can be heads of these PrPs, e. g.: *definir* (Eng. to define), *denominar* (Eng. to denominate), *conocer* (Eng. to know), and others, as shown in table 1.

The following examples show analytical definitions using these verbs:

1. *La [conjuntivitis]* $_{Term}$ *es una [inflamación]* $_{Genus}$ *de la conjuntiva del ojo.* (Eng. [Conjunctivitis] $_{Term}$ is an [inflammation] $_{Genus}$ of the conjunctiva of the eye).
2. *Se define [conjuntivitis]* $_{Term}$ *como una [inflamación]* $_{Genus}$ *de la conjuntiva del ojo.* (Eng. It is defined [conjunctivitis] $_{Term}$ as an [inflammation] $_{Genus}$ of the conjunctiva of the eye).

In (1) and (2), we observe terms and analytical definitions linked through PrPs whose heads are the verbs *to be* and *define*. In both cases, the term *conjunctivitis* is conceived as *an inflammation*, for this reason the *genus* of these definitions is the term *inflammation*. According to Wilks *et al.* (1995), these cases are a canonical example of hyponymy-hypernymy relations into analytical definitions. Generally, term and *genus* in analytical definitions correspond to hyponym-hyperonym pairs of items.

LEXICAL RELATIONS

Lexical Relation Approach

Lexical relationships represent an approach from the structural semantics for organizing a conceptual space. If we assume words, or lexical units, represent concepts, then structural semantics proposes to organize a conceptual space by means of lexical relationships such as hyponymy-hypernymy, synonymy, meronymy-holonymy, and antonymy. Lexicons, thesaurus and ontologies are resources where these relationships are used.

According to Hirst (2009), a lexicon is a linguistic object consisting in a list of words in a language along with some knowledge of how each word is used. A good example of a computational lexicon of English widely used is WordNet (Fellbaum, 1998). On the other hand, an ontology is not a linguistic object, but rather, it is a set of categories of objects or ideas in the world, along with certain relationships among them. The Gene Ontology provides a good example of ontology where defined terms represent gene product properties. Such ontology covers three domains: cellular component, molecular function and biological process.

Currently, given the increasing amount of information available in the Web, digital libraries, and so on, there is a great interest by automatically exploiting such digital resources for building taxonomies and ontologies. As Poesio (2005) notes, this interest originated from a cognitive perspective:

"A second, cognitive school argued that the best way to identify epistemological primitives was to study concept formation, semantic priming and learning in humans, whereas the best approach to the construction of domain ontologies was to use (generally, unsupervised) machine learning techniques to automatically extract such ontologies from language corpora and other data. This approach found its philosophical foundations in the work of Wittgenstein, whereas from a psychological perspective, it was rooted in the work of Rosch" (p. 2)

The previous perspective coincided with the adoption of statistical approaches at the beginning of the 90's. In turn, NLP researchers focused on machine learning with the goal of automating the knowledge acquisition process in order to cope with the fact that knowledge changes continuously.

Therefore, considering needs mentioned above and regularity of the language for expressing relations in texts, lexical relationships are an approach suitable for exploiting text sources with the goal of extracting knowledge.

Hyponymy-Hypernymy Relation

Hyponymy is a relation of inclusion. Croft and Cruse (2004) distinguish between two kinds of relations of inclusion: simple hyponymy linguistically exemplified by expression *An X is a Y*, and taxonomy, more discriminating than hyponymy, whose characteristic linguistic expression is *An X is a kind/type of Y*. As Croft and Cruse also point out, expression *a kind/type of* exerts some type of selectional pressure on pairs of items.

An important issue derived from this division is: all of the subordinate categories of a hyperonym can be good hyponyms, but not all of them can be good taxonyms of a hyperonym. An example where a good hyponym is not a good taxonym is concept *stallion*. *Stallion* can be considered a good hyponym of *horse* (*stallion is a male horse*), but *stallion* is not a good taxonym of *horse* because feature *male* found in its definition highlights a sexual profile and it would create non-optimal categories. Authors note that a division of the domain of animals into males and females would create categories with too little internal cohesion and too little external distinctiveness, therefore, little information. According to this analysis, features modifying a hyperonym may be a useful element in order to determine how a division in sub-categories or subordinate categories is being made.

Croft and Cruse (2004) argue that an important number of good taxonyms are natural kinds (e.g., animals, and naturally occurring materials, such as water, oil, rock, and so on), and their definitions often require encyclopedic characterization, so, it is difficult to define them by means of a hyperonym plus a single feature. On the other hand, there are cases where a good taxonym could be found adding features implicit in a single modifier of the hyperonym. For example, *spoon* can be divided by *teaspoon*, *coffee-spoon*, *soup-spoon*, and so on. In this case, *spoon* is taxonomized on the basis of what they are used in connection with and resultant taxonomy seems to be more useful than previous example. Another example of division by single-feature is: large/metal/round/deep spoon, but, in this case, subdivision does not seem to be a useful taxonomy of *spoon*.

Finally, the linguistic expression *A kind/type of* used as a diagnostic test in the taxonymy relation is treated by Wierzbicka (1996) as a lexical expression of semantic primitives for representing taxonomy. In general terms, semantic primitives are considered as a set of words specifying concepts, where it is not possible these concepts being defined by other concepts. According to Wierzbicka, all humans, independently of language, possess the same basic set of semantic primitives or innate concepts and they encode them in words.

Characterizing Taxonymy

According to Croft and Cruse (2004), taxonomizing is not only to divide a larger class into smaller classes. Subclasses or categories must be good taxonomies of the larger class. For determining goodness of subcategories, Cruse suggests to take into account the nature of the resultant sub-categories and their relations to one another, in the light of the purpose of taxonomization. With respect to this particular point, he argues:

"Taxonomy exists to articulate a domain in the most efficient way. This requires good categories, which are a) internally cohesive, b) externally distinctive, and c) maximally informative" (Croft and Cruse, 2004, p. 148)

The three properties mentioned above are supported by basic level categories. An example of taxonomy where a hyponym is defined by its hyperonym plus a modifier is *Nephrotic Syndrome is a renal disease*. These modifiers have a set of features implicit, rather than only single feature. According to Croft and Cruse (2004), there are many natural kinds requiring encyclopedic definitions where a definition by means of a hyperonym plus a single-feature is not always possible. For example, how to define *horse* in terms of its hyperonym *animal* plus a single feature? Cruse noted that good taxonyms of a larger class may be identified by means of the nature of the features jointly used with hyperonyms. Some features such as large/round are conceptually simple, and others can be more complex, for example, those representing functionality or some other relevant characteristic. So the question that remains is: complex features may be better able to support taxonymy?

According to Cruse (1994), taxonym and hyperonym must share the same perspective. For example, *stallion* is not a good taxonym of *horse* because it has a sexual perspective, while *horse* does not. This issue is interesting, but, unfortunately, it results somewhat vague if we want to automate recognition of perspectives in a set of hyponyms o subordinate categories from the hyperonym.

Table 2. Terminological patterns

Pattern	Example
Noun + Adjective (Spanish) Adjective + Noun (Eng.)	Enfermedad cardiovascular Cardiovascular disease
Noun + Prepositional Phrase (Spanish)	Enfermedad de Alzheimer Alzheimer's disease Disease of the heart
Noun + Noun	Diabetes mellitus
Acronyms	ONU
Noun + Letter	Vitamin A
Letter + Noun	H Pylori

LINGUISTIC STRUCTURE OF TERMS

Term Structure

In tasks of term extraction for Catalan (Estopà, 2003) and Spanish (Vivaldi, 2004), patterns with preposition *de (Eng. of/from)* and adjectives are the most common for structuring terms in specialized domains. Table 2 shows patterns of construction of terms considered in this work. In this table modifiers of a noun, such as prepositional phrases with *de* and adjectives configure more specific terms are showed.

In this work, for the case of hyponyms derived from hyperonyms, we only consider adjectives.

Adjectives

According to Demonte (1999) adjective is a grammatical category modifying a noun. Adjectives have very precise formal characteristics: there is a kind of meaning preferably expressed by means of adjectives.

Adjectives represent a very important element in building terms, for example, cases such as *inguinal hernia, venereal disease* are considered terms or subordinate categories in a medical domain, but *rare disease, serious disease* seem more evaluative judgments to a context than terms or specific categories. Therefore, not all of the adjectives are relevant, so that it is necessary to explore its general characteristics in order to propose a set of heuristics that allow filter out non-relevant adjectives.

There are two kinds of adjectives assigning properties to nouns. The difference between these two classes of adjectives consists on the number of properties implied by each of them, and ways of link them with the noun. On the one hand, adjectives referring to a constitutive feature of the modified noun. This feature is exhibited or characterized by means of a single physical property: color, form, character, predisposition, sound: *libro azul* (blue book), *señora delgada* (slim lady), *hombre simpatico* (nice man). On the other hand, relational adjectives assign a set of properties (in the following examples, all of the characteristics jointly defining names like *sea* or *field*): *Puerto marítimo* (maritime port), *paseo campestre* (campestral walking).

Given mentioned above, in this work we focused on relational adjectives because of we consider provide a relevant set of hyponyms or subordinate categories to hyperonyms in specialized domains. In order to discern between relational and evaluative adjectives we took into account three criteria formulated in Demonte (1999). Having in mind these criteria, we extracted a set of evaluative adjectives from the

Table 3. Criteria for discerning between relational and evaluative adjectives

Criterion	Regular expression
Adjective used predicatively: The *method is important*	<VSFIN><ADJ>
Adjective used in comparisons, so that its meaning is modified by adverbs of degree: *relatively fast.*	<ADV><ADJ>
Precedence of adjective respect to the noun: *A serious disease.*	<ADJ><NC>

same collection of texts under study, so that a fixed stop list is avoided. Table 3 shows criteria considered and its implementation by means of a chunking phase. Tags correspond to TreeTagger tags (Schmid, 1994), where VSFIN is *to be* finite verb, ADJ is adjective, ADV is adverb and NC is common noun.

Finally, the linking of relational adjectives and nouns with which they share semantic content is very important in lexicons such as WordNet (Fellbaum, 1998). In WordNet, adjectives are linked by means of a network of antonyms, but the most of relational adjectives have not obvious antonyms, so that simply are linked with the noun with which they share semantic content.

DESCRIPTION OF THE METHODOLOGY

Our methodology is based on exploiting a set of *genus* (hypernyms) extracted from DCs. This subset is used both as a filter in order to select most relevant DCs, and as a *seed set* in a bootstrapping step for extracting a great deal of hyponyms or subordinate categories from hypernyms. Steps required by the methodology are presented in figure 2. We briefly describe the steps of methodology:

1. Preprocessing of text collection consist on removing some non-relevant elements such as tables, emails, links, information in parentheses, and so on. Additionally, a process of sentence segmentation before part of speech tagged is done. Then, lemmas and tags are corrected considering information found within the corpus. Finally, a step of normalization of a tag subset is carried out.
2. Conceptual extraction consists on application of a grammar of regular expressions that take into account the most common syntactical behavior of elements in a DC. Then, candidate DCs are input to an additional process of filter out of nouns indicating meronymy-holonymy and causality relations.

Terms

According to this description, a term can be represented in the following way:

$$T : \langle art \mid fsp \rangle \langle nc \mid np \mid alfs \mid acrnm \rangle +$$
$$\langle adj \mid nc \mid np \mid alfs \mid vladj \rangle *$$
$$\left(\begin{array}{l} \langle pdel \rangle \langle nc \mid np \mid adj \mid alfs \mid acrnm \rangle + \\ \langle adj \mid nc \mid np \mid alfs \rangle * \end{array} \right) *$$

Figure 2. Methodology proposed

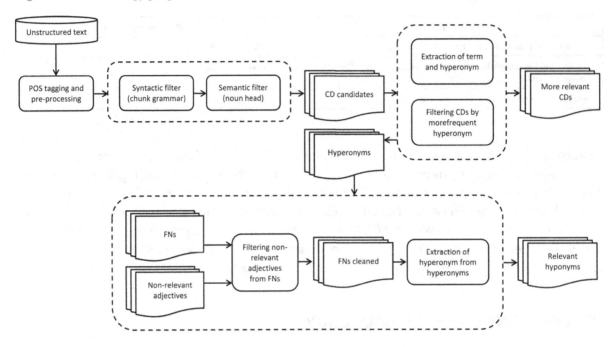

An obligatory article <art> or dot <fsp> were included in order to reduce noise and to extract the more relevant results. On the other hand, items such as <alfs> or <acrnm> allow increasing recall of DCs to cases such as: vitamin A (<nc><alfs>), ONU (<acrnm>).

Noun Phrase with Hypernym (HP)

It is a relatively common situation to find empty heads (any, type, kind, and so on) in noun phrases where hypernym can be found. So, we consider noun phrases with prepositional phrases with head *of*.

$$HP1 : \langle ART | QU \rangle ? \langle NC | NP \rangle + \left\langle \begin{array}{c} ADJ | NC | VLADJ | \\ CARD \end{array} \right\rangle *$$

$$(\langle ADV \rangle \langle ADJ \rangle) ? (\langle PDEL \rangle \langle NC | NP \rangle + \langle ADJ \rangle *) *$$

$$HP2 : \langle CARD | QU \rangle (\langle ADV \rangle \langle ADJ \rangle) ?$$

$$(\langle PDEL \rangle \langle ADV \rangle ? \langle NC | NP | CARD | ADJ \rangle +) +$$

$$HP3 : \langle DM | ART \rangle \langle CQUE | REL \rangle \langle NC \rangle ?$$

$$\langle ADJ \rangle *$$

Expressions HP1 and HP2 are evaluated in order to extract hypernym more related with the term being defined. This is done filtering either empty heads as well as indicative of other relations. The latter regular expression (HP3) includes cases where we have a demonstrative <dm> or article <art> and a relative expression where it is possible that a noun is missing:

Sp. La [energía primaria]$_{Term}$ *es [aquella]*$_{hypernym}$ *que no ha sido afectada por alguna transformación, con la excepción de su extracción.*

(Eng. The [primary energy]$_{Term}$ *is [that]*$_{hypernym}$ *that has not been affected for any transformation, with the exception of its extraction.)*

Synonyms (Syn)

Between a term and a verbal pattern other items can be introduced, for example, punctuation signs, adverbs, relative items and synonyms of the term being defined:

1. [Erythropsia]$_{Term}$ [or red vision]$_{Syn}$ is [a [condition]$_{hypernym}$ in which all objects are seen tinged with red.]$_{Definition}$
2. [Devic disease]$_{Term}$, [also known as Neuromyelitis Optica, or Devic's syndrome]$_{Syn}$ is [an inflammatory [disease]$_{hypernym}$ of the central nervous system.]$_{Definition}$

This kind of element was considered in our chunk grammar in order to enhance scope to fragments that deviates its behavior from the canonical:

Syn1:(<CM>?<CCO><ART>?<NC|NP|ACRNM>+<ADJ|ALFS|NC|NP>*(<PDEL><NP|NC>+ <ADJ>*)?)+

Syn2:((<CM>)?<CCO>?<CQUE>?<ADV|VLFIND>+<CSUBX>?<ART>?<NC|NP|ACRNM>+ <ADJ|ALFS|NC|NP>*(<PDEL><NP|NC>+<ADJ>*)?)

Contextual Patterns of DCs

Verbal patterns present in DCs can give clues about position of the term and hypernym. For instance, when verb *to be* is present in DCs, generally term can be found in the left side of verb and hypernym after verb, that is, we have the next syntactical configuration: (T)<vsfin>(HP1)(Def), where term (T), verb to be <vsfin>, noun phrase of the hypernym (HP1) and rest of definition (Def). Table 4 shows some contextual patterns of analytical fragments extracted from candidate DCs. Elements within parentheses represent constituents and those in angular parentheses POS tags.

Heuristics for Extraction of Hypernyms

Lexical relationships represent an approach from the structural semantics for organizing a conceptual space. If we assume words represent concepts, then structural semantics proposes to organize a conceptual space by means of lexical relationships such as hyponymy-hypernymy, synonymy, meronymy-holonymy, and antonymy. Lexicons and ontologies are resources where these relationships are useful.

Table 4. Contextual patterns of DCs

Fragment of DC
1. Smog is a kind of air pollution…
2.Macular edema is the cause of vision loss …
3. Intestine is part of digestive system …
7. Invasive tumor is that that is extended to surrounding areas …
8. Digestive apparatus is a set of organs …
9. A tableware is a set of dishes, glasses and cups …

Once the inclusion of patterns for terms and hypernyms as well as common verbal patterns in analytical definitions is presented, we propose the extraction of hypernyms from DCs by applying the following heuristics:

1. Division of a DC fragment according to the verb pattern. For instance, if contextual pattern of DC is (T) <vsfin>(HP1), then a string of text is divided into two segments with respect to <vsfin>. For example, in Python code this is done by: fragm.split("ser/vsfin")
2. Filtering empty heads such as *any, one, type, kind* and noun heads indicative of other relations (part-whole and causal relations) in noun phrase of hypernym. Cases in table 5 represent examples. Noun heads indicative of hyponymy are: *Type, kind, subtype, class, subclass, form, specie, example, version, field, subfield, discipline, subdiscipline.*

When one of these heads is found, hypernym is located after preposition *of*. However, if there is no prepositional phrase after empty head, hypernym is left empty. On the other hand, if noun heads indicative of causal or part-whole relations are found, DC is considered non-relevant. Noun heads of causal and part-whole relations are:

Part-Whole: part, piece, constituent, fragment, component, portion, segment, fraction.
Causal: cause, consequence, effect, result, product, reason, origin.

3. Noun heads such as *set, subset, group and family* are filtered as indicative of hyponymy, but we considered it important to analyze the rest of the sentence with the goal of discarding the presence of a list of elements. For example, in case (5) noun head *organs* can be considered as a hypernym, but in case (6), *dish* is not a hypernym because there is a list of elements indicating another type of relation, in this case, a part-whole relation.
4. When, there is no noun head and only a determinant as *that* followed by a relative as *that* or *which*, hypernym is extracted from noun phrase of the term, that is, noun head of noun phrase of term is considered as hypernym. If noun phrase of term has only one noun, then hypernym is left empty. An example of this heuristic is case (4), here hypernym corresponds to *tumor*.

Table 5. Examples of non-hypernym heads

Contextual Patterns
(T) (Syn1| Syn2)?<VSFIN> (HP1|HP2|HP3)(Def)
<SE>?<PPC>?<VLFIND><CSUBX>? (T) (Syn1| Syn2)?<PA|PAL> (HP1|HP2|HP3) (Def)
(HP1|HP2) <VLFIND> <CSUBX>?(T)

Setting Thresholds for Improving Precision

With the goal of improving precision in extraction of DCs, we proposed an additional filter phase. This phase takes into account the occurrence frequency of hypernyms obtained. We assumed that more frequent hypernym candidates have a higher probability of being true hypernyms than those less frequent. So, it is possible to determine a threshold of frequency in order to get the most relevant results.

Extracting Hyponyms from Hyperonyms

Extraction of hyponyms from hyperonyms consist on extracting hyperonyms plus a relational adjective as candidates to terms or subordinate categories. In order to achieve this goal, the most frequent subset of hyperonyms is utilized for extracting these adjective modifiers.

RESULTS

Source of Textual Information

The source of textual information is constituted by a set of documents of the medical domain, basically human body diseases and related topics (surgeries, treatments, and so on). These documents were collected from MedlinePlus in Spanish. MedlinePlus is a site with a goal to provide information about diseases, treatments, and conditions that is easy to understand.

The kind of communication used in this textual source can be considered as expert-beginner because the information is intended for patients, families, and it is created by various health institutes. Taking into account that each knowledge area has a different lexical set, this kind of communicative situation will be most explanatory using definitions where the meaning of the lexical set must be clarified.

The size of the corpus is 1.2 million of words. We chose a medical domain for reasons of availability of textual resources in digital format. Furthermore, we assume that the choice of this domain does not suppose a very strong constraint for generalization of results to other domains.

Computational Tools

The programming language used in order to automate all tasks required was Python version 3.4 as well as the NLTK module (Bird, Klein, & Loper, 2009). NLTK module constitutes a very valuable resource for research and development in natural language processing.

Table 6. Precision, recall and F-measure

Phase	Recall	Precision	F-measure
Baseline	87%	17%	28%
Chunk Grammar	58%	62%	60%
Filter 1	57%	68%	61%
Filter 2, Freq ≥ 5	42%	80%	55%
Filter 2, Freq ≥ 6	40%	81%	54%
Filter 2, Freq ≥ 10	35%	84%	49%
Filter 2, Freq ≥ 20	27%	90%	42%

Analysis of Results

Chunk grammar is a method in order to extract patterns from texts. DCs are text fragments following a more or less regular structure where this kind of resources can be used with an acceptable performance. Table 6 shows results of precision, recall and F-measure obtained with our method in medicine corpus. Our baseline consists of extracting candidate DCs by considering presence of verbs shown in table 1 within sentences delimited by dot.

Results in table 6 show that chunk grammar achieved a recall of 58% and a precision of 62%. Applying first filter (filter 1) of relations causal and part-whole, a precision of 68% with a reduction of recall to 57% was obtained. On the other hand, the application of frequency thresholds of occurrence of hypernyms shows best results in precision, but as thresholds are increased, recall is significantly reduced. Therefore, if a high precision is an important issue in results, we can apply this kind of heuristics in order to get the best DCs.

Comparing with Other Works

There are significant works about task of conceptual extraction for various languages: French, English, German and Spanish. Specifically for Spanish, there are very few studies. Alarcón (2009) proposed a method of conceptual extraction for Spanish and it is considered a relevant work in this kind of tasks. The proposed method considers verbal patterns in order to extract DCs from texts as well as restriction rules for filtering non-relevant DCs. Verb heads used by Alarcón are reported in table 1 and they are the same considered in this work.

We compared both methods by applying the extraction system designed by Alarcón, named Ecode (Extractor de contextos definitorios), and our program to the medicine corpus. Only for analytical definitions, Ecode achieved a recall of 46%, while with our method we obtained a 58%. On the other hand, our precision of 62% was higher than Ecode (41%).

Results show a significant advantage with respect to proposed method by Alarcón, but we think it would be appropriate to apply our method to corpora of other domains in order to determine stability of our results.

CONCLUSION

We present a method to extract DCs and hyponymy-hypernymy relations from restricted domains. DCs are a rich source in knowledge with respect to a specific domain and they are useful in order to build from dictionaries to ontologies. Our method considers the extraction of lexical relations of hypernymy for filtering non-relevant DCs under the assumption that more frequent hypernyms have a higher probability of being true hypernyms. Hence, candidate DCs with most frequent hypernyms will have a higher probability of being true DCs.

Our results show that precision can be improved by setting frequency thresholds for more frequent hypernyms. So, if precision in results is required, heuristics as proposed in this work can give very useful results.

Despite the difficulty of defining most of concepts in terms of necessary and sufficient conditions, we considered definitions represent a point of view agreed about a concept in specialized domains, and they are useful in order to extract lexical relations and other kinds of relations (attributives, part-whole, thematic roles, and so on).

ACKNOWLEDGMENT

This work has been supported by the National Commission for Scientific and Technological Research (CONICYT) of Chile, Project Numbers: 3140332 and 11130565.

REFERENCES

Acosta, O., Sierra, G., & Aguilar, C. (2011). Extraction of Definitional Contexts using Lexical Relations. *International Journal of Computers and Applications, 34*(6), 46–53.

Aguilar, C. (n. d.). *Análisis lingüístico de definiciones en contextos definitorios* [Unpublished doctoral dissertation] UNAM, Mexico.

Alarcon, R. (2009). *Descripción y evaluación de un sistema basado en reglas para la extracción automática de contextos definitorios* [Unpublished doctoral dissertation]. IULA-UPF, Barcelona.

Alshawi, H. (1987). Processing Dictionary Definitions with Phrasal Pattern Hierarchies. *Computational Linguistics, 13*(3-4), 195–202.

Berlin, B. (1992). *Ethnobiological classification: principles of categorization of plants and animals in traditional societies*. Princeton, N.J.: Princeton University Press. doi:10.1515/9781400862597

Bird, S., Klein, E., & Loper, E. (2009). *Natural Language Processing whit Python*. Sebastropol, Cal.: O'Reilly.

Buitelaar, P., & Cimiano, P. (2008). *Ontology learning and population: bridging the gap between text and knowledge*. Amsterdam: IOS Press.

Buitelaar, P., Cimiano, P., & Magnini, B. (2005). *Ontology learning from text*. Amsterdam: IOS Press.

Calzolari, N. (1984). Detecting patterns in a lexical data base. In *Proceedings of the 22nd Annual Meeting of the Association for Computational Linguistics.* (pp.170-173). Stanford, CA: ACL Publications. doi:10.3115/980491.980527

Cimiano, Ph., Pivk, A., Schmidt, L., & Staab, S. (2004). Learning Taxonomic Relations from Heterogeneous Sources of Evidence. In *Proceedings of the ECAI 2004 Ontology Learning and Population*, Valencia, Spain.

Cohen, H., & Lefebvre, C. (2005). *Handbook of Categorization and Cognitive Science.* Amsterdam: Elsevier.

Collins, M., & Quillian, M. (1969). Retrieval time from semantic memory. *Journal of Verbal Learning and Verbal Behavior, 8*(2), 241–248. doi:10.1016/S0022-5371(69)80069-1

Croft, W., & Cruse, A. (2004). *Cognitive Linguistics.* Cambridge: Cambridge University Press. doi:10.1017/CBO9780511803864

Cruse, D. A. (1986). *Lexical Semantics.* Cambridge: Cambridge University Press.

Demonte, V. (1999). El adjetivo. Clases y usos. La posición del adjetivo en el sintagma nominal. In Bosque, I., & Demonte, V. (Eds.), Gramática descriptiva de la lengua Española. (pp. 129-215). Madrid: Espasa-Calpe.

Dolan, W., Vanderwende, L., & Richardson, S. (1993). Automatically deriving structured knowledge bases form online dictionaries. In *Proceedings of the Pacific Association for Computational Linguistic.* (pp. 5-14).

Estopà, R. (2003). *Extracció de terminologia: elements per a la construcció d'un SEACUSE* [Ph. D. Dissertation]. IULA-UPF, Barcelona.

Evans, V., & Green, M. (2006). *Cognitive Linguistics: An Introduction.* Mahwah, NJ: LEA Publications.

Faure, D., & Nedellec, C. (1998). A Corpus-based Conceptual Clustering Method for Verb Frames and Ontologies. In: *Proceedings of the LREC Workshop on adapting lexical and corpus resources to sublanguages and applications.* (pp. 5-12). Granada, Spain.

Fellbaum, C. (1998). *WordNet: An Electronic Lexical Database.* Cambridge, Mass.: The MIT Press.

Hearst, M. (1992). Automatic Acquisition of Hyponyms from Large Text Corpora. [Nantes, France.]. *Proceedings of, COLING-92*, 539–545.

Hirst, G. (2009). Ontology and the lexicon. In S. Staab & R. Studer (Eds.), *Handbook on Ontologies.* (pp. 269–292). Berlin: Springer. doi:10.1007/978-3-540-92673-3_12

Minsky, M. (1974). *A Framework for Representig Knowledge. Department of Artificial Intelligence.* Cambridge, Mass.: MIT.

Montes, M., Ortega, R., & Villaseñor, L. (2007). Using Lexical Patterns for Extracting Hyponyms from the Web. In MICAI 2007. Advances in Artificial Intelligence, 4827. (pp.904-911). Berlin: Springer.

Murphy, G. (2002). *The Big Book of Concepts.* Cambridge, Mass.: MIT Press.

Murphy, L. (2003). *Semantic Relations and the Lexicon: Antonymy, Synonymy and other Paradigms*. Cambridge: Cambridge University Press. doi:10.1017/CBO9780511486494

Pantel, P., & Pennacchiotti, M. (2006): Espresso: Leveraging Generic Patterns for Automatically Harvesting Semantic Relations. In *Proceedings of Conference on Computational Linguistics*. (pp. 113-120). Sydney, Australia: ACL Publications. doi:10.3115/1220175.1220190

Pereira, F., Lee, L., & Tishby, N. (1993). Distributional Clustering of English Words. In *Proceedings of the 31st Annual Meeting of the Association for Computational Linguistics*. (pp. 183-190). Columbus, Ohio: Ohio State University. doi:10.3115/981574.981598

Pinker, S. (1999). *Words and Rules*. London: Weindefeld & Nicholson.

Poesio, M. (2005). Domain Modelling and NLP: Formal Ontologies? Lexica? Or a Bit of Both? *Applied Ontology*, *1*(1), 27–33.

Rosch, E. (1978). Principles of categorization. In E. Rosh & B. Lloyd (Eds.), *Cognition and Categorization*. (pp. 27–48). Hillsdale, N.J.: LEA Publications.

Rosh, E., Mervis, C., Gray, W., Johnson, D., & Boyes, P. (1976). Basic objects in natural categories. *Cognitive Psychology*, *8*(3), 382–439. doi:10.1016/0010-0285(76)90013-X

Ryu, K., & Choy, P. (2005). An Information-Theoretic Approach to Taxonomy Extraction for Ontology Learning. In P. Buitelaar, P. Cimiano, & B. Magnini (Eds.), *Ontology Learning from Text: Methods, Evaluation and Applications*. (pp. 15–28). Amsterdam: IOS Press.

Sager, J. C. (1990). *A Practical Course in Terminology Processing*. Philadelphia, Amsterdam: John Benjamins Publishing. doi:10.1075/z.44

Schmid, H. (1994). Probabilistic Part-of-Speech Tagging Using Decision Trees. In *Proceedings of International Conference on New Methods in Language Processing*. Retrieved from www.cis.uni-muenchen. de/~schmid/tools/TreeTagger/data/tree-tagger1.pdf

Sierra, G., Alarcon, R., Aguilar, C., & Bach, C. (2008). Definitional verbal patterns for semantic relation extraction. *Terminology*, *14*(1), 74–98. doi:10.1075/term.14.1.05sie

Smith, B. (2003). Ontology. In L. Floridi (Ed.), *Blackwell Guide to the Philosophy of Computing and Information*. (pp. 155–166). Oxford: Blackwell.

Smith, E., & Medin, D. (1981). *Categories and concepts*. Cambridge, Mass.: Harvard University Press. doi:10.4159/harvard.9780674866270

Snow, R., Jurafsky, D., & Ng, A. (2006). Semantic Taxonomy Induction from Heterogenous Evidence. In *Proceedings of the 21st International Conference on Computational Linguistics and 44th Annual Meeting of the ACL*. (pp. 801–808). Sydney: ACL Publications. doi:10.3115/1220175.1220276

Sowa, J. (2005). Categorization in Cognitive Computer Science. In H. Cohen & C. Lefebvre (Eds.), *Handbook of Categorization and Cognitive Science*. (pp. 141–163). Amsterdam: Elsevier. doi:10.1016/B978-008044612-7/50061-5

Tanaka, J., & Taylor, M. (1991). Object Categories and Expertise: Is the Basic Level in the Eye of the Beholder? *Cognitive Psychology*, *23*(3), 457–482. doi:10.1016/0010-0285(91)90016-H

Ungerer, F., & Schmid, H. (1996). *An introduction to cognitive linguistics*. New York: Logman.

Vivaldi, J. (2004). *Extracción de candidatos a términos mediante la combinación de estrategias heterogéneas* [Ph. D. Dissertation]. IULA-UPF, Barcelona.

Wierzbicka, A. (1996). *Semantics: Primes and Universals*. Oxford: Oxford University Press.

Wilks, Y., Slator, B., & Guthrie, L. (1996). *Electric Words*. Cambridge, Mass.: MIT Press.

Wittgenstein, L. (1953). *Philosophical Investigations*. London: Blackwell.

ADDITIONAL READING

Acosta, O., Aguilar, C., & Sierra, G. (2013). Using Relational Adjectives for Extracting Hyponyms from Medical Texts. In Lieto, A. & Cruciani, M. (edts.). In *Proceedings of the First International Workshop on Artificial Intelligence and Cognition* (pp. 33-44). Torino, Italy: CEUR Workshop Proceedings.

Acosta, O., Aguilar, C., & Sierra, G. (2013). Comparación de dos enfoques para la extracción de hipónimos relevantes derivados de hiperónimos. In Sanz I. Berlanga R. & Pérez M. (Eds.). *Memorias del XVIII Congreso de la Sociedad Española para el Procesamiento del Lenguaje Natural* (pp. 80-88), Colección e-Treballs d'informàtica i tecnologia, No. 12, Castellón, Spain: Universitat Jaume I.

Alshawi, H. (1989). Analysing the dictionary definitions. In B. Boguraev & E. Briscoe (Eds.), *Computational Lexicography for Natural Language Processing* (pp. 153–169). London, New York: Longman.

Amsler, R. (1989). Research Toward the Development of a Lexical Knowledge Base for Natural Language Processing. In N. Belkin, & C. van Rijsbergen (Eds.), *Proceedings of 12th International Conference on Research and Development in Information Retrieval* (pp. 242-249). Cambridge, Mass.: ACM. doi:10.1145/75334.75360

Auger, A. (1997). *Repérage des énonces d'intérêt définitoire dans les bases de données textuelles*. Unpublished doctoral dissertation. Neuchâtel, Switzerland: University of Neuchâtel.

Barsalou, L., Simmons, W., Barbey, A., & Wilson, C. (2003). Grounding conceptual knowledge in modality-specific systems. *Trends in Cognitive Sciences*, *7*(2), 84–91. doi:10.1016/S1364-6613(02)00029-3 PMID:12584027

Berland, M., & Charniak, E. (1999). Finding parts in very large corpora. In: *Proceedings of the 37th annual meeting of the Association for Computational Linguistics* (pp. 57-64). Orlando, Florida: ACL Publications. doi:10.3115/1034678.1034697

Boguraev, B., & Briscoe, E. (1989). *Computational Lexicography for Natural Language Processing*. London, New York: Longman.

Boguraev, B., & Pustejovsky, J. (1996). *Corpus Processing for Lexical Acquisition*. Cambridge, Mass.: MIT Press.

Fillmore, Ch. (1985). Frames and the semantics of understanding. *Quaderni di semantica, 6*, 222–254.

Gruber, T. (1993). Translation Approach to Portable Ontology Specifications. *Knowledge Acquisition, 5*(2), 199–220. doi:10.1006/knac.1993.1008

Guarino, N. (1995). Formal Ontology, Conceptual Analysis and Knowledge Representation. *International Journal of Human-Computer Studies, 43*(5/6), 625–640. doi:10.1006/ijhc.1995.1066

Malaisé, V., Zweigenbaum, P., & Bachimont, B. (2005). Mining defining contexts to help structuring differential ontologies. *Terminology, 11*(1), 21–53. doi:10.1075/term.11.1.03mal

Meyer, I. (2001). Extracting a knowledge-rich contexts for terminography: A conceptual and methodological framework. In D. Bourigault, Ch. Jacquemin, & M. C. L'Homme (Eds.), *Recent Advances in Computational Terminology* (pp. 279–302). Amsterdam, Philadelphia: John Benjamins. doi:10.1075/nlp.2.15mey

Rebeyrolle, J. (2000). *Forme et fonction de la définition en discours*. Unpublished doctoral dissertation. Toulouse, France: Université Toulouse-Le Mirail.

Riegel, M. (1987). Définition directe et indirecte dans le langage ordinaire: les énoncés définitoires copulatifs. *Langue française, 73*, 29-53.

Rips, L., & Medin, D. (2005). Concepts, Categories, and Semantic Memory. In K. Holyoak & R. Morrison (Eds.), *Cambridge Handbook of Thinking and Reasoning*. Cambridge: Cambridge University Press.

Rosch, E., & Lloyd, B. (1978). *Cognition and categorization*. Hillsdale, N. Y.: Lawrence Erlbaum Associates.

Rosch, E., & Mervis, C. (1975). Family resemblances. Studies in the internal structure of categories. *Cognitive Psychology, 7*(4), 573–605. doi:10.1016/0010-0285(75)90024-9

Rosh, E., Mervis, C., Gray, W., Johnson, D., & Boyes, P. (1976). Basic objects in natural categories. *Cognitive Psychology, 8*(3), 382–439. doi:10.1016/0010-0285(76)90013-X

Sager, J., & Ndi-Kimbi, A. (1995). The conceptual structure of terminological definition and their linguistic realisations: A report on research in progress. *Terminology, 2*(1), 61–85. doi:10.1075/term.2.1.04sag

Sierra, G. (2009). Extracción de contextos definitorios en textos de especialidad a partir del reconocimiento de patrones lingüísticos. *Linguamática, 1*(2), 13–37.

Sierra, G., Alarcón, R., Aguilar, C., & Bach, C. (2010). Definitional verbal patterns for semantic relation extraction. In A. Auger & C. Barrière (Eds.), *Probing Semantic Relations. Exploration and Identification in Specialized Texts* (pp. 73–96). Amsterdam, Philadelphia: John Benjamins Publishing. doi:10.1075/bct.23.04sie

Vossen, P., & Copestake, A. (1993). Defaults in lexical representation. In T. Briscoe, V. Paiva, & A. Copestake (Eds.), *Inheritance, Defaults and the Lexicon* (pp. 246–274). Cambridge: Cambridge University Press.

KEY TERMS AND DEFINITIONS

Category: A set of entities grouped and organized under certain criteria established.

Categorization: A cognitive mechanism to organize information obtained from our interaction with our world.

Concept: A mental construction which contains information about a specific entity based on our knowledge and our experience.

Definitional Context: A discursive fragment constituted by a term, a definition, and linguistic or metalinguistic connector as predicative phrases, typographical markers or pragmatic patterns.

Hyponymy-Hypernymy: A kind of hierarchical lexical relation where is established a conceptual subordination between the meaning of two or more words, e. g.: a robin (hyponym) is a kind of bird (hypernym).

Lexical Relation: A conceptual link established between words grouped around a lexicon.

Prototype Theory: A theoretical model situated in the framework of cognitive science, formulated by Eleanor Rosch (1938). This theory proposes methods for graduating the process of categorization of concepts, considering some members of a category are more central than others.

Taxonomy: A system of classified concepts associated by specific criteria. This classification can be expressed through lexical relations as hyponymy-hyperonymy.

Term: A word or compound words that designates an specific entity, event or relation into the framework of a scientific or technical knowledge domain.

Chapter 4
Revealing Groups of Semantically Close Textual Documents by Clustering:
Problems and Possibilities

František Dařena
Mendel University in Brno, Czech Republic

Jan Žižka
Mendel University in Brno, Czech Republic

ABSTRACT

The chapter introduces clustering as a family of algorithms that can be successfully used to organize text documents into groups without prior knowledge of these groups. The chapter also demonstrates using unsupervised clustering to group large amount of unlabeled textual data (customer reviews written informally in five natural languages) so it can be used later for further analysis. The attention is paid to the process of selecting clustering algorithms, their parameters, methods of data preprocessing, and to the methods of evaluating the results by a human expert with an assistance of computers, too. The feasibility has been demonstrated by a number of experiments with external evaluation using known labels and expert validation with an assistance of a computer. It has been found that it is possible to apply the same procedures, including clustering, cluster validation, and detection of topics and significant words for different natural languages with satisfactory results.

INTRODUCTION

People and companies have many opportunities to express their opinions related to a wide variety of topics. The media used for such communication include personal web pages and blogs, social networks, discussion boards, e-mail, instant messages, and others. Various subjects can benefit from a high availability of information, which also demands bigger involvement, knowledge, information processing and decision making skills. Due to huge volumes of data that is often freely available for many different

DOI: 10.4018/978-1-4666-8690-8.ch004

subjects there is a need for approaches that enable to use the data for decision making. Since most of the data is available in an unstructured textual form, disciplines focusing on this type of data have gained on their significance during the last few years (Miner at al., 2012).

Because of inadequate time and effort that would be needed in order to reveal the knowledge hidden in the data, the processing cannot be often done manually by humans. Instead, the application of computer based automated methods is a more desirable choice. This is enabled by the availability of increased computational speed and memory sizes of ordinary computers as well as by the development of new algorithms that are able to address various needs and problems. Instead of a traditional methodology employing human operators for reading the documents, statistical analysis, and data mining techniques based on the non-linguistic structure of the documents (Dini & Mazzini, 2010), intelligent computer-based analysis called text mining might arrive at new and unforeseen results.

Text mining is a branch of computer science that uses techniques from data mining, information retrieval, machine learning, statistics, natural language processing, and knowledge management (Berry & Kogan, 2010). The greatest potential of text mining applications is in the areas where large quantities of textual data are generated and collected. These areas include, besides others, categorization of newspaper articles or web pages, e-mail filtering, organization of a library, customer complaints (or feedback) handling, marketing focus group programs, competitive intelligence, market prediction, extraction of topic trends in text streams, discovering semantic relations between events, or customer satisfaction analysis (Cao et al., 2014; Koteswara Rao & Dey, 2011; Miner at al., 2012; Nassirtoussi, 2014; Weiss et al., 2010). Text mining involves tasks such as text categorization, term extraction, single- or multi-document document summarization, clustering, association rules mining, or sentiment analysis (Feldman & Sanger, 2007).

At the end of the last century, machine learning gained on its popularity and became a dominant approach to text mining (Sebastiani, 2002). *Machine learning* is a discipline that focuses on modification or adaptation of computer behavior based on the past experience (the data in this case) so the behavior gets better in the future. Such an adaptation depends on whether there is the right behavior specified. If there is, it means that there is a set of examples with correct answers (actions) provided. In this case we talk about *supervised learning*. During the learning process a computer tries to generalize the knowledge to be able to react correctly to all, even previously unseen inputs. When the correct responses are not provided, a computer tries to find some patterns based on similarities between the inputs. This approach is known as *unsupervised learning* (Marsland, 2009). The common goal of both approaches is to achieve accuracy comparable to that achieved by human experts.

Supervised learning which is the most common type of learning problem (Dittrich, 1995) is also popular in text mining (Sebastiani, 2002). Therefore many text mining tasks require that the data items to be processed have assigned labels that categorize the data. Then the classifier, which is a function that generalizes the knowledge about how to assign correct labels to the data, uses the labels in the process of learning. In some cases, especially when the learned model suffers from high variance (it is too much fit to the exemplar data), having more labeled data is a possible direction of further improvements (Cawley & Talbot, 2010).

Unfortunately, unavailability of the labeled data is often a major problem. As new data constantly occurs, it is nearly impossible to have the labels assigned to the data in a reasonable time and in reasonable amounts. The labeling process itself is also very demanding. Reading just tens or hundreds of documents and assigning the labels correctly requires effort of many people for many hours. Even when the people (annotators) are experts in the given field, resulting quality of the labeled data collection is not obliged to be high because there does not have to be a complete agreement of the annotators (Saratlija, Šnajder & Dalbelo Bašić, 2011).

Clustering, as the most common form of unsupervised learning, enables automatic grouping of un-labeled documents into subsets called clusters. The clusters are coherent internally and must be clearly different from each other to express their own distinct information. If the clusters are good and reliable with respect to the given goal, they can be successfully used as classes. Thus, clustering has been many times successfully used for organizing and searching large text collections, for example, in automatic creation of ontologies, summarizing, disambiguating, and navigating the results retrieved by a search engine, patent analysis, detecting crime patterns and many others (Bsoul, Salim & Zakaria, 2013; Dhillon & Modha, 1999; Guo & Zhang, 2009; Tseng, Lin & Lin, 2007).

While supervised learning tasks usually follow a well-defined goal, for example, minimizing the generalization error in classification, there are no such definitive criteria for unsupervised learning. Instead, interesting structures within the samples are expected to be found (Seeger, 2001) and the evaluation must be often done by a human expert. Only in the case when the labels are available (which is a kind of external information representing a certain goal), it might be revealed whether the created clusters contain objects that belong mostly to one class. However, this, due to the clustering process nature, does not have to be a right measure of the clustering quality.

The goal of the chapter is to introduce clustering as a family of algorithms that can be successfully used to organize text documents into groups without prior knowledge of these groups. The chapter also demonstrates how unsupervised clustering might be used to group large amount of unlabeled textual data so it can be used later for further text mining tasks with the goal of revealing hidden information. The focus is on the data that is quite common today – rather short messages created in an informal manner by various types of people. The attention is paid to the process of selecting clustering algorithms, their parameters, inevitable methods of data preprocessing, and to the methods of evaluating the results by a human expert with an assistance of computers, too.

CLUSTERING

Clustering has gained on its importance during the last few years with the increasing amounts of data available. It covers a wide variety of algorithms rooted in statistics, computer science, computational intelligence, and machine learning with applications in many disciplines (Xu & Wunsch, 2009). The goal of clustering is to organize the data into groups where the entities in each group are similar and entities in different groups are not similar. The cluster might be also defined using a projection of the entities into a n-dimensional feature space (n is the number of features/attributes of the objects). A cluster is then a subspace with high density separated from other clusters by regions with lower density. We might also say that distances between the objects in one cluster are less than distances between objects in the cluster and not in the cluster (Everitt et al., 2011).

Clustering algorithms usually operate on two types of structures. The first type represents the objects to be clustered as sequences of attributes (variables, features) of the objects in the form of vectors. All objects then form an object-by-variable matrix. The second structure is a collection of proximities that have to be available for all pairs of the objects. The proximities are then represented by a square object-to-object matrix containing similarities or dissimilarities of the objects (Kaufmann & Rousseeuw, 2005).

Types of Clustering and the Algorithms

Having a set of objects to be clustered $X = \{x_1, x_2, ..., x_n\}$ where each object is described by a feature vector $x_i = \{x_{i1}, x_{i2}, ..., x_{in}\}$, *partitional (flat) clustering* seeks a k-partition $C = \{C_1, C_2, ..., C_k\}$, $k \leq n$ of X such that

$$C_i = \varnothing, i = 1, 2, ..., k; \bigcup_{i=1}^{k} C_i = X; C_i \cap C_j = \varnothing, i, j = 1, 2, ..., k \text{ and } i \neq j.$$

Hierarchical clustering constructs a tree like, nested structure partition of X, $H = \{H_1, H_2, ..., H_k\}$, $k < n$, such that $C_i \in H_m$, $C_j \in H_l$ and $m > l$ imply $C_i \subset C_j$ or $C_i \cap C_j = \varnothing$ for all $i, j \neq i$, $m, l = 1, 2, ..., k$ (Xu & Wunsch, 2009).

When each object belongs exactly to one cluster, we talk about *hard* clustering. It is also possible to have each object associated with each cluster with a degree of membership in the interval [0, 1]. This approach is known as *soft* or *fuzzy* clustering (Feldman & Sanger, 2007).

There exist a large number of clustering algorithms and their variations. Different clustering algorithms usually lead to different clustering solutions. Moreover, clustering algorithms always produce a partition of the data even when no structure in the data really exists (Xu & Wunsch, 2009).

No matter what algorithm is used, the clustering optimization is a very hard task. For example, for a hard, flat clustering of n elements into k clusters there exist $k^n/k!$ possible clustering solutions. Thus, some kind of a greedy approximation algorithm is usually used (Feldman, Sanger, 2007).

Hierarchical Clustering

Hierarchical clustering methods include top-down (divisive) and bottom-up (agglomerative) methods. The result of their application is a dendrogram representing nesting of the clusters into a hierarchical, tree-like structure.

In the *agglomerative methods*, each item to be clustered is considered to be a single cluster at the beginning. In each of the following steps, two most similar clusters are joined together until all objects are in one cluster. The result is thus a binary tree representing hierarchical dependencies between the clusters. By cutting the dendrogram, one can obtain a certain number of clusters. Cutting the tree closer to the root leads to a lower number of clusters whereas cutting the tree further from the root leads to a higher number of clusters (Myatt & Johnson, 2009), see Figure 1.

Using the single linkage clustering method (SLINK), the clusters are merged according to the similarity of the most similar objects from the clusters. The antithesis to SLINK, known as the complete linkage clustering method (CLINK), determines the similarity according to the similarity of two most dissimilar objects. In the Unweighted Pair Group Method with Arithmetic Mean (UPGMA), the distance between two clusters is calculated as the average of all distances between pairs of objects in both clusters (that is, the mean distance between elements of each cluster). The Weighted Pair Group Method with Arithmetic Mean (WPGMA) assigns higher importance to the objects added to the clusters later. In centroid methods, e.g., the Unweighted or Weighted Pair Group Method with Centroid (UPGMC or WPGMC), the similarity of the clusters is measured using the cluster centroids (Romesburg, 2004; Jain & Dubes, 1988).

Figure 1. A dendrogram as a result of agglomerative hierarchical clustering of objects C1, C2, ..., C6. By performing the cut A four clusters, {C1, C2}, {C3}, {C4, C5}, and {C6}, are obtained (dashed line). The cut B divides the objects into two clusters, {C1, C2, C3}, and {C4, C5, C6} (dotted line).

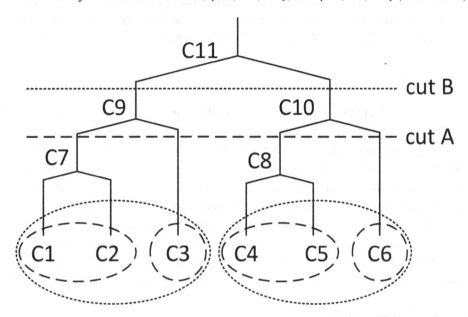

In *divisive methods*, all data is put into one cluster. In the following steps, the data is split into several clusters, typically using a flat method. The same step is then recursively repeated for the new clusters according to some criteria. The procedure finishes when a given number of clusters is found or when there are clusters containing only single objects. An example of divisive clustering method is the bisecting k-means algorithm. The objects creating one cluster are split into two clusters using the basic k-means algorithm, see below. Then, the cluster with a higher number of objects or with the largest variance is selected and split again. The selection and splitting steps are repeated until a desired number of clusters is reached (Cimiano, Hotho & Staab, 2004). It has been found that the bisecting k-means is generally better for higher numbers of clusters than the direct k-means method (Karypis, 2003).

Partitioning Clustering

Partitioning clustering methods do not consider any explicit structure between the clusters. Their result is a set of k clusters, where k is given or automatically determined. In recent years, it has been found that partitioning clustering algorithms are well suited for clustering large document data sets due to their relatively low computational requirements (Zhao & Karypis, 2001).

K-means is the most widely used flat clustering algorithm. In the first step, k randomly selected cluster centers (the seed) are selected (very often, k randomly selected objects). Then, all objects are assigned to a cluster which is the closest in order to minimize the residual sum of squares (squared distance of each object from the centroid summed over all objects). In the following step, the cluster centroids are re-computed according to the positions of the objects in the clusters. The steps of assignment of the objects to the clusters and re-computation of cluster centroids are repeated until a stopping criterion has been met. This condition might be a fixed number of iterations or, most commonly, the situation when the cluster centroid positions do not change between iterations. Because the result does not have to be optimal (the algorithm arrives to a local optimum), several strategies might be chosen. For example, the entire process might be repeated several times with a different seed and the best solution is chosen, outliers might be excluded from the seed set, or the seed might be obtained from another method, such as hierarchical clustering (Manning, Raghavan & Schütze, 2008).

Graph Partitioning

Instead of using vector document representation, graph based methods work with the collection of documents in the form of a graph. In the *similarity graph* the documents are represented by vertices of a graph where the edges that exist between each pair of the nodes are quantified according to the similarity between the documents. Then, a way how to partition the graph is searched so the edge-cut is minimized.

An alternate model using graphs considers the documents and the terms contained in them. The graph is then a bipartite graph where its set of vertices consists of two sets – a set of documents V_d and a set of terms V_t. If a document contains a term, then the vertex in V_d, representing the document, and the vertex in V_t, representing the term, are connected by an edge. The weights of the edges are set using *tf-idf* measure. During the clustering process, documents as well as terms associated with these documents are assigned to the clusters while the edge-cut is optimized (Zhao & Karypis, 2001).

Clustering Text Documents

Clustering might be successfully applied also to collections of text documents. The goal of document clustering is to partition the documents into clusters (subsets, groups) so the documents in each cluster are more similar to each other than to documents in other subsets. In other words, the similarity of the documents in a cluster is high whereas the similarity of the documents between different clusters is low.

This process has, however, several unique characteristics that must be taken into consideration. Usually, documents have very complex internal structure given by the natural language in which the documents are written. Thus, processing such collections usually requires massive computational power,

Figure 2. Distribution of unique words (after removing very rare words) in positive and negative reviews compared with the distribution in the mixed set of documents for different languages.

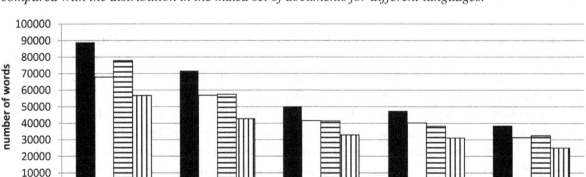

especially for some algorithms. Also, the evaluation of text clustering and assigning meaningful labels to the clusters is a complicated task (Feldman & Sanger, 2007).

When handling the documents simply as a bag of words and using simple comparisons of the words in different documents (often employing vector document representation), the imperfectness of various methods is caused by the fact that the majority of words appear in all classes of documents, see Figure 2 for an example of word distribution in a collection of documents containing positive and negative reviews of hotel services.

It is also worth showing that the text processing problem, based on words without keeping their original mutual connections or succession that provide the right meaning of phrases, is not an easy task. Consider, for example, the phrases *"quite bad accommodation"* and *"not so bad accommodation"* that share about a half of the words while having completely different meaning. Figure 3 illustrates it well: for a random selection of 5,000 reviews from each class (positive and negative reviews), a reader can see that both classes contain the same frequent words. For example, the positive terms like *good, clean, comfortable*, and so on, can be also contained in negative reviews. However, the right meaning is naturally given by connections with other terms.

Figure 3. The most frequent words that appear in both the negative (the dashed curve) and positive (the solid curve) reviews. The occurrence (frequency) can sometimes be similar, sometimes different, however, it itself is not the only decisive factor. Source: Žižka, Burda and Dařena (2012).

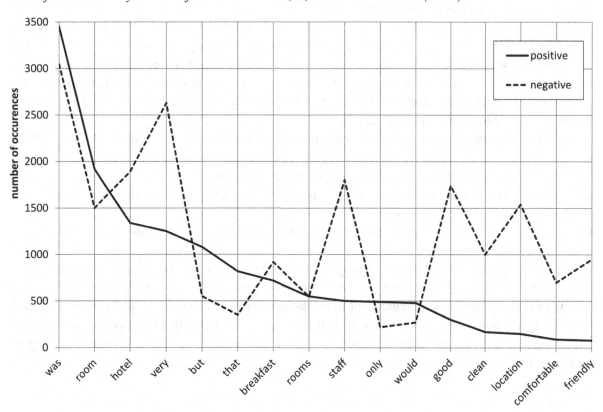

Representation of Text Documents

Generally, text data is freely written having no explicit structure. In order to be able to process the data using, for example, machine learning algorithms, it must be transformed to a representation suitable for the given algorithm and the particular task. Textual data might be generally structured according to the level at which the data is analyzed, from the sub-word level (decomposition of words and their morphology) to the pragmatic level (the meaning of the text with respect to its context and situation). Ambiguities at each level can be resolved at the following higher level (e.g., the syntactic level can help decide whether a word is a noun or a verb). Generally, the higher the level is, the more details about the text are captured and the higher is the complexity of automatic creation of the representation. In many cases, words are meaningful units of little ambiguity even without considering the context and therefore they are the basis for most work in text mining. A big advantage of word-based representations is their simplicity and the straightforward process of their creation. The texts are simply transformed to a bag of words, a sequence of words where the ordering is irrelevant. A widely used format for representing the documents is the vector space model proposed by Salton (Salton, Wong & Yang, 1975). Each document is then represented by a vector, $x_i = (x_{i1}, x_{i2}, ..., x_{im})$, where individual dimensions represent values of individual attributes of the text. Commonly, each word is treated as such one attribute (Joachims, 2002). The entire document collection is represented by an $n \times m$ matrix where n is a number of all documents (that is, a number of rows) and m is the number of unique words (that is, a number of columns) in the collection. Such a set of unique words (or other features) is known as the dictionary (Weiss et al., 2010). Then, every matrix word element, x_{ij}, is a binary, integer, or real number depending on the applied representation of words. Zero elements in the matrix mean that the word (or another document feature) representing the column is not present in the text.

Having a large collection of text documents, there is one additional problem. As the vocabulary of a natural language is large, vectors representing the documents have many dimensions (see Figure 4) and the vectors are very sparse (the number of unique words in a document is very small compared to the total number of words in the dictionary). High dimensionality and sparseness of the data increase the computational complexity and may lead to lower classification accuracy with normal machine learning methods (Phan, Nguyen & Horiguchi, 2008).

The weights of every term are generally determined by three components (Salton & McGill, 1983):

- local weight representing the frequency in every single document,
- global weight reflecting the discriminative ability of the terms, based on the distribution of the terms over the entire document collection,
- normalization factor correcting the impact of different lengths of documents.

The most popular methods for determining the local weights of the words include *term presence (tp)* – the weights are binary (0 or 1), representing the presence or absence of the term, and *term frequency (tf)* – the weights correspond to numbers of times the word appeared in the text. Most commonly used global weight is *inverse document frequency (idf)* with the general idea that the less the word is common among all texts, the more specific and thus more important it is. Inverse document frequency of the term x_i can be calculated as

Figure 4. Numbers of unique words for collections of text documents of different sizes. The documents represent customer reviews written in different natural languages.

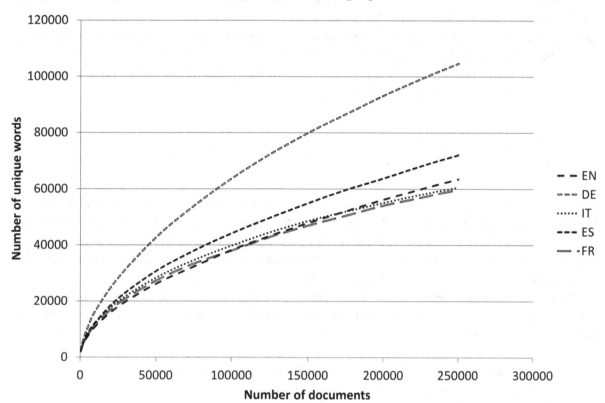

$$idf\left(t_i\right) = \log\frac{N}{n\left(x_i\right)},$$

where N is the number of documents in the collection, and $n(x_i)$, also called document frequency, is the number of documents containing the term x_i. The local weight *tf* is often combined with the global weight *idf* into a weight called *term frequency–inverse document frequency, tf-idf* (Cummins & O'Riordan, 2006).

The quality of vector representation can be increased by using n-grams, enhancing by semantics, removing the very frequent of very infrequent words, removing stop words, application of stemming, and others. Although using n-grams, syntactical phrases, stemming, and stop words removal can influence the results of text mining algorithms, their effects on the quality of text mining tasks are often marginal (Figueiredo et al., 2011).

Document Similarity

Document similarity is the only endogenous information that is available in the clustering process. The similarity can be measured between individual documents, between groups of documents, or between a document and a group of documents. This depends on the applied clustering algorithm. For instance, some algorithms measure the similarity between two clusters in terms of the similarity of the most similar objects (single linkage clustering method, SLINK) or two most dissimilar objects (complete linkage clustering method, CLINK). In the k-means algorithm the objects are moved to the closest cluster; the objects are compared to the centroids of the clusters for this assignment. In agglomerative centroid methods, each cluster is represented by a centroid and the similarity is calculated between these centroids (Romesburg, 2004; Jain, Dubes, 1988).

A group of documents C might be represented by a vector C_C that can be calculated as the mean of vectors representing all documents x in the group:

$$C_C = \frac{\sum_{x \in C} x}{|C|} = \left(C_{C1}, C_{C2}, \ldots, C_{Cm} \right),$$

where $\sum_{x \in C} x$ is a vector the elements of which contain sums of corresponding elements of all documents from the group C, and $|C|$ is the size of the set C_C, i.e., the number of documents in C; C_{Ci} are thus average values calculated from elements of all vectors from group C. This vector can be seen as a fictive composite object. Then, comparison of two documents, of a document and a cluster, or of two clusters might be done in the same way (Weiss et al., 2010).

There exist many possibilities of how to measure the similarity between documents. In order to consider a measure $d(A, B)$ measuring the similarity/distance between objects A and B, a correct metric the following criteria must be fulfilled (Schaeffer, 2007):

- if A and B are identical, the distance between them must be zero: $d(A, A) = 0$,
- the distance must be symmetrical: $d(A, B) = d(B, A)$,
- the triangle inequality holds: $d(A, B) \leq d(A, C) + d(C, B)$.

The similarity of a document pair is often represented by a value that reflects the positions of the multidimensional points created by individual items. Generally, the closer the points appear, the more similar the text items are (Srivastava & Sahami, 2009). The similarity computation depends on a specific situation. In text mining tasks, *cosine similarity* based on the angle between vector pairs (Duda, Hart & Stork, 2001) is often used:

$$L_C(A, B) = \frac{A \cdot B}{A * B} = \frac{\sum_{i=1}^{m} A_i * B_i}{\sqrt{\sum_{i=1}^{m} (A_i)^2} * \sqrt{\sum_{i=1}^{m} (B_i)^2}},$$

where $A = (A_1, A_2, \ldots, A_m)$ and $B = (B_1, B_2, \ldots, B_m)$ are vectors representing the documents, m is the number of attributes, and $A \cdot B$ is the scalar product of vectors A and B. The values of L_C range between 0 and 1; the more similar the documents are, the smaller angle between their vectors is and the higher the value of this measure is.

Another simple computation employs the *Euclidean distance* between two text documents A and B:

$$L_E\left(A,B\right)=\sqrt{\sum_{i=1}^{m}\left(A_i-B_i\right)^2}$$

The closer the documents located in the *m*-dimensional space are, the smaller the value of L_C is.

Jaccard coefficient measures the similarity in terms of intersection of two sets divided by their union. For text documents, the Jaccard coefficient compares the sum of weights of shared terms to the sum of weights of terms that are present in either of the two documents but are not the shared terms (Huang, 2008):

$$L_J\left(A,B\right)=\frac{A\cdot B}{A+B-A\cdot B}=\frac{\sum_{i=1}^{m}A_i*B_i}{\sqrt{\sum_{i=1}^{m}\left(A_i\right)^2}+\sqrt{\sum_{i=1}^{m}\left(B_i\right)^2}-\sum_{i=1}^{m}A_i*B_i}$$

Depending on a specific task or data, other distance measures might be applied, for example, Minkowski, Manhattan, Chebyshev, Hamming, Mahalanobis, Pearson's correlation coefficient and others, see, for instance, (Kaufman & Rousseeuw, 2005; Huang, 2008).

Some of the above mentioned similarity measures might be used for construction of a similarity graph (see above) that is used for graph based clustering (Schaeffer, 2007).

Criterion Functions in Partitioning Clustering

During assigning the documents into the clusters, a particular clustering criterion (objective) function defined over the entire clustering solution is optimized (i.e., minimized or maximized). Zhao and Karypis (2001) define internal, external, hybrid, and graph-based criterion functions.

Internal criterion functions try to maximize the similarity of documents in individual clusters while not considering the documents in different clusters. The first internal criterion function I_1 maximizes the sum of average pairwise similarities between the documents assigned to each cluster, weighted according to the size of each cluster. When cosine similarity measure is used the I_1 function is defined as follows:

$$I_1=\sum_{r=1}^{k}n_r\left(\frac{1}{n_r^2}\sum_{x_i,x_j\in S_r}\cos\left(x_i,x_j\right)\right)$$

The second internal criterion function I_2 maximizes the similarity between individual documents and the centroids C_r of the clusters where the documents are assigned. The value of I_2 is for cosine similarity calculated as

$$I_2=\sum_{r=1}^{k}\sum_{x_i\in S_r}\cos\left(x_i,C_r\right)$$

External criterion function E_1 focuses on optimization of dissimilarity of individual clusters. Thus, using this function, the documents of each cluster are separated from the entire collection:

$$E_1 = \sum_{r=1}^{k} n_r \cos\left(C_r, C\right)$$

where C is the centroid of the entire document collection. The value of E_1 is being minimized, which means that the angle of vectors C_r and C is the biggest possible.

Hybrid criterion functions do not optimize only one criterion but more of them. Instead of focusing only on intra-cluster similarity of the clustering solution – while not taking into account documents in different clusters or focusing only on the distinctness of the clusters – hybrid functions combine both internal and external criteria. The two hybrid criterion functions combine the external function E_1 with I_1 or I_2 respectively:

$$H_1 = \frac{I_1}{E_1} \qquad H_2 = \frac{I_2}{E_1}$$

Both internal functions I_1 and I_2 are normally maximized. Although E_1 is normally minimized, hybrid functions H_1 and H_2 are maximized because their values are inversely related to E_1.

Graph based criterion function MinMaxCut (Ding et al., 2001) minimizes the edge-cut between the vertices representing documents in different clusters in a *similarity graph S_r*, scaled by the sum of the internal edges. The edge-cut is defined as the sum of the edges connecting vertices in one cluster to vertices in the other cluster:

$$\sum_{r=1}^{k} \frac{\operatorname{cut}\left(S_r, S - S_r\right)}{\sum_{x_i, x_j \in S_r} \operatorname{sim}\left(x_i, x_j\right)},$$

where $cut(S_r, S-S_r)$ is the edge-cut between the vertices in S_r to the rest of the vertices in the graph $S-S_r$.

When the cosine similarity measure is used, the G_1 criterion function is defined as

$$G_1 = \sum_{r=1}^{k} \frac{\sum_{x_i \in S_r, x_j \in S-S_r} \cos\left(x_i, x_j\right)}{\sum_{x_i, x_j \in S_r} \cos\left(x_i, x_j\right)}$$

Because in this process both internal and external similarities are considered, this criterion function G_1 might be seen as a hybrid one.

The normalized cut criterion function working on a *bipartite graph* (vertices represent documents and terms, edges correspond to the presence of terms in the documents) looks for an optimal edge-cut. The normalized cut (Zha et al., 2001) criterion function is defined as

$$G_2 = \sum_{r=1}^{k} \frac{\mathrm{cut}\left(V_r, V - V_r\right)}{W\left(V_r\right)},$$

where V_r is the set of vertices assigned to the rth cluster, and $W(V_r)$ is the sum of the weights of the adjacency lists of the vertices assigned to the rth cluster (rth cluster contains both documents as well as terms).

Evaluating the Clustering Process

In the supervised learning approach the known labels are used in the process of generalizing the knowledge. Such generalization is usually not perfect. Large input space and noise caused, for example, by spelling and grammar errors are typical for textual data written in a natural language. This causes many problems when building a classifier and implies a higher classification error (Joachims, 2002). However, supervised approaches generally provide the lowest error rate among the machine learning methods.

Using an unsupervised approach, the perfectness of the output is usually expected to be much lower that desired. The reason is the fact that the missing labels must be assigned automatically without having any prior knowledge of the data. Thus, the labels might be finally assigned differently than a human expert would assign them because only he or she has a clear objective and can use some additional, external information (Weiss et al., 2010).

Sufficiently high quality (acceptable for a user) of clusters is essential for the success of the entire process. It is obvious that having only one cluster is unacceptable because there is no structure visible in

Figure 5. Quality of clustering solutions with different numbers of clusters measured by the Purity criterion.

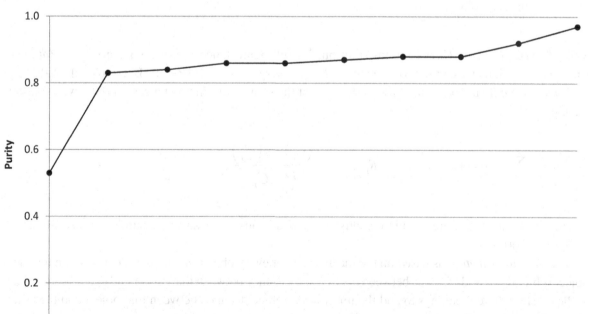

the data. On the other hand, having the same number of clusters and instances (i.e., each cluster contains only one object) lacks any generalization although the clusters are perfect in terms of all measures of cluster quality. The relation between the number of clusters and the quality of the clusters was demonstrated by an experiment based on clustering textual documents representing customer reviews (see the description of the data below). Figure 5 contains information about the quality of clustering solutions for different numbers of clusters for the given specific data. It is obvious that with the increasing number of the clusters the quality expressed in terms of purity of the clusters (for an explanation see below) approaches to 1 (which represents a perfect clustering solution).

Internal Evaluation Measures

Using internal measures the clusters are evaluated according to the characteristics derived from the data itself. They are usually based on the criteria of compactness and separation. *Compactness* measures how much the objects are in a cluster related to each other. Lower variance measured, e.g., in terms of pairwise or center-based distances in the cluster, signifies higher compactness. Separation evaluates how a cluster is separated from other clusters. Measures using distances between cluster centers, pairwise distances between objects from different clusters, or measures based on density might be applied (Liu et al., 2010).

Various aspects of the internal quality can be combined to a single measure, e.g. the Dunn Index, Davies-Bouldin index, or the Silhouette index.

The *Dunn index* measures cluster to cluster distances against cluster diameters:

$$I\left(C\right) = \frac{\min_{i \neq j}\left\{\delta\left(C_i, C_j\right)\right\}}{\max_{1 < l < k}\left\{\Delta\left(C_l\right)\right\}},$$

where $C = \{C_1, C_2, ..., C_k\}$ is a clustering solution, δ is a cluster distance measure, e.g., $min_{x \in Ci, y \in Cj}\{d(x,y)\}$, and $\Delta(C_l)$ is a diameter measure of the cluster l, e.g., $max_{x,y \in Cl}\{d(x,y)\}$ (Rivera-Borroto et al., 2012).

Davies-Bouldin index is a function of the ratio of the sum of within-cluster scatter to between cluster separation:

$$\left(C\right) = \frac{1}{k} * \sum_{i=1}^{k} R_i, \text{where} R_i = \max_{j=1..n, i \neq j} R_{ij}, R_{ij} = \frac{s\left(C_i\right) + s\left(C_j\right)}{\delta\left(C_i, C_j\right)},$$

where s measures the scatter within the cluster and δ is a cluster distance measure (Stein, zu Eissen & Wißbrock, 2003).

The *Silhouette method* is based on the mean score for every object in the data set. The score for each object is based on the difference between the average distance between that object and every other object in the cluster where it belongs to and the minimum average distance between that object and the other objects in all of the other clusters. The difference is divided by a normalizing term, which is the greater of the two averages:

$$S = \frac{1}{n} \sum_{i=1}^{n} \frac{b_i - a_i}{\max\{a_i, b_i\}},$$

where n is the number of objects to be clustered, a_i is the average distance (dissimilarity) between the object i and all other objects in the same cluster like i, and b_i is the minimum average distance (dissimilarity) between i and the objects in other clusters than i belongs to. The index ranges from -1 to 1 where higher values indicate better clustering solutions (Guerra et al., 2012).

External Evaluation Measures

External measures for evaluating the quality of clustering solutions can be used when the class labels (ground truth) for the data to be clustered are available apriori. It is therefore an objective evaluation measuring the extent of how many objects are assigned to a "wrong" cluster.

Entropy, as proposed by Shannon, measures the average amount of information that is received in incoming messages (Balian, 2003). This measure can be also successfully used for measuring the quality of clusters (Steinbach, Karypis & Kumar, 2000). The lowest entropy (value 0) and thus the best quality of a cluster is achieved when the cluster contains instances solely from one class. The highest entropy (value $log(c)$, where c is the number of classes) and thus the worst quality of a cluster is achieved when there are instances of more classes in the cluster and the classes are equally distributed. When there are instances of more classes in one cluster, probabilities of distributions of the data among the classes must be calculated first in order to compute the entropy. The value p_{ij} represents the probability that a member of the cluster j belongs to the class i. The entropy of the cluster j is then calculated as

$$E_j = -\sum_i p_{ij} \log p_{ij},$$

where the sum is taken over all classes in the given cluster. Considering more clusters the entropy of the entire clustering solution might be calculated as the sum of the entropies of all clusters weighted according to the size of the clusters:

$$E = \sum_{j=1}^{k} \frac{n_j E_j}{n},$$

where k is the number of clusters, n_j is the size of the cluster j, and n is the number of instances to be clustered.

Another measure that is often used in information retrieval and classification is known as the *F-measure*. It combines values of precision (the fraction of instances that are from a desired, i.e., relevant class) and recall (the fraction of relevant instances that are retrieved). It is obvious that both values are always calculated with respect to the given class. Precision for the class i in the cluster j can be calculated as

$$Prec\left(i,j\right) = \frac{n_{ij}}{n_j},$$

where n_{ij} is the number of instances of the class i in the cluster j, and n_j is the total number of instances in the cluster j. Recall for the class i in the cluster j can be calculated as

$$Rec\left(i,j\right) = \frac{n_{ij}}{n_i},$$

where n_{ij} is the number of instances of the class i in the cluster j, and n_i is the total number of instances of the class i. The value of F-measure is typically calculated as the harmonic mean of precision and recall:

$$F\left(i,j\right) = 2 * \frac{Prec\left(i,j\right) * Rec\left(i,j\right)}{Prec\left(i,j\right) + Rec\left(i,j\right)}$$

The F-measure for the entire clustering solution is the averaged F-measure for all classes distributed over all clusters (Stein & zu Eissen, 2003):

$$F = \sum_{i=1}^{l} \frac{n_i}{n} * \max_{j=1..k} F\left(i,j\right),$$

where l is the number of classes, n_i is the number of instances from the class i, n is the number of all instances, and k is the number of clusters.

Measure called *Purity* measures how pure individual clusters are, i.e., to which extent the clusters contain instances from one class (Zaki & Wagner, 2014). The Purity for the cluster j can be calculated as

$$P_j = \frac{1}{n_j} * \max_{i=1..l} n_{ij},$$

where n_j is the number of instances in the cluster j, n_{ij} is the number of instances of the class i in the cluster j, and l is the number of classes. The Purity of the entire clustering solution is an average of purities for all clusters weighted according to their sizes (Zhao & Karypis, 2001):

$$P = \sum_{j=1}^{k} \frac{n_j}{n} * P_j,$$

where n_j is the number of instances in the cluster j, n is the total number of all instances, P_j is the purity of the cluster j, and k is the number of clusters.

Evaluation Based on Expert Opinion

This kind of validation is carried out by human experts and is suitable under many circumstances (Mendes, Cardoso, 2006). It may reveal new insight into the data, but is generally very expensive and demanding. The results that are subjectively influenced are also not very well comparable (Färber et al., 2010).

The objects to be clustered are characterized by some attributes and their values – each object can be thus seen as a multidimensional vector. These objects are located in a multidimensional space (where the number of dimensions is equal to the number of attributes) according to the values of the vectors. Intuitively, the clusters can be defined as sub-spaces containing the objects that are clearly separated from the other sub-spaces. This identification can be thus done visually by a human expert. However, the problem is when the number of dimensions is greater than three. There exist methods that are able to project objects from a multidimensional space to 2D or 3D space. This enables the users to examine visually whether the created clusters correspond to the clusters that they can see. Such an approach is based on the principle that groups of objects that are separated in 2D (or 3D space) are also separated in a space with many dimensions (Huang, Ng & Cheung, 2001). This kind of evaluation is, however, difficult to use for data with a very high number of dimensions, which is the case of textual document collections.

The experts might also examine the objects in individual clusters and consider to which extent such an arrangement contributes to the objective that they have specified. In the case that many objects are being automatically categorized, such a manual process would be very difficult and thus infeasible. In that case it is possible to consider not all of the documents but examine only some of them. There exist several approaches of how to choose the representative documents (Gelbukh et al., 2003). A user might be presented with a document which is:

- an average document – the document lies most closely to the remaining documents in the cluster, i.e., it is located near the centroid of the cluster;
- the least typical element – the document is close the border of the cluster, closely to the remaining clusters; it is most similar to the documents in the other clusters;
- the most typical – the document is located near the border of the cluster, far from the other clusters; it is the most different from all of the documents in the collection and thus most specific.

The results of the last two methods might be difficult to interpret especially in the case that there are many clusters in the clustering solution. Therefore, choosing a document that is located in the center of the cluster seems to be a suitable method. Sometimes, one document does not have to be informative enough. Therefore, more documents selected using the same criterion might be used. In that situation, the documents will be ranked according to the given criterion and a few documents that lie at the top of such a list of ranked documents are selected.

Evaluation Based on Expert Opinion with Advanced Machine Learning Support

The documents that are categorized using the clustering process are often represented by means of a bag of word which ignores the order of the words in the documents and thus loses some important information. Such a distortion might also negatively influence the semantic meaning of the document. A reconstruction of the original document from the bag of words representation, especially when further preprocessing steps are applied, is often impossible. It is therefore beneficial to maintain both representations of each document – the original and vector representations. When it is not possible to have both versions of the documents available, it is beneficial to apply a procedure that will filter and present only relevant attributes that sufficiently well characterize the documents in the clusters.

The procedure presented below is based on the assumption that the semantic content of the generated clusters is given by words (terms) that are significant for expressing the meanings; such words can be revealed by the application of some data mining techniques. Certain important terms relate to a specific topic while other significant words to different ones. Žižka & Dařena (2011a) and Dařena & Žižka (2011) applied a generator of decision trees that provided a ranked list of attributes the values of which were decisive for minimizing the entropy during the documents classification. The main idea was to find such document elements that were important from the correct classification viewpoint. It was also assumed that these elements could say what a document was talking about. Such important attributes –present here, the words, were called significant words.

A decision tree is in fact a directed graph where exactly one vertex, called the root, is connected only to outgoing edges and some of the vertices, called leaves, are associated only with incoming edges. Additionally, there exists exactly one path between the root and each leaf; the graph naturally does not contain loops. The decision tree is used in order to give an answer to the given problem – here the answer is the category of the object to be classified based on the values of attributes characterizing the object. Vertices (also the nodes) of the tree, except the leaves, represent questions that must be answered (for example: whether the document contains the word *location* or not). According to an answer to the question, one of the outgoing edges (also the links) is selected, which moves us to a following node. This node contains either another question or – in the case of the leaves – the answer to the entire problem, i.e., the category into which the object should be placed. In a text mining problem, the documents are characterized by attributes that are functions of the words appearing in the documents. The questions in a decision tree generally incorporate a value that is a function of a certain word (similarly in our approach when we worked only with single words) or word combinations (e.g., n-grams). Typically, the value has three components – a local weight based on the frequency of the word in a single document, a global weight reflecting the distribution of the word in all documents, and a normalization factor reducing the effects of different document lengths (Chrisholm & Kolda, 1999). An example of a fragment of a decision tree that might be used for classification of documents into categories Positive and Negative reviews can be found in Figure 6. The function of the words is here denoted as *f(word)*. Because the value is numeric, it is compared to a numeric value. Very often, due to low frequency of words in single documents, it is only important whether the word is in the document (i.e., $f(word) > 0$) or is not in the document ($f(word) = 0$).

The decision tree is built with utilization of labeled data. Selecting the attributes that best contribute to splitting, a heterogeneous set of instances mixed from different classes between more homogeneous subsets representing instances belonging to more specific classes, the tree is continuously built from the top while decreasing the entropy of the new sets in the lower levels (Quinlan, 1993).

The tree is able to provide a list of attributes the values of which are relevant for assigning every document instance to some of the predefined classes. These words can be found in the nodes of the decision tree as parts of the questions. Other words that are certainly contained in the documents as well have no or marginal effect in the classification. The most significant word, in terms of its contribution to decreasing entropy in the sets that are characterized by the common value of the given attribute, is in

Figure 6. An example of a fragment of a decision tree that might be used for the classification of English reviews into classes Positive (+) and Negative (-). Source: Žižka and Dařena (2011b).

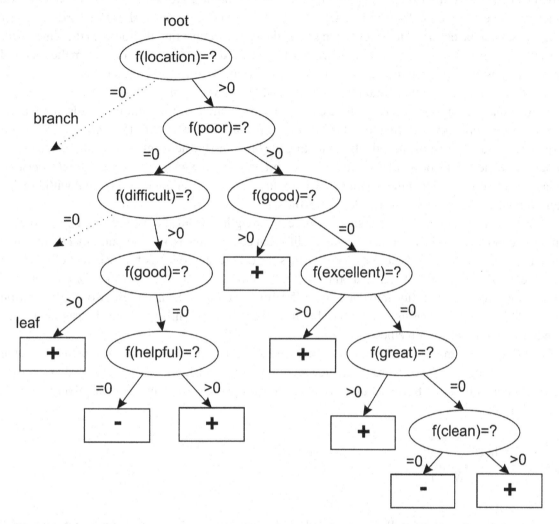

the root of the decision tree. It is because the tree asks each time for the value of the attribute representing the word. Other words in the rank get gradually lower significance according to their importance for decreasing entropy with respect to the classification accuracy. As it was shown in Žižka and Dařena (2011b), those significant words (and phrases composed from them) corresponded very well to a reader's point of view. For the presented data type, such words represent the semantic contents of the clusters.

The words appearing in the decision tree create a dictionary composed of only the significant words. Their number is a small fraction of all the words used in the reviews, typically a couple of hundreds from tens of thousands. For example, for a set of 50,000 reviews written in English, around 200 significant words (from the total number of about 26,500) relevant to the classification into twenty classes were found. The classification using the decision tree worked with a relatively small accuracy error. It was, applying 10-fold cross-validation testing, around 10%. Although classification accuracy was not the main goal of this task, it shows that the words are indeed relevant with respect to the predefined categories.

The significant words, however, do not tell anything about how relevant they are with respect to individual classes – some words are typical for one class while they are quite rare for the other classes. Sometimes, one word might frequently appear in reviews from more groups. How the words are related to the classes can be observed in the decision tree and its paths connecting the root and the leaves. Here, the leaves represent individual classes and the words contained in each branch (path from the root to the leaf) of the classification tree represent combinations of terms leading to a certain class.

If a branch ending in a leaf contains words that lead exclusively to that class, such words are typical just for that class. Branches leading to different classes may contain some identical words, for example, *always – good – breakfast* (leading to a class positively evaluating the breakfast), or *always – not – good – breakfast* (leading to a class negatively evaluating the breakfast), where only the word *not* makes a difference while the other words are the same. Another branch can contain *always – not – good – personnel* (a class negatively criticising the personnel) where the semantic meaning does not deal with breakfast at all even when there are also some identical words.

Thus, there is a problem how to assign a degree of strength to words pointing correctly (in combinations with other words) via different branches to different classes, that is, to different semantic meanings. For example, a word W_1, *bad*, can be used 30 times for correct and 0 times for incorrect classification into the class B (bad breakfasts), and another word W_2, *always*, can be used 30 times for correct and 20 times for incorrect classification into that class B (50 times in total). Which of these two words contribute more to B? The word W_1 was used less times but in 100% correctly, while the word W_2 was used 5 times more but with only 60% correctness.

According to the method described in Dařena and Žižka (2011), the frequencies of the correct and incorrect directing by a given word in the tree were represented using a two-dimensional vector space to introduce a weight that balanced those two frequencies. The word weight w_w was given by the following formula:

$$w_w = \frac{N_C}{N_N} * \frac{\ln \sqrt{N_C^2 + N_N^2}}{\ln \left(N_{max} \right)},$$

where N_{max} is the maximum of $N_{correct}$ (the number of a word usages for correct classifications) and N_{all} (the sum of a word usages for all classifications). The logarithms dampen the influence of big values. The calculated weight then determines the importance of a word in relation to a given class – higher numbers mean greater relevancy. The weight w_w might be also modified using a multiplication factor l that takes into consideration the level of the word (corresponding node) in the decision tree. The higher (closer to the root) the word in the decision tree is, the less specific for a particular class it is. For example, the word in the root of the tree is relevant for a large portion of the documents and thus it is not too specific with respect to just one class. The weight then might be calculated as $w_w' = l * w$, where the value of l increases with the distance from the root.

Using the information from the decision tree, lists of significant words together with their relevance measures (as expressed by the weight w_w) with relation to predefined classes might be obtained. These words then should characterize the semantic meanings of most of the categories.

Labeling the Clusters

Sometimes, not only the labels for the data are not assigned to the documents but the labels also do not have to exist. We might consider a company selling some products or providing some services. On some web pages the customers have a possibility to talk about them, evaluate them, or simply send complaints electronically, everything freely written using a natural language. Reading thousands of such messages by a human expert and identifying the major topics that are mentioned would be infeasible. Instead of that, a computer might try to find some groups of documents that are somehow similar and distinguished from the other groups. We might expect that these groups will be more or less related to individual aspects of the product or service. Subsequently these groups might be further processed so typical representatives of the groups or keywords characterizing the groups can be retrieved and used, e.g., for improving the business quality.

According to Ferraro & Wanner (2012) two main strategies of document cluster labeling can be identified. In internal cluster labeling, which is usually quite a simple approach, the label of the cluster is based solely on the content of the cluster. The title of a representative document or a list of words that appear with a sufficient frequency might be used. In differential cluster labeling the label is determined by contrasting the cluster with other clusters. When a candidate label depends on a cluster more than on the other clusters, it is considered a good label for that cluster. Several statistical measures, such as Mutual Information, Information Gain, or χ^2 might be applied.

HOTEL SERVICE MULTILINGUAL REVIEWS: A CASE STUDY

To demonstrate how clustering might be useful in the process of mining knowledge from textual data, the above mentioned procedures were applied to real world data representing customer opinions regarding accommodation services.

The Data Used in the Experiments

The text data used in the experiments contained opinions in many languages of several millions of customers who – via the on-line Internet service – booked accommodations in different hotels and countries worldwide. Besides the information about the hotel prices, facilities, policies, terms, and conditions, the web contains user reviews related to their stays in a given hotel. The reviews cannot be entered by any person but only by the people that made a reservation through the web and stayed in the hotel. Each review consists of an identification of the reviewer, his or her overall evaluation (a number on a ten point scale) and the text of the review. The identification of the user includes the country and city where the reviewer comes from – this information was used for determining the language of the review. Each review text has two parts – a negative and positive experience in the hotel, both written in a natural language. Because of the policies of the hotel reservation web, the samples are labeled as positive and negative relatively carefully and by people who really stayed in the hotel. On one hand, the reviews are often written quite formally; on the other hand, most of them embody all deficiencies typical for texts written in natural languages (mistyping, transposed letters, missing letters, grammar errors, sometimes combinations of two languages in one item, and so on). Often, languages that normally use diacritic (for example, Czech, French, Spanish, and others) are used sometimes with and sometimes without it.

The data was collected from more than 100 countries, 108,000 hotels, and contained about 5,000,000 reviews written in many languages. Such a big number of labeled examples enabled to create data sets with sufficient sizes where an automated approach to processing is indeed beneficial. Also, such data sets could be created for an interesting number of different languages. In out experiments, we focused on widespread languages with high number of reviews, i.e., English (EN), German (DE), Spanish (ES), French (FR), and Italian (IT).

Labeling the reviews by the country of the reviewer enabled to extract texts originated in different countries automatically. However, belonging to a particular country does not necessarily mean that the reviewer used the language of that country. This means that some reviews mixed together sentences in two or more languages. This is, on the other hand, something that is relatively common.

Clustering the Documents

The software package CLUTO was used for automatic categorization of the documents into clusters. CLUTO can be applied to clustering low- and high-dimensional data sets and for analyzing the characteristics of the various clusters. It provides a wide variety of clustering algorithms, similarity (or distance) functions, extensive cluster visualization capabilities and output options, or methods for effectively summarizing the clusters (see http://glaros.dtc.umn.edu/gkhome/views/cluto).

Firstly, the documents were converted to their vector representations where the words that appeared less than three times in the entire collection were always filtered out. The reason is that such very rare words (very often just errors caused by misspelling or typographical errors) represent the noise in the data that negatively influences the results and increases computational complexity of text mining tasks. They also do not add anything to the similarity computations which are used in most clustering methods (Aggarwal & Zhai, 2012).

Subsequently, the collections of documents of different sizes and written in different natural languages were clustered using different algorithms and their parameters, according to the given goal. Figure 7 illustrates quite a common situation. Here it is demonstrated how the original sets of reviews for individual languages were relatively split among ten cluster groups (ten clusters for each investigated language). After looking at the size of the last cluster, its size is considerably bigger. The reason is that for some of the reviews it was difficult to assign them to a cluster with a clearly defined topic. Thus this cluster typically contained reviews with no obvious topic or with mixed topic, often not too important. After looking at the generated significant words for this cluster (see below), the cluster was semantically indifferent. Other clusters mostly represented prevailing topics. The situation was very similar for other numbers of clusters in the clustering solutions; only the lower numbers (below five) did not show big differences in the numbers of reviews distributions between clusters, especially for the minimum given by two clusters. The semantically relevant clusters had very close sizes within each group (see cluster 1 to cluster 9).

Evaluating the Results of Clustering by External Validity Measures

Generally, it is not possible to say what clustering methods, their parameters, criterion functions, similarity measures etc. are the best for the given purpose and for the given data. Thus, evaluation for the given data and objective must be performed. Because the processed data was also labeled, it was possible to evaluate the results of clustering using external evaluation measures. The labels indicating whether the

Figure 7. The distribution of relative sizes of ten individual clusters for the five investigated natural languages. The last cluster 10 represents a mixture of several different topics where none of them prevails semantically the others.

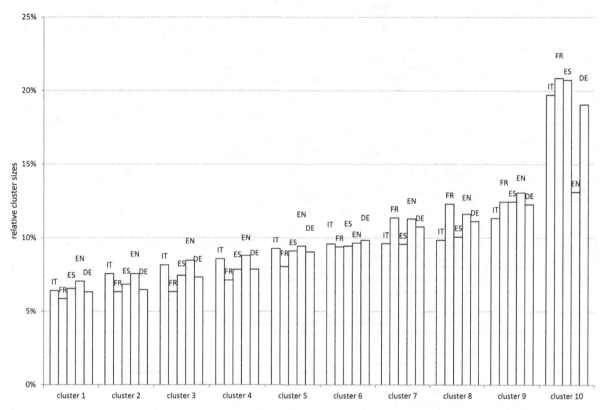

review was considered as positive or negative enabled to evaluate the quality of clustering with respect to the reviews categorization according to their sentiment polarity.

Because the type and character of the processed data is different from many classical document collections, such as the Reuters corpus, it was interesting to find out what methods would be suitable for clustering such a data item. In order to reveal the efficiency of different strategies, some of the combinations provided by the CLUTO package were used for document collections of different sizes. In order to find out whether the language of the documents plays a role in the process of selecting the optimal parameters, different language sets were processed as well.

The CLUTO package offers a wide variety of clustering methods, criterion functions, similarity measures, column weighting models, and others. See Table 1 for the parameters that were investigated (note that not all of the combinations are allowable). In addition, stop words removal was applied to the data and both original and modified data were clustered. During the transformation of the original text data to a vector representation a utility *doc2mat* distributed together with CLUTO enables removing stop words. However, the internal list of stop words is only in English. Thus lists of general stop words for other languages needed to be provided as well (the Snowball project, see http://snowball.tartarus. org, contains language resources, e.g., rules for stemming and also lists of stop words for different languages; these lists were used in our experiments). In order to determine the impact of different number of clusters on the quality of clustering **solution, the** data was split into 2, 5, 10, 20, and 50 clusters. We

Table 1. Investigated parameters of clustering available in CLUTO package.

The Method Used for Clustering (Parameter *–clmethod*)	
rb	Repeated bisection method.
rbr	The solution is determined with the application of repeated bisection and subsequently it is further optimized.
direct	CLUTO's variation of the k-means algorithm.
graph	A method operating on a graph representing the document collection.
agglo	Agglomerative paradigm for clustering is chosen.
bagglo	Agglomerative clustering that is biased by adding new features that are initially found by the repeated bisection method.
Criterion Functions (Parameter *–crfun*)	
i1,iI2	Functions focusing on intra-cluster similarity; they are maximized during the clustering process.
e1	A function focusing on inter-cluster similarity; it is minimized during the clustering process.
h1, h2	Functions combining both intra- and inter-cluster similarity; they are maximized during the clustering process.
g1, g1p	Functions focusing on the edge-cut on the graphs representing the documents/terms and their similarities; they are minimized during the clustering process.
slink, wslink, clink,wclink, upgma	Traditional criterion functions used for hierarchical clustering: single-link, cluster-weighted single link, complete link, cluster-weighted complete link, and the Unweighted Pair Group Method with Arithmetic Mean
Similarity Measures (Parameter *–sim*)	
cos	Cosine similarity measure.
dist	The similarity is inversely proportional to Euclidean distance and is used for graph based clustering.
jacc	The similarity is computed using extended Jaccard coefficient and is used for graph based clustering.
Column weighting model (parameter *–colmodel*)	
none	No scaling is used for the columns of the document-term matrix.
idf	The columns of the document-term matrix are scaled according to the inverse document frequency (idf) weighting scheme.

also processed data sets of different sizes – the sets contained 10,000, 25,000, 50,000, 100,000, and 250,000 documents.

As a result of the experiments with external validity measure (labels assigning the reviews to a set of positive or negative ones) values of clustering performance, including the Purity and Entropy, were obtained. For the analysis of the impact of clustering parameters on the quality of clustering solutions contingency tables were applied. A contingency table is a matrix containing frequencies from multiple classifications. The simplest form is a table representing a classification based on two attributes. The rows correspond to the possible values of one attribute and the columns correspond to the possible values of the other attribute. The cells in the two-way table represent the frequencies (numbers) of items classified according to the particular values of both attributes. The table often contains aggregate values for the rows and columns, too (Weerahandi, 2003). The values and aggregate values might, in addition to frequencies (counts), express also sums, averages, minimal or maximal values, variance, and others (in the tables below, the aggregate value is always mentioned in the table caption; it is the arithmetic average in all cases). A contingency table might also display dependencies between more than just two attributes.

Table 2 contains information about the impact of selected clustering methods and criterion functions on the quality of clustering of English reviews into two, five, ten, twenty five, and fifty groups. Similar analysis, this time for the German language, considering **a** number of documents instead of **a** number of clusters is reported in table 3. Cluster quality expressed in terms of the Entropy was correlated to the quality expressed by the Purity of the clusters (higher Purity corresponded to lower Entropy). Thus only, one of these measures is presented.

It is obvious that the overall performance in terms of the quality of clustering methods is very comparable, almost the same – expressed using the average Purity value, around 75%. Similar numbers were obtained for all of the processed natural languages. The best results were systematically achieved with the application of the external criterion function *e1*, internal function *i2*, and hybrid function *h2* (combining external function *e1* and internal *i2*). Slightly worse results were demonstrated with reviews written in Spanish.

A strong positive impact on the clustering quality had application of global weighting using inverse document frequency (*idf*). The biggest improvement of *idf* weighting was observed for the repeated bisection method whereas no relation to the used criterion function was noticeable.

Table 2. The average Purity of clusters of reviews written in English using selected parameters. The table displays the values for combinations of three clustering methods (direct method, repeated bisection, and repeated bisection refined), five criterion functions (internal – i1, i2, external e1, and hybrid – h1, h2), and the number of clusters.

Clustering Method Criterion Function	Number of clusters					Aggregate
	2	5	10	20	50	
direct	**0.71**	**0.74**	**0.74**	**0.76**	**0.77**	**0.74**
e1	0.76	0.76	0.76	0.77	0.78	**0.77**
h1	0.70	0.75	0.75	0.76	0.77	**0.75**
h2	0.75	0.76	0.76	0.77	0.77	**0.76**
i1	0.63	0.68	0.69	0.73	0.75	**0.69**
i2	0.73	0.76	0.75	0.76	0.77	**0.75**
rb	**0.71**	**0.73**	**0.75**	**0.77**	**0.79**	**0.75**
e1	0.76	0.77	0.78	0.79	0.80	**0.78**
h1	0.70	0.72	0.73	0.75	0.78	**0.74**
h2	0.75	0.76	0.77	0.78	0.80	**0.77**
i1	0.63	0.66	0.70	0.74	0.76	**0.70**
i2	0.73	0.75	0.76	0.78	0.79	**0.76**
rbr	**0.71**	**0.74**	**0.75**	**0.76**	**0.77**	**0.75**
e1	0.76	0.76	0.76	0.78	0.79	**0.77**
h1	0.70	0.75	0.76	0.76	0.77	**0.75**
h2	0.75	0.76	0.76	0.77	0.78	**0.77**
i1	0.63	0.68	0.71	0.74	0.76	**0.70**
i2	0.73	0.75	0.75	0.77	0.77	**0.75**
Aggregate	**0.71**	**0.74**	**0.75**	**0.76**	**0.78**	**0.75**

Table 3. The average Purity of clusters of reviews written in German using selected parameters. The table displays the values for combinations of three clustering methods (direct method, repeated bisection, and repeated bisection refined), five criterion functions (internal – i1, i2, external e1, and hybrid – h1, h2), and the number of clustered documents.

Clustering Method Criterion Function	Number of Documents					Aggregate
	10,000	25,000	50,000	100,000	250,000	
direct	**0.75**	**0.74**	**0.75**	**0.75**	**0.74**	**0.75**
e1	0.76	0.76	0.77	0.77	0.75	**0.76**
h1	0.75	0.75	0.75	0.75	0.75	**0.75**
h2	0.76	0.76	0.77	0.76	0.76	**0.76**
i1	0.71	0.70	0.70	0.70	0.69	**0.70**
i2	0.75	0.76	0.76	0.76	0.75	**0.76**
rb	**0.75**	**0.75**	**0.75**	**0.75**	**0.74**	**0.75**
e1	0.76	0.77	0.77	0.77	0.75	**0.77**
h1	0.75	0.74	0.74	0.74	0.73	**0.74**
h2	0.77	0.77	0.77	0.77	0.76	**0.77**
i1	0.71	0.71	0.70	0.70	0.69	**0.70**
i2	0.77	0.77	0.78	0.78	0.76	**0.77**
rbr	**0.75**	**0.75**	**0.75**	**0.75**	**0.74**	**0.75**
e1	0.76	0.77	0.77	0.77	0.75	**0.76**
h1	0.75	0.75	0.75	0.75	0.74	**0.75**
h2	0.77	0.76	0.77	0.77	0.75	**0.76**
i1	0.70	0.71	0.70	0.70	0.70	**0.70**
i2	0.76	0.76	0.76	0.77	0.76	**0.76**
Aggregate	**0.75**	**0.75**	**0.75**	**0.75**	**0.74**	**0.75**

In table 5, times (durations) needed for clustering the documents using an ordinary personal computer can be found. The time increases linearly for the investigated combinations of methods with the increasing number of documents. The direction (slope) of the line approximating the growth ranged between $7*10^{-5}$ and $3*10^{-4}$ for the processed data. Relating clustering methods (the table is not included) and criterion functions with numbers of clusters, an exponential growth is noticeable for the direct method while as for the bisecting approach the increase of time needed for the clustering is nearly linear. The time needed for creating two clusters was about 2 seconds on average for all data set sizes for the direct method; creating 50 clusters took about 64 seconds on average. As for repeated bisection or repeated bisection refined, the time increased from about 2 seconds (two clusters) to about 13 seconds or 19 seconds on average.

Removing stop words had a small positive impact on the quality of clustering expressed in terms of the Purity. There was no obvious dependence on the used clustering method, criterion function, data set size, or number of clusters. The only exception was a noticeable smaller improvement when using I_1 criterion function. The improvement was different for different languages – the biggest improvement can be noted for English. The biggest reduction of time needed for clustering was also achieved for this language. The detailed numbers can be found in Table 6.

Table 4. The average Purity of clusters of reviews written in French using and not using global weighting for three clustering methods (direct method, repeated bisection, and repeated bisection refined), different numbers of clusters and clustered documents.

Number of Documents Number of Clusters	Global Weighting							
	idf				none			
	Clustering Method			Aggreg.	Clustering Method			Aggreg.
	direct	rb	rbr		direct	rb	rbr	
10,000	**0.79**	**0.81**	**0.79**	**0.80**	**0.69**	**0.68**	**0.68**	**0.68**
2	0.80	0.80	0.80	**0.80**	0.62	0.62	0.62	**0.62**
5	0.80	0.80	0.80	**0.80**	0.66	0.66	0.65	**0.66**
10	0.79	0.81	0.79	**0.80**	0.70	0.68	0.69	**0.69**
20	0.78	0.81	0.79	**0.79**	0.71	0.70	0.71	**0.71**
50	0.79	0.82	0.79	**0.80**	0.74	0.72	0.74	**0.73**
25,000	**0.79**	**0.81**	**0.79**	**0.80**	**0.69**	**0.68**	**0.69**	**0.68**
2	0.79	0.79	0.79	**0.79**	0.63	0.63	0.63	**0.63**
5	0.80	0.80	0.80	**0.80**	0.65	0.65	0.65	**0.65**
10	0.79	0.81	0.79	**0.80**	0.69	0.68	0.69	**0.69**
20	0.78	0.81	0.79	**0.80**	0.72	0.69	0.72	**0.71**
50	0.79	0.82	0.80	**0.80**	0.74	0.73	0.74	**0.74**
50,000	**0.79**	**0.81**	**0.79**	**0.79**	**0.69**	**0.68**	**0.69**	**0.69**
2	0.79	0.79	0.79	**0.79**	0.63	0.63	0.63	**0.63**
5	0.80	0.80	0.79	**0.80**	0.66	0.66	0.66	**0.66**
10	0.78	0.80	0.78	**0.79**	0.69	0.68	0.70	**0.69**
20	0.77	0.81	0.78	**0.79**	0.72	0.69	0.72	**0.71**
50	0.79	0.82	0.80	**0.80**	0.75	0.73	0.75	**0.74**
100,000	**0.79**	**0.81**	**0.79**	**0.80**	**0.69**	**0.68**	**0.69**	**0.68**
2	0.79	0.79	0.79	**0.79**	0.63	0.63	0.63	**0.63**
5	0.80	0.80	0.79	**0.80**	0.65	0.66	0.65	**0.65**
10	0.78	0.81	0.79	**0.79**	0.70	0.69	0.70	**0.69**
20	0.78	0.81	0.78	**0.79**	0.71	0.70	0.72	**0.71**
50	0.78	0.82	0.79	**0.80**	0.75	0.73	0.74	**0.74**
250,000	**0.79**	**0.81**	**0.79**	**0.79**	**0.69**	**0.67**	**0.69**	**0.68**
2	0.79	0.79	0.79	**0.79**	0.62	0.62	0.62	**0.62**
5	0.80	0.80	0.79	**0.80**	0.66	0.66	0.66	**0.66**
10	0.79	0.81	0.78	**0.79**	0.69	0.68	0.70	**0.69**
20	0.78	0.81	0.78	**0.79**	0.71	0.69	0.72	**0.71**
50	0.79	0.82	0.79	**0.80**	0.75	0.73	0.74	**0.74**
Aggregate	**0.79**	**0.81**	**0.79**	**0.80**	**0.69**	**0.68**	**0.69**	**0.68**

Table 5. Average time needed for clustering reviews written in Italian for three clustering methods (direct method, repeated bisection, and repeated bisection refined), five criterion functions (internal – i1, i2, external e1, and hybrid – h1, h2), and different numbers of clustered documents.

Clustering Method Criterion Function	Number of Documents					Aggregate
	10,000	25,000	50,000	100,000	250,000	
direct	**2.19**	**4.87**	**10.00**	**20.99**	**63.64**	**20.34**
e1	2.43	5.34	10.91	22.70	67.75	**21.82**
h1	2.80	6.27	12.79	26.95	79.16	**25.59**
h2	2.79	6.20	12.65	26.27	76.96	**24.97**
i1	1.13	2.53	5.38	11.70	40.82	**12.31**
i2	1.81	4.02	8.27	17.36	53.50	**16.99**
rb	**0.78**	**1.93**	**4.09**	**8.82**	**22.70**	**7.66**
e1	0.82	2.00	4.10	8.93	23.58	**7.89**
h1	0.90	2.21	4.74	10.17	27.07	**9.02**
h2	0.86	2.19	4.55	10.14	25.79	**8.70**
i1	0.64	1.59	3.57	7.43	19.03	**6.45**
i2	0.66	1.67	3.47	7.41	18.05	**6.25**
rbr	**0.95**	**2.32**	**4.98**	**10.65**	**28.37**	**9.46**
e1	1.02	2.41	5.10	10.96	29.57	**9.81**
h1	1.15	2.78	5.92	12.60	34.24	**11.34**
h2	1.11	2.70	5.71	12.35	32.69	**10.91**
i1	0.69	1.75	4.01	8.41	22.60	**7.49**
i2	0.80	1.96	4.18	8.94	22.75	**7.73**
Aggregate	**1.31**	**3.04**	**6.36**	**13.49**	**38.24**	**12.49**

Table 6. The average Purity of clustering (using methods direct, rb, and rbr, for all data set sizes, and numbers of clusters) the reviews with and without stop words; the table also contains the portion of the original time needed for clustering with excluding the stop words.

Language	Average Purity		Time Without Stop Words
	Stop Words Preserved	Stop Words Removed	
EN	0.72	0.77	79%
DE	0.74	0.76	81%
ES	0.71	0.72	82%
FR	0.73	0.74	82%
IT	0.75	0.75	83%

When using *graph representation* of the clustered documents, other similarity measures, besides cosine similarity, were available – the Euclidean distance and Jaccard index. When using Jaccard index as a similarity measure, slightly worse results were achieved than in the case of cosine similarity or the Euclidean distance. This difference was decreasing with the increased number of clusters (cosine similarity also showed the least dependence on the number of clusters). The Euclidean distance outperformed cosine similarity with the increasing number of clusters; as for two clusters there were their values almost the same. In term of computational complexity, using the Euclidean distance required more time (e.g., about 15% for English) compared to other two similarity measures. Compared, e.g., to direct or repeated bisection clustering methods, the time needed for graph based clustering was significantly longer (about 5-10 times compared to the direct method, about 20-30 times to the repeated bisection method).

Examination of *agglomerative hierarchical clustering methods* was not carried out to the extent of examination of repeated bisection and direct methods due to high computational complexity and memory consumption. Especially when using *i1, i2, e1, h1,* and *h2* criterion functions, the time needed for clustering the documents was inadequate, even for very small data sets. When clustering only 10,000 English reviews, slightly better quality was achieved with the application of the biased agglomerative method (*bagglo*) compared to ordinary agglomerative clustering (*agglo*). The Purity increased from 0.63 to 0.72 for *upmga* criterion function and from 0.63 to 0.66 for *wlink*. With increasing the number of clusters, the quality of the clustering remained the same for *slink* and *wslink* criterion functions; as for the remaining ones the quality of clustering increases as reported, e.g., in Figure 5. The time needed for clustering was significantly longer compared to repeated bisection, direct, and graph based methods. However, it remained almost the same with the increasing number of clusters unlike for the other methods. Because of a low number of experiments that have been carried out, sufficiently relevant and legitimate conclusions regarding the application of agglomerative hierarchical clustering cannot be made.

As it was mentioned above, the quality of the clusters also increases with the increasing number of clusters. Figure 8 illustrates how the quality changes with the increasing number of documents. It is interesting to see that there exists a certain boundary from which the values of the Entropy and Purity oscillate and do not change much with the increasing number of documents. This boundary is visible at the point where the data set contains about 10,000 documents. This means, that having a relatively low number of documents for clustering, the quality of the clustering solution might be lower (or not too stable) as in the case of larger data sets. This phenomenon is demonstrated on clustering balanced collections of positive and negative reviews of different sizes into five clusters; with increasing the number of clusters, the oscillation on the left side of the graph is not that obvious.

Figure 8. The Purity and Entropy for clustering solutions containing five clusters for different balanced data set sizes of English positive and negative reviews. The clustering was performed using the direct method, h2 criterion function, tf-idf weighting, and cosine similarity measure.

Evaluating the Results of Clustering by Examining Central Representatives

The first method used for evaluating the results of clustering by human experts is based on examination of a feasible amount of good representatives of individual clusters. The documents that were located near the center of the clusters were selected as the representatives. They might be therefore seen as average documents that contain a meaning most typical for the given group of documents.

This procedure can be rationalized by the research results of Dařena & Zižka (2013). The authors presented an approach called automated biased selection for selecting a set of sample documents that were subsequently used for text mining tasks (document ranking and classification). This method, as an alternative to manual selection and evaluation of potential textual samples, also relied on selecting documents close to the center of a group of all documents considered to be samples. The experiments showed that the measures of classifier quality for the presented classification were close or better than for the classification based on manual data preparation. Also the documents retrieved and filtered using the presented method based on ranking by similarity showed higher similarity.

Generally, the document collections contain reviews that might be characterized by some unknown number of topics. The goal of clustering is to organize the documents into groups that share common topics. The quality of characteristic of the topics depends on the homogeneity of the documents in the clusters. As it was mentioned, there is generally higher homogeneity in clustering solutions with a higher number of clusters. Thus, what topics and how well identified they were depended on the number of the created clusters.

In the clustering solution with 20 clusters, one cluster clearly discussing the *quietness* of the hotel and rooms could be identified (for example, reviews like *"very quiet and not very atmopsheric when I was there"*, or *"the room was quiet"*). In solutions with 10 or 50 clusters such clearly focused groups could not be found. In clustering solutions with 10 and 20 clusters two clusters related to staff were found (for example, with reviews like *"the staff was very nice"*, or *"staff very friendly"*). When 50 clusters were created, about nine groups more or less discussing the staff could be found.

In general, with the increasing number of the clusters new, more clearly separated topics might become apparent. These topics were previously hidden, i.e., they were either distributed across more clusters or were not represented by reviews in the centers of the clusters. In the clustering solution with 20 clusters, new topics related to *price* (e.g., *"for the price I can't ask for more"*, or *"nothing to say for this price"*) or *services* (e.g., *"the service was not the best"*, or *"service could be better"*) appeared.

With more clusters, one topic is usually spread among more clusters and is often more detailed. For example, the topic *location* is quite generally discussed in one of the clusters (*"as always the location is good"*, *"very good location"*) among 10 created clusters. In 20 clusters, two groups slightly more specific could be found (*"yes, great location"*, *"no everything was just great for the location"*, and *"easy to get around"*, *"location this was very easy to find"*). In 50 clusters, **a s**ignificantly higher number of clusters concerned with location is obvious. These clusters discuss the location sometimes from a more specific perspective – for example, with relation to the train station (*"it is near train station"*, *"it was quite far from the train station"*) or airport (*"it is very near to the airport"*, *"near by to airport"*), together with other aspects of the hotel (*"location, cleanliness"*, *"the staff, location and cleanliness"*), emphasizing centrality of the location (*"the very central location"*, *"it was central location"*), or walking distance (*"nothing outside the hotel within walking distance"*, *"the location was good everything in walking distance"*).

Evaluating the Results of Clustering by Application of a Decision Tree Generator

By application of a decision tree generator for identification of the significant words, lists of words ordered according to their relevance to individual classes (corresponding with the clusters created in the previous step) were created. By examination of the first words at the top of the lists, the prevailing topic could be identified in most of the cases. If the following example, the identification of a topic according to first ten significant words (only two from the total number of ten clusters) for each of the processed language is demonstrated (translations of non-English words is included):

- English:
  - *comfortable, spacious, clean, bed, modern, quiet, room, large, lovely, well:* identified topic *room positives;*
  - *bit, too, small, noisy, noise, little, bathroom, old, dated, rather:* identified topic *room negatives;*
- German:
  - *Lage (location), nähe (near), zentrale (central), freundliches (friendly), ruhige (quiet), gute (good), nettes (nice), zum (for), direct (directly), Flughafen (airport):* identified topic *location;*
  - *Atmosphere (atmosphere), freundliche (friendly), mitarbeiter (employee), nette (nice), freundlicher (friendly), the, betreuung (care), zuvorkommende (courteous), netter (nice), service (service):* identified topic *atmosphere;*
- Spanish:
  - *poco (little), falta (lack), desayuno (breakfast), caro (expensive), algo (something), buffet (buffet), antiguo (old), poca (little), un (a), escaso (poor):* identified topic *general negatives;*
  - *baño (bath), pequeño (small), diseño (design), bañera (bathtub), habitación (room), cama (bed), pequeña (small), ducha (shower), baños (bathrooms), cuarto (room):* identified topic *rooms;*
- French:
  - *proximité (proximity), ville (city), centre (center), proche (close), metro (metro), plage (beach), parking (parking), proximite (proximity), gare (station), mer (sea):* identified topic *location;*
  - *sale (room), peu (little), trop (too), manqué (lack), absence (absence), odeur (smell), insonorisation (soundproofing), douche (shower), bruit (noise), chamber (room):* identified topic *room negatives;*
- Italian:
  - *cortesia (courtesy), gentilezza (kindness), disponibilità (availabilitz), personale (staff), tranquillità (tranquility), del (of), pulizia (cleanliness), cordialità (friendliness), accoglienza (welcome), silenzio (silence):* identified topic *pleasantness;*
  - *rapport (relation), prezzo (price), qualità (quality), ottimo (excellent), o (or), buon (good), buono (good), ristorante (restaurant), servizio (service), qualita (quality):* identified topic *good quality.*

As it was mentioned above, there were several clusters where the topic could not be easily determined according to the list of significant words. Examples of such lists for some of the investigated languages follow: English – *I, nothing, my, have, like, didn't, that, would, they*; Spanish – *no (not), que (that), hay (there is), por (for), ya (already), más (more), a (to), al (to the), se (self), noche (night)*; or German – *keine (no), etwas (something), kein (no), im (in), zu (to), klein (small), könnte (could), laut (loud), parkplätze (parking place), hellhörig (poorly soundproofed).*

Table 7 contains examples of identified prevailing topics for all of the clusters for each of the processed natural languages. It is obvious that clustering with subsequent analysis of the cluster contents

Table 7. The revealed prevailing semantic contents (for ten generated clusters) based on significant words in individual reviews for the five tested languages. N/A means that no specific topic could be derived from the significant words and the cluster represented a mixture of several topics approximately balanced. The cluster numbers are not important.

Cluster	Language				
	English	**German**	**Spanish**	**French**	**Italian**
1	value	general positives	rooms	breakfast, facilities	location
2	hotel facilities	N/A	environment	N/A	staff, facilities
3	N/A	location	location (no diacritic)	environment	rooms
4	room positives	N/A	N/A	Room negatives	N/A
5	room negatives	breakfast	location (with diacritic)	location	pleasantness
6	N/A	general positives	general negatives	N/A	room facilities
7	staff	atmosphere	N/A	location	location
8	room facilities	quality/price	rooms	price, quality	N/A
9	location	room positives	quality/price	N/A	good quality
10	N/A	N/A	location	comfort	room positives

enabled to identify the topics of most of the clusters so the documents from these clusters could be later used for a specific task with additional knowledge of the topic. It can be noticed that the topics are more or less similar across all of the languages, which supports the applicability of this procedure. Some of the clusters, where the topics could not be identified, could be further analysed or simply excluded from further processing. In this example the datasets, each containing 50,000 documents, were clustered into 10 categories. When more clusters were created, some topics were likely to repeat; with a low number of clusters the decision about the prevailing topic was usually more complicated.

FUTURE RESEARCH DIRECTIONS

The following research work aims at deeper analysis of the clustering procedure, including more languages, and more sophisticated data preparation (including analysis of the impact of stop words removal and applying a kind of stemming). A big problem is subsequently (in bulk, after writing reviews) correcting mistyping of very large data volumes. The application of different approaches to clustering, e.g., hierarchical (top-down) partitioning without a given number of clusters, driven by a measure of internal coherence of the clusters, and subsequent evaluation of the clusters might be also investigated. A possibility of eliminating the problem of having the same significant words in more than one cluster by giving higher weights to more specific words (words appearing in fewer groups of documents) could be examined as well. All this should lead to an improved separation of individual aspects of the data and better characterization of it. It should be also investigated how (and in which) the various number of requested clusters differs and for what number of clusters the suggested method begins to be useless due to the loss of generality.

Sometimes automatic categorization of the documents does not lead to sufficiently homogeneous solutions. This is often caused by many topics mentioned in single documents. To solve this problem, Dařena, Žižka & Přichystal (2014), in their research focused on opinion mining from unlabeled data, first split the documents (customer complaints) into individual sentences. Their subsequent categorization reduced this problem and increased the quality of knowledge extracted from the data. Thus, a special attention should be paid to the process of data segmentation.

A semi-supervised learning procedure represents a trade-off between the supervised and unsupervised learning. It works initially with usually a small set of instances with known labels, which positively supports the supplementary labeling of a much larger remainder of unlabeled instances. Clustering might be successfully used as a part of some semi-supervised techniques. For example, clustering might be useful under assumptions that distribution of the labels of the objects corresponds to the distribution of the objects across some structure, for example, across the generated clusters. Using this semi-supervised approach, known as *cluster-and-label*, new labels for the objects that share the same cluster with available labeled objects might be generated (Su et al., 2010). In a similar fashion, Dařena & Žižka (2013) used clustering as a part on a novel algorithm called *SuDoC* (Semi-unsupervised Document Classification). The method consists of two steps – preparing clustering solutions of the entire data to be labeled with different numbers of clusters, and labels spreading from initially labeled document instances within at least two clustering solutions, starting with a clustering solution with a higher number of clusters and continuing with one or more clustering solutions having less clusters. Using this procedure, better values of the chosen classification performance metrics than in the case of traditional supervised classifiers were achieved.

In the recent days, new clustering algorithms that use some auxiliary information that has to be preserved in the clustering solution have been developed. The auxiliary information can have a form of explicit must-link and cannot-link constraints (Wagstaff et al., 2001), information about relationships between multiple data sets to be clustered (Rinsurongkawong & Eick, 2010), or relationships between the objects that are considered in addition to the attributes of the objects (Neville, Adle &, Jensen, 2003). The additional information that is used for modification of the criterion (objective) function might be very useful and improves the results of automatic categorization (Tadepalli, Ramakrishnan & Watson, 2009).

As the dimensionality of vectors representing textual documents is a serious problem, the application of methods of dimensionality reduction is one of the directions of the future research. The reduction might take place locally (deleting unimportant elements in every single document) or globally, which reduces the feature space. Popular global dimensionality reduction techniques for text mining include, e.g., Latent Semantic Indexing (Feldman & Sanger, 2007), or term clustering (Li, 2002).

CONCLUSION

The chapter presented methods that can be used for automatic categorization of collections of text documents with special emphasis on disclosing semantic contents of the groups. The presented research aimed at particular large real-world data sets, looking for an uncomplicated method applicable to not only one specific language.

The experiments that were carried out with a very large volume of untagged textual documents written in five different natural languages demonstrated that it was possible to use successfully a support of a computer. The feasibility was demonstrated by a number of experiments using external and expert evaluation measures for validation of the clusters. It has been found that some combinations of the clustering methods and their parameters provide acceptable results (expressed by the Purity values of 75% or higher). The created clusters might thus be used for subsequent text mining tasks, especially for classification using the labels assigned in the clustering process.

Discovering the semantic contents of the clusters was carried out using two methods. The first one needed examination of some portion of the documents from each cluster. The presented documents were located near the centroids of the clusters so they represented average or typical documents. According to them, a user might determine the given topic quite well. In order to specify what is typical (words and their combinations) for the documents expressing a given topic, a supervised machine learning support was used. Through the decision trees application a computer was able to help in revealing the meaning of groups of textual documents considerably by the extraction of significant words.

It has been found that it is possible to apply the same procedures, including clustering, cluster validation, and detection of topics and significant words for different natural languages with satisfactory results, small differences being given by different nature of various languages. When analyzing the semantics of the groups of documents created automatically in an unsupervised manner, it has been found that the identified topics (semantic meaning) are often very similar. On one hand, this was quite predictable since the documents discussed the same kind of services; on the other hand, this supported the applicability of the methods for multilingual collections of documents.

Unfortunately, comparing and evaluating different similar systems is extremely difficult because of the different used data sets, preprocessing methods, algorithms and their parameters, and knowledge resources adopted. Text-mining belongs among strongly data-driven areas from the machine learning viewpoint and the inductively obtained results often depend on particular data (Sebastiani, 2002).

ACKNOWLEDGMENT

This work was supported by the research grant IGA of Mendel University in Brno No. 16/2014.

REFERENCES

Aggarwal, C. C., & Zhai, C. (2012). A survey of text clustering algorithms. In C. C. Aggarwal & C. Zhai (Eds.), *Mining text data.* (pp. 77–128). New York, NY: Springer. doi:10.1007/978-1-4614-3223-4_4

Balian, R. (2013). Entropy, a Protean concept. *Séminaire Poincaré, 2,* 13–27.

Berry, M. W., & Kogan, J. (2010). *Text Mining: Applications and Theory.* Chichester: Wiley. doi:10.1002/9780470689646

Bsoul, Q., Salim, J., & Zakaria, L. Q. (2013). An Intelligent Document Clustering Approach to Detect Crime Patterns. *Procedia Technology (4th International Conference on Electrical Engineering and Informatics, ICEEI 2013), 11,* 1181–1187.

Cao, Y., Zhang, P., Guo, J., & Guo, L. (2014). Mining Large-scale Event Knowledge from Web Text. *Procedia Computer Science (2014 International Conference on Computational Science), 29,* 478–487.

Cawley, G. C., & Talbot, N. L. C. (2010). On Over-fitting in Model Selection and Subsequent Selection Bias in Performance Evaluation. *Journal of Machine Learning Research, 11*, 2079–2107.

Chrisholm, E., & Kolda, T. G. (1999). *New term weighting formulas for the vector space method in information retrieval* [Technical Report No. ORNL/TM-13756]. Computer Science and Mathematics Division – Oak Ridge National Laboratory.

Cimiano, P., Hotho, A., & Staab, S. (2004). *Comparing Conceptual.* Divisive and Agglomerative Clustering for Learning Taxonomies from Text.

Cummins, R., & O'Riordan, C. (2006). Evolving local and global weighting schemes in information retrieval. *Information Retrieval, 9*(3), 311–330. doi:10.1007/s10791-006-1682-6

Dařena, F., & Žižka, J. (2011). Text Mining-based Formation of Dictionaries Expressing Opinions in Natural Languages. In *Mendel 2011: 17th International Conference on Soft Computing.* (pp. 374-381). Brno: University of Technology.

Dařena, F., & Žižka, J. (2013). SuDoC: Semi-unsupervised Classification of Text Document Opinions Using a Few Labeled Examples and Clustering. In *Flexible Query Answering Systems.* (pp. 625–636). Heidelberg: Springer. doi:10.1007/978-3-642-40769-7_54

Dařena, F., Žižka, J., & Přichystal, J. (2014). Clients' freely written assessment as the source of automatically mined opinions. *Proceedings of Procedia Economics and Finance (Enterprise and the Competitive Environment 2014 conference, ECE 2014,), 12*(1), 103-110. Brno, Czech Republic.

Dhillon, I. S., & Modha, D. S. (1999). Concept decompositions for large sparse text data using clustering. *Machine Learning, 42*(1/2), 143–175. doi:10.1023/A:1007612920971

Dietterich, T. (1995). Overfitting and Undercomputing in Machine Learning. *Computing Surveys, 27*(3), 326–327. doi:10.1145/212094.212114

Ding, C., He, X., Zha, H., Gu, M., & Simon, H. (2001). Spectral min-max cut for graph partitioning and data clustering. In *ICDM '01 Proceedings of the 2001 IEEE International Conference on Data Mining.* (pp. 107-114). Washington: IEEE Computer Society.

Dini, L., & Mazzini, G. (2010). Real Time Customer Opinion Monitoring. In S. Sirmakessis (Ed.), *Text Mining and its Applications: Results of the NEMIS Launch Conference.* (pp. 159–168). Berlin: Springer.

Duda, R. O., Hart, P. E., & Stork, D. G. (2001). *Pattern Classification.* New York, NY: Wiley.

Everitt, B. S., Landau, S., Leese, M., & Stahl, S. (2011). *Cluster analysis.* Chichester: Wiley. doi:10.1002/9780470977811

Färber, I., Günnemann, S., Kriegel, H., Kröger, P., Müller, E., & Schubert, E. et al. (2010). On Using Class-Labels in Evaluation of Clusterings. In *Proceedings of the 1st International Workshop on Discovering, Summarizing and Using Multiple Clusterings (MultiClust 2010) in conjunction with 16th ACM SIGKDD Conference on Knowledge Discovery and Data Mining (KDD 2010).* Washington.

Feldman, R., & Sanger, J. (2007). *The Text Mining Handbook: Advanced Approaches in Analyzing Unstructured Data.* New York, NY: Cambridge University Press.

Ferrano, G., & Wanner, L. (2012). Labeling Semantically Motivated Clusters of Verbal Relations. *Procesamiento del Lenguaje Natural*, *49*, 129–138.

Figueiredo, F., Rocha, L., Couto, T., Salles, T., Goncalves, M. A., & Meira, W. Jr. (2011). Word co-occurrence features for text classification. *Information Systems*, *36*(5), 843–858. doi:10.1016/j.is.2011.02.002

Gelbukh, A. F., Alexandrov, M., Bourek, A., & Makagonov, P. (2003). Selection of Representative Documents for Clusters in a Document Collection. In *Proceedings of Natural Language Processing and Information Systems, 8th International Conference on Applications of Natural Language to Information Systems*. (pp.120-126).

Guerra, L., Robles, V., Bielza, C., & Larrañaga, P. (2012). A comparison of clustering quality indices using outliers and noise. *Intelligent Data Analysis*, *16*, 703–715.

Guo, Q., & Zhang, M. (2009). Multi-documents Automatic Abstracting based on text clustering and semantic analysis. *Knowledge-Based Systems*, *22*(6), 482–485. doi:10.1016/j.knosys.2009.06.010

Huang, A. (2008). Similarity Measures for Text Document Clustering. In *Proceedings of the Sixth New Zealand Computer Science Research Student Conference*. (pp. 49-56).

Huang, Z., Ng, M. K., & Cheung, D. W.-L. (2001). An empirical study on the visual cluster validation method with fastmap. In *Proceedings of the 7th international conference on database systems for advanced applications (DASFAA 2001)*. (pp. 84-91). Hong-Kong: Springer. doi:10.1109/DASFAA.2001.916368

Jain, A. K., & Dubes, R. C. (1988). *Algorithms for Clustering Data*. Engelwood Cliffs, NJ: Prentice Hall.

Joachims, T. (2002). *Learning to classify text using support vector machines*. Norwell, MA: Kluwer Academic Publishers. doi:10.1007/978-1-4615-0907-3

Karypis, G. (2003). *CLUTO: A Clustering Toolkit*. Minneapolis: University of Minnesota, Department of Computer Science.

Kaufmann, L., & Rousseeuw, P. J. (2005). *Finding Groups in Data: An Introduction to Cluster Analysis*. Hoboken, NJ: Wiley.

Koteswara Rao, G., & Dey, S. (2011). Decision support for e-governance: A text mining approach. *International Journal of Managing Information Technology*, *3*(3), 73–91. doi:10.5121/ijmit.2011.3307

Li, H. (2002). Word clustering and disambiguation based on co-occurrence data. *Natural Language Engineering*, *8*(1), 25–42. doi:10.1017/S1351324902002838

Liu, Y., Li, Z., Xiong, H., Gao, X., & Wu, J. (2010). Understanding of Internal Clustering Validation Measures. In *Proceedings of ICDM 2010, The 10th IEEE International Conference on Data Mining*. (pp. 911-916). doi:10.1109/ICDM.2010.35

Manning, C. D., Raghavan, P., & Schütze, H. (2008). *Introduction to Information Retrieval*. Cambridge: Cambridge University Press. doi:10.1017/CBO9780511809071

Marsland, S. (2009). *Machine Learning: An algorithmic perspective*. Boca Raton, FL: Chapman & Hall/CRC.

Mendes, A. B., & Cardoso, M. G. M. S. (2006). Clustering supermarkets: The role of experts. *Journal of Retailing and Consumer Services*, *13*(4), 231–247. doi:10.1016/j.jretconser.2004.11.005

Miner, G., Elder, J., Hill, T., Nisbet, R., Delen, D., & Fast, A. (2012). *Practical Text Mining and Statistical Analysis for Non-structured Text Data Applications*. Waltham, MA: Academic Press.

Myatt, G. J., & Johnson, W. P. (2009). *Making Sense of Data II: A Practical Guide to Data Visualization, Advanced Data Mining Methods, and Applications*. Hoboken, NJ: Wiley. doi:10.1002/9780470417409

Nassirtoussi, A. K., Wah, T. Y., Aghabozorgi, S. R., & Ling, D. N. C. (2014). Text mining for market prediction: A systematic review. *Expert Systems with Applications*, *41*(16), 7653–7670. doi:10.1016/j.eswa.2014.06.009

Neville, J., Adler, M., & Jensen, D. (2003). Clustering relational data using attribute and link information. In *Proceedings of the Text Mining and Link Analysis Workshop, 18th International Joint Conference on Artificial Intelligence*.

Phan, X. H., Nguyen, L. M., & Horiguchi, S. (2008). Learning to Classify Short and Sparse Text & Web with Hidden Topics from Large-scale Data Collections. In *Proceeding of the 17th international conference on World Wide Web.* (pp. 91-100). New York: ACM. doi:10.1145/1367497.1367510

Quinlan, J. R. (1993). *C4.5: Programs for Machine Learning*. San Francisco, CA: Morgan Kaufmann.

Rinsurongkawong, V., & Eick, C. F. (2010). Correspondence Clustering: An Approach to Cluster Multiple Related Spatial Datasets. In *Proceedings of Asia-Pacific Conference on Knowledge Discovery and Data Mining (PAKDD)*. doi:10.1007/978-3-642-13657-3_25

Rivera-Borroto, O. M., Rabassa-Gutiérrez, M., Grau-Ábalo, R. C., Marrero-Ponce, Y., & García-de la Vega, J. M. (2012). Dunn's index for cluster tendency assessment of pharmacological data sets. *Canadian Journal of Physiology and Pharmacology*, *90*(4), 425–433. doi:10.1139/y2012-002 PMID:22443093

Romesburg, H. C. (2004). *Cluster analysis for researchers*. Raleigh, NC: Lulu Press.

Salton, G., & McGill, M. J. (1983). *Introduction to Modern Information Retrieval*. New York, NY: McGraw-Hill.

Salton, G., Wong, A., & Yang, C. (1975). A Vector Space Model for Automatic Indexing. *Communications of the ACM*, *18*(11), 613–620. doi:10.1145/361219.361220

Saratlija, J., Šnajder, J., & Dalbelo Bašić, B. (2011). Unsupervised Topic-Oriented Keyphrase Extraction and its Application to Croatian. In *Lecture Notes in Artificial Intelligence (14th International Conference on Text, Speech and Dialogue)*. (pp. 340–347). doi:10.1007/978-3-642-23538-2_43

Schaeffer, S. E. (2007). Graph clustering. *Computer Science Review*, *1*(1), 27–64. doi:10.1016/j.cosrev.2007.05.001

Sebastiani, F. (2002). Machine Learning in Automated Text categorization. *ACM Computing Surveys*, *1*(1), 1–47. doi:10.1145/505282.505283

Seeger, M. (2001). *Learning with labeled and unlabeled data. Technical report*. University of Edinburgh.

Stein, B., & zu Eissen, S. M. (2003). Automatic Document Categorization: Interpreting the Performance of Clustering Algorithms. In KI. (pp. 254-266). Springer.

Stein, B., zu Eissen, S. M., & Wißbrock, F. (2003). On Cluster Validity and the Information Need of Users. In *Proceedings of the 3rd International Conference on Artificial Intelligence and Applications (AIA 03).* (pp. 2165-221).

Steinbach, M., Karypis, G., & Kumar, V. (2000). A Comparison of Document Clustering Techniques. In *Proceedings of the KDD Workshop on Text Mining.*

Su, H., Chen, L., Ye, Y., Sun, Z., & Wu, Q. (2010). A Refinement Approach to Handling Model Misfit in Semi-supervised Learning. In Advanced Data Mining and Applications, Lecture Notes in Computer Science. (pp. 75-86). doi:10.1007/978-3-642-17313-4_8

Tadepalli, S., Ramakrishnan, N., & Watson, L. T. (2009). *Clustering constrained by dependencies.* [Technical Report TR-09-12]. Computer Science and Mathematics, Virginia Tech.

Tseng, Y.-H., Lin, C.-J., & Lin, Y. (2007). Text mining techniques for patent analysis. *Information Processing & Management, 43*(5), 1216–1247. doi:10.1016/j.ipm.2006.11.011

Wagstaff, K., Cardie, C., Rogers, S., & Schroedl, S. (2001). Constrained K-means Clustering with Background Knowledge. In *Proceedings of the Eighteenth International Conference on Machine Learning.* (pp. 577-584).

Weerahandi, S. (2003). *Exact Statistical Methods for Data Analysis.* New York, NY: Springer.

Weiss, S. M., Indurkhya, N., Zhang, T., & Damerau, F. J. (2010). *Text Mining: Predictive Methods for Analyzing Unstructured Information.* New York, NY: Springer.

Xu, R., & Wunsch, D. C. (2009). *Clustering.* Hoboken, NJ: Wiley.

Zaki, M. J., & Wagner, M. (2014). *Data Mining and Analysis: Fundamental Concepts and Algorithms.* Cambridge: Cambridge University Press.

Zha, H., He, X., Ding, C. H. Q., Gu, M., & Simon, H. D. (2001). Bipartite Graph Partitioning and Data Clustering. In *Proceedings of the 2001 ACM CIKM International Conference on Information and Knowledge Management.* (pp. 25-32). ACM.

Zhao, Y., & Karypis, G. (2001). Criterion Functions for Document Clustering: Experiments and Analysis. [Technical Report #01-40]. University of Minnesota, Department of Computer Science.

Žižka, J., Burda, K., & Dařena, F. (2012). Clustering a very large number of textual unstructured customers' reviews in English. In *Proceedings of Artificial Intelligence: Methodology, Systems, and Applications.* Heidelberg: Springer. doi:10.1007/978-3-642-33185-5_5

Žižka, J., & Dařena, F. (2011a). Mining Significant Words from Customer Opinions Written in Different Natural Languages. In *Proceedings of the 14th International Conference on Text, Speech and Dialogue, Lecture Notes in Artificial Intelligence.* (pp. 211-218). Heidelberg: Springer.

Žižka, J., & Dařena, F. (2011b). Mining Textual Significant Expressions Reflecting Opinions in Natural Languages. In *Proceedings of the 11th International Conference on Intelligent Systems Design and Applications.* doi:10.1109/ISDA.2011.6121644

ADDITIONAL READING

Abbasi, A., Chen, H., & Salem, A. (2008). Sentiment analysis in multiple languages: Feature selection for opinion classification in Web forums. *ACM Transactions on Information Systems*, *26*(3), 1–34. doi:10.1145/1361684.1361685

Abney, S. P. (2008). *Semisupervised Learning for Computational Linguistics*. Boca Raton, FL: Chapman & Hall/CRC.

Aizawa, A. (2003). An information-theoretic perspective of tf–idf measures. *Information Processing & Management*, *39*(1), 45–65. doi:10.1016/S0306-4573(02)00021-3

Aue, A., & Gamon, M. (2005). *Customizing sentiment classifiers to new domains: a case study. Technical report*. Microsoft Research.

Basu, S., Davidson, I., & Wagstaff, K. (Eds.). (2009). *Constrained Clustering: Advances in Algorithms, Theory, and Applications*. Boca Raton, FL: Chapman & Hall/CRC.

Bekkerman, R., El-Yaniv, R., Tishby, N., & Winter, Y. (2003). Distributional Word Clusters vs. Words for Text Categorization. *Journal of Machine Learning Research*, *3*, 1183–1208.

Bishop, C. M. (2007). *Pattern Recognition and Machine Learning*. Heidelberg: Springer.

Boiy, E., & Moens, M. F. (2009, October). Machine Learning Approach to Sentiment Analysis in Multilingual Web Texts. *Information Retrieval*, *12*(5), 526–558. doi:10.1007/s10791-008-9070-z

Chang, M., & Poon, C. K. (2009). Using phrases as features in email classification. *Journal of Systems and Software*, *82*(6), 1036–1045. doi:10.1016/j.jss.2009.01.013

Dařena, F., Žižka, J., & Burda, K. (2012). Grouping of Customer Opinions Written in Natural Language Using Unsupervised Machine Learning. In *Proceedings of the 14th International Symposium on Symbolic and Numeric Algorithms for scientific Computing SYNASC*. (pp. 265–270). doi:10.1109/SYNASC.2012.29

Dhillon, I. S., & Modha, D. S. (1999). Concept decompositions for large sparse text data using clustering. *Machine Learning*, *42*(1/2), 143–175. doi:10.1023/A:1007612920971

Ghosh, J., & Strehl, A. (2006). Similarity-Based Text Clustering: A Comparative Study. In *Grouping Multidimensional Data*. (pp. 73–97). Berlin: Springer. doi:10.1007/3-540-28349-8_3

Gu, Q., Zhu, L., & Cai, Z. (2009). Evaluation Measures of the Classification Performance of Imbalanced Data Sets. *ISICA*, *51*, 461–471.

Hastie, T., Tibshirani, R., & Friedman, J. (2009). *The Elements of Statistical Learning: Data Mining, Inference, and Prediction*. (2nd Ed.). Berlin: Springer. doi:10.1007/978-0-387-84858-7

Howland, P., & Park, H. (2004). Cluster-Preserving Dimension Reduction Methods for Efficient Classification of Text Data. In M. W. Berry (Ed.), *Survey of text mining: clustering, classification, and retrieval* (pp. 3–23). New York, NY: Springer. doi:10.1007/978-1-4757-4305-0_1

Jackson, P., & Moulinier, I. (2007). *Natural language processing for online applications: Text retrieval, extraction and categorization*. Amsterdam: John Benjamins. doi:10.1075/nlp.5

Li, Y., Chung, S. M., & Holt, J. D. (2008). Text document clustering based on frequent word meaning sequences. *Data & Knowledge Engineering, 64*(1), 381–404. doi:10.1016/j.datak.2007.08.001

Lin, D. (1998). An information-theoretic definition of similarity. In *Proceedings of the 15th International Conference on Machine Learning.* (pp. 296—304). San Francisco, CA: Morgan Kaufman.

Mladenic, D., & Grobelnik, M. (1998). Word sequences as features in text-learning. In *Proceedings of the ERK-98, the Seventh Electrotechnical and Computer Science Conference.* (pp. 145-148).

Nie, J. Y. (2010). Cross-Language Information Retrieval. *Synthesis Lectures on Human Language Technologies, 3*(1), 1–125. doi:10.2200/S00266ED1V01Y201005HLT008

Pang, B., & Lee, L. (2008). Opinion mining and sentiment analysis. *Foundations and Trends in Information Retrieval, 2*(1-2), 1–135. doi:10.1561/1500000011

Pons-Porrata, A., Berlanga-Llavori, R., & Ruiz-Shulcloper, J. (2007). Topic discovery based on text mining techniques. *Information Processing & Management, 43*(3), 752–768. doi:10.1016/j.ipm.2006.06.001

Rusell, S., & Norvig, P. (2010). *Artificial intelligence: A modern approach.* Upper Saddle River, NJ: Pearson Education.

Schaeffer, S. E. (2007). Graph clustering. *Computer Science Review, 1*(1), 27–64. doi:10.1016/j.cosrev.2007.05.001

Srivastava, A. N., & Sahami, M. (Eds.). (2009). *Text Mining: Classification, Clustering, and Applications.* Boca Raton, FL: Chapman & Hall/CRC. doi:10.1201/9781420059458

Zhang, Y., Jin, R., & Zhou, Z. (2010). Understanding bag-of-words model: A statistical framework. *International Journal of Machine Learning and Cybernetics, 1*(1), 43–52. doi:10.1007/s13042-010-0001-0

KEY TERMS AND DEFINITIONS

Cluster Validation: Clustering validation is a technique used to evaluate the quality (goodness) of the clusters created in a clustering process. The quality should be evaluated with respect to a given goal (purpose). External validation uses external information (typically the true clusters) that is not present in the data; internal validation relies solely of the information in the data.

Clustering Criterion Function: Clustering criterion function is a function that quantifies a clustering solution in terms of its quality. It might take into account similarities of objects within the clusters, dissimilarities of the objects between the clusters, or both. This function is optimized (minimized or maximized) during the clustering process.

Clustering: Clustering is an unsupervised problem of dividing a set of objects into groups (known as the clusters) according to the properties of the objects. Objects in one group are similar while objects in different groups are distinct.

Expert Opinion: Expert opinion is an opinion or a decision of a human expert. This decision is based on the preferences, experience, qualification, or skills of the expert.

Machine Learning: Machine learning is a branch of artificial intelligence (subfield of computer science) that focuses on studying and developing algorithms that can learn from data. Machine learning enables making decisions that are not based on explicitly programmed instructions and thus improving performance of machines based on past experience. It covers a wide variety of tasks that can be distinguished according to the information that is available to the machine during learning. The main categories include supervised learning (learning from examples where the machine is presented some inputs and corresponding desired outputs), unsupervised learning (the machine must find the structure in the data without external information), semi-supervised learning (learning, where the machine has only a small number of good examples), and reinforcement learning (the machine tries to maximize some kind of reward in the form of a feedback).

Opinion Analysis: Opinion (or sentiment) analysis is a subfield of text mining. It focuses on finding subjective information in text data. This information can have a form of an attitude towards a subject (or a topic) or an overall emotional state. Typical sentiment analysis tasks include identification of subjectivity, classification of sentiment polarity or emotional states, or feature-based sentiment analysis.

Text Mining: Text mining (sometimes also text data mining) is a discipline that focuses on extraction of useful knowledge from text data. It relies on the methods similar to those from data mining but includes also specialized methods that need to be applied to texts before employment of the data mining algorithms. Typical text mining tasks include document classification, information retrieval, document clustering, or information extraction. Text mining uses methods and techniques from artificial intelligence, machine learning, natural language processing, linguistics, statistics, and many others.

Chapter 5
Semantics–Based Document Categorization Employing Semi–Supervised Learning

Jan Žižka
Mendel University in Brno, Czech Republic

František Dařena
Mendel University in Brno, Czech Republic

ABSTRACT

The automated categorization of unstructured textual documents according to their semantic contents plays important role particularly linked with the ever growing volume of such data originating from the Internet. Having a sufficient number of labeled examples, a suitable supervised machine learning-based classifier can be trained. When no labeling is available, an unsupervised learning method can be applied, however, the missing label information often leads to worse classification results. This chapter demonstrates a method based on semi-supervised learning when a smallish set of manually labeled examples improves the categorization process in comparison with clustering, and the results are comparable with the supervised learning output. For the illustration, a real-world dataset coming from the Internet is used as the input of the supervised, unsupervised, and semi-supervised learning. The results are shown for different number of the starting labeled samples used as "seeds" to automatically label the remaining volume of unlabeled items.

INTRODUCTION

Let us imagine a common problem: Having a small set of textual documents as samples of certain semantic categories, where each document is correctly labeled by its category, it is necessary to categorize a very big mountain of remaining unlabeled documents where their category is not known but can be determined by the semantic contents. It is possible by reading those documents; however, it can take a very long time and expenses. Today's possibility is to employ machines, computers, which could do it for us via *machine learning*. If there is a sufficiently high number of labeled samples, a classification

DOI: 10.4018/978-1-4666-8690-8.ch005

algorithm can be inductively trained using the specific labeled samples and then applied to labeling the unlabeled documents – a procedure known as *supervised learning* where a supervisor (teacher) is a process that monitors the training process from the minimization of the classification error point of view. Lowering the error is achieved by gradual modification of particular parameters of the selected algorithm.

When no training samples are available, *unsupervised learning* (clustering) can be applied but the missing information – provided by the labeled samples during the supervised learning – mostly later leads to somehow inferior classification results because that absent feedback between the teacher and learner influences the training process negatively. The missing labels might be compensated by manual labeling but it could be unacceptable due to a very high necessary effort, which is inevitable for large data.

As a certain kind of trade-off, the above mentioned possibility of having a small set of training samples as the starting point looks appealingly because the limited labeling can be performed manually. Then, using it for the right aiming, that "seed" training set can be applied to labeling of the uncategorized documents which may be gradually added to the training set. The classifier can be repeatedly retrained as the training set size is growing and the expected result may be better than in the case of the unsupervised learning because more training information is progressively available. Such an approach is known as *semi-supervised learning*. Naturally, the quality of the semi-supervised learning depends on the ability to correctly label the samples that are supposed to strengthen the training set, which is usually given by a specific application, its data, and the method of the labeling correctness evaluation.

Using real-world data, this chapter's goal is to demonstrate how the semi-supervised learning can work. In addition, the results of the semi-supervised approach are compared with outputs of the unsupervised as well as supervised learning employing the same data. The substance of experiments aimed at the classification of textual documents from their semantic point of view, which was satisfaction or dissatisfaction with hotel services. People who used the hotel services could then express their opinion by writing a not too long review using a www portal with the help of the Internet and a browser in their computer (PC). The opinions were not placed at hotel web-pages; they were published by an agency that enables on-line booking of accommodation. Such opinions can later serve for other potential customers as well as directly for the service providers. The reviews were written freely, with no requested structure, using any natural language, and for the experiments described in the following sections, those textual items were divided into two categories: positive and negative ones. As it is shown, all three training methods provided positive results in accordance with the information that was available either by no, or limited, or full labeling.

TEXT MINING USING MACHINE LEARNING APPROACH

In accordance with this chapter pointing, and without any exact definition, the concept *text mining* is generally comprehended as a specialized branch of *data mining*. Data mining is the computational process of discovering knowledge in large data sets of any type involving methods at the intersection of artificial intelligence, machine learning, statistics, and database systems. Text mining area focuses on revealing knowledge in large *text data*, namely analyzing text in natural languages, which are (or, for some old languages, were) used by human beings. People use their spoken and written natural languages for communicating pieces of knowledge or information to each other. The current technology enables storing textual data in very large volumes using the computer technology; however, such storages – databases – make sense only when the *data* may be later somehow utilized: retrieving its part – *information* – relevant to carrying out a particular task and acquiring *knowledge* hidden in it.

We can understand the accumulated data as a representation of a collection of concrete items, observed individual facts. Through its generalization using induction, certain knowledge, that is patterns, can be discovered. For large data sets, machines must be employed; it is typical, for example, for analyzing semantic contents of various blogs, discussion groups, and so like, with thousands or millions contributions in the course of time. When the data is not large, the analysis can be performed 'manually' by humans within an acceptable stretch of time. On the other hand, it can be justifiably expected that more data means usually more and better knowledge buried in it provided that the data is not just a collection of random values. Similar facts and reasoning has led to the birth of data and text mining using the rapidly developing computer technology. However, it is not quite obvious how machines could simply replace humans in such non-machine areas like understanding natural languages, which does not belong to problems that can be easily modeled by traditional tried-and-tested tools as mathematics. An interesting inspiration is learning because people can learn languages and use them.

The *inductive machine-learning* branch of artificial intelligence, based on generalization of concrete samples, provides today tens of algorithms and methods for training computers (Alpaydin, 2009). In short, sufficient number of good samples enables a computer to automatically reveal something general, typical.

Based on the information provided by the available individual data items used as training samples, three fundamental learning methods are today recognized:

- supervised learning (learning with a teacher who provides feedback),
- unsupervised learning (learning without a teacher and feedback),
- semi-supervised learning (learning with a limited teacher's support and feedback).

Supervised Learning-Based Text Mining

Among the three mentioned learning methods, the *supervised learning* takes advantage of having the largest information volume available. This means that every observed fact has its own label that says what a specific group (class, category) the fact belongs to – or, if the task does not constitute classification using discrete classes but a regression problem, the label is a continuous numeric value representing the output of an unknown, searched for function. The supervised learning-based algorithms analyze available training samples knowing which sample is a member of which class, thus having a good possibility to reveal what is for a given class typical and what marks the investigated classes off – it depends on the data inner, not quite obvious, structure.

Provided that the training examples are correctly labeled, useful knowledge may be mined. For example, having a large collection of customers' opinions related to goods purchased on-line at electronic commerce companies (like the popular *amazon.com* or others), the Internet-based retailers can reveal what the customers like when give five stars or dislike when assign one or two only. The number of stars – one to five – defines five gradually different classes, and the following-up analysis can discover what are the characteristic features of goods or services connected to five-star items and what for one-star ones: Which words or phrases? High quality? Low price? Fast delivery? Or some combinations of them? Each customer expresses her or his opinion writing text in natural language, which is understandable by human readers but makes troubles for machines. However, as the practice has demonstrated many times, see, for example, (Dean, 2014), machines can be trained relatively well, simulating human experts to a certain degree – especially from the large data volumes point of view.

The training process – which means setting a specific chosen algorithm's parameters according to the particular training data – is supervised: the teacher has the labeled samples of classes, knowing what sample is a member of what class. Those samples *without* the labels are presented to a selected trained algorithm (a trainee), which returns its assumed classification projection. The supervising teacher knows the labels, so it is possible to check the trainee's progress. If the trainee's classification is correct, nothing is necessary to change; otherwise, as the kind of feedback from its teacher, the algorithm receives instructions concerning the needed change of its parameters that are responsible for assigning a right class, decreasing the existing classification error. For example, the widely popular decision tree algorithms *c4.5* and *c5* (Quinlan, 1993) tries – as its parameters – to find specific words leading to the categorization with the lowest entropy (that is, disorder), dividing the original heterogeneous data-set (all samples are mixed in one set) into as much homogenous subsets as possible (ideally containing only members of one class). Sometimes, decision tree algorithms are called "divide et impera," divide and rule, from the data management point of view.

This chapter can not describe here the details because machine learning is today a very extensive scientific area but interested readers may familiarize themselves with deep as well as wide knowledge in a lot of good books dealing with this data mining branch on various theoretical and practical levels. For example, an interested reader can find a lot of very useful deep information in literature like (Bishop, 2007), (Marsland, 2009), (Mohri et al., 2012), and many others – it cannot be covered just in a chapter. Because this chapter aims at demonstrating the capabilities of the related training methods known as semi-supervised learning, the subsequent subchapters compare results obtained by several different techniques using the same data.

Unsupervised Learning-Based Text Mining

Unlike the supervised learning, the *unsupervised* one does not have information (the labels) about the appropriate belonging of collected facts (text data) to correct classes simply because the classes are not known; therefore such a kind of feedback like in the supervised case can not be provided for tuning the classification algorithms' parameters. The unsupervised learning applies one of several available methods (Bishop, 2007) that look for potential similarities between the analyzed facts, revealing the hidden structure. Groups (or *clusters*) of the facts, which are – to a certain predefined level – similar enough, then create the classes. The unsupervised data/text mining branch (also known as *clustering*) is described in this book in the chapter "*Revealing groups of semantically close textual documents by clustering: Problems and possibilities*" where a reader can find also many additional appropriate references to relevant literature. In this chapter, to show and compare the possibilities of the unsupervised learning procedure applied to the same data, a reader may also look at the results presented in this chapter below – the application of the popular and effective modification of the well known algorithm *k-means* (Bishop, 2007) compared with the supervised and semi-supervised methods' results.

Semi-Supervised Learning-Based Text Mining

The main point of this chapter is the *semi-supervised learning*. As its name suggests, it is neither supervised, nor unsupervised one – approximately, something between. The main idea behind this approach, interestingly and well described in (Søgaard, 2013) and, form the text mining point of view, also in (Blum & Mitchell, 1998), may come from the situation when there is only a limited number of labeled samples. Such a number is not enough for a reliable supervised training procedure, however, there is also a lot of unlabeled samples, which could considerably make the training data-set stronger to support the supervised training. The question is: How to enlarge that small set of labeled samples with the unlabeled items? According to the literature (Abney, 2008), there is not the only one possibility. On one side, it is good because a user can choose for her or his specific data the most effective procedure; on the other side, the typical problem is that it is not easy to say which one would work as well as possible. Similarly like in many other machine learning applications, it is often necessary to look for the best method and algorithm experimentally, especially if there is a new, not time-tested problem, without a verified solution.

At first glance, the unlabeled samples might be separated between groups using the unsupervised learning. The problem is that the automatically generated clusters do not have to fit the already known classes defined by the labeled samples. Thus, it is necessary to find an answer to the following question: How to sort out the unlabeled cases between the existing classes defined by known labeling, so that all the samples (labeled *and* unlabeled) can be used for the training process?

To answer the given question, several ways based on the semi-supervised learning comes into consideration. The main idea uses the fact that even not too many, still some labeled training samples are available. Those samples may be generalized and thus converted into knowledge, which – in spite of its possible imperfectness due to the low number of labeled training samples – may be used for the subsequent labeling of the waiting unlabeled cases. Consequently, the number of labeled samples increases and – provided that the labeling was correct – the classifier can be gradually retrained using more and more training samples.

Obviously, the suggested procedure strongly depends on the quality of the initial labeled training samples because this is what influences the resulting classification accuracy. As it was said above, the more training samples are available, the better learning degree can generally be expected. However, also in this case it is necessary to use correctly labeled samples, otherwise the classifier would not work well despite the big number of the samples. Intuitively, having a small set of very good training samples playing the role of flawless representatives, a good classifier with just a low percentage of accuracy errors may be expected, and as a result, the unlabeled samples can get correct labels. In reality, it is not always possible to use only good labeled samples because everything depends on what data are at the moment available. Should it be possible to prepare a small but good initial training set, the expected results might be justifiably better than the outputs of the clustering procedures – the reason is grounded in the fact that the semi-supervised learning method can use more information taking advantage from the existing handful of labeled training samples.

The up-to-date literature, for example, (Albalate & Minker, 2011) offers several alternative semi-supervised learning procedures. Their selection depends on a specific application and data, thus also in this case it is not always easy to exactly predict what course of action should be used to reach optimal results. For a given data, a set of carefully designed experiments and their evaluated results can indicate which steps should be for an intended application employed. In the following part of the chapter, this couple of relatively simple semi-supervised learning methods suggested itself:

- *self-training*, and
- *co-training*.

The self-training method, see, for example, (Chapelle et al., 2010), is able to take advantage of the information that is – in spite of the missing labels – incorporated in the unlabeled cases and after the classification, which assigns them the labels, appends them actually to the original training set, thus building an effective classifier ready for an intended application. Still, the situation is not in actual fact so straightforward because the initial training set containing the "true" labeled cases can mislabel some of the unlabeled ones and such inaccuracy can expectedly and gradually increase as the not always correct labeling continues.

A CASE STUDY: SEMI-SUPERVISED LEARNING FROM SERVICE REVIEWS

The possibilities of the semi-supervised learning are in this chapter demonstrated using a collection of real-world data, which is the set of many reviews of hotel service customers. Such data are publicly available via the Internet. This specific data comes from one of the popular *booking.com* web service, where people can book an accommodation simply using the Internet connection. After using the hotel service, customers can – again via the Internet – write down their review how they ware (dis)satisfied with the service, what was good and what wrong, using their natural language and keyboard. The reviews have a simple unstructured textual form, often contain mistyping and various errors, and are typically not very long (the accessed data has some 21 words on average; the shortest reviews have just one word, the longest ones rarely up to 140). A reader can find there reviews in far more than 35 languages where English dominates, however, many reviews are written also in alternative 'big' languages like Spanish, French, German, and so like. As a curiosity, someone (probably a linguist dealing with very old languages) wrote a review using a very long time dead language unintelligible for a common man. Some reviews are even written in two languages: English (which is today a kind of international language) plus her/his native one. In addition, a reviewer can add one (very bad) to five (very good) stars, which can lead to a certain type of classification. Some more data details can be found in (Žižka & Dařena, 2011a).

In this chapter, the authors used reviews in English because it guaranteed a sufficient number of reviews. At the time of the data collection, the English language had 1,931,824 reviews that could be labeled either as positive (1,191,367 having 4 or 5 stars) or negative (740,457 having 1 or 2 stars), while the reviews with 3 stars were omitted as neither positive nor negative. This report deals with the mentioned binary categorization only. The original intention has been to mine knowledge from that data, for example, what is typical for positive and negative reviews from the semantic point of view, and so like. An interested reader can find more in (Dařena & Žižka, 2013) and (Dařena et al., 2014).

Altogether, the used English reviews have almost 200,000 unique terms, which is the size of the data dictionary. However, such a high number of unique terms is to a certain degree given by the existence of many mistyping that generate 'artificial' words, thus negatively increasing the vocabulary. Such words play a role of noise, unfavorably influencing the data correctness and strongly increasing the computational complexity. Due to the very large number of reviews, the data cleaning is practically out of the question. Here is one of many examples what various forms a word *accommodation* (and its derivatives) acquired in the written real-world text: accom, accomadate, accomadated, accomadating, accomadation, accomadations, acommodate, accomaddation, accomandating, ...

Each review represented one textual document using the UTF-8 encoding (Universal character set Transformation Format 8-bit). It was necessary and very useful to prepare the data for the text-mining process applying several common, in practice tried and tested steps. In the similar cases, many experiments of many researchers showed that certain terms do not generally provide any useful semantic information. Therefore, all numbers, punctuation, and special characters (for example, €, $, #, &, @, and so like) were removed. In addition, all words having one or two alphabetic characters were removed as well; the practice shows that – for English – such a simple procedure eliminates most of the irrelevant attributes from the classification point of view. It is possible to go farther and apply additional filtering, however, here the authors intentionally limited the preparation phase to just the simplest steps because the previous experiments aimed at various different goals demonstrated that the results for the given data were practically not noticeable, sometimes even harmful (for example, stemming, or stop-words removing). In any case, it is necessary to know that the procedures used here describe results for the given data – in this text-mining area, it is good to be careful before generalizing because many steps are heuristic. Sometimes the procedures that work for certain data do not work for different data, and vice versa. Experimenting usually helps reveal what is useful and what is not.

Each remaining review word was represented by its frequency in a document. The method described here used the popular matrix (or vector) format of textual documents, which can be shown as a table where a column represents one attribute (that is, a unique word) and a row stands for a document. A table cell typically contains a chosen numerical representation of a word frequency (or its modification) in a given document, which may be either a binary number (1/0, a word is/isn't in a certain document) or integer one (the frequency itself) or real one (for example, a relative frequency as term frequency times inverse document frequency), or anything suitable for the solved problem, (Sebastiani, 2002). Such a simple representation (or its similar clones) is also known as CSV (comma separated values) and now commonly accepted by many free or commercial software tools applicable to data/text mining. The last column is mostly conventionally devoted to nominal class names or (for regression tasks) values of the output variable. This chapter works with nominal classes, *positive* and *negative* customers' evaluation of the used hotel services.

Let us look anew at the problem investigated in one of the chapters of this book, "Revealing Groups of Semantically Close Documents by Clustering: Problems and Possibilities." The clustering process was able to automatically find documents that belonged to specific groups, which were distinguished by their certain prevailing topics. Generally, it is not always easy to say in advance how many groups should be created – various documents can be reciprocally more or less similar. Usually, insisting on higher similarity may lead to more groups containing less documents, and vice versa. Thus, the number of generated groups depends strongly on a value of a selected similarity parameter the value of which typically symbolizes a distance – or separation – between the documents. Such a distance is given by the mutual (dis)similarity based on terms contained in the documents, and the terms (that is, their semantics) are responsible for the document meaning. Because the natural language is not based on exact mathematical definitions and proofs, it is often very difficult to strictly say when a needed numerical value of the calculated document similarity degree denotes either *it is* or *it is not* similar enough to be (or not to be) included in a specific group. One of possible solving of that problem is allowing being a member of more than only one group to various degrees, as can be found, for example, in (Puri, 2011).

The main problem comes from the fact that sometimes there is not information enough to correctly navigate the document categorization – simply due to the unawareness of which categories should be taken into consideration. Unlike the supervised learning, the unsupervised one must learn from unlabeled examples where the lack of the information provided by knowing the corresponding category for each training sample strongly supports drawing the general knowledge out of many particular labeled samples. Working on the right assumption that the correct training-sample labeling makes the mining of the text semantic-content recognition significantly stronger, the idea of assigning labels to the unlabeled documents (before starting the training process of a classifier) suggests itself. If there is not too high number of unlabeled documents, such a task may be performed manually by human experts within an acceptable time (including corresponding expenses). However, for a large volume of text documents, which is today typical in the areas like social networks, blogs, Internet discussion groups, and similar ones, such a solution is unaccomplishable – there is simply no time to read and subsequently label millions, billions, or more of the available samples to discover knowledge hidden in them and apply it later to the next documents incoming in the future. Unquestionably, the manual processing of just a small part of the unlabeled documents would be possible but in such a case there is a certain risk of the loss of valuable information hidden in the many skipped items. When there is the training material enough, why not to use it? During the inductive learning process, when specific samples are generalized to obtain knowledge, the practice shows that more particular documents cover the investigated area better, for example, (Žižka & Dařena, 2012).

Eventually, such above-mentioned reasoning resulted in a quite novel idea – *semi-supervised learning* – inspired by a thought that an initial, not very large set of (possibly manually) labeled samples might be used for establishing of the suitable, expected categories of the documents (Abney, 2008). The *semi-supervised learning* means a kind of learning somewhere between the *unsupervised* (without the feedback from a teacher when the training examples are unlabeled) and *supervised* one (a teacher knows correct example labels, so the feedback is possible), as the term itself tells. After predefining the categories of the selected (or just available) initial 'starting' documents that would play a role of a certain 'seed', the following incoming, yet unlabeled documents can consecutively and automatically get their appropriate labels depending on the similarity degree to the already labeled ones. Therefore, such a process is able to transform the original large set of items, which – from the categorization point of view – misses the important kind of information, into the set of labeled samples. Then, that set could be used, for example, for the following process of a classifier training because the training classes are created in this way, or simply just for the basic categorization of the future incoming unlabeled documents using the initially chosen similarity metrics. Naturally, the 'artificially' added information about the originally missing categorization might be lower or less correct than in the case when the authentic labels are known. Anyway, it can be rightfully expected that such information, even if maybe not always quite correct, would better support the classification or prediction process – especially in the cases when *unsupervised learning* has to face the problem connected with the ignorance of existing categories of the large volume of the documents. The initial, even if limited, completion of the information by human experts within an acceptable time can provide important progress particularly in the area (natural language processing) related to humans but calling for the machine help because of too big data.

In the literature, for example, (Albalate & Minker, 2011), (Chapelle et al., 2010), and (Xu et al., 2010), a reader may find several possible semi-supervised methods. This chapter concentrates on the two ones (here used as heuristics), today probably in practice representing the main semi-supervised stream, which can demonstrate possible principles of applying the mentioned idea:

- *self-training*, and
- *co-training*.

To compare the results of the semi-supervised learning with the output of other possible methods, the outcomes of the performed experiments show also following two approaches, given the same textual data:

- *unsupervised learning* – clustering (the document labels were removed), and
- *supervised learning* – training of common classifiers (the document labels were used).

Self-Training Semi-Supervised Method

The self-training algorithm is today very popular because it works well and its fundamental idea is not complicated. The mathematical theory, which is behind the algorithm, is not here analyzed and for interested readers can be found in, for example, (Hastie et al., 2013). This chapter aims at demonstrating the practical possibilities, so the following sections bring only verbal description of the basic principles.

Firstly, using a small training "seed" set of labeled data samples, a classifier is trained via the supervised approach: Each training-set item has a known class label at its disposal. Secondly, provided that the classifier classifies reliably with an acceptable low misclassification error, it is progressively applied to unlabeled items with the goal to assign appropriate class labels to them. If a label is assigned to an unlabeled item with *acceptable confidence* (see below), the item is appended to the existing training set and the classifier is retrained using such enlarged input information source – that is why the algorithm is called *self-training* because it autonomously inductively extends its knowledge by generalization of the increasing number of specific samples. This second step is repeated until reaching a certain stopping criterion, for example, a predefined number of training samples or cycles, or classification accuracy, or when the accuracy stops its increase after achieving a given increment between two (or more) cycle steps. Then, the classifier is ready for its application.

Generally, any classification algorithm may be used under the condition that after assigning a label to an unlabeled item, it also returns a value, which says how much that labeling is reliable. Such an *acceptable confidence* value can, for example, be the probability score, which is provided by the naïve Bayes classifier (Duda et al., 2001) and (Barber, 2012), the distance from the closest neighbor provided by the k-nearest neighbor algorithm, the distance from the classes' border when using support vector machines, and so like – more information and theory can an interested reader find in (Cristianini & Shave-Taylor, 2000). If the acceptable confidence value of a performed labeling is equal or better than a predefined threshold, such a labeled item is accepted for enlarging the training set.

Theoretically all the unlabeled items may be accepted, however, in practice, only part of them is satisfying the predefined criteria. When the accepted number of labeled items is not sufficient, it is necessary to weaken the criteria or collect more unlabeled items, if possible. It is mostly very difficult to predict exactly all the necessary parameters for the described procedure and experimenting can help exclude unsuitable situations – this is a price a user has to pay when no exact mathematical solution is available, but for all that, a solution can be finally found.

Summarizing the self-training requirements, it is necessary to have a seed training set, an algorithm returning the reliability of assigning a label, a predefined value of the accept/reject threshold, and a stopping criterion.

Co-Training Semi-Supervised Method

As the name itself indicates, the co-training algorithm employs cooperating classifiers. The original idea (Blum & Mitchell, 1998) comes from a vision that more classifiers can be used provided that each of them has a *different, mutually independent* view on the same data-set. If the combined different views lead (to a given degree) to the same labeling, an unlabeled item can get that label. Afterwards, the labeled item extends the training set and the classifiers may be retrained and used like in the self-training case. Usually only two classifiers are used because one of problems is to define those different independent views at data, which is easier for just two aspects. Unfortunately, there is no common straightforward way to define those different views – it depends on the application itself. In (Blum & Mitchell, 1998), the authors describe their experiments with web pages from departments of computer science at several universities. The first view on the textual contents of web pages was using all words that were there except the underlined ones, which were included in links and created the second view. In (Wang & Zhou, 2007), several possible alternatives are suggested, for example:

- an artificial random separation of the training items into halves,
- applying two different classification algorithms instead of using two same ones,
- the same classification algorithm with two different setting of parameters,
- and some others.

In the experiments executed by the chapter authors, yet another approach was applied: The reviews were simply divided into halves where one half contained documents with higher word number ("long" documents) and the other one had reviews with lower number of words ("short" documents). The mutual independence precondition was abided by the fact that a review was represented by the bag-of-words method where no mutual dependence of words exists, thus the long and short reviews were – from this point of view – mutually independent, too. In addition, both classes contained long and short reviews practically evenly (the minimum, maximum, and average number of words were almost the same).

The co-training method, used in the demonstrated case, was implemented in a standard way, which was described above. The goal of that implementation was the demonstration of the main basic possibilities provided by the fundamental idea: Having no teacher feedback, train itself with the help of some initial, non-zero starting position given a small set of labeled samples (pre-labeled by human experts, if possible). Here, a classifier was trained using the randomly selected labeled samples and then applied to unlabeled ones, assigning them appropriate labels (classes), thus gradually enlarging the number of the labeled ones. As a result, the set of labeled samples could be used for subsequent supervised learning provided that the up-to-now classification accuracy was acceptable for a given application – a user had definitely to decide it.

The case demonstrated in this chapter worked with just pure textual documents represented as the known and received *bag-of-words* (Sebastiani, 2002). The terms (words) were the only contents. The *bag-of-words* representation assumes the plain mutual independence of the word occurrence: a position of a word in a document does not depend on positions of other words, which significantly decreases the otherwise very high, steeply non-linearly increasing computational complexity given by the unique-word (that is, attribute) number in the dictionary generated from all used textual documents of the investigated application. The basic word representation was their frequency, which was used for defining the two necessary views. The whole dictionary was sorted out according to the individual word frequencies and then divided into two parts where one contained the 50% of words with higher frequencies and the other one the remaining 50% with lower frequencies. The reason of such separation was that frequent words play usually a different role than infrequent ones. It is not easy to exactly analyze and support such an assumption, especially when the data volume is large. Very frequent words may be significant for the categorization but it depends on their occurrence in specific classes. For example, the word *good*, if very frequent, may play a significant role when occurring very often in a class with something positive (and very rarely in a negative class) but when it is very often in more classes, its significance can be quite negligible. Similarly, the role of rare words is equivocal, too, because they can be quite insignificant due to their very low number in documents, but sometimes they can be important, especially when combined with other words. Other experiments with the data (Žižka & Dařena, 2011b), which were used also here, revealed that there were only less than 200 words relevant for the correct classification (from several tens of thousands words in the collected almost 2,000,000 English documents). Thus, two disjunctive subsets of words (that is, views) were available for two independent classifiers.

One classifier was trained employing the first view, the other one employing the second view. The resulting classification was given by the combination of both results. Here is an uncomplicated example how the combination was carried out: Let us have two classifiers, C_1 and C_2 for example, the popular probability-based naïve Bayes, which assumes the conditional independence, a textual document D_i, and two classes, A and B. Take please note of the fact that each of the two classifiers looks at the data differently and mutually independently. The question is: to which class does D_i belong, A or B? Let C_1 says that the probability P_1 of D_i's belonging to A is $P_1(A)$, and C_2 says that the probability P_2 of D_i's belonging to A is $P_2(A)$. Then, the resulting classification is given by the combination of both results, that is, how much C_1 *and* C_2 together assign the class A to D_i:

$$P(A) = P_1(A) \cdot P_2(A).$$

Similarly, the membership degree of D_i to B is computed, too, and the higher numerical result is accepted. Generally, the two (or more) collaborating classifiers can be of the same or different type but a user has to define the intersection of their particular results.

Unsupervised Learning – Clustering

To test efficiency (accuracy) of the unsupervised learning method, a software tool *Cluto* (Zhao & Karypsis, 2004) was chosen. *Cluto* is a well known, publicly accessible system that enables applying various clustering methods with a large scale of parametrization. Based on previous large experimental testing (Žižka, Burda, & Dařena, 2012), a popular clustering method known as k-means (Kaufman & Rousseeuw, 2005) was selected (in *Cluto*, the name of this method was "direct"). The k parameter – the number of generated clusters – was set to 2 to receive the positive and negative clusters of reviews. After finishing the clustering process, the contents of both created clusters could be exactly verified because in fact the labels of all reviews were known, thus it was easy to compute the resulting accuracy based on the correct and incorrect incorporation of reviews into the clusters taken finally as the "positive" and "negative" class representation.

Supervised Learning

For the comparison of the semi-supervised and supervised learning method, four to a great extend used algorithms from the family of the broadly verified supervised-learning ones were selected here; for the details of those algorithms, see for example (Witten et al., 2011), (Alpaydin, 2009), and (Hastie et al., 2013). The algorithms included probabilistic naïve Bayes and multinomial naïve Bayes (this modification works with word frequencies considering which words are in the investigated classes), k-nearest neighbors (known as one of the "lazy" algorithms), and support vector machines, SVM, which looks for an optimal linear class separation within a space with enlarged number of dimensions using kernel functions (Bottou et al., 2007). As an SVM tool, a publicly accessible implementation known as SVMLight (Joachims, 2002) was employed for this case.

The naïve Bayes algorithm family supposes (not always quite correctly) that all input variables (here, words) describing a data item are mutually independent – in practice, it is often inevitable due to otherwise too high computational complexity coming from the enormous number of all possible combinations of attribute values (pairs, triplets, quadruplets, and so on). The "naivety" is in the assumption that a word's position and its relation to other words does not have to be taken into consideration (using the bag-of-words method). Then, the probability that a specific word set containing n words (that is, their numerical representation, e.g., frequency), x_1, x_2,..., x_n, belongs to a certain class, C_k, can be computed much more effortlessly as a conditional probability based on the simplified Bayes theorem:

$$p(C_k \mid x_1, x_2, \ldots, x_n) \doteq p(C_k) \prod_{i=1}^{n} p(x_i \mid C_k),$$

for words occurring in the investigated classes, where $p(x_i \mid C_k)$ is the *a posteriori* conditional probability (likelihood) of an *i*-th word that it belongs to C_k, and $p(C_k)$ is an *a priori* probability of C_k. After computing the left-sided probabilities for all given classes, the class with the highest probability is selected. Despite the certain incorrectness, naïve Bayes in practice works very well, which empirically means that the mutual attribute dependency is usually none or very low.

The *k*-nearest neighbors method is "lazy" because it does not compute anything during the collection of the labeled samples – they are plainly stored in a database. When an unlabeled sample has to be classified, its *k* nearest neighbors in the database vote for the label ($k \geq 1$). The distance to a neighbor is usually computed as the Euclidean one between two points in a hyper-plane, however, it can be whatever suitable metric for a given application and its kind of space. In fact, the distance is the measure of the similarity between two items (the zero distance means the identity of two or more items). A point is a document the coordinates of which are defined by its words.

The SVM procedure (non-probabilistic binary linear classifier) uses those items (supporting vectors) that define a linear border belt where the class separating line lies in the middle (an optimal linear separation of two classes). Finding the vectors is computationally demanding but in the end only the (usually small) set of supporting vectors has to be saved and the future classifications are fast. The linear border is looked for in a higher-dimensional space comparing with the original one, therefore a suitable kernel function has to be mostly experimentally found; typically a linear, polynomial, or Gaussian radial basic function are applied. If there are more than two classes, more SVM binary classifiers have to be trained for each class against others.

DESCRIPTION OF THE REVIEW DATA SET

Table 1 provides brief information about the data-set used in the experiments.

To illustrate the real-world textual data used for the text mining described in this book section, a couple of examples might be interesting for a reader, just to elucidate the situation. Here are some randomly selected examples of the **positive** reviews, including the possible original mistyping, misspelling, or

Table 1. The basic statistical characteristic of the English collection of customers' reviews. The ratio negative/positive number is approximately 62% while the average length, minimum, maximum, and variance are very similar or almost the same

	Positive Reviews	Negative Reviews
Total number of reviews	1,190,949	741,092
Maximal review length in words	391	396
Minimal review length in words	1	2
Average number of review words	22	26
Variance (σ^2)	403	618

grammatical errors, as well as a bilingual case (which was not the only one – this one combines Polish and English, but in the downloaded data, there were several hundreds of such cases, often "matching" either Chinese or Japanese with English). The errors that a reader can see below are just copied from the originals. More than a couple of reviews are demonstrated here in order to emphasize the variedness; still, certain common service attributes can be revealed even here (*food, quiet hours, transport, cleanness, …*). Anyway, a question remains open: Is such a small random selection representative enough? From the statistical point, it is not. A handful of samples can be processed easily but to get reliable knowledge concerning the service quality, at least thousands (or much more) reviews are necessary. Well, the illustration is here:

- everything was great in this hotel, the staff, the swimming pool, the size of the room, the kitchen with microwave, coffee maker, toaster, and a hair dryer in the bathroom. although it is in a very relaxing area, there were bars and supermarkets around the hotel and it was very convenient. there are lots of activities for small kids and excellent size of swimming pool. definitely recommendable.
- i like your location not far from old town
- clean room and friendly staff, good for costal walk with easy access to local shops and restaraunts
- w oliwkowym gaju nieduża hacjenda z dopracowanymi dodatkami dała nam wyciszenie, nasłonecznienie i pyszne jedzenie. in the olive grove the small hacienda with supplements touched up gave us the calm, the solar exposure and the delicious food.
- excellent.
- i thought it was very good value for money and considering it's only a two star we got more than expected. we had a large room with balcony and flat screen tv which had a couple of english channels. fresh fruit and hot drinks were available for free all day and the continental breakfast had plenty of choice. the staff were very friendly and helpful, giving us recommendations of places to visit. the location was good you just need to get tram 25 from central station which stops virtually straight outside the hotel. overall excellent!
- near roma ciampino airport.
- walking distance to the beach and shopping areas. the variety of food is good.
- i've stayed in the hotel for 8 nights in a double room traveling for tourism. everything was fine: very clean room (fresh towels, sheets every day), nice breakfast buffet with many choices (kept full throughout the serving time), professional and hospitable staff speaking good english and free wifi. the hotel is located in a small, quite street very close to sirkeci train and tramway station,

within walking distance to most touristic attractions (10' to top kapi palace, 15' to agia sophia, blue mosque, 5' to egyptian market). the only minor issue is that the hotel has very little view but being out all day long it didn't really bothered us. i very much enjoyed my stay in hotellino and fully recommend it for either business or pleasure.

- thai cozy house, is situated in a great location very close to koh san rd but not too close to be invaded by noise, we just recently returned to thai cozy house and the standard of the rooms was basic compared to a tourist hotel yet for back packer is ideal english movie channels, clean sheets every day, air conditioning and extremely low cost compared to what else is out there. the tailor on site " overseas tailor" is amazing quality and i have just purchased another 2 suits from there bringing the total i have bought so far to 5 suits and 10 shirts all of impeccable quality and while priced a little higher than other tailors in bangkok the quality is immeasurably higher.
- nice and quiet place.
- super b&b hotel. billed as a 2*, hotel, but i have stayed in worse 5* rooms. rooms were bright, refreshingly clean and had good quality bed linen. the bathrooms were very chic with large walk in showers. the owners who run the hotel were really helpful and friendly providing a professional but personal touch. what a lovely change to be able to take our dog into a clean room and not be hived off into an old run down one. breakfast was also great.
- only jaccuzi
- anya, the housekeeper, she was brilliant, nothing was too much trouble, and the room was serviced to an exceedingly high standard. breakfast could sink a battleship!!!!!!!!!!!
- we really enjoyed our stay at vincci capitol hotel as it was comfortable with a great cental location. a really good breakfast. also veryfriendly and helpful staff.
- biutiful place natural golf hors pool
- i like everithing.
- location was excellent, close to everything. great room for the price. will definetly stay again.
- we had a "superior room", which was spacious, very clean & comfortable. the cooked breakfast was great & the owners were very friendly & welcoming !

Similarly, some examples of the negative reviews can be seen here. It includes also a strange case marked as a *negative review* (having just one star) even if "all was pleasant" could be considered as being a *positive review*, which means that also such kind of errors may be encountered in the real-world data sets – therefore, it is not generally possible to expect a perfect classifier (100% accuracy) when the data is not perfect. Because of the really large volumes of the real data, it is extremely difficult, maybe impossible, to exclude such kind of errors; however, when the errors do not prevail, they also do not play a deciding factor. Possible comments are identical with those ones mentioned with the positive samples above. Here are the **negative** samples:

- terrible! very unclean. first. upon arrival we were told that we could not have a non smoking room (which we had booked months ago). if this was not to our liking we could swap the next day! second. room was not clean, and of course smelt of smokers. third. we found a cockroach in the room. fourth. internet was charged at $24.95 per 24 hours, but was given to us free after mentioning that my booking through booking.com said it was free......should i go on?
- rom 3 was next to the breakfast room & the terrace ovrlooked the next door farm yard but the front terrce looking over to the alps was stunning

- dining room
- tv channels poor, i cant immagine a 4 stars hotel with no one helped us to get our luggeges to the room the reciptionest was very rude by saying u hav to take ur luggege to ur room!!
- i am afraid the outer windows of my room (they were double glazed) were extremely dirty and spoiled the view. my other criticism would be that radio 2 was played in the brasserie throughout breakfast. the incessant chattering of chris evans and guests is very annoying when you are trying to read a newspaper or arrange your thoughts for the day. I don't think radio is appropriate in such a setting. selected background music - if anything - would be more acceptable.
- the room we booked was an executive room - it was fine, but it was nothing special. i certainly didn't feel that the price we paid had been worth it for the extravegant treat.... was left feeling quite disappointed. i only used the spa for a leg wax, and was glad i didn't have anything 'relaxing' done because again, this was a big let down. the staff were, again, wonderful - but the facilities and rooms (small, cramped and cluttered) were not four star by any stretch of the imagination. the only other thing to add was that breakfast was also a little disappointing - the quality of the food and service was excellent, but 2 out of 3 times we went for breakfast there was plenty missing from the hot buffet and the continental buffet! oops!
- sauna was broken
- all was pleasant
- i asked for smoking but didn't get it.didn't have resturant open all day.internet isn't same as north american,so i didn't know how to use it and language barrier seemed to far apart to get help that i needed.
- too few towels.
- the rooms could do with some renovation. in the bathroom the shower was leaking quite badly and the hot/cold water was irregular in temperature. the wallpaper was loosening in some places. its not horrible, but could be a lot better.
- small beach
- we got some problems with 2 bedrooms where it was stinky 'coz of the drain of bathroom. so the staffs were efficient. something else is a bit annoying if you aim to stay there for a long while: the breakfast. it's definitely the same every morning. we were happy because it's included into the price but if they could change a bit, not so much, each couple days, it would be great. the "b" ochanomizu has also a problem with their dryer what takes a long long time to dry your clothes. it would be super if they could write the washer and dryer's notice in english too.
- the man at the hotel lacks service. he refused to give me blankets. even though i asked for a clean quiet room, i got a room which was loud all night. also the ceiling had water stain - which i can deal with but the wall paper had mold due to the water leak- i suppose. i sneezed for awhile until i got used to the mold. since there was not too many comments about loudness I wasn't too worried. my friend had a very stinky loud room.
- i would never stay in this hotel more. the rooms were not renovated since the hotel was built. the furniture was old fashioned. the bathroom had mold problems. the room was stinking mold. our clothes smelled mold many days after staying the hotel. the room's floors were unclean and sandy. the staff was unprofessional and could hardly speak english. at the check in they played so loud music at the launch so we hardly could have a conversation. at the evening the access to the beach was closed.

- toilet stink maybe because of the moist tiles & no ventilation. kettle not provided but tea, coffee etc available.

- sloppy service, overworked staff. meals definitely not worth the cost. we were overcharged on three occasions. two mornings we were charged for breakfast for 4 people (we were three) thats 26 extra euro! we were overcharged for one of the nights we stayed, thats another 27 euros! we were also charged for food we ordered that did not arrive, another 3 euros. make sure you check your bills! we were refunded the money without problems, but had we not checked we would have been 56 euro out of pocket. we would go back again, however, as the hotel is lovely and in a beautiful area. we eventually found a place called mersil st pierre on the lakeside and an inexpensive italian pizzeria. very good food overlooking the lake.

- never will i stay here again. no water in the rooms. and no where to buy water. went to bar and was charged £4 for a bottle of water. only 200ml's. ordered food to the room, waited over 45 mins. when it came it was awful.something i would not even feed my dog. the worse thing about it, that it cost more than the room it self. air con was not working. bed was very uncomfortable. sheets were dirty. bathroom was not clean. water from the taps was brown. shower head was very dirty. carpet had stains. this is not a four star hotel. i would not even class it at a one star. the worst hotel i have ever stayed at!!!!

- many bugs inside the room and very dirty

- the hotel says it is 4 or 5 stars but it does not have a swimming pool which I find very unusual. i had quite an uncomfortable stay at your hotel.thank you,cara greene.

And so like, and so on. Sometimes, both the positive as well as negative opinion was included in a review, however, the final decision – the degree of negativity (or positivity) – was assigned by a reviewer, including her/his possible mistyping. Of course, such reviews are very subjective, however, this is what a hotel keeper might be interested in as it plays the decisive role whether a guest would recommend or visit that hotel. Having a lot of such reviews is very useful but reading them all and gaining common knowledge could be impossible due to the inevitable too long time. So, as it was said, the automatic processing of this data type could be very helpful.

Sometimes, when reading a review, one can not be sure if it is irony or an evaluation mistake; see, please, the last negative review example (probably the ironic *thank you,cara greene*). Irony – it is also another, not easy topic waiting for its solution, (Carvalho et al., 2009), but this chapter does not deal with it. The possible mistakes of assigning an incorrect class of a document, or even introducing irony, may produce lowering the sense of certain, otherwise unambiguous words expressing the "agreed" meaning. People can meet such kind of communication problems, too, and it is not always facile to "decrypt" some messages even for us – human beings. When using trained machines for revealing the semantic contents, it is inevitable to apply a good testing process – based on high-quality data – before starting a real application of them to the real-world data.

The results in this chapter are based on testing using randomly selected samples from the positive and negative data-sets provided that – from the statistical point of view – an overwhelming majority of the reviews simply express the positivity or negativity and there are not too many ironic or wrongly assigned reviews. From this point of view, a certain classification imperfection must be accepted if it is not too high from a user point of view. The degree of the imperfection cannot be strictly defined; it is up to the classifier user what inaccuracy might be accepted for her or him. Quite generally, it is possible to say that an error lower than 50% can be accepted because it is better than a random guessing – the base line for the comparison is that random guessing that depends on the number of classes and the number of their members. So called *zero-rule classifier*, which predicts simply the mean (for a numeric class) or the mode (for a nominal class), can serve well for providing such a base-line. Another applicable approach to overcome the high classification error can be *boosting*, for example, the popular procedure known as *Adaboost* (adaptive boosting) where a group of "weak learners" are trained and their collective (sometimes weighted) voting may give very good results. Adaboost is based on the idea that if a learner is good for a certain samples and bad for other ones, another learner can be trained on that difficult part, and the number of such trainees can be gradually increased. Some introducing information can be found in (Witten et al., 2011), including also corresponding references to other literature.

THE SEMI-SUPERVISED PROCEDURE PARAMETERIZATION

In the following subchapters, a reader can look at results obtained for different training and testing data volumes for several learning algorithms. The data was prepared and used so that the semi-supervised procedure imitated the supposed future utilization

Initial Preparation of the 'Seed' Training Samples and Their Gradual Increasing

For the quite initial training starter of samples, which should be carefully selected to support the additional search for similar and dissimilar cases as good as possible, the number of prototypal positive and negative samples was given by supposed data volumes that a human expert would be able to prepare within not a long time – no more than tens or hundreds of samples. Moreover, the starting samples were selected in order to balance the both used classes (positive and negative reviews) by their number of members because unbalanced training sets usually present a problem: the more one class prevails another one, the worse training results can be expected as many experiments and theoretical outcomes may show (Menardi & Torelli, 2010). However, the following automated training phase employed the data as it was, without any artificial balancing because the goal was to simulate the reality. To avoid a possible influence of a specific training sample order on the result, the samples were randomly aligned in each of the experimental phase. The experiments did not use manually selected seed samples in order to avoid a possible bias towards some review attributes that might immediately come into the mind, as *price, cleanness, food,* and so like – what if there would be something more or different? Thus, only the random selection was employed, even if it could be interesting to investigate the various bias influences.

After creating the starting set of labeled samples (with known classes, supervised training), an initial classifier was trained to generalize them, inducing certain information (labeling) that supports classification. At this phase, the first step was finished.

In the second step, the randomly aligned unlabeled reviews were classified as they were arriving. Every review was classified, and if its classification reached a higher accuracy than a given threshold value, that sample was assigned to its appropriate class, that is, it was labeled, and added to the gradually enlarged training set (here subsequently called as *testing/training*). Then, the classifier was retrained and went on in this repeated process until all the accepted unlabeled cases (with "hidden" class membership for the training process) were categorized taking into consideration the starter. Because both the real classes were not balanced 50%: 50%, see Table 1 above, the ratio of the randomly selected unlabeled (hidden labels) testing/training samples preserved approximately the ratio of the original, from 23% for

Table 2. The results of parametrized semi-supervised self-training algorithm for 30 positive and 30 negative starting samples, plus 823 testing/training samples (77% positive, 23% negative) with hidden labels (taken as unlabeled)

Threshold %	Balancing	Throttling %	Average accuracy %
80	no	no	77
80	yes	no	76
80	no	80	78
95	no	no	79
95	yes	80	78
95	no	80	78
99	no	no	78
99	yes	no	78
99	no	80	78

negative and 77% for positive representatives up to 20% and 80% ones. That semi-supervised learning method is illustrated in Figure 2. The results for four different negative/positive rates, compared with the results of supervised and unsupervised learning, can be seen in Table 3, 4, 5, and 6.

Self-Training Algorithm's Parameterization

For the illustration, Table 2 shows results provided by the self-training algorithm with the data characterized by the starter containing 60 labeled reviews (50% positive and 50% negative ones, that is, 30^+ and 30^-) plus 823 unlabeled testing/training samples (77% positive, 23% negative). This step was a preliminary one aimed at experimentally finding the convenient semi-supervised learning algorithm's parameters for the given data; more general parameter details can be found in (Abney, 2008):

- threshold: the level of acceptance/rejection of a new potential training sample; see also the explanation above of the term *acceptable confidence*,
- balancing: the original (77%: 23%) balancing modified to 50%: 50% (positive and negative class ratio), and
- throttling: the percentage of accepted new training samples from all those that meet the threshold (may be used for preventing a large influx of newly labeled instances from overwhelming the influence of the previously labeled instances in early iterations).

All the experiments described in this chapter, counting this step, were repeated four times, each time with quite different randomly selected reviews (including the subsets for the starter data) to prevent a possible influence of a particular data subset on the results.

The demonstrated outcomes implicate a surmise that for the given natural-language data the specific parametrization of the self-training algorithm has practically no big importance. Such a surmise was supported also by additional experiments with various data size and ratios – from the accuracy point of view, the results were invariable, too. Interestingly, the balancing parameter played no role as well

Table 3. Classification accuracy acquired by the seed 30⁺ and 30⁻ for 823 testing samples

Starter 30⁺ and 30⁻, 823 testing (77⁺ and 23⁻ %)						
Learning	Algorithm	Accuracy %				Average %
Supervised	**NB**	84	80	81	84	**82.25**
	MNB	80	80	81	80	80.25
	k-NN	37	37	37	68	44.75
	SVM	75	65	74	73	71.75
Clustering	k-means	71	71	71	71	**71.00**
Semi-supervised self-training	**NB**	83	74	78	79	**78.50**
	MNB	80	80	72	74	76.50
	k-NN	37	37	37	68	44.75
	SVM	75	65	74	68	70.50
Semi-supervised co-training	**NB**	77	79	78	80	**78.50**
	MNB	69	79	80	78	76.50
	k-NN*)	-	-	-	-	-
	SVM	62	61	70	68	65.25

*) Co-training k-NN could not be computed because the used software (the static library ANN for C++) was not able to work with such a large input data-set.

Table 4. Classification accuracy acquired by the seed 40⁺ and 40⁻ for 1002 testing samples

Starter 40⁺ and 40⁻, 1002 testing (57⁺ and 43⁻ %)						
Learning	Algorithm	Accuracy %				Average %
Supervised	NB	71	75	74	81	75.25
	MNB	79	82	81	82	81.00
	k-NN	39	35	37	63	43.50
	SVM	82	84	84	83	**83.25**
Clustering	k-means	80	83	84	86	**83.25**
Semi-supervised self-training	NB	80	84	88	89	**85.25**
	MNB	77	80	81	82	80.00
	k-NN	37	37	37	63	43.50
	SVM	82	84	84	85	83.75
Semi-supervised co-training	NB	72	75	74	76	74.25
	MNB	77	73	72	80	75.5
	k-NN*)	-	-	-	-	-
	SVM	79	78	77	77	**77.75**

*) Co-training k-NN could not be computed because the used software (the static library ANN for C++) was not able to work with such a large input data-set

Table 5. Classification accuracy acquired by the seed 255⁺ and 255⁻ for 11,6321 testing samples

Starter 255⁺ and 255⁻, 11632 testing (74⁺ and 26⁻ %)						
Learning	Algorithm	Accuracy %				Average %
Supervised	**NB**	89	89	89	86	**88.25**
	MNB	87	87	89	87	87.50
	k-NN*)	-	-	-	-	-
	SVM	82	82	81	80	81.25
Clustering	k-means	73	70	73	72	**72.00**
Semi-supervised self-training	**NB**	83	89	89	86	**86.75**
	MNB	87	87	86	86	86.50
	k-NN*)	-	-	-	-	-
	SVM	82	82	81	80	81.25
Semi-supervised co-training	**NB**	88	88	85	85	**86.50**
	MNB	86	87	86	85	86.00
	k-NN*)	-	-	-	-	-
	SVM	71	72	74	79	74.00

*) Co-training k-NN could not be computed because the used software (the static library ANN for C++) was not able to work with such a large input data-set.

Table 6. Classification accuracy acquired by the seed 255⁺ and 255⁻ for 32,191 testing samples

Starter 255⁺ and 255⁻, 32191 testing (74⁺ and 26⁻ %)						
Learning	Algorithm	Accuracy %				Average %
Supervised	**NB**	88	88	87	85	**87.00**
	MNB	87	86	84	85	85.50
	k-NN*)	-	-	-	-	-
	SVM	80	79	82	81	80.50
Clustering	k-means	73	70	71	71	**71.25**
Semi-supervised Self-training	NB	82	83	82	84	82.75
	MNB	83	84	84	83	**83.50**
	k-NN*)	-	-	-	-	-
	SVM	80	80	82	81	80.75
Semi-supervised co-training	NB	86	84	87	82	**84.75**
	MNB	86	85	87	84	85.50
	k-NN*)	-	-	-	-	-
	SVM	70	73	71	72	71.50

*) Co-training k-NN could not be computed because the used software (the static library ANN for C++) was not able to work with such a large input data-set.

even if the positive/negative percentage ratio was rather far from 50:50 (here, 77:23). And the throttling parameter was also quite irrelevant. Therefore, the applied parameter values finally were like this:

- threshold 95%,
- balancing not used,
- throttling not used.

Co-Training Algorithm's Parameterization

At the beginning, in this case, it was not quite clear what *two independent views* on the data should be selected. The reviews contained only pure text, and several attempts – like using statistically prevailing either positive or negative contradictory words (good-bad, big-small, etc.) – gave no reasonable results. It was expected because individual words use to have often smaller meaning than collocations that may even turn the meaning over (good/not good, etc.). Maybe, from this point of view, it would be interesting to enlarge the research to find if such a method, based on n-grams and/or synonyms, could be applicable. Eventually, co-training used the reviews' dictionary simply divided into two halves: 50% of words having higher frequencies and the remaining 50% of words with lower frequencies on the frequency scale for the given set of English reviews.

Alternatively, the authors of this chapter tried to generate the independent views by splitting the generated dictionary down the middle via the random selection of words, however, the repeated experiments showed that the results were very nondeterministic – the resulting classifier accuracy fluctuated up to 15% during the testing phase. Therefore, those results were here omitted.

COMPARING UNSUPERVISED, SEMI-SUPERVISED, AND SUPERVISED LEARNING

In this subchapter, a reader can look at the results of experiments the goal of which was to compare the semi-supervised algorithms *self-training* (ST) and *co-training* (CT) with outcomes of several other popular text-mining methods. For the experiments, the same data-sets were used as the input of the supervised-learning algorithms *naïve Bayes* (NB), *multinomial naïve Bayes* (MNB), *k nearest neighbors* (k-NN), and *support vector machines* (SVM). At the same time, it would be interesting to know what the unsupervised learning can accomplish; in this case, the *clustering* algorithm known as *k-means* was chosen based on certain previous experience (Žižka et al., 2012). Altogether, seven machine-learning algorithms were used in the experiments described here. To summarize the different understanding of the data by the three groups of learning:

- *Unsupervised learning* used only unlabeled reviews for generating the mentioned two classes and the results – which reviews were labeled as positive and negative – were compared with the known (but here for the algorithm hidden) labels. The accuracy was simply given by the ratio of the correctly and incorrectly labeled cases because it was known.
- *Semi-supervised learning* employed the starter labeled data for training, and then the testing data was gradually classified and when the threshold was positively exceeded, the sample was included into the suggested class, with the following retraining of the classifier.

- *Supervised learning* used the same labeled training samples as the semi-supervised approach and the accuracy was checked using also the same testing subsets.

To demonstrate the most significant outcomes, this chapter presents the four following representative results of four-times repeated experiments with the different positive/negative review ratios. The *average* accuracy value (in the last table columns) is the arithmetic mean obtained from the four experiments.

- In the first experiment group, the starter contained 60 labeled reviews (50% positive and 50% negative ones, that is, 30^+ and 30^-) plus 823 unlabeled testing/training samples (77% positive, 23% negative). It was also used for the parameterization of the semi-supervised methods. See also Table 3 and Figure 1.
- The second experiment group used 80 labeled (40^+ and 40^-) plus 1002 unlabeled (57% positive and 43% negative). See also Table 4 and Figure 2.
- The third experiment group used 500 labeled (250^+ and 250^-) plus 11,632 unlabeled (74% positive and 26% negative). See also Table 5 and Figure 3.
- The fourth experiment group worked with 500 labeled (250^+ and 250^-) plus 32,191 unlabeled (74% positive and 26% negative). See also Table 6 and Figure 4.

In the area of the semi-supervised training methods, another interesting point is how a classifier's accuracy progresses during accepting unlabeled samples when their similarity degree (taking into consideration the labeled ones) is equal or better than a certain predefined threshold value. The experiments demonstrated that the accuracy rate changes were appreciable, sometimes quite noticeably. As an illustration, the following graph Figure 5 shows several iteration steps for four different, randomly selected 60 starting labeled textual datasets (data 1, 2, 3, and 4), 30^+ and 30^-, each time using the same 823 testing cases (divided between 77^+ and 23^- %) randomly selected at the beginning so that the miscellaneous starting training samples' effects can be mutually compared.

Here, a reader can see the results of the self-training method with the application of the popular naïve Bayes classifier. In fact, the first iteration step is equivalent to the supervised learning procedure because the starting dataset contains only labeled samples, 30 positive and 30 negative ones. In all the investigated cases, the final accuracy was worse than at the very beginning. The graph shows that the step number 2 is much worse, in tens of per cent. However, in the following iteration steps, the accuracy increased again as the additionally labeled training samples were added to the starter. Two experiments terminated after the fourth step, and other two ones after the fifth step – the reason was that no extra reviews could be included into the gradually increasing training dataset because the set threshold value did not allow it anymore.

CONCLUSION

As it can be seen, the best results were obtained – expectedly – using the traditional supervised learning procedure. However, the semi-supervised learning acquired surprisingly good values that were close to the supervised learning. Larger sets of the starter samples gave better results but the difference was not too significant as the tables and graphs demonstrate. From the algorithm selection point of view, naïve Bayes was the best method but other algorithms (SVM and MNB) worked well, too. The clustering

Figure 1. The graphical illustration of the average values in Table 3

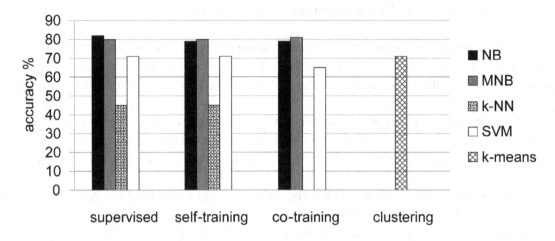

Figure 2. The graphical illustration of the average values in Table 4

Figure 3. The graphical illustration of the average values in Table 5

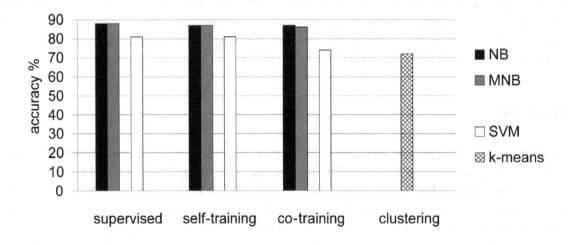

Figure 4. The graphical illustration of the average values in Table 6

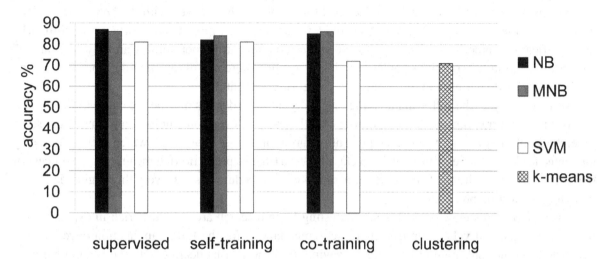

Figure 5. The accuracy development influenced by gradually adding new samples and retraining the classifier (naïve Bayes)

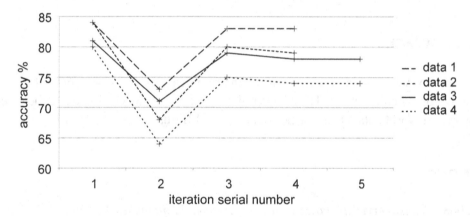

procedure could be used as well, however, the results were inferior due to the missing initial information provided by the starter sets.

It is necessary to realize that machine learning methods need to be tailored for a specific application and data. It would be interesting to see how much could the results demonstrated here differ from results obtained from another type of textual documents like scientific papers and so like. The hotel service reviews are typical for short ones provided on-line by customers but it is a question to what degree it would differ from various blogs, discussion groups, and so like. And there is also one more important question: What if the opinions change during time? How much a starter can help when the future development of textual messages is not stable? Maybe, it would be necessary to monitor the classification system behavior and from time to time to retrain it; or, to look for algorithms that would be able to adapt to the time-based changes and modify the parameters. The naïve Bayes algorithm can be used also in such situations as the contemporary research shows, see, for example, (Bifet et al., 2010) and (Read et al., 2012) – massive on-line analysis.

The performed experiments revealed that the correct parametrization of the semi-supervised procedure was not easy and the suitable values had to be apparently received with the help of trials. The initial size of the starter as well as the threshold level undoubtedly played an important role. Similarly, the significant parameter is what samples the starter contains at its root point. Carefully, "manually" labeled selected initial training samples certainly introduce more useful information – but very likely, too few samples do not have to represent their categories adequately.

On the other side, the following arriving originally unlabeled cases may be the cause of the disruption of the initial training set stability, introducing diversity or even some noise – anyway, at the same time, the result may be more general, representing larger or deeper knowledge, which in the future may guarantee finding more relevant results via classification (that is, prediction). It means that the process of building a classifier with the help of the semi-supervised procedure has to be very thoroughly designed, including the testing procedure.

This area presents unquestionably an interesting large research area possibly rich in expected new results, findings, and valuable prospective recommendations for the future application development, connected (but not only) with the Internet growing use or any tasks dealing with the accumulation of textual documents oriented also to their automatic semantic investigation. Beyond reasonable doubt, this area is also predestined for merging with the arising branch of processing of so called "Big Data," see (Kitchin, 2014).

ACKNOWLEDGMENT

The work on this chapter was supported in part by the research grant IGA No. 16/2014 of the Mendel University in Brno, Czech Republic. This chapter also benefited from carrying out some extensive experiments with real-world data by our former student Karel Burda.

REFERENCES

Abney, S. (2008). *Semisupervised Learning for Computational Linguistics*. London: Chapman and Hall/CRC.

Albalate, A., & Minker, W. (2011). *Semi-Supervised and Unsupervised Machine Learning: Novel Strategies*. Hoboken: Wiley.

Alpaydin, E. (2009). *Introduction to Machine Learning. (Adaptive Computation and Machine Learning series)*. Cambridge: The MIT Press.

Barber, D. (2012). *Bayesian Reasoning and Machine Learning*. Cambridge: Cambridge University Press.

Bifet, A., Holmes, G., Kirkby, R., & Pfahringer, B. (2010). MOA: Massive online analysis. *Journal of Machine Learning Research, 99*, 1601–1604.

Bishop, C. M. (2007). *Pattern Recognition and Machine Learning. (Information Science and Statistics)*. New York: Springer.

Blum, A., & Mitchell, T. (1998). Combining labeled and unlabeled data with co-training. In: *COLT: Proceedings of the Workshop on Computational Learning Theory* (pp. 92-100). Morgan Kaufmann. doi:10.1145/279943.279962

Carvalho, P., Sarmento, L., Silva, M. J., & De Oliveira, E. (2009). Clues for Detecting Irony in User-Generated Contents: Oh...!! It's so easy. In *Text Sentiment Analysis TSA'09*. ACM Press. doi:10.1145/1651461.1651471

Chapelle, O., Schölkopf, B., & Zien, A. (Eds.). (2010). *Semi-Supervised Learning. (Adaptive Computation and Machine Learning series)*. Cambridge: The MIT Press.

Cristianini, N., & Shawe-Taylor, J. (2000). *An Introduction to Support Vector Machines and Other Kernel-based Learning Methods*. Cambridge: Cambridge University Press. doi:10.1017/CBO9780511801389

Dařena, F., & Žižka, J. (2013). SuDoC: Semi-unsupervised Classification of Text Document Opinions Using a Few Labeled Examples and Clustering. In *Flexible Query Answering Systems* (pp. 625–636). Springer. doi:10.1007/978-3-642-40769-7_54

Dařena, F., Žižka, J., & Přichystal, J. (2014). Clients' freely written assessment as the source of automatically mined opinions. Proceedings of Procedia Economics and Finance, 12(1), Conference Enterprise and the Competitive Environment 2014, ECE-2014 (pp. 103-110). Elsevier Science Bv.

Dean, J. (2014). *Big Data, Data Mining, and Machine Learning: Value Creation for Business Leaders and Practitioners. (Wiley and SAS Business Series)*. Hoboken: Wiley. doi:10.1002/9781118691786

Duda, R. O., Hart, P. E., & Stork, D. G. (2001). *Pattern Classification* (2nd Ed.). New York: John Wiley & Sons.

Hastie, T., Tibshirani, R., & Friedman, J. (2013). *The Elements of Statistical Learning: Data Mining, Inference, and Prediction* (2nd Ed.). New York: Springer.

Joachims, T. (2002). *Learning to Classify Text Using Support Vector Machines. (The Springer International Series in Engineering and Computer Science)*. Boston: Kluwer academic Publishers. doi:10.1007/978-1-4615-0907-3

Kaufman, L., & Rousseeuw, P. J. (2005). *Finding Groups in Data: An Introduction to Cluster Analysis. (Probability and Statistics)*. Hoboken: Wiley.

Kitchin, R. (2014). *The Data Revolution: Big Data, Open Data, Data Infrastructures and Their Consequences*. London: SAGE Publications.

Marsland, S. (2009). *Machine Learning: An Algorithmic Perspective. (Machine Learning & Pattern Recognition)*. Boca Raton: Chapman & Hall/CRC.

Menardi, G., & Torelli, N. (2012). Training and assessing classification rules with imbalanced data. *Data Mining and Knowledge Discovery*, 28(1), 92–122. doi:10.1007/s10618-012-0295-5

Puri, S. (2011). A Fuzzy Similarity Based Concept Mining Model for Text Classification: Text Document Categorization Based on Fuzzy Similarity Analyzer and Support Vector Machine Classifier. *International Journal of Advanced Computer Science and Applications*, 2(11), 115–121. doi:10.14569/IJACSA.2011.021119

Quinlan, J. R. (1993). *C4.5: Programs for Machine Learning*. San Mateo: Morgan Kaufmann.

Read, J., Bifet, A., Holmes, G., & Pfahringer, B. (2012). Scalable and efficient multi-label classification for evolving data streams. *Machine Learning*, 88(1-2), 243–272. doi:10.1007/s10994-012-5279-6

Sebastiani, F. (2002). Machine Learning in Automated Text Categorization. *ACM Computing Surveys*, 34(1), 1–47. doi:10.1145/505282.505283

Søgaard, A. (2013). *Semi-Supervised Learning and Domain Adaptation in Natural Language Processing. (Synthesis Lectures on Human Language Technologies)*. Morgan & Claypool Publishers.

Wang, W., & Zhou, Z. (2007). Analyzing co-training style algorithms. Proceedings of Machine Learning: ECML 2007 (pp. 454-465). Springer. doi:10.1007/978-3-540-74958-5_42

Witten, I. H., Frank, E., & Hall, M. A. (2011). Data Mining: Practical Machine Learning Tools and Techniques. Third Edition. (The Morgan Kaufmann Series in Data Management Systems). Morgan Kaufmann.

Zhao, Y., & Karypsis, G. (2004). Empirical and Theoretical Comparisons of Selected Criterion Functions for Document Clustering. *Machine Learning*, 55(3), 311–331. doi:10.1023/B:MACH.0000027785.44527.d6

Žižka, J., Burda, K., & Dařena, F. (2012a). Clustering a very large number of textual unstructured customers' reviews in English. In: Artificial Intelligence: Methodology, Systems, and Applications (pp. 38-47). Springer.

Žižka, J., & Dařena, F. (2011a). Mining Significant Words from Customer Opinions Written in Different Languages. In: *Proceedings of the 14th International Conference on Text, Speech and Dialogue, Lecture Notes in Artificial Intelligence* (pp. 211-218). Springer.

Žižka, J., & Dařena, F. (2011b). Mining Textual Significant Expressions Reflecting Opinions in Natural Languages. In *Intelligent Systems Design and Applications* (pp. 136–141). IEEE. doi:10.1109/ISDA.2011.6121644

Žižka, J., & Dařena, F. (2012). Parallel Processing of Very Many Textual Customers' Reviews Freely Written Down in Natural Languages. In: *IMMM 2012: The Second International Conference on Advances in Information Mining and Management* (pp. 147-153). IARIA XPS Press.

ADDITIONAL READING

Abdel-Hady, M. F. (2011). *Semi-Supervised Learning with Committees: Exploiting Unlabeled Data using Ensemble Learning Algorithms*. Südwestdeutscher Verlag für Hochschulschriften.

Aggarwal, C. C., & Zhai, C. X. (Eds.). (2014). *Mining Text Data*. Heidelberg: Springer.

Biemann, C., & Mehler, A. (Eds.). (2014). *Text Mining: From Ontology Learning to Automated Text Processing Applications. (Theory and Applications of Natural Language Processing)*. Cham: Springer. doi:10.1007/978-3-319-12655-5

Bottou, L., Chapelle, O., & DeCoste, D. (Eds.). (2007). *Large-Scale Kernel Machines. (Neural Information Processing series)*. Cambridge: The MIT Press.

Brown, M. S. (2014). *Data Mining For Dummies*. Hoboken: Wiley.

Cimiano, P., Unger, C., & McCrae, J. (2014). *Ontology-Based Interpretation of Natural Language. (Synthesis Lectures on Human Language Technologies)*. Morgan & Claypool Publishers.

Cioffi-Revilla, C. (2014). *Introduction to Computational Social Science: Principles and Applications. (Texts in Computer Science)*. London: Springer. doi:10.1007/978-1-4471-5661-1

Clark, A., Fox, C., & Lappin, S. (Eds.). (2012). *The Handbook of Computational Linguistics and Natural Language Processing*. Chichester: Wiley-Blackwell.

Herbrich, R. (2001). *Learning Kernel Classifiers: Theory and Algorithms. (Adaptive Computation and Machine Learning)*. Cambridge: The MIT Press.

Indurkhya, N., & Damerau, F. J. (Eds.). (2010). Handbook of Natural Language Processing. Second Edition. (Machine Learning & Pattern Recognition). Chapman and Hall/CRC.

Ingersoll, G. S., Morton, T. S., & Farris, A. L. (2013). *Taming Text: How to Find, Organize, and Manipulate It*. Shelter Island: Manning Publications.

Kao, A., & Poteet, S. T. (Eds.). (2006). *Natural Language Processing and Text Mining*. London: Springer.

Larose, D. T. (2014). *Discovering Knowledge in Data: An Introduction to Data Mining. (Wiley Series on Methods and Applications in Data Mining)*. New York: Wiley. doi:10.1002/9781118874059

Liu, B. (2011). Web Data Mining: Exploring Hyperlinks, Contents, and Usage Data. Second Edition. (Data-Centric Systems and Applications). Heidelberg: Springer. doi:10.1007/978-3-642-19460-3

Liu, B. (2012). *Sentiment Analysis and Opinion Mining. (Synthesis Lectures on Human Language Technologies)*. Morgan & Claypool Publishers.

Miner, G., Elder, J. I. V., & Hill, T. (2012). *Practical Text Mining and Statistical Analysis for Non-structured Text Data Applications*. Waltham: Elsevier.

Mohri, M., Rostamizadeh, A., & Talwalkar, A. (2012). *Foundations of Machine Learning. (Adaptive Computation and Machine Learning series)*. Cambridge: The MIT Press.

Peng, W.-C., Wang, H., & Bailey, J. (Eds.). (2014). *Trends and Applications in Knowledge Discovery and Data Mining: PAKDD 2014 International Workshops. (Lecture Notes in Artificial Intelligence)*. Springer. doi:10.1007/978-3-319-13186-3

Pustejovsky, J., & Stubbs, A. (2012). *Natural Language Annotation for Machine Learning*. Sebastopol: O'Reilly Media.

Russell, M. A. (2013). *Mining the Social Web: Data Mining Facebook, Twitter, LinkedIn, Google+, GitHub, and More* (2nd Ed.). Sebastopol: O'Reilly Media.

Schölkopf, B., & Smola, A. J. (2001). *Learning with Kernels: Support Vector Machines, Regularization, Optimization, and Beyond. (Adaptive Computation and Machine Learning)*. Cambridge: The MIT Press.

Xu, Z., King, I., & Lyu, M. R. (2010). *More Than Semi-supervised Learning: A unified view on Learning with Labeled and Unlabeled Data*. Colne: LAP LAMBERT Academic Publishing.

KEY TERMS AND DEFINITIONS

Classification Accuracy: The rate between the sum of the number of true positives + true negatives and the sum of true positives + false positives + true negatives + false negatives, when answering questions (that is, classifying).

Data Mining: Discovering patterns and knowledge, which is not apparent and is hidden in data. The knowledge discovery by analyzing data is not trivial.

Inductive Learning: Transforming the attributes of a set containing specific individual data samples into general knowledge.

Information: A subset of data samples, which is relevant for generalization related to a particular problem or application.

Machine Learning: A procedure that mainly inductively learns from data. The learning is based on generalization of specific samples. The goal is to find appropriate parameters for a given learning algorithm due to data.

Semi-Supervised Learning: A learning method (algorithm), which has available only a limited support (few labeled samples) to learn correct answers (labels of unlabeled data samples) to questions. When an answer is correct (the right label is assigned), the labeled sample can be added to the training set, thus reinforcing the training process.

Supervised Learning: A learning method (algorithm), which uses a feedback between a trainer and trainee. The trainer knows the right answers (data labels) while the trainee learns the correct answers using the feedback for corrections to eliminate its mistakes.

Text Mining: Revealing knowledge from a specific kind of data – textual data.

Unsupervised Learning: A learning method (algorithm), which cannot use any feedback and has to find right answers itself. Unsupervised learning generates clusters of mutually similar items that differ from items in other clusters.

Chapter 6

Natural Language Processing as Feature Extraction Method for Building Better Predictive Models

Goran Klepac
Raiffeisen Bank Austria d.d., Croatia

Marko Velić
University of Zagreb, Croatia

ABSTRACT

This chapter covers natural language processing techniques and their application in predicitve models development. Two case studies are presented. First case describes a project where textual descriptions of various situations in call center of one telecommunication company were processed in order to predict churn. Second case describes sentiment analysis of business news and describes practical and testing issues in text mining projects. Both case studies depict different approaches and are implemented in different tools. Language of the texts processed in these projects is Croatian which belongs to the Slavic group of languages with more complex morphologies and grammar rules than English. Chapter concludes with several points on the future research possible in this domain.

INTRODUCTION

In big data era, predictive models development should not be based on internal data from structured relation databases as the only disposable data sources for model development. Growing trend of unstructured data gives us opportunity to use potentials from unstructured data sources.

This does not mean that traditional methodology for predictive model development should be neglected; it means that it should be improved with patterns from unstructured data for better performance of the models. For the business problems solving, like churn prediction, fraud detection or other predictive

DOI: 10.4018/978-1-4666-8690-8.ch006

model development in business, introducing elements (patterns) found by natural language processing into predictive business model development introduces gains on model reliability and efficiency.

Traditional approach to predictive model development does not consider textual data as valuable data source for model constructions. Textual data sources like customer comments in call centers or similar data sources are excluded from model development sample, even if it could contain valuable information in domain of churn understanding/ prediction, fraud understanding/ prediction, customer needs for the next best offer modeling etc. Main reason for that is unclear methodology and idea how to use it, beside common attitude that this type of data is useless for predictive business statistical model development based on Bayesian networks, logistic regression, neural networks or similar.

Croatian language is a member of the Slavic group of languages together with Bosnian, Slovenian, Serbian, Macedonian, Russian, Czech, Polish, Ukrainian etc. Altogether Slavic group counts 18 different languages and is spoken by more than 200 million people.

Slavic languages are similar in the roots of the many words and different in grammar rules. Considering natural language processing techniques that try to mitigate problems with grammatical and different morphological word features it is reasonable to assume that it is worth experimenting with models on different languages. More on this will be covered in final sections of this chapter.

Chapter will give solutions on how unstructured data (different kind of text data) with natural language processing could be used as the elements for building better business predictive models. This will be illustrated with two cases.

First case will describe a scenario where a telecom company wants to develop churn predictive model. Case will show how this company used textual data from call center (customer comments written by operators in call center). Collected textual data contains variety of information, questions, and comments from customers entered into textual fields by operators. It contains questions about new services/ products, notifications about equipment failure, questions about bills etc. Natural language processing showed some patterns within textual data, which showed strong impact on churn commitment. Recognized textual pattern leads company to conclusion about churn nature and causes. Characteristic of this case is relying on internal data sources – structured and unstructured, where recognized textual pattern could be joined to unique customer, which is important when we want to make predictive business data mining models on customer level.

Second case will show different scenario – developing predictive models for stock market. In this case, public text data will be used for predictive model developing purposes. Stock market predictions are often based on previous price trends (technical analysis) and company's financial reports (fundamental analysis). There are systems that include collaborative filtering methods (also known as Wisdom of the Crowds) where many users rate stocks, similar to rating movies or books on popular online systems. In addition, there are advancements in sentiment analysis where stock market news or social network messages are being processed to identify possible future trends. This section will show one case where technical analysis, fundamental analysis and collaborative filtering are already in use on one Croatian stock market web portal. In addition, chapter will present development of the sentiment analysis module for mining business news. In the effort to collect annotated dataset that would allow for sentiment analysis, experts (brokers) are asked to annotate more than 500 business news i.e. RSS abstracts of the news collected by the portal's web parsers.

RSS news include headings, abstracts, date and the link to the source. Experts' inputs are companies that news relates to and the overall sentiment for the particular company. Sentiment can be positive, neutral or negative. Relation news-stock-sentiment is important since the same news can be positive for one company and in the same time negative for the other (consider the impact of oil price raise on the oil company and electricity company). Since the Croatian stock market is relatively small, impact of the particular news on the price trend can be significant and examples for these events will be shown.

Chapter will cover all the steps needed for successful implementation of the text mining techniques to develop sentiment analysis module. These steps include parsing, case reasoning, stop words, lemmatization, features creation (named entities, bag of words, word n-grams), features selection (association measures, term frequency, term-document frequency etc.) and finally predictive model development and testing. Since not all companies are covered in the media in the same way (with the same frequency), the dataset is very asymmetrical so this problem will be covered in more detail.

Existing literature presents some findings in sentiment analysis for the English language but covering Slavic group of languages is limited so this chapter will contribute in that way since the Croatian language will be used and it is very similar to other South and East Europe languages. Research is implemented in one open-source data-mining tool (Python programming language).

BACKGROUND

Natural language processing is often observed as special area which does not have much in common with traditional data mining on structured data (Berry, 2010), (Abney, 2008), (Bird, 2009). A data mining solution in business often demands creative way of solving problems, which is not often prescribed and uniform (Klepac, 2010), (Klepac, 2013). Text mining and natural language processing is one possible direction that can be applied for solving problems like churn or fraud detection. Natural language processing has its own methodology (Agirre, 2007), (Berry, 2010) which should be respected and covered during development phase. Usual text mining applications are solving problems like vector space methods (Chisholm, 1999), text categorization (Debole, 2003), analyzing text streams (Engel, 2009), text clustering (Hotho, 2009) and similar. Here we cover business problems like fraud, churn or other predictive modeling in business. Well-knowm methodology from this area and new researches in domain of text categorization (Bell, 2003), keyword extraction from textual sources (Feldman, 2007), text classification (Li, 2003), document summarization (Mirchev, 2014), (Soucy, 2003), text pattern recognition (Whitney, 2009) could be valuable sources for finding new approaches for business problem solving. Unrevealed text patterns could be valuable source of information for developing predictive models, because unstructured data could contain hidden information that could help in better understanding causes of the observed problems. Structured data contain predefined information and it is no guarantee that those predefined pieces of data will be useful in situation where company should find main reasons for increasing churn rate or decreasing sales. In that situation, using unstructured data as additional data sources along with structured data for predictive model development could result with much more reliable predictive models. Recognized patterns could be used for building better predictive models as well as better understanding the roots of the observed problem, and for hypothesis acceptance or rejections. As it will be presented, often existing methodology which is mainly concentrated on pure text mining problems should be adopted for those purposes.

Text mining, natural language processing and text information retrieval used to be observed as areas of data mining (Han, 2006) which does not have lot in common with traditional predictive business models.

BUILDING BETTER PREDICTIVE MODELS BY INFORMATION RETRIEVAL FROM CALL CENTER DATA

Problem Description and Motivation for Information Text Retrieval

Telecommunication company faced a problem of raising churn rate, i.e. increased number of customers leaving the network. Management of the company decided to implement knowledge discovery to mitigate this problem. For achieving that aim, project was divided in two phases. In the first phase, model for customer prospective value calculation based on fuzzy expert system has been developed. By using the model, customers worth for keeping in portfolio were selected. Second phase was concentrated on developing predictive churn model based on data sample of most valuable customers selected by fuzzy expert system usage. Presented approach is used frequently for similar problems and described in details in (Klepac, 2014). Predictive churn models give assessment about churn probability in the future. They calculate the probability that certain subscriber/buyer will commit the churn in determined future period. These types of models are often widely accepted as synonyms for churn models. Important stage of predictive churn modeling is attribute relevance analysis. Attribute relevance analysis is key activity in model development process. It assures right variable selection and reduces irrelevant attributes that can cause models with unpredictable outputs, unusable in churn prediction. Besides this purpose, attribute relevance analysis has important role in understanding of key churn factors. It does not mean that this stage in modeling will provide all the answers important for churn understanding, but it for sure raises right questions and opens horizons in understanding of churn nature for specific portfolio. For the purpose of attribute relevance analysis weight of evidence measure and information value measure were used.

$$WoE = ln\left(\frac{Dnc}{Dc}\right)$$

$$IV = \sum_{i=1}^{n}\left(Dnc_i - Dc_i\right) * ln\left(\frac{Dnc_i}{Dc_i}\right)$$

Weight of evidence is calculated as a natural logarithm of ratio between the number of non-churners (Dnc) and churners (Dc) in distribution spans. Information value is calculated as sum of differences between distribution of non-churners and churners in distribution spans and product of corresponding weight of evidence. Results given by weight of evidence measure and information value measure were crucial as motivation for information text retrieval. Analysis showed several strong predictors by information values, which were related to client behavior and profile characteristics. One of the strongest predictors revealed through analysis was "call in call center" during observation period, in which model was used for evaluation of committing churn. Weight of evidence showed the following rule. If client calls call center in some period before churn was observed, it shows higher probability for committing churn than client that did not called call center. Challenge was to find potential useful patterns within textual (memo) fields made by call center operators during call with clients, for finding potential reason why clients made churn within observed period.

Call center in company is organized in departments responsible and competent for different areas like:

- Technical support
- Contract renewal and new contracts
- Information about new products
- Common information
- Complaints

Attribute relevance analysis was performed without differentiation regarding departments (areas). Another question was, is there any difference regarding the relevance of attribute "call in call center" among calls to specific call center department. Detailed additional attribute relevance analysis showed that there was significant difference regarding relevance of attribute "call in call center" depending on which specific call center department was called. Clients that called call center departments: complaints, common information, and technical support by information value showed significantly higher churn rate than clients that called other call center departments. Callers that called regarding contract renewal or new contracts, or information about new products by information value showed negligible intention for committing churn within observed period. Due to these findings, further analysis regarding information retrieval from call center textual data was concentrated on data from complaints department, common information department, and technical support department.

Text Data – Preliminary Analysis and Preparation

For text processing, Python programming language and Natural Language Toolkit (NLTK) were used. NLTK was originally created by Department of Computer and Information Science at the University of Pennsylvania. It has been developed and expanded with the help of dozens of contributors, and serves as the basis of many research projects, as well as for commercial projects.

Disposable text data from call centers has never been analyzed. Heads of these departments had blur picture about main reasons of customer's calls. Those situation initiated strategy of initial exploration of textual data set on consolidated level. Initial exploration of textual data set included consolidation and purification.

Consolidation was performed in a way to produce the data structure described in Table 1.

Presented structure was the base for all further analytical activities. Existing data from call center within observed period has been loaded into described data structure via an ETL process. This data structure assured good initial point for further analytical activities. It contains diversification by department, diversification by call, and diversification by customer ID that is important for future predictive churn modeling. After consolidation, initial text purification has been done as tokenization, text normalization and removing stop words (mostly conjunctions and adverbs). These steps were performed in Python programming language and Natural Language Toolkit library. These steps allow us to reduce the number of words and word morphology variations and calculate significance of the particular words more accurately. In this way, we are selecting informative words i.e. words with significant meaning (Bird, 2009). Let assume that we would like to find the words from the vocabulary of the text that are more than 10 characters long. Let it be property P, so that P(w) is true if and only if w is more than 5 characters long. Now we can express the words of interest as (Bird, 2009):

$\{w \mid w \in V \ \& \ P(w)\}$
[w for w in V if p(w)]

Table 1. Base data structure for analysis

Date
Department ID
Call ID
Customer ID
Textual notes related to call filled by operator

"The set of all w such that w is an element of V (the vocabulary) and w has property P." (Bird, 2009). In that way, most of the conjunctions, adverbs, and pronouns were removed from the text.

Identified conjunctions and adverbs were stored into Python list along with predefined stop words. Presented technique was used for effective stop word recognition, along with predefined stops words defined by analysts. Generated lists, give opportunity for potential removing of some short words that have deeper meaning and could be useful for further analyses. It is important to mention that operators in call center in this case used simplified language for making notes. They have been mostly concentrated on writing key points recognized as important regarding the specific call. That fact was important for making analytical strategy. Firstly, it was important to find out most frequent words (before making any stemming because it is unknown text set and custom made stemming was done after performing this step). Frequent word analysis was done on department level, by using NLTK library on tokenized text (tokenized by using NLTK library) with excluded stop words.

Analytical strategy was to perform information retrieval on department level for departments:

- complaints
- common information
- technical support

due to the fact that clients which called those three departments within observed period of time shoved higher churn rate than others which called other departments. Table 2 shows recognized stop words.

Instead of using predefined stemmers, this cycle of frequent word recognition shoved frequent words in cases, and final preprocessing procedure was based on manual word stemming based on recognized frequent nouns in cases, and frequent verbs as well as other word types. As an illustration, Table 3 shows some of recognized frequent words before stemming process for technical support department in Croatian language.

After frequent word recognition, it was evident which word are more frequent, and for finding same words in cases recognized frequent words were sorted within Python's lists. That helps analysts to define roots of most frequent words and to avoid appearance of word in cases. As result, same frequent words in cases were substituted with mutual root word.

For example: each of the words (*prekid, prekida, prekidom, prekidima*) were substituted with *prekid* (Eng. interruption).

Each of the words (*Titra, titranje, titranjem, titrajući*) were substituted with *Titra* (Eng. flicker).

Each of the words (*Pregrijava, grije, grijati, zagrijan, pregrijan*) was substituted with *grije* (Eng. heated).

Each of the words (*Vruć, vrući, vrućem, vrućega*) were substituted with *vruć* (Eng. hot).

Table 2. Recognized stop words

Recognized stop words
a, ako, ali, bi, bih, bio, bismo, biste, biti, da, do, duž, ga, hoće, hoću, i, iako, ih, ili, iz, ja, je, jedna, jer, jesam, još, ju, kada, kako, koja, koje, koji, kojima, li, me, mene, meni, mi, moj, moja, moje, mu, na, nad, nakon, nam, nama, nas, naš, naša, naše, našeg, ne, neće, nećemo, nećete, neću, nešto, ni, nije, njemu, njezin, njezina, njih, njihov, njima, o, od, on , ona, oni, ono, ova, pa, pod, pored, s, sa, se, sebe, sebi, si, smo, ste, su, sve, svi, svog, svoj, ta, tada, taj, tako, te, tebe, ti, to, toj, tome, tu, u, uz, vam, vama, vas, vaš, vasa, vase, već, vi, vrlo, za, zar, će, ćemo, ćete, ćeš, ću, što

Table 3. Some of recognized frequent words before stemming process

Some of Recognized Frequent Word Before Stemming Process
Prekid, prekida, prekidom, prekidima
Titra, titranje, titranjem, titrajući
Pregrijava, grije, grijati, zagrijan, pregrijan,
Vruć, vrući, vrućem, vrućega,
…

Next step was focused on recognition of different words with same or similar meaning, like heated and hot, because after reading transcripts of few calls it was evident that both was related to heating problems of installed modems. There were several similar situations.

After that, substitution (stemming) has been done based on defined root words and synonyms substitution. Final stage in data preparation was collocation discovery by using class from NLTK on previously prepared textual data. As results few collocations were discovered like "*prekid vez*" root words for (Eng. signal interruption) and "titra slik", (Eng. picture flicker) Substitution has been done based on discovered collocations. It was done on data for each call center department, and data was ready for information retrieval.

Redesigned SMART Model for Retrieving Patterns

Inspiration for information retrieval model was Cornell SMART system. It uses following formula to compute the (normalized) term frequency (TF), inverse document frequency (IDF) and TF-IDF measure (Han, 2006):

$$TF(d;t) = \begin{cases} 0 & if\ freq(d;t) = 0 \\ 1 + \log\left(1 + \log\left(\frac{freq}{d};t\right)\right) & otherwise \end{cases}$$

$$IDF(t) = \log\frac{1 + |d|}{|d_t|}$$

$$TF\text{-}IDF(d;t) = TF(d;t)*IDF(t)$$

Freq(d; t) shows how frequent term t occurs in the document d. "Inverse document frequency (IDF), represents the scaling factor, or the importance, of a term *t*. If a term *t* occurs in many documents, its importance will be scaled down due to its reduced discriminative power. For example, the term „database systems" may likely be less important if it occurs in many research papers in a database system conference." (Han, 2006) TF-IDF measure gives unique measure, which represents importance of some term within the set of documents. Our intention is to find importance of some term used during calls within call center department. Taking in consider presented facts, we should modify existing Cornell SMART system to fit our needs. Segment is specific business area within call center like complaints, common information and technical support (departments within call center).

$$STF(s;t) = \begin{cases} 0 & if\, freq\left(cs_i;t\right) = 0 \\ 1 + \log\left[1 + \log\left(\sum_{i=1}^{n} freq\left(cs_i;t\right)\right)\right] & otherwise \end{cases}$$

n – number of calls within one segment

cs_i – i-th call within observed segment

freq(csi; t) – number of occurrences of term *t* within *i*-th call

STF(s;*t*) – term frequency *t* within segment

$$SCTP(t) = \begin{cases} 0 & if\left(cs_t\right) = 0 \\ 1 + \log\left(\dfrac{|cs_t|}{|cs|} + 1\right) & otherwise \end{cases}$$

cs_t – number of calls within segment containing term *t*

cs – number of calls within segment

SCTP(t) – call term ponder within segment

STF(s;t)-SCTP(t) = STF(t)*SCTP(t)

STF(s;t)-SCTP(t) measure – shows strength of the term *t* within segment

That means that calls should be treated as documents and *Inverse document frequency* measure should be substituted with more convenient measure regarding our analytical needs. Basic idea is that for churn detection in call departments where it is evident that previous call has an influence on future churn if a term *t* occurs in many calls its importance, should not be scaled down. Its importance should be increased. With respect to above mentioned, we designed measure *STF(s;t)-SCTP(t)* which consolidates

Table 4. Most relevant terms by STF(s;t)-SCTP(t) for technical support

Term	STF(s;t)-SCTP(t)
Grije	2,521276
Titra slik	2,311935
Prekid vez	1,654524
Pad nap	1,453213
Slik	1,236745

term frequency t within segment STF(s;*t*) and *call term ponder within segment SCTP(t).* Constructed *call term ponder within segment* measure has lower influence than *term frequency t within segment* within model, because intention was to make higher stress on term frequency than on occurrence of term *t* within calls. It still has significant influence on the result, but its importance is lower than importance of *term frequency t within segment.* This could be changed depending on analytical aims. Consolidated within the single value this shows importance of some term within observed department.

Applying Redesigned SMART Model on Data

Main idea was to find relevant terms, those that frequently occur within calls, and relevance of term could raise depending of term frequency within calls as well as term occurrence within calls, with slightly higher impact on term frequency within calls. Reason for that is discovering relevant terms for measuring impact on churn due to fact that it was obvious that previous call has an influence on future churn. *STF(t)-SCTP(t) measure* was calculated for all three segments recognized as important. Table 4. shows most relevant terms by STF(s;t)-SCTP(t) for technical support.

It is important to stress out that for example term *Grije* (eng. Heating) high *STF(s;t)-SCTP(t)* measure was caused by high occurrence of term frequency within segment as well as because of high *call term ponder.* Further analysis showed that same clients made several calls frequently regarding the heating problems with equipment. Similar was with Titra *slik,* picture flickering, with lower occurrence of term frequency within segment and lower *call term ponder.* Calculated *STF(s;t)-SCTP(t)* measures for all three segments became base for additional attribute relevance analysis for churn modeling purposes. Attribute relevance analysis showed high relevance by Information value (IV) for all three segments. Technical support has the highest IV of 0.98, complaints had lower but still high IV of 0.67, and common information had IV of 0.49. Table 5 shows detailed WoE measure for technical support calls.

Regarding the WoE, it is evident that if caller used word *Grije* (heating equipment problems) it has strong impact on committing churn in near future. Similar is with *titra slik,* flickering picture problems. Line interruption *Prekid vez* has also impact on committing churn in near future. Same analysis was done for remaining three segments, where other patterns, which influence the churn, were discovered.

Comparison of Predictive Churn Model Developed with and Without Text Patterns from Redesigned SMART Model

For measuring influence of recognized textual patterns on churn, two models were developed on different data samples. Predictive models were based on Bayesian network and neural network.

Table 5. WoE measure for relevant terms in technical support calls

Term	WoE
Grije	-2.34
Titra slik	-1.79
Prekid vez	-0.75
Pad nap	0.13
Slik	0.18
Frequent word not used	1.43
Did not call	2.36

Table 6. Comparison by ROC area under the curve

Model	ROC AUC withouth text patterns	ROC AUC with text patterns
Bayesian network	0.803	0.922
Neural network	0.801	0.920

Firstly, Bayesian network and neural network were developed on development sample, which did not contain recognized textual patterns. Reliability based on ROC was high and almost similar for both models. Secondly, Bayesian network and neural network were developed on development sample, which contained recognized textual patterns. Reliability based on ROC was increased and it was as well almost similar for both models.

That confirms hypothesis about potential improvement of predictive models by using results from text information retrieval. The most important result is that along with better predictive model performance, company discovered potential key factors of rising churn rate which are related to (mostly repeating) technical problems with equipment. Hypotheses are that these are the key factors, which motivate users for breaking contracts. Detailed analysis could include observing churn rate by districts (hypothesis could be that maybe some technical problems especially picture flickering are caused by location or servers for IP TV). It could include other type of additional analysis, which is out of the scope of this chapter. However, it is important to emphasize that this approach is useful for solving concrete business problems, as well as digging for hidden knowledge useful for further decision process.

SENTIMENT ANALYSIS CASE STUDY

This section will present one case study implemented on a real world problem of natural language processing. Goal of the research is predictive model development for news sentiment analysis. Section will present various theoretical as well as practical issues. Topics covered are data acquisition, data preprocessing methods, unbalanced data problems considerations, predictive model building and testing approaches. Special emphasis is put on the handling of the unbalanced datasets and issues arising in evaluating this kind of models. Text may serve as a tutorial for building similar predictive models realised on any kind of data, not just text-specific, because problems that are tackled here exit in analyses of data from other domains.

Case Study Settings

Case presented in this section is an implementation of natural language processing techniques on the data from one Croatian financial web portal – *icapital.hr*. This portal targets at small financial investors and besides many technical and fundamental analyses shown, it aggregates business related news from various sources via RSS feeds. Currently, portal implements technical analysis with various indicators derived from the stock price values time series and fundamental analyses including various financial indicators calculated from the companies' financial reports and current stock valuations. Besides this, portal also includes one artificial intelligence (AI) module – The Stock Detective, that implements so called "Wisdom of the Crowds" or "Collaborative Filtering" algorithm (Velić et al, 2013). Considering this context of already existent modules, sentiment analysis module can be considered as additional piece of the future AI puzzle that aims to achieve benefit for portal's users. This benefit could mean some kind of investment advice or prediction regarding the future stock-price movement based on these modules.

Research Motivation, Goal and Global Picture

Goal of the research project presented here is to enable for automatic sentiment classification of news collected from other business portals during the day. Research task of this project is part of the more complex process as shown in Figure 1.

If experiments resulting from this project were successful, the given module could be used as an integral part of a broader more advanced AI process as shown on Figure 2. To enable this broader AI process, sentiment analysis module should be developed, resulting with accurate and reliable sentiment classifications. Goal of this research is to achieve automatic recognition of *negative* and *positive* news that relate to certain stocks. Thus, results from technical, fundamental analysis, collaborative filtering and sentiment analysis could be used as inputs for a global predictive model. Furthermore, sentiment analysis module could be used as a content generator for various alerts that will alert users if positive or negative news occur for stocks on their watchlist.

Considering all that has been said in this chapter it is evident that sentiment analysis has strong practical motivation. Scientific motivation for this research is covered in next section.

Sentiment Analysis State of the Art

Regarding the scientific context of this research it is worth to note that sentiment analysis is not a new problem in information and computer science but as this research is focused on the analysis of content written in Croatian language it is a challenging task. Sentiment analysis of the texts in English is covered in works such as (Whitehead and Yaeger, 2010), (Aase et al, 2011), (Delmonte and Pallotta, 2011) and (Nagar and Hahsler, 2012). Sentiment analysis as a feature extraction method that can enable predictive models regarding the stock prices movements is covered in (Han, 2012), (Jacob et al 2012), (Tulankar et al. 2013). Sentiment analysis of texts written in Croatian is presented in (Agić et al, 2010). In this research, achieved accuracy reaches 0.63 measured by the F1-score.

Considering sentiment analysis and even natural language processing in general, analysis of Croatian language is somewhat more complex problem that analysis of English content. Croatian language is much more complicated in grammar rules and various morphological forms. Due to this complexity,

Figure 1. Existing modules of the portal

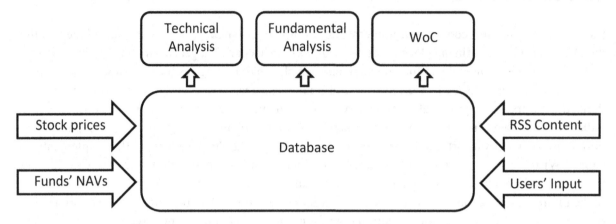

Figure 2. Possible future AI process

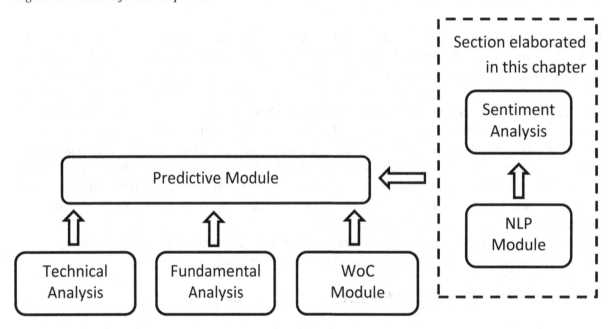

classifying documents written in Croatian is much more demanding both in terms of computational costs and in terms of classification accuracy (Šilić et al, 2007.).

Analysis and modelling presented in the next sections is conducted in Orange data mining tool (Demšar et al, 20013) including the Orange Text Mining Add-On (Župan et al.). This Add-On implements features for Croatian language such as lemmatization and stop words list. Add-on was developed in cooperation with Bojana Dalbelo Basic, Sasa Petrovic, Frane Sarisc Mladen Kolar (all Faculty of Electrical Engineering and Computing, University of Zagreb, Croatia), Annie Morin (IRISA, Université Rennes 1, Rennes, France), and Jean-Hugues Chauchat (Université Lyon, ERIC-Lyon2, Bron Cedex, France). Additional argument for this Add-On is its compatibility with other Orange modules and Widgets that will be useful in this study since we will combine natural language processing methods with traditional data mining techniques.

Dataset

Data used in this research is an annotated dataset of business news and sentiments and it consists of 776 manually annotated RSS news abstracts. Dataset is created by InterCapital Plc as an integral part of the iCapital.hr business portal. Among other administrative features of the portal, experts (stockbrokers and portal administrators) were given one form that enables quick and easy annotation of the news. Annotation consists of two parts. First feature is stock-news matching where experts can indicate if the news is related to one or more specific companies i.e. stocks. Second part is sentiment marking where expert can choose if the news has negative, positive or neutral sentiment for particular stock. Both of this is covered with one GUI feature that enables quick and easy user experience. It is important to indicate that one news in this setting can be at the same time positive for one stock (company) and negative for the other (others). Experts are annotating news on daily basis since 11th of August 2011 and until the time of writing this text (18th of March 2014, i.e., more than two and a half years) exactly 776 news were annotated. Final annotated RSS news include ticker annotation, sentiment annotation, heading, abstract, date and the link to the source i.e. fulltext. Practical motivation for correct news annotation is one graph on the website that shows stock price timeseries together with markings for annotated news. This feature is widely used by the portal's users that can report any discrepancies on the portal's forum publically and due to that and the expertise of the annotators, we can consider this dataset being reliable.

Some dataset characteristics can be observed in the following distribution analysis.

Dataset used in this research has one symptomatic characteristic and that is very asymmetrical not-normal distribution. In the literature, this kind of data is often called unbalanced. There are few stocks that have a lot of news annotated and many stocks with few news. This is somewhat expected since Croatian market involves similar distribution considering sales volumes i.e. few stocks are very popular among investors. It is very interesting to observe that two stocks that have the most news (accidentally the same number of news for each of them) are actually two most popular companies that were once in national ownership and in 2006 and 2007 caused a lot of media attention during their IPOs (Initial Public Offer). As can be seen in the distribution analysis presented in Table 8, dataset includes many stocks with few accompanying news texts. This could yield a problem in our model. Consider for example one stock that has only four news and all of them annotated as *positive*. These stocks could introduce a bias in our classifier and in that way artificially increase the importance of the ticker itself. News distribution with respect to orientation is shown on Figure 3.

Table 7. Dataset variables

Variable	Meaning	Type
ID	Unique identifier of the data instance	Integer
ticker	Stock ticker	Text
date	New date and time	Date
heading	Heading of the news	Text
text	RSS text - actually abstract of the news from 3rd party source (business portal)	Text
orientation	Whether the news is positive, neutral or negative	Nominal
link	Hyperlink to the source and news fulltext	Text

Figure 3. News distribution regarding the sentiment

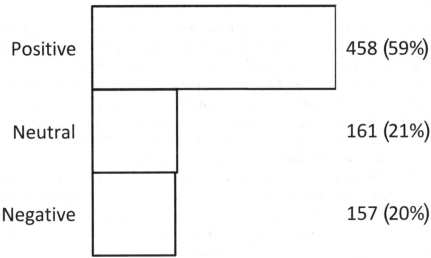

Positive   458 (59%)

Neutral   161 (21%)

Negative   157 (20%)

Data Preprocessing

Textual data is not formatted data. Any news considered in our example can be of any length and consisted of any number of words. Raw textual data is not useful as an input for classic machine learning algorithms. Thus, data has to be preprocessed and features need to be extracted.

Our data preprocessing included removal of the Croatian specific letters i.e. replacement with standard ASCII letter due to the problems with utf-8 encoding and software compatibilities. Detailed inspection of the dataset revealed that due to the unknown reasons some texts were missing from the dataset although heading were present. Concatenation of the headings and news texts due to some missing data in the texts was the next preprocessing step. All of the aforementioned preprocessing steps were conducted without any specialised software, just using the text editor. For this kind of preprocessing one should use advanced text editors which are capable of processing big data files and advanced text manipulations such as encoding conversions, regular expression operations etc. Second strategy is to write your own scripts for preprocessing tasks in easy to learn languages like Python that allows for for rapid prototyping.

Features Extraction – Natural Language Features Problems

As with any other data, regarding the preparation for machine learning tasks, features extraction from textual data are one of the most important steps in predictive model building. To clear the terminology here, features are actually variables or attributes for machine learning algorithms. In regular tabular data (e.g. data instances are measurements of the height and weight of the patient), the table columns are features. If we consider bunch of text as a data instance, feature (ie. variable) definition is not so obvious. One approach is to use the whole text as one original feature but this is not feasible due to the unlimited variety of values this feature could hold. We want to extract significant words and phrases that carry information about the text sentiment. Approach that is being widely used in natural language processing tasks is extracting the particular words and phrases from the text and then somehow quantifying

Table 8. News distribution regarding the stock they relate to

Ticker	News Count	Ticker	News Count
HT-R-A	61	PDBA-R-A	4
INA-R-A	61	VLHO-R-A	4
DLKV-R-A	40	VPIK-R-A	4
DDJH-R-A	30	ATPL-R-A	3
CROS-R-A	26	BPBA-R-A	3
ATGR-R-A	25	IGH-R-A	3
DIOK-R-A	25	JDBA-R-A	3
ADRS-P-A	24	LURA-R-A	3
PODR-R-A	24	RIZO-R-A	3
LEDO-R-A	23	TNPL-R-A	3
KORF-R-A	22	ZVZD-R-A	3
ADRS-R-A	20	HDEL-R-A	2
PTKM-R-A	20	HGSP-R-A	2
KOEI-R-A	19	INDG-R-A	2
CROS-P-A	18	JDPL-R-A	2
ADPL-R-A	15	KODT-P-A	2
KRAS-R-A	15	KODT-R-A	2
LKRI-R-A	15	LKPC-R-A	2
ULPL-R-A	15	MDKA-R-A	2
ERNT-R-A	14	MGMA-R-A	2
INGR-R-A	13	MIV-R-A	2
TISK-R-A	13	SNBA-R-A	2
ZABA-R-A	13	VLEN-R-B	2
PBZ-R-A	12	ARNT-R-A	1
VIRO-R-A	12	ELPR-R-A	1
RIVP-R-A	11	HCVT-R-A	1
BD62-R-A	10	HIMR-R-A	1
BLJE-R-A	10	HJDR-R-A	1
OPTE-R-A	9	HMST-R-A	1
ACI-R-A	8	KABA-R-A	1
THNK-R-A	8	KOKA-R-A	1
VDKT-R-A	8	MLNR-R-A	1
HPB-R-A	7	PIVK-R-A	1
JMNC-R-A	7	PLAG-R-A	1
JNAF-R-A	7	SAPN-R-A	1
MAIS-R-A	7	SLDM-R-A	1
VART-R-1	7	SUNH-R-A	1
LRH-R-A	6	TNKC-R-A	1

Table 8. Continued

Ticker	News Count	Ticker	News Count
ULJN-R-A	6	TUHO-R-A	1
3MAJ-R-A	4	ZLAR-R-A	1
CRAL-R-A	4	ZTNJ-R-A	1
FRNK-R-A	4		

the amount of information and relevance of the each particular feature by some mathematical operation (calculating term frequency or any other measure described in the previous case study).

Result of this approach applied on textual data is one huge and sparse data table. Table columns are actually words and phrases and rows are textual instances. Each row has only smaller part of columns filled and the rest of the data fields are actually missing values or encoded as 0 (zero). Thus we say that this kind of data is very high dimensional.

Both unbalanced datasets and high dimensionality are typical for natural language processing problems. In the following sections, we will cover mitigation strategies for these problems.

Features

Previous case study presented SMART methodology for natural language processing using the NLTK software package. Case study presented here will offer slightly different approach and use a different tool.

Bag of Words

Bag of Words are one of the most popular structured representations of textual data. Literally, the method name already describes the essence of it. Consider dividing a text into a set of words and then putting every word into a bag. Counting the occurrence of the each word and making a list for every text in the dataset is exactly the output of the Bag of Words method.

Morphological Normalisation

Since Bag of Words analysis of the text can yield a very wide data table with columns of every single word form in the text there is a method for reducing the table size and still conserve most of the information. This method is called morphological normalisation. Goal of the morphological normalisation process is to bring down various forms of the same word to only one form. E.g. words *price*, *pricing*, *prices* can be represented with a single word form like *price* and the general meaning can be still preserved. It is evident that this process will mostly serve beneficially for complex languages where words can have many forms in various grammar contexts. Approaches often used are Stemming and Lemmatization. Stemming is a process of reducing a word to its root (stem or base). Lemmatization a similar process but more complex where different grammar rules and reducing methods are applied for different word parts. Many stemming and lemmatization algorithms are presented in the literature and these are often included in software packages for natural language processing.

N-Grams, Named Instances and Combined Features

N-grams are combinations of *n* items like characters, phonemes, words etc. If n is 1 then it is called *unigram*, if n is 2 then we cay say it is *bigram* or *digram* and if n is 3 then it is called *trigram*, for 4 it is four-gram and so on. Quantification of n-gram occurance in the text can be tackled in the same way as of word sin bag of words model. Obiously n-grams' information quantification can benefit from normalisation steps done before n-grams extracting. Another interesting way of feature extraction from text are *Named instances*. This is similar to n-gram but not limited to certain number of items captured. The method here is to include in the feature sequence of words starting with capital letter. Approach used here is to preprocess the same text several times and in each iteration extract different kind of features. Later the most informative features can be used to represent feature vector of the text e.g. the most important words from bag of words model, the most important bigrams etc. These we call the *Combined features*.

Handling Unbalanced Dataset

As it is mentioned earlier, unbalanced data is a common problem in textual data analysis. Unbalanced data is data that consists of disproportional number of observations of a particular class. Often, unbalanced data is found in medicine domain where many patients included in study are healthy and few of them show some disease symptoms. Since the many of the machine learning algorithms inherently try to optimize general prediction accuracy it is obvious that this can be significantly influenced by class disproportion. The model can be built in favor of the major class (or classes) or minor class variance can be insufficiently included in the training set.

Besides model building issues, there are problems with evaluating these models. Consider an example where 100 patients are included in the study. If 99 of them are healthy and the one is sick, we can build predictive model that will always predict a healthy patient. In testing phase, this model will be accurate 99% of time, but model will miss that crucial one. Literature presents several approaches for handling the unbalanced datasets. Overall, these approaches can be split into two main groups. Solutions on algorithm level and solutions on data level. Solutions on algorithm level can include so called "cost sensitive" classifiers where costs of specific misclassifications can be different and in that way classifier can be "artificially biased" in favor of specific classifications i.e. errors (Kotsiantis et al. 2006). There are also some algorithm specific solutions e.g. hyperplane positioning with corrected distance from a particular class if the Support Vector Machines (SVM) classifier is used. Furthermore, different probability thresholds for classifications of the particular classes can be used to support the inference in favor of the undersampled class.

Regarding the unsupervised learning problems, possible solution is putting weights on distances between members of a particular cluster and in that way spread or shrink the cluster area in hyperspace and enable fair chances of cluster membership for new observations, if this is a goal of the clustering model.

Solutions on data level (applied in this research) mostly mean some form of undersampling process. The simplest method is random undersampling of the majority class (Kotsiantis et al 2003). New sample that is derived from this process has equally distributed classes and is ready for training. This method is simplest but with some drawbacks. Most notably, variance of the majority class will be lost due to the undersampling that discards some data. This can be reflected in lower model accuracy. Second big drawback is the inability of the classifier to correctly predict probability distributions of the classes since the sample is not random anymore. There are many more methods presented in the literature like duplicating examples of the minority class, interpolation of the new artificial examples based on the distances between members of the same class etc. Researcher should be careful to prevent overfitting when applying these techniques.

Identifying Good Features – Morphological Normalisation

Since Croatian language is very morphologically complex, normalization is a first step in the analysis. As it is described earlier, goal of the morphological normalisation process is to bring down various forms of the same word to only one form. For this experiment, we have used lemmatization method that is implemented in the Preprocess module of the Orange Text mining Add-On.

Stop Words and Features

Stop words removal has its pros and cons. Consider following example phrases: oil price is rising, oil price is rising rapidly, and oil price is not rising. Stop words removal in first two phrases ensures capturing of three important words if 3-gram is extracted. On the other hand, if the „not" is treated as a stop word, first and third phrase will have the same meaning but actually these are opposites.

Exploring the dataset, we have noticed that there are some news with only headings or heading plus one sentence and others with few sentences. For the Bag of Words feature set, we have experimented with the additional normalisation to cover the different lengths of the texts (news). In this research, there were no significant differences in model performance but it is worth experimenting with models that include length normalisation and without it.

Table 9 presents the most important words and n-grams. The table is sorted by the Information gain value descendingly. Actual information gain value range from 0.180 to 0.027 for words and from 0.015 to 0.180 for 2-grams.

Predictive Models and Results

Model presented in the following text was built using the four main sources for features. Entire datased was preprocessed four times and thus bag of words, unigrams, digrams, trigrams and four-grams were extracted as four feature groups. Since these procedures result in vast numbers of features, only top 10 percent from each group measured by occurance frequency were used. After that, information gain scores were calculated on the top 10 percent from each group. Top 200 features were selected from each group and then again, information gain on all of them combined was calculated resulting in final 300 features which included features from every group.

After preprocessing, bag of words and n-grams extracting and features selection, we were ready to utilize machine learning algorithms for building the predictive model. We have experimented with several classifiers and Naive Bayes prove to be the most succesful one. Testing methodology was crossvalidation with five folds and results are presented in Table 10. These results reflect process with lemmatization, stop words removal and Naive Bayes classifier.

Following this we can calculate standard performance measures. Classification accuracy calculated as $(TP+TN)/(TP+TN+FP+FN)$ is $CA = 0.8014$. Sensitivity or Recall calculated as TP/P or $TP/(TP+FN)$ is 0.8244, specificity TN/N or $TN/(TN+FP)$ equals 0.7786. Area under the ROC curve equals 0.8580,

Table 9. The top 20 most important features after extracting words and 2-grams

Rank	Croatian word	English translation of the word	Croatian 2-gram	English translation of the 2-gram
1	ticker	ticker	ticker	ticker
2	gubitak	loss	uzrok slab	cause weak
3	moći	to be capable of	spominjati lose	to mention bad
4	vrijednost	value	ljetan sezona	summer season
5	vis	Vis (Island)	turisticku sezona	tourist season
6	vrijeme	weather	pun znacajnije	full more significant
7	diokija	Dioki (company)	lose vrijeme	bad weather
8	rast	growth	znacajnije problem	more significant problem
9	vlada	government	travanjski rezultat	April result
10	interes	interest (concern)	zabrinjavajucih znakov	worrying signs
11	nagodba	settlement (agreement)	kasti uzrok	cause
12	petrokemija	Petrokemija (company)	raspored praznik	holidays schedule
13	minus	minus	rezultat najcesce	result usually
14	potpisati	to sign	sezona analiza	analysis of the season
15	kamata	interest (rate)	otkriti pun	to reveal whole
16	dostaviti	to deliver	slab travanjski	poor in April
17	problem	problem	nepovoljan raspored	unfavorable schedule
18	nepovoljan	unfavorable	godina iznositi	year amount (total)
19	lose	bad	put zagrebacke	way Zagreb (capital)
20	predsezona	preseason	bruto dobiti	gross profit

Table 10. Confusion matrix after crossvalidation test

	Negative	Positive	Total
Negative	102	29	**131**
Positive	23	108	**131**
Total	**125**	**137**	**262**

F1 measure equals 0.8060 and Precision equals 0.7883. These are high values but the following chapter will inspect this in more detail.

Not So Fast

This section will cover some pitfalls that are not obvious at the first glance. One must be careful when designing this kind of models and sincere when reporting results. Natural language processing is a difficult task and it should be carried out and reported carefully. This section will explain why previously reported results may be and actually are biased.

Repeating Experiments

Due to the characteristics and problems of the natural language processing described earlier, we will repeat subsampling few times and then compare results. Although, through the process of feature extraction described in the text, we tried to build robust and stable model, it is reasonable to assume that due to so many possible combinations these results on different samples will differ. Is it obvious that random subsampling can affect model performance. This is due to the very big variance in the natural language dataset and relatively small dataset that results from the undersampling process. It is not just subsampling preprocessing that can introduce randomness in the process but also the mechanisms of some classifiers used. Example for this can be utilization of the model slike Random Forest that inherently involve randomization in the model-building phase. This is additional reason to repeat experoiments and report few results or calculate the average success measures.

Experimenting with natural language processing methods involves lot of trials and errors with many parameters in the whole pipeline that can be fine-tuned to build a good final model.

This schema has many widgets that can be configured with different algorithm settings and four main flows to enable experiments with Bag of Words and n-grams. This representation of the pipeline within easy to use GUI is very effective for running experiments and prototyping the final solution. This specific tool enables scripting in Python language once the final model has been assembled.

Separate Test Data

Although we used cross validation as a testing method it is a reasonable question to ask what would happen if we feed the previously excluded data (due to the unbalanced dataset) to the trained classifier. Feeding the very new data to the classifier for testing purposes is always a good robustness test. This data of course includes only positive news but it is a still good testing ground for our method. Table 11 summarizes results of this experiment.

Since there are no Negative examples (we used all of them for model creation) we can calculate only following measures CA = 0.6859 and thus Sensitivity = 0.6859. Yet another pitfall here is the data that is excluded at the very beginning - the news that relate to rare mentioned stocks. These data even include negative news. After including it into the testing set, results are still worse but more realistic.

These results are obviously lower at it is worth to note why is it so. Cross validation method is a good testing method in classical machine learning problems when we have relatively small dataset and we want to make the best possible precision estimate in a reasonable execution time (if *leave one out* method takes too long). In this particular case, we have conducted cross validation test after the feature extraction methods, described earlier, done their job. This is also bias since the feature importance methods used the whole dataset (i.e. balanced subset). Therefore, testing with this completely new data is some kind

Table 11. Confusion matrix for separate test set not included in subsample

	Negative	Positive	Total
Negative	0	0	**0**
Positive	87	190	**277**
Total	**87**	**190**	**277**

Table 12. Confusion matrix for separate test set which includes those related to the excluded stocks:

	Negative	Positive	Total
Negative	13	10	23
Positive	135	186	321
Total	148	196	344

of an ultimate accuracy test that simulates a situation in practice when there are news coming that our model (nor any part of the analysis performed including feature selection steps) has never seen before.

Inspecting Errors

Whenever the one is building predictive models, it is worth of the effort to explore the errors. Table 13 presents one news that was classified incorrectly in the latest described experiment (one with the separate testing set).

This news relates to a company called *Petrokemija* (ticker: PTKM-R-A) from Kutina. News dates from 22nd of November 2012. 15:31:00. This news is marked as a positive one, but our classifier recognized it as a negative one. Problem is that this news is really a positive one, since the company's management reports about the increased production that will try to compensate losses caused by the bad weather in the recent past. Classifier is misled here since the news actually describes the bed event (losses caused by the storms).

Solutions and Recommendations

Considering stability problems i.e. different results of particular model instances based on generated data sample one could ask for more evidence by using more data. In addition, although we have tried to incorporate only those news that relate to more popular stocks (i.e. stocks with more news) relative importance of the *ticker* variable could still be indicator of a bias. Next experiments will involve build models on the samples that are balanced for each stock present in the database. Testing should be performed on the whole set (together with excluded news).

Careful reader probably picked up the variable *ticker* as one of the most important variables. If we have not excluded stocks with very few news in the beginning this could mean significant bias in our model. Since this problem is solved as a part of preprocessing stage, this could simply mean that there are stocks that generally tend to connote positive or negative sentiment in the media. For our model to be realistic, we need news that are already matched with stocks. This is present at some of the data sources

Table 13. Errorneous classification

Original news	Petrokemija: Otpremljena milijunta tona gnojiva KUTINA - "Uz velike napore Petrokemija nadoknadjuje izgubljene kolicine tijekom ovih nepogoda i nastoji sustici planirane ciljeve", navode iz kutinske tvrtke.
English translation	Petrokemija: The millionth ton of fertilizer is dispatched KUTINA - "With huge efforts Petrokemija is compensating the quantities lost during these storms and tries to catch up the planned goals", it is reported from the company.

i.e. some business portals add a ticker at the time of writing the news, but not all of them. In our dataset this was carried out by the experts. For future use, some kind of automatism is needed. Thus, future research could aim to build a model that will be capable to automatically assign certain stock to news and through this case we will introduce some new concepts for natural language processing e.g. named instances as a feature extraction method to capture all important names related to company.

FUTURE RESEARCH DIRECTIONS

There is plenty of research opportunities for predictive models improvement by using the results from text information retrieval. Future research could be aimed on discovering potential of Latent semantic Indexing (LSI) method and their adoption for improvement of predictive models.

Another direction could be aimed on discovering potentials of methods like Bayesian networks for better model development in way of attribute relevance analysis between existing variables, especially textual patterns for connection purposes inside network. It could result with better prediction power along with discovering patterns related to business logic.

Experiments considered in the sentiment analysis case study included only RSS abstracts of business news. Possible future direction is following links and parsing original websites to collect news full text. It is reasonable to suppose that more text used in the preprocessing phase will result with features that are more relevant. This in turn can result with models that are more reliable.

In this text, we have shown how to combine natural language processing methods with traditional data mining techniques such as Information gain method for attribute selection. As it is described earlier, high dimensionality of the data is one of the most notable problems in text mining and dimensionality reduction techniques like Principal Components Singular Value Decomposition are widely used in similar research. Implementation of these methods before classification step is also planned for future work.

Since analysis and modelling of the content written in Croatian is resulting with promising results one of the possible future experiments is development of models that will perform well on different Slavic languages.

Combining structured data as a traditional data mining information source with unstructured data as it is shown in this chapter is not the only way of improving predictive business models. Following research experiments could be focused on additional data sources like social networks. Thus, social network analysis (SNA) methods could be used to yield new sources of information like identifying the most influential customers and applying sentiment analysis procedures on the user generated textual data. Company can build an online community of customers on social networks or track tagged messages on e.g. Twitter or blogs.

CONCLUSION

Although natural laguage processing is still not widely accepted as a valuable information source, it is evident that knowledge retrieved from this kind of data can improve accuracy of the predictive business models.

It is possible in cases when there is strong relation between observed event and some hidden text pattern that can be revealed by using systems like adopted SMART system. Regarding the fact that unstructured data more and more plays important role in data analytics and problems like churn, fraud, segmentation are still in focus in everyday business, this approach could contribute in model reliability and precision.

This chapter presented two case studies with interesting results achieved. First study used NLP methods in order to identify churn in telecommunication industry. Interesting results are achieved in analysis of the call centre data. Company got a new valuable information source that has not been utilized before. This is presented with development and testing of the predictive models with and without textual data as feature source. Second case study presented sentiment analysis research where business news were used as an information source regarding the stock price movement.

As it is described, there are some practical and testing considerations that should be taken into account when processing natural language like wise use of existing data, feature design, unbalanced data, normalisation, testing scenarios etc. If features are carefuly desinged by using the natural language processing techniques and if models are tested in realistic way than predictive models can be improved by using the text as an unstructured data source.

REFERENCES

Aase, K. (2011). *Text Mining of News Articles for Stock Price Predictions*. Norwegian University of Science and Technology.

Abney, S. (2008). *Semisupervised Learning for Computational Linguistics*. Chapman and Hall.

Agić, Ž., Ljubešić, N., & Tadić, M. (2010). Towards sentiment analysis of financial texts in Croatian. In *Poceedings of the Seventh International Conference on Language Resources and Evaluation.*

Agirre, E., & Edmonds, P. (2007). *Word Sense Disambiguation: Algorithms and Applications*. Springer. doi:10.1007/978-1-4020-4809-8

Bel, N., Koster, C. H., & Villegas, M. (2003). Cross-Lingual Text Categorization. In *Proceedings of ECDL-03, 7th European Conference on Research and Advanced Technology for Digital Libraries* (pp.126–139). Trodheim, Norway. Springer-Verlag, Heidelberg. doi:10.1007/978-3-540-45175-4_13

Berry, M. W., & Kogan, J. (2010). *Text mining applications and theory*. Chichester: Wiley. doi:10.1002/9780470689646

Bird, S., Klein, E., & Loper, E. (2009). *Natural Language Processing with Python*. Sebastopol: O'Reilly.

Chisholm, E., & Kolda, T. G. (1999). *New term weighting formulas for the vector space method in information retrieval* [Technical Report ORNL-TM-13756]. Oak Ridge National Laboratory, Oak Ridge, TN.

Debole, F., & Sebastiani, F. (2003). Supervised Term Weighting for Automated Text Categorization. In *Proceedings of SAC-03, 18th ACM Symposium on Applied Computing* (pp. 784–788). Melbourne, FL. ACM Press. doi:10.1145/952532.952688

Delmonte, R., & Pallotta, V. (2011). Opinion Mining and Sentiment Analysis Need Text Understanding. Advances in Distributed Agent-Based Retrieval Tools Studies in Computational Intelligence, 361, 81–95. Berlin: Springer-Verlag.

Demšar, J., Curk, T., & Erjavec, A. (2013). Orange: Data Mining Toolbox in Python. *Journal of Machine Learning Research, 14*, 2349–2353.

Engel, D., Whitney, P., Calapristi, A., & Brockman, F. (2009). Mining for emerging technologies within text streams and documents. In *Proceedings of the Ninth SIAM International Conference on Data Mining*.

Feldman, R., & Sagner, J. (2007). *The Text Mining Handbook*. Cambridge: Cambridge University Press.

Han, J., & Kamber, M. (2006). *Data Mining: Concepts and Techniques*. San Francisco: Morgan Kaufmann.

Han, Z. (2012). *Data and text mining of financial markets using news and social media*. MSc thesis, University of Manchester.

Hotho, A., Staab, S., & Stumme, G. (2003). *Text Clustering Based on Background Knowledge. Institute of Applied Informatics and Formal Descriptive Methods* (pp. 1–35). Germany: University of Karlsruhe.

Jacob, B., Feldman, R., Kogan, S., & Richardson, M. (2012). *Which News Moves Stock Prices*. Working Paper.

Klepac, G. (2010). Preparing for New Competition in the Retail Industry. In A. Syvajarvi & J. Stenvall (Eds.), *Data Mining in Public and Private Sectors: Organizational and Government Applications* (pp. 245–266). Hershey, PA: Information Science Reference; doi:10.4018/978-1-60566-906-9.ch013

Klepac, G. (2013). Risk Evaluation in the Insurance Company Using REFII Model. In S. Dehuri, M. Patra, B. M., & A. Jagadev (Eds.) Intelligent Techniques in Recommendation Systems: Contextual Advancements and New Methods (pp. 84–104). Hershey, PA: Information Science Reference. doi:10.4018/978-1-4666-2542-6.ch005

Klepac, G. (2014). Data Mining Models as a Tool for Churn Reduction and Custom Product Development in Telecommunication Industries. In P. Vasant (Ed.), *Handbook of Research on Novel Soft Computing Intelligent Algorithms: Theory and Practical Applications* (pp. 511–537). Hershey, PA: Information Science Reference; doi:10.4018/978-1-4666-4450-2.ch017

Kotsiantis, S., Kanellopoulos, D., & Pintelas, P. et al. (2006). Handling imbalanced datasets: A review. *GESTS International Transactions on Computer Science and Engineering, 30*(1), 25–36.

Kotsiantis, S., & Pintelas, P. (2003). Mixture of expert agents for handling imbalanced data sets. *Annals of Mathematics. Computing & Teleinformatics, 1*, 46–55.

Li, C., Wen, J.-R., & Li, H. (2003). Text Classification Using Stochastic Keyword Generation. In *Proceedings of ICML-03, 20th International Conference on Machine Learning* (pp. 469–471). Washington, DC, Morgan Kaufmann Publishers, San Francisco.

Matsuo, Y., & Ishizuka, M. (2004). Keyword extraction from a single document using word co-occurrence statistical information. *International Journal of Artificial Intelligence Tools, 13*(1), 157–169. doi:10.1142/S0218213004001466

Miner, G. (2012). *Practical Text Mining and Statistical Analysis for Non-structured Text Data Applications*. Oxford: Academic Press.

Mirchev, U., & Last, M. (2014). Multi-Document Summarization by Extended Graph Text Representation and Importance Refinement. In A. Fiori (Ed.), *Innovative Document Summarization Techniques: Revolutionizing Knowledge Understanding* (pp. 28–53). Hershey, PA: Information Science Reference; doi:10.4018/978-1-4666-5019-0.ch002

Nagar, A., & Hahsler, M. (2012). Using Text and Data Mining Techniques to extract Stock Market Sentiment from Live News Streams. In *International Conference on Computer Technology and Science (ICCTS 2012)*, IACSIT Press, Singapore.

Šilić, A., Chauchat, J., Dalbelo Bašić, B., & Morin, A. (2007). N-Grams and Morphological Normalization in Text Classification: A Comparison on a Croatian-English Parallel Corpus. *Progress in Artificial Intelligence –. Lecture Notes in Computer Science, 4874*, 671–682. doi:10.1007/978-3-540-77002-2_56

Soucy, P., & Mineau, G. W. (2003). Feature Selection Strategies for Text Categorization. In *Proceedings of* Y. Xiang and B. Chaib-Draa (Eds.), *CSCSI-03, 16th Conference of the Canadian Society for Computational Studies of Intelligence* (pp. 505–509). Halifax.

Tulankar, S., Athale, R., & Bhujbal, S. (2013). Sentiment Analysis of Equities using Data Mining Techniques and Visualizing the Trends. *IJCSI International Journal of Computer Science Issues, 10*(4).

Velic, M., Grzinic, T., & Padavic, I. (2013, June 24-27). Wisdom of Crowds Algorithm for Stock Market Predictions. In *International Conference on Information Technology Interfaces ITI 2013*. Cavtat/Dubrovnik, Croatia.

Whitehead, M., & Yaeger, L. (2010). Sentiment Mining Using Ensemble Classification Models. In *Innovations and Advances in Computer Sciences and Engineering* (pp. 509–514). Springer Netherlands. doi:10.1007/978-90-481-3658-2_89

Whitney, P., Engel, D., & Cramer, N. (2009). Mining for surprise events within text streams. In *Proceedings of the Ninth SIAM International Conference on Data Mining* (pp. 617–627). Society for Industrial and Applied Mathematics. doi:10.1137/1.9781611972795.53

Zupan, B., Demšar, J., Petrović, S., Kolar, M, Šarić, F., & Dalbelo Bašić, B. (2008). *orngTxt: Orange data mining tool, Add-On for Text mining* [Computer software].

ADDITIONAL READING

Jurafsky, D., & Martin, J. H. (2009). *Speech and Language Processing*. Englewood Cliffs, NJ: Prentice Hall.

Manning, C., & Schütze, H. (1999). *Foundations of Statistical Natural Language Processing*. Cambridge, MA: MIT Press.

NLTK Project. (2015). NLTK 3.0 documentation. Retrieved from http://www.nltk.org/

Python Software Foundation. (2015). Python. Retrieved from https://www.python.org

Weiss, S. M., Indurkhya, N., Zhang, T., & Damerau, F. J. (2010). *Text Mining: Predictive Methods for Analyzing Unstructured Information*. New York, NY: Springer.

KEY TERMS AND DEFINITIONS

Churn: When used in business context it referes to quitting some service or leaving e.g. telecommunications subscription (contract).

Feature: In machine learning context it refers to variable. Other synonims include attribute, independent variable, descriptor etc.

N-gram: Part of text that consists of *n* items.

NLP: Natural Language Processing – using computer to automatically process text written in natural language and to extract information and knowledge from it.

SMART: System for coputing the information measure of specific text items.

TF/IDF: Term Frequency / Inverse Document Frequency – measures for computing textual items importance, i.e., information.

Variable Importance: Measure of the variable (feature) relevancy. Often indication information that variable carries or power of distinction between two classes.

Chapter 7
Departing the Ontology Layer Cake

Abel Browarnik
Tel Aviv University, Israel

Oded Maimon
Tel Aviv University, Israel

ABSTRACT

In this chapter we analyze Ontology Learning and its goals, as well as the input expected when learning ontologies - peer-reviewed scientific papers in English. After reviewing the Ontology Learning Layer Cake model's shortcomings we suggest an alternative model based on linguistic knowledge. The suggested model would find the meaning of simple components of text – statements. From them it is easy to derive cases and roles that map the reality as a set of entities and relationships or RDF triples, somehow equivalent to Entity-relationship diagrams. Time complexity for the suggested ontology learning framework is constant (O(1)) for a sentence, and O(n) for an ontology with n sentences. We conclude that the Ontology Learning Layer Cake is not adequate for Ontology Learning from text.

INTRODUCTION

An ontology is defined in our context as a formal, explicit specification of a shared conceptualization. *Formal* refers to the fact that the ontology should be machine readable (therefore ruling out natural language). *Explicit* means that the type of concepts used, and the constraints on their use are explicitly defined. *Shared* reflects the notion that an ontology captures consensual knowledge, that is, it is not private to some individual, but accepted by a group.

Most available ontologies are crafted and maintained with human intervention. Ontologies represent reality, and as such, require frequent updates, turning it into a resource that is both costly and difficult to obtain *and* maintain. To overcome this problem the discipline of *Ontology Learning* has emerged. *Learning* is interpreted in the literature as the process of creating the ontology and populating it. In our work, the goal of Ontology Learning is the (at least semi) automatic extraction of knowledge, possibly

DOI: 10.4018/978-1-4666-8690-8.ch007

structured as simple or composite statements, from a given corpus of textual documents, to form an ontology.

Surveys have been conducted since the early days of Ontology Learning showing the different approaches used to tackle the problem. In fact, most, if not all, the approaches follow a model named the *Ontology Learning Layer Cake* and share many features such as statistical based information retrieval, machine learning and data and text mining, making resort to linguistics based techniques for certain tasks. The approaches include multiple steps towards learning an ontology, namely term extraction, concept formation, creation of a taxonomy of concepts, relation extraction and finally rules extraction. Usually, big corpora are required to obtain good results. Web textual data is often the target of choice, due to its abundance.

Our work includes the following items:

Analysis of the Goals of Ontology Learning from Text

An ontology represents in our view a "portion" of the world that we are looking at. As an example, the toxicity of engineered nanoparticles (or nanotoxicity) domain is something that we would like to model. Many organizations, among them the European Commission, are endorsing and financing research projects on the subject (See for instance NHECD – Browarnik et al., 2009). The nanotoxicity domain is relatively new and dynamic. Every new paper published on the subject may add a new detail to the nanotoxicity model (i.e., a new concept, or a new relation between concepts). Hence, we see Ontology Learning as a tool for modeling a domain and to keep it up-to-date.

Analysis of the Input Used to Learn Ontologies

The input used for modeling a domain is dependent on the domain itself. What matters when considering the input used is whether the input consists of well-formed text or not. Modeling scientific domains such as nanotoxicity would certainly be based on peer-reviewed papers or other kinds of scientific articles or books. These are texts that can be deemed well-formed and quality checked. We may safely estimate that a domain is *not* learnt from sources such as email or new media (such as posts in Facebook or Tweeter) because these media often contain ill-formed text. While it could be used for tasks such as sentiment analysis, the media itself seems inappropriate for Ontology Learning from text. Indeed, the quality of the input is one of the parameters to be taken into account when devising an ontology learning framework.

Analysis of the Ontology Learning Layer Cake Model

The Ontology Learning Layer Cake model (or OLC) aims at learning ontologies by using a multistep approach. It first extracts terms from text. Some methods driven on OLC try to find, at this point, synonyms to the terms. The next step consists of building a hierarchy of terms. Upon building this hierarchy, which can be called a taxonomy, OLC methods point at relations, including non-taxonomic relations. The last stage is the rules or inference stage.

Most OLC driven methods recur, at least at some stage, to statistics or machine learning, the basis for unsupervised learning methods, either to extract terms, to build taxonomies or to extract relations and rules. This choice of unsupervised methods results, probably, from the fact that unsupervised methods are robust and often require less human resources than supervised methods.

Each individual step in OLC driven methods is evaluated using precision and recall measures. Precision and recall for these individual are generally lower than the optimum (i.e., 100%). The sequential nature of OLC driven methods results in a low overall performance for the whole process, caused by the bound performance of each individual step.

Moreover, some of the methods invest efforts to find intermediate results (such as terms, the result of the first layer) using Linguistics. It seems that this is too high an investment for a rather modest result. For example, using syntax is a way of using the structure of a sentence to find a (partial, at least) result. But then the structure so laboriously found is dismissed. This is certainly true if two or more steps in the OLC method repeat syntactic/semantic efforts, only to obtain intermediate results that are then used in the non-structural analysis made by the OLC method.

Alternative Models for Ontology Learning

We will argue that Ontology Learning could be tackled in a different way. The objective is to model domains. As mentioned above, many of the domains are defined by papers that contain well-formed text. English language *structure* remains constant, in spite of the fact that the language itself evolves. That is, English sentences are formed by functional words and lexical words. The structure is dictated by functional words, something that seldom changes. Lexical words do change often, but these changes have very small impact, if any, on sentence structure. On these grounds, we advocate for a structural approach towards Ontology Learning.

These conclusions lead us to suggest an alternative way to learn ontologies. We present a, modular, linguistic based, experimental framework for ontology learning that builds on existing, wide coverage syntactical, lexical and semantic resources. We depart from the OLC approach, proposing to model the domain, which is equivalent to learning the ontology, by finding the meaning of simple components of text – namely statements, the basic unit of text carrying meaning. From these statements the framework derives cases and roles that map the reality as a set of entities and relationships, much in the same way as Entity-relationship diagrams do.

ONTOLOGY AND ONTOLOGY LEARNING: A REVIEW

The amount of digitally stored information has grown exponentially with the introduction of the World Wide Web. This information includes textual data as well as other formats (such as voice or video). Most of the information is unstructured and cannot be manipulated manually because there is so much of it that it becomes intractable. Even search engines such as Google can only filter information in a rather simple way, relying on keywords, some linguistic and semantic features such as synonymy and its proprietary algorithms, such as PageRank, Panda and Penguin.

Natural Language is the tool used by humans to communicate, process and record information. Enabling non-human agents (e.g., computers) to use Natural Language would allow these agents to perform tasks such as translation, textual data processing, understanding and even reasoning. Those tasks are otherwise out of reach for non-human agents. To allow machines to manipulate information intelligently, to communicate with each other and with humans the idea of the Semantic Web raised (Berners-Lee, Hendler, & Lassila, 2001).

One of the requisites of the Semantic Web, as well as of Natural Language understanding by machines, is the need to make reference to large amounts of *real world knowledge*, sometimes referred to as common-sense knowledge. For this purpose a knowledge representation scheme is needed. Without it, no search or inference would be possible. Ontologies are among the artifacts used to represent such knowledge and to let all involved parties understand each other.

Ontologies

Gruber (1973) defines an ontology as an explicit specification of a conceptualization. The term is borrowed from philosophy, where ontology is a systematic account of what exists. For knowledge-based systems, what "exists" is exactly that which can be represented. Studer, Benjamins, &Fensel (1998) define it as a formal, explicit specification of a shared conceptualization. A conceptualization refers to an abstract model of some phenomenon in the world by having identified the relevant concepts of that phenomenon. Explicit means that the type of concepts used, and the constraints on their use are explicitly defined. Formal refers to the fact that the ontology should be machine readable, which excludes natural language. Shared reflects the notion that an ontology captures consensual knowledge, that is, it is not private to some individual, but accepted by a group.

Buitelaar, Cimiano, Grobelnik, & Sintek (2005) classify ontologies following their use:

- Ontologies referring to high level concepts such as time, space, and event are classified as "top-level" ontologies and are generally domain independent. It makes sense to speak about unified, top-level ontologies.
- Ontologies describing the vocabulary related to a generic domain by specializing the concepts introduced in the top-level ontology are "domain ontologies".
- A description of the vocabulary related to a generic task or activity by specializing the top-level ontologies is a "task ontology".
- Finally, there are application ontologies. These are the most specific ontologies. Concepts in application ontologies often correspond to roles played by domain entities while performing a certain activity.

Top level ontologies, also called "upper" or "foundation" ontologies, were most likely constructed, at least initially, with human intervention. This is evidenced by Shah et al. (2006) for Cyc, Masolo, Borgo, Gangemi, Guarino, & Oltramari (2003) for DOLCE, and Niles and Pease (2001) for SUMO. It is worth noting that there are only a few upper ontologies and their rate of change is allegedly low.

Human intervention becomes an issue for the other types of ontologies. Those ontologies are numerous and potentially large. Moreover, these ontologies evolve often. The benefits of automatically (or at least semi-automatically) learning ontologies are one of the motivations behind ontology learning research. In this context, learning an ontology means both the construction of the ontology's skeleton (classes and subclasses in object oriented parlance) and the facts that describe the domain (instances).

It is interesting to note that there are several points of view when it comes to defining or classifying ontologies. As an example, Feldman and Sanger (2007) define an ontology as "*a tuple O:=(C, ≤ c) consisting of a set …[of] concepts and a partial order…labeled a concept hierarchy or taxonomy*". But an ontology should include non-hierarchic relationships. This is because in the real world hierarchic relation are only "a part of the story". Thus, an ontology can't be seen as a taxonomy, unless in the particular domain there are only hierarchic relations.

Uschold and Gruninger (2004) and Wong, Liu, and Bennamoun (2012) provide a different opinion on ontologies, by underlining the differences between lightweight ontologies, as compared to heavyweight (or formal) ontologies. Ontologies represent different kinds of things represented by classes. These classes are organized in networks of classes and subclasses. An ontology together with the specific instances of its classes or subclasses forms a knowledge base. The classes and the relationships constitute the ontology. Within the spectrum of ontologies, lightweight ontologies stand at one end, with only basic information such as terms. At the other end stand rigorously formalized logical theories. Formality increases from lightweight to heavyweight ontologies. The degree of formality has an influence on how the ontology is represented, e.g., its representation scheme.

Most of the syntactic/semantic constructs are touted Ontology or contain the word Ontology within their name. Such diverse constructs can be represented by a myriad of knowledge representation devices, textual or graphical. For instance, a glossary can be a text file without any further indexing method, while a UML data model is best described by a standardized graphic representation.

Vrandecic (2010) aggregates the types of ontologies into five categories, according to the semantic spectrum:

- catalogs / sets of IDs
- glossaries / sets of term definitions
- thesauri / sets of informal is-a relations
- formal taxonomies / sets of formal is-a relations
- proper ontologies / sets of general logical constraints

In fact, only the last category deserves being classified as an ontology. The first two are sets without relations, the third and the fourth are taxonomies (i.e., sets of IS-A relations).

Sowa and Majumdar (2003) list a number of knowledge representation artifacts used in Artificial Intelligence. The list includes "Lexical Semantics", (with WordNet as an example), "Axiomatized Semantics" (exemplified by several domain-dependent knowledge bases, as well as by Cyc), "Statistical approaches" (used for tasks such as deriving grammar rules from a corpus, or extracting relations from text), "Knowledge Soup" (Sowa, 1990; Sowa, 2000), *"What distinguishes knowledge soup from systems such as Cyc is the absence of a predefined, monolithic organization of the knowledge base. Instead, the knowledge can be developed and organized incrementally in an open-ended lattice of theories, each of which is consistent by itself, but possibly inconsistent with other theories in the same lattice"*) and Task-Oriented Semantic Interpretation, a simplification of the "Knowledge Soup".

It is interesting to note that many of the authors cited above refer to ontologies as being declarative, as opposed to procedural, in the sense that one associates generally to programming languages, and therefore cannot be just compiled and run as most other software artifacts. Yet, there are declarative languages, generally related to Artificial Intelligence, such as Prolog (Shapiro & Sterling, 1994), that in spite of being declarative implement many interesting developments and systems.

Ontology Representation: Resource Description Framework (RDF)

The Resource Description Framework (RDF) is a set of specifications originally designed as a metadata data model. It is generally used as a method for conceptual description or modeling of information.

The RDF data model defined in W3C (1999) resembles modeling approaches such as Entity-Relationship or Class diagrams. It makes statements about resources (in particular Web resources) in the form of subject-predicate-object expressions. These expressions are known as triples in RDF terminology. The subject denotes the resource, and the predicate denotes traits or aspects of the resource and expresses a relationship between the subject and the object.

On top of RDF we found RDF Schema, or RDFS. RDFS is defined as a set of classes with certain properties, intended to structure RDF resources. Everything in RDFS is a resource.

The main RDFS constructs are classes, properties, and utility properties. A class is a resource. In other words we can say that a class is a subclass of a resource.

Ontology Representation Schemes: Web Ontology Language (OWL2)

The Web Ontology Language (OWL), defined in Patel-Schneider and Horrocks (2004), is a set of knowledge representation languages for authoring ontologies. The languages are characterized by formal semantics and RDF/XML-based serializations for the Semantic Web.

OWL2, defined by W3C (2009), is an extended and revised version of OWL, the Web Ontology Language developed by the W3C (World Wide Web Consortium) Web Ontology Working Group and published in 2004. Ontologies are, in W3C parlance, formalized vocabularies of terms, often covering a specific domain and shared by a community of users. These vocabularies define terms by describing their relationships with other terms in the ontology. The aim of OWL2 is to facilitate ontology development and sharing via the Web, with the ultimate goal of making Web content more accessible to machines.

OWL2 ontologies provide classes, properties, individuals, and data values and are stored as Semantic Web documents. OWL2 ontologies can be used along with information written in RDF, and OWL2 ontologies themselves are primarily exchanged as RDF documents.

OWL2 is a knowledge representation language, designed to formulate, exchange and reason with knowledge about a domain of interest. The basic building blocks of OWL2 are:

- Axioms: basic statements expressed by an OWL ontology
- Entities: elements used to refer to real-world objects
- Expressions: combinations of entities to form complex descriptions from basic ones

In the framework of this research we assume that knowledge consists of statements or propositions, such as "knowledge consists of statements" or "reality is complex". An OWL2 ontology is essentially a collection of such basic "pieces of knowledge." Statements in an ontology are called axioms in OWL2, and the ontology asserts that its axioms are true. OWL statements might be either true or false given a certain state of affairs. It should be noted that OWL makes an "open world assumption". This means that facts that can't be confirmed are undefined, not false.

When humans think, they draw conclusions from their knowledge. An important feature of OWL is that it captures this aspect of human intelligence for the forms of knowledge that it can represent. But what does it mean, generally speaking, that a statement is a consequence of other statements? Essentially it means that this statement is true whenever the other statements are. In OWL terms: we say, a set of statements A entails a statement a if in any state of affairs wherein all statements from A are true, also a is true. Moreover, a set of statements may be consistent (that is, there is a possible state of affairs in which all the statements in the set are jointly true) or inconsistent (there is no such state of affairs). The formal semantics of OWL specifies, in essence, for which possible "states of affairs" a particular set of OWL statements is true.

Statements normally refer to objects of the world and describe them e.g. by putting them into categories (like "Mary is female") or saying something about their relation ("John and Mary are married"). All atomic constituents of statements, be they objects (John, Mary), categories (female) or relations (married) are called entities. In OWL2, objects are called individuals, categories are classes and relations are properties. Properties in OWL2 are further subdivided. Object properties relate objects to objects (like a person to their spouse), while datatype properties assign data values to objects (like an age to a person). Annotation properties are used to encode information about (parts of) the ontology itself (like the author and creation date of an axiom) instead of the domain of interest.

As a central feature of OWL, names of entities can be combined into expressions using so called constructors. As a basic example, the atomic classes "female" and "professor" could be combined conjunctively to describe the class of female professors. The latter would be described by an OWL class expression that could be used in statements or in other expressions. In this sense, expressions can be seen as new entities which are defined by their structure. In OWL, the constructors for each sort of entity vary greatly. The expression language for classes is very rich and sophisticated, whereas the expression language for properties is much less so.

There are two alternative ways of assigning meaning to ontologies in OWL2, Direct Semantics ("OWL2 DL") and RDF-Based Semantics ("OWL2 Full"). Not every OWL2 ontology qualifies as an OWL2 DL ontology. The direct model-theoretic semantics provides a meaning for OWL2 in a Description Logic style. The RDF-Based Semantics is an extension of the semantics for RDFS and is based on viewing OWL2 ontologies as RDF graphs. The two main differences are that under the direct model-theoretic semantics annotations have no formal meaning and under the RDF-Based Semantics there are some extra inferences that arise from the RDF view of the universe.

There are three additional "profiles" of OWL2 intended mainly (though not strictly) for specific domains. These domains are OWL2 EL, designed with bio-health ontologies in mind, OWL2 QL, which expressively can represent key features of Entity-relationship and UML diagrams, and OWL2 RL, aimed at applications that require scalable reasoning without sacrificing too much expressive power.

Hitzler, Krotzsch, and Rudolph (2009) summarize OWL as follows:

- OWL: an expressive ontology language with practical impact
- Structurally representable in RDF
- Reasoning typical based on extensional ("direct") semantics:
  - closely related to description logics and first-order logic (with equality)
  - different from RDF semantics, but compatible for many purposes
- Various flavors for different applications:
  - OWL Full provides RDF-based semantics (undecidable)
  - OWL DL decidable but complex (N2ExpTime)
  - OWL profiles for light-weight reasoning (in PTime)

Ontology Learning from Text

Ontology Learning from text, the task of obtaining knowledge on a specific domain, is often seen as the extraction of ontologies by applying natural language analysis techniques to texts.

Some of the well-known ontology learning approaches for this task follow:

- Association rules were initially defined on the database field. *"Given a set of transactions, where each transaction is a set of literals (called items), an association rule is an expression of the form X implies Y, where X and Y are sets of items. The intuitive meaning of such a rule is that transactions of the database which contain X tend to contain Y"* (Agrawal, Imieliński, & Swami, 1993). The association rules method for ontology learning have been originally described and evaluated in Maedche and Staab (2000). Maedche and Staab (2003) used it to discover non–taxonomic relations between concepts, using a concept hierarchy as background knowledge.
- Conceptual clustering (Faure & Nedellec, 1999): Concepts are grouped according to the semantic distance between each other to make up hierarchies. Calculation of semantic distance between two concepts may depend on different factors and must be provided.
- Ontology pruning (Kietz, Maedche, & Volz, 2000): Ontology pruning aims at building domain ontologies based on different heterogeneous sources. First, a generic, core ontology is used as a top level structure for the domain-specific ontology. Second, a dictionary which contains important domain terms described in natural language is used to acquire domain concepts. These concepts are classified into the generic core ontology. Third, domain-specific and general corpora of texts are used to remove concepts that were not domain specific. Concept removal follows the heuristic that domain-specific concepts should be more frequent in a domain-specific corpus than in generic texts.
- Concept learning (Hahn, Romacker, & Schulz, 2000): A given taxonomy is incrementally updated as new concepts are acquired from real-world texts.

Following Buitelaar, Cimiano, and Magnini (2005), *"...the process of defining and instantiating a knowledge base is referred to as knowledge markup or ontology population, whereas (semi-)automatic support in ontology development is usually referred to as ontology learning"*.

Cimiano (2006) describes the tasks involved in Ontology Learning as forming a layer cake. The layers are, from bottom to top, *terms, synonyms, concepts, concept hierarchies, relations* and *rules*.

This approach can be seen as a cornerstone in Ontology Learning. It is the dominant approach in the domain, and will be reviewed further on this chapter.

It assumes that terms (gathered through term extraction methods) are the basic building blocks for the task of ontology learning. There are many methods of term extraction (Bourigault & Jacquemin, (1999), Kozakov et al (2004), Wermter & Hahn (2005)) and many tools are publicly available (Baroni & Bernardini (2004), Navigli & Velardi (2004), Sclano & Velardi (2007)).

The synonym layer is either based on ready-available sets such as WordNet synsets (after sense disambiguation), on clustering techniques or other similar methods, or on web-based knowledge acquisition.

The concept layer is unclear, due to the fact that no consensual definition of what a concept is exists. The prevailing opinion is that it should include: an intentional (intentional, n. d.) definition of the concept, a set of concept instances, i.e. its extension, and a set of linguistic realizations, i.e. (multilingual) terms for this concept.

The concept hierarchy level (i.e., the taxonomic level) uses one of three paradigms to induce taxonomies from text:

- the application of lexico-syntactic patterns to detect hyponymy relations (Hearst, 1992). This approach is known to have reasonable precision but very low recall.
- the exploitation of hierarchical clustering algorithms to automatically derive term hierarchies from text, based on the Harris' distributional hypothesis, that terms are similar in meaning to the extent in which they share syntactic contexts (Harris, 1968).
- The third paradigm stems from the information retrieval community and relies on a document-based notion of term subsumption as proposed for example in Sanderson and Croft (1999). Salient words and phrases extracted from the documents are organized hierarchically using a type of co-occurrence known as subsumption. The resulting structure is displayed as a series of hierarchical menus.

The relation level has been addressed primarily within the biomedical field. The goal is to discover new relationships between known concepts (such as symptoms, drugs, and diseases) by analyzing large quantities of biomedical scientific articles.

Relation extraction through text mining for ontology development was introduced in work on association rules in Maedche and Staab (2000). Recent efforts in relation extraction from text have been carried on under the ACE (Automatic Content Extraction) program (NIST, n.d.), where entities (i.e. individuals) are distinguished from their mentions, and normalization, the process of establishing links between mentions in a document and individual entities represented in a ontology, is part of the task for certain kind of mentions (e.g. temporal expressions).

The rule level is at an early stage (Lin & Pantel, 2001). The EU-funded project Pascal textual entailment challenge (Dagan, Glickman, & Magnini, 2006), a related task, has driven attention to this problem.

Ontology Learning Layer Cake shortcomings are reviewed by Chen and Wu (2005), who cite, among others, Gómez-Pérez and Manzano-Macho (2003). These shortcomings are:

a) the transition from the syntactic to the semantic layers does not fully take into account the semantic information of the sentences,
b) the methods rely mainly on WordNet,
c) the semantic information on the input corpus is not fully utilized,
d) relation extraction is not based on semantics, and
e) there are limitations to the pattern methods used.

Our analysis of Ontology Learning (OL) focuses on the works by Wong (2009) and Wong et al. (2012). They define OL from text as aiming to turn facts and patterns from an ever growing body of information into shareable high-level constructs for enhancing everyday applications (e.g., Web search) and enabling intelligent systems (e.g., Semantic Web). Following the usual view of the subject, OL from text is essentially the process of deriving high-level concepts and relations as well as the occasional axioms from information to form an ontology. Hence, the bottleneck in handcrafting structured knowledge sources (e.g., dictionaries, taxonomies, knowledge bases) and training data (e.g., annotated text corpora) remains an obstacle towards large-scale deployment of OL systems, a necessity if we are to minimize human efforts in the learning process. The authors advocate for an approach that would focus on learning lightweight ontologies first and extend them later if possible. This strategy should bring about a gradual rise in the adoption of ontologies across many domains that require knowledge engineering, in particular, interoperability of semantics in their applications (e.g., document retrieval, image retrieval, bioinformatics, manufacturing, industrial safety, law, environment, disaster management, e-Government, e-Commerce, and tourism).

The following remarks are derived from the consensus among Ontology Learning reviews:

- The fully automatic learning of ontologies may not be possible
- A common evaluation platforms for ontologies is needed
- The results for discovery of relations between concepts are less than satisfactory
- The more recent literature (i.e., second part of the decade) points at the increase in interest on the Web to address the knowledge acquisition bottleneck and to make ontology learning operational on a Web-scale

Remarks on Ontology Learning Techniques

Term extraction and concept formation have been tackled, since the inception of ontology learning from text, in a myriad of ways (Sclano & Velardi (2007), Wermter & Hahn (2005), Wong, Liu, & Bennamoun (2009), Zhang & Ciravegna (2011), Massey & Wong (2011), Yeh & Yang (2008)).

Relation discovery, on the other hand, remains an open problem. Wong et al. (2012) cite the work by Specia and Motta (2006). This work introduces a pipeline of existing tools for the extraction of semantic relations between pairs of entities. From the description of the work it seems that a domain ontology and a predefined set of patterns are necessary to obtain the relations. Ciaramita, Gangemi, Ratsch, Šarić, and Rojas (2008) use syntactic dependencies as potential relations.

Many researches have turned to the web as a source for large scale corpora to be used for statistics and machine learning based methods for relations learning. Sombatsrisomboon, Matsuo, and Ishizuka (2003) proposed a simple three-step technique for discovering taxonomic relations (i.e., hypernym/hyponym) between pairs of terms using search engines. Sanchez and Moreno (2008) developed a technique for learning domain patterns using domain-relevant verb phrases extracted from webpages provided by search engines, sometimes leading to non-taxonomic relation discovery. Rosenfeld and Feldman (2006) devised URES (Unsupervised Relation Extraction System), which extracts relations from the Web in a totally unsupervised way. Feldman and Sanger (2007) work further, enhancing relation extraction by using named entity recognition (NER). Etzioni, Banko, Soderland, and Weld (2008) developed TextRunner to extract information across different domains from the Web. TextRunner is a two-phase process. The first phase uses a conditional random field-based model to label the constituents in the input strings as either entities or relationships. An extractor is then used in the second phase to extract triples to capture the relationships between entities. Pei, Nakayama, Hara, and Nishio (2008) proposed a two-step technique (name mapping followed by logic-based mapping) to deduce the type of relations between concepts in Wikipedia. Liu, Xu, Zhang, Wang, Yu, and Pan (2008) developed Catriple, a system to automatically extracting triples using Wikipedia's categorical system. Suchanek, Kasneci, and Weikum (2007) developed Yago, an ontology built on top of both WordNet and Wikipedia, containing (in 2007) more than 1 million entities and 5 million facts. The semantic relations include the Is-A hierarchy as well as non-taxonomic relations between entities. The rationale behind Yago is the fact that many applications (Semantic Web, machine translation, word sense disambiguation, etc.) could profit from an always updated, open knowledge base containing both mundane facts and semantic information and links, with an accuracy close to 100%, comparable to the accuracy of an encyclopedia. Suchanek, Kasneci, and Weikum compare their work to the work by Ruiz-Casado, Alfonseca, and Castells (2005) as well as to KnowitAll (Etzioni et al., 2004), saying that

"Although these approaches have recently improved the quality of their results considerably, the quality is still significantly below that of a man-made knowledge base. Typical results contain many false positives (e.g., IsA(Aachen Cathedral, City), to give one example from KnowItAll). Furthermore, obtaining a recall above 90 percent for a closed domain typically entails a drastic loss of precision in return. Thus, information extraction approaches are only of little use for applications that need near-perfect ontologies (e.g. for automated reasoning). Furthermore, they typically do not have an explicit (logic-based) knowledge representation model."

Yago is followed by Yago2 (Hoffart, Suchanek, Berberich, & Weikum, 2012), an ontology based on Wikipedia, WordNet and GeoNames, a geographical database that covers all countries and contains over eight million placenames. Yago2 has knowledge of more than 10 million entities (like persons, organizations, cities, etc.) and contains more than 120 million facts about these entities. The accuracy of YAGO is manually evaluated, with an accuracy reported by the authors to be 95%. Every relation is annotated with its confidence value. Other efforts by Weber and Buitelaar (2006) .Wong (2009) and Mintz, Bills, Snow, and Jurafsky (2009) are also based on web resources.

ONTOLOGY LEARNING FROM TEXT – THE OBJECTIVE, THE INPUT

Domain ontologies are used to describe a domain. A domain ontology plays a role similar to that of the conceptual layer of an Entity-Relationship Diagram (or ERD) in the area of system analysis. In both we point at entities, attributes, relationships and more.

System analysis is performed by humans – system analysts – that gather information from humans involved in the domain, together with environmental details, to create the conceptual layer of an ERD for that domain. An ERD has two additional layers, the logical layer and the physical layer. These two layers deal with implementation details and therefore are not relevant to our discussion. From now on, when we refer to ERD we mean the conceptual layer of an ERD. We say that an ERD is equivalent to an ontology because an ERD of the domain represents conceptually the entities involved and the relations between the entities. An ontology is an explicit specification of a conceptualization, a systematic account of what exists.

Ontology Learning is, hence, the task of gathering the information and building the ontology of the domain. This task is similar to building an ERD.

The main difference between preparing an ERD for a business and learning an ontology for a domain such as nanotoxicity is that the nanotoxicity domain is derived from a corpus of scientific papers that are a strong basis for a learning process without human intervention (except for paper writing), while preparing an ERD for an enterprise requirements planning (or ERP) system relies on knowledge that is seldom written, let aside formalized. Yet, in both cases we target a model of the domain. Hence, ontology learning is in fact a modeling technique and its goal is to obtain a model of the domain.

We should consider the sources of text used towards learning ontologies, and its quality. To this end we could think of a Martian visiting Earth. The visitor could find himself browsing the New York Time website on November 21st, 2013. He could see there that *"Applicants Find Health Website Is Improving, but Not Fast Enough "* (Goodnough, 2013). Having no worldly knowledge he would not understand that this issue is related to the US health reform named *Obamacare*. This is where an ontology comes of use. An ontology of US politics would provide the visitor with the background knowledge he would need to understand the newspaper. The source for this ontology learning task would be newspapers and books. As we deal with learning ontologies from text we do not consider video or audio sources. We do not consider new media (such as *Tweeter*, email or *Facebook*) either, because newspapers, magazines and books would most probably cover all the requirements. And because of the linguistic quality of the input. Language quality in new media cannot be taken for granted. Newspapers, magazines and books undergo editing which is a sort of quality control. This is not to say that there is no use for new media. It can be used for less formal tasks, as is the case with sentiment analysis.

Our opinion is that most existing methods for ontology learning from text recur to well-formed text. There is no clear information on this issue. Our review revels that ASIUM, OntoLearn and CRCTool perform term extraction using sentence parsing. Text-to-Onto, TextStorm/Clouds and Syndikate perform term extraction using syntactic structure analysis and other techniques. OntoGain uses shallow parsing for term extraction. These tasks would be unfeasible with ill-formed text.

Thus, we assume that the input for Ontology Learning from text consists of well-formed text.

ANALYSIS OF THE ONTOLOGY LEARNING LAYER CAKE MODEL

Methods that use the Ontology Learning Layer Cake model divide Ontology Learning into up to five sequential steps, obtaining *terms*, *concepts*, *taxonomic relations*, *non-taxonomic relations* and *axioms*.

Some methods perform all the steps, but some perform only part of it. The results shown by the methods are dissimilar. ASIUM, Text-to-Onto, Ontolearn and Ontogain do not provide an overall figure of precision and recall for the whole ontology learning process. TextStorm/Clouds cites an average result of 52%. Syndikate mentions high precision (94 to 97% for different domains) and low recall (31 to 57% correspondingly, for the same domains). CRCTool report a figure of 90.3% for simple sentences and 68.6% for complex sentences. We assume that these figures represent the harmonic mean (F measure) of the method.

The main characteristics shared by methods based on the OLC model are:

- The method is split into sequential steps. The output of step i is the input for step $i + 1$ (even though there may be additional inputs from other sources).
- If 'collateral' output is obtained from step i it is not passed to step $i + 1$.
- A method has four or five sequential steps. Each step depends on the previous one. If every step has precision and recall (and therefore harmonic mean, the F measure) bound by p ($p < 1$), then the method's recall and precision bound is p^n (n is the number of steps). As an example, if we assume the F measure of every step to be 0.8, the F measure of the whole ontology learning method with 4 steps would be 0.41.

- If a step makes resort to statistical or machine learning methods it requires considerable amounts of data to give significant results. In general, it also requires the data to be split into a training set and a test set.
- Statistical and machine learning methods have to beware of the danger of over fitting and wrong choices of training and test sets. These may bring about to output distortion.
- Ontology Layer Cake model-based methods recur to statistical evidence regarding knowledge on the area being studied. Thus, features such as co-occurrence of terms or words may induce conclusions that make no sense to subject experts.
- The statistical nature of the some steps makes it impossible to trace back specific results. As an example, a method may find a relation between two concepts following the co-occurrence of the two concepts in the same sentence or paragraph in different portions of text or even in different documents, without being able to find the reason for the relation found.

The unsupervised nature of statistical or machine learning methods are an incentive to choose such methods as lesser human effort is required, as compared to methods that try to understand the subject matter. Such understanding is critical for the success of non-statistical, non-machine learning methods. The human efforts and the fact that results are sometimes similar for both supervised and unsupervised methods boosts the inclination to choose unsupervised methods.

In this case, however, we see that OLC methods use sometimes techniques – to some extent – supervised. Such may be the case, for example, in TextStorm/Clouds. This method uses part of speech tagging (using WordNet), syntactic structure analysis and Anaphora resolution for term extraction and for taxonomic and non-taxonomic relation learning. Yet, this is an OLC method with its "cascading" nature.

Another point to be considered is the reason to choose a sequential, "cascading" method. It is possible that the OLC approach was inspired by the "divide and conquer" algorithm design paradigm. A divide and conquer algorithm works by breaking down a problem into two or more sub-problems, breaking down the sub-problems again until these become simple enough to be solved directly. The solutions to the sub-problems are then combined to give a solution to the original problem. Problems in data mining are often solved using "cascading" algorithms that are built on the divide and conquer paradigm. The fact that data mining was followed by textual data mining which in turn inspired Ontology Learning may be one of the reasons for the choice.

ENGLISH STRUCTURE FROM AN ONTOLOGY LEARNING OPTIC

English Language Structure

The Longman Grammar of Spoken and Written English (in short, LGSWE) (Biber, Johansson, Leech, Conrad, & Finegan, 1999) defines a spectrum of grammatical units (or classes) forming a hierarchy.

A class is made out of one or more constituents of lower level classes. Discourse is made of one or more sentences, made, in turn, of one or more clauses. Clauses are made of one or more phrases. Phrases are constituted by one or more words that are themselves constituted by morphemes. We could describe discourse in terms of morphemes or words, but this would be a very complex way to describe a language. Using hierarchical structures, the task becomes more tractable. We will focus on four types of grammatical units, namely words, phrases, clauses and sentences.

Words

- Lexical words – the main carrier of meaning in a text. Lexical words are numerous and form an open class, meaning that words can be added as needed. Words can be nouns, verbs, adjectives and adverbs (sometimes one word belongs to more than one class).
- Function words – indicate relationships between lexical words or larger units, or indicate how to interpret a lexical word or larger unit. Function words form a closed class (i.e., function words are very seldom added to the language). A function word may belong to one or more of the following subclasses:
  - Determiners – used to narrow down the reference of a noun
  - Pronouns – used instead of full noun phrases
  - Primary auxiliaries (be, have, do) – used to build complex verb phrases
  - Modal auxiliaries (can, could, may, might, must, shall, should, will, would) – used to build complex verb phrases. There are also semi-modals such as dare, need and others.
  - Prepositions – used to introduce prepositional phrases. Examples of prepositions: about, after, around, as, at, by, down, for, from, in, into, like, of, off, on, round, since, than, to, towards, with, without, such as, as far as, and more.
  - Adverbial particles – used mainly to give a meaning of motion or result. Examples: about, across, along, around, away, back, by, down, forth, home, in, off, out, over, past, through, under, up, etc.
  - Coordinators – used to build coordinate structures – both phrases and clauses. The main coordinators are *and, but* and *or*. Other coordinators for special cases are *nor, either* and *neither*.
  - Subordinators – used to introduce dependent clauses. There are three main subclasses of subordinators:
    - Used to introduce adverbial clauses: after, as, because, if, since, although, whether, while and more.
    - Used to introduce degree clauses: *as, than, that*.
    - Used to introduce complement clauses: *if, that, whether*.
  - Wh-words – used to introduce clauses. Except for how and that wh-words begin with wh. Wh-words are used as interrogative clause markers (as in "***What** do they* want") or as relativizers (as in "*the car **which** she had abandoned*").
  - Existential *there* – often described as an anticipatory subject (as in "*there is no other option*").
  - The negator *not* – used mainly to negate clauses
  - The infinitive marker *to* – used mainly as a complementizer preceding infinitive forms of verbs.
  - Numerals – generally either ordinals (the answer to which) or cardinals (the answer to how many).
- Inserts – a type of word inserted freely on text, carrying often emotional and interactional meaning, especially frequent in spoken text.

Table 1 shows the differences between lexical and function words.

Words can belong to more than one class. A single word such as *like* can be a lexical word (noun, verb, adjective or adverb) or a function word (a preposition or a subordinator).

Table 1. Typical differences between lexical and function words

Features	Lexical words	Function words
Frequency	Low	High
head of phrase	Yes	No
Length	Long	Short
lexical meaning	Yes	No
Morphology	Variable	Invariable
Openness	Open	Closed
Number	Large	Small
Stress	Strong	Week

Phrases

Phrases are constituted by one or more words. A phrase may embed other phrases at different levels. Such an embedding may result in more than one meaning for the whole construct. Following the example on Biber et al. (1999), p. 94, the phrase *"Mr Adamec threatened to quit last night"* can be interpreted in two ways:

a. [Mr Adamec] [threatened] [to quit] [last night]
b. [Mr Adamec] [threatened] [to quit [last night]]

Phrases are indicated by brackets. The first interpretation means that *Mr Adamec expressed last night his threat to quit sometime in the future*, while the second interpretation means that *Mr Adamec threatened to quit last night*. The different levels of embedding are exemplified by the phrase *[last night]*, which is embedded more deeply in *b* than in *a*.

There are several types of phrases, the major types being noun phrases, verb phrases, adjective phrases, adverb phrases and prepositional phrases.

- Noun phrases – a phrase that consists of a noun alone or accompanied by a determiner, and possibly followed by complements to complete the meaning of the phrase. A complex noun phrase can even be discontinuous, as in the following sentence (the noun phrase fractions appear in bold): *"In this chapter **a description** will be given **of the food assistance programs that address the needs of the family**"*
- Verb phrases – a phrase with a lexical verb or a primary verb as head or main verb, either alone or accompanied by auxiliaries. Verb phrases in our context do not include accompanying elements such as objects and predicatives. Verb phrases are often discontinuous, as in the following (verb phrase fractions appear in bold): *"The current year **has** definitely **started** well"*
  - Adjective phrases – a phrase containing an adjective as head, probably accompanied by modifiers. Adjective phrases can be discontinuous as in the following (fractions appear in bold): *"You couldn't have a **better** name **than that**"*
  - Adverb phrases – a phrase headed by an adverb, possibly with modifiers.

Table 2. Rank scale of grammatical analysis

Rank	Structure	Constituents	Realization
1	Clause	S V C A	Phrases
2	Phrase	PRM H POM	Words
3	Word	Pf R Sf	Morphemes

　◦　Prepositional phrases – it consists of a preposition and a complement. It may be viewed as a noun phrase extended by a link showing relationship to surrounding structures.

Clauses

Biber et al (1999) define a clause as a unit structured around a verb phrase. The lexical verb in the verb phrase denotes an action (drive, run, shout, etc.) or a state (know, seem, resemble, etc.). The verb phrase appears with one or more elements denoting the participants involved in the action, state, etc. (agent, affected, recipient, etc.), the attendant circumstances (time, place, manner, etc.), the relationship of the clause to the surrounding structures, etc. Together with the verb phrase, these are the clause elements. The clause elements are realized by phrases or by embedded clauses.

A clause may be divided into two main parts: a subject and a predicate. The subject is generally a nominal part, while the predicate is mainly a verbal nucleus.

Preisler (1997) focuses on three of the grammatical structures we defined so far: clauses, phrases and words. A clause in this context contains the constituents <u>S</u>ubject, <u>V</u>erbal, <u>C</u>omplement and <u>A</u>dverbial, all or some of them. Each of the constituents is in fact a phrase (there are several phrase types). A phrase is constituted by a head (H) and a modifiers, either a premodifier (PRM) or a postmodifier (POM), or any combination of such constituents. In turn, words are also made of a root and affixes, either prefixes (Pf), suffixes (Sf) or a combination. Preisler summarizes the constructs in a rank scale as shown in Table 2:

Yet, there is a variation, for example, where a phrase constituent can be another phrase (as in "*a ridiculously low price*"), instead of a word, as we would expect, or even a clause that may be a constituent of a phrase (as in "*The Lady sitting on the couch*"). Such a behavior is called rank shifting (see (Preisler, 1997), p. 22). Rank shifting adds complexity to the task of extracting semantic representation, because the automatic detection of clause boundaries that is essential to the decomposition of sentences becomes a very complex task. In this context, rankshifted clauses are called subclauses, while non-rankshifted clauses are called main clauses.

Clauses appearing together in a larger unit (generally sentences, but possibly phrases in the event of a rank-shifted clause) are linked by structural links, the principal types being *coordinators*, *subordinators* and *wh-words*. These were already mentioned in the function word section above. Coordinators create coordinated clauses. On the other hand, *subordinators* and *wh-words* create embedded clauses.

Sentences

Preisler (1997) defines a sentence as one or more main clauses, corresponding to units which in written language are bounded by the punctuation mark. SIL (SIL, n.d.) defines a sentence as a grammatical unit that is composed of one or more clauses. Jones, Horning, and Morrow (1922) state that a sentence is a word or a group of words expressing a complete thought. This definition is, at least, ambiguous. How does one characterize a complete thought? Moreover, a complete thought may require much more than a single sentence.

Wikipedia (2015) classifies sentences as follows:

By Structure

- A simple sentence consists of a single independent clause with no dependent clauses.
- A compound sentence consists of multiple independent clauses with no dependent clauses. These clauses are joined together using conjunctions, punctuation, or both.
- A complex sentence consists of at least one independent clause and one dependent clause.
- A complex-compound sentence (or compound-complex sentence) consists of multiple independent clauses, at least one of which has at least one dependent clause.

By Purpose

- A declarative sentence or declaration, the most common type, commonly makes a statement: *I am going home*.
- An interrogative sentence or question is commonly used to request information — *When are you going to work?* — but sometimes not
- An exclamative sentence or exclamation is generally a more emphatic form of statement expressing emotion: *What a wonderful day this is!*
- An imperative sentence or command tells someone to do something: *"Go to work at 7:30 in the morning"*.

Subsentence

Browarnik and Maimon (2012) introduce another construct that may be used towards the extraction of semantic contents from text, a subsentence. To define a subsentence a verbal construct (or VC in short) is first defined. A VC is a sequence of one or more verbal words, as in "is/VBZ" or in "may/MD have/VB been/VBN". A subsentence is a sentence fragment with no more than one verbal construct (VC).

English Linguistic Resources

WordNet

WordNet (Fellbaum, 1998; Miller, Beckwith, Fellbaum, Gross, & Miller 1990) is one of the most widely used resources in NLP. Sometimes called an ontology, sometimes a semantic network, and even an augmented thesaurus or a taxonomy, *"WordNet is an on-line lexical reference system whose design is inspired by current psycholinguistic theories of human lexical memory. English nouns, verbs, and adjectives are organized into synonym sets, each representing one underlying lexical concept. Different relations link the synonym sets."* (Miller et al., 1990).

Wordnet is based on a **lexical matrix**. At its base is the concept *"...that a word is a conventional association between a lexicalized concept and an utterance that plays a syntactic role."* (Miller et al., 1990).

This architecture is very appropriate for finding synonymy and polysemy. Every row in the lexical matrix is a synonym set or *synset*. In order to accommodate other semantic relations Wordnet makes use of pointers between synsets.

Verbnet

Verbs often express the main ideas of a sentence. It is therefore natural to emphasize the importance of a verbal resource for text understanding in general, and for ontology learning in particular.

VerbNet (Kipper Schuler, 2005) is a hierarchical verb lexicon with syntactic and semantic information for English verbs, using Levin verb classes (Levin, 1993) to systematically construct lexical entries. It uses verb classes to capture generalizations about verb behavior. The first level in the hierarchy consists of the original Levin classes, with each class subsequently refined to account for further semantic and syntactic differences within a class. Each node in the hierarchy is characterized extensionally by its set of verbs, and intentionally by a list of the arguments of those verbs and syntactic and semantic information about the verbs. The argument list consists of thematic roles and possible selectional restrictions on the arguments expressed using binary predicates. The syntactic information maps the list of thematic arguments to deep-syntactic arguments (i.e., normalized for voice alternations, and transformations). The semantic predicates describe the participants during various stages of the event described by the syntactic frame.

Kipper Schuler (2005) compares in her dissertation the differences between VerbNet and other linguistic resources such as Wordnet and Framenet, among others. A linkage between VerbNet and other resources is also referred to.

Framenet

FrameNet is a computational lexicography project that extracts information about the linked semantic and syntactic properties of English words from large electronic text corpora, using both manual and automatic procedures. The name 'FrameNet', inspired by 'WordNet', reflects the fact that the project is based on the theory of Frame Semantics, and that it is concerned with networks of meaning in which words participate (Fillmore, Johnson, & Petruck, 2003)

The basic idea is that one cannot understand the meaning of a single word without access to all the essential knowledge that relates to that word. For example, one would not be able to understand the word "sell" without knowing anything about the situation of commercial transfer, which also involves, among other things, a seller, a buyer, goods, money, the relation between the money and the goods, the relations between the seller and the goods and the money, the relation between the buyer and the goods and the money and so on.

Thus, a word activates, or evokes, a frame of semantic knowledge relating to the specific concept it refers to (or highlights, in frame semantic terminology). A semantic frame is defined as a coherent structure of related concepts that are related such that without knowledge of all of them, one does not have complete knowledge of one of the either, and are in that sense types of gestalt. Frames are based on recurring experiences. So the commercial transaction frame is based on recurring experiences of commercial transaction.

Words not only highlight individual concepts, but also specify a certain perspective in which the frame is viewed. For example "sell" views the situation from the perspective of the seller and "buy" from the perspective of the buyer. This, according to Fillmore, explains the observed asymmetries in many lexical relations (Wikipedia, 2014).

A lexical unit (LU) is a pairing of a word with a meaning. Typically, each sense of a polysemous word belongs to a different semantic frame, a script-like conceptual structure describing a particular type of situation, object, or event and the participants and props involved in it. For example, the Apply_heat frame describes a common situation involving a Cook, some Food, and a Heating_Instrument, and is evoked by words such as *bake, blanch, boil, broil, brown, simmer, steam*, etc. These are frame elements (FEs) and the frame-evoking words are LUs in the Apply_heat frame. Some frames are more abstract, such as Change_position_on_a_scale, evoked by LUs such as *decline, decrease, gain, plummet, rise*, etc., with FEs such as Item, Attribute, Initial_value and Final_value.

Framenet contains, to date (Framenet, 2012), more than 10,000 word senses and more than 170,000 manually annotated sentences. It includes more than 12,600 lexical units, more than 8,100 of which are fully annotated, in more than 1,100 semantic frames.

In addition to LUs, FE's and the relationships described above, FrameNet also defines relationships between frames (i.e., inheritance, etc.) as well as links between frame elements.

ALTERNATIVE MODELS FOR ONTOLOGY LEARNING

Can Ontology Learning Profit from Linguistic Modelling?

The approaches and methods reviewed above stem mainly from Cimiano's Ontology Learning Layer Cake model (Cimiano, 2006). That is, there is consensus about the fact that first one has to gather terms (and probably also synonyms), then concepts, and finally extract relations (taxonomic for all the systems, with some of the systems and approaches aiming also at non-taxonomic relations, with a variable degree of success). To conclude, few systems also cross the reasoning threshold. Some of the methods are purely statistic; most of them use a mixture of statistical, linguistic and Natural Language Processing (NLP) methods, with Statistics taking an important role. The reason for this may be based on Brants (2003) conjecture. Brants argues that NLP contribution to Information Retrieval related tasks is rather ineffective.

This is the place to ask whether this is the only way to proceed. We ask two questions:

- Would it be possible to start, for example, by gathering relations (any relation, not necessarily taxonomic) and then proceed to the other layers mentioned in the ontology layer cake?
- If we want to store knowledge in RDF or RDFS is there any requirement that the order should respect the ontology layer cake order?

Another point worth mentioning is that even the linguistic or NLP based methods may rely on corpora as the basis for their analysis. It is said that the most promising trend is to look for the web as the corpus of choice due to its extent and coverage. And this is where we must ask a second question:

- As we are dealing with a specific subject – Ontology Learning – would it be appropriate to deal with text in a purely linguistic, even linguistic-theoretical manner? In other words, do we have to recur to corpora, or can we use language modeling to obtain results?

The answer to the questions above is based on our analysis of English language structure. English is the language of choice because many of the texts that we would like to use towards Ontology Learning are in English (even though an ontology, at least a formal one, should be language neutral).

Extracting Semantic Representation from Text

Many Psycholinguistics and Neurolinguistics researchers looked at how humans gather information from text (see for example Caplan, 2003). It is rather consensual that humans gather information from text at the sentence level or even at the clause level, and not at the document (or corpus) level. Thus, extracting the semantic payload of text would ideally include deep parsing, semantic labeling of the text and a process of knowledge accumulation. From a practical point of view we may not – yet – be able to follow this path. To overcome these limitations, researchers apply practical approaches based on heuristics and partial methods.

The literature shows several attempts to gather information from text at the sentence level. The model proposed by Chen and Wu (2005) makes extensive use of FrameNet (Fillmore, 1976). A semantic frame can be thought of as a concept with a script. It is used to describe an object, state or event. Chen and Wu avoid the need to deep-parse the sentences forming the text by using Framenet:

Given a tagged sentence as input, the syntactic parser produces a phrase-structure tree as output. The semantic role-labeling task can identify the semantic relationships, or semantic roles, filled by constituents of a sentence within a semantic frame based on the syntactic parsing tree. The whole process will generate the syntactic-semantic mapping structure.

Chaumartin (2005) presents another attempt to tackle the semantic representation issues. Instead of using Framenet, the lexical-semantic transition uses VerbNet (Kipper Schuler, 2005). Antelope (Chaumartin, 2008) is an implementation of Chaumartin's work.

Both methods (Chen & Wu (2005), Chaumartin (2005)) deal with text at the sentence level. Chen does not provide a tool to showcase the capabilities of his approach, except for an example on the paper: *"They had to journey from Heathrow to Edinburgh by overnight coach. ".* The example is assigned Framenet's frame *Travel* with all its elements (traveler, source and goal).

Chaumartin presents a full-fledged toolbox to test the capabilities of his approach. The system includes an example. The result is a clear semantic representation of the sentence in terms of VerbNet classes and all the accompanying constraints. The representation includes all the semantic details necessary to assess the situation and allow for higher order activities such as question answering, reasoning and maybe automatic translation. Yet, for other sentences results are not satisfactory, as in *"Most of these therapeutic agents require intracellular uptake for their therapeutic effect because their site of action is within the cell"* or *"Here is a word w which is the head word of a constituent in the sentence and is not recognized by the traditional method when finding its associated concept"*. The examples above yield no result (i.e., no VerbNet class is recognized and therefore no semantic representation is extracted). One of the reasons that may lead the systems above to fail to discover the semantic contents of complex or compound sentences is that such a sentence structure requires more than one frame or verb class to be found. The internals of Antelope may require too many computations for such sentences. As a result, an acceptable coverage of multi-frame or multi-verb sentences may be beyond the reach of Antelope. In order to improve the ability to extract the semantic content from text (and obtain a semantic representation), it seems necessary to look deeper into the structure of the language.

From Clauses or Subsentences to RDF Triples and RDFS

As mentioned before, LGSWE (Biber, 1999) defines a clause as a unit structured around a verb phrase. The lexical verb in the verb phrase denotes an action (drive, run, shout, etc.) or a state (know, seem, resemble, etc.). The verb phrase appears with one or more elements denoting the participants involved in the action, state, etc. (agent, affected, recipient, etc.), the attendant circumstances (time, place, manner, etc.), the relationship of the clause to the surrounding structures, etc. Together with the verb phrase, these are the clause elements. The clause elements are realized by phrases or by embedded clauses. A clause may be divided into two main parts: a subject and a predicate. The subject is generally a nominal part, while the predicate is mainly a verbal nucleus. Preisler (1997) states that a clause contains the constituents Subject, Verbal, Complement and Adverbial, all or some of them. Rank shifting adds complexity to the subject. In this context, rankshifted clauses are called subclauses, while non-rankshifted clauses are called main clauses.

Clauses appearing together in a larger unit (generally sentences, but possibly phrases in the event of a rank-shifted clause) are linked by structural links, the principal types being *coordinators*, *subordinators* and *wh-words*. Coordinators create coordinated clauses. On the other hand, *subordinators* and *wh-words* create embedded clauses.

Subsentences, the concept introduced by Browarnik and Maimon (2012) sometimes overlap with clauses. Yet, subsentences keep the construct simpler because of the restriction to the number of verbal constructs (VC) per subsentence.

The above definitions give as a clue as to the possibility of representing knowledge extracted by linguistic modelling by using RDF constructs, e.g., a RDF triple and a clause or a subsentence seem to represent entities and relationships. In other words, knowledge extracted from a clause or a subsentence can be represented by a RDF triple. Generally a RDF triple is defined by a RDF scheme. In our case, where we start from knowledge extracted from a clause or a subsentence to obtain a RDF triple, the RDF scheme (or RDFS) should be obtained from a generalization of the RDF triples obtained, in a bottom-up fashion.

Statistical Methods vs. Linguistic-Based Methods

Most methods for Natural Language Processing (NLP), especially the methods used for Ontology Learning, rely on Statistics. To mention only the most prominent Ontology Learning systems, we see that:

- ASIUM uses agglomerative clustering for taxonomy relations discovery
- Text-To-Onto uses agglomerative clustering, hypernyms from WordNet and lexico-syntactic patterns for taxonomic relation extraction. Non-taxonomic relations are extracted using association rule mining
- In TextStorm/Clouds both taxonomic and non-taxonomic relations are obtained using part of speech tagging using WordNet, syntactic structure analysis and anaphora resolution
- Syndikate implements semantic templates and domain knowledge for relations extraction

- OntoLearn's relation extraction relies on hypernyms from WordNet (relations extracted are only taxonomic)
- CRCTOL does relation extraction (taxonomic and non-taxonomic) using lexico-syntactic patterns and syntactic structure analysis
- OntoGain applies aglomerative clustering and formal concept analysis to extract taxonomic relations and Association rule mining for non-taxonomic relations

Moreover, for most of the reviewed Ontology Learning methods and systems even the term and concept layers (stemming from Cimiano's Ontology Learning Layer Cake model) are extracted using statistical methods.

The linguistic modelling approach for Ontology Learning from text is based on the following facts:

- An ontology can be represented by RDF triples.
- RDF triples are subject-predicate-object expressions.
- Clauses are components of sentences and include a subject, a verbal part, a complement and an adverbial part, all or some of them. Subsentences are a textual passage built around one verbal construct.
- RDF triples are equivalent to clauses or subsentences.

Therefore, a RDF triple can be constructed from a clause or a subsentence. But how does one extract the triple from a clause? And how does one find a clause from a sentence?

Clause boundary detection (or CBD) was addressed by Abney (1996), Ejerhed (1996) and others. There is evidence that the problem was satisfactorily solved using diverse methods ranging from finite state automata to probabilistic methods, with close to linear time complexity. Therefore we can say that it is possible to obtain clauses from sentences. Subsentence detection was addressed by Browarnik and Maimon (2012) showing that subsentences can be obtained with the $O(1)$ time complexity.

Chaumartin (2005) shows how to extract a kind of role based frame from a sentence, even though, as we indicated above, working at the sentence level has succeeded only partially.

Yet, statistical methods are very useful and should by no means be neglected. Constructing resources such as POS taggers, WordNet, VerbNet or FrameNet do profit from statistical methods. Based on these resources one can try to create a somehow theoretical linguistic model that would not recur to corpora in order to extract clauses or subsentences from sentences, and in turn convert it into RDF triples, thus learning an ontology with no – direct – use of corpora.

Conclusions from Previous Work

At the beginning of this section we asked three questions:

- Would it be possible to start, for example, by gathering relations (any relation, not necessarily taxonomic) and then proceed to the other layers mentioned in the Ontology Learning Layer Cake model?
- If we want to store knowledge in RDF or RDFS is there any requirement that the order should respect the Ontology Learning Layer Cake order?

- As we are dealing with a specific – Ontology Learning – would it be appropriate to deal with text in a purely linguistic, even linguistic-theoretical manner? In other words, do we have to recur to corpora, or can we use language modeling to obtain results?

After reviewing the structure of the language we deal with (English in our context), the apparent equivalence between RDF and clauses or subsentences, and the differences between statistical and linguistic-based methods, we conclude that a framework for Ontology Learning can be based on linguistic modeling.

Background

Ontology Learning from text converts unstructured information into a structured body of knowledge. It should be achieved at the lowest possible cost. By cost we refer to time complexity and human resources investment. This structured body of knowledge can be formulated, as an example, in RDF or RDFs.

One of the objectives of our work is to show that it is possible to devise an alternative to the Ontology Learning Layer Cake model for Ontology Learning from text. We look at the task with the intention to avoid using (directly) corpora to learn an ontology. We also try to learn ontologies using linguistic modelling, and not making resort to statistical findings, as would be the case if we wanted to learn about the cause-effect relation between two entities on the basis of the number of times the two entities co-occur.

The widely accepted Ontology Learning Layer Cake may well be the result of the decision to tackle Ontology Learning by statistical methods. The Ontology Learning Layer Cake states that first one learns terms. Afterwards come (generally) concepts, proceeding then to taxonomic relations, non-taxonomic relations and finally, when possible, reasoning instruments.

But how does one extract terms or concepts from text that comes without any structure? It seems that one has to recur to corpora. If a word once appeared in text and was identified then one can reuse the results. The vast quantity of text available today makes it possible to argue that almost any word representing a term already appeared in text and therefore the result is assured. Yet, this is only circumstantial and not precise. Once the basic layer has been obtained one proceeds to the subsequent layers, working on the same paradigm that was used for the basic layer.

Our review of Ontology Learning methods has shown results that can be deemed satisfactory, mainly if one takes into account the complexity of the task. The tasks make heavy use of computational resources, yet there is still room (and need) for improvement.

We will depart from this paradigm using the formulations that follow.

The Alternative, Experimental Ontology Learning Framework

We now turn to suggest an alternative framework for Ontology Learning that departs from the Ontology Learning Layer Cake (OLC) paradigm. OLC is, as mentioned above, a bottom-up strategy. We propose a top-down approach as follows:

- Split sentences into clauses or subsentences
- For each clause or subsentence find a verbal class that best matches the clause or subsentence
- Based on the hints given by the pattern of the verbal class (e.g., the VerbNet verb frame) classify the components according to VerbNet thematic roles

- Using WordNet verify selectional restrictions set by the VerbNet verb frame
- Create the resulting frame

Following our analysis of language structure we conclude that a sentence may include one or more clauses or subsentences. A RDF triple has a close relationship to a clause or a subsentence, as shown in our analysis. Therefore, we argue that the first step towards Ontology Learning should be splitting a sentence to obtain basic components. It has been shown that sentence decomposition algorithms using regular expressions achieve very good results (above 90% success).

Chaumartin (2005) introduces a sentence based framework that obtains frames from a sentence. As mentioned before, the fact that Chaumartin's system targets sentences and not clauses or subsentences results in a low rate of success. What is clear, though, is that the same methods applied by Chaumartin to a sentence can be applied to a clause or subsentence. In other words, given a subsentence or clause with a word tagged as a verbal component, it is required to find a pattern out of all the patterns proposed by VerbNet. Chaumartin performs the matching using a Prolog implementation of VerbNet. His choice is based on the features offered by Prolog, such as unification. The system assigns thematic roles and selectional restrictions to the components. When more than one frame is suitable the systems picks the frame matching the highest number of thematic roles. The following example shows the procedure for the (single-clause) sentence *"The cultivator eliminated the beetles with pesticide"* (taken from Chaumartin, 2005).

There are two suitable verb classes (murder and remove). Together with the thematic roles it becomes four possible interpretations:

1. "murder#1" the cultivator$_{(Agent)}$ eliminated$_{(Verb)}$ the beetles$_{(Patient)}$ with pesticide$_{(Instrument)}$ (SR: cultivator$_{(animate+concrete)}$ beetles$_{(animate)}$)
2. "remove#1" the cultivator$_{(Agent)}$ eliminated$_{(Verb)}$ the beetles$_{(Theme)}$ with pesticide (SR: cultivator$_{(internal\ control)}$)
3. "murder#2" the cultivator$_{(Agent)}$ eliminated$_{(Verb)}$ the beetles$_{(Patient)}$ with pesticide (SR: cultivator$_{(animate+concrete)}$ beetles$_{(animate)}$)
4. "remove#2" the cultivator$_{(Agent)}$ eliminated$_{(Verb)}$ the beetles$_{(Theme)}$ with pesticide (SR: cultivator$_{(internal\_control)}$)

Based on the hypothesis that the likelihood of a semantic interpretation is proportional to the number of identified thematic roles murder#1 is chosen, thus identifying the Agent as "the cultivator", the Patient as "the beetles" and the Instrument as " pesticide". As a reference, VerbNet specifies the frame as shown in Table 3.

The last row in Table 3 specifies semantic information that can be used for reasoning. For instance, if a sentence is classified as corresponding to this frame then it can be derived that the patient was alive before the event and not alive after the event.

The Alternative Framework in Terms of Subsentences

From this point onward we will refer to subsentences. While it is possible to formulate the algorithm in term of clauses, subsentences are linear in nature and do not include nesting or embedding and therefore are simpler.

Table 3. Murder#1

NP V NP PP.instrument	
example	"Caesar killed Brutus with a knife."
syntax	Agent V Patient {with} Instrument
semantics	cause(Agent, E) alive(start(E), Patient) not(alive(result(E), Patient)) use(during(E), Agent, Instrument)

In the preprocess step sequences of successive verbs are reduced to a single "verbal token". As an example, the input *"The/DT words/NNS have/VBP been/VBN spoken/VBN"* becomes *"The/DT words/ NNS {have/VBP_been/VBN_spoken/VBN}/VC"* (VC stands for "verbal construct").

The algorithm follows:

For each sentence:

First step: split sentence into subsentences

Input: single sentence

Process: split sentence

Output: set of subsentences

Second step: get verbal frame

Input: subsentences, VerbNet, WordNet

Process: For each subsentence:

If there is no verbal component in the subsentence

Skip the following steps and go back to the next subsentence.

Else

Using each of the verbal words that form the verbal component find all verbal classes V' in VerbNet with any of the words (transformed to infinitive) included in the verbal construct in the list of member verbs.

Create an empty list of matches.

For each verbal class v'∈ V'

Match the subsentence components to the verbal class structure. To this end use the syntactic frame sf contained in the verbal class and the part of speech assigned to each component of the subsentence.

Evaluate the number of thematic roles matched. This number is dictated by the verbal class frame chosen.

For every word (or words) with a thematic role assignment check if the concept (represented by the word - or words - that were assigned the thematic role) complies with the selectional restrictions on these thematic roles. To this end look for the word in the subsentence at the relevant part of Wordnet (using the part of speech of the word).

If the selectional restriction is violated

Drop the current match.

Else

Add the match with all the findings (i.e., number and detail of thematic roles matched) to the list of results.

End

Output: Three possible outcomes:

1. No match – no addition to the ontology learning task
2. One match with highest number of thematic roles assigned – add the frame to the ontology learning task
3. More than one match with highest number of thematic roles assigned – not decidable. Report for further research.

Time Complexity of the Proposed Framework

In order to evaluate the complexity of the proposed algorithm we briefly underline the algorithm and comment on the complexity of every subtask.

1. Pre-process sentence – The preprocessing step consists of checking the input sentence against a predefined set of rules. Currently the set contains 45 rules. Therefore the complexity of the pre-processing step is $O(1)$.
2. Split sentence into subsentence – The time complexity is $O(1)$ with a constant overhead that may be high but bound. This complexity is explained as follows:
   a. Sigurd, Eeg-Olofsson, and Van Weijer (2004) show that sentence length has a predicted behavior (as function of L, the number of words) of $f_{exp} = 1.1 * L^1 * 0.90L$. It follows that the majority of sentences have 50 words or less. The number of sentences longer than 51 words decreases asymptotically. Elia (2009) writes that the average length of a sentence found in resources such as Britannica and Wikipedia is less than 23 words. LGSWE (Biber, 1999) suggests, based on the analysis of its annotated corpus, that it would be unusual to find a sentence

with more than three levels of embedding or nesting in written, academic text. Some of the registers, i.e. CONV or NEWS, show even lower levels of embedding. **Therefore we assume that the length of a sentence is bound and lower than a given arbitrary constant.**

    b.   Every word in a sentence is checked at least once, by at most the whole set of rules (currently 20 rules),

    c.   If a rule matches, the word is processed again against at most 20 rules.

    d.   The number of fragments is bound, as is the number of words in a sentence – for any practical purpose. Therefore a constant c can be found as an upper bound for the number of fragments, from which stems the maximum number of passes.

3.   For each subsentence do:

    a.   Find all verbal classes that match (all or part of) the verbal construct (in infinitive form) in the subsentence. To estimate this subtask we will assume the infinitive form is given. The process of finding the verbal forms that appear in the subsentence on every possible verbal class in VerbNet requires a scan of all verbs in all verbal classes. The number of verbs is 6272. The number of classes and subclasses is 472. This task is time consuming, yet it is not influenced by the structure of the subsentence. In other words, the complexity is $O(1)$, even though the constant associated with it may be bigger than usual.

    b.   For each verbal class found do:

    For every syntactic frame in the verbal class do:

        i.   Match the thematic roles in the syntactic frame to the components of the subsentence

        ii.   Count number of thematic roles matched

        iii.   Check if word matching thematic role complies with given selectional restriction. If not compliant - drop

        iv.   Add match to list of candidates

This action takes as input a given syntax frame and a set of POS-tagged words. To check the match between the syntactic frame and the set of words one must, at most, check every word to every thematic role. Both the number of thematic roles and words in the subsentence are bound. Moreover, we can argue that the worst case would be a sentence with a single subsentence, and as seen before, the length of a sentence, l, is bound. The worst case can safely be assessed as being proportional to l^2. The value l is bound and therefore we have another case of $O(1)$, probably with a high value of the constant value involved. It is worth noting that these steps were performed by Chaumartin (2005) in his Antelope framework. One of the remarks in Chaumartin's paper is that the framework has limitations related to the structure of the sentences being considered. The framework proposed in this chapter overcomes these difficulties.

    c.   Choose best match. If single match proceed. Else drop.

All the steps in the algorithm are $O(1)$. The overall complexity of the algorithm requires that we estimate the number of verbal classes that are matched by a subsentence and the number of syntactic frames by verbal class. We adopt the following assumptions:

- We assume that the number of verbal classes matched by the verbal words in a subsentence is low. It is certainly bound.
- We assume that the number of syntactic frames per verbal frame is lower than 10. This assumption can be easily verified.

Under these assumptions the overall complexity of the algorithm is $O(1)$ for every sentence. If the input has n sentences then the time complexity of the whole task is $O(n)$.

CONCLUSION AND FURTHER RESEARCH

The Suggested Framework Compared to OLC Methods

The comparison between the suggested linguistic modeling framework and Ontology Layer Cake based methods requires an evaluation of features found in the different approaches.

OLC Methods

OLC methods, as mentioned above, perform some or all of the following tasks:

- Extracting terms from the text
- Obtaining concepts on the basis of the terms
- Learning taxonomic relations
- Learning non-taxonomic relations

Most OLC methods are based on corpora analysis. To this end a corpus is obtained and split into a training set and a test set. In order to obtain statistically significant results OLC methods recur to big corpora. This need results in resource intensive computations.

Besides resource consumption, the adequacy of the corpus used to the subject being learned is not granted. Moreover, the statistical methods may suffer from flaws such as over fitting.

Most modern methods – at least those analyzed in this chapter – are largely unsupervised. Unsupervised methods normally require less human intervention than supervised or rule based methods. When compared to rule based methods, unsupervised methods are also more robust - a rule based method may become unusable if the rules of the problem change. Statistical or machine learning methods are more stable, possibly due to the fact that the size of the corpora being used makes the results harder to contradict.

The methods are evaluated using recall and precision measures. The harmonic mean of any single step of any OLC method will not be higher than .95. The fact that every step build on the previous step results in an upper bound of .81 for any OLC method. This figure is based on the optimistic assumption of every single step having an harmonic mean (F_1 measure) of .95. In many cases F_1 is lower and carries a lower overall result. Our review showed that a four step method will probably be below 0.5.

OLC methods use statistical features found in text, such as co-occurrence of words or patterns obtained from a training set, either using supervised or unsupervised methods. It is thus clear that the relations extracted are often the result of circumstantial co-occurrences of words and do not necessarily reflect real relationships.

The fact that the methods are not language-specific makes it possible to port the methods to other languages.

The Suggested Framework

The framework relies on the following resources:

- Part-of-speech taggers
- WordNet
- VerbNet

There is a wide choice of part of speech (POS) taggers, such as the Brill POS tagger, the Link Grammar Parser, Maximum Entropy POS taggers, Hidden Markov Model POS taggers and more. Some of these taggers use corpora to classify the parts of speech. WordNet and VerbNet were built and are maintained using human resources.

Except for the above resources, the suggested framework does not make resort to any additional external resource. It does not use corpora. Instead, it is the result of thoroughly examining the structure of English sentences.

Every subsentence is converted into a RDF graph (or an equivalent set of RDF triples). Therefore, there is a clear link between a RDF graph and the subsentence, allowing for back and forth references, useful for the evaluation of the algorithm. If an assertion (a RDF graph) is found erroneous, it is possible to trace back how the graph was obtained and to correct it.

This framework efficiency cannot be measured by recall or precision in the same way used to measure OLC methods. A subsentence is translated into a RDF graph. It may be right or wrong (and it can be corrected). Yet, if a subsentence is present, a RDF graph will be created. This would mean a 100% recall in any case. This makes recall trivial. Precision in this context would measure how good subsentences are translated into RDF graphs. The option to trace back translations adds correction capabilities in a way that is not achievable for OLC methods.

The stability of the framework is a function of English sentence structure stability. We argue that English structure remains largely unchanged over time. There is a constant addition of lexical words (such as nouns and verbs), but the core English structure, reflected in (and implemented by) function words, seldom changes.

The framework is language-specific. While an RDF triple is language neutral, obtaining it from a sentence in languages other than English requires the framework to be adapted to every language. After all, it builds on the insight obtained into the structure of a given language (English in our case). In other words, Part-of-speech algorithms, WordNet and VerbNet have to be available for the target language, and the subsentence method has to be re-engineered.

Open and Unresolved Issues of the Alternative Framework

The suggested framework is one of the possible options to tackle Ontology Learning from text. Deep parsing coupled with a mechanism to transform the parsed sentence into RDF graphs could be suitable as well.

There are many developments necessary to enhance the framework and make it more robust.

The framework currently uses subsentences, yet it could be adapted to use clauses instead. While the algorithm to automatically detect subsentences is linear and splits sentences into simple structures that do not include nesting or embedding, using clauses may be appropriate because of the body of knowledge accumulated around clauses.

The framework does not link, at this stage, between subsentences. For instance, in the last example,

[Most of these therapeutic agents require intracellular uptake for their therapeutic effect] because [their site of action is within the cell]

the two subsentences are linked by a causal link, *because*. The system finds two RDF graphs, one per subsentence. In fact, there is an additional graph, stating that subsentence 1 occurs *because* subsentence 2. At this stage the framework does not deal with this feature that would require being able to link between RDF graphs. Yet, it is essential to answer this question and should be addressed.

The framework does not deal with elliptic references or anaphora resolution, an issue that will enhance the knowledge extracted from text.

The framework aims at obtaining RDF graphs. Obtaining RDFS, instead, requires a further layer to generalize or make abstractions about the RDF graphs. This task requires further research. We can point at the possibility of generalizing RDF graphs such as the one obtained from *"the cultivator eliminated the beetles with pesticide"*. Using WordNet's hypernymy we can find facts about 'the cultivator', 'the beetles' and 'pesticide'. Using these features we could, for instance, obtain a pattern of higher abstraction level such as *'persons eliminate insects with chemical substances'*.

Yet, it is clear that further research is needed for this issue.

CONCLUSION

Ontology Learning from text using OLC based methods does not profit from the fact that the text used is well-formed. OLC based methods harmonic mean is bound by its sequential, cascading nature. No correcting mechanism can be implemented because there is no linkage between a given input and the output.

An Ontology Learning framework based on language structure can be devised to overcome most of these shortcomings.

REFERENCES

Abney, S. (1996). Partial parsing via finite-state cascades. *Nat. Lang. Eng. 2*(4), 337-344. doi:.10.1017/S1351324997001599

Agrawal, R., Imieliński, T., & Swami, A. (1993). Mining association rules between sets of items in large databases. [ACM.]. *SIGMOD Record, 22*(2), 207–216. doi:10.1145/170036.170072

Baroni, M., & Bernardini, S. (2004). BootCaT: Bootstrapping corpora and terms from the web. In *Proceedings of LREC, 4*.

Berners-Lee, T., Hendler, J., & Lassila, O. (2001). The semantic web. *Scientific American, 284*(5), 28–37. doi:10.1038/scientificamerican0501-34 PMID:11341160

Biber, D., Johansson, S., Leech, G., Conrad, S., & Finegan, E. (1999). *Longman Grammar of Spoken and Written English*. Longman Publications Group.

Bourigault, D., & Jacquemin, C. (1999). Term extraction+ term clustering: An integrated platform for computer-aided terminology. In *Proceedings of the ninth conference on European chapter of the Association for Computational Linguistics* (pp. 15-22). Association for Computational Linguistics. doi:10.3115/977035.977039

Brants, T. (2003). Natural Language Processing in Information Retrieval. In B. Decadt, V. Hoste, & G. De Pauw (Eds.)(2003, December 19), Computational Linguistics in the Netherlands. Centre for Dutch Language and Speech, University of Antwerp.

Browarnik, A., et al. (2009, June 2-5). Creation of a critical and commented database on the health, safety and environmental impact of nanoparticles – challenges and objectives. *Presentation at the NHECD networking meeting on the occasion of EuroNanoForum*. Prague. Retrieved from http://www.nhecd-fp7.eu

Browarnik, A., & Maimon, O. (2012, April). Subsentence Detection with Regular Expressions. *Presented at the XXX AESLA International Conference*. Lleida.

Buitelaar, P., Cimiano, P., Grobelnik, M., & Sintek, M. (2005, October 3). Ontology Learning from Text In *European Conference on Machine Learning*. Porto, Portugal.

Buitelaar, P., Cimiano, P., & Magnini, B. (2005). Ontology Learning from Texts: An Overview. In P. Buitelaar, P. Cimiano, & B. Magnini. *Ontology Learning from Text: Methods, Evaluation and Applications*. In *Frontiers in Artificial Intelligence and Applications, 123*. IOS Press.

Caplan, D. (2003). Neurolinguistics. In *The Handbook of Linguistics*. UK: Blackwell Publishing. doi:10.1002/9780470756409.ch24

Chaumartin, F. R. (2005). *Conception et réalisation d'une interface syntaxe / sémantique utilisant des ressources de large couverture en langue anglaise. Master de Recherche en Linguistique et Informatique* (in French).

Chaumartin, F. R. (2008). Antelope: Une plate-forme industrielle de traitement linguistique. *TAL, 49*(2), 1–10.

Chen, E., & Wu, G. (2005). *An Ontology Learning Method Enhanced by Frame Semantics* (pp. 374–382). ISM.

Ciaramita, M., Gangemi, A., Ratsch, E., Šarić, J., & Rojas, I. (2008). Unsupervised learning of semantic relations for molecular biology ontologies. In *Proceeding of the 2008 conference on Ontology Learning and Population: Bridging the Gap between Text and Knowledge* (pp. 91-104).

Cimiano, P. (2006). *Ontology Learning and Population from Text.Algorithms, Evaluation and Applications*. Springer.

Dagan, I., Glickman, O., & Magnini, B. (2006). The PASCAL Recognising Textual Entailment Challenge. *Lecture Notes in Computer Science, 3944*, 177–190. doi:10.1007/11736790_9

Ejerhed, E. I. (1996). Finite state segmentation of discourse into clauses. *Natural Language Engineering*, *2*(4), 355–364. doi:10.1017/S1351324997001629

Elia, A. (2009). Quantitative Data and Graphics on Lexical Specificity and Index of Readability: The Case of Wikipedia. Revista Electronica de Linguistica aplicada, 8, 248-271.

Etzioni, O., Banko, M., Soderland, S., & Weld, D. S. (2008). Open information extraction from the web. *Communications of the ACM*, *51*(12), 68–74. doi:10.1145/1409360.1409378

Etzioni, O., Cafarella, M. J., Downey, D., Kok, S., Popescu, A.-M., Shaked, T., et al. (2004). Web-scale information extraction. Proceedings of KnowItAll. Retrieved from http://portal.acm.org/ft_gateway.cf m?id=988687&type=pdf&coll=&dl=ACM&CFID=15151515&CFTOKEN=6184618

Faure, D., & Nedellec, C. (1999). Knowledge acquisition of predicate argument structures from technical texts using machine learning. In *The system ASIUM* (pp. 329–334). Knowledge Acquisition, Modeling and Management. doi:10.1007/3-540-48775-1_22

Feldman, R., & Sanger, J. (2007). *Text Mining Handbook: Advanced Approaches in Analyzing Unstructured Data*. Cambridge University Press.

Fellbaum, C. (Ed.). (1998). *WordNet: An Electronic Lexical Database*. Cambridge: MIT Press.

Fillmore, C. J. (1976). Frame semantics and the nature of language. *Annals of the New York Academy of Sciences*, *280*(1 Origins and E), 20–32. doi:10.1111/j.1749-6632.1976.tb25467.x

Fillmore, C. J., Johnson, C. R., & Petruck, M. R. (2003). Background to framenet. *International journal of lexicography, 16*(3), 235-250.

Framenet. (2012). Current Project Status. Retrieved from https://framenet.icsi.berkeley.edu/fndrupal/current_status

GeoNames.org. (n.d.). *GeoNames*. Retrieved from http://www.geonames.org/

Gómez-Pérez, A., & Manzano-Macho, D. (Eds.). (2003). *Deliverable 1.5: A Survey of Ontology Learning Methods and Tools, OntoWeb deliverable*. Retrieved from http://www.sti-innsbruck.at/fileadmin/documents/deliverables/Ontoweb/D1.5.pdf

Goodnough, A. (2013). Applicants Find Health Website Is Improving, but Not Fast Enough. *The New York Times*. Retrieved from http://www.nytimes.com/2013/11/21/us/politics/applicants-find-health-website-is-improving-but-not-fast-enough.html?hp&_r=0

Gruber, T. R. (1993). A Translation Approach to Portable Ontology Specifications. *Knowledge Acquisition, 5*(2), 199–220. doi:10.1006/knac.1993.1008

Hahn, U., Romacker, M., & Schulz, S. (2000). MedSynDiKATe – design considerations for an ontology-based medical text understanding system. In *Proceedings of the AMIA Symposium* (p. 330). American Medical Informatics Association.

Harris, Z. (1968). *Mathematical Structures of Language*. John Wiley & Sons.

Hearst, M. A. (1992). Automatic acquisition of hyponyms from large text corpora. In *Proceedings of the 14th conference on Computational linguistics-Volume 2* (pp. 539-545). doi:10.3115/992133.992154

Hitzler, P., Krotzsch, M., & Rudolph, S. (2009). Knowledge Representation for the Semantic Web. In KI 2009.

Hoffart, J., Suchanek, F. M., Berberich, K., & Weikum, G. (2012). YAGO2: A spatially and temporally enhanced knowledge base from Wikipedia. *Artificial Intelligence, 194*, 28–61. doi:10.1016/j. artint.2012.06.001

Intentional. (n. d.). *Dictionary.com Unabridged*. Retrieved from [[REMOVED HYPERLINK FIELD] http://dictionary.reference.com/browse/intentional

Jones, G. M., Horning, L. E., & Morrow, J. D. (1922). *A High School English Grammar*. Toronto, London: J. M Dent & Sons.

Kietz, J. U., Maedche, A., & Volz, R. (2000). A method for semi-automatic ontology acquisition from a corporate intranet. In Workshop Ontologies and text.

Kipper Schuler, K. (2005). *VerbNet – a broad-coverage, comprehensive verb lexicon* [PhD thesis]. University of Pennsylvania. Retrieved from http://verbs.colorado.edu/~kipper/Papers/dissertation.pdf

Kozakov, L., Park, Y., Fin, T., Drissi, Y., Doganata, Y., & Cofino, T. (2004). Glossary extraction and utilization in the information search and delivery system for IBM Technical Support. *IBM Systems Journal, 43*(3), 546–563. doi:10.1147/sj.433.0546

Levin, B. (1993). *English Verb Classes and Alternation, A Preliminary Investigation*. The University of Chicago Press.

Lin, D., & Pantel, P. (2001). DIRT – Discovery of Inference Rules from Text. In *Proceedings of the ACM SIGKDD Conference on Knowledge Discovery and Data Mining 2001* (pp. 323-328). doi:10.1145/502512.502559

Liu, Q., Xu, K., Zhang, L., Wang, H., Yu, Y., & Pan, Y. (2008). Catriple: Extracting triples from Wikipedia categories. In The Semantic Web (pp. 330-344).

Maedche, A., & Staab, S. (2000). Discovering conceptual relations from text. In W. Horn (Ed.), *Proceedings of the 14th European Conference on Artificial Intelligence (ECAI'2000)*.

Maedche, A., & Staab, S. (2003). Ontology Learning. In S. Staab & R. Studer (Eds.), *Handbook on Ontologies in Information Systems*. Springer.

Masolo, C., Borgo, S., Gangemi, A., Guarino, N., & Oltramari, A. (2003). *WonderWeb Deliverable D18*. Ontology Library.

Massey, L., & Wong, W. (2011). A cognitive-based approach to identify topics in text using the Web as a knowledge source. In *Ontology Learning and Knowledge Discovery Using the Web*. Challenges and Recent Advances. doi:10.4018/978-1-60960-625-1.ch004

Miller, G. A., Beckwith, R., Fellbaum, C., Gross, D., & Miller, K. J. (1990). Introduction to WordNet: An On-line Lexical Database. *International Journal of Lexicography, 3*(4), 235–244. doi:10.1093/ijl/3.4.235

Mintz, M., Bills, S., Snow, R., & Jurafsky, D. (2009). Distant supervision for relation extraction without labeled data. In *Proceedings of the Joint Conference of the 47th Annual Meeting of the ACL and the 4th International Joint Conference on Natural Language Processing of the AFNLP: Volume 2-Volume 2* (pp. 1003-1011). Association for Computational Linguistics. doi:10.3115/1690219.1690287

Navigli, R., & Velardi, P. (2004). Learning Domain Ontologies from Document Warehouses and Dedicated Websites. *Computational Linguistics*, *30*(2), 151–179. doi:10.1162/089120104323093276

Niles, I., & Pease, A. (2001). Towards a standard upper ontology. In *Proceedings of the international Conference on Formal ontology in information Systems* - Volume 2001, Ogunquit, Maine, USA, October 17-19, 2001 (pp. 2-9). New York, NY: ACM Press.

NIST. (n. d.). *Automatic Content Extraction*. Retrieved from http://www.itl.nist.gov/iad/894.01/tests/ace/

Pascal. (n. d.) *About Pascal*. Retrieved from http://www.pascal-network.org/

Patel-Schneider, P. F., & Horrocks, I. (2004). *OWL Web Ontology Language Semantics and Abstract Syntax: Section 2. Abstract Syntax*. Retrieved from http://www.w3.org/TR/2004/REC-owl-semantics-20040210/syntax.html

Pei, M., Nakayama, K., Hara, T., & Nishio, S. (2008). Constructing a global ontology by concept mapping using wikipedia thesaurus. In Advanced Information Networking and Applications-Workshops, 2008. AINAW 2008 (pp. 1205-1210). doi:10.1109/WAINA.2008.117

Preisler, B. (1997). *A Handbook of English Grammar on Functional Principles*. Aarhus University Press.

Resource Description Framework (RDF) Model and Syntax Specification. (1999). *W3C*. Retrieved from http://www.w3.org/TR/PR-rdf-syntax/

Rosenfeld, B., & Feldman, R. (2006). URES: an unsupervised web relation extraction system. In *Proceedings of the COLING/ACL on Main conference poster sessions* (pp. 667-674). Association for Computational Linguistics. doi:10.3115/1273073.1273159

Ruiz-Casado, M., Alfonseca, E., & Castells, P. (2005). Automatic Extraction of Semantic Relationships for WordNet by means of Pattern Learning from Wikipedia. In *10th International Conference on Application of Natural Language to Information Systems (NLDB 2005)*. Alicante, Spain, June 2005. Lecture Notes in Computer Science, 3513, 67-79. Springer Verlag. doi:10.1007/11428817_7

Sánchez, D., & Moreno, A. (2008). Learning non-taxonomic relationships from web documents for domain ontology construction. *Data & Knowledge Engineering*, *64*(3), 600–623. doi:10.1016/j.datak.2007.10.001

Sanderson, M., & Croft, B. (1999). Deriving concept hierarchies from text. In Research and Development in Information Retrieval (pp. 206–213). doi:10.1145/312624.312679

Sclano, F., & Velardi, P. (2007). TermExtractor: a Web Application to Learn the Shared Terminology of Emergent Web Communities. In *Proc. of the 3rd International Conference on Interoperability for Enterprise Software and Applications (I-ESA 2007)*. Funchal (Madeira Island), Portugal, March 28–30th, 2007. doi:10.1007/978-1-84628-858-6_32

Shah, P., Schneider, D., Matuszek, C., Kahlert, R. C., Aldag, B., Baxter, D., et al. (2006). Automatic Population of Cyc: Extracting Information about Named-entities from the Web. In *Proceedings FLAIRS 2006* (pp. 153-158). Melbourne Beach, Florida May 11-13, 2006.

Shapiro, E. Y., & Sterling, L. (1994). *The art of Prolog: advanced programming techniques.* Cambridge, Mass: MIT Press.

Sigurd, B., Eeg-Olofsson, M., & Van Weijer, J. (2004). Word length, sentence length and frequency – Zipf revisited. *Studia Linguistica, 58*(1), 37–52. doi:10.1111/j.0039-3193.2004.00109.x

SIL. (n. d.). *SIL*. Retrieved from http://www.sil.org/

Sombatsrisomboon, R., Matsuo, Y., & Ishizuka, M. (2003). Acquisition of hypernyms and hyponyms from the WWW. In *Proceedings of the 2nd International Workshop on Active Mining*.

Sowa, J. F. (1990). Crystallizing theories out of knowledge soup. In Z. W. Ras & M. Zemankova (Eds.), *Intelligent Systems: State of the Art and Future Directions* (pp. 456–487). London: Ellis Horwood Ltd.

Sowa, J. F. (2000). *Knowledge Representation: Logical, Philosophical, and Computational Foundations*. Pacific Grove, CA: Brooks/Cole Publishing.

Sowa, J. F., & Majumdar, A. K. (2003). Task-*Oriented Semantic Interpretation*. Retrieved from http://www.jfsowa.com/pubs/tosi.htm

Specia, L., & Motta, E. (2006). A hybrid approach for relation extraction aimed at the semantic web. In Flexible Query Answering Systems (564-576). doi:10.1007/11766254_48

Studer, R., Benjamins, V. R., & Fensel, D. (1998). Knowledge engineering: Principles and methods. *Data & Knowledge Engineering, 25*(1), 161–197. doi:10.1016/S0169-023X(97)00056-6

Suchanek, F. M., Kasneci, G., & Weikum, G. (2007). Yago - A Core of Semantic Knowledge, Unifying WordNet and Wikipedia. In *16th international conference on World Wide Web (WWW 2007)*.

Uschold, M., & Gruninger, M. (2004). Ontologies and semantics for seamless connectivity. *SIGMOD Record, 33*(4), 58–64. doi:10.1145/1041410.1041420

Vrandecic, D. (2010). *Ontology Evaluation* [PhD thesis]. KIT, Fakult. Wirtschaftswissenschaften, Karlsruhe.

Weber, N., & Buitelaar, P. (2006). Web-based ontology learning with isolde. In *Proc. of the Workshop on Web Content Mining with Human Language at the International Semantic Web Conference*, (Vol. 11). Athens GA, USA.

Wermter, J., & Hahn, U. (2005). Finding new terminology in very large corpora. In *Proceedings of the 3rd international conference on Knowledge capture* (pp. 137-144). ACM. doi:10.1145/1088622.1088648

Frame semantics (linguistics). (2014). Wikipedia. Retrieved from http://en.wikipedia.org/wiki/Frame_semantics_%28linguistics%29

W3C. (2009). *OWL 2 Web Ontology Language: Document Overview*. Retrieved from http://www.w3.org/TR/2009/REC-owl2-overview-20091027/

Wikipedia. (2015). Sentence (linguistics). Retrieved from http://en.wikipedia.org/wiki/Sentence_(linguistics)

Wong, W., Liu, W., & Bennamoun, M. (2009). A probabilistic framework for automatic term recognition. *Intelligent Data Analysis*, *13*(4), 499–539.

Wong, W., Liu, W., & Bennamoun, M. (2012). Ontology Learning from Text: A Look back and into the Future. [CSUR]. *ACM Computing Surveys*, *44*(4), 20. doi:10.1145/2333112.2333115

Wong, W. Y. (2009). *Learning lightweight ontologies from text across different domains using the web as background knowledge* (Doctoral dissertation, University of Western Australia).

Yeh, J. H., & Yang, N. (2008). Ontology construction based on latent topic extraction in a digital library. In *Digital Libraries* (pp. 93–103). Universal and Ubiquitous Access to Information. doi:10.1007/978-3-540-89533-6_10

Zhang, Z., & Ciravegna, F. (2011). Named entity recognition for ontology population using background knowledge from Wikipedia. In *Ontology Learning and Knowledge Discovery Using the Web: Challenges and Recent Advances*. Hershey: IGI Global. doi:10.4018/978-1-60960-625-1.ch005

KEY TERMS AND DEFINITIONS

Clause: a unit structured around a verb phrase. The lexical verb in the verb phrase denotes an action (drive, run, shout, etc.) or a state (know, seem, resemble, etc.). The verb phrase appears with one or more elements denoting the participants involved in the action, state, etc. (agent, affected, recipient, etc.), the attendant circumstances (time, place, manner, etc.), the relationship of the clause to the surrounding structures, etc. Together with the verb phrase, these are the clause elements. The clause elements are realized by phrases or by embedded clauses. A clause may be divided into two main parts: a subject and a predicate. The subject is generally a nominal part, while the predicate is mainly a verbal nucleus.

Entity-Relationship Diagram: an entity–relationship model or diagram is a data model for describing the data or information aspects of a domain or its process requirements, in an abstract way that lends itself to ultimately being implemented in a database such as a relational database. The main components of ER models are entities (things) and the relationships that can exist among them, and databases.

Ontology Learning Layer Cake Model: A model for Ontology Learning that splits the overall task into sub-tasks or layers, with each layer building on the previous layer. The lower layer obtains terms that contribute towards obtaining concepts. These are used in turn to construct concept hierarchies, relations, relations hierarchies and sometimes axioms.

Ontology Learning: the process of creating the ontology and populating it.

Ontology: a formal, explicit specification of a shared conceptualization. Formal refers to the fact that the ontology should be machine readable (therefore ruling out natural language). Explicit means that the type of concepts used, and the constraints on their use are explicitly defined. Shared reflects the notion that an ontology captures consensual knowledge, that is, it is not private to some individual, but accepted by a group.

RDF: The Resource Description Framework (RDF) is a set of specifications originally designed as a metadata data model. It is generally used as a method for conceptual description or modeling of information. It makes statements about resources (in particular Web resources) in the form of subject-predicate-object expressions. These expressions are known as triples in RDF terminology. The subject denotes the resource, and the predicate denotes traits or aspects of the resource and expresses a relationship between the subject and the object.

Subsentence: A subsentence is a sentence fragment with no more than one verbal construct (VC). A VC is a sequence of one or more verbal words, as in "is/VBZ" or in "may/MD have/VB been/VBN".

VerbNet: a hierarchical verb lexicon with syntactic and semantic information for English verbs, using Levin verb classes to systematically construct lexical entries. It uses verb classes to capture generalizations about verb behavior. The first level in the hierarchy consists of the original Levin classes, with each class subsequently refined to account for further semantic and syntactic differences within a class.

Chapter 8
Semantics of Techno-Social Spaces

Sergey Maruev
Russian Presidential Academy of National Economy and Public Administration, Russia

Dmitry Stefanovskyi
Russian Presidential Academy of National Economy and Public Administration, Russia

Alexander Troussov
Russian Presidential Academy of National Economy and Public Administration, Russia

ABSTRACT

Nowadays, most of the digital content is generated within techno-social systems like Facebook or Twitter where people are connected to other people and to artefacts such as documents and concepts. These networks provide rich context for understanding the role of particular nodes. It is widely agreed that one of the most important principles in the philosophy of language is Frege's context principle, which states that words have meaning only in the context of a sentence. This chapter puts forward the hypothesis that semantics of the content of techno-social systems should be also analysed in the context of the whole system. The hypothesis is substantiated by the introduction of a method for formal modelling and mining of techno-social systems and is corroborated by a discussion on the nature of meaning in philosophy. In addition we provide an overview of recent trends in knowledge production and management within the context of our hypothesis.

INTRODUCTION

Nowadays, most of the digital content is generated within public and enterprise techno-social systems like Facebook, Twitter, blogs, wiki systems, and other web-based collaboration and hosting tools, office suites, and project management tools, including Google Docs, SlideShare, Trello and Basecamp. These applications have transformed the Web from a mere document collection into a highly interconnected social space, where documents are actively exchanged, filtered, organized, discussed and edited collaboratively. In these techno-social systems "everything is deeply intertwingled" using the term coined by

DOI: 10.4018/978-1-4666-8690-8.ch008

the pioneer of information technologies Ted Nelson (Nelson, 1974): people are connected to other people and to "non-human agents" such as documents, datasets, analytic tools and concepts. These networks become increasingly multidimensional (Contractor, 2007), providing rich context for understanding the role of particular nodes that represent both people and abstract concepts.

In techno-social systems infrastructures are composed of many layers (such as Internet communication protocols, markup languages, metadata models, knowledge representation languages which have spanned over two decades) and interoperate within a social context that drives their everyday use and development. Abstract concepts become the foci of social interactions. The ability to automatically grasp context and, from context, to infer meaning, becomes very attractive.

It is widely agreed that one of the most important principles in the philosophy of language is Frege's context principle, which states that words have meaning only in the context of a sentence, that a philosopher should "never ... ask for the meaning of a word in isolation, but only in the context of a proposition" (Frege, 1884). The context principle also figures prominently in the work of Bertrand Russell and Ludwig Wittgenstein. In this chapter we put forward the hypothesis that semantics of the content of techno-social systems should be analysed in the context of the whole techno-social system; not only in the context of one sentence or even the corpus of all textual information in the systems, but based on the whole structure of the techno-social space which includes actors and various artefacts, and the relations between actors and the thing they create and do.

We substantiate our hypothesis by describing a method of formal modelling of techno-social systems and use of graph-based methods for mining such models, and demonstrate applicability of our method for traditional tasks of natural language processing (including term disambiguation and finding semantic foci of a document), as well as for applications in various recommender systems based on a hybrid approach when textual analysis is combined with link analysis.

Nodes in the network represent people, concepts, annotations, projects etc. Links represent social relations (such as friendship, kinship, social roles, etc.), relations in social spaces (such as *hasSchool* or *hasProject*), and semantic relations (*isA, instanceOf, hasPart*, etc.). Socio-semantic relations can be perceived as knowledge in the same way as semantic relations in semantic networks. From the point of view of the traditional dichotomy between top-down and bottom-up approaches to knowledge production and management, network models of techno-social systems can be regarded as bottom-up created social knowledge. When contrasted with ontologies, such networks represent a weaker type of knowledge that lacks conceptualization and cannot be readily used for inferencing. Correspondingly, the potential of this knowledge can be revealed only through the use of robust methods of "soft computing" such as soft clustering and fuzzy inferencing that are tolerant to errors and incompleteness of data, which is endemic in any user-centric knowledge system.

We will provide an overview of a particular class of algorithms suitable for mining massive multidimensional networks which is a generalization of the spreading activation methods. The first spreading activation models were used in cognitive psychology to model processes of memory retrieval (Collins & Loftus, 1975; Anderson, 1983). This framework was later exploited in Artificial Intelligence (AI) (Crestani, 1997; Aleman-Meza et al., 2003; Rocha et al., 2004) as a processing framework for semantic networks and ontologies, and applied to Information Retrieval (Schumacher et al. 2008). The reason that we do not discuss other algorithms is based mainly on the fact that this computational scheme is scalable and efficient, and the observation that many popular algorithms actually fall into this class of algorithms. This class of algorithms also covers network flow algorithms, which are at the heart of centralization methods in social network analysis (see Borgatti, 2005; Everett & Borgatti, 2005; Borgatti & Everett, 2006).

We demonstrate the ability of the discussed class of algorithms to model very complex phenomena taking into account the inherently imprecise dimensions of nuanced empirical reality. We show the applications of these algorithms to the traditional tasks of natural language processing (such as ontology-based semantic annotation and disambiguation), as well as for navigation and recommendation in techno-social systems (Kinsella et al., 2008).

ON THE NATURE OF MEANING IN PHYLOSOPHY

"The apple is violet" might be a wrong assertion, but a correct answer at an optical test. Terms like *Smartphones* or *iPhone 5* are related to electronic goods, and when met in customs declarations for commercial goods might entail premium customs duties and the assignment of a security escort for the shipment. Textual descriptions of goods in customs declarations, as well as many other texts on the web, are short and are not always grammatically correct; therefore it might be seen as rather unexpected, that a rudimentary (in terms of the use of linguistic tools and linguistic data, such as ontologies) text processing used in the paper (Maruev et al., 2014b) can easily learn from data that terms like *"Cases for iPhones"* have essentially nothing to do with *electronics* when it concerns the functioning of the international trade. To stress why this is surprising, we need to point out that the expression *"Cases for iPhones"* is semantically compositional (that is, the meaning of this expression is determined mostly by its constituents), and syntactically stands in the same relation *N Prep N* to *iPhones*, as the expression *"Bullets for Guns"* stands to *Guns*. The reason of that success is that semantics of words or expressions in this paper has been derived from the data, and has been expressed in the form of relations between terms and other artefacts of the system (including customs duties and assignment of a security escort for the shipment).

In this chapter we argue for the advantages provided by analysing semantics of the content of techno-social systems in the context of the whole system, especially in the relations between terms mentioned and the actors and artefacts of the system. In this section, we show that our hypothesis is in line with recent advances in the philosophy of language. We believe that the availability of big data, combined with the recent advances in methods of mining such data, in regard to certain problems (for instance, mining of customs declarations to provide recommendations), allows us to achieve, what Bertrand Russell aspired to acquire using mathematical logic: "to achieve definite answers, which have the quality of science rather than of philosophy" (Russell, 1945).

It is widely agreed that one of the most important principles in the philosophy of language (and in semantics) is Frege's **context principle**, which states that words have meaning only in the context of a sentence in that a philosopher should "never ... ask for the meaning of a word in isolation, but only in the context of a proposition" (Frege, 1953). In this chapter we put forward the hypothesis that semantics of the content within techno-social spaces (and possibly the meaning of separate words and terms used in this content) should be analysed in the context of the whole techno-social system; not only in the context of one sentence or even the corpus of all textual information in the systems, but also in the context of the structure of the specific system, i.e. relations between authors of sentences and the things such authors create and do.

By no means has this thesis contradicts the Frege's context principle such that the context of a specific proposition plays a special role in understanding the meaning of words. However, in many cases the meaning of words transpires only in a larger context. At Frege's times, there were no real opportunities to exploit computational approaches whereby *the bigger* context could be processed for our formal reason. Nowadays, in case of techno-social systems, the context is present as computer data.

We substantiate our hypothesis by describing method to model such systems formally and the use of graph-based methods for mining such models. We demonstrate the applicability of our method for traditional tasks of natural language processing (including term disambiguation and finding semantic foci of a document), as well for applications in various recommender systems based on a hybrid approach when textual analysis is combined with link analysis.

Our hypothesis about the extension of the context is in line with the modern trends in philosophy. In this section, we will outline the so called ordinary language philosophy that holds "the view of meaningfulness of words in sentences as being primarily determined by the ways in which they were put to use in our practical activity and the role they played in a broader context of our form of life" (Bragg, 2013). The nature of meaning has been always in the focus of the philosophy, as one of the major problems of the philosophy of language. Computational methods of linguistic have already influenced philosophy: "The experimental philosophy movement has recently gained some momentum in the philosophical community. The movement's basic idea is to introduce experimental methods (other than thought experiments) or, more broadly conceived, empirical methods to philosophy" (Bluhm, 2013). To understand the emerging tasks in semantics it is useful to have a wide outlook at the approaches to semantics in linguistics and, more broadly, in the philosophy. In this section, we argue that in both cases there is a trend to look at the meanings of words in a broader context.

In the 19th century the philosophy of language became so pervasive that for a time, in analytic philosophy circles, philosophy as a whole was understood to be a matter of philosophy of language. In the 20th century, "language" became an even more central theme within the most diverse traditions of philosophy. The phrase "the linguistic turn" was used to describe the noteworthy emphasis that modern-day philosophers put upon language (Marconi, 1981). The linguistic turn is the birth of analytic philosophy, the moment when philosophical approaches could be linked to the computational approaches. Friedrich Ludwig Gottlob Frege (1848–1925) is generally considered to be the father of analytic philosophy. Giuseppe Peano (1858–1932) and Bertrand Russell (1872–1970) introduced his work to later generations of logicians and philosophers.

Analytic philosophy introduced empirical methods to philosophy. According to Bertrand Russell: "Modern analytical empiricism ... differs from that of Locke, Berkeley, and Hume by its incorporation of mathematics and its development of a powerful logical technique. It is thus able, in regard to certain problems, to achieve definite answers, which have the quality of science rather than of philosophy. It has the advantage, in comparison with the philosophies of the system-builders, of being able to tackle its problems one at a time, instead of having to invent at one stroke a block theory of the whole universe. Its methods, in this respect, resemble those of science. I have no doubt that, in so far as philosophical knowledge is possible, it is by such methods that it must be sought; I have also no doubt that, by these methods, many ancient problems are completely soluble." (Russell, 1945).

Definitions and descriptions of analytic philosophy often include a focus on conceptual analysis; A.P. Martinich draws an analogy between analytic philosophy's interest in conceptual analysis and analytic chemistry, which "aims at determining chemical compositions" (Marconi, 1981).

The Ordinary Language Philosophy was a school of thought which emerged in Oxford in the year following World War II and since that time was the dominant mode in British philosophy until the 1970th. Philosophers associated with the school include some of the most distinguished British thinkers of the 20th century, such as Gilbert Ryle and J.L. Austin.

The ordinary language philosophy has continuity with the analytical tradition to consider that many philosophical propositions turn out not to be mistaken but are nonsensical or empty. With its roots in the work of Ludwig Wittgenstein, Ordinary Language Philosophy is concerned with the meaning of words as used in everyday speech. Its adherents believed that many philosophical problems were created by the misuse of words, and that if such 'ordinary language' were correctly analysed, such problems would disappear.

The ordinary language philosophy can be considered as a late phase in the history of the analytical tradition in philosophy which began at the begging of 20th century and it resembles the earlier phases in that tradition in that it takes its primary business to be the clarification of the nature and the structure of our means of representing reality and the assumption is that if we do engage in that clarificatory job we'll actually discover something of that the nature of that reality.

The ordinary language philosophy is different from its predecessors that in order to engage in the process of the clarification of the nature and the structure of our means of representing reality it focuses on "the normal ways" competent speakers use language, not on the employing a formal language of modern logic. One of the reasons why they were so confident that that medium is going to suffice for their purposes was that they have a radically different view of what language was from their analytical predecessors. They understood their predecessor's viewing the meaningfulness of language as essentially a matter of it being a system of propositions that corresponded of failed to correspond to reality. In ordinary language philosophy holds the "the view of meaningfulness of words in sentences as being primarily determined by the ways in which they were put to use in our practical activity and the role they played in a broader context of our form of life" (Bragg, 2013).

MULTIDIMENSIONAL NETWORKS – AN EXAMPLE

The sheer volume of data in techno-social systems (which are web services by standard definitions) requires the use of scalable methods for modelling suitable for aggregation of heterogeneous information, such as multidimensional networks, to model the data, which form techno-social space. In this section, we illustrate the notion and the use of multidimensional networks with a simple example taken from the paper by Troussov et al. (2011), entitled "Social Context as Machine-Processable Knowledge".

The idea of modelling techno-social systems by multidimensional networks naturally comes from the view that the content of techno-social systems could be viewed as knowledge, and the networks are a traditional way of knowledge representation. Various types of knowledge could be modelled by networks – from the knowledge codified in ontologies to the data such as "who did what" gathered from the log files of web services. The nodes in these networks could represent concepts, facts, documents, people, projects, organizations, timestamps, etc. The links could represent semantic relations between concepts, ties between people, affiliations, etc. To corroborate our interpretation of the social context, constituted by the realities of techno-social systems, as machine processable knowledge let us consider a contrived network depicted on the Fig. 1.

Figure 1. A contrived example of a network, which could be interpreted as a part of ontology, or as a snapshot from a social site (log-files of techno-social systems keep track about who did what; triples could be aggregated into a network). The shape of nodes indicates the type of nodes: geographical artefacts, actors, meetings and projects.

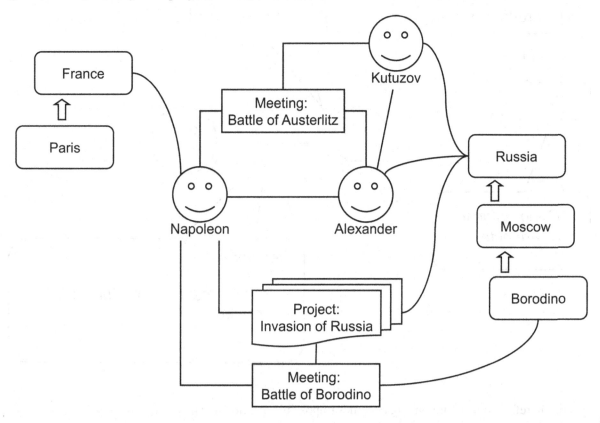

This network is a multidimensional network, that is the nodes and links are typed, as it is depicted on the next figure. Nodes and links are usually provided with labels written in a natural language, such as *France, Napoleon, Alexander*, etc.

A network depicted at Fig. 1 might be originated as an instantiation of ontology related to the events of Napoleonic wars, or as a network of collocations between terms in Leo Tolstoy's novel "War and Peace". At the same time, the same network might be just created from the log files of techno-social systems modelling business activities of *a French businessman Napoleon* related to his business in *Russia* (of course, in this case words *Battle* and *Invasion* would be replaced by business terms, like *Fact-finding meeting at Borodino*).

From the point of view of the traditional dichotomy between codification and collaboration approaches to knowledge management, the social context could be considered as bottom-up created knowledge. Graphs are one of the traditional means of knowledge representation having advantages of extensibility, and the ease of merging heterogeneous information. One can use the nodes of a graph for representing facts, concepts, people, organizations, etc., and the arcs to represent binary relationships between them. However, the knowledge represented by multidimensional networks like depicted of the Fig. 1 could be considered as "weak" knowledge, since it lacks conceptualization and nodes and links are "weakly"

Figure 2. In multidimensional networks nodes and links are typed, "semantics" of types usually does not allow using logical inferencing. Nodes and links are provided with labels written in a natural language, which allows enriching the network with lexical layer.

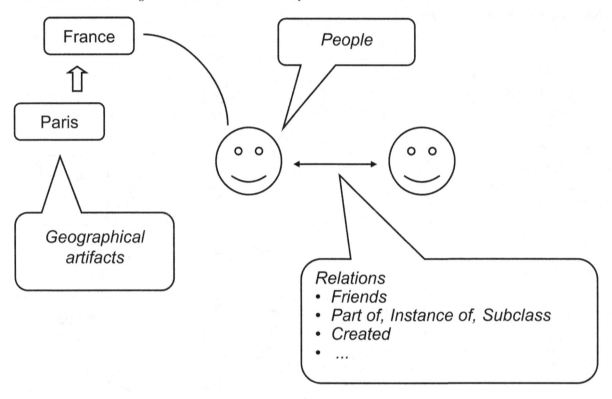

typed. Therefore logical inferencing becomes impossible. At the same time methods of soft mathematics could be used on multidimensional networks, as we will show in the rest of this section. These networks can be treated as a "weak" knowledge, which nevertheless might be used accurate recommendations and even for such traditional applications as knowledge-based text processing.

Let us consider a particular task of recommendation; for instance, *Napoleon* is planning a new *Fact-finding meeting at Borodino,* codenamed *Battle of Borodino*, he needs recommendations whom to invite to this meeting. The task of recommendation requires various considerations, including "Who needs to be there?", "Will they accept the invitation?", etc. From the point view of the application of graph-based methods, this task and its computational solution are explained of the Fig 3.

The problem of recommendation can be solved by application of graph-based methods, such as spreading activation, working on the data modelled by a multidimensional network. Intuitively, actors who might be useful at the meeting are those who are experts in the fields related to the meeting (such as *Russia*), it might be important that they are somehow related to Napoleon, or were his business partners in the past (which generates trust and make it more probable that they will accept the invitation to the meeting).

Propagation algorithms and their generalizations, discussed in section "Mining Using Processes on Networks", offer a tool to formally recognize this intuition and to adequately express it in a precise yet flexible operational form. To start search, one needs to select a set of nodes (a fuzzy set, or, more generally, a function on nodes), the initial conditions of the task: the recommendations are about the meeting,

Figure 3. The problem of recommendation can be solved by application of graph-based methods, such as spreading activation, working on the data modelled by a multidimensional network (for instance, to find people whom to invite to the next meeting scheduled by Napoleon).

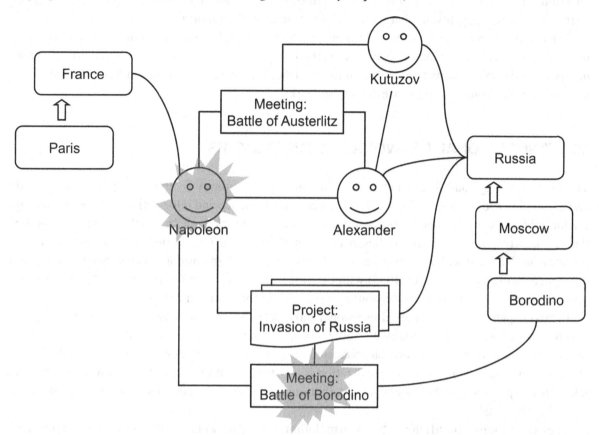

the recommendations are prepared for *Napoleon*, etc. On the Fig. 3 two nodes are marked as the initial conditions: *Napoleon* and *The Meeting*. The task of the graph-mining has two objectives: to find candidates and to rank them according to their "proximity" to the initial conditions and to their "structural importance". We call this task a local dynamic ranking. Propagation algorithms allow to perform both tasks in one go: to combine breadth-first search with ranking. Ranks of nodes are computed iteratively, on each iteration taking into account the topology of the expending vicinity of the area around the initial conditions.

Computation of the structural importance of nodes is one of the core tasks of network analysis, especially in the well-established area of the social network analysis. Quantification of "the proximity" to the initial set of nodes is not clear; in view of the analysis of methods of centralization in (Borgatti, 2005; Everett & Borgatti, 2005; Borgatti & Everett, 2006) we assume that quantification should be based on the number and shortness of the paths between the initial set and the node in question.

To perform local dynamic ranking one can use iterations of spreading activation method to propagate the initial activation to neighbour nodes. After the algorithm finish, the level of activation could be considered as local ranking of nodes induced by the initial activation. Nodes, which have high level of activation, and at the same time represent people (which is the requirement of the task), could be used for the recommendation. For instance, nodes labelled as *Alexander* and *Kutuzov* will have high level of activation since from the Fig. 3 it is clear that they are connected with *Napoleon* and various artefacts related to the meeting by many short paths. Both of the nodes *Alexander* and *Kutuzov* have high out-degree, therefore it is plausible that these nodes are structurally important.

The Fig. 3 shows a generic scheme of mining multidimensional networks and the application of iterative computations (like spreading activation method) for recommendation, where initial conditions are modelled as the initial activation. A formal mathematical construct for this scheme is provided in next section entitled "Mining using Processes on Networks".

MULTIDIMENSIONAL NETWORKS AS ONTOLOGIES

The term "ontology" has different meanings. In philosophy, ontology is "the metaphysical study of the nature of being and existence" (Peirce, 1893). In computer science and information science, an ontology is a formal framework for representing knowledge. This framework names and defines the types, properties, and interrelationships of the entities in a domain of discourse. The entities are conceptualizations of phenomena. The most widely used definition of the ontology is "An ontology is an explicit specification of a conceptualization." (Gruber, 1993) with Guarino's clarifications (Guarino, 1998): "… engineering artefact, constituted by a specific vocabulary used to describe a certain reality… "

In this chapter, we position multidimensional networks as a formal framework of representing reality; as a framework, particularly suitable for representing bottom-up created knowledge, shifting the focus of representation from specification and conceptualization to capturing empirical data about the objects at the instantiation level. The conceptualization is substituted with limited abstractions of phenomena taken from a particular techno-social system (but modification of the network by knowledge engineers might be beneficial).

The explanation of the difference between multidimensional networks and traditional ontologies needs clarifications and involves a discussion on what is knowledge. To make such philosophical digression short, we will substitute the discussion by summarizing the parable from (Nietzsche, 1873):

On a remote planet there was once a clever animal that invented knowledge. The remote planet is Earth; the clever animal is human beings. But that knowledge was not about how things really were, that knowledge was a way of organizing and understanding of the universe to support the continuing life of that animal. The knowledge was a form of adaptation to ensure biological survival. This knowledge was not about truth, truth - what seems to be truth - is actually all about survival and the will to power.

Of course, we do not accept the model of the relationships between the will to truth and the will to power, proposed by Nietzsche. But this metaphysical world picture urges us to think that reason had a history, that reason was not something just eternal, it was something which took different forms in different cultures.

There is a traditional dichotomy of two approaches to knowledge production and management; both are important and complementary to each other. Recently, this dichotomy has been widely acknowledged by philosophers and by IT scientists and practitioners. Following (Fonseca, 2009), one can name this dichotomy as "To Codify or To Collaborate". Codification is an objectivist view of knowledge management as codification of knowledge in databases. Collaboration here is the limited behaviourist view of knowledge as communication and collaboration tools in support of social practices.

For a several decades, knowledge management (KM) has been strongly aligned with the codification: KM was technocentric, driven by information technologies to capture unstructured information to store it in databases in a top down fashion. However, this monolithic approach failed to leave to its expectations (Gurteen, 2007). The pendulum swung in the other direction, from *Codification* to *Collaboration*, to decentralized social knowledge management, to management (centralized or decentralized) of bottom-up created knowledge. The social knowledge is accumulated mainly through *Collaboration* on the layer of limited abstractions of phenomena provided by web services; this knowledge which is created in a bottom up fashion is managed collaboratively, but can be optionally "managed", or "improved" by knowledge engineers in a top down manner. The term social knowledge management can receive at least two linguistic interpretations; we believe that it should be considered as the agglomeration of two interpretations:

SOCIAL KNOWLEDGE MANAGEMENT =

= {SOCIAL} KNOWLEDGE MANAGEMENT + {SOCIAL KNOWLEDGE} MANAGEMENT

In a short term, the dominance of bottom-up approached to knowledge management will probably continue, mainly because *the codification* (a prescriptive approach) is a long term investment, while *the collaboration* (descriptive approach), has immediate gain in the true spirit of Web 2.0 business models. Authors of (Troussov & Nevidomsky, 2011) provided the considerations regarding "Codification vs. Use (business practices)". Traditionally, business looks for local benefits, while the state provides infrastructures for the common good. Codification creates the infrastructure that doesn't produce local short term benefits. For instance, the popular lexical database WordNet provides benefits for its user, not necessarily to its creators. Private companies have not enough incentives to invest in the codification (at least in situations where these enterprises don't have the monopoly). The codification can be very efficient and beneficial for its creators, when it is done by a monopolist. The state has monopoly on the common good, so one can expect that states will continue to fund research projects related to the codification, and the results of these projects will be beneficial for the common good, and, probably, will come into business use.

From the point of view of the dichotomy between the codification and the collaboration, the social context, the space formed by the artefacts of techno-social systems, could be considered as a bottom-up created social knowledge. In our times, proliferation of social networking tools, blogs and microblogs, user-generated content sites, and other social services have transformed the way people communicate and consume information, resulting in the accumulation of unprecedented amounts of data about human actions and behaviour. This "big data" revolution has created a new type of exploitable machine-processable knowledge. These fundamental changes shape our views on the palette of approaches to formal reasoning methods and automatic reasoning tools.

We view multidimensional networks as a direct analogue of traditional ontologies as far as it concerns the networked form of knowledge representation and the ease of applicability of formal methods (although, not necessarily based on the mathematical logic), allowing in regard to certain problems, to achieve definite answers, with quantifiable certainty. In case of multidimensional networks this certainty could be close to full certainty, but only if the network has enough data to address the problem in question.

The differences between multidimensional networks and other types of ontologies are listed below:

1.   Multidimensional networks lack conceptualization and the nodes and links are weekly typed.
2.   Knowledge codified in ontologies makes it possible to use mathematical logic, to make inferencing. Multidimensional networks could be considered as a "weak" knowledge, inferencing is usually not possible; however, inferencing can be substituted by propagation methods which agglomerate the information about the lengths of various paths between nodes, and quantify the strength of the connections.
3.   Graph-based methods, introduced in this chapter, can be perceived as a kind of "fuzzy inferencing", allowing solving certain problems based on noisy and incomplete data. The sheer volume of the data in techno-social systems could make these conclusions the same definite as conclusions achieved by the traditional logical tools (especially if we take into account that the knowledge encoded in ontologies is never *the truth, the whole truth, and nothing but the truth*).
4.   In terms of the traditional dichotomy between two approaches to knowledge production and knowledge management, ontologies are usually based on *"codified"* knowledge, while multidimensional networks represent bottom-up created knowledge, *"collaboration based"* knowledge.
5.   The performance of knowledge based processing for interpreting words and sentences in texts created in a particular techno-social system, hinges primarily on the ability to map concepts mentioned in texts to the artefacts of the system, which essentially determines the domain of the discourse. Therefore "semantic" models of such systems should be enriched with a corresponding lexical layer. Automated creation of such layers successfully converts multidimensional networks into lexico-semantic resources, as it has been demonstrated in (Troussov et al., 2008b). The method of conversion has been further developed in (Davis et al., 2008; Troussov et al., 2009a).

MODELLING USING MULTIDIMENSIONAL NETWORKS

We illustrate the practicality of our approach to the semantics of techno-social spaces by introducing a method for formal modelling of techno-social systems, which allows for efficient graph-mining.

Representation, Modelling, and Adequacy-for-Purpose

In this subsection we briefly discuss those aspects of modelling process which are relevant to our discussion about the semantics of social spaces.

The English verb *to represent* frequently means *to bring forward to somebody's attention*. This verb could be also used also in the sense *to be a sign or symbol of something*. For instance, if one puts a tuber of potato on a map of Paris, the tuber may represent the Eiffel tower; at the same time, from a naïve common sense point of view, a tuber cannot model the Eiffel tower. Representation involves thinking about something in a particular way.

The term "model" in computer sciences usually means a mathematical model which is a description of a system using mathematical concepts and language. Mathematical models are used in the natural sciences, in engineering disciplines, and many other fields including economics and sociology. A model may help to explain a system, to study the effects of different components, and to make predictions about the behaviour of the system.

Frequently, representation leads to modelling. However, the same ideas in representation could be realized by different mathematical constructs. In both representation and modelling "the question is not whether a scientific model is true, nor whether it is probably true, but whether it is adequate for the purposes for which it is to be used." (Parker, 2011).

Below we list several items which one needs to keep in mind when modelling techno-social systems:

1. Terminology used in the representation and in the modelling should reflect (and usually reflects) various aspects of real life data and the methodology of different sciences. For instance, networks and graphs are similar mathematical concepts, but these terms are used in different domains of modelling (while studying semantic networks it might be suitable to use the network terminology, not the graph-theoretic terminology).
2. Terminology used in the representation might be misleading for modelling. For instance, the traffic at a junction of two roads could be represented by two dimensional vectors where each component keeps records regarding the traffic alongside along one road. However such records are not "vectors" which are subjects of linear algebra, and such records do not show how many cars bump into the buildings at the corners of the cross-road.
3. The same representation could be *modelled* by various mathematical constructs. For instance, the some network could be modelled by graphs or by hyper-graphs.
4. The choice of one or another construct could bring misleading direction into the research. For instance, graphs could be modelled by matrixes (incidence matrixes) and the matrix form is a powerful method to study graphs, even so linear algebra is not necessarily an adequate tool to process the data modelled by the graph.

Ubiquity of Modelling by Networks

There are many areas of research and development where network modelling is widely used. For apparent reason, this includes study of real-life networks, including communication and transport networks, web modelling, and social network analysis. Knowledge based natural language processing also heavily relies on the use of network models of knowledge, including taxonomies and ontologies.

We briefly outlined the application of network modelling to model the data from techno-social systems in subsection "Multidimensional Networks – an Example". Here, the modelling nodes represent actors and the various artefacts they create and do. How well does the network modelling suit for modelling those artefacts?

Apparently, a collection of customs declarations has a different nature than the documents which are exchanged, filtered, organized, discussed and edited collaboratively in public techno-social systems. However, deep mining of customs declarations involves the same tasks as in the mining of techno-social spaces: discovery of patterns of relations between the actors (such as traders, carriers, insurers, customs officers), the artefacts of the international trade (such as the nomenclature of goods, taxation, convoying of transports, etc.), and the term used in goods description.

In recent papers (Maruev et al., 2014a) and (Maruev et al., 2014b) network modelling has been applied to model customs declarations data. In the rest of this section we summarize the results of these papers and show their importance to semantic applications.

"Big data frequently come in tabular form of rows and columns of numbers, special codes and short textual descriptions, in strict structured, disciplined formats generated by a variety of transactional and operational business systems" (Maruev et al., 2014b). Customs declarations for commercial goods are essentially a prototypical case of tabular data where each column describes a particular feature of the declaration, including the vendor, the carrier, the type of the goods, etc. In both papers the authors used the network models where a collection of customs declarations is represented by a network. Fig.4 shows a fragment of the network constructed in (Maruev et al., 2014b). The network has been from the original tabular data in the reduced feature space, where only the nomenclature codes of the commodity and words from textual descriptions are used.

There are two types of nodes on this figure. Those labelled by numbers represent commodity codes for goods; nodes labelled by strings of alphabetical characters represent words used in textual descriptions. Links are weighted; weights show the statistical "strength" of connections. This network shows, for example, that the word *"dlja" ("for"* in English) has been met in many goods descriptions and with many goods codes. Most of the formal methods, used to compute structural importance of the nodes in the network, will rate this word very high; one can also wrongly assume that this word could be a good predictor for the nomenclature code. Since this is a frequently used word, statistical methods will also assume the high importance of this word. By removing of such words, using the empirical procedure known as "stop words removal", we will have negative results on the mining since it will remove from the data important syntactic information which the algorithm might use to sense the presence of multi-word terms like *"Cases for iPhone"*.

In (Maruev et al., 2014a) and (Maruev et al., 2014b) the modelling has been done using linguistically light methods: only a standard stemming (The Porter Stemmer for Russian) has been applied. This pre-processing deemed to be needed to conflate various grammatical forms of related words in highly inflected Russian language. The removal of stop words had not been done for the reason explained above. The recognition of multiword terms has not been performed for the reasons listed below:

1.   Recognition of multiword terms world require significant language-specific work;
2.   The results of such recognition will be poor since the textual snippets are very short and are not always grammatically correct;
3.   Recognition of multiword units as one term would be beneficial mostly for idiomatic or non compositional terms like *"The Holy Roman Empire"*, which "was neither *holy*, nor *Roman*, nor an *empire"*, as Voltaire remarked.

The network model of a collection of customs declarations for commercial goods keeps track only about collocations of pair of the words ("cases", iPhone, "for", etc.). However, as it transpires from (Maruev et al., 2014a) and (Maruev et al., 2014b), propagation based algorithms are sensitive to the presence of multiword terms in the initial data. At the same time, these algorithms can prevent the nodes with large number of connections, like the nodes corresponding to function words, to dominate the results of the mining.

The rationale of the network modelling for tabular data has been explained in the paper (Maruev et al., 2014b) by analogy with the use of finite state representation in computer processing of morphology in terms of the approach to the modelling and to the veracity-for-purpose, where the purpose is the discovery of hidden patterns in data.

Many data in office applications comes as "tables", and are processed by spreadsheet applications such as Microsoft Excel. Data which are perceived as networks, such as social networks, in many cases

Figure 4. Network modelling has been used for mining of customs declarations in (Maruev et al., 2014a) and (Maruev et al., 2014b). This figure shows a fragment of a collection of customs declarations for commercial goods represented as a network. Textual descriptions of goods depicted on this fragment include "Blocknotes for Records" and "Bluzons for Girls" ("Bloknot dlja Zapis" and "Bluzon dlja Devochek" in Russian after stemming). The labels on nodes are stems of Russian words (transliterated from Cyrillic to Latin script) used in textual descriptions of goods. The nodes representing the nomenclature codes of commercial goods have digital labels. Link weights show the statistical "strength" of connections between nodes.

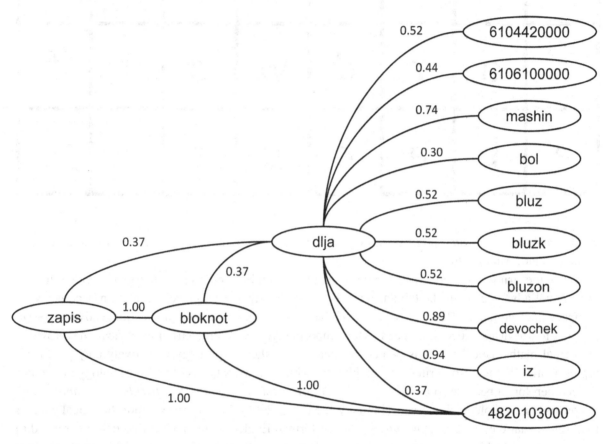

are converted to "a table", that is the incidence matrix and are processed using linear algebra methods (in mathematics, an incidence matrix is a matrix that shows the relationship between two classes of objects.).

However, linear algebra provides only a subclass of useful graph-mining techniques. Authors of (Maruev et al., 2014b) argue that the usefulness of graph-based methods for mining of unstructured heterogeneous data (usually represented as tabular data) is underappreciated. This statement is somewhat similar to the ideas which led to the coinage of the term "graph databases" (Rodriguez, 2011), although in (Maruev et al., 2014b) the emphasize is solely on the data representation and mining algorithms which navigate though the network using links between neighbours, not on the methods of spars matrix storage.

The method of modelling tabular data by networks can be explained by analogy with the use of finite state representation in computational morphology. Many lists of common English words start from the

Figure 5. The rationale behind modelling tabular data (including customs declarations) by networks could be explained by analogy with the network representation of dictionaries. This figure show the list of a few English words represented in a tabular form.
The same table could be redrawn as a graph where nodes represent letters.

a	a	r	d	v	a	r	k
a	a	r	d	w	o	l	f
a	b	a	c	u	s		

words *aardvark, aardwolf,* and *abacus*. For solving crosswords, in might be suitable to model the list in the tabular form like this:

When the strings are words from a natural language, graph-based representation of data has at least one crucial advantage over the tabular representation. Firstly, the graph representation becomes very compact since common affixes of words are conflated, and this leads to non-functional advantages (in memory footprint and processing speed). More importantly, even when such compactification is provided by formal mathematical methods, which are unaware of the morphology, effectively they produce a representation of the list of strings in a graph form which shows patterns of the morphology of the language; therefore it becomes possible to process out-of-vocabulary words, like *trichloroisocyanuric*, and to construct morphological guessers (Jurafsky & Martin, 2009). For instance, a morphological guesser might infer that the word *ontologisation* is a well formed English noun, and to find that it is related to the noun ontology. Moreover, using graph-representation one can infer that the relation between the pair of words *ontology-ontologisation* is the same as the relation between words *industry-industrialization* (see, for instance, Troussov & O'Donovan, 2003).

The procedure of the processing out of vocabulary words, like the word *ontologisation*, can be summarized in the following diagram:

Input: a new word: ontologisation →

→ Network model of existing words →

→ Patterns which the input follows

Figure 6. The list of English words from the Fig. 5 could be visualized as a graph.
If this graph is used to construct a computer dictionary, it can be compactified to the following form:

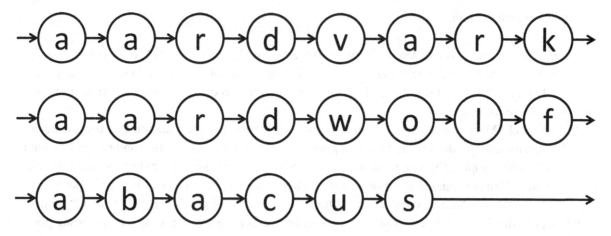

According to this diagram, a new word, like *ontologisation*, is mapped into the network representing known words. The exact mapping is not possible for out-of-vocabulary words, but morphological parts of the word, including prefixes, roots, and suffixes) will be mapped to corresponding strings of symbols (like *ontolog-* and *-isation*). Graph-based methods are used to provide such mapping and to "to connect the dots" between parts of the of the word *ontologisation*.

The same diagram has been used for mining of customs declarations. When the network model of customs declaration has been already constructed, the scheme of processing new declarations is the same as it is in the above mentioned morphological applications:

Input: a new customs declaration record →

Figure 7. The graph from the previous Fig. 6 could be compactified to the graph shown on this figure and usually referred to as the Mealy finite-state machine. Yet both graphs have exactly the same data as the original list of common English words, shown on the Fig. 5 in the tabular form. While the tabular representation might be convenient for solving crosswords, graph representation shown on this figure is suited for natural language applications since it helps to reveal morphological patterns.

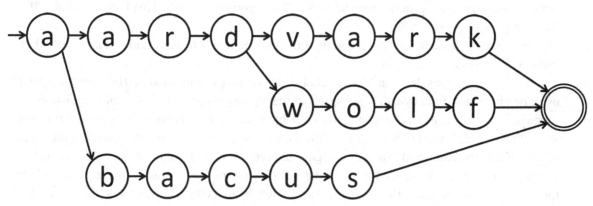

→ Network model of customs declaration data →

→ Patterns which the input follows

There is also a significant difference between these two use cases. Patterns of the language could be discovered using the human insight and techniques for computational linguistics. In streams of big data, patterns dynamically vary at run time, which requires real-time processing, which could be performed only by scalable methods.

Maruev et al. (Maruev et al., 2014a; Maruev et al., 2014b) use the same data sets of customs declarations for commercial goods collected at checkpoints between Russian Federation and one of EU countries. Both papers employ the same methods of modelling the data using multidimensional networks, the same algorithms for mining the models for two use cases which were identified by experts in the field as practically important – checking if the textual description of goods is consistent with the other parameters of the declaration, and assigning of a security escort vehicle for a truck transporting goods to the Russian Federation.

Validation of the approach has been carried out on the real world data that were not used in building the models; in both scenarios the achieved accuracy was 100 percent in most important use cases.

The lowest reported accuracy was 90.5 percent, but the data used were insufficient for the completion of the task (the data had no time stamps, while customs codes for fruits imported to Russian Federation, such as tomato, frequently depend on the season). However, the accuracy measured in top two results, was 100 percent.

The graph algorithm used was a generic computational procedure on graphs as it has been described in (Troussov et al., 2009). However, in (Maruev et al., 2014a) and (Maruev et al., 2014b) the fuzzy logic has been injected into this scheme; that is the affect that neighbour nodes produce on a node is considered as a logical operation AND. The logical operation used in (Maruev et al., 2014a) and (Maruev et al., 2014b) has a parameter which allows to regulate how well parameters of operation can compensate each other. To explain this phrase one can use the direct analogy between fuzzy logic operation AND and the operation used in arithmetic to compute means of several numbers. The case of full compensation corresponds to arithmetic mean, which is if one of the arguments will be increased by a certain value, and the other will be decreased by the same value, the results will be the same. However, in very many practical applications arithmetic mean is not an appropriate method for calculating an average, and other methods, including geometric mean, are used. The experimental results strongly confirmed that:

1. Graph mining using the generic spreading activation algorithm described in (Troussov et al., 2009) does not provide good results;
2. Injection of fuzzy logic makes the spreading activation method, which is a wide class of algorithms, suitable for both cases;
3. The two use cases considered in Maruev et al., 2014a) and (Maruev et al., 2014b) are "the polar" use cases in terms of the essential properties of the algorithms providing accurate prediction.
4. In the task of security escort assigning, most reliable features should dominate the results trumping less reliable predictors; which in terms of fuzzy logic operations could be expressed as follows: the results of the operation AND should be highly skewed towards the value of the bigger operand.
5. The logical aggregation skewed towards the value of the bigger operand spectacularly fails for the other use case, which is the prediction the nomenclature code of goods based on the words in

the textual description. Authors demonstrated that for this use case, significant number of weak predictors easily overrules the judgment based on strong predictors.

6.   There is a one parametric family of logical AND operations, which covers both polar use cases discussed above. The value of the parameter which provides the best solution for a particular use case can be automatically learned from the data (and the formal description of the task modelled by subsets of nodes).

The significance of these results to the topic of our chapter can be perceived as follow:

1.   Network models are capable to represent various contexts and for many cases have high degree of veracity-for-purpose.
2.   The meaning of words in the textual description of commercial goods could be better understood in the context of a data set of customs declarations.
3.   In mining of customs declarations for tasks which strongly relate to "understanding" of words in the description of goods, excellent results were achieved using linguistically light approach (only standard stemming has been used); which indicates that "understanding" of words has been achieved by using the extended context.
4.   Of the shelf graph mining methods might not work for mining multidimensional networks.
5.   At the same time the generic iterative computational procedure on graphs described in (Troussov et al., 2010) might perform well provided that the formula of aggregation is modified according to the properties of the network and the task of mining.

In section entitled "Mining using Processes on Networks" we provide more generic description of graph-based methods which takes into account "the lessons" listed above.

Building Network Models of Techno-Social Systems

In this section, we describe the process of building network models of techno-social systems. Since the adequacy-for-purpose of models is intrinsically interconnected with the methods of mining intended to be applied for models, we discuss the modelling in the general framework of the research and developments related to the study of techno-social systems. Our exposition is mainly based on the paper (Troussov et al., 2013), and the published and unpublished work done in collaboration with Dr. J. Žižka and Dr. F. Dařena at Mendel University in Brno (Dařena et al., 2010; Troussov et al., 2011).

Cycles of Modelling

We describe the life-cycle of development of scientific or commercial software for mining and navigation in techno-social systems: *Real-life System – Models – Methods of Mining – Software – Applications*. We will focus on the first three stages, for the discussion on the other stages (*Software* and *Applications*) see (Troussov et al., 2013). The emphasis on the technical details of modelling and mining is needed to substantiate our hypothesis about the advantages of the extension of the context: mining big data is a difficult task, and the discussion about the extension of the context has practical interest only if there is a path for solving related technical problems, and the use of the extended context is computationally feasible.

We use three-tier architecture of modelling, introduced in (Troussov, 2009) and further developed in (Troussov et al., 2013). The idea of three-tier modelling is based on the use of patterns of the Rational Unified Process, which is an iterative software development process framework created by the Rational Software Corporation, a division of IBM since 2003. The use of this methodology allows to focus on the goals of the research, the expected use cases, the foreseeable changes in the goals, on separation of stages and the structure of the research. It permits however the production of componentized software.

With respect to modelling, one needs firstly to study certain techno-social systems (Facebook, Twitter, etc) or a class of such systems, like microblogging. It is important to determine the availability of methods for collection of information, problems experienced by users in search and navigation, problems of developers of such systems, problems in analysis of the system and making social and economic conclusions based on the results of the study. For instance, in case of social networks, important tasks are the identification of on-line communities and the structural importance of actors in the network. Deriving ontologies from the data might be an important task. Creation of recommender engines for users and system analytics might also be commercially important task.

Network modelling is way of converting the techno-social data into a knowledge, which can be exploited using formal methods. Social and semantic networks are an example of such models, while multidimensional networks allow for modelling various interconnected artefacts of techno-social systems. On Fig. 8 the initial stage of investigating techno-social systems is depicted in the left-down corner.

Stage 1: Modelling Techno-Social Systems by Multidimensional Networks, where Real-Life Phenomena are represented by Abstract Networks

Below is the description of the stages of modelling on Fig. 8. The sequence *Real-life system – Model – Methods – Software – Applications –* is based on the use of constructions (which software developers call patterns) of the Rational Unified Process.

Multidimensional network models allow accurate modelling of the system and its artefacts, up to high-fidelity modelling using log files of the systems (the files which have records who did what etc. To simplify mining, one can omit some of the aspects of data, for instance, such as temporal aspects by ignoring time-stamps. There are always chances to miss some important properties of the data without taking into consideration that the users use the systems for their convenience, and not always as it was intended by the system. For instance, the users of folksonomies might use the tags which will remind them that the paper is needed to complete a task, instead of tags which will provide accurate semantic metadata.

Progressing towards higher level of abstraction, one needs to keep track of those properties of real techno-social systems which might be of importance for future interpretation of the results of mining.

Stage 2: Modelling Networks by Graphs

We model real-world techno-social systems by multidimensional networks. To apply abstract algorithms one needs to convert the network into the next level of abstractions, such as graphs. Although there are many common elements in networks and graphs, they belong to different domains: networks are closer to real life, graphs are used in mathematics. Below we list main differences between network modelling and graph modelling:

1.   Network modelling is used to create a detailed model suitable for a wide class of tasks.

Figure 8. Cycles of modelling: Real-life system – Model – Methods – Software – Applications. This diagram shows three-tier modelling of techno-social systems and the process of development of applications for mining that systems. Moving clock-wise along this diagram we explain the sequence of actions, starting from the analysis and modelling, moving towards applications of formal methods and construction of software applications.

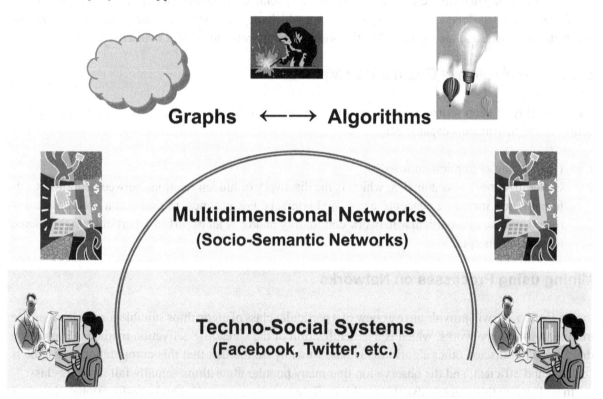

2. Graph models are generated from network models taking into account a specific task and the properties of graph mining methods.

3. The same network could be represented by different graphs. For instance, the structure of data from folksonomies could be represented as a graph with four types of vertices, of as a hypergraph (in mathematics, a hypergraph is a generalization of a graph in which an edge can connect any number of vertices) with three types of vertices (Hotho, et al., 2006; Jaschke, et al., 2007).

4. The distinction between two levels of abstraction is also important for multidisciplinary study of techno-social systems:

   a. Formal description of the network should be clear for linguists and sociologists. For instance, in the network the nodes and the links are typed, and the labels used are *User, Academy, Part-Of, Works-In.,* etc. Translation of these types into parameters of the graph (directions, weights of links) might depend of the methods of graph-mining

   b. The results of the graph-mining should be eventually presented using the network labels

To illustrate the need for two-step modelling of network graphs, we provide an additional example i.e. *A wheel is a part of the car, the car has wheels.* Assumptions like these can be aggregated into a semantic network, which has relations of meronymy and holonymy (A-Part-Of, Has-A). At time of modelling, the quantification of the importance of various relations cannot be expressed by the weight of links in a graph since: a) the importance of various relations for particular tasks of mining is not known yet; b) different graph-mining algorithms treat weights differently. Therefore network models serve to represent the observed reality in terms "convenient" to domain specialists. Network models are converted to more formal graph models depending on the purposes for which they will be used – task of the mining and the graph-mining tools, and are expressed in the abstract form "convenient" for mathematicians.

Stage 3: Application of Graph-based Methods

The feasibility of deep semantic analysis of the content of techno-social systems depend on the availability of the instruments capable of:

1. Discovering of implicit knowledge;
2. Generalization across domains, which is the discovery of hidden relations between entities of different types, including concepts, actors and artefacts. For instance, to find that a specific actor is representative of a particular network community and/or is an expert in a particular field related to certain concepts.

Mining using Processes on Networks

In this section, we will provide an overview of a particular class of algorithms suitable for mining massive multidimensional networks, which is a generalization of the spreading activation methods. The reason that we do not discuss other algorithms is based mainly on the fact that this computational scheme is scalable and efficient, and the observation that many popular algorithms actually fall into this class.

In addition to this crucial advantage, which might be seen as technical and non-functional, this class also covers network flow algorithms, which are at the heart of centralization methods in social network analysis (see Wasserman & Faust, 1994; Hanneman & Riddle, 2005), according to recent observations by Borgatti and Everett in (Borgatti, 2005), (Everett & Borgatti, 2005) and (Borgatti & Everett, 2006), that in social network analysis all the current approaches to structural importance are based on the idea that something is flowing between the nodes across the links. Authors of this chapter hold the view that in many tasks related to the mining of massive networks the structural prominence of nodes, as well as other parameters of local topology indeed could be explained and computed in terms of incoming, outcoming and passing through traffic; authors also argue that the notions of *traffic* and *network flow* could be, and should be, replaced by more general notion of the abstract processes on the networks which happen in the absence of long-distance forces. In other words, the essence of Borgatti and Everett's observation might be useful for mining networks where interactions happen only between neighbors (or, more accurately, other interactions are simply not captured in the network model), where interactions are compared with contact forces in physics as opposed to long range forces (like electric forces); apparently, in some cases this interactions can be explained by "a flow" thought the links, and in other cases such explanation is not possible, not needed, and might be confusing.

Propagation Algorithms and their Use

Formally, the solution of many network data mining tasks reduces to the following problem: given an initial function $F_0(v)$ on the network nodes, construct the function $F_{lim}(v)$ which provides the answer.

In different domains the function F_0 could be referred to as the initial conditions, the initial activation, semantic model of a text, etc. In ontology based language processing, the initial function F_0 is the semantic model of a text w.r.t. to the knowledge: for instance, $F_0(v)=0$ if the concept v is not mentioned in the text, $F_0(v) =n$ if the concept v is mentioned n times. The function $F_{lim}(v)$ should show the foci of the text; for instance, $\text{Argmax}(F_{lim})$ is the most important focus of the text, while $F_{lim}(\text{Argmax}(F_{lim}))$ is the numerical value of the "relevancy". In IR, the link analysis, such as Google's PageRank (Brin & Page, 1998; Langville & Meyer, 2006), ranks web pages based on the global topology of the network by computing $F_{lim}(v)$ using the iterative procedure where the initial condition is that all web pages are equally "important" ($F_0(v) \equiv 1$).

Computationally efficient and scalable algorithms usually compute the function F_{lim} using iterations: on each iteration the value of $F_{n+1}(v)$ is computed depending on the values of the function F_n on the nodes connected to the node v. This iterative scheme is used in a very broad range of different algorithms, including Google's PageRank, spreading activation, computation of eigenvector centrality using the adjacency matrix.

Most of the mathematical algorithms behind such iterative computations are propagation algorithms known widely as "network flow" algorithms: they are based on the idea that something is flowing between the nodes across the links, and the structural prominence of nodes could be explained and computed in terms of incoming, outcoming and passing through traffic.

Similar iterative computational schemes have been used for long time in finite element analysis to solve physical problems including propagation of heat, of mechanical tensions, oscillations, etc. Although finite element analysis automata usually perform on rectangular (cubic, etc.) grids, the extension to arbitrary networks is feasible.

However, the interaction between the material points in mechanics could not always be described as a flow, and such interactions could model more complex processes than diffusion. For instance, one dimensional heat transfer equations can be numerically simulated on a one-dimensional mesh by iterations. On each iteration recomputation is based on the formula below:

$$F_{new}(v) = (F(\text{RightNeighbour}(v)) + F(\text{LeftNeighbour}(v))) / 2.$$

This linear equation confirms the perception of the heat transfer as a flow: on each iteration the heat – the value of the function F – flows from nodes to the neighbour nodes. In physics, a conservation law states that the amount of heat in an isolated physical system does not change as the system evolves, so "move mechanism" in heat propagation is a transfer. In network theory applications, network flow could be also done by "copy mechanism", such as replication in spread of deceases.

At the same time, in physics, many processes cannot be interpreted as a flow and cannot be described by a function of one real variable. For instance, to simulate the behaviour of an oscillating string one needs to operate with three values at each node - position, mass and velocity of the material point corresponding to the node. And none of these properties "flow" to the neighbours.

Using the terminology of functional analysis, each iteration used to compute the function F_{lim} is an operator T which converts a function $x_1(v)$ on the nodes of the graph to another function on the nodes of the same graph. Linear systems, like the process describing the heat transfer, can be described by linear operators, that is

$$T\{A{\cdot}x(v)+B{\cdot}y(v)\} = A{\cdot}T\{x(v)\}+B{\cdot}T\{y(v)\},$$

for any constants A and B, and functions x(v) and y(v).

With a caution, one can say that most of the network flow processes, the processes that were used as examples by Borgatti and Everett, are "linear" processes and are described by linear operators. In other words, most of the popular algorithms mentioned before in this chapter, are essentially "linear". Apparently, linear operators cannot model the behaviour of complex systems, where the whole is more than the sum of the component, and we can tentatively assume that essential processes in techno-social spaces are complex processes.

Methodical Approach to the Construction of Propagation Algorithms

A methodical, systematic approach to designing the propagation algorithms for particular applications should include considerations on:

1. the desirable outcomes for nodes
2. the network processes that produce the desirable effect
3. taking into account data properties (like small world phenomena properties)

The idea of the desirable outcome for nodes is clearly stated in social network analysis, where one of the most important tasks is ranking of nodes according to their structural importance in the topology of the network. The process of ranking is called centralization, and centralization is one of the most spectacular applications of network flow algorithms. For instance, Google's PageRank could be explained in terms of random walking – "PageRank is a probability distribution used to represent the likelihood that a person randomly clicking on links will arrive at any particular page" (Wikipedia). Other traditional approaches to find structurally prominent nodes include spectral graph-based methods and spreading activation.

Beyond the Network Flow Algorithms: Abstract Processes on Network

Network flow algorithms have certain drawbacks. One of them is that "the results are not sensitive to the initial conditions" (in information retrieval applications these would mean that the search results do not depend on the query), without introducing additional empirical mechanisms such as constraints on the number of iterations. Another drawback is that nodes with many links are usually "overrated" since on each iteration the activations accumulated in such nodes flashes back and forward between such nodes and their neighbours, leading to the permanent increase of the level of activation in nodes with numerous connections. The results of network flow algorithms are also not sensitive enough to the clustering structure of the network and the network flow algorithms cannot detect network sub-structures (clusters, communities, etc.). These drawbacks are caused by the linear nature of the network flow algorithms. Network flow algorithms may be not suitable for modelling complex processes *where the whole is more than the sum of its parts*.

To overcome the limitations of network flow methods, while simultaneously maintaining the iterative computational framework, one can replace diffusion like isolated interactions between neighbour nodes by more complex network processes. The key observation here is that the iterative computational procedures described above were used long before in numerical simulation in physics, mechanics, chemistry and engineering sciences (Morton & Mayers, 2005; Rübenkönig, 2006). Therefore, the iterations could be viewed as "the finite difference methods on networks" (Troussov et al., 2009, Troussov et al., 2011). Another directions include the drawing from cellular automata (Schiff, 2008), as it was noticed in (Troussov et al., 2009), and fuzzy logic (Chen, 1996).

APPLICATIONS TO NATURAL LANGUAGE PROCESSING

According to (Ou et al., 2006) "It is an established fact that knowledge plays a vital role in the comprehension and production of discourse. The process of interpreting words, sentences, and the whole discourse involves an enormous amount of knowledge which forms our background and contextual awareness. However, how various types of knowledge can be organized in a computer system and applied to the comprehension process is still a major challenge for semantic interpretation systems used in natural language processing". The knowledge about relations between of the artefacts of techno-social system is arguable the most important knowledge for semantic processing of texts created in this system.

In this chapter we demonstrated how to build models of techno-social systems in the form of multidimensional networks, which can be viewed as "semantic" networks. The applicability of the knowledge encoded in semantic network or ontologies to text processing hinges on the ability to map concepts mentioned in texts to the nodes of the network. Automatic creation of such layers to convert multidimensional networks into lexico-semantic resources is feasible, as it has been demonstrated in (Troussov et al., 2009a) among others.

Methods of network modelling and mining presented in this chapter, as well as methods of lexical enrichment of such models, have been successfully applied for several use cases of mining real-world data and construction of various recommender engines. In this section, we will provide a quick overview of related papers where the social context has been efficiently used for well understood tasks in natural language processing (such as context-dependent automated, large scale semantic annotation, term disambiguation, search of similar documents), as well as for novel applications such as social recommender systems, which aim to alleviate information overload for social media users by presenting the most attractive and relevant content.

Recall, the network models used in the above described papers are multidimensional, although some of them are essentially semantic, or social, socio-semantic networks. Network models of customs declarations introduced in (Maruev et al., 2014a) were used in (Maruev et al., 2014a) to clarify semantics of words used in textual descriptions of goods. These networks capture elements of distributional semantics (collocation of words used in textual description), however the bulk of the network constitute non-linguistics artefacts (such as alpha-numeric codes of goods).

Network Flow Methods for Natural Text Processing

Spreading activation algorithms were used for knowledge based natural language (text) processing in (Judge et al., 2007), (Judge et al., 2008), (Troussov et al., 2009), (Troussov et al., 2008a), (Troussov et al., 2009b). In these papers the text has been modelled as "a cloud" of concepts in a semantic network and graph-based operations were used for mining of text models. The rationale and the intended goals of graph-based methods described in these papers could be recounted as follows.

We assume that the source text is coherent and cohesive as opposed to random list of words. Therefore if some concept are relevant to the text, as indicated by the big value of M, the "neighbour" concepts are also somehow relevant to the text, since the neighbourhood of nodes is defined by links which represent semantic relations between concepts such as synonymy, "is-a", "part-of" etc. We also assume that the keywords (subject terms, subject headings, descriptors), defined in information retrieval as terms that capture the essence of the topic of a document, should have a special position within the clustering structure of the text models (for instance, they hardly exist outside of strong clusters induced by the terms mentioned in the document).

Finding the key terms is done by spreading the activation from concepts mentioned in the text to other concepts in a semantic network. As an end-to-end solution the knowledge based semantic processing of a text is the transformation of the seed (concepts mentioned in a text) to a larger set of concepts ranked according to their relevance to the initial seed.

Hybrid Recommender System in the Activity Centric Environment Nepomuk-Simple

In this section, we will outline the hybrid recommender system in the activity centric environment Nepomuk-Simple (EU 6th Framework Project NEPOMUK), see (Decker & Frank, 2004; Sauermann, 2005; Sauermann et al., 2005; Groza et al., 2007; Sauermann et al. 2009).

"Real" desktops usually have piles of things on them where the users (consciously or unconsciously) group together items which are related to each other or to a task (Malone, 1983). The so called Pile User Interface, used in the Nepomuk-Simple imitates this type of data and metadata organization which helps to avoid premature categorization and reduces the retention of useless documents (Troussov et al., 2009b; Nepomuk PSEW Recommendation, 2009).

Metadata describing user data is stored in the Nepomuk Personal Information Management Ontology (PIMO). Proper recommendations, such as recommendations for additional items to add to the pile, apparently should be based on the textual content of the items in the pile. Although methods of natural language processing for information retrieval could be useful, the most important type of textual processing are those which allow us to relate concepts in PIMO to the processed texts. Since any given PIMO will change over time, this type of natural language processing cannot be performed as pre-processing of all textual context related to the user. Hybrid recommendation needs on-the-fly textual processing with the ability to aggregate the current instantiation of PIMO with the results of textual processing.

Modelling this ontology as a multidimensional network allows the augmentation of the ontology with new information, such as the "semantic" content of the textual information in user documents. Recommendations in Nepomuk-Simple are computed on the fly by network flow methods performing in the unified multidimensional network of concepts from PIMO augmented with concepts extracted from the documents pertaining to the activity in question (Troussov et al., 2008b).

CONCLUSION

In this chapter we argued that that semantics of the textual content of techno-social systems should be analysed in the context of the whole system, taking into account the relations between terms and the actors and artefacts of the system. This allows essentially for "knowledge-based" language processing, but using not the knowledge codified in ontologies, but instead the bottom up created knowledge in the form of relations between terms and artefacts of the system. We demonstrated that this hypothesis is in line with the Frege's context principle and recent advances in the philosophy of language. Putting forward this hypothesis is of current importance and is pressing due to the emergence of techno-social systems, which have transformed the Web from a mere document collection into a highly interconnected space.

We demonstrated feasibility of useful language engineering applications developed based on this hypothesis by introducing the method of modelling techno-social systems, which is also applicable to modelling collections of documents such as customs declarations for commercial goods, where semantics of terms is related to various codes and goods nomenclature. In these techno-social systems people are connected to other people and to artefacts such as documents, datasets, analytic tools and concepts.

Since the volume of data in most of the techno-social system falls into category of Big Data, in this chapter we provided a short overview of only those network mining methods which are scalable. We demonstrated that computationally efficient and scalable algorithms usually are based on the iterative computational scheme where on each iteration only connections between neighbour nodes are used. We discussed papers where these interactions were interpreted as network flow, and presented a generalization where the network flow is substituted with more generic processes based on the local (in the absence long range forces) interactions.

We theorise that the future development of algorithms used in the iterative computational framework might be driven by "physics-inspired" and "logic-inspired" algorithms. Physics inspired algorithms have roots in numerical simulation of various physics phenomena, particularly by finite-difference methods. Logic inspired algorithms could be based on lessons from the use of cellular automata and on the injection of fuzzy-logic into the computational scheme.

REFERENCES

Aleman-Meza, B., Halaschek, C., Arpinar, I., & Sheth, A. (2003). Context-Aware Semantic Association Ranking. In *Proceedings of SWDB'03, Berlin, Germany* (pp. 33-50).

Anderson, J. (1983). A Spreading Activation Theory of Memory. *Journal of Verbal Learning and Verbal Behavior*, 22(3), 261–295. doi:10.1016/S0022-5371(83)90201-3

Bluhm, R. (2013). *Empirical Methods of Linguistics in Philosophy*. Retrieved from http://philevents.org/event/show/11885

Borgatti, S. (2005). Centrality and network flow. *Social Networks*, 27(1), 55–71. doi:10.1016/j.socnet.2004.11.008

Borgatti, S., & Everett, M. (2006). A graph-theoretic perspective on centrality. *Social Networks*, 28(4), 466–484. doi:10.1016/j.socnet.2005.11.005

Bragg, M. (2013). *Ordinary Language Philosophy*. BBC Podcast. Retrieved from http://www.bbc.co.uk/programmes/b03ggc19

Brin, S., & Page, L. (1998). The Anatomy of a Large-Scale Hypertextual Web Search Engine. In *Seventh International World-Wide Web Conference (WWW 1998)*, April 14-18, 1998, Brisbane, Australia. doi:10.1016/S0169-7552(98)00110-X

Chen, C. H. (Ed.). (1996). *Fuzzy Logic and Neural Network Handbook*. McGraw-Hill.

Collins, A. M., & Loftus, E. F. (1975). A spreading-activation theory of semantic processing. *Psychological Review*, *82*(6), 407–428. doi:10.1037/0033-295X.82.6.407

Contractor, N. (2008). *The Emergence of Multidimensional Networks*. Retrieved from http://www.hctd.net/newsletters/fall2007/Noshir Contractor.pdf

Crestani, F. (1997). Application of Spreading Activation Techniques in Information Retrieval. *Artificial Intelligence Review*, *11*(6), 453–482. doi:10.1023/A:1006569829653

Dařena, F., Troussov, A., & Žižka, J. (2010). Simulating activation propagation in social networks using the graph theory. *Acta Universitatis Agriculturae et Silviculturae Mendelianae Brunensis*, *LVIII*(3), 21–28. doi:10.11118/actaun201058030021

Davis, B., Handschuh, S., Troussov, A., Judge, J., & Sogrin, M. (2008, May 26-June 1). Linguistically Light Lexical Extensions for Ontologies. In *Proceedings of the 6th edition of the Language Resources and Evaluation Conference (LREC) in Marrakech, Morocco*.

Decker, S., & Frank, M. (2004). The Social Semantic Desktop. *Technical Report DERI-TR-2004-05-02, Digital Enterprise Research Institute (DERI)*. Retrieved from http://www.deri.ie/fileadmin/documents/DERI-TR-2004-05-02.pdf

Everett, M. G., & Borgatti, S. P. (2005). Extending centrality. In Carrington, P. J., Scott, J., & Wasserman (Eds.), Models and Methods in Social Network Analysis (pp. 181-201). Cambridge University Press. doi:10.1017/CBO9780511811395.004

Fonseca, F., & Martin, J. (2009). Beyond Newspeak: Three arguments for the persistence of the informal in the creation and use of computational ontologies. *Knowledge Management Research & Practice*, *7*(3), 196–205. doi:10.1057/kmrp.2009.16

Frege, G. (1884). *The Foundations of Arithmetic: a logico-mathematical enquiry into the concept of number. English translation by J. L. Austin, B. H* (revised edition 1953). Oxford: Blackwell.

Groza, T., Handschuh, S., Moeller, K., Grimnes, G., Sauermann, L., Minack, E., et al. (2007, September 5-7). The NEPOMUK Project – On the way to the Social Semantic Desktop. In *Proceedings of International Conferences on new Media technology (I-MEDIA-2007) and Semantic Systems (I-SEMANTICS-07)* (pp. 201-210). Graz, Austria..

Gruber, T. R. (1993). A translation approach to portable ontologies. *Knowledge Acquisition*, *5*(2), 199–220. doi:10.1006/knac.1993.1008

Guarino, N. (1998). Formal Ontology in Information Systems. In *Proceedings of FOIS'98* (pp. 3-15). Trento, Italy, 6-8 June 1998. Amsterdam: IOS Press.

Gurteen, D. (2007). *KM 2.0: KM goes Social*. Retrieved from http://www.gurteen.com/gurteen/gurteen. nsf/id/km-goes-social

Hanneman, R. A., & Riddle, M. (2005). *Introduction to social network methods.* Riverside, CA: University of California. Retrieved from http://faculty.ucr.edu/~hanneman/)

Hotho, A., Jaschke, R., Schmitz, C., & Stumme, G. (2006). Information retrieval in folksonomies: Search and ranking. *Lecture Notes in Computer Science, 4011*, 411–426. doi:10.1007/11762256_31

Jaschke, R., Marinho, L., Hotho, A., Schmidt-Thieme, L., & Stumme, G. (2007). Tag Recommendations in Folksonomies. In *Proceedings of the 11th European Conference on Principles and Practice of Knowledge Discovery in Databases PKDD*, Warsaw, Poland.

Judge, J., Nakayama, A., Sogrin, M., & Troussov, A. (2008). *Method and System for Finding a Focus of a Document*. Patent Application US 20080/263038 Kind Code: A1. Filing Date: 02/26/2008.

Judge, J., Sogrin, M., & Troussov, A. (2007, September 26-28, 2007). Galaxy: IBM Ontological Network Miner. In *Proceedings of the 1st Conference on Social Semantic Web (CSSW)*. Leipzig, Germany.

Jurafsky, D., & Martin, J. H. (2009). *Speech and Language Processing: An Introduction to Natural Language Processing, Speech Recognition, and Computational Linguistics* (2nd Ed.). Prentice-Hall.

Kinsella, S., Harth, A., Troussov, A., Sogrin, M., Judge, J., Hayes, C., & Breslin, J. G. (2008). Navigating and Annotating Semantically-Enabled Networks of People and Associated Objects. In T. Friemel (Ed.), *Why Context Matters: Applications of Social Network Analysis* (pp. 79–96). VS Verlag. doi:10.1007/978-3-531-91184-7_5

Langville, A. N., & Meyer, C. (2006). *Google's PageRank and Beyond: The Science of Search Engine Rankings*. Princeton: Princeton University Press.

Malone, T. W. (1983). How do people organize their desks? Implications for designing office information systems. *ACM Transactions on Office Information Systems, 1*(1), 99–112. doi:10.1145/357423.357430

Marconi, D. (1981). Storia della Filosofia del Linguaggio. In G. Vattimo (Ed.), *L'Enciclopedia Garzantina della Filosofia*. Milan: Garzanti Editori.

Maruev, S., Stefanovsky, D., Frolov, A., Troussov, A., & Curry, J. (2014a). Deep Mining of Custom Declarations for Commercial Goods. *Procedia Economics and Finance, 12*(1), 397–402.

Maruev, S., Stefanovsky, D., Frolov, A., Troussov, A., & Curry, J. (2014b). Multidimensional Networks for Heterogeneous Data Modeling. In *Proceedings of the International Conference on Intelligent Information and Engineering Systems INFOS 2014*, (pp. 67-77). Rzeszów - Polańczyk, Poland.

Morton, K. W., & Mayers, D. F. (2005). *Numerical Solution of Partial Differential Equations, An Introduction*. Cambridge: Cambridge University Press. doi:10.1017/CBO9780511812248

Nelson, T. (1974). *Computer Lib/Dream Machines*. sixth printing (May 1978). Nepomuk. Retrieved from http://dev.nepomuk.semanticdesktop.org/wiki/UsingPsewRecommendations

Nietzsche, F. (1873). *On Truth and Lies in an Extra-Moral Sense.*

Ou, W., Elsayed, A., & Hartley, R. (2005). Towards ontology-based semantic processing for multimodal active presentation. In *Games Computing and Creative Technologies.* Conference Papers.

Parker, W. (2011). *Scientific Models and Adequacy-for-Purpose.* Retrieved from www.lorentzcenter.nl/lc/web/2011/460/presentations/Parker.pdf

Peirce, C. S. (1893). Extension of the Aristotelian syllogistic. Grand Logic. Princeton University (1997).

Rocha, C., Schwabe, D., & Poggi de Aragao, M. (2004). A Hybrid Approach for Searching in the Semantic Web. In *Proceedings of the 13th international conference on World Wide Web* (pp. 374-383). May 17-20, 2004, New York, NY, USA. doi:10.1145/988672.988723

Rodriguez, M. (2011). Knowledge Representation and Reasoning with Graph Databases. Retrieved from http://markorodriguez.com/2011/02/23/knowledge-representation-and-reasoning-with-graph-databases/

Rübenkönig, O. (2006). *The Finite Difference Method (FDM) – An introduction.* Albert Ludwigs University of Freiburg.

Russell, B. (1945). *A History of Western Philosophy.* New York: Simon & Schuster.

Sauermann, L. (2005). The semantic desktop – a basis for personal knowledge management. In *Maurer, H., Calude, C., Salomaa, A., & Tochtermann, K. (Eds.), Proceedings of the I-KNOW 05. 5th International Conference on Knowledge Management* (pp. 294–301).

Sauermann, L., Bernardi, A., & Dengel, A. (2005). Overview and outlook on the semantic desktop. In S. Decker, J. Park, D. Quan, & L. Sauermann *(Eds.), Proceedings of the First Semantic Desktop Workshop at the ISWC Conference 2005* (pp. 1–18).

Sauermann, L., Kiesel, M., Schumacher, K., & Bernardi, A. (2009). Semantic Desktop. *Social Semantic Web, 2009,* 337–362. doi:10.1007/978-3-540-72216-8_17

Schiff, J. L. (2008). *Cellular automata; a discrete view of the world.* Hoboken: Wiley-Interscience.

Schumacher, K., Sintek, M., & Sauermann, L. (2008, June 1-5). Combining Fact and Document Retrieval with Spreading Activation for Semantic Desktop Search. The Semantic Web: Research and Applications. *Proceedings of 5th European Semantic Web Conference, ESWC 2008* (pp. 569-583) *Tenerife, Canary Islands, Spain.*

Troussov, A., Dařena, F., Žižka, J., Parra, D., & Brusilovsky, P. (2011). Vectorised Spreading Activation Algorithm for Centrality Measurement. *Acta Universitatis Agriculturae et Silviculturae Mendelianae Brunensis, LIX*(7), 469–476. doi:10.11118/actaun201159070469

Troussov, A., Judge, J., Alexandrov, M., & Levner, E. (2011). Social Context as Machine-Processable Knowledge. In *Proceedings of the International Conference on Intelligent Information and Engineering Systems INFOS* (pp. 104-114). Rzeszów - Polańczyk, Poland.

Troussov, A., Judge, J., Sogrin, M., Akrout, A., Davis, B., & Handschuh, S. (2009a). A Linguistic Light Approach to Multilingualism in Lexical Layers for Ontologies. In G. Demanko, K. Jassem, & S. Szpakowicz (Eds.), *SLT,* 12). Polish Phonetics Association.

Troussov, A., Judge, J., Sogrin, M., Bogdan, C., Edlund, H., & Sundblad, Y. (2008b). Navigating Networked Data using Polycentric Fuzzy Queries and the Pile UI Metaphor Navigation. In *Proceedings of the International SoNet Workshop* (pp. 5-12).

Troussov, A., Levner, E., Bogdan, C., Judge, J., & Botvich, D. (2009). Spreading Activation Methods. In A. Shawkat & Y. Xiang (Eds.), *Dynamic and Advanced Data Mining for Progressing Technological Development*. Hershey: IGI Global.

Troussov, A., Maruev, S., Stefanovsky, D., & Tischenko, S. (2013). *Models and analysis of Techno-Social Environments of Business. RANEPA* [Preprint. In Russian.]. Moscow, Russia.

Troussov, A., & Nevidomsky, A. (2011). Solving Problems on Graphs with Propagation Algorithms. *An intvited talk at the International Conference on Intelligent Information and Engineering Systems INFOS.* Rzeszów-Polańczyk, Poland.

Troussov, A., & O'Donovan, B. (2003). Morphosyntactic Annotation and Lemmatization Based on the Finite-State Dictionary of Wordformation Elements. *Proceeding of the International Conference Speech and Computer (SPECOM' 2003)*, October 27-29 2003, Moscow, Russia.

Wasserman, S., & Faust, K. (1994). Social Network Analysis: Methods and Applications. New York: Cambridge University Press. doi:10.1017/CBO9780511815478

KEY TERMS AND DEFINITIONS

Adequacy-for-Purpose: In representation and modeling, the adequacy-for-purpose is the concern with the question if the model is adequate for the purposes for which it is to be used.

Frege: Friedrich Ludwig Gottlob Frege (1848–1925), is generally considered to be the father of analytic philosophy.

Frege's Contextual Principle: The most important principle in the philosophy of language, which says that words have meaning only in the context of a sentence, that a philosopher should "never ... ask for the meaning of a word in isolation, but only in the context of a proposition" (Frege, 1953).

Multidimensional Networks: Networks suitable for aggregation of heterogeneous information; when used in modeling the data from techno-social systems, the nodes represent actors and various artifacts they create and do.

NEPOMUK: Networked Environment for Personal, Ontology-based Management of Unified Knowledge; EU 6th Framework Project concerned with the development of a social semantic desktop.

Network-Flow Algorithms: Algorithms on graphs based on the idea that something is flowing between the nodes across the links; subclass of the category of "Processes on Networks" algorithms.

Processes on Networks: A wide class of algorithms on graphs suitable for simulation of processes where interactions happen only between neighbor nodes; generalization of network-flow algorithms.

Russell: Bertrand Russell (1872–1970). A British philosopher, logician and mathematician, one of the founders of analytic philosophy.

Spreading Activation Method: A class of algorithms containing most of the network-flow algorithms. Originated in cognitive psychology to model processes of memory retrieval, later has been widely used in Artificial Intelligence, Information Retrieval. Recently has been applied for navigation and recommendation on multidimensional networks.

Techno-Social Space: The term introduced in this book to describe the data from techno-social systems (which are usually web services).

Techno-Social Systems: Public and enterprise systems where content is exchanged, filtered, organized, discussed and edited collaboratively. Facebook, Twitter and LinkedIn are among most known techno-social systems.

The Ordinary Language Philosophy: A school of philosophy of the analytical tradition which holds the view that meaningfulness of words in sentences is being primarily determined by the ways in which they were put to use in practical activities.

Wittgenstein: Ludwig Josef Johann Wittgenstein (1889–1951). An Austrian-British philosopher who worked in logic, the philosophy of mathematics, the philosophy of mind, and the philosophy of language, who significantly influenced the analytical philosophy and the Oxford "ordinary language" school of philosophy.

Chapter 9

Translational Mismatches Involving Clitics (Illustrated from Serbian ~ Catalan Language Pair)

Jasmina Milićević
Dalhousie University, Canada

Àngels Catena
Universitat Autònoma de Barcelona, Spain

ABSTRACT

Translation of sentences featuring clitics often poses a problem to machine translation systems. In this chapter, we illustrate, on the material from a Serbian ~ Catalan parallel corpus, a rule-based approach to solving translational structural mismatches between linguistic representations that underlie source- and target language sentences containing clitics. Unlike most studies in this field, which make use of phrase structure formalisms, ours has been conducted within the dependency framework of the Meaning-Text linguistic theory. We start by providing a brief description of Catalan and Serbian clitic systems, then introduce the basics of our framework to finally illustrate Serbian ~ Catalan translational mismatches involving the operations of clitic doubling, clitic climbing, and clitic possessor raising.

INTRODUCTION

This chapter focuses on translational mismatches between Serbian and Catalan sentences featuring clitics.

A *clitic* is a deficient wordform in that it lacks inherent stress and has to lean prosodically on a stressed wordform (or phrase) in the clause, called the *host* of this clitic. Prototypical examples of clitics are clitic pronouns, but there are also clitic auxiliaries, conjunctions, particles, etc. In addition to having outstanding phonological behavior, clitics can be set apart form "normal" wordforms by their morphonology (special inflection and/or external sandhis) and syntax (clustering, rigid linear placement even in so called free word-order languages). The literature on clitics is huge; for a general and typological

DOI: 10.4018/978-1-4666-8690-8.ch009

Figure 1. SSyntSs of sentences (1)

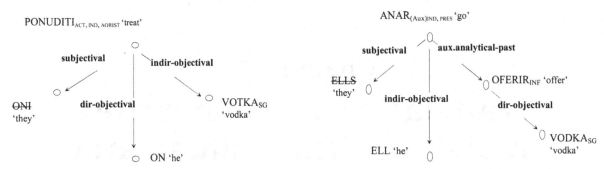

perspective on clitics, see in particular Zwicky (1977), Klavans (1995), Halpern (1995) and Spencer and Louis (2012); for work on Serbian and Catalan clitics, as well as for illustrative examples, see below.

By *translational mismatches*, or *divergences*, we mean non-trivial correspondences between linguistic representations that underlie a source language sentence and its equivalent in the target language. More specifically, we are interested in *structural mismatches*, which represent cases of violation of *isomorphism* between linguistic representations (Mel'čuk 2006, pp. 105-106). Two linguistic representations, say two syntactic dependency trees, are *isomorphic* if 1) all their nodes are in one-to-one correspondence based on the identity or semantic equivalence of their lexical labels, and 2) the dependency inside any two corresponding pairs of nodes has the same direction (i.e., there is no inversion of subordination, or head-switching). An influential typology of structural mismatches was proposed in Dorr (1993, 1994) and further developed in Mel'čuk and Wanner (2006); more on this will be said in due course.

For example, the (surface) syntactic structures of the Serbian sentence (1a) and its Catalan equivalent (1b) feature a structural mismatch involving clitic pronouns (boldfaced); for the structures themselves, see Figure 1:[1]

(1)	a.	*Ponudiše*	*ga*	*votkom*	'They treated him with.vodka'.
		they.treated	he-ACC.SG	vodka-INSTR.SG	
	b.	***Li***	*van*	*oferir vodka*	'They offered him vodka'.
		he-DAT.SG	they.go	offer vodka	

While the Serbian verb takes the Recipient (= the person getting the offer) as the DirO, for its Catalan equivalent the same complement is an IndirO, which results in different case assignment to the clitics (accusative *vs.* dative). Moreover, in the Catalan sentence, the IndirO clitic is raised to the past auxiliary, *van*, and linearly positioned with respect to it. Roughly speaking, *raising* is a syntactic operation whereby a syntactic dependent changes its governor for one that is higher up in the syntactic hierarchy (in our case, the dative clitic *li*, a dependent of the verb *oferir*, becomes a dependent of the governor of *oferir*).[2]

Translation of clitic sequences represents a difficult NLP task, as can be concluded from many publications dealing with text generation or machine translation in which the problem is mentioned, among others, Russo (2010), Larasati (2012) and Din (2013). A major clitic related problem encountered when processing the source language is the identification of the source/referent of the pronominal clitic, on the basis of contextual information. Also, pronominal clitics often require morphological and syntactic disambiguation. During generation of the target language sentence, a correct linear position must be chosen for the clitics, taking into account several levels of linguistic analysis.

The diversity of NLP approaches to this problem reflects the diversity of takes on the clitics in theoretical linguistics, where even the notion of clitic is controversial (are clitics wordforms, affixes, or a third type of linguistic entity?). Another aspect of diversity concerns the general theoretical orientation of clitic descriptions, most evident, again, in syntax, where the two main stances are phrase-structure syntax and dependency syntax; for a comparison of the corresponding formalisms, see Rambow and Joshi (1997) and Mel'čuk (2009, pp. 83-95).

We approach the issue from a contrastive perspective: by analyzing clitic-involving mismatches observed in a parallel corpus consisting of a Serbian novel (Kiš, 1979) and its translation into Catalan (Škrabec, 2003). The mismatches we found in the corpus are not exclusively related to or triggered by clitics: since clitics are "pro-words," substitute elements *par excellence*, inter-linguistic mismatches between them can only be symptomatic of discrepancies happening at deeper representation levels, where clitics do not appear at all. But due to their obligatoriness and concomitant high frequency in texts, clitics make the mismatches in which they are featured "fly in your face," and so help reveal some general characteristics of the languages compared. Thus, we were able to observe interesting differences between Serbian and Catalan, concerning pronominalization patterns, obligatory/optional implementation of actants, allowed government pattern ($\approx$ subcategorization frame) alternations, preferences for possessor raising, preferences for the use of verbal voices, etc.

Our description is carried out from the viewpoint of a dependency-based linguistic theory, the Meaning-Text theory (Mel'čuk 1974, 2012, 2013; Kahane 2003), in particular the MTT dependency syntax (Mel'čuk 1988, Mel'čuk & Polguère (eds) 2009). In this framework, translation is viewed as a particular case of paraphrasing (= production of paraphrases, or semantically equivalent sentences), i.e., *inter-linguistic* paraphrasing. This makes it possible to use for translation essentially the same linguistic tools needed for intra-linguistic paraphrasing. The MTT framework has been used in a number of rule- and transfer-based machine translation applications (as opposed to statistical and interlingua-based ones), for instance Nasr, Rambow, Palmer and Rosenzweig (1997), Lavoie, Kittredge, Korelsky and Rambow (2000) and Apresjan et al. (2003).

Our approach is not computational as such but is relatively easy to implement. Even though the translation of clitics is not primarily a semantic problem, owing to the above-mentioned ubiquity of clitics in texts, it is revealing of many relevant properties of participating languages at all levels of linguistic description, including semantics.

In sum, the chapter's goal is to present an NLP challenging task—translation of clitic sequences (from Serbian into Catalan)—within a particular dependency-based framework that offers an elegant and economical solution to the problem through a re-use of existing linguistic resources.

BACKGROUND

We start by briefly describing the Serbian and Catalan clitic systems, representative of two major varieties of clitics—second-position [= 2P] and ad-verbal clitics, as well as presenting our corpus data.

Table 1. Serbian clitic cluster template

LI Interr/Emphatic	AUX <Copula,Loc>≠ *je* 'is'	PRON -DAT	PRON -ACC/GEN	REFL	AUX <Copula,Loc>=*je* 'is'
1	2	3	4	5	6

Then we expound the Meaning-Text approach to translation and highlight its advantages in a cursory comparison with alternative approaches.

We will consider only the clitics that have special properties, in particular special linear placement properties, with respect to other wordforms; in other words, clitic prepositions and conjunctions, as well as all other *simple clitics* in the sense of Zwicky (1977), will be left out.

Serbian and Catalan Clitics Compared

To our knowledge, this is the first comparison of a second-position clitic system and an ad-verbal clitic system within a dependency framework, and the first dependency-oriented account of Catalan clitics, abundantly described within phrase-structure approaches to syntax, for example, in Bonet (2002), Bonet and Lloret (2005), and Martín (2012). Dependency-based accounts of Serbian clitics are found in Čamdžić and Hudson (2002), and Milićević (2009a); "mainstream" accounts are, among others, Browne (1975), Progovac (1996), Radanović-Kocić (1996), and Bošković (2004).

Serbian clitics are 2P, or Wackernagel, clitics. That is, they are necessarily *enclitics* and follow, roughly speaking, the first phrase or the first full-fledged word of their clause (there are some more complex placement options, which involve so called *skipping* of clause constituents, but we cannot go into an explanation of these). All clitics of the clause are gathered into a *cluster* and linearly placed together within the clause. The structure of the clitic cluster is specified by the template given in Table 1 (not all of the positions in the template can be filled at the same time; several co-occurrence restrictions apply which we will not detail here).

As we can see, Serbian clitic cluster consists of rather heterogeneous items: interrogative and emphatic particles, auxiliary and copular/locative verbs, personal pronouns, and a reflexive adjunct, used to mark some verbal voices and inherently reflexive verbs. Here are examples of Serbian sentences containing clitics (the clitics are boldfaced, the host is underlined):

(2) a. *Kad* *li* *sam* *mu* *je* *poslao* 'When on earth did I send her/it to him?'

             1   2   3   4

    when EMPH am to.him her having-sent

  b. *Juče* *sam* *mu* *je* *poslao* 'I sent her/it to him yesterday'.

                2   3   4

    yesterday am to.him her having-sent

  c. *Posla*== *ću* *mu* *je* 'I will send her/it to him'.

                    3   4

    Send will-1SG to.him her

Table 2. Catalan clitic cluster template

PRON$_{REFL}$	PRON$_{-2P}$	PRON$_{-1P}$	PRON$_{-3P, DAT}$	PRON$_{-3P, ACC}$	PRON$_{PARTITIVE}$	PRON$_{LOCATIVE}$
1	2	3	4	5	6	7

The host of a 2P clitic (= the clause element the clitic leans on in an actual sentence) and its syntactic governor (= the lexeme in the syntactic structure of this sentence to which the clitic is subordinated) do not necessarily coincide. Thus, neither of the clitics in (2a) or (2b) is syntactically governed by their host, the interrogative adverb KAD 'when' and the temporal adverb JUČE 'yesterday', respectively. In fact, these hosts are themselves syntactically governed by one of the clitics—the auxiliary *sam* '[I] am', which functions as the absolute head of its clause (Milićević, 2009b). In (2c), only the pronominal clitics are syntactically governed by the host, the lexical verb POSLATI '(to) send', this verb being itself syntactically subordinated to the future auxiliary *ću* '[I] will'.[3]

As for Catalan clitics, they are all pronouns: personal, adverbial and reflexive (a marker of voice and inherently reflexive verbs). They too are grouped into a cluster, specified by the template in Table 2.

The host of a Catalan clitic is necessarily the verb that plays the role of its (surface) syntactic governor; this is the case with all ad-verbal clitics.[4] Depending on context, these clitics can appear as *proclitics* or *enclitics*; thus, they are proclitics to the verb in the indicative mood in (3a), but they encliticize to the verb in the infinitive in (3b).

(3)	a.	*Ens*	*la*	*porten*		'They bring her/it to us'.
		2	5			
		to.us	her	they.bring		
	b.	*Volen*	*portar-*	*nos-*	*la*	'They wanted to bring her/it to us'.
				2	5	
		They.want	bring	to.us	her	

In Serbian, there are no corresponding elements for the Catalan partitive and locative clitics, while Catalan has no clitic auxiliaries or particles. Such discordances will not be considered in this paper. More interesting are the discordances related to the operations of *clitic doubling* and *clitic raising*, or *climbing* (cf. Endnote 2) widespread in Catalan and non-existent in Serbian,[5] as well as those resulting from *possessor raising*, common in both languages but not necessarily resorted to in the same contexts. These three types of mismatching contexts will be the main focus of this paper.

Meaning-Text Approach to Translation

Meaning-text linguistic theory is a framework for the construction of models of natural languages, called *Meaning-Text models*, or MTMs. An MTM is a multi-stratal, lexicalist, dependency-based and synthesis-oriented model; it consists of a set of rules that carry out mappings between (representations of) meanings and their possible expressions, including lexical rules, stored in a dictionary of a particular type—explanatory-combinatorial dictionary, or ECD. A lexical entry in an ECD comprises a full-fledged periphrastic definition of the lexical unit L, a specification of L's government pattern and a description of its restricted lexical co-occurrence (collocations and semantic derivations) in terms of *lexical functions* (Wanner, 1996). The rules are grouped into modules, each operating between two adjacent levels of representation of utterances: semantic, deep/surface syntactic, deep/surface morphological, deep/surface phonological. There are two basic rule types, correspondence (= expression) rules and equivalence (= paraphrasing) rules.

The basic structure at the semantic level of representation is a *semantic network*, at the two syntactic sub-levels it is a *dependency tree* (for details, see below), while in morphology and phonology it is a string (of wordforms and phonemes, respectively); these formalisms are universal, i.e., cross-linguistically valid.

As already stressed, the notion of dependency is central to the approach: this is a hierarchical relation between two linguistic items, the *governor* and the *dependent*, such that the linguistic behavior of the latter—its presence in the sentence, its linear position, its morphological form—is determined by the former. Dependencies are of three types: semantic, syntactic and morphological (Mel'čuk, 2009); in this paper, we will be mostly interested in syntactic dependencies.

Clitics appear at the surface-syntactic/deep-morphological representation levels, as a result of the operations of *pronominalization* and *cliticization*, licensed under rather complex (communicative and other) conditions that may be different in Catalan and Serbian. These operations are not considered here.

Meaning-Text approach to translation (Kulagina & Mel'čuk, 1967; Mel'čuk & Wanner, 2001, 2006, 2008; Nasr et al. 1997; Kahane, 2007) strives to simplify as much as possible the transfer phase of the translation process while not making its other phases, i.e., the analysis of sentences in the source language and the synthesis of those in the target language, more complex. To do so, it relies on the notion of *deep-syntactic structure* [= DSyntS], a cross-linguistically valid, generalized representation of sentence organization, where differences between individual languages are maximally reduced. It is at this representation level that the transfer from the source- to target language is performed, with the aid of 1) monolingual dictionaries of ECD type for the two languages, "augmented" by a bi-lingual index of correspondences between them, and 2) a set of paraphrasing rules. The idea is brilliantly simple: some divergences appearing at a closer-to-surface representation level, namely the surface-syntactic level, are resolved "automatically", so to speak, as soon as we pass to the deep-syntactic representation level; such divergences, due to surface-syntactic idiosyncrasies, are called *pseudo-mismatches*. The divergences that remain at the deep-syntactic level are genuine mismatches that are taken care of by the existing paraphrasing system (Žolkovskij & Mel'čuk, 1967; Mel'čuk, 1974, 2013; Milićević, 2007, pp. 245-335). This is possible because the types of structural divergences between two semantically equivalent DSyntSs are the same intra- and inter-linguistically. Once the transfer is performed, the rules of the target language, that are needed independently, for other applications, are used to synthetize the target sentences. Thus, translation is performed with a minimal additional investment of linguistic resources. Compared to most other approaches to machine translation, this approach is more economical, owing to the fact that it uses the universally valid formalism of deep-syntactic structure as an interlingua of sorts (cf. the title of the paper Nasr et al., 1997).

A Meaning-Text based translation system is capable of handling all logically possible types of structural mismatches (Mel'čuk & Wanner, 2006, pp. 106-114). There are 3 major types of structural mismatches: mismatches involving lexical units, those involving grammemes (= inflectional values), and those involving syntactic relations; the latter, which are particularly interesting in the present context, can arise

Figure 2. DSynSs of sentences (1)

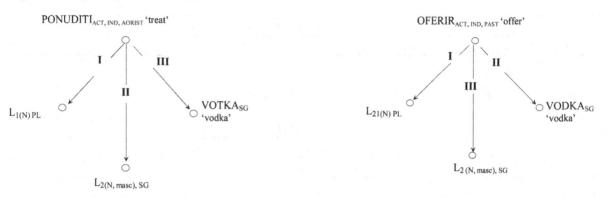

in connection with the following 4 operations (on syntactic dependency trees): 1) branch labeling; 2) branch inversion; 3) branch transposition (raising/lowering), and 4) node fission/fusion.

Let us illustrate this approach by showing how the mismatches between the structures of sentences (1) above are resolved. At the surface-syntactic level, the structures underlying these sentences display two branch labeling mismatches, one branch transposition mismatch and one node fusion/fission mismatch; cf. the surface-syntactic structures [= SSyntSs] in Figure 1.

The SSyntS of a sentence is a dependency tree whose nodes are labeled with all the lexemes of the sentence (including auxiliary and structural words, such as governed prepositions and conjunctions) and whose branches are labeled with the names of language-specific surface-syntactic relations—a hundred or so per language.

The items involved in labeling mismatches are, on the one hand, a pronominal (future clitic) DirO in Serbian *vs.* IndirO in Catalan and, on the other hand, a nominal IndirO in Serbian *vs.* a nominal DirO in Catalan. The branch transposition mismatch is caused by the fact that the IndirO in the Catalan structure hangs from the auxiliary node, as a result of the operation of clitic climbing, while in the Serbian structure it hangs from the node labeled with the lexical verb. The node fission mismatch is caused by the fact that the Serbian verb is in the simple past and the Catalan one in the compound past tense: we see one verbal node, V_{lex}, in the Serbian structure *vs.* a sub-tree "$V_{aux} + V_{lex}$" on the Catalan side. (In both structures, the Subject node is marked for deletion, both Serbian and Catalan being PRO-drop languages; this is indicated by a strikethrough of the name of the Subject lexeme.)

At the deep-syntactic representation level, only the two labeling mismatches remain, as shown in Figure 2.

The Deep-Syntactic Structure of a sentence is a dependency tree whose nodes are labeled with the semantically full lexemes of the sentence (structural words, i.e., analytical realizations of inflectional values such as auxiliaries, as well as governed prepositions/conjuctions and substitute pronouns are excluded) and whose branches carry the names of deep-syntactic dependency relations. These relations, language independent and few in number, are of two major types: subordinating (actantial relations, from **I** to **VI**, **ATTR**(ibutive), **APPEND**(itive)) and coordinating (**COORD**(inative)).

The mismatches in Figure 2 are due to the diverging Government Patterns of the verbs PONUDITI '(to) treat' and OFERIR '(to) offer'(cf. Table 3). They are resolved during transfer, with the aid of the information contained in the index of correspondences between the Serbian and Catalan ECDs.

This information is used as a link between the full-fledged GPs of the two verbs, given in Table 4.

Table 3. An entry in the index of correspondences between Serbian and Catalan ECDs

PONUDITI ⇔ OFERIR
GP: $Y_{Theme} = III \Leftrightarrow Y_{Theme} = II$; $Z_{Recipient} = II \Leftrightarrow Z_{Recipient} = III$

Table 4. GPs of the verbs PONUDITI '(to) treat'/OFERIR '(to) offer'

PONUDITI		
X ⇔ I (Actor)	Y ⇔ III (Theme)	Z ⇔ II (Recipient)
1. –subjectival→N_{NOM}	1. –indir.objectival→N_{INSTR}	1. –dir.objectival→N_{ACC}
oferir		
X ⇔ I (Actor)	Y ⇔ II (Theme)	Z ⇔ III (Recipient)
1. –subjectival→N	1. –dir.objectival→N	1. –indir.objectival→a N; $Pron_{CLIT, DAT}$

The analysis of the Serbian SSyntS, which uses the GP of PONUDITI, yields the corresponding DSyntS (left-hand side of Figure 2), with the sources of pronominal elements, noted $L(exeme)_1$ and $L(exeme)_2$, partially reconstructed (the full reconstruction requires looking up contextual information). Then, it suffices to match PONUDITI with OFERIR and let the rules of Catalan construct the DSyntS of the Catalan sentence (right-hand side of Figure 2), using the GP of OFERIR.

The other two SSynt level structural divergences turn out to be pseudo-mismatches, automatically resolved at the DSynt level thanks to its more general character.

The node fission SSynt-level mismatch disappears because all verbal analytical constructions are reduced to their DSynt sources—inflectional values (= grammemes), attached to corresponding lexical nodes.

As for the branch attachment SSynt-level mismatch, it does not show at the DSynt-level because the corresponding clitic climbing operation is performed in the transition DSyntS ⇒ SSyntS. This means that the Catalan DSyntS in Figure 2 can be mapped to two SSyntSs: one with the clitic raised to the auxiliary, which yields the SSyntS in the right-hand side of *Figure 1*, and one with the clitic remaining *in situ*, i.e., attached to the lexical verb, not shown here, corresponding to the sentence *Van offerir-li vodka*.

In the case of sentences (1), the transfer is performed without recourse to paraphrasing rules, using only lexicographic information form the Serbian ~ Catalan index of correspondences. For an illustration of the use of paraphrasing rules in transfer, see **Example 1** below.

RESOLUTION OF TRANSLATIONAL MISMATHCES INVOLVING CLITICS IN A MEANING-TEXT LINGUISTIC MODEL: ILLUSTRATIVE EXAMPLES

In what follows, we illustrate mismatches between Catalan and Serbian involving the operations of clitic doubling, clitic climbing and (clitic) possessor raising. As mentioned previously, the first two operations do not exist in Serbian; the third one does exist, but the preferences for raising the possessor or leaving it *in situ* may be different in the two languages.

Out of 108 pairs of sentences with mismatches involving clitics found in our parallel corpus, 28 were instances of clitic doubling in Catalan *vs.* no doubling in Serbian, 8 concerned clitic climbing in Catalan with no corresponding operation in Serbian, and 4 were due to the use of a raised possessor *vs.* a possessive adjective (2 cases of raised possessor in Serbian *vs.* possessive adjective in Catalan and 2 cases of possessive adjective in Serbian *vs.* raised possessor in Catalan). The remaining discordances correspond to pronominal passives in Catalan (10) *vs.* analytical passives in Serbian (13), and those due to the inexistence of some clitic types in Serbian (22), respectively in Catalan (23), that we decided not to consider in this paper.

Example 1: A Mismatch Involving Clitic Doubling in Catalan

(4) a.

Novski	*je*	*bio*	*zamoljen*	*telefonom*	*da hitno*	*dođe*	*u centralu*
Novski	is	being.been	asked	by.telephone	That urgently	he.comes	to central.bureau

'Novski was asked by telephone to come urgently to the central bureau'.

b.

A Novski	*li van*	*demanar per telèfon*	*que*	*anés*	*urgentment*	*a la central*
to Novski	to.him they.go	to.ask by telephone	that	he.should.go	urgently	to the central.bureau

'They asked of Novski by telephone to come urgently to the central bureau'.

The Serbian sentence is in the passive voice, with the proper noun *Novski* as the SSynt-Subject and no expression of the Agent Complement. The Catalan sentence is in the active, with a phonetically null but semantically full subject—a 3PL indefinite lexeme meaning 'some people' (cf. the 3PL agreement of the auxiliary, *van*), and the phrase *a Novski* functioning as the *fronted* indirect object *doubled* by the dative clitic pronoun *li*. Fronting is a syntactic operation that "moves" a clause element, an object of a circumstantial of the main verb, in the clause-initial position because of some communicative factors; in our case, the IndirO is fronted because it expresses the Theme ($\approx$ Topic) of the sentence and in Catalan such an element is always sentence-initial.[6] Clitic doubling is an operation whereby a verbal nominal complement is "reinforced" by another one in the form of a clitic pronoun (Anagnostopoulou, 2006). While clitic doubling exists in some Slavic languages, namely Macedonian and Bulgarian, it is not present in Serbian. Catalan, along with some other Romance languages, such as Spanish, has both optional and obligatory clitic doubling (Forcadell & Vallduví, 2000). In this particular case, doubling of the IndirO is obligatory, triggered by the fronting of this complement.

The SyntSs of sentences (4) are given in Figure 3 (for simplicity's sake the circumstantials 'by.telephone' and 'urgently', irrelevant for the discussion, are omitted; the zero subject in the Catalan SSynS is represented as Ø$_{'people'}$—not to be confounded with the subject marked for deletion, which is indicated by means of a strikethrough).

These structures feature the following mismatches:

- **Branch labeling mismatches,** caused by different verbal voices: passive in Serbian, with NOVSKY as the subject depending on the top node and the Agent Complement unexpressed, *vs.* active in Catalan, with the indefinite 3PL zero pronoun fulfilling the role of the Subject and the prepositional phrase A NOVSKY 'to Novsky' functioning as the IndirO of the lexical verb. Additionally, we see here a communicative mismatch since these two syntactically divergent ele-

Figure 3. SSyntSs of sentences (4)

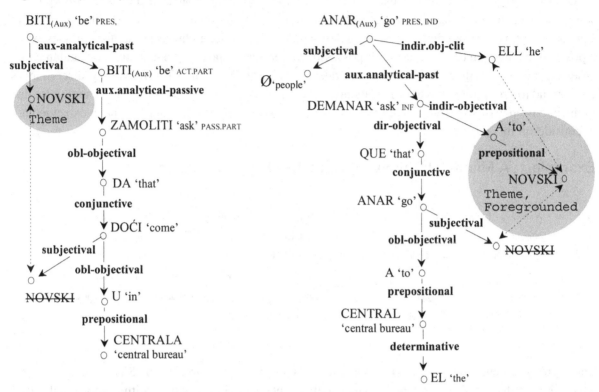

ments (the Serbian Subject and the Catalan IndirO) also have slightly diverging communicative roles: that of the Theme and Foregrounded Theme, respectively.

- **Node fission mismatch**, caused, again, by different verbal voices: passive past in Serbian, with two auxiliary verbs, *vs.* active past in Catalan, with only one auxiliary.
- **Mismatch caused by clitic doubling** in Catalan (Solà, 2002): nothing in the Serbian SSyntS corresponds to the (future clitic) pronoun ELL 'he' depending on the auxiliary ANAR in the Catalan SSyntS.[7]

At the DSynt-level, only the branch labeling mismatches and the related communicative mismatch remain; cf. the DSyntSs of the two sentences, Figure 4. (In the DSyntS of the Serbian sentence, the Agent Complement node—the one linked to the top node by the SSyntRel **II**—is reconstructed in order to facilitate the transfer.)

These mismatches are resolved in two steps. First, a paraphrasing rule is applied to the DSyntS of (4a), and the DSyntS of a synonymous Serbian sentence (4c), given in *Figure 5*, is constructed. This sentence has the verb in the active voice with a zero 3PL indefinite subject—since the Communicator (= the person or persons who did the asking) is unknown—and the noun NOVSKI in the position of the fronted DirO:

(4c) *Novskog   su   zamolili   (telefonom)   da (hitno)   dođe   u centralu*

Novski-ACC   are   having.asked-3PL.MASC   by.telephone   that urgently   he.comes to central.bureau

'Novsky was asked by telephone to come urgently to the central bureau'.

Figure 4. DSyntSs of sentences (4a) and (4b)

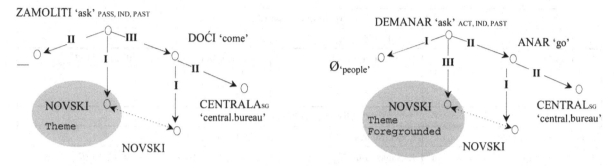

Figure 5. DSyntSs of sentence (4c)

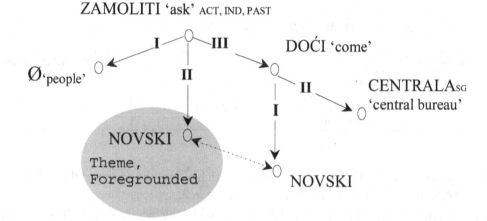

The paraphrasing rule linking the DSyntSs of sentences (4a) and (4c) is given in Table 5; it describes a syntactic conversion (= passivization) for a di-transitive communication verb:

The rule in Table 5 allows us to re-label the actancial branches stemming from the verbal node in such a way that DSyntA **I** becomes DSyntA **II**, DSyntA **II** becomes DSyntA **I** and DSyntA **III** stays in place; this amounts to changing the verb's diathesis from the passive to the active one;[8] cf. Table 6. The lexical identity of the verb does not change, the passive ~ active opposition being inflectional, i.e., concerning the wordforms of the same lexeme.

Once the conversion rule has been applied, it is the DSyntA **II** of the verb that expresses the Theme; to ensure its clause-initial positioning (at a later stage of synthesis—more precisely, in the SSynt ⇒DMorph transition), it has to be additionally marked as Foregrounded. This amounts to eliminating the communicative mismatch that the source and the target syntactic structures displayed at the outset.

As the second step, the resulting Serbian DSyntS, structurally much closer to the target structure than the starting one, is transferred into Catalan using the information in the Serbian ~ Catalan bi-lingual

Table 5. A Syntactic conversion (= passivization) paraphrasing rule

$$L_{(V)PASS} \equiv Conv_{213}(L_{(V)ACT})$$

Table 6. GP of the Serbian verb ZAMOLITI '(to) ask'

Active (basic) diathesis		
X ⇔ I (Communicator)	Y ⇔ II (Addressee)	Z ⇔ III (Message)
1. –subjectival→N_{NOM}	1. –dir.objectival→N_{ACC}	1. –oblique.objectival→$da_{(Conj)}$ 'that' $CLAUSE_{PRES}$ 2. –oblique.objectival→V_{INF} 3. –oblique.objectival→za 'for' N_{ACC} 4. –oblique.objectival→N_{ACC}
Passive (derived) diathesis		
X ⇔ II (Communicator)	Y ⇔ I (Addressee)	Z ⇔ III (Message)
1. –agentive.passive→od *(strane)* 'from (part)' N_{GEN}	1. –subjectival→N_{NOM}	1. –oblique.objectival $da_{(Conj)}$ 'that' $CLAUSE_{PRES}$ 2. –oblique.objectival V_{INF} 3. –oblique.objectival za 'for' N_{ACC} 4. –oblique.objectival N_{ACC}

Table 7. GP of the Catalan verb DEMANAR '(to) ask' (with the active diathesis)

X ⇔ I (Communicator)	Y ⇔ II (Message)	Z ⇔ III (Addressee)
1. –subjectival→N	OBLIGATORY 1. –dir.objectival→N 2. –dir.objectival→$que_{(Conj)}$ 'that' *CLAUSE*SUBJ 3. –inf.objectival→de 'of' *VINF*	1. –indir.objectival→a 'to' N

index of correspondences (like that in Table 3 above), which allows the access to the GP of the Catalan equivalent of ZAMOLITI in the Catalan ECD given in Table 7.

As one can see, the branch labeling mismatch was caused by the fact that the Addressee is the second deep-syntactic actant of ZAMOLITI and the third of DEMANAR, while Message is the third deep-syntactic actant of the Serbian verb and second of the Catalan verb.

As for the SSynt mismatch caused by the obligatory doubling of the IndirO by the clitic pronoun *li* 'to.him', it does not show at the SSynt-level, since the corresponding operation is performed in the DSynt ⇒ SSynt transition.

Example 2: A Mismatch Involving Clitic Climbing in Catalan

(5) a. *I krenuše*   [*da **ga** traže*]$_{Completive Cl.}$ 'And they set out to look for him'.

      And they.set out   that him   look.for

   b. *I van*   *decidir d'anar==**lo**[a buscar]*$_{Inf. Phrase}$ 'And they decided to go and look for him'

      and they.go   decide   of go-INF him to look.for

In Serbian the clitic DirO (*ga*) of the "lower" verb (*traže*) is in the subordinate clause, this being the only placement option possible,[9] but its Catalan counterpart (*lo*) climbs out of the infinitival phrase to become a dependent of the "higher" verb (*anar*), with respect to which it is then linearly positioned.

Figure 6. SSyntSs of sentences (5)

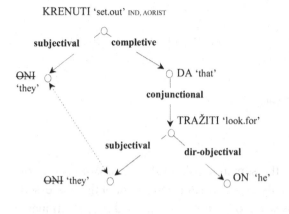
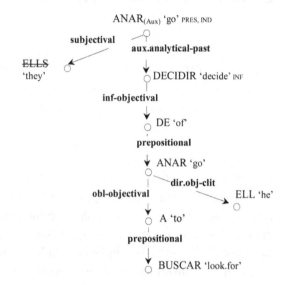

Figure 7. DSyntSs of sentences (5)

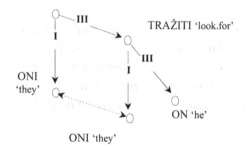
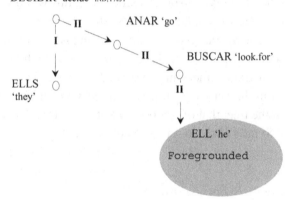

This climbing is optional (unlike the one illustrated in example (4)), but for stylistic reasons it is highly preferred over leaving the clitic DirO *in situ* (*I van decidir d'anar a buscar==lo*).[10]

Figures 6 and 7 show the SSyntSs and DSyntSs of these sentences.[11]

This SSynt-level mismatch caused by the climbing of the Catalan clitic does not appear at the DSynt-level, since, as was shown above, the operation of clitic climbing intervenes in the DSyntS ⇒ SSyntS transition. The climbing of the clitic is triggered by the communicative mark Foregrounded characterizing the node labeled with the pronoun ELL 'he' in the DSyntS of sentence (5b).

Example 3: A Mismatch Involving Possessor Raising in Serbian

(6)	a.	*Drže ći*	***mu***	*srebrni*	*krst*	*iznad čela,...*	'Keeping the silver cross above his forehead, …'
		Keeping	to.him	silver	cross	above forehead, ...	
	b.	*Aguantant*	*la creu*	*de plata*	*sobre*	*el seu front, ...*	Idem.
		Keeping	the cross	of silver	above	the his forehead…'	

Possessor raising refers to a situation where an item in the semantic role of the *Possessor*—a person owing a body part, a house, etc., i.e., the *Possessed*, normally expressed as a dependent of the Possessed, raises to the verb governing the noun in the role of Possessed to become its clitic IndirO (traditionally called "Possessor Dative"); see Figure 8. Possessor raising is common in both Serbian and Catalan, but inexistent in English; the English examples in the right hand part of Figure 8 are constructed.

In (6), Serbian sentence features possessor raising, while its Catalan counterpart does not. Expressing the possessor by the possessive adjective is possible in Serbian, but this option is communicatively (and stylistically) marked. The situation is actually identical in Catalan, i.e., possessor raising is the default case in this language as well. However, in this particular context, the translator chose the *in situ* expression of the Possessor; we believe that this was done in order to mark a contrast (the agent is keeping the cross above someone else's forehead).

The operation of possessor raising is performed in the transition from the semantic to deep-syntactic representation level. Therefore, the mismatch between (6a) and (6b) shows at the DSynt-level; it is a branch attachment mismatch: in the Serbian DSyntS, the pronoun ON 'he'—the future dative clitic—hangs from the verbal top node via the DSyntRel **III**, while its Catalan equivalent occupies a lower position in the tree, that of a dependent of a nominal dependent of the verb (an indirect dependent, at that). The DSyntSs of these sentences in Figure 9.

Figure 8. Possessor Raising

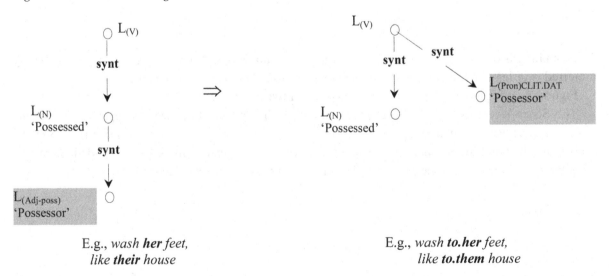

E.g., *wash **her** feet,*
*like **their** house*

E.g., *wash **to.her** feet,*
*like **to.them** house*

Figure 9. DSyntSs of sentences (6)

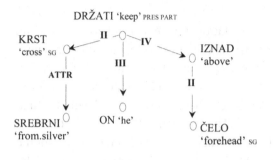
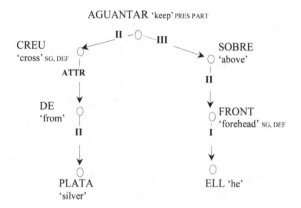

Figure 10. SemSs of sentences (6)

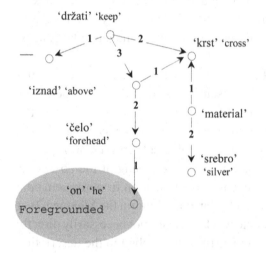
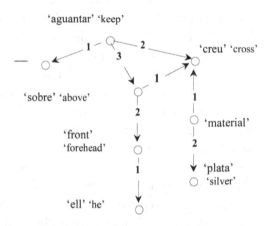

The raising of the Possessor to the position of DSyntA **III** (= the future IndirO) of the verb provokes the demotion of the DSyntA expressing the Location (which should be numbered **III**, as in the Catalan structure), which amounts to a branch-labeling mismatch: **IV** in the Serbian structure *vs.* **III** in its Catalan equivalent.

Semantic Structures [= SemSs] of sentences (6) are given in Figure 10; the structures are incomplete, since the grammatical meanings are not represented:

The SemS (of a sentence) is a network whose nodes are labeled with semantemes (= lexical meanings of the language) and whose arcs are labeled with distinctive numbers indicating semantic dependency relations between a predicative semanteme and the semantemes functioning as its arguments (in the logical sense).

As we can see, at Sem-level of representation the "Possessor ~ Possessed relationship" is encoded in the same way in both languages, the semanteme in the role of the Possessor ('on'/'ell') being the argument of that appearing in the role of the Possessed ('čelo'/'front'). The raising of the Possessor, intervening in the Sem ⇒ DSynt transition, is licensed by the communicative mark Foregrounded characterizing the corresponding semanteme.[12]

CONCLUSION

This chapter has illustrated a technique for the resolution of translational mismatches between Serbian and Catalan sentences containing clitics, used within a Meaning-Text linguistic model—a dependency-based, stratificational model of language in which translation is treated as inter-linguistic paraphrasing and proceeds with a minimal additional investment of linguistic resources. This is possible thanks to the cross-linguistically valid formalism of deep syntactic structure, the representation level at which the transfer from the source- to the target language is performed. The generalized character of the deep syntactic structure allows for a maximal reduction of differences between representations of source and target sentences, thus automatically eliminating many of the structural divergences caused by idiosyncratic features of individual languages, visible at closer-to-surface representational levels. For example, a surface-syntactic level mismatch caused by the climbing of a Catalan clitic does not appear at the deep-syntactic level since the operation of clitic climbing intervenes in the DSyntS $\Rightarrow$ SSyntS transition. The remaining divergences are taken care of in the transfer phase by means of monolingual source- and target language dictionaries, needed independently, with a minimal addition of an index of correspondences between them, and the paraphrasing system, also needed independently. All the operations preceding and following the transfer are performed by the rules of the source and target languages, necessary for other applications.

We have compared the Serbian and Catalan clitics as they appear in parallel texts, concentrating on structural divergences between corresponding linguistic representations related to the operations of clitic climbing, clitic doubling and (clitic) possessor raising, the first two inexistent in Serbian, the third one represented in both languages but resorted to in different contexts. As our analysis has shown, even though the clitics appear only at the surface-syntactic/deep-morphological representation levels, their description is often linked to deeper levels of representation. Thus, the raising of the possessor, which eventually appears in the sentence as a dative clitic, happens in the transition from the semantic to deep-syntactic representation levels. Contrasting Serbian and Catalan clitics within the Meaning-Text framework has revealed some interesting differences between the two languages, not necessarily directly related to or triggered by the clitics. The same technique could be fruitfully applied to the description of other linguistic phenomena and other language pairs.

ACKNOWLEDGMENT

We extend our heartfelt gratitude to Igor Mel'čuk for his most helpful remarks on a pre-final version of this paper.

REFERENCES

Anagnostopoulou, E. (2006). Clitic doubling. In M. Everaert & H. Riemsdijk (Eds.), *The Blackwell Companion to Syntax* (pp. 519–581). Malden, MA: Blackwell Publishing. doi:10.1002/9780470996591.ch14

Apresjan, J., Boguslavksij, I., Iomdin, L., Lazurskij, A., Sannikov, V., Sizov, V., & Tsinman, L. (2003). ETAP-3 Linguistics processor: A full-fledged NLP implementation of the MTT. In *Proceedings of the 1st International Conference on the Meaning-Text Theory.* (pp. 279-288). Paris: École Normale Supérieure.

Bonet, E. (2002). Cliticització. In J. Solà, M. R. Lloret, J. Mascaró, & M. P. Saldanya (Eds.), *Gramàtica del català contemporani.* (pp. 933–989). Barcelona: Empúries.

Bonet, E., & Lloret, M. R. (2005). More on alignment as an alternative to domains: The syllabification of Catalan clitics. *Probus. International Journal of Latin and Romance Linguistics, 17*(3), 37–78.

Bošković, Ž. (2004). Clitic placement in South Slavic. *Journal of Slavic Linguistics, 12,* 39–90.

Browne, W. (1975). Serbo-Croatian enclitics for English-speaking learners. In R. Filipovic (Ed.), Kontrastivna analiza engleskog i hrvatskog ili srpskog jezika. (pp. 105-134). Zagreb: Institut za lingvistiku Filozofskog fakulteta.

Čamdžić, A., & Hudson, R. (2002). Serbo-Croat-Bosnian clitics and word grammar. *UCL Working Papers in Linguistics, 14,* 321-353.

Din, A. (2013). Cliticization and endoclitics generation of Pashto language. In *Proceedings of the 4*[th] *Workshop on South and Southeast Asian NLP.* (pp 77-82). Nagoya: Asian Federation of Natural Language Processing.

Dorr, B. (1993). *Machine translation. A view from the lexicon.* Cambridge, MA: The MIT Press.

Dorr, B. (1994). Machine translation divergences: A formal description and proposed solution. *Computational Linguistics, 20*(4), 579–633.

Forcadell, M., & Vallduví, E. (2000). Duplicación clítica: el caso catalán. In J. Ruiz de Mendoza, M. Fornés, J. M. Molina, & L. Pérez (Eds.), *Panorama actual de la lingüística aplicada: conocimiento, procesamiento y uso del lenguaje.* (pp. 679–689). Logroño: Universidad de La Rioja.

Halpern, A. (1995). *On the placement and morphology of clitics.* Stanford, CA: CSLI Publications.

Heringer, H. J., & Lobin, H. (Eds.), *Dependency and valency. An international handbook of contemporary research*, 1. (pp. 546–570). Berlin, New York: De Gruyter.

Kahane, S. (2003). The Meaning-Text Theory. In V. Agel, L.M. Eichinger, H-W. Eroms, P. Hellwig,

Kahane, S. (2007). A formalism for machine translation in MTT (including syntactic restructuring). In *Wiener Slawistischer Almanach,* 69, *Proceedings of the 3*[rd] *International Conference on Meaning-Text Linguistics.* (pp. 229-238). Munich: Kubon & Sagner.

Kiš, D. (1979). *Grobnica za Borisa Davidoviča.* Beograd: BIGZ.

Kis, D. (2003). *Una tomba per a Boris Davidovič* [S. Škrabec Translated] [Original work published 1976]. Manresa: Angle.

Klavans, J. (1995). *On clitics and cliticization: The interaction of morphology, phonology and syntax.* New York, London: Garden Publishing Inc.

Kulagina, O., & Mel'čuk, I. (1967). Automatic translation: Some theoretical aspects and the design of a translation system. In A. D. Booth (Ed.), *Machine Translation.* (pp. 139–171). Amsterdam: North-Holland Publishing Company.

Larasati, S. D. (2012). Handling Indonesian clitics: A dataset comparison for an Indonesian-English statistical machine translation system.In *Proceedings of the 26*[th] *Pacific Asia Conference on Language, Information and Computation.* (pp. 146-152). Bali: Faculty of Computer Science, Universitas Indonesia.

Lavoie, B., Kittredge, R., Korelsky, T., & Rambow, O. (2000). A framework for MT and multilingual NLG systems based on uniform lexico-structural processing. In *ANLC 2000. Proceedings of the 6*th *Conference on Applied Natural Language Processing.* (pp. 60-67). Stroudsburg, PA: Association for Computational Linguistics. doi:10.3115/974147.974156

Martín, F. J. (2012). *Deconstructing Catalan object clitics.* Ann Arbor, MI: UMI Dissertation Publishing.

Mel'čuk, I. (1974). *Opyt teorii lingvističeskix modelej Smysl ~ Tekst.* Moskva: Nauka.

Mel'čuk, I. (1988). *Dependency syntax: Theory and practice.* Albany, NY: State University of New York Press.

Mel'čuk, I. (2001). *Communicative organization in natural language.* Amsterdam, Philadelphia: John Benjamins Publishing Company. doi:10.1075/slcs.57

Mel'čuk, I. (2006). *Aspects of the theory of morphology.* Berlin, New York: Mouton De Gruyter.

Mel'čuk, I. (2009). Dependency in natural language. In I. Mel'čuk & A. Polguère (Eds.), *Dependency in Linguistic Description* (pp. 1–110). Amsterdam, Philadelphia: John Benjamins Publishing Company. doi:10.1075/slcs.111.03mel

Mel'čuk, I. (2012). *Semantics: From meaning to text* (Vol. 1). Amsterdam, Philadelphia: John Benjamins Publishing Company. doi:10.1075/slcs.129

Mel'čuk, I. (2013). *Semantics: From meaning to text* (Vol. 2). Amsterdam, Philadelphia: John Benjamins Publishing Company. doi:10.1075/slcs.135

Mel'čuk, I., & Polguère, A. (Eds.). (2009). Dependency in linguistic description. Amsterdam/Philadelphia: John Benjamins Publishing Company.

Mel'čuk, I., & Wanner, L. (2001). Towards a Lexicographic Approach to Lexical Transfer in Machine Translation (Illustrated by the German ~ Russian Language Pair). *Machine Translation, 16*(1), 21–87. doi:10.1023/A:1013136005350

Mel'čuk, I., & Wanner, L. (2006). Syntactic Mismatches in Machine Translation. *Machine Translation, 20*(2), 81–138. doi:10.1007/s10590-006-9013-7

Mel'čuk, I., & Wanner, L. (2008). Morphological mismatches in Machine Translation. *Machine Translation, 22*(3), 101–152. doi:10.1007/s10590-009-9051-z

Milićević, J. (2007). *La paraphrase. Modélisation de la paraphrase langagière.* Bern: Peter Lang.

Milićević, J. (2009a). Linear placement of Serbian clitics in a syntactic dependency framework. In I. Mel'čuk & A. Polguère (Eds.), *Dependency in Linguistic Description.* (pp. 235–277). Amsterdam: John Benjamins Publishing Company. doi:10.1075/slcs.111.06mil

Milićević, J. (2009b). Serbian auxiliary verbs: Syntactic heads or dependents? In W. Cichocki (Ed.), *Proceedings of the 31st Annual Conference of the Atlantic Provinces Linguistic Association, PAMAPLA, 31.* (pp. 43-53). Brunswick: University of New Brunswick.

Nasr, A., Rambow, O., Palmer, M., & Rosenzweig, J. (1997). Enriching lexical transfer with cross-linguistic semantic features or how to do interlingua without interlingua. In *Proceedings of the Interlingua Workshop at the MT Summit*. Retrieved from ResearchGate Database.

Progovac, L. (1996). Clitics in Serbian/Croatian: Comp as the second position. In A. Halpern & A. Zwicky (Eds.), *Approaching second: Second position clitics and related phenomena*. (pp. 411–428). Stanford, CA: CSLI Publications.

Radanović-Kocić, V. (1996). The placement of Serbo-Croatian clitics: A prosodic approach. In A. Halpern & A. Zwicky (Eds.), *Approaching second: Second position clitics and related phenomena*. (pp. 429–446). Stanford, CA: CSLI Publications.

Rambow, O., & Joshi, A. (1997). A formal look at dependency grammars and phrase-structure grammars, with special consideration of word-order phenomena. In L. Wanner (Ed.), *Recent Trends in Meaning-Text Theory*. (pp. 167–190). Amsterdam, Philadelphia: John Benjamins Publishing Company.

Russo, L. (2010). The Automatic Translation of Clitic Pronouns: The ITS-2 System. *Generative Grammar in Geneva*, *6*, 203–220.

Solà, J. (2002). Clitic Climbing and Null Subject Languages. *Catalan Journal of Linguistics*, *1*, 225–255.

Spencer, A., & Louis, A. (2012). *Clitics. An introduction*. Cambridge: Cambridge University Press. doi:10.1017/CBO9781139033763

Wanner, L. (Ed.). (1996). *Lexical functions in lexicography and natural language processing*. Amsterdam, Philadelphia: John Benjamins Publishing Company. doi:10.1075/slcs.31

Žolkovskij, A., & Mel'čuk, I. (1967). O semantičeskom sinteze. *Problemy Kibernetiki*, *19*, 177–238.

Zwicky, A. (1977). *On clitics*. Bloomington, IN: Indiana University Linguistics Club.

KEY TERMS AND DEFINITIONS

Clitic Climbing: A syntactic operation whereby a clitic lexeme (in a dependency tree) changes its syntactic governor G_1 for a governor G_2 that is higher up in the syntactic hierarchy (G_2 normally being the governor of the clitic's former governor G_1); G_2 then becomes the host of the climbed clitic. Typical example (the host is underlined, the clitic is in boldface): Romance pronominal clitic climbing, as in Spanish *Te quiero ver* 'you[SG]-ACC I.wish to.see' (vs. *Quiero verte* 'I.wish to.see you[SG]-ACC', with the clitic staying *in situ*). See also *(syntactic) raising*.

Clitic Doubling [i.e., Doubling by a Clitic]: A syntactic operation whereby a verbal nominal complement is "reinforced" by a *resumptive* pronominal clitic. A typical example (the doubled complement is underlined, the doubling clitic is in boldface): Romance pronominal clitic doubling, as in Spanish *A mi me gusta bailar* 'To me to.me is.pleasing to.dance' = 'As for me, I like dancing'.

Clitic: A *wordform* that lacks inherent stress and has to lean prosodically on a stressed wordform in the clause, acting as the *host* of this clitic. A typical example: Romance pronominal clitics, taking a verb as their host, as in French *Maman la leur raconte* lit. 'Mum her to.them is telling [e.g., a story (feminine gender) to the children]'.

Dependency Tree: A formalism used to represent the syntactic structure of a sentence in dependency-oriented linguistic models. This is a connected, directed and fully labeled graph, with the nodes carrying lexical labels and the branches labeled with the names of syntactic-dependency relations; this graph is subject to two additional constraints: 1) one of its nodes, called the *top node* (or *root*) of the tree, does not receive any entering branches; 2) every other node receives one and only one entering branch. The nodes of a dependency tree are not linearly ordered, since their linear ordering is a function of dependency relations between them.

Paraphrasing Rule [= Reformulation Rule]: An equivalence rule, that is, a rule that operates between two linguistic representations of the same level (two semantic representations, or two syntactic representations, etc.) and allows for a meaning-preserving lexical and/or structural modification of the source representation. A typical example: $V \equiv$ light V + de-verbal N(V). This paraphrasing rule allows for a replacement of a verbal lexeme by a construction consisting of the corresponding de-verbal noun and a support verb of this noun; it underlies, for instance, the following paraphrases: *The lab technician **analyzed** the samples. ~ The lab technician **performed** an **analysis** of the samples.* Many paraphrasing rules are cross-linguistically valid and can be used in translation ($\approx$ inter-linguistic paraphrasing); thus, the following French translation of the starting English sentence is obtained by the application of the paraphrasing rule adduced above: *Le technicien chimiste a **effectué** l'**analyse** des échantillons.*

Possessor Raising: A linguistic operation whereby $N_{\text{'Possessor'}}$, a noun in the semantic role of the *Possessor* (a person owing a body part, a house, etc.), normally expressed as a dependent of a noun in the role of the *Possessed* (the body part, the house in question), is raised to the verb governing the $N_{\text{'Possessed'}}$ to become its clitic Indirect Object (traditionally called *Possessor Dative*): $V \rightarrow N_{\text{'Possessed'}} \rightarrow N_{\text{'Possessssor'}} \Rightarrow$ Pron.clit$_{\text{'Possessssor'}} \leftarrow V \rightarrow N_{\text{'Possessed'}}$. A typical example: Possessor Raising in the languages of the Balkans, as in Serbian. *Kako **ti** je otac?* 'How to.you$_{[SG]}$ is father?' = 'How is your father?' (vs. the marked variant with the non raised possessor *Kako je **tvoj** otac?* 'How is your father?'). Possessor Raising can be modeled as a semantic operation, by means of a Semantic-to-Syntax correspondence rule, or as a syntactic operation, making use of a Syntax-to-Syntax equivalence (restructuring) rule.

Syntactic Dependency Relation: A hierarchical relation between two lexemes in a syntactic structure, L_{governor}**-synt**$\rightarrow L_{\text{dependent}}$, such that the governing lexeme determines the syntactic behavior of the dependent lexeme: its linear position in the corresponding sentence, its inflectional form, etc. Technically speaking, L_{governor} determines to a greater extent than $L_{\text{dependent}}$ the *passive syntactic valence* of the entire construction, that is, the external syntactic links of the latter. A typical example: in English, in the construction Adj—N (*red wine, Canadian winter*), the syntactic governor in the noun, since the entire construction fits into larger constructions in the way a single noun does (rather than a single adjective): *I like **red wine** ~ I like **wine** ~ *I like **red***. The noun can appear in the sentence without the adjective, the converse not being the case, and the adjective is linearly positioned with respect to the noun (to its left), not vice versa.

Translational Mismatch [= Translational Divergence]: A non-trivial correspondence between linguistic representations that underlie a source language sentence and its equivalent in the target language. Roughly speaking, this is a lack of one-to-one correspondence between some lexical elements in the representations and/or dependency relations holding between lexical elements. A typical example: the reversal of syntactic dependency, or *head-switching*, taking place in the translation of Eng. *He **swam**-**synt**→**across** the river* to Fr. *Il **traversa**-[la rivière]-**synt**→à la nage* lit. 'He crossed the river swimming'.

ENDNOTES

[1]   The following abbreviations and symbols are used in the paper: ACC: accusative (nominal case); ACT: active (verbal voice); DAT: dative (nominal case); DirO: Direct Object; GEN: genitive (nominal case); GP: Government Pattern (of a lexical unit); IND: indicative (verbal mood); INF: infinitive (verbal finiteness); IndirO: Indirect Object; INSTR: instrumental (nominal case); OBL: oblique (nominal case); PL: plural (nominal/verbal number); PRES: present (verbal tense); SG: singular (nominal/verbal number); SUBJ: subjunctive (verbal mood); ==: boundary between a clitic and its host where they are traditionally spelled without a space.

[2]   When speaking of a raising operation that involves clitics, it is customary to use the term (clitic) climbing; we will follow this usage in the paper.

[3]   Note the affix-like behavior of the future auxiliary, which provokes the truncation of the infinitive suffix (-*ti*) of the lexical verb: *posla+ti ću* ⇒ *posla==ću*.

[4]   Clitic climbing, illustrated in (1b) above, complicates the picture insofar the climbing clitic changes its syntactic governor, but then this new governor becomes its host, so that the rule "the governor of the clitic = the host of this clitic" is observed.

[5]   Serbian has an operation similar to but distinct from clitic climbing: clitic *pseudo-climbing* (Milićević, 2009, pp. 242-243), restricted almost exclusively to clitics' moving out of an infinitival phrase and much less prominent than genuine climbing of the Romance type; see footnote 9 for an example.

[6]   We cannot present here the Meaning-Text approach to the communicative structure, a.k.a. information structure, of sentences. For the communicative markers used in this paper—Theme and Foregrounded—as well as the full range of communicative markers the theory foresees, see Mel'čuk (2001).

[7]   There is another SSyntS mismatch, not related to the clitics in any way and turning out to be a pseudo-mismatch at the DSynt-level: the absence of an article in Serbian *vs.* EL 'the' depending on the noun CENTRAL 'central.bureau' in Catalan. Such discordances will no longer be mentioned.

[8]   Diathesis of a lexical unit L is the correspondence between L's semantic actants [= arguments of the logical predicate expressed by L) and L's deep syntactic actants [≈ its syntactic complements]; the concepts is similar to but distinct from that of *linking*, used in some other frameworks. On Meaning-Text approach to grammatical voice, see Mel'čuk (2006).

[9]   Clitic pseudo climbing out of a subordinate clause gives an ungrammatical result: **Onda **ga** krenuše [da traže]*; it is however possible out of an infinitival phrase: *Onda **ga** krenuše [tražiti]*; this option is actually preferred over leaving the clitic *in situ*: *Onda krenuše [tražiti **ga**]*. (In order to show these placement options, we replaced here the conjunction I 'and/'so', which cannot host the clitics, with the adverb ONDA 'then', which can.)

[10]   There is also a lexical addition in Catalan: the verb DECIDIR 'to decide' that does not correspond to anything in the Serbian sentence; we will not discuss this addition.

[11]   Strictly speaking, it is illegitimate to feature pronominal elements in a DSyntS (as well as in a SemS); how-ever, we will allow ourselves this liberty for the sake of simplicity.

[12]   Possessor raising can also be performed at the DSynt-level (rather than in the SemS ⇒ DSyntS transition), by means of an equivalence rule that looks much like what is represented in *Figure 8*.

Chapter 10
Machine Translation within Commercial Companies

Tomáš Hudík
Teradata Corporation, Czech Republic

ABSTRACT

This chapter gives a short introduction to machine translation (MT) and its use within commercial companies with special focus on the localization industry. Although MT is not a new field, many scientists and researchers are still interested in this field and are frequently coming up with challenges, discoveries and novel approaches. Commercial companies need to keep track with them and their R&D departments are making good progress with the integration of MT within their complicated workflows as well as minor improvements in core MT in order to gain a competitive advantage. The chapter describes differences in research within university and commercial environments. Furthermore, there will be given the main obstacles in the deployment of new technologies and typical way in which a new technology can be deployed in corporate environment.

INTRODUCTION

Machine translation is a part of computational linguistic. Its aim is to use machines for easier, faster and cheaper translations. There are more areas which closely correlate with MT. For example, Computer Aided Translation (CAT) which uses software tools to facilitate the translation process, spell checkers, terminologies, concordances, translation memories tools etc. There have already been developed software packages which wrap all these small applications into one big program like SDL Trados, Déjà Vu, MemSource and many others. The 1990s witnessed the expansion of the CAT tools market by making the software affordable to small businesses and freelance translators, but prices and the resource requirements were still too high. The introduction of the Internet and the possibility for translators to exchange data worldwide required adaptation and the introduction of generally acceptable standards. Translation memories represented such a standard, and their adoption was soon followed by an exponential growth of the market for CAT software (Gocci, 2009).

DOI: 10.4018/978-1-4666-8690-8.ch010

The main difference between MT and CAT tools is that while MT programs are used for the translation process itself, CAT tools tend to help a human translator. In the real world projects, both of them are used in parallel. CAT tools for preparing the translation process and MT for the translation itself, then CAT tools are used again for the evaluation, post-editing done by humans and finally for shipment to original format.

In this chapter, the focus is on machine translation of natural languages (e.g., from English to Russian), we will not describe various types of translators translating artificial languages such as programming languages or automata.

The history of machine translation can be traced back to the 17th century when Leibnitz and Descartes laid theoretical aspects of the first translators based on mechanical devices; however, those theories have never been implemented. In the 1930s, some interesting works, such as Mechanical Brain patent, dealing with MT appeared. The first suggestion that electronic computers could be used to translate from one natural language into another was written by Andrew D. Booth and Warren Weaver in 1948. As the computer era started, two main MT paradigms appeared. They have been up to now in use. The first is rule-based where humans are trying to identify various language rules and the second is called statistical MT where rules are identified by computers themselves based on statistics applied to big training sets. In the 1950s and early 1960s, MT became very popular, expectations were high and research was heavily funded. The constant threat of the Cold War caused euphoria in government and military circles regarding the anticipated possibilities of MT. Until 1966, great amounts of money were spent in order to develop MT systems, mostly for the English-Russian language constellation. Mainly rule-based MT was popular in those days. It was the preferred paradigm since there were not enough bilingual training sets for statistical MT and also computers were not powerful enough to provide complex math operations on large datasets. On the other hand, rule-based MT requires two professions – a linguist who creates rules and a programmer coding the rules into the machine. People have continually realized that acquired results were not good enough and MT hype started to decrease. With the publication of the Automatic Language Processing Advisory Committee (ALPAC) – report in 1964, by the request of the US administration, the CIA and the National Science Foundation, the funding decreased immediately, due to the prognosis that MT is neither useful nor does it seem to provide any considerable advance or meaningful progress. With the exception of some practically oriented teams in Europe and the USA, research and development of MT expired.

Since the 1970s, MT research was slowly revitalized and headed to a continuously increasing popularity from the beginning of the 1980s (Stein, 2013). Due to rapid development of computer hardware and computer technologies, statistical machine translation became a more significant branch of MT since 1990. This era started with the invention of IBM translation models in the '80s (Brown, Pietra, Pietra, & Mercer, 1993). Nowadays there can be seen another big wave of interest in MT with many people involved and researching in the field. There are many conferences, projects and grants like MT Marathons, International Association for Machine Translation (IAMT), The Prague Bulletin of Mathematical Linguistics (PBML) and many others. Contrary to the hype in the 1960s, at this time also the private sector (many translation companies) is using and enjoying benefits of MT.

The main branches of MT are:

1. *Rule-based (RBMT)* – it is an original form of MT, based on linguistic information and dictionaries. In general, it is not a good choice for translation companies since they would need at least one extra person per language to train an MT engine. The advantage of RBMT is that there are

some already pre-trained engines ready to be used; however, most of them are built only for non-commercial purposes. The most popular RBMT project is Apertium which has been developed at the University of Alicante (Spain) and has a good community support. Other important products are Systran (the first commercial product in MT), Gramtrans, etc.

2. *Example-based (EBMT)* – it is a form of example-based learning derived from machine learning. EBMT is based on analogy with previous translations. A segment is translated according to already translated sub-segment parts. As a general MT tool, it is rarely used; however, it can be useful for smaller projects like determining sentence context. The known protagonists are: Cunei or CMU Example-Based Machine Translation System.

3. *Statistical MT (SMT)* – is the most popular MT branch. It deploys statistics which is trying to infer rules from huge bilingual content (training set). In general, the more training data are used the better results are produced. Currently the most popular MT tool is Moses. It is used almost exclusively within the translation industry as no native linguist is required and already translated projects can be used for training. The main developer is the University of Edinburgh (UK), although, there is a huge developer and user community from universities as well as private companies. The tool recently started to be developed as a professional software package with major releases and pre-built binaries. There is also a mailing list with fast reliable responses and a big number of various conferences and projects. In the next section, we will also stick to SMT and Moses. Other SMT packages are Joshua, Stanford Phrasal, cdec, or Jane.

4. *Hybrid MT (HMT)* – leverages the strengths of statistical and rule-based translation methodologies. In fact, almost all of the already described RBMT and SMT tools should be labeled as HMT since they use at least a bit from the other technology: Moses can work with the same basic rules while Apertium implements some kind of statistics. Commercial companies like Asia Online or PROMT usually claim that they belong to this category because they are trying to improve the original open source RBMT or SMT packages by applying techniques from the other methodology.

Statistical Machine Translation

Texts need to be preprocessed before they enter SMT; this is true for the training as well as translation phase. Since SMT is based on statistics and many tasks can be automated, the preprocessing is relatively straightforward. This is especially true for Moses where many preprocessing tools are already included and used directly within the translation process. For example casing, MT is still just about machines which do not understand the text. Therefore they cannot distinguish when an uppercase character is used because of the beginning of a sentence or it is used in the name of a company (e.g., IBM). Moses processes characters as they are in the original text, that means, for instance, words "Me" or "me" are treated like two different words. Therefore it is needed to unify casing in all texts entering SMT. Moses uses a script called lowercase.perl which lowercase texts as a part of data preprocessing step.

Proper selection of training texts is one of the most important tasks. The training texts (data) have to be close to the ones which will be translated through MT. This is a similar assumption as the one of machine learning (ML) algorithms: the more similar training and testing data are the better results testing data will be produced.

SMT has more similarities with machine learning and it also uses many algorithms from ML. In general, the overall SMT process is very close to an ML task. It is needed to have initial training data which is used for training a model that is used for processing test (unseen) data. In SMT, this model

Figure 1. Simplified typical SMT process. First, MT engine needs to be created from preprocessed training texts (bilingual and monolingual). Then, translated (target) texts are getting from Moses where source texts (testing data) are translated by the trained MT engine.

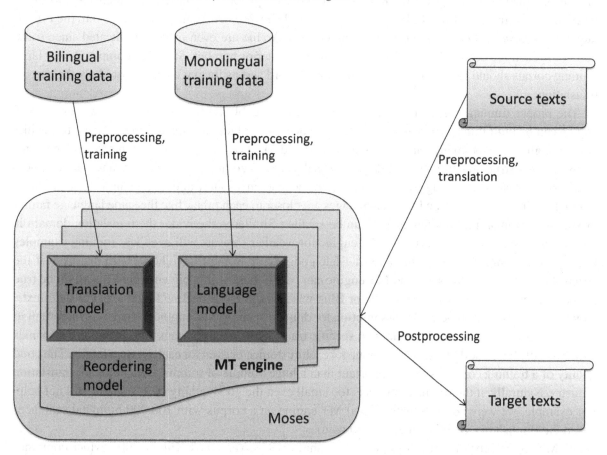

is called MT engine, however, many researchers use different names like MT system, or MT machine. Programmers can think of an MT engine as a library or equation which needs to be built before it can be used on testing data. When the MT engine is created, real translation tasks can start (Figure 1). So the translation is a process which applies the trained model on the testing data.

As it has already been written, the preprocessing step (e.g., lowercasing) is needed for both – training data and translation data. Similarly, it is needed to postprocess data coming from Moses. However, postprocessing is done only on testing (target) data. Fixing of casing is required during data postprocessing. Moses provides two ways how to guess the correct case for each word; unfortunately none of them works without errors. Postprocessing tasks are usually case by case specific. Numbers or named entities are often different in the source and target language. For example: 10,000 versus 10.000 or 10 000; Microsoft Inc. vs. Microsoft Gmbh. Such eventualities are not often recognized by an MT engine and it is better to hard-code them as the rules applied during data postprocessing.

The original idea of SMT was to translate words as the basic units of a text. This approach is called *a word-based or lexical translation*. The first project was *IBM Candidate* built in the late 1980s. The Candidate translates every word to its equivalent in the target language. Even though this approach is already obsolete many techniques and methodologies developed in this early stage are still in use. The statistics is used to identify the correct target word and its form. Usually, a source word (a word from an original language which is going to be translated) has multiple possible target equivalents and forms (a target word is a translated word). For example, the English word *hello* can be translated into the French target as: *bonjour*, *allô* or *coucou*. Slavic languages or Arabic are even more complicated since some parts of speech are declined according to case, state, gender or number. Statistics computed over large training corpus should give a highest score to a target word and its form which is most likely the correct translation.

The proper training corpus is the most critical and valuable part of any SMT. A successful MT engine can be built if the corpus is big enough and does not contain too many errors. Vague terms like "big enough" and "too many" are common in NLP and MT because they deal with natural languages whose formal structures are still not deeply formally described and understood by any mathematical apparatus. In case of a training corpus, vague terms depend on a source and target language and a translation domain. If the source and target languages are closer to each other, like the same language family or similar grammar, the training corpus can be smaller. Similarly, the wider the translation domain is the bigger corpus will be needed. An MT engine for weather forecast will need less training examples than a general-purpose MT engine like translate.google.com Some researchers claim that even if the corpus contains more errors, a good MT engine can be still built if it is big enough. This might be true for general-purpose engines like Google, or Bing where users are expecting to get a gist of their texts. However, it turned out to be a false assumption for domain specific MT engines where it is important to have the precise translation. These domain specific translations are important for translation companies which usually have one dedicated MT engine for each customer, or even for each product family. The good quality of a training corpus is more important than a huge volume of training data holds for translation industry. Naturally, if the training corpus is too small even the good quality of its content will not help. For example, we were able to create a good MT engine on a corpus with 100.000 bilingual sentences (from the English to Czech language, IT domain).

An MT engine is based on a noisy-channel (Shannon, 1948; Yamada & Knight, 2001) which combines the translation and language models. The basic equation is:

$$\text{argmax}_e\ p(e|f) = \text{argmax}_e\ p(f|e)\ p(e),$$

where *e* represents an English target segment, *f* is a foreign language sentence (source) and a candidate with the highest score will be chosen. The terms source and target are common nowadays, however, the terms English (referring to the target) and a foreign (source) which were used in literature in the past. (Koehn, 2010) gives a deeper formal description of the whole SMT process.

Translation model (TM) – In this section TM refers to the translation model, however, it is better known as the translation memory which was shortly described with CAT tools in the beginning of this chapter. Generally speaking, TM is supposed to find the best translation candidate based on the source language (Koehn, 2010). It has to be trained on bilingual well-aligned data from the same domain as our intentional translations.

Language model (LM) is a statistical description of a language. It is trained from a monolingual corpus and used for selection of the most probable target segment based on the statistical characteristic of the target language. In contrary to TM, LM data does not have to be from the same domain. Usually, LM is trained on a mix composed of target language texts taken from the TM training corpus and some other target language texts. If the LM training data is taken from different domains, the rule of thumb says: when a MT engine is built, test it to see whether the translations are correct. For example, if a MT engine is trained for an IT domain and LM training data contains too many segments from law, translations can have correct terminology but used in weird law way (vague, sentences are longer than those in IT usually are or are more formal). It is also good to consider what kind of data is acquired in LM. For instance, texts in various forums on the Internet often contain many errors, they can be written by non-native speakers and the style is informal. If the MT engine's output is supposed to be in a proper language, it is better to use only verified sources such as books, formal reports etc.

Later, it was realized that there are often cases where one source word is translated into multiple target words or vice-versa. Therefore the word-based turned out to be not enough. A hot scientific topic became the *phrase-based* approach where statistical methods identify phrases. A phrase is a small set of words grouped according to an n-gram. The n-gram (usually 1-3gram) is a contiguous sequence of n words from a given sequence. Although some newer approaches like the syntax-based one have already been developed, the phrase-based SMT is still giving good and stable results for majority of language pairs and therefore it is widely used across the localization industry.

MT in Universities and in the Business Environment

As it was stated earlier MT has already been in use within commercial environment since the 1980s. A pioneer was Systran which was developed already in 1968. A commercial MT research can be dated back into the '80s as well. While university research (both: basic or applied) is focused mainly on publication records and the aim is to come up with completely new ideas, corporate research (almost exclusively applied) is mostly about applying small new pieces in order to improve or upgrade existing systems and workflows. In general, the university research covers much wider area of topics. On the other hand, it is common to do a research on some subject and then switch into something else, eventually to solve the initial task from a different point of view. This is hardly imaginable in the corporate world which has more rigid structures and is driven by profit.

Because of these reasons, the MT research is different in university and corporate environment. MT means the machine translation done on natural languages themselves (translate text strings or voices from one language into another) in a university research while in a business environment it means the machine translation of some content (e.g., text with pictures and formatting) from one natural language into another in the business environment.

Let's describe some easily interchangeable and overlapping terms (Since all names are long, acronyms have been created. For example, L10N – starts with L, followed by 10 letters and ends with N mean Localization. Similar acronyms are for Internalization – I13N and Globalization – G13N):

- *Translation* – standard translation of strings.
- *Localization (L10N)* – Localization industry generally means LSPs (Language Service Providers) and companies that support LSPs in some way. LSPs are managing the entire translation process: working with translators, editors, and proofreaders or posteditors. They often offer design and publishing services for the translated content as well.
- *Internationalization (I18N)* – evolved out of translation and localization. The goal is as for the original content to be international-ready. For example, all modern compilers such as GNU GCC or .NET framework, can work with special files or tools which contain translations into multiple

languages. Then, the compiled program uses only strings for a language chosen by the end user. Deployment of I18N should be considered strategically at the beginning of content development.

- *Globalization (G11N)* – is the result of internalization and localization.

For further details see (gala-global.org, 2014) or (Pawlowski, 2008; Bert, 2000).

Basically, LSPs are translating the content containing various meta information. Such meta information deals with fonts, formatting, keyboard shortcuts, currencies, date format, invisible notes, national holidays etc., which cannot be encoded in a standard text format. LSPs have developed complicated and specific file formats which are capable to handle this meta information effectively. *TMX (Translation Memory eXchange)* and *XLIFF (XML Localization Interchange File Format)* are used most often nowadays. Fortunately, these formats are standard XML files developed by open consortiums such as OASES or W3C without proprietary features, so they are easily readable and modifiable.

The translation of a localization content instead of a standard text is still a challenging topic with various opinions and publications. Jinhua Du in (Du, Roturier, & Way, 2010) compares three different approaches:

1. trying to place meta information on proper places in target,
2. no modification (translate whole content as it is),
3. group meta information into some categories, and then keep the categories as a word or token.

Interestingly, method 3 tightly followed by method 2 turned to be the best solution. This could work if there is only a small amount of meta information, however, the meta information is produced by CAT tools and therefore it is hard to control what percentage of it will be included in the localization file. The meta information can be easily 2—5 times bigger than the standard text. This is common when a localization workflow contains multiple CAT tools. If the second or third method were used with such a big amount of meta information, weird meta information would pop-up randomly throughout the translated texts. Another possibility would be to remove meta information completely, however, it would be difficult to insert the translated text back to the original localization file, or completely new formatting and design would be needed. All those approaches are inefficient if the amount of meta data is unknown in advance. They can be used for some ad-hoc tasks where it is known that incoming input will contain only a small portion of the meta information.

Our analyses showed that we need to choose the first method. Likely, other LSPs came to the same conclusion. Unfortunately, the research and development of this method turned to be very difficult and long-term. The biggest obstacle was to find a proper placement for the meta information in the target language. There are many strange hurdles which are not visible at the first sight. For example:

- Will meta information persist without any change? If the meta information is about the writing direction and if the translation is from English to Arabic which has different writing directions (right to left), the meta information will be changed during the translation process.
- How to identify after (or before) which target word the meta information should be placed. Remember, the number of words in a translated string can be different and words are usually re-ordered.
- If a source sentence has a pair tag <b><b/> where should it be placed in a target string? For example, a source string: 1 <b>2 3</b> 4 is translated into a target string 4 3 1 2. Where the tag

<b> should be placed – 4 <b>3</b> 1 <b>2</b> or 4 <b>3 1 2</b>? Note, phrase 1 in the source segment is translated into phrase 1 in the target language (in this case the number of source and target words is the same, just the word-ordering differs).

- Should the meta information be bind to the start of the segment, or to a particular word instead? For example: string <kl/> 1 2 3 is translated as 4 2 1 3. The correct placement of the tag should be: <kl/> 4 2 1 3, or 4 2 <kl/>1 3?
- Etc.

An open source project *m4loc* http://code.google.com/p/m4loc/ (Hudík & Ruopp, 2011) has been created to develop a solution for a better meta information placement. The work has continued for three years now and still not all the problems have been solved or even covered successfully. However, the tool gives acceptable results for most standard cases. A winning scenario was to use *Okapi Tikal* (http://www.opentag.com/okapi/wiki/index.php?title=Tikal) tool which converts all common input formats (TMX, XLIFF, PO, HTML, etc.) into much simpler XML-like file or stream where only a few tags are allowed. Tikal has simplified the task a lot since it substitutes any number of diverse tags substitute for a single or pair tag. Then, a chain of small Perl scripts together with Moses segmentation trace option (-t) are used to identify target phrases which are likely to be tag holders. Finally, Tikal is used for the converting those simple tags back into their original form and re-inserting translated (target) segments back into the original localization file.

Major Challenges of MT Deployment within a Commercial Company

While testing and deployment of new MT technologies within a university environment is usually easy and straightforward in terms of number of people engaged and ways how to incorporate changes within existing workflows, it is quite an opposite for business. The major challenges are

- employees' resistance,
- scientific outcomes are often buggy, are not tested enough, or for all eventualities,
- many works exist only as described theoretical models (no prototype),
- majority papers describe positive aspects only,
- novelty tools are often working well only for very a specific problem, or a specific test set,
- marketing claims which are hiding important technical problems,
- etc.

Employees' resistance is probably the biggest problem. This resistance is understandable and natural since those people are mostly working in operations where all the tasks have to be done precisely, repeatedly and in a timely manner (usually strict deadlines) – no time for failures or tests. Often, even the upper management is more prone to a change, or test a new technology than the production. Note, while *operations management* is focused on planning and administration of production services or goods and tries to minimize the resources and at the same time to increase output, *production management* is concerned with input/output and churning out products in the shape of a desired finished product (Murthy, 2005).

Production and operation employees hate all changes even if they know that such change can provide them with benefits. Just a simple evaluation of a new technology could pose problems because of people who might be feeling that the new technology could threaten them in some way. They can be afraid of losing their jobs, losing their uniqueness, necessity to learn new things, not meeting some requirements because of the change. Such fears are irrational in many cases. Feared employees are trying to undermine the new technology in every possible way. They are trying to falsify results (e.g., time or accuracy), when they are asked to fill a questionnaire all questions dealing with subjective issues are filled in favor of the original technique.

The progress in NLP gives interesting examples how it could be difficult to transfer any scientific novelty into companies. In the 1990s, companies were evaluating and deploying CAT tools into their workflows. During these years, so-called *translation memories* (TM) started to be widely used. In short, a translation memory is a set or a database of segments built up from a former translation. TMs are especially useful when translating a new version of a product, since both versions (old and new) will likely contain many identical and similar segments. The translators do not have to re-translate the same segments again and again. This is also true for terminology. It is likely that both versions will use the same terminology, or whenever there is just a slight change it will be carefully emphasized by a client. Although the benefits are obvious, many translators were in deep oppositions since they were afraid of losing their prestige and jobs. After time and enormous press from the localization companies, they have realized that machines just make their work faster and easier and have finally accepted it.

Another example is CAT tools in general. They are especially useful when complex products like software packages are being translated. It is due to the need to make the translation into multiple target languages. The whole process (i.e., creates a sub-project for each language and creates tasks for each translator depending on his/her contract and time-availability, delivering the small tasks to the translators all over the world. When they are finished – those small tasks need to be unified into one language package and the package is inserted as a language mutation to the original software which is sent back to the client) is done by CAT tools like SDL Trados or MemoQ. Nowadays, no translator would like to have this process done manually. CAT tools have changed localization industry a lot. Old-fashioned translators refusing any changes have moved from "everyday" translations to an art (prose, or poetry) or some other field where machines still do not make much sense. The rest have learned how to use CAT tools and the whole translation process is much faster, done mainly by native speakers located anywhere in the world and in big volumes. Imagine, writing a document without spell checker, a translator looking for a specific term in a paper dictionary, or a translator who is making up the same phrase for multiple times. The negative aspect of the change is that people are forced to be more specialized and do more monotonous tasks. Unfortunately, this has been true for every automation process since the Industrial Revolution.

In these days, there is similar fear due to the progress in machine translation. Translators are afraid of being replaced by the science and machines. Even though, the machines are still a way behind humans. Basically, we can think of the MT engine as an improved translation memory (TM). Often, if TM is good enough, MT cannot compete. MT is especially useful when there is not any translation memory which would be very close to intended translation texts. While a new technology is being deployed, it is important to talk a lot and iteratively with the production employees. Even better than talking to them, it is to try so-called shadowing (watching people while they are working). Unfortunately, the shadowing is problematic since people are not feeling comfortable when their work is watched closely and management does not like it as well because it usually takes some extra time which is very important during real-world projects.

Such talks and shadowing can avoid a lot of information noise, stress and lead to more accurate results while the new technique is evaluated. An interesting evaluation was done in the European Union project

Let'sMT! We needed to evaluate how good our MT engines are for multiple domains and languages. All documents were MT translated and handed over to translators. Before they started to work, we had several meetings where all technical details were explained. During these talks we found out that the translators do not like when they are supposed to fix errors done by MT machine. The problem was that their role was changed from the translator to the post editor. They preferred to be the ones who have the power to decide (choose different translation) and to be creative not just to fix errors. Therefore we changed the workflow and put our MT translated documents into CAT tools (SDL Trados and MemoQ) just as MT suggestions together with some other translation memories. Each translation task was composed of two variations. The first one was as it was described (1x MT translation and several MTs) and the second one did not contain MT suggestions (just several TMs). The translators did not know what variations they are translating. Instead of measuring how many errors the MT did, we have focused on:

1. How often a translator used a MT translated segment instead of a segment taken from a TM,
2. Whether the first variation (with MT) was translated faster than the variation without MT,
3. What kind of errors MT did the most often (grammatical, semantic, etc.).

These questions are more suitable for real projects than just measuring number of MT errors. The results were interesting – in average, translations with MT segments were approximately 25 – 30% faster than translation without MT (Lībiete, Skadiņš, Šarman, & Hudík, 2012; Skadiņš, Skadiņa, Pinnis, Vasiļjevs, & Hudík, 2014).

Scientific outcomes are another reason why companies are adopting MT slower than they can. However, this is rather a general problem in the university environment today. There are many conferences and each gives many papers. Unfortunately, majority of them do not have high scientific value since authors are in rush to have as many publications as possible and so the research quality is decreasing. Often, proposed approaches are not tested enough, or they are not well-written so it is hard to create a prototype based on the paper. If the prototype has been created, it is often buggy or the usage and parameters are not well described so it is better to create one of your own at the end.

MT departments researchers are going through the published papers and are trying to filter out those that could give some interesting results. It is a long and difficult journey from a paper to successful business application. An MT expert needs to understand the paper correctly, needs to think for what project types, or language pairs the novelty could bring some benefits. Normally, if a novel approach makes better results only for some target languages and gives worst outcomes for some other languages it is not to be implemented. Do not forget, LSPs are usually supposed to make translation into multiple languages per project. It would be demanding to have multiple parallel workflows per project just because some target languages might have slightly better results if a special setup or a tool is used. This is one of the reasons why LSPs are still using an older phrase-based approach instead of the newer tree-based one. The tree-based one can give better results for some Asian languages, or some specific language pairs, but results for other languages are usually worse (Chiang, 2005; Durran, Fraser, Schmid, & Hoang, 2013). This fact reveals how important it is to public also "negative results" or comparative studies that would indicate under what criteria some technique will not work well enough, or is inferior to another. Such researches could be of the same value for engineers as a paper describing a "winning strategy".

Finding enough skilled MT researchers and engineers is also one of the big challenges. The field is relatively young and is constantly changing. MT departments need people who are able and willing to learn new things all the time.

Mainly in the past, the training data represented another big issue. For the translation model, it is needed to have big amount of correctly aligned bi- or multi-lingual texts. Today, the situation is much better and many repositories with correctly aligned texts can be found. Even though, these resources are mainly for academic purposes only and their domains usually do not match with domains required by the LSP clients. There is also the sensitive ethical and law question whether it is possible to train an MT engine on different client's content (i.e., create an MT engine for the client A on translations done for the client B) While the translation was done by LSP, this company should be able to use its translation for another client. On the other hand, the client A provided the whole content for the translation. LSP is usually forced to sign a contract which forbids the use of the client's content for any other task.

Deployment of a New MT Feature – Typical Scenario

Currently, all bigger LSPs are working or experiencing with MT. Note that even though almost all of the bigger localization companies claim that they are using MT within their workflows, in some cases such a claim is still more marketing than reality. On the other hand, there are some big corporations from different fields which are using MT to pre-translate their products in order to decrease overall price of the translation. It is difficult to find how many companies are really using MT solutions and on what maturity level since no private company would allow any foreigner to look closely at their workflows and know-how. The majority of those who are using MT for real have implemented Moses or use some service based on Moses system (KantanMT, Let'sMT!, Precision Translation Tools, etc.).

Companies which have technically experienced employees are trying to implement MT on their own as it should be cheaper, many options can be adjusted and do not have to trust a third party. However, it requires having at least one MT expert dedicated to MT solely. Having full-time MT experts is very important because they are monitoring research in the field and whenever a new feature appears they test whether it can improve the translation process. If the tests are successful, they need to create a prototype. Then, it is needed to persuade all involved parties, oversee and evaluate the whole deployment of the prototype within workflow. Afterwards, it is needed to communicate the results with management and probably to try to improve (bug fixing) the whole process iteratively. Since there are not enough good technicians who would also be good communicators, department managers usually negotiate results and persuade involved parties.

If a localization company does not have skilled MT experts, it can use a service from some MT provider (some of them are listed in the first paragraph of this section). Even if the price can be tempting, it is good to think about it carefully. There are clients (especially in IT and life sciences) who are extremely sensitive about their data. Such client is reluctant to give a job to an LSP who will send its content to a third company. They usually prefer bigger LSPs with their own MT department and established processes. Another disadvantage of outsourced MT is that you still need someone from the management personally interested and involved in the process to communicate, persuade and motivate people within the company. Otherwise, the LSP is risking that its operations or translators (they are not usually company's employees but rather suppliers or partners) will refuse MT. They can refuse, avoid or diminish the use of MT mainly because of claims about poor MT performance. Therefore LSP needs some manager with a good knowledge of MT who would decide whether those claims are reasonable. If they are reasonable MT provider should try to improve its results. If the results are OK the manager needs to press on production line and explain that the results are correct and they have to use MT as it was agreed.

A big advantage of companies offering MT services (MT providers) is that they can provide good advice/policies since MT is their core business. Their software and provided services are supposed to be upgraded and improved on regular basis so LSP can work with the latest technologies.

Let's look closer at the deployment of a new MT feature. When an interesting idea which could improve the translation process is found, it is needed to create a prototype. The prototype should be deployed in the identical environment as your production system. Needless to say, using a production system for testing is dangerous. Virtualization software (e.g., VMware or VirtualBox) can help and emulate the production system. Please note, even if the virtualization can help a lot with prototyping and testing, it is not a good option for the production systems themselves because MT software is resource demanding. For instance, Moses is using system resources heavily (difficult statistics requires multiple passes through huge data), therefore it is better to have it installed on real hardware.

Prototype testing and evaluation should be done carefully. More kinds of evaluation have to be provided. The prototype needs to run smoothly without any crashes on every possible input. Then it is needed to make sure that the novel approach (prototype) is giving better MT outputs. If it gives better results only on some particular languages or translation domain (IT, weather, etc.), engineers need to make sure that the prototype does not give worse results than the current system (baseline) on the rest. In the case that prototype gives exceptional results on specific languages but underperforms the rest, specific workflow for specific languages can be created. Keep in mind that multiple workflows demand more effort and much more problematic bug fixing might be needed

Prototype Evaluation

The evaluation of translation is tricky since there is not only one correct translation of a segment. All translators, humans or MT engines, can translate a segment differently and there is no single number which would indicate what translation is closer to the source. Therefore the evaluation of a translation is something between art and science. In general, MT can be evaluated automatically (e.g., Bleu, Meteor, Nist etc.) or by so-called *human evaluation*.

Even the automatic MT evaluation needs input from humans. However, it is still cheaper and easier to achieve than the real human evaluation since some older, already translated texts can be used. LSPs usually use automatic evaluation for testing or ranking of various MT engines and for common tasks related to MT. The human evaluation is not used very often. It is often used when the automatic evaluation approves an MT engine. However, we still need some better assessment of how good an MT engine is.

The tests of a translation are done by *post-editor* or *proofreader*. These roles are similar and many people do not distinguish between them. While a proofreader repairs errors in human translated texts the post-editor repairs errors in MT-generated texts. A proofreader approves that a translation is correct or good-enough (depends on a contract) and can be shipped to a customer. Bigger LSPs have thousands of translators from various cultures and standards all around the world and their evaluations or performance assessments are needed quite often. These tasks are done by proofreaders. These people should be trustworthy senior translators. Proofreaders usually do also post-editing tasks.

Industry standard for the automatic evaluation is *Bleu* (Bilingual Evaluation Understudy) (Papineni, Roukos, Ward, & Zhu, 2002) in these days. It computes n-gram precision, which is the ratio of correct n-grams in relation to the total number of n-grams. It computes precision but there is no mechanism for recall.

A newer evaluation technique is Meteor (Lavie & Agarwal, 2005). The metric was designed to fix some of the Bleu problems. It is based on the harmonic mean of unigram precision and recall, with recall weighted higher than precision. In other words, recall was missing in Bleu and its use should move the evaluation score closer to human judgment.

Meteor has already been constantly developed for years (available on GitHub), has many interesting advanced features such as graphical output, comparison of multiple MT engines, paraphrase matching, i.e., synonyms or stemming and tuned parameters for a set of European languages. However, if a general evaluation metric is needed (for any language), it is better to stick to the basic version without any enhanced features. Otherwise, the tuned parameters would lead to unpredictable skewed results of unsupported languages.

Some older version of a product– since the new version is supposed to be translated– is usually used for the automatic evaluation. Simply put, it is good to make the evaluation on texts which are as close to the texts we want to translate later as possible. These texts should be translated very well and proof-edited by humans. They also need to be in segment-by-segment format, that means two textual files, one with the source language where one line is one segment and the second file with the translated target language where again one line represents one segment. Naturally, both files need to have the same number of lines. This target file creates a *human translation*. Then, source texts are translated by the MT engine – an *MT translation* is created. So we have:

1. source texts (sometimes called as *reference*),
2. human translation,
3. MT translation (MT engine's output).

Two sources: MT and human translation can be input for Bleu, NIST, or basics Meteor results. All three sources are needed for full Meteor results. Meteor will give a score for each particular segment, i.e., for each triple composed of the source segment, the MT translated segment and the human translated segment. And it will also give an overall picture of the test set. Figure 2 gives an example of a very small test set (some 50 segments). It can be seen the translation was exceptionally good. More than a half of the segments was translated with the accuracy higher than 90%.

Human evaluation is more difficult since we need trusted human experts that would decide how good a translation is. Such evaluation is usually done by post-editors who need to be carefully trained. While the automatic translation results are given as accuracy measured in per cents, the human evaluators give scales, e.g., 1–5:

5 flawless
4 good
3 non-native
2 disfluent
1 incomprehensible

Naturally, there are many more possible ways how to provide human evaluation (e.g., measuring of various types of errors such as: grammatical, lexical, typos, semantic, etc.) (Graham, Baldwin, Moffat, & Zobel, 2013) However, variations on a simple scale are used within the commercial sector mostly. It is important to make sure that post-editors are professionals (not resistant to changes) and trustworthy

Figure 2. Meteor results. X-axis represents score ranges, e.g., 20-30% and Y-axis shows number of segments. For example, some 5 segments have been translated with accuracy of 80-90%. And more than 25 segments have been translated with accuracy higher than 90%

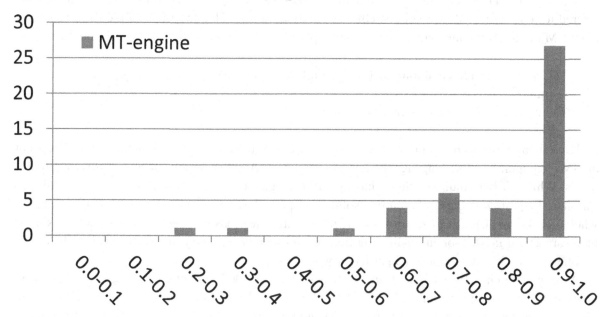

employees. To suppress the human factor it is possible to make two versions where only one would contain MT, post-editors should not know which version they are evaluating. Other possibilities: the evaluation can be done multiple times, or by engaging more post-editors who would evaluate the same part.

This will evaluate how good the prototype is from the technical point of view. Based on all previous tests if there is still belief that it will outperform the current workflow (think of whole workflow not just the number of errors done by the MT engine) a pilot project can be prepared.

Pilot Project

While the pilot is being deployed, it is important to identify and talk with all affected people. It is necessary to explain reasonably what this change can mean to them. How it will affect them, what negatives and benefits they should experience. Be honest and identify negative aspects as well can save time and disappointments.

Whenever possible, it is good if there is a way how to jump back smoothly to original workflow in case of any serious problem. When the pilot is over, it is again needed to interview all the affected people and do a small research whether the assumptions were correct. Such talks can give a better picture of the change and make people more open for future cooperation.

CHALLENGES AND FUTURE DIRECTIONS

As it was described in this chapter MT and also MT in business environment is a fast evolving and research oriented area. There are many initiatives, however, only a few of them will turn out to be successful.

For some time now, there has been a discussion under what circumstances it would be better having so-called on-line translation workflow. Off-line solution is a standard batch-based solution, where localization files are MT pre-translated and then in the form of a pre-translated text or as an MT suggestion offered to translators and post editors. On-line solution means MT translation on the run. It requires having MT engines running while the translation phase of a project is active. This could be great for

- MT engine's incremental training (Sankaran, Grewal, & Sarkar, 2010), i.e., internal incremental re-training.
- There is not enough time to train MT engine in advance.

Even though, the incremental training is still more research than a real production feature and not all SMT components (like language models) do support it. Another disadvantage is hardware requirements. While off-line solution requires having an MT engine running in RAM only for time needed to translate the particular batch; the on-line solution requires having the MT engine running during the whole translation phase. If there are 10 parallel translation sessions it is needed to have 10 times same hardware as it is needed for an off-line solution. Therefore it is necessary to think carefully whether an on-line solution is suitable for some particular workflow.

Among other challenges belong factored models (Hoang, 2007) or better re-ordering (Goh, Onishi, & Sumita, 2011; Braune, Gojun, & Fraser, 2012). Better reordering would be especially useful for more distant languages (different syntactic structures) and for translation of longer sentences where a placement of a source and target words is significantly different.

Currently, mainly Europe is funding MT research projects because it spends approximately 1% of its overall annual budget on the translations into all 24 official European languages. The European Union heavily supports Moses. For example, the European Commission uses Moses in house to aid human translators. Interesting projects are an older EuroMatrix and newer EuroMatrix Plus which collected and aligned various corpuses.

MT and internationalization is becoming a part of widely-used standards like W3C. *Internationalization Tag Set (ITS)* represents wide selection of methodologies facilitating internalization process. There are several so-called categories (e.g., *provenance*) which are supposed to be used throughout the life-cycle of a multilingual content. Some of them are used to keep separated texts produced by humans and texts that are automatically generated by, for example, MT engines.

For a further academic type of research it is good to follow MT Marathons www.statmt.org/moses/?n=Moses.Marathons and keep an eye on the particular MT methodology like Moses, or Apertium. For an industrial type of research, there is a big specialized conference called Localization World and the dedicated journal MultiLingual.

REFERENCES

Bert, E. (2000). *A Practical Guide to Localization. Benjamins.* John Publishing Company.

Braune, F., Gojun, A., & Fraser, A. (2012). Long-distance reordering during search for hierarchical phrase-based SMT. In *Proceedings of the 16th Annual Conference of the European Association for Machine Translation*, (pp. 177–184). Trento.

Brown, P. F., Pietra, V. J., Pietra, S. A., & Mercer, R. L. (1993). The Mathematics of Statistical Machine Translation: Parameter Estimation. *Computational Linguistics*, *19*(2), 263–311.

Chiang, D. (2005). A hierarchical phrase-based model for statistical machine translation. In *Proceedings of the 43rd Annual Meeting on Association for Computational Linguistics*. Stroudsburg, PA, USA: Association for Computational Linguistics. doi:10.3115/1219840.1219873

Du, J., Roturier, J., & Way, A. (2010). TMX markup: a challenge when adapting SMT to the localisation environment. *In: EAMT 2010 – 14th Annual Conference of the European Association for Machine Translation*.

Durran, I. N., Fraser, A., Schmid, H., & Hoang, H. (2013). Can Markov Models Over Minimal Translation Units Help Phrase-Based SMT. In *Proceedings of the 51st Annual Meeting of the Association for Computational Linguistics*. Retrieved from https://www.gala-global.org/what-localization

Gocci, L. (2009). CAT Tools for Beginners. *Translation Journal*, *13*(4), 133–147.

Goh, C.-L., Onishi, T., & Sumita, E. (2011). Rule-based reordering constraints for phrase-based SMT. In *proceedings of the 15th conference of the European Association for Machine Translation*. (pp. 113–120).

Graham, Y., Baldwin, T., Moffat, A., & Zobel, J. (2013). Continuous Measurement Scales in Human Evaluation of Machine Translation. In *Proceedings of the 7th Linguistic Annotation Workshop & Interoperability with Discourse*. (pp. 33–41). Sofia: Association for Computational Linguistics.

Hoang, H. (2007). Factored translation models. In *Proceedings of the 2007 Joint Conference on Empirical Methods in Natural Language Processing and Computational Natural Language Learning*. (pp. 868–876).

Hudík, T., & Ruopp, A. (2011). The integration of Moses into localisation industry. *Proceedings of the 15th conference of the European Association for Machine Translation*. (pp. 47–53).

Hutchins, W. J. (1986). *Machine translation: past, present, future*. New York: John Wiley & Sons.

Khalilov, M., & Fonollosa, J. A. (2009). N-gram-based Statistical Machine Translation Versus Syntax Augmented Machine Translation: Comparison and System Combination. In *Proceedings of the 12th Conference of the European Chapter of the Association for Computational Linguistics*. (pp. 424–432). Athens, Greece. doi:10.3115/1609067.1609114

Koehn, P. (2010). *Statistical Machine Translation*. Cambridge: Cambridge University Press.

Lavie, A., & Agarwal, A. (2005). METEOR: An Automatic Metric for MT Evaluation with Improved Correlation with Human Judgments. In *Proceedings of the ACL Workshop on Intrinsic and Extrinsic Evaluation Measures for Machine Translation*. (pp. 65–72). Association for Computational Linguistics.

Lībiete, N., Skadiņš, R., Šarman, J., & Hudík, T. (2012). *Deliverable D6.4 Evaluation of integration in CAT tools*.

Murthy, P. R. (2005). *Production And Operations Management*. New Age International.

Papineni, K., Roukos, S., Ward, T., & Zhu, W.-J. (2002). BLEU: a Method for Automatic Evaluation of Machine Translation. In *Proceedings of the 40th Annual Meeting on Association for Computational Linguistics*. (pp. 311–318). Association for Computational Linguistics.

Pawlowski, J. (2008). Culture Profiles: Facilitating Global Learning and Knowledge Sharing. In *16th International Conference on Computers in Education (ICCE)*. Taipei.

Sankaran, B., Grewal, A., & Sarkar, A. (2010). Incremental Decoding for Phrase-based Statistical Machine Translation. In *Proceedings of the Joint Fifth Workshop on Statistical Machine Translation and MetricsMATR*. (pp. 216–223). Uppsala: Association for Computational Linguistics.

Shannon, C. (1948). A mathematical theory of communication. *The Bell System Technical Journal*, *27*(3), 379–423. doi:10.1002/j.1538-7305.1948.tb01338.x

Skadiņš, R., Skadiņa, I., Pinnis, M., Vasiļjevs, A., & Hudík, T. (2014). Application of Machine Translation in Localization into low-resourced languages. *Proceedings of the 18th conference of the European Association for Machine Translation*.

Stein, D. (2013). Machine Translation – Past, Present, and Future. *Translation: Computation, Corpora. Cognition*, *3*(1).

Yamada, K., & Knight, K. (2001). A Syntax-based Statistical Translation Model. In *Proceedings of the 39th Annual Meeting on Association for Computational Linguistics*. (pp. 523–530). Toulouse, France.

KEY TERMS AND DEFINITIONS

CAT Tools: Computer Aided Translation – specialized software used by human translators providing functions to facilitate the translation process.

Localization Industry: Companies the core business of which is localization. By this term we generally refer to LSP companies.

LSP: Language Service Provider: A company that is able to manage the entire process of complex translation tasks, i.e., the translations into multiple languages working with native translators and proofreaders. These companies are offering also design and publishing services for the translated content.

MT: Machine Translation: Translation of a natural language by a machine.

NLP: Natural Language Processing: Is a shared scientific field of field of computer science, artificial intelligence, and linguistics dealing with interactions between the human and computers.

SMT: Statistical Machine Translation: Statistical Machine translation – machine translation based on statistical analysis of a natural language.

Source Language/Segment: A language/segment that will be translated.

Target Language/Segment: A language to which the translation is done. Translated segment.

Chapter 11
A Corpus–Stylistic Approach of the Treatises of Great Athanasius About Idolatry

Georgios Alexandropoulos
National and Kapodistrian University of Athens, Greece

ABSTRACT

This research focuses on the corpus stylistic analysis of the treatises of Great Athanasius. In this interdisciplinary study classical texts are approached through linguistic tools and the main purpose is to describe the style of Great Athanasius in these treatises, after having extracted all these quantitative data utilizing computational tools. The language Great Athanasius uses is a language that expresses intensely his speculations on the achievement of religious change and restructuration. His language expresses his religious ideology. His speeches are persuasive, ideological and represent the rhetorician's opinion. They are based on the speaker's intentionality; it directs him to the specific rhetorical framework, since he aims at one and unique inspirational result, that is, persuasion.

PURPOSE OF RESEARCH AND METHODOLOGY

In this chapter we are going to describe the significance of corpus linguistics when combined with the analysis of classical texts. Alexandropoulos (2013ab, 2014abc) tries to approach the byzantine texts in a new rhetorical way using rhetorical theories and corpus analysis tools. Corpus linguistics (Kennedy, 1992; Atkins, Clear, & Ostler, 1992; Leech & Fligelstone, 1992) can help us understand the use and repetition of some words or lexical bundles, fixed and semi-fixed multi-word combinations; these formulaic sentences can contain one word or many words. Corpus linguistics gives us the opportunity to use text-handling tools as a concordance, word frequency counts (per % or per ‰) or wordlists, keyword analysis, cluster analysis and lexico-grammatical profiles; in this way, we can extract and study longer sequences of words in discourse statistically; this enables us to focus more on what is frequent, instead of examining what stands out following the traditional Aristotelian rhetoric approach. (Nowadays corpus processing and linguistics focus on lexical bundles and many researchers of the linguistic discipline try

DOI: 10.4018/978-1-4666-8690-8.ch011

Table 1. Constituents of corpora of Great Athanasius

Texts	Words tokens count
Contra Gentes	19,580
De incarnatione verbi	21,410

to recognize some high frequency multiword sets. Mainly, some linguists, such as Baker (2006), Biber & Barbieri (2007), Biber, Conrad & Cortes (2004), Cortes (2004), Hyland (2008ab) focus on lexical bundles and try to describe their structure and their functions into the texts.) Halmari (2005) utilizes computational tools also in order to describe the style of Reagan and Clinton. Alexandropoulos (2014c) describes the most frequently used intertextualistic sources in the political speeches of Julian using also corpus analysis tools. Alexandropoulos (2014ab) examines also the classical texts combining rhetoric analysis with corpus stylistic tools. After extracting all these quantitative data from the corpus we can go even further, following a qualitative interpretation of them, because, as Biber et al. (1998) support, corpus-based research also aims to uncover patterns of language use through the analysis of these results.

The issue of this research is based on the idea of defining and studying the rhetorical and linguistic practice of Great Athanasius, who expresses his disagreement with the Ethnics and his religious view. Until now, we can find a lot of traditional studies in literature review in reference with byzantine, classical texts, based on the Aristotelian concept of rhetoric (Brédif, 1879; Cameron, 1994; Hunger, 1978; Kennedy, 1994; Mirhady, 2007; Nesselrath, 1997; Pernot, 2000; Roberts, 1984; Ross, 1974; Wolf, 2008). Corpus linguistics can be combined with and serve the goal of this interdisciplinary research. The above combination enables us to have clear results, based on quantitative and qualitative data. The perceptual salience is not always enough to approach texts.

The main objectives of this research can be reflected in the following questions:

i)   What are the most frequently used words, adjectives, pronouns, verbs and lexical bundles?
ii) What are the differences and similarities between the two speeches?
iii) How the most frequently used elements serve the speaker's ideological goal and define his style?

Our research is relied on two texts of Great Athanasius (295– 2 May 373) – who was the twentieth bishop of Alexandria – concerning his beliefs about idolatry (Bardy, 1914; Brakke, 1995; Cavallera, 1914; Cross, 1945; Dragas, 1980; Kannengiesser, 1991; Lauchert, 1911; Meijering, 1968; Pettersen, 1990; Roldanus, 1968; Thompson, 1971). Great Athanasius was a great Father of the Church and a pillar of Orthodoxy. It is believed that he was one of the most important theologians as he contributed to the formation of the Trinitarian dogma. The texts (for the translation of these speeches please visit Elpenor (n.d.)) for the corpora were typed in computer and for their form we relied on Migne (1857-1866).

A variety of models and methodological tools are adopted in this study. Actually, for the extraction of the most frequently used words, lexical bundles etc. the Antconc (Anthony, 2006) program is adopted. For the study of the lexical bundles, Biber et al (2004) and Hyland (2008ab) models are adopted. For the study of the rhetorical relations, Mann & Thompson theory is adopted in accordance with the context (Malinowski, 1923; Firth, 1957; Austin, 1962; Hymes, 1964, 1974) following Hymes (1964, 1974). For the interpretation of the speech acts, we rely on Searle's (1969·1979·1994·1996ab) categorization. For the study of the intertextualistic sources, some models such as Fairclough (1992), van Leeuwen (1996),

Caldas & Coulthard (1997), Leech (1980) are also adopted. Incorporated discourse's modes and forms of representation are going to be examined on the basis of the typology's mechanisms of Thompson (1996).

CONTRA GENTES

Context of the Speech

This speech is the first speech of Great Athanasius and it refers to the error of idolatry. The orator tries to reveal that Greek mythology is sunk in superstition. This speech is divided into two parts: in the first part, the orator talks about the error of idolatry and in the second part he tries to persuade the audience about the existence of one only God. It is believed that in his speech the orator expresses his deep faith and love for the humans who have lost their way. He expresses also the thought that God is revealed to the people through the Holy Scriptures and through what He has created. He believes that we can acquire the knowledge of the real God only if we rely on the doctrines of the Holy Fathers. If we follow this tactic, we can support our faith and compare it with everyone who has a different opinion, like the supporters of idolatry who scoff at religion. Because of this behavior, the certain people are much to be pitied, since they cannot accept that the faith to Christian theology is superior to others. The springboard of idolatry for the orator is the arrogance and the sensualism of the people; people have lost their way and believe in materialism and not in spiritualism. Going ahead to the end of his speech, the orator attacks the polytheism and makes an attempt to prove that everything obeys to the will of God. The structure (Robertson, 1892) of this text is the following:

1. Introduction: The purpose of this treatise is a vindication of the Christian doctrine, and especially of the Cross, against the scoffing objection of Gentiles. The effects of this doctrine are its main vindication.
2. Evil is no part of the essential nature of things; the original creation and constitution of man in grace and in knowledge of God.
3. The decline of man from the above condition, owing to his absorption in material things.
4. The gradual abasement of the Soul from Truth to Falsehood by the abuse of its freedom of Choice.
5. Evil, then, is based essentially on the choice of what is lower in preference to what is higher.
6. False views of the nature of evil.
7. Refutation of dualism from reason. Impossibility of two Gods. The truth as to evil is that which the Church teaches: it originates, and resides, in the perverted choice of the darkened soul.
8. The origin of idolatry is similar to it. The soul, materialized by forgetting God and engrossed in earthly things, transforms them into gods. The race of men descends into a hopeless depth of delusion and superstition.
9. The various developments of idolatry: worship of the heavenly bodies, the elements, natural objects, fabulous creatures and personified lusts, men living and dead. The case of Antinous and the deified Emperors.
10. Similar human origin of the Greek gods, by decree of Theseus. The process through which mortals became deified.
11. The deeds of heathen deities and particularly of Zeus.

12. Other shameful actions ascribed to heathen deities. All prove that they are but men of former times, and not even good men.
13. The folly of image worship and its dishonor to art.
14. Image worship condemned by Scripture.
15. The details about the gods, conveyed in their representations by poets and artists, show that they are without life and that they are neither gods, nor decent men and women.
16. Heathen arguments in palliation of the above: and (1) 'the poets are responsible for these unedifying tales.' But are the names and existence of the gods any better authenticated? Both stand or fall together. Either the actions must be defended or the deity of the gods be given up. And the heroes are not credited with acts inconsistent with their nature, as, on this plea, the gods are.
17. The truth probably is that the scandalous tales are true, while the divine attributes ascribed to them are due to the flattery of the poets.
18. Heathen defense continued. (2) 'The gods are worshipped for having invented the Arts of Life.' But this is a human and natural, not a divine, achievement. And why, on this principle, are not all inventors deified?
19. The inconsistency of image worship. Arguments in palliation. (1) The divine nature must be expressed in a visible sign. (2) The image a means of supernatural communications to men through angels.
20. But where does this supposed virtue of the image reside? In the material essence, in the form or in the maker's skill? Untenability of all these views.
21. The idea of communications through angels involves an even wilder inconsistency and it does not, even if true, justify the worship of the image.
22. The image cannot represent the true form of God, since in this case God would be corruptible.
23. The variety of idolatrous cults proves that they are false.
24. The so-called gods of one place are used as victims in another.
25. Human sacrifice. Its absurdity. Its prevalence. Its calamitous results.
26. The moral corruptions of Paganism all admittedly originated from the gods.
27. The refutation of popular Paganism being taken as a conclusive element; we reach the higher form of nature-worship. How Nature witnesses God through the mutual dependence of all its parts, which forbid us to think of anyone of them as the supreme God. This is shown analytically.
28. But neither can the cosmic organism be God. For that would make God consist of dissimilar parts, and subject Him to possible dissolution.
29. The balance of powers in Nature shows that it is not God, either collectively or in parts.
30. The soul of man, being intellectual can know God of itself, if it be true to its own nature.
31. Proof of the existence of the rational soul.
32. The body cannot originate such phenomena; and in fact the action of the rational soul is seen in its ruling over the instincts of the bodily organs.
33. The soul immortal.
34. The soul, then, if it gets rid of the stains of sin is able to know God directly; its own rational nature imaging back the Word of God, after whose image it was created. But even if it cannot pierce the cloud which sin draws over its vision, it is confronted with the witness of creation to God.
35. Creation is a revelation of God; especially in the order and harmony pervading the whole.
36. This is the most striking part, if we consider the opposing forces out of which this order is produced.
37. The same subject is continued.

Table 2. The most frequent words (‰) without stemming and exclusion criteria

77.7 καὶ /and	17.1 τὴν / the	16.1 δὲ / but	14.76 τοῦ / of the
12.97 τῶν / of the	12.16 τὰ / the	11.65 τὸ / the	11.1 τὸν / the
11.03 τῆς / of	10.72 γὰρ /for one	9.19 ἐν / in	8.9 ὁ / the

38. The Unity of God shown by the Harmony of the order of Nature.
39. Impossibility of a plurality of Gods.
40. The rationality and order of the Universe proves that it is the work of the Reason or Word of God.
41. The Presence of the Word in nature is necessary, not only for its original Creation, but also for its permanence.
42. This function of the Word is described comprehensively.
43. Three similes to illustrate the Word's relation to the Universe.
44. The similes are applied to the whole Universe, seen and unseen. Finally, the orator extracts some conclusions and he supports that it is necessary to return to the Word, if our corrupt nature is to be restored.

Frequency Words List

In Table 2 we can have a general picture of the most frequent words with no stemming and exclusion criteria. It is noted that this table contains mostly articles (ὁ/ *the*, τῆς/ *the*), conjunctions (καὶ/ *and*), particles (γὰρ/ *for one*), prepositions (ἐν/ *in*), etc.

Table 3 provides us with the most frequently used words of emotional value.

Great Athanasius utilizes a lot of words with emotional value. These words urge us to say that god plays an important role in his speech as a corollary of its theocratic content and orientation.

*1. τούτῳ τῷ Θεῷ Λόγῳ πειθόμενα τὰ μὲν ἐπὶ γῆς ζωογονεῖται, τὰ δὲ ἐν οὐρανοῖς συνίσταται. καὶ διὰ τοῦτον θάλαττα μὲν πᾶσα καὶ ὁ μέγας ὠκεανὸς ὅροις ἰδίοις ἔχουσι τὴν ἑαυτῶν κίνησιν· ἡ δὲ ξηρὰ πᾶσα χλοηφορεῖ καὶ κομᾷ παντοίοις καὶ διαφόροις φυτοῖς, ὡς προεῖπον. / Obeying Him, even **God the Word**, things on earth have life and things in the heaven have their order. By reason of Him all the sea, and the great ocean, move within their proper bounds, while, as we said above, the dry land grows grasses and is clothed with all manner of diverse plants. (42)*

In this part of his speech, Great Athanasius presents into representative speech acts the divine power of the god. The whole nature obeys to Him and He gives life to things we see as a driving force.

Use of Verbs

We are about to shed some light on the most frequently used verbs. To this purpose, we rely again on the frequency wordlist extracted via the Antconc program. This is going to give us the ability to analyze thoroughly the rhetorical style of Great Athanasius.

Table 4 helps us to understand that Great Athanasius utilizes more verbs in third singular reference.

*2. Οὐδὲ γὰρ πολλοὺς εἶναι **δεῖ** νομίζειν τοὺς τῆς κτίσεως ἄρχοντας καὶ ποιητάς, ἀλλὰ πρὸς εὐσέβειαν ἀκριβῆ καὶ ἀλήθειαν ἕνα τὸν ταύτης δημιουργὸν πιστεύειν προσήκει· καὶ τοῦτο τῆς κτίσεως αὐτῆς ἐμφανῶς δεικνυούσης./ For **we must not think** there is more than one ruler and maker*

Table 3. Words of emotional value with stemming

Word	Frequency ‰
Θεός / God	14.86
Λόγος /Word	3.065
Πατήρ / Father	2.76
Ψυχή / soul	2.50
Χριστός / Christ	12.25
εἴδωλο / Idol	1.073
ἀλήθεια / truth	0.77

of Creation; but it belongs to correct and true religion to believe that its Artificer is one, while Creation herself clearly points to this. (39)

In this example, the orator utilizes a verb of deontic character (into a directive speech act) with a purpose to direct the audience to follow his religious ideology about the rulers and makers of Creation. It is also noted that after the conjunction ἀλλὰ *(but)* he utilizes one more verb of deontic character προσήκει *(it deserves)* in order to persuade the audience that the Artificer is one and they should believe in Him. It is also worth mentioning that the orator promotes his view utilizing the rhetorical relation of antithesis (following Mann & Thompson Rhetorical Structure Theory) and the nucleus of his message is presented after the conjunction ἀλλὰ, because he wants the hearers to focus on what they should do in their lives on the issue of faith.

In addition to the use of the previous verb, it is useful to study the functions of one more verb that is very common to ancient and byzantine Greek in elliptical sentences. The verb ἐστι *(is)* can be sometimes used into impersonal syntaxes (as a means of detachment, see Chafe (1982)) accompanied by the adjective ἄξιον *(7repeats-0.36‰)* as a directive speech act.

3. ταῦτα δὲ καὶ τὰ τοιαῦτα πράσσοντες, ὁμολογοῦσι καὶ ἐλέγχουσι καὶ τοὺς λεγομένους αὐτῶν θεοὺς τοιοῦτον ἐσχηκέναι τὸν βίον. ἐκ μὲν γὰρ Διὸς τὴν παιδοφθορίαν καὶ τὴν μοιχείαν, ἐκ δὲ Ἀφροδίτης τὴν πορνείαν, καὶ ἐκ μὲν Ῥέας τὴν ἀσέλγειαν, ἐκ δὲ Ἄρεος τοὺς φόνους, καὶ ἐξ ἄλλων ἄλλα τοιαῦτα μεμαθήκασιν, ἃ οἱ νόμοι μὲν κολάζουσι, πᾶς δὲ σώφρων ἀνὴρ ἀποστρέφεται. ἆρ᾽ οὖν **ἄξιον** ἔτι τούτους νομίζειν εἶναι θεούς, τοὺς τὰ τοιαῦτα ποιοῦντας, καὶ μὴ μᾶλλον τῶν ἀλόγων

Table 4. The most frequent verbs

Word	Frequency ‰
ἐστι / is	6.33
ἔχουσι / have	0.012
ἔδει / must	0.97
γέγονε / become	0.56
δεῖ / must	0.56
κινεῖται / move	0.51
λέγω / say	0.46
γέγονεν/ had become	0.41

ἀλογωτέρους ἡγεῖσθαι τούτους διὰ τὴν ἀσέλγειαν τῶν τρόπων; ἄρα ἄξιον τοὺς θρησκεύοντας αὐτοὺς νομίζειν ἀνθρώπους, καὶ μὴ μᾶλλον ὡς ἀλόγων ἀλογωτέρους, καὶ τῶν ἀψύχων ἀψυχοτέρους, οἰκτείρειν; εἰ γὰρ ἐλογίζοντο τῆς ἑαυτῶν ψυχῆς τὸν νοῦν, οὐκ ἂν ἐν τούτοις κατεπεπτώκεισαν ὅλοι πρηνεῖς, καὶ τὸν ἀληθινὸν ἠρνοῦντο τοῦ Χριστοῦ Πατέρα Θεόν./ But acting in this and in like ways, they admit and prove that the life of their so-called gods was of the same kind. For from Zeus they have learned corruption of youth and adultery, from Aphrodite fornication, from Rhea licentiousness, from Ares murders, and from other gods other like things, which the laws punish and from which every sober man turns away. **Does it then remain fit** to consider them gods who do such things, instead of reckoning them, for the licentiousness of their ways, more irrational than the brutes? **Is it fit** to consider their worshippers human beings, instead of pitying them as more irrational than the brutes, and more soul-less than inanimate things? For had they considered the intellectual part of their soul they would not have plunged headlong into these things, nor have denied the true God, the Father of Christ. (26)

In this part of his speech Great Athanasius utilizes the impersonal syntax of the certain elliptical expression into a directive speech act. The double use of this expression into directive speech acts has as a goal to motivate the thought of the audience and lead them to a certain pathway of religious faith and ideology, rejecting the Ethnics.

Use of Adjectives

Adjectives can also operate as a means for the speaker either to describe or evaluate entities of the text. In this speech, we noted that some nouns, such as γραφή, θεός are accompanied with certain adjectives promoting the value of the certain entities (see Table 5).

Attack to the Opponent

Great Athanasius also utilizes the adjectives ψευδῆ (*false*) and ἄφρονες (*foolish*) in order to attack the Ethnics. He states that their doctrines are false because they are based on lies. Some examples:

*4. ἐὰν δέ τις ἐξετάσῃ τὸν λόγον μετ' ἐπιμελείας, εὑρήσει τούτων οὐκ ἔλαττον τῶν πρότερον δειχθέντων τὴν δόξαν εἶναι **ψευδῆ**. /But if one examines the argument with care, he will find that the opinion of these persons also, not less than that of those previously spoken of, is **false**. (19)*

*5. ὅμοιον γὰρ ὡς εἴ τις τὰ ἔργα πρὸ τοῦ τεχνίτου θαυμάσειε, καὶ τὰ ἐν τῇ πόλει δημιουργήματα καταπλαγείς, τὸν τούτων δημιουργὸν καταπατοίη· ἢ ὡς εἴ τις τὸ μὲν μουσικὸν ὄργανον ἐπαινοίη, τὸν δὲ συνθέντα καὶ ἁρμοσάμενον ἐκβάλλοι. **ἄφρονες** καὶ πολὺ τὸν ὀφθαλμὸν πεπηρωμένοι./ For it is just as if one were to admire the works more than the workman, and being awestruck at the public works in the city, were to make light of their builder, or as if one were to praise a musical instrument but to despise the man who made and tuned it. **Foolish** and sadly disabled in eyesight! (47)*

Use of Pronouns

In general it noted that Great Athanasius utilizes more frequently the personal pronoun in the first singular and plural reference (as a means of involvement, see Chafe (1982)) and not in the second (see Table 6). In this way, it could be said that Great Athanasius speaks as a delegate of his religious ideology.

6. Πρὶν δὲ ἡμᾶς ἰδεῖν καὶ τῆς ἀποδείξεως ἄρξασθαι, ἀρκεῖ τὴν κτίσιν αὐτὴν κατ' αὐτῶν μονονουχὶ βοῆσαι, καὶ δεῖξαι τὸν αὐτῆς ποιητὴν καὶ δημιουργὸν θεόν, τὸν καὶ ταύτης καὶ τοῦ παντὸς βασιλεύοντα

Table 5. Synapses of nouns

Θεός / God	Γραφή / Scripture
ἄφθαρτος / incorruptible	θεόπνευστοι, -ος / inspired by God
ἀθάνατος / immortal	ἅγιαι / Holy
Ἀγαθὸς /good	ἱεραὶ / Holy
φιλάνθρωπος / philanthropist	θεῖα/ divine, Holy

τὸν Πατέρα τοῦ Κυρίου ἡμῶν Ἰησοῦ Χριστοῦ· ὃν ἀποστρέφονται μὲν οἱ δοκησίσοφοι, τὴν δὲ παρ' αὐτοῦ γενομένην κτίσιν προσκυνοῦσι καὶ θεοποιοῦσι, καίτοι προσκυνοῦσαν καὶ αὐτὴν καὶ ὁμολογοῦσαν ὃν ἐκεῖνοι δι' αὐτὴν ἀρνοῦνται Κύριον. / But before we look, or begin our demonstration, it suffices that Creation almost raises its voice against them, and points to God as its Maker and Artificer, Who reigns over Creation and over all things, even the Father of **our** Lord Jesus Christ; Whom the would-be philosophers turn from to worship and deify the Creation which proceeded from Him, which yet itself worships and confesses the Lord Whom they deny on its account. (27)

In this example, the personal pronoun ἡμῶν helps Great Athanasius to intensify the content of his message promoting his and his supporters faith in their God, who is the Maker and Artificer. The certain part of speech, where this personal pronoun is included, is contrasted with the faith of the Ethnics who are the would-be philosophers according to the orator.

In his speech, Great Athanasius utilizes the demonstrative pronoun (see Table 7) so as to bring to the surface the previous entities of their speech through the demonstrative reference or to specify the reason that something happens.

7. ἐν αὐτῷ δὲ καὶ δι' αὐτοῦ, καὶ ἑαυτὸν ἐμφαίνει, καθὼς ὁ Σωτὴρ φησιν· Ἐγὼ ἐν τῷ Πατρὶ καὶ ὁ Πατὴρ ἐν ἐμοί· ὥστε ἐξ ἀνάγκης εἶναι τὸν Λόγον ἐν τῷ γεννήσαντι, καὶ τὸν γεννηθέντα σὺν τῷ Πατρὶ διαιωνίζειν. **Τούτων** δὲ οὕτως ἐχόντων, καὶ οὐδενὸς ἔξωθεν αὐτοῦ τυγχάνοντος, ἀλλὰ καὶ οὐρανοῦ καὶ γῆς, καὶ πάντων τῶν ἐν αὐτοῖς ἐξηρτημένων αὐτοῦ, ὅμως ἄνθρωποι παράφρονες, παραγκωνισάμενοι τὴν πρὸς τοῦτον γνῶσιν καὶ εὐσέβειαν, τὰ οὐκ ὄντα πρὸ τῶν ὄντων ἐτίμησαν· καὶ ἀντὶ τοῦ ὄντως ὄντος Θεοῦ τὰ μὴ ὄντα ἐθεοποίησαν, τῇ κτίσει παρὰ τὸν κτίσαντα λατρεύοντες, πρᾶγμα πάσχοντες ἀνόητον καὶ δυσσεβές./ But in and through Him He reveals Himself also, as the Savior says: I in the Father and the Father in Me:" so that it follows that the Word is in Him that begat Him, and that He that is begotten lives eternally with the Father. But **this** being so, and nothing being outside Him, but both heaven and earth and all that in them is being dependent on Him, yet men in their folly have set aside the knowledge and service of Him, and honored things that are not instead of things that are; and instead of the real and true God deified things that were not, "serving the creature rather than the Creator," thus involving themselves in foolishness and impiety. (47)

The demonstrative pronoun, into a representative speech act, helps the orator to introduce again into the speech the message of the previous sentences, in order to extract a conclusion about what happens now in the religious life, even though the Savior said that He in the Father and the Father is in Him. The summarization gives us the general picture of the society on the issues of religious life, since people are impious and do not care about the real God of the world.

Table 6. Personal pronouns used

Pronouns	Repeats	Frequency ‰
1st person sg reference ἐγώ / I, me	3	0.15
ἐμοῦ, μοῦ / I, me	1	0.051
ἐμοί (ἔμοιγε), μοι / I, me	1	0.051
ἐμέ, με / I, me	0	0
Total amount	5	0.26
1st person pl reference ἡμεῖς / we, us	3	0.15
ἡμῶν / we, us	15	0.77
ἡμῖν / we, us	6	0.31
ἡμᾶς / we, us	7	0.36
Total amount	31	1.58
2nd person sg reference σύ / you	2	0.10
σοῦ, σου / you	0	0
σοί, σοι / you	0	0
σε, σε / you	0	0
Total amount	2	0.10
2nd person pl reference ὑμεῖς / you	1	0.051
ὑμῶν / you	2	0.10
ὑμῖν / you	3	0.15
ὑμᾶς/ you	1	0.051
Total amount	7	0.36
Total of all 1st and 2nd personal pronouns	45	2.3

Lexical Bundles

Table 8 helps us to comprehend that Great Athanasius focuses more on his text organization and production and, therefore, his lexical bundles are oriented to the text. We do not meet lexical bundles of personal stance, because of the fact that the orator prefers mostly to attack his opponents through objec-

Table 7. Demonstrative pronouns

Pronouns	Repeats	Frequency ‰
τούτων/ of these	75	3.83
τοῦτο/ this	63	3.21
ταῦτα/ these	59	3.01

Table 8. Lexical bundles

Frequency ‰	Lexical bundle	Function (according to Biber)	Function (according to Hyland)
3.56	καὶ διὰ τοῦτο/ and for this reason	Reference expression	Text oriented
0.31	καὶ δι' αὐτοῦ/ and through him	Reference expression	Text oriented
0.2	ἐν τῷ σώματι / in body	Reference expression	Text oriented
0.2	διὰ τοῦτο γοῦν / for this reason	Reference expression	Text oriented
0.2	διὰ τοῦτο γὰρ / for this reason	Reference expression	Text oriented
0.2	εἰ μὲν οὖν / if	Discourse organizer	Text oriented
0.2	καὶ οἱ μὲν / and the ones	Discourse organizer	Text oriented
0.2	πρὸς τὸν Θεόν / for the God	Reference expression	Text oriented

tive arguments without any kind of personal subjective opinion. The theocratic character of his speech is also reflected in the lexical bundle *πρὸς τὸν Θεόν,* which operates as a reference expression.

8. Ταύτας δὲ καὶ τὰς τοιαύτας τῆς εἰδωλομανίας εὑρέσεις ἄνωθεν καὶ πρὸ πολλοῦ προεδίδασκεν ἡ γραφὴ λέγουσα· Ἀρχὴ πορνείας ἐπίνοια εἰδώλων· εὕρεσις δὲ αὐτῶν φθορὰ ζωῆς. οὔτε γὰρ ἦν ἀπ' ἀρχῆς, οὔτε εἰς τὸν αἰῶνα ἔσται. κενοδοξία γὰρ ἀνθρώπων ἦλθεν εἰς τὸν κόσμον, **καὶ διὰ τοῦτο** σύντομον αὐτῶν τέλος ἐπενοήθη./ But of these and such like inventions of idolatrous madness, Scripture taught us beforehand long ago, when it said, "The devising of idols was the beginning of fornication, and the invention of them, the corruption of life. For neither were they from the beginning, neither shall they be forever. For the vainglory of men they entered into the world, and **therefore** shall they come shortly to an end. (11)

In the aforementioned example, the orator utilizes the lexical bundle *καὶ διὰ τοῦτο* into representative speech acts, in order to extract a conclusion that the invention of idols is a product of vanity and it will have as a result the short end.

Intertextuality

Introducing Lexical Items of the Integrated Speech

In this point of our research, we focus on the findings of the introducing lexical types of the integrated speech (see Table 9). To this purpose, we use the Antconc program and a concordance list, so as to have clear results for our research. When applying this program to the certain speech it is noted that the certain orator introduces the intertextualistic sources through assertive and neutral reporting verbs or particles, according to Caldas-Coulthard (1997), so as to interpret the intertextualistic source and prove that the first person speaking appears to express his degree of conviction, as far as the truth of his words is concerned or with neutral reporting verbs, as a means of neutral objectivity.

It is noted that Great Athanasius uses the aforementioned reporting verbs and particles in combination with sources from the religious system in which he believes. When he uses intertextualistic sources from the Greek philosophy and way of thinking, he also uses reporting verbs such as *ἀπεφήναντο* (1

Table 9. Introducing lexical items of the intertextualistic sources

Lexical elements	Frequency %	Function
Φησίν/ asserts	0.61%	assertive reporting verb
Λέγουσα/ saying	0.30%	neutral reporting particle
εἶπεν / said	0.26%	neutral reporting verb
Λέγων/ saying	0.21%	neutral reporting particle
Λέγουσιν/ say	0.10%	neutral reporting verb
Λεγούσης/ saying	0.10%	neutral reporting particle
Ἔλεγεν/ said	0.10%	neutral reporting verb

repeat), ἐξηγήσαντο (1 repeat). These propositional introducing reporting verbs, according to Leech (1980), give us the chance to learn how Great Athanasius realizes the integrated part of the speech. They also have a strong charge of subjectivity about the real view of the first speaker instead of the neutral or assertive reporting verbs.

Kind of Intertextualistic Sources

It is noted that Great Athanasius uses mostly sources form the theological system he supports, than from the philosophical and religious system of the Greek people (see Table 10). The integrated parts of the speech are retrieved from books such as the *Holy Bible, Psalms, Deyteronomion, Genesis, Exodus* etc. and letters such as the *Letter to Corinthians, Letter to Romans, Letter to Timothy.*

9. *...ὅτι δι᾽ αὐτοῦ καὶ ἐν αὐτῷ συνέστηκε τὰ πάντα τά τε ὁρατὰ καὶ τὰ ἀόρατα, καὶ αὐτός ἐστιν ἡ κεφαλὴ τῆς Ἐκκλησίας, ὡς οἱ τῆς ἀληθείας διάκονοι διδάσκουσιν ἐν ἁγίοις γράμμασιν./ ...for through Him and in Him all things consist, things visible and things invisible, and He is the Head of the Church," as the ministers of truth teach in their holy writings (41) .*

In the aforementioned example, Great Athanasius integrates into his speech an intertextualistic source through a parabolic sentence, in order to give proof to what he says about the power of God as He is the Maker of all visible and invisible things.

DE INCARNATIONE VERBI

Context of the Speech

This treatise was written around 317–319 AD by Great Athanasius in order to examine the event of the Incarnation of the Word. The first part of the speech analyzes the dual purpose of the Incarnation of the Word: a) the return of mankind in the state of immortality lost as a result of the original sin, and b) giving people the ability to know the true God. The second part of this treatise describes the means by which they achieve the dual purpose of the Incarnation: the works of Christ, death and resurrection. The third part of the speech refutes the objections of the Jews and the Greeks (pagans) for the Incarnation of the Word. The objections of the Jews invalidated by their prophetic tradition. The objections of the

Table 10. The most frequent intertextualistic sources

Name of the source	Frequency %
ἡ γραφὴ / αἱ γραφαἰ/ Holy Scripure	0.046%
ὁ Κύριος / Lord	0.15%
ὁ Σωτὴρ / Savior	0.15%
ὁ Παῦλος / Saint Paul	0.15%
τὸ Πνεῦμα / Holy Wit	0.10%
ὁ θεολόγος ἀνήρ / οἱ θεολόγοι ἄνδρες/ theologians	0.10%

pagans invalidated by logical reasoning. Finally, the orator states that the completion of the doctrine of the Incarnation of salvation requires two things: study of the Holy Bible and life ignorance.

The structure (Robertson, 1892) of this treatise is the following:

1. Introduction of the subject of this treatise: the humiliation and incarnation of the Word.
2. Erroneous views of Creation are rejected.
3. The true doctrine. Creation out of nothing; out of God's lavish bounty of being. Man created above the rest, but incapable of independent perseverance. Hence, the exceptional and supra-natural gift of being in God's Image, with the promise of bliss conditionally upon his perseverance in grace.
4. Our creation and God's Incarnation are most intimately connected. As by the Word man was called from non-existence into being and further received the grace of a divine life; so, by that first fault, which forfeited that life and incurred corruption, untold sin and misery filled the world.
5. Because God has not only made us out of nothing, but also He gave us freely, by the Grace of the Word, a life in correspondence with God. But men, having rejected eternal things, and, by counsel of the devil, turned to things of corruption, became the cause of their own corruption in death, being, as I said before, by nature corruptible, but destined, by the grace of the Word, to have escaped their natural state, had they remained good.
6. The human race was then wasted, God's image was being effaced, and His work was ruined. Either, then, God must forego His spoken word by which man had incurred ruins; or that which had shared in the being of the Word must sink back again into destruction, in which case God's design would be defeated. What then? Was God's goodness to suffer this? But if so, why had man been made? It could have been weakness, not goodness on God's part.
7. On the other hand, there was the consistency of God's nature, not to be sacrificed for our profit. Were men, then, to be called upon to repent? But repentance cannot avert the execution of a law; still less can it remedy a fallen nature. We have incurred corruption and need to be restored to the Grace of God's Image. None could renew us, but He Who had created us.
8. The Word, then, visited that earth in which He was yet always present; and saw all these evils. He takes a body of our Nature, and that of a spotless Virgin, in whose womb He makes it His own, wherein to reveal Himself, conquers death, and restores life.
9. The Word, since death alone could stay as a plague, took a mortal body which, united with Him, should avail for all, and by partaking of His immortality stays as the corruption of the Race. By being above all, He made His Flesh an offering for our souls; by being one of us, he clothed us with immortality.

10. By a similar simile, the reasonableness of the work of redemption is shown. How Christ wiped away our ruins and provided an antidote through His own teaching. Scripture proofs of the Incarnation of the Word and of the Sacrifice He wrought.

11. Second reason for the Incarnation. God, knowing that man was not by nature sufficient to know Him, gave him, in order that he might have some profit in being, a knowledge of Himself. He made them in the Image of the Word, that thus they might know the Word and through Him the Father. Yet man, despising this, fell into idolatry, leaving the unseen God for magic and astrology; and all this in spite of God's manifold revelation of Himself.

12. For though man was created in grace, God, foreseeing his forgetfulness, also provided the works of the creation to remind man of him. Yet further, He ordained a Law and Prophets, whose ministry was meant for the entire world. Yet men heeded only their own lusts.

13. Here again, was God to keep silence? To allow to false gods the worship He made us render to Himself? A king whose subjects had revolted would, after sending letters and messages, go to them in person. How much more shall God restore in us the grace of His image? These men, not themselves but copies, could not do. Hence the Word Himself must come (1) to recreate, (2) to destroy death of the Body.

14. A portrait once effaced must be restored from the original. Thus the Son of the Father came to seek, save and regenerate. No other way was possible. Blinded himself, man could not see to heal. The witness of creation had failed to preserve him and could not bring him back. The Word alone could do so. But how? Only by revealing Himself as a Man.

15. Thus, the Word condescended to the man's engrossment in corporeal things, by even taking a body. All man's superstitions He met halfway; whether men were inclined to worship Nature, Man, Demons or the dead, He proved Himself Lord of all these.

16. He came then to attract man's sense-bound attention to Himself as a man, and so to lead him on to recognize Him as God.

17. How the Incarnation did not limit the ubiquity of the Word, nor diminish His Purity.

18. How the Word and Power of God works in His human actions: by casting out devils, by Miracles, by His Birth of the Virgin.

19. Man, unmoved by nature, was to be taught to know God by that sacred Manhood, Whose deity all nature confessed, especially in His Death.

20. None, then, could bestow incorruption, but He Who had made, none restore the likeness of God, save His Own Image, none quicken, but the Life, none teach, but the Word. And He, in order to pay our debt of death, must also die for us, and rise again as our first-fruits from the grave. Mortal therefore His Body must be; corruptible, His Body could not be.

21. Death brought to naught by the death of the Christ. Why, then, did not Christ die privately or in a more honorable way? He was not subject to natural death, but had to die at the hands of others. Why then did He die? Nay but for that purpose He came, and but for that, He could not have risen.

22. But why did He not withdraw His body from the Jews and, thus, guard its immortality? (1) It became Him not to inflict death on Himself, and yet not to shun it. (2) He came to receive death as the due of others; therefore it should come to Him from without. (3) His death must be certain, so as to guarantee the truth of His Resurrection. In addition, He could not die from infirmity, lest He should be mocked in His healing of others.

23. Necessity of a public death for the doctrine of the Resurrection.

24. Further objections anticipated. He did not choose His way of death; for He was to prove himself Conqueror of death in all or any of its forms: (simile of a good wrestler). The death chosen to disgrace Him proved the Trophy against death: moreover it preserved His body undivided.

25. Why the Cross, of all deaths? (1) He had to bear the curse for us. (2) On it He held out His hands to unite all, Jews and Gentiles, in Himself. (3) He defeated the Prince of the powers of the air in His own region, clearing the way to heaven and opening for us the everlasting doors.

26. Reasons for His rising on the Third Day. (1) Not sooner for else His real death would be denied, nor (2) later; to (a) guard the identity of His body, (b) not to keep His disciples too long in suspense, nor (c) to wait till the witnesses of His death were dispersed, or its memory faded.

27. The change wrought by the Cross in the relation of Death to Man.

28. This exceptional fact must be tested by experience. Let those who doubt it become Christians.

29. Here then wonderful effects are presented, and a sufficient cause, the Cross, accounts for them, as the sunrise accounts for daylight.

30. The reality of the resurrection is proved by facts: (1) the victory over death is described above: (2) the Wonders of Grace are the work of One Living, of One who is God: (3) if the gods be (as alleged) real and living, a fortiori He Who shatters their power is alive.

31. If Power is the sign of life, what do we learn from the impotence of idols, for good or evil, the constraining power of Christ and the Sign of the Cross? Death and the demons are by this proved to have lost their sovereignty. Coincidence of the above argument from facts with that from the Personality of Christ.

32. But who is to see Him risen, so as to believe? Nay, God is ever invisible and known by His works only: and here the works cry out in proof. If you do not believe, look at those who do, and perceive the Godhead of Christ. The demons see this, though men are blind. Summary of the argument so far.

33. Unbelief of the Jews and scoffing of the Greeks. The former confounded by their own Scriptures. Prophecies of His coming as God and as a Man.

34. Prophecies of His passion and death in all its circumstances.

35. Prophecies of the Cross. How these prophecies are satisfied in Christ alone.

36. Prophecies of Christ's sovereignty, flight into Egypt, etc.

37. Psalm 22:16, etc. Majesty of His birth and death. Confusion of oracles and demons in Egypt.

38. Other clear prophecies of the coming of God in the flesh. Christ's miracles unprecedented.

39. Do you look for another? But Daniel foretells the exact time. Objections to this removed.

40. Argument (1) from the withdrawal of prophecy and destruction of Jerusalem, (2) from the conversion of the Gentiles, and that to the God of Moses. What more remains for the Messiah to do that Christ has not done?

41. Answer to the Greeks. Do they recognize the Logos? If He manifests Himself in the organism of the Universe, why not in one Body? For a human body is a part of the same whole.

42. His union with the body is based upon His relation to Creation as a whole. He used a human body, since to man it was that He wished to reveal Himself.

43. He came in human rather than in any nobler form, because (I) He came to save, not to impress; (2) man alone of creatures had sinned. As men would not recognize His works in the Universe, He came and worked among them as Man; in the sphere to which they had limited themselves.

44. As God made man by a word, why not restore him by a word? But (1) creation out of nothing is different from reparation of what already exists. (2) Man was there with a definite need, calling

for a definite remedy. Death was ingrained in man's nature: He then must wind life closely to human nature. Therefore, the Word became Incarnate that He might meet and conquer death in His usurped territory. (Simile of straw and asbestos.)

45. Thus once again every part of creation manifests the glory of God. Nature, the witness to its Creator, yields (by miracles) a second testimony to God Incarnate. The witness of Nature, perverted by man's sin, was thus forced back to the truth. If these reasons suffice not, let the Greeks look at facts.

46. Discredit, from the date of the Incarnation, of idol-cults, oracles, mythologies, demoniacal energy, magic, and Gentile philosophy. And whereas the old cults were strictly local and independent, the worship of Christ is catholic and uniform.

47. The numerous oracles—fancied apparitions in sacred places, etc., dispelled by the sign of the Cross. The old gods prove to have been mere men. Magic is exposed. And whereas Philosophy could only persuade selected and local cliques of Immortality, as well as goodness—men of little intellect have infused into the multitudes of the churches the principle of a supernatural life.

48. Further facts. Christian continence of virgins and ascetics. Martyrs. The power of the Cross against demons and magic. Christ by His Power shows Himself more than a man, more than a magician, more than a spirit. For all these are totally subject to Him. Therefore He is the Word of God.

49. His Birth and Miracles. You call Asclepius, Heracles and Dionysus gods for their works. Contrast their works with His and the wonders at His death, etc.

50. Impotence and rivalries of the Sophists put to shame by the Death of Christ. His Resurrection unparalleled even in Greek legends.

51. The new virtue of continence. Revolution of the Society, purified and pacified by Christianity.

52. Wars, etc., roused by demons, lulled by Christianity.

53. The whole fabric of Gentiles leveled at a blow by Christ secretly addressing the conscience of Man.

54. The Word Incarnate, as is the case with the Invisible God, is known to us by His works. Through them we recognize His deifying mission. Let us be content to enumerate a few of them, leaving their dazzling plentitude to him who will behold.

55. Summary of foregoing. Cessation of pagan oracles, etc.: propagation of the faith. The true King has come forth and silenced all usurpers.

56. Search then, the Scriptures, if you can, and so fill up this sketch. Learn to look for the Second Advent and Judgment.

57. Above all, so live that you may have the right to eat of this tree of knowledge and life, and so come to eternal joys. Doxology.

Frequency Word List

Table 11 provides some information about the most frequently used words in this speech. Articles (ὁ, τοῦ), conjunctions (καὶ) and particles (γὰρ) come first in use. After applying stemming criteria, we can see that in this speech the orator uses some words of emotional value (see Table 12) in high frequency level as a part of his ideological language.

*10. Οὕτως μὲν οὖν ὁ **Θεὸς** τὸν ἄνθρωπον πεποίηκε, καὶ μένειν ἠθέλησεν ἐν ἀφθαρσίᾳ· ἄνθρωποι δὲ κατολιγωρήσαντες καὶ ἀποστραφέντες τὴν πρὸς τὸν **Θεὸν** κατανόησιν, λογισάμενοι δὲ καὶ ἐπινοήσαντες ἑαυτοῖς τὴν κακίαν, ὥσπερ ἐν τοῖς πρώτοις ἐλέχθη, ἔσχον τὴν προαπειληθεῖσαν τοῦ **θανάτου** κατάκρισιν, καὶ λοιπὸν οὐκ ἔτι ὡς γεγόνασι διέμενον· ἀλλ' ὡς ἐλογίζοντο διεφθείροντο· καὶ ὁ **θάνατος** αὐτῶν ἐκράτει βασιλεύων./ Thus, then, **God** has made man, and willed that he should abide*

Table 11. The most frequent words (‰) without stemming and exclusion criteria

61. 7 καὶ / and	22.2 τοῦ / of the	16.96 τὴν / the	14.38 δὲ/ but
13.9 τὸν / the	12.7 τῶν / of the	12.66 τῆς / the	11.77 ἐν/ in
11.72 ὁ / the	10.88 γὰρ / for one	10.46 τὸ / the	7.8 μὲν/ in the one hand

*in incorruption; but men, having despised and rejected the contemplation of **God**, and devised and contrived evil for themselves (as was said in the former treatise), received the condemnation of **death** with which they had been threatened; and from thenceforth no longer remained as they were made, but were being corrupted according to their devices; and **death** had the mastery over them as king. (4)*

The partial repetition of the words θάνατος/death, θεός / god into representative speech acts helps the orator to promote his view about the fact of the death. The fact of the death is the direct corollary of the will of men to despise and reject the contemplation of God. Now in their lives death prevails and not incorruption.

Use of Verbs

By applying again the Antconc program, we are going to extract some quantitative data about the most frequently used verbs in this speech (see Table 13).

Table 13 helps us to understand that Great Athanasius utilizes more verbs in a third singular reference. His verbal choices reveal that he refers to past events and he tries to promote his view about what they should have done in certain occasions and issues. The verb ἐστι(ν)/is is used more as personal verb, into representative speech acts, and not into impersonal syntaxes.

11. Εἰ γὰρ αὐτομάτως τὰ πάντα χωρὶς προνοίας κατ' αὐτοὺς γέγονεν, ἔδει τὰ πάντα ἁπλῶς γεγενῆσθαι καὶ ὅμοια εἶναι καὶ μὴ διάφορα. Ὡς γὰρ ἐπὶ σώματος ἑνὸς ἔδει τὰ πάντα εἶναι ἥλιον ἢ σελήνην, καὶ ἐπὶ τῶν ἀνθρώπων ἔδει τὸ ὅλον εἶναι χεῖρα, ἢ ὀφθαλμόν, ἢ πόδα. Νῦν δὲ οὐκ ἔστι μὲν οὕτως· ὁρῶμεν δὲ τὸ μέν, ἥλιον· τὸ δέ, σελήνην· τὸ δέ, γῆν· καὶ πάλιν ἐπὶ τῶν ἀνθρωπίνων σωμάτων, τὸ μέν, πόδα· τὸ δέ, χεῖρα· τὸ δέ, κεφαλήν./ For if, as they say, everything has had its beginning of itself, and independently of purpose, it would follow that everything had come into mere being, so as to be alike and not distinct. For it would follow in virtue of the unity of body that everything **must be** sun or moon, and in the case of men it would follow that the whole must be hand, or eye, or foot. But as it

Table 12. Words of emotional value with stemming

Word	Frequency ‰
Θεός / God	13.6
Λόγος / Word	6.17
θάνατος / death	5.8
Χριστός / Christ	4.72
πατήρ / Father	3.41
Σωτήρ / Savior	3.18
ζωή / life	13.55

Table 13. The most frequent verbs

Word	Frequency ‰
ἐστι (ν) / is	3.83
γέγονε / had become	1.5
ἔδει / must be	1.83

is this is not so. On the contrary, we see a distinction of sun, moon, and earth; and again, in the case of human bodies, of foot, hand, and head. (2)

At this point of his speech Great Athanasius informs us through representative speech acts on the arguments of the Ethics about the creation of the world. The basic cause of the creation is for the orator the God. The orator wonders about the accuracy of the syllogism of the Ethics and the verb ἔδει, in a past tense, aids him in what he should have done in order this syllogism to be confirmed. The following sentence in the negative form rejects the previous syllogism and makes clear into the thought of the audience the fact that the argumentative syllogism of the Ethics is indefensible.

Use of Adjectives

Adjectives can also operate as a means for the speaker either to describe, evaluate entities of the text. In this speech, we noted that some nouns, such as γραφή, θεός are accompanied with certain adjectives promoting the value of the certain entities (see Table 14).

The orator utilizes some adjectives before nouns with religious value. The certain adjectives present the entities of the religious system that the orator supports, providing to them particular and special worth.

12. ...ἀλλὰ γὰρ χάριτι Θεοῦ σημάναντες ὀλίγα καὶ περὶ τῆς θειότητος τοῦ Λόγου τοῦ Πατρὸς καὶ τῆς εἰς πάντα προνοίας καὶ δυνάμεως αὐτοῦ· καὶ ὅτι ὁ **ἀγαθὸς Πατὴρ** τούτῳ τὰ πάντα διακοσμεῖ καὶ τὰ πάντα ὑπ᾽ αὐτοῦ κινεῖται καὶ ἐν αὐτῷ ζωοποιεῖται·/ ...and whereas we have by God's grace noted somewhat also of the divinity of the Word of the Father, and of His universal Providence and power, and that the **Good Father** through Him orders all things, and all things are moved by Him, and in Him are quickened. (2)

In this example, the orator presents his and his supporters' God as a divine entity who cares about everyone, orders all things and all things are moved by him. He is the Maker and he has the power of life.

Some other adjectives also operate as elliptical impersonal syntaxes (see Table 15). The omitted verb that accompanies these adjectives is the verb ἐστι/is.

13. Εἰ τοίνυν ἐν τῷ κόσμῳ σώματι ὄντι ὁ τοῦ Θεοῦ Λόγος ἐστί, καὶ ἐν ὅλοις καὶ τοῖς κατὰ μέρος αὐτοῦ πᾶσιν ἐπιβέβηκε, τί **θαυμαστὸν** ἢ τί **ἄτοπον** εἰ καὶ ἐν ἀνθρώπῳ φαμὲν αὐτὸν ἐπιβεβηκέναι; Εἰ γὰρ **ἄτοπον** ὅλως ἐν σώματι αὐτὸν γενέσθαι, **ἄτοπον** ἂν εἴη καὶ ἐν τῷ παντὶ τοῦτον ἐπιβεβηκέναι, καὶ τὰ πάντα τῇ προνοίᾳ ἑαυτοῦ φωτίζειν καὶ κινεῖν· σῶμα γάρ ἐστι καὶ τὸ ὅλον. Εἰ δὲ τῷ κόσμῳ τοῦτον ἐπιβαίνειν καὶ ἐν ὅλῳ αὐτὸν γνωρίζεσθαι πρέπει, πρέποι ἂν καὶ ἐν ἀνθρωπίνῳ σώματι αὐτὸν ἐπιφαίνεσθαι, καὶ ὑπ᾽ αὐτοῦ τοῦτο φωτίζεσθαι καὶ ἐνεργεῖν. Μέρος γὰρ τοῦ παντὸς καὶ τὸ ἀνθρώπων ἐστὶ γένος. Καὶ εἰ τὸ μέρος ἀπρεπές ἐστιν ὄργανον αὐτοῦ γίνεσθαι πρὸς τὴν τῆς θεότητος γνῶσιν, **ἀτοπώτατον** ἂν εἴη καὶ δι᾽ ὅλου τοῦ κόσμου γνωρίζεσθαι τὸν τοιοῦτον./ If, then, the Word of God is in the Universe, which is a body, and has united Himself with the whole and with all its parts, what is there **surprising** or **absurd** if we say that He has united Himself with man also. For if it were **absurd** for

Table 14. Synapses of nouns

Θεός	Γραφή	Πατήρ
ἄφθαρτος / incorruptible	θεία /Holy	ἀγαθὸς/ good

*Him to have been in a body at all, it would be **absurd** for Him to be united with the whole either, and to be giving light and movement to all things by His providence. For the whole also is a body. But if it beseems Him to unite Himself with the universe, and to be made known in the whole, it must beseem Him also to appear in a human body, and that by Him it should be illumined and work. For mankind is part of the whole as well as the rest. And if it be unseemly for a part to have been adopted as His instrument to teach men of His Godhead, it must be **most absurd** that He should be made known even by the whole universe. (41)*

In this example, Great Athanasius tries to motivate the thought of the audience through the question, by creating in their mind a mental problem. (Rhetorical questions and questions of directive character are included into the stylistic choices of the orators, because in this way they motivate the thought of the audience and direct to a particular way of action. According to Spurgin (1994:303) 'the rhetorical question, because it invites assent, can provide a persuasive conclusion to the argument'. For more details about the way of persuasion see Borg (2007).) The answer to this question of directive character, with the aid of adjective elliptical phrases, has as a purpose to make an evaluation and reveal the thought of the speaker about God: His union with the body is based upon His relation to Creation as a whole. He used a human body, since to man it was that the way He wished to reveal Himself. In the last sentence of this example, the speaker utilizes one more time the same adjective ἄτοπον in a superlative degree, since he desires to prove that something like that can be supported and it is an indefensible argument.

Attack to the Opponent

The way of attacking against the opponent builds up the arguments of the speaker. The speaker expresses his evaluation and disagreement for the opponent in both ways: negative evaluative adjectives and rhetorical relation of contrast.

14. Τοσαύτης οὖν οὔσης τῆς τοῦ Θεοῦ ἀγαθότητος καὶ φιλανθρωπίας, ὅμως οἱ ἄνθρωποι, νικώμενοι ταῖς παραυτίκα ἡδοναῖς καὶ ταῖς παρὰ δαιμόνων φαντασίαις καὶ ἀπάταις, οὐκ ἀνένευσαν πρὸς τὴν ἀλήθειαν· ἀλλ᾽ ἑαυτοὺς πλείοσι κακοῖς καὶ ἁμαρτήμασιν ἐνεφόρησαν, ὡς μηκέτι δοκεῖν αὐτοὺς λογικούς, ἀλλὰ ἀλόγους ἐκ τῶν τρόπων νομίζεσθαι./ God's goodness then and loving-kindness being so great— men nevertheless, overcome by the pleasures of the moment and by the illusions and deceits

Table 15. The most frequent adjectives

Word	Frequency ‰
ἄτοπον / absurd	0.7
θαυμαστόν /surprising	0.42

sent by demons, did not raise their heads toward the truth, but loaded themselves the more with evils and sins, so as no longer to seem rational, but from their ways **to be reckoned void of reason**. *(12)*

15. Περὶ δὲ τῆς Ἑλληνικῆς σοφίας καὶ τῆς τῶν φιλοσόφων μεγαλοφωνίας, νομίζω μηδένα τοῦ παρ᾽ ἡμῶν δεῖσθαι λόγου, ἐπ᾽ ὄψει πάντων ὄντος τοῦ θαύματος, ὅτι τοσαῦτα γραψάντων τῶν παρ᾽ Ἕλλησι σοφῶν καὶ μὴ δυνηθέντων πεῖσαι κἂν ὀλίγους ἐκ τῶν πλησίον τόπων περὶ ἀθανασίας καὶ τοῦ κατ᾽ ἀρετὴν βίου, **μόνος ὁ Χριστὸς** *δι᾽ εὐτελῶν ῥημάτων, καὶ δι᾽ ἀνθρώπων οὐ κατὰ τὴν γλῶτταν σοφῶν, κατὰ πᾶσαν τὴν οἰκουμένην παμπληθεῖς ἐκκλησίας ἔπεισεν ἀνθρώπων καταφρονεῖν μὲν θανάτου, φρονεῖν δὲ ἀθάνατα, καὶ τὰ μὲν πρόσκαιρα παρορᾶν, εἰς δὲ τὰ αἰώνια ἀποβλέπειν, καὶ μηδὲν μὲν ἡγεῖσθαι τὴν ἐπὶ γῆς δόξαν, μόνης δὲ τῆς ἀθανασίας ἀντιποιεῖσθαι./ But as to Gentile wisdom, and the sounding pretensions of the philosophers, I think none can need our argument, since the wonder is before the eyes of all, that while the wise among the Greeks had written so much, and were unable to persuade even a few from their own neighbourhood, concerning immortality and a virtuous life,* **Christ alone**, *by ordinary language, and by men not clever with the tongue, has throughout all the world persuaded whole churches full of men to despise death, and to mind the things of immortality; to overlook what is temporal and to turn their eyes to what is eternal; to think nothing of earthly glory and to strive only for the heavenly. (47)*

In the aforementioned example (14), we observe that the speaker tries to promote his view and the religious system he supports through evaluative adjectives regarding the character of the opponents: ἀλόγους and through the adversative conjunction ὅμως in order to reveal what they do and how they behave instead of God, those who ignore God's goodness and loving-kindness. In the example (15) the speaker promotes, through the rhetorical relation of contrast, Christ as the only one who managed to persuade everyone to despise death and to mind the things of immortality; to overlook what is temporal and to turn their eyes to what is eternal; to think nothing of earthly glory and to strive only for the heavenly.

Use of Pronouns

In general it is remarked that in this speech the orator utilizes more personal pronouns than in *Contra Gentes*. He utilizes a lot of pronouns in first plural reference (see Table 16), a fact that certifies that he speaks as a delegate of the religious system that he supports.

16. ...ἣν Ἰουδαῖοι μὲν διαβάλλουσιν, Ἕλληνες δὲ χλευάζουσιν, **ἡμεῖς** *δὲ προσκυνοῦμεν.../... and to His divine Appearing among us, which Jews traduce and Greeks laugh to scorn, but* **we** *worship...(1)*

In this example, Great Athanasius contrasts through the rhetorical relation of contrast (on the level of coherence) the entities of the Jews and the Greeks with his ideological group and separates the crowd into two groups, the faithful and the unfaithful men. The personal pronoun ἡμεῖς promotes his and his supporters way of thinking about the incarnation of the Word.

17. Ἔπειτα καὶ **τοῦτο** *ἰστέον, ὅτι ἡ γενομένη φθορὰ οὐκ ἔξωθεν ἦν τοῦ σώματος, ἀλλ᾽ αὐτῷ προσεγεγόνει, καὶ ἀνάγκη ἦν ἀντὶ τῆς φθορᾶς ζωὴν αὐτῷ προσπλακῆναι, ἵνα ὥσπερ ἐν τῷ σώματι γέγονεν ὁ θάνατος, οὕτως ἐν αὐτῷ γένηται καὶ ἡ ζωή. / Secondly, you must know* **this** *also, that the corruption which had set in was not external to the body, but had become attached to it; and it was required that, instead of corruption, life should cleave to it; so that, just as death has been engendered in the body, so life may be engendered in it also. (44)*

In this example, the pronoun τοῦτο (see the frequency of this pronoun in Table 17) helps the orator to organize the cohesion of his text and lead us to the next thematic pole of his argumentative route concerning the corruption of the body.

Table 16. Personal pronouns used

Pronouns	Repeats	Frequency ‰
1st person sg reference ἐγώ / I, me	3	0.14
ἐμοῦ, μοῦ / I, me	0	0
ἐμοί (ἔμοιγε), μοι / I, me	0	0
ἐμέ, με / I, me	0	0
Total amount	3	0.14
1st person pl reference ἡμεῖς / we	13	0.61
ἡμῶν / we	46	2.15
ἡμῖν / we	12	0.56
ἡμᾶς / we	25	1.17
Total amount	96	4.48
2nd person sg reference σύ / you	1	0.046
σοῦ, σου / you	0	0
σοί, σοι / you	2	0.093
σε, σέ / you	0	0
Total amount	3	0.14
2nd person pl reference ὑμεῖς / you	1	0.046
ὑμῶν / you	5	0.233
ὑμῖν / you	1	0.046
ὑμᾶς / you	0	0
Total amount	7	0.33
Total of all 1st and 2nd personal pronouns	109	5.09

Lexical Bundles

In this speech Great Athanasius utilizes mainly lexical bundles oriented to the text (see Table 18). Only one lexical bundle operates as a means of expressing a personal stance. The lexical bundle ὁ τοῦ Θεοῦ Λόγος contains words of emotional value, such as Θεός, Λόγος.

18. Ὅθεν ὁ **τοῦ Θεοῦ Λόγος** δι' ἑαυτοῦ παρεγένετο, ἵνα ὡς Εἰκὼν ὢν τοῦ Πατρὸς τὸν κατ' εἰκόνα ἄνθρωπον ἀνακτίσαι δυνηθῇ./ Whence **the Word of God** came in His own person, that, as He was the Image of the Father, He might be able to create afresh the man after the image. (13)

This lexical bundle aids the speaker empower his arguments about the significance of the Word of God on the issue of Incarnation.

Table 17. Demonstrative pronoun τοῦτο

Pronoun	Frequency ‰
τοῦτο / this	4.4

Intertextuality

Introducing Lexical Items of the Integrated Speech

By applying this program to this speech it is noted that the certain orator introduces the intertextualistic sources through assertive and neutral reporting verbs or particles (see Table 19), according to Caldas-Coulthard (1997), so as to interpret the intertextualistic source and display that the first person speaking appears to express his degree of conviction, as far as the truth of his words is concerned or with neutral reporting verbs, as a means of neutral objectivity.

It is noted that Great Athanasius uses the aforementioned reporting verbs and particles in combination with sources from the religious system in which he believes. In general, neutral reporting verbs are much more than the assertive reporting verbs. This confirms to us that the speaker integrates the intertextuality into his speech in an objective way without interpreting the stance of the first speaker who puts forward the integrated message.

Kind of Intertextualistic Sources

It is observed that Great Athanasius uses mostly sources from the theological system he supports (see Table 20). The integrated parts of the speech are retrieved from books such as *Genesis,* and letters such as the *Letter to Corinthians.*

19. εἰ δὲ παραβαῖεν καὶ στραφέντες γένοιντο φαῦλοι, γινώσκοιεν ἑαυτοὺς τὴν ἐν θανάτῳ κατὰ φύσιν φθορὰν ὑπομένειν, καὶ μηκέτι μὲν ἐν παραδείσῳ ζῆν, ἔξω δὲ τούτου λοιπὸν ἀποθνήσκοντας μένειν

Table 18. Lexical bundles

Frequency ‰	Lexical bundle	Function (according to Biber)	Function (according to Hyland)
0.56	ἐν τῷ σώματι / in body	Reference expression	Text oriented
0.51	κατὰ τοῦ θανάτου/ against the death	Discourse organizer	Text oriented
0.47	ὁ τοῦ Θεοῦ Λόγος / the Word of God	Reference expression	Text oriented
0.42	ἐκ τῶν ἔργων / from the actions	Reference expression	Text oriented
0.32	Εἰ μὲν οὖν / if	Discourse organizer	Text oriented
0.28	διὰ τοῦ σώματος/ though the body	Reference expression	Text oriented
0.28	περὶ τῆς ἀναστάσεως / about the resurrection	Discourse organizer	Text oriented
0.23	οἷόν τε ἦν / it was possible	Personal Stance	Speaker oriented

Table 19. Introducing lexical items of the intertextualistic sources

Lexical elements	Frequency %	Function
Φησίν/ asserts	0.09	assertive reporting verb
Λέγων/ saying	0.06	neutral reporting particle
Λέγοντες/ saying	0.056	neutral reporting verb
Λέγουσα/saying	0.028	neutral reporting particle

ἐν τῷ θανάτῳ καὶ ἐν τῇ φθορᾷ. Τοῦτο δὲ καὶ ἡ θεία γραφὴ προσημαίνει λέγουσα ἐκ προσώπου τοῦ Θεοῦ· "Ἀπὸ **παντὸς ξύλου τοῦ ἐν τῷ παραδείσῳ βρώσει φαγῇ· ἀπὸ δὲ τοῦ ξύλου τοῦ γινώσκειν καλὸν καὶ πονηρὸν οὐ φάγεσθε ἀπ᾽ αὐτοῦ· ᾗ δ᾽ ἂν ἡμέρᾳ φάγησθε, θανάτῳ ἀποθανεῖσθε.**" Τὸ δὲ θανάτῳ ἀποθανεῖσθε", τί ἂν ἄλλο εἴη ἢ τὸ μὴ μόνον ἀποθνήσκειν, ἀλλὰ καὶ ἐν τῇ τοῦ θανάτου φθορᾷ διαμένειν;/ but that if they transgressed and turned back, and became evil, they might know that they were incurring that corruption in death which was theirs by nature; no longer to live in paradise, but cast out of it from that time forth to die and to abide in death and in corruption. Now this is that of which Holy Writ also gives warning, saying in the Person of God: **Of every tree that is in the garden, eating you shall eat: but of the tree of the knowledge of good and evil, you shall not eat of it, but on the day that you eat, dying you shall die.** But by dying you shall die, what else could be meant than not dying merely, but also abiding ever in the corruption of death? (3)

The integrated speech in quoting operates as a means for the speaker to prove that what he said in the previous lines is true; so, according to the Holy Writ, if everyone lives in paradise, then he must accept the corruption of death.

CONCLUSION

In general, it is noted that Great Athanasius utilizes particular stylistic mechanisms, so as to persuade the audience on these theological issues. He utilizes more words of theocratic character as he speaks about God, the Word. He also utilizes some words with emotional value, such as death and life. The use of the epistemic verbs is strictly restricted and he tries to present his view using more impersonal syntaxes of elliptical expressions with deontic modality (ἄτοπον ἐστί/ *it is absurd*, ἄξιον ἐστί/ *it deserves, it fits*); he uses verbs with deontic modality (ἔδει/ *must be*) about what they should have done. He utilizes some certain adjectives, so as to define his and his supporters' God, such as ἄφθαρτος/ *incorruptible*, ἀθάνατος/ *immortal*, ἅγιος/Saint, φιλάνθρωπος / *philanthropist*, since in this way he evaluates the worth of his God or the integrated source that he incorporates into his speech as to persuade about his way of view. He also uses some adjectives, so as to attack the opponent; these adjectives are not repeated,

Table 20. The most frequent intertextualistic sources

Name of the source	Frequency
ἡ γραφὴ / αἱ γραφαί/ *Holy Scripture*	0.089
ὁ Μωϋσῆς / *Moses*	0.051

but the orator invents new ones as he is an orator with a rich vocabulary and knows very well to use the language choices, since he also utilizes some verbs and participles, such as μυθολογοῦσιν / *they tell tales,* μυθολογήσαντες / *telling tales,* πολὺ τὸν ὀφθαλμὸν πεπηρωμένοι / *Foolish and sadly disabled in eyesight,* in order to describe the character of his opponent. He utilizes more personal pronouns in the second speech as this speech is a presentation of his religious system he supports and promotes. Therefore, he gives emphasis to his and his supporters' view and he uses personal pronoun of plural reference, since he speaks as a delegate. He also utilizes demonstrative pronouns in order to empower the demonstrative reference, making simultaneously the necessary clarifications. With reference to his lexical bundles, he proves that he is an orator who organizes his thought and his texts very well, because he utilizes more lexical bundles oriented to the text, either as discourse organizers or as reference expressions. With regard to intertextuality (Bazerman & Prior, 2004) (Alexandropoulos (2013a) adopted the above model in the analysis of the political speeches of Julian the emperor and he defined certain functions after the after the recontextualization such as support, proof etc.), he incorporates more sources from his religious system and he uses more assertive or neutral reporting verbs, giving in this way the sense that he presents the view of the intertextualistic source in an objective way without any kind of interpretation regarding the thought of the first speaker. Last but not least, it could be supported that these speeches are ideological speeches (Hodge and Kress (1993) support, "the relation of language and ideology is presented unbreakable in the degree that the language allows the externalization of ideology, but also the control of the handled messages and ideas") and their stylistic choices have as a purpose the promotion of the beliefs of the speaker and his supporters (through certain words of theological character and through personal pronouns that divide the crowd into supporters and non-supporters), the evaluation of the opponent (through adjectives) and the motivation of the audience (through directive speech acts).

REFERENCES

Alexandropoulos, G. (2013a). *Text and context in Flavius Claudius Julian's political speeches: coherence, intertextuality and communicative goal* [PhD Thesis]. University of Athens. Munich: Lincom.

Alexandropoulos, G. (2013b). Stylistic approach of Julian the emperor and Gregory Nazianzean. *The Buckingham Journal of Language and Linguistics, 6,* 1–13.

Alexandropoulos, G. (2014a). *Christians against the Ethnics.* Munich: Lincom.

Alexandropoulos, G. (2014b). *The epitaphs of Gregory of Nazianzus: a stylistic approach.* Munich: Lincom.

Alexandropoulos, G. (2014c, May 22-24). Julian's political speeches: rhetorical and computational approach. *6th International Conference on Corpus Linguistics.* Las Palmas de Gran Canaria, Universidad de Las Palmas de Gran Canaria.

Anthony, L. (2006). Developing a freeware, multiplatform corpus analysis toolkit for the technical writing classroom. *IEEE Transactions on Professional Communication, 49*(3), 275–286. doi:10.1109/TPC.2006.880753

Atkins, S., Clear, J., & Ostler, N. (1992). Corpus design criteria. *Journal of Literary and Linguistic Computing, 7*(1), 1–16. doi:10.1093/llc/7.1.1

Austin, J. (1962). *How to Do Things with Words.* Oxford: Oxford University Press.

Baker, P. (2006). *Using Corpora in Discourse Analysis.* London: Continuum.

Bardy, G. (1914). *Saint Athanase.* Paris.

Bazerman, C., & Prior, P. (2004). *What Writing Does and How It Does It.* NJ: Erlbaum.

Biber, D., & Barbieri, F. (2007). Lexical bundles in university spoken and written registers. *English for Specific Purposes, 26*(3), 263–286. doi:10.1016/j.esp.2006.08.003

Biber, D., Conrad, S., & Cortes, V. (2003). Lexical bundles in speech and writing: An initial taxonomy. In: A. Wilson, P. Rayson, & T. McEnery (Eds.), Corpus linguistics by the lune. (pp. 71-93). Frankfurt/ Main: Peter Lang.

Biber, D., Conrad, S., & Cortes, V. (2004). If you look at...: Lexical bundles in university teaching and textbooks. *Applied Linguistics, 25*(3), 371–405. doi:10.1093/applin/25.3.371

Biber, D., Conrad, S., & Reppen, R. (1998). *Corpus linguistics: Investigating language structure and use.* Cambridge: Cambridge University Press. doi:10.1017/CBO9780511804489

Borg, J. (2007). *Persuasion – The Art of Influencing People.* London: Pearson / Prentice Hall.

Brakke, D. (1955). *Athanasius and the politics of Ascetism.* Oxford: Clarendon Press.

Brédif, L. (1879). *Demosthene: L'eloquence politique en Grèce.* Paris: Librairie Hachette.

Caldas-Coulthard, C. R. (1997). *News as Social Practice: A Study in Critical Discourse Analysis.* Florianopolis: Advanced Research in English Series.

Cameron, A. (1994). *Christianity and the rhetoric of empire.* Berkeley: University of California Press.

Cavallera, F. (1914). *Saint Athanase.* Paris: Librairie Bloud.

Chafe, W. (1982). Integration and involvement in speaking, writing and oral literature. In: Tannen, D. (Ed.), Spoken and written language. (pp. 35-55). Notwood: Ablex.

Cortes, V. (2004). Lexical bundles in published and student disciplinary writing: Examples from history and biology. *English for Specific Purposes, 23*(4), 397–423. doi:10.1016/j.esp.2003.12.001

Cross, F. L. (1945). *The studies of Athanasius.* Oxford.

Dragas, G. (1980). *Athanasiana: essays in the theology of Saint Athanasius.* London.

Fairclough, N. (1992). *Discourse and social change.* Cambridge: Polity Press.

Firth, J. R. (1951/1957). *Papers in Linguistics, 1934-1951.* London: Oxford University Press.

Halmari, H. C. (2005). In search of "successful" political persuasion. A comparison of the styles of Bill Clinton and Ronald Reagan. In: Hari, H. & T. Virtanen (Eds.), Persuasion across genres. A linguistic approach. (pp. 105-134). Amsterdam / Philadelpia: John Benjamins Publishing Company.

Hodge, R., & Kress, G. (1993). ²). *Language as Ideology.* London: Routledge.

Hunger, H. (1978). *Die hochsprachliche profane Literatur der Byzantiner*. Munchen: Beck.

Hyland, K. (2008a). As can be seen: Lexical bundles and disciplinary variation. *English for Specific Purposes, 27*(1), 4–21. doi:10.1016/j.esp.2007.06.001

Hyland, K. (2008b). Academic clusters: Text patterning in published and postgraduate writing. *International Journal of Applied Linguistics, 18*(1), 41–62. doi:10.1111/j.1473-4192.2008.00178.x

Hymes, D. (1964). Towards Ethnographies of Communication: The Analysis of Communicative Events. *American Anthropologist, 66*(6), 12–25.

Hymes, D. (1974). *Foundations of Sociolinguistics: An Ethnographic Approach*. Philadelphia: University of Pennsylvania Press.

Kannengiesser, C. (1991). *Arius and Athanasius: two Alexandrian theologians*. Hampshire: Gower Publications.

Kennedy, G. (1992). Preferred ways of putting things. In J. Svartvik (Ed.), *Directions in Corpus Linguistics*. (pp. 335–373). Berlin: Mouton de Gruyter. doi:10.1515/9783110867275.335

Kennedy, G. A. (1994). *New History of Classical Rhetoric*. Princeton, NJ: Princeton, University Press.

Lauchert, F. (1911). *Leben des hl*. Köln: Athanasius des Grossen.

Leech, G., & Fligelstone, S. (1992). Computers and corpus analysis. In C. S. Butler (Ed.), *Computers and Written Texts*. (pp. 115–140). Oxford: Blackwell.

Leech, G. N. (1980). *Explorations in Semantics and Pragmatics*. Amsterdam: Benjamins B.V. doi:10.1075/pb.i.5

Malinowski, B. (1923). The problem of meaning in primitive languages. In C. K. Ogden & I. A. Richards (Eds.), The Meaning of Meaning. London: Routledge & Kegan Paul. (pp. 296-336).

Mann, W. C., Matthiesen, C. M., & Thompson, S. A. (1992). Rhetorical Structure theory and text analysis. In W. C. Mann & S. A. Thompson (Eds.), *Text description: diverse analyses of a fund raising text*. Amsterdam: John Benjamins. doi:10.1075/pbns.16.04man

Mann, W. C., & Thompson, S. A. (1986). Relational propositions in discourse. *Discourse Processes, 9*(1), 57–90. doi:10.1080/01638538609544632

Mann, W. C., & Thompson, S. A. (1988). Rhetorical Structure Theory: Towards a functional theory of text organization. *Text—Interdisciplinary Journal for the Study of Discourse, 8*(3), 243–281. doi:10.1515/text.1.1988.8.3.243

Meijering, E. P. (1968). *Orthodoxy and Platonism in Athanasius*. Leiden.

Migne, J. P. (1857-1866). *Patrologiae Graecae Cursus Completu*.

Mirhady, D. C. (2007). *Influences on Peripatetic Rhetoric. Essays in honor of W.W. Fortenbaugh*. Brill. doi:10.1163/ej.9789004156685.i-286

Nesselrath, H. G. (1997). *Einleitung in die Griechische Phillogie.* Leipzig: B. G. Teubner. doi:10.1007/978-3-663-12074-2

Pernot, L. (2000). *La Rhétorique dans l'Antiquité.* Paris: Librairie Générale Française.

Pettersen, A. (1990). *Athanasius and the human body.* Bristol: Bristol Press.

Roberts, W. R. (1984). *The Rhetoric and the poetics of Aristotle.* New York: The Modern Library.

Robertson, A. (1892) *On the Incarnation of the Word.* In K. Knight (Ed.), Nicene and Post-Nicene Fathers, Second Series, Vol. 4. Buffalo, NY: Christian Literature Publishing Co. Retrieved from http://www.newadvent.org/fathers/2802.htm

Roldanus, J. (1968). *Le Christ et l' home dans la theologie d'Athanase d'Alexandrie.* Leiden.

Ross, D. (1974). *Aristotle.* London: Methuen.

Searle, J. (1969). *Speech Acts: An Essay in the Philosophy of language.* Cambridge: Cambridge University Press. doi:10.1017/CBO9781139173438

Searle, J. R. (1979). *Expression and Meaning. Studies in the Theory of Speech Acts.* Cambridge: Cambridge University Press. doi:10.1017/CBO9780511609213

Searle, J. R. (1994). How Performatives Work. In R. M. Harnish (Ed.), *Basic Topics in the Philosophy of Language.* (pp. 75–95). London: Harvester Wheatsheaf.

Searle, J. R. (1996a). What is a Speech Act? In A. P. Martinich (Ed.), *The Philosophy of Language.* (pp. 130–140). Oxford: Oxford University Press.

Searle, J. R. (1996b). Indirect Speech Acts. In A. P. Martinich (Ed.), *The Philosophy of Language.* (pp. 168–182). Oxford: Oxford University Press.

De Witt Spurgin, S. (1994). The power to persuade: A rhetoric and reader for argumentative writing. NJ: Prentice Hall.

St Athanasius the Great. (n. d.). Elpenor. Retrieved from http://www.elpenor.org/athanasius/

Thompson, G. (1996). Voices in the text: Discourse perspectives on language Reports. *Applied Linguistics, 17*(4), 501–530. doi:10.1093/applin/17.4.501

Thompson, R. (1971). *Athanasius Contra Gentes and De Incarnatione.* Oxford: Clarendon Press.

van Leeuwen, T. (1996). The representation of social actors. In C. R. Caldas-Coulthard & M. Coulthard (Eds.), *Texts and Practices: Readings in Critical Discourse Analysis.* (pp. 32–70). London: Routledge.

Wolf, F. (2008). *Aristotle et la politique.* Presses Universitaires de France.

ADDITIONAL READING

Mc Enery, T., & Wilson, A. (1996). *Corpus Linguistics.* Edinburgh: University Press.

Semino, E., & Short, M. H. (2004). *Corpus stylistics: speech, writing and thought presentation in a corpus of English writing*. London: Routledge.

Weinandy, T. (2007). *A Theological Introduction*. England: Ashgate Publishing Company.

KEY TERMS AND DEFINITIONS

Coherence: It is a linguistic mechanism which is based on the continuity of senses.

Cohesion: It is divided into grammatical cohesion which is based on structure, and lexical cohesion which is based on our lexical knowledge.

Corpus Linguistics: A new discipline of linguistics and studies the texts through large collections of machine-readable texts (corpora).

Idolatry: It is the worship of an idol or a physical object as a representation of a god.

Intertextuality: It is the integration of other opinions into the text production.

Lexical Bundles: The are groups of words that occur together and help to the organization of the message over the text production.

Style: The way we utilize our language as to persuade and lead the audience to certain actions. It is based on the personal linguistic choices of each orator over his speech or text production.

Compilation of References

Aase, K. (2011). *Text Mining of News Articles for Stock Price Predictions*. Norwegian University of Science and Technology.

Abney, S. (1996). Partial parsing via finite-state cascades. *Nat. Lang. Eng. 2*(4), 337-344. doi:.10.1017/S1351324997001599

Abney, S. (2008). *Semisupervised Learning for Computational Linguistics*. London: Chapman and Hall/CRC.

Acosta, O., Sierra, G., & Aguilar, C. (2011). Extraction of Definitional Contexts using Lexical Relations. *International Journal of Computers and Applications, 34*(6), 46–53.

Adamic, L. A., & Huberman, B. A. (2002). Zipf's law and the Internet. *Glottometrics, 3*, 143–150.

Aggarwal, C. C., & Cheng, X. Z. (2012). *Mining Text Data*. New York, USA: Springer. doi:10.1007/978-1-4614-3223-4

Aggarwal, C. C., & Zhai, C. (2012). A survey of text clustering algorithms. In C. C. Aggarwal & C. Zhai (Eds.), *Mining text data*. (pp. 77–128). New York, NY: Springer. doi:10.1007/978-1-4614-3223-4_4

Agić, Ž., Ljubešić, N., & Tadić, M. (2010). Towards sentiment analysis of financial texts in Croatian. In *Poceedings of the Seventh International Conference on Language Resources and Evaluation*.

Agirre, E., & Edmonds, P. (2007). *Word Sense Disambiguation: Algorithms and Applications*. Springer. doi:10.1007/978-1-4020-4809-8

Agrawal, R., Imieliński, T., & Swami, A. (1993). Mining association rules between sets of items in large databases. [ACM.]. *SIGMOD Record, 22*(2), 207–216. doi:10.1145/170036.170072

Aguilar, C. (n. d.). *Análisis lingüístico de definiciones en contextos definitorios* [Unpublished doctoral dissertation] UNAM, Mexico.

Alarcon, R. (2009). *Descripción y evaluación de un sistema basado en reglas para la extracción automática de contextos definitorios* [Unpublished doctoral dissertation]. IULA-UPF, Barcelona.

Albalate, A., & Minker, W. (2011). *Semi-Supervised and Unsupervised Machine Learning: Novel Strategies*. Hoboken: Wiley.

Albee, A. (2010). eMarketing Strategies for the Complex Sale Marketing Interactions. New York, USA: Mv Graw Hill.

Aleman-Meza, B., Halaschek, C., Arpinar, I., & Sheth, A. (2003). Context-Aware Semantic Association Ranking. In *Proceedings of SWDB'03, Berlin, Germany* (pp. 33-50).

Alexandropoulos, G. (2013a). *Text and context in Flavius Claudius Julian's political speeches: coherence, intertextuality and communicative goal* [PhD Thesis]. University of Athens. Munich: Lincom.

Alexandropoulos, G. (2014c, May 22-24). Julian's political speeches: rhetorical and computational approach. *6th International Conference on Corpus Linguistics*. Las Palmas de Gran Canaria, Universidad de Las Palmas de Gran Canaria.

Alexandropoulos, G. (2013b). Stylistic approach of Julian the emperor and Gregory Nazianzean. *The Buckingham Journal of Language and Linguistics*, *6*, 1–13.

Alexandropoulos, G. (2014a). *Christians against the Ethnics*. Munich: Lincom.

Alexandropoulos, G. (2014b). *The epitaphs of Gregory of Nazianzus: a stylistic approach*. Munich: Lincom.

Alpaydin, E. (2009). *Introduction to Machine Learning. (Adaptive Computation and Machine Learning series)*. Cambridge: The MIT Press.

Alshawi, H. (1987). Processing Dictionary Definitions with Phrasal Pattern Hierarchies. *Computational Linguistics*, *13*(3-4), 195–202.

Anagnostopoulou, E. (2006). Clitic doubling. In M. Everaert & H. Riemsdijk (Eds.), *The Blackwell Companion to Syntax* (pp. 519–581). Malden, MA: Blackwell Publishing. doi:10.1002/9780470996591.ch14

Anderson, J. (1983). A Spreading Activation Theory of Memory. *Journal of Verbal Learning and Verbal Behavior*, *22*(3), 261–295. doi:10.1016/S0022-5371(83)90201-3

Anthony, L. (2006). Developing a freeware, multiplatform corpus analysis toolkit for the technical writing classroom. *IEEE Transactions on Professional Communication*, *49*(3), 275–286. doi:10.1109/TPC.2006.880753

Apresjan, J., Boguslavksij, I., Iomdin, L., Lazurskij, A., Sannikov, V., Sizov, V., & Tsinman, L. (2003). ETAP-3 Linguistics processor: A full-fledged NLP implementation of the MTT. In *Proceedings of the 1ˢᵗ International Conference on the Meaning-Text Theory*. (pp. 279-288). Paris: École Normale Supérieure.

Atkins, S., Clear, J., & Ostler, N. (1992). Corpus design criteria. *Journal of Literary and Linguistic Computing*, *7*(1), 1–16. doi:10.1093/llc/7.1.1

Auerbach, F. (1913). Das Gesetz der Bevolkerungskonzentration. *Petermanns Geographische Mitteilungen*, *LIX*, 73–76.

Austin, J. (1962). *How to Do Things with Words*. Oxford: Oxford University Press.

Axtell, R. L. (2001). Zipf distribution of US firm sizes. *Science*, *293*(5536), 1818–1820. doi:10.1126/science.1062081 PMID:11546870

Babenko, L. G., & Kazarin, Y. V. (2004). The Linguistic Analysis of the Literary Text. Theory and Practice Manual. Moscow: Flinta: Nauka.

Baker, P. (2006). *Using Corpora in Discourse Analysis*. London: Continuum.

Balian, R. (2013). Entropy, a Protean concept. *Séminaire Poincaré*, *2*, 13–27.

Barber, D. (2012). *Bayesian Reasoning and Machine Learning*. Cambridge: Cambridge University Press.

Bardy, G. (1914). *Saint Athanase*. Paris.

Baroni, M., & Bernardini, S. (2004). BootCaT: Bootstrapping corpora and terms from the web. In *Proceedings of LREC*, 4.

Bazerman, C., & Prior, P. (2004). *What Writing Does and How It Does It*. NJ: Erlbaum.

Bel, N., Koster, C. H., & Villegas, M. (2003). Cross-Lingual Text Categorization. In *Proceedings of ECDL-03, 7th European Conference on Research and Advanced Technology for Digital Libraries* (pp.126–139). Trodheim, Norway. Springer-Verlag, Heidelberg. doi:10.1007/978-3-540-45175-4_13

Berlin, B. (1992). *Ethnobiological classification: principles of categorization of plants and animals in traditional societies*. Princeton, N.J.: Princeton University Press. doi:10.1515/9781400862597

Berners-Lee, T., Hendler, J., & Lassila, O. (2001). The semantic web. *Scientific American, 284*(5), 28–37. doi:10.1038/scientificamerican0501-34 PMID:11341160

Berry, M. W., & Kogan, J. (2010). *Text Mining: Applications and Theory*. Chichester: Wiley. doi:10.1002/9780470689646

Bert, E. (2000). *A Practical Guide to Localization. Benjamins*. John Publishing Company.

Biber, D., Conrad, S., & Cortes, V. (2003). Lexical bundles in speech and writing: An initial taxonomy. In: A. Wilson, P. Rayson, & T. McEnery (Eds.), Corpus linguistics by the lune. (pp. 71-93). Frankfurt/Main: Peter Lang.

Biber, D., & Barbieri, F. (2007). Lexical bundles in university spoken and written registers. *English for Specific Purposes, 26*(3), 263–286. doi:10.1016/j.esp.2006.08.003

Biber, D., Conrad, S., & Cortes, V. (2004). If you look at...: Lexical bundles in university teaching and textbooks. *Applied Linguistics, 25*(3), 371–405. doi:10.1093/applin/25.3.371

Biber, D., Conrad, S., & Reppen, R. (1998). *Corpus linguistics: Investigating language structure and use*. Cambridge: Cambridge University Press. doi:10.1017/CBO9780511804489

Biber, D., Johansson, S., Leech, G., Conrad, S., & Finegan, E. (1999). *Longman Grammar of Spoken and Written English*. Longman Publications Group.

Bifet, A., Holmes, G., Kirkby, R., & Pfahringer, B. (2010). MOA: Massive online analysis. *Journal of Machine Learning Research, 99*, 1601–1604.

Binali, H., Wu, C., & Potdar, V. (2010). Computational approaches for emotion detection in text. In Pro*ceeding of the 4th IEEE International Conference of Digital Ecosystems and Technologies (DEST)*. Dubai, United Arab Emirates. doi:10.1109/DEST.2010.5610650

Bird, S., Klein, E., & Loper, E. (2009). *Natural Language Processing whit Python*. Sebastropol, Cal.: O'Reilly.

Bishop, C. M. (2007). *Pattern Recognition and Machine Learning. (Information Science and Statistics)*. New York: Springer.

Bluhm, R. (2013). *Empirical Methods of Linguistics in Philosophy*. Retrieved from http://philevents.org/event/show/11885

Blum, A., & Mitchell, T. (1998). Combining labeled and unlabeled data with co-training. In: *COLT: Proceedings of the Workshop on Computational Learning Theory* (pp. 92-100). Morgan Kaufmann. doi:10.1145/279943.279962

Bonet, E. (2002). Cliticització. In J. Solà, M. R. Lloret, J. Mascaró, & M. P. Saldanya (Eds.), *Gramàtica del català contemporani.* (pp. 933–989). Barcelona: Empúries.

Bonet, E., & Lloret, M. R. (2005). More on alignment as an alternative to domains: The syllabification of Catalan clitics. *Probus. International Journal of Latin and Romance Linguistics, 17*(3), 37–78.

Borgatti, S. (2005). Centrality and network flow. *Social Networks, 27*(1), 55–71. doi:10.1016/j.socnet.2004.11.008

Borgatti, S., & Everett, M. (2006). A graph-theoretic perspective on centrality. *Social Networks, 28*(4), 466–484. doi:10.1016/j.socnet.2005.11.005

Borg, J. (2007). *Persuasion – The Art of Influencing People*. London: Pearson / Prentice Hall.

Bošković, Ž. (2004). Clitic placement in South Slavic. *Journal of Slavic Linguistics, 12*, 39–90.

Bourigault, D., & Jacquemin, C. (1999). Term extraction+ term clustering: An integrated platform for computer-aided terminology. In *Proceedings of the ninth conference on European chapter of the Association for Computational Linguistics* (pp. 15-22). Association for Computational Linguistics. doi:10.3115/977035.977039

Bozkir, A. S., Mazman, S. G., & Sezer, E. A. (2011). Identification of User Patterns in Social Networks by Data Mining Techniques: Facebook Case. In *Proceedings of the Technological Convergence and Social Networks in Information Management Conference (IMCW) 2010*. Ankara, Turkey.

Bragg, M. (2013). *Ordinary Language Philosophy*. BBC Podcast. Retrieved from http://www.bbc.co.uk/programmes/b03ggc19

Brakke, D. (1955). *Athanasius and the politics of Ascetism*. Oxford: Clarendon Press.

Brants, T. (2003). Natural Language Processing in Information Retrieval. In B. Decadt, V. Hoste, & G. De Pauw (Eds.) (2003, December 19), Computational Linguistics in the Netherlands. Centre for Dutch Language and Speech, University of Antwerp.

Braune, F., Gojun, A., & Fraser, A. (2012). Long-distance reordering during search for hierarchical phrase-based SMT. In *Proceedings of the 16th Annual Conference of the European Association for Machine Translation*, (pp. 177–184). Trento.

Brédif, L. (1879). *Demosthene: L'eloquence politique en Grèce*. Paris: Librairie Hachette.

Brin, S., & Page, L. (1998). The Anatomy of a Large-Scale Hypertextual Web Search Engine. In *Seventh International World-Wide Web Conference (WWW 1998)*, April 14-18, 1998, Brisbane, Australia. doi:10.1016/S0169-7552(98)00110-X

Browarnik, A., & Maimon, O. (2012, April). Subsentence Detection with Regular Expressions. *Presented at the XXX AESLA International Conference*. Lleida.

Browarnik, A., et al. (2009, June 2-5). Creation of a critical and commented database on the health, safety and environmental impact of nanoparticles – challenges and objectives. *Presentation at the NHECD networking meeting on the occasion of EuroNanoForum*. Prague. Retrieved from http://www.nhecd-fp7.eu

Browne, W. (1975). Serbo-Croatian enclitics for English-speaking learners. In R. Filipovic (Ed.), Kontrastivna analiza engleskog i hrvatskog ili srpskog jezika. (pp. 105-134). Zagreb: Institut za lingvistiku Filozofskog fakulteta.

Brown, P. F., Pietra, V. J., Pietra, S. A., & Mercer, R. L. (1993). The Mathematics of Statistical Machine Translation: Parameter Estimation. *Computational Linguistics, 19*(2), 263–311.

Bsoul, Q., Salim, J., & Zakaria, L. Q. (2013). An Intelligent Document Clustering Approach to Detect Crime Patterns. *Procedia Technology (4th International Conference on Electrical Engineering and Informatics, ICEEI 2013), 11*, 1181–1187.

Buitelaar, P., & Cimiano, P. (2008). *Ontology learning and population: bridging the gap between text and knowledge*. Amsterdam: IOS Press.

Buitelaar, P., Cimiano, P., Grobelnik, M., & Sintek, M. (2005, October 3). Ontology Learning from Text In *European Conference on Machine Learning*. Porto, Portugal.

Buitelaar, P., Cimiano, P., & Magnini, B. (2005). Ontology Learning from Texts: An Overview. In P. Buitelaar, P. Cimiano, & B. Magnini. *Ontology Learning from Text: Methods, Evaluation and Applications*. In *Frontiers in Artificial Intelligence and Applications, 123*. IOS Press.

Caldas-Coulthard, C. R. (1997). *News as Social Practice: A Study in Critical Discourse Analysis*. Florianopolis: Advanced Research in English Series.

Calzolari, N. (1984). Detecting patterns in a lexical data base. In *Proceedings of the 22nd Annual Meeting of the Association for Computational Linguistics*. (pp.170-173). Stanford, CA: ACL Publications. doi:10.3115/980491.980527

Čamdžić, A., & Hudson, R. (2002). Serbo-Croat-Bosnian clitics and word grammar. *UCL Working Papers in Linguistics, 14*, 321-353.

Cameron, A. (1994). *Christianity and the rhetoric of empire*. Berkeley: University of California Press.

Cao, Y., Zhang, P., Guo, J., & Guo, L. (2014). Mining Large-scale Event Knowledge from Web Text. *Procedia Computer Science (2014 International Conference on Computational Science), 29*, 478–487.

Caplan, D. (2003). Neurolinguistics. In *The Handbook of Linguistics*. UK: Blackwell Publishing. doi:10.1002/9780470756409.ch24

Caroll, L. (2003). Alicia En El País De Las Maravillas. Ediciones del Sur. Retrieved from http://www.ucm.es/data/cont/docs/119-2014-02-19-Carroll.AliciaEnElPaisDeLasMaravillas.pdf

Carpenter, B. (2005). Scaling high-order character language models to gigabytes. In *Proceedings of the association for computational linguistics software workshop*. Ann Arbor, Michigan, USA. doi:10.3115/1626315.1626322

Carvalho, P., Sarmento, L., Silva, M. J., & De Oliveira, E. (2009). Clues for Detecting Irony in User-Generated Contents: Oh...!! It's so easy. In *Text Sentiment Analysis TSA'09*. ACM Press. doi:10.1145/1651461.1651471

Cawley, G. C., & Talbot, N. L. C. (2010). On Over-fitting in Model Selection and Subsequent Selection Bias in Performance Evaluation. *Journal of Machine Learning Research, 11*, 2079–2107.

Chafe, W. (1982). Integration and involvement in speaking, writing and oral literature. In: Tannen, D. (Ed.), Spoken and written language. (pp. 35-55). Notwood: Ablex.

Chapelle, O., Schölkopf, B., & Zien, A. (Eds.). (2010). *Semi-Supervised Learning. (Adaptive Computation and Machine Learning series)*. Cambridge: The MIT Press.

Chaumartin, F. R. (2005). *Conception et réalisation d'une interface syntaxe / sémantique utilisant des ressources de large couverture en langue anglaise. Master de Recherche en Linguistique et Informatique* (in French).

Chaumartin, F. R. (2008). Antelope: Une plate-forme industrielle de traitement linguistique. *TAL, 49*(2), 1–10.

Chen, C. H. (Ed.). (1996). *Fuzzy Logic and Neural Network Handbook*. McGraw-Hill.

Chen, E., & Wu, G. (2005). *An Ontology Learning Method Enhanced by Frame Semantics* (pp. 374–382). ISM.

Chiang, D. (2005). A hierarchical phrase-based model for statistical machine translation. In *Proceedings of the 43rd Annual Meeting on Association for Computational Linguistics*. Stroudsburg, PA, USA: Association for Computational Linguistics. doi:10.3115/1219840.1219873

Chisholm, E., & Kolda, T. G. (1999). *New term weighting formulas for the vector space method in information retrieval* [Technical Report ORNL-TM-13756]. Oak Ridge National Laboratory, Oak Ridge, TN.

Ciaramita, M., Gangemi, A., Ratsch, E., Šarić, J., & Rojas, I. (2008). Unsupervised learning of semantic relations for molecular biology ontologies. In *Proceeding of the 2008 conference on Ontology Learning and Population: Bridging the Gap between Text and Knowledge* (pp. 91-104).

Cimiano, P. (2006). *Ontology Learning and Population from Text.Algorithms, Evaluation and Applications*. Springer.

Cimiano, P., Hotho, A., & Staab, S. (2004). *Comparing Conceptual.* Divisive and Agglomerative Clustering for Learning Taxonomies from Text.

Cimiano, Ph., Pivk, A., Schmidt, L., & Staab, S. (2004). Learning Taxonomic Relations from Heterogeneous Sources of Evidence. In *Proceedings of the ECAI 2004 Ontology Learning and Population*, Valencia, Spain.

Cohen, H., & Lefebvre, C. (2005). *Handbook of Categorization and Cognitive Science.* Amsterdam: Elsevier.

Collins, A. M., & Loftus, E. F. (1975). A spreading-activation theory of semantic processing. *Psychological Review,* *82*(6), 407–428. doi:10.1037/0033-295X.82.6.407

Collins, M., & Quillian, M. (1969). Retrieval time from semantic memory. *Journal of Verbal Learning and Verbal Behavior, 8*(2), 241–248. doi:10.1016/S0022-5371(69)80069-1

Contractor, N. (2008). *The Emergence of Multidimensional Networks.* Retrieved from http://www.hctd.net/newsletters/fall2007/Noshir Contractor.pdf

Cortes, V. (2004). Lexical bundles in published and student disciplinary writing: Examples from history and biology. *English for Specific Purposes, 23*(4), 397–423. doi:10.1016/j.esp.2003.12.001

Coussement, K., & Poel, D. V. (2008). Integrating the voice of customers through call center emails into a decision support system for churn prediction. *Journal of International Management, 45*(3), 164–174.

Crestani, F. (1997). Application of Spreading Activation Techniques in Information Retrieval. *Artificial Intelligence Review, 11*(6), 453–482. doi:10.1023/A:1006569829653

Cristianini, N., & Shawe-Taylor, J. (2000). *An Introduction to Support Vector Machines and Other Kernel-based Learning Methods.* Cambridge: Cambridge University Press. doi:10.1017/CBO9780511801389

Croft, W., & Cruse, A. (2004). *Cognitive Linguistics.* Cambridge: Cambridge University Press. doi:10.1017/CBO9780511803864

Cross, F. L. (1945). *The studies of Athanasius.* Oxford.

Cruse, D. A. (1986). *Lexical Semantics.* Cambridge: Cambridge University Press.

Cummins, R., & O'Riordan, C. (2006). Evolving local and global weighting schemes in information retrieval. *Information Retrieval, 9*(3), 311–330. doi:10.1007/s10791-006-1682-6

Dagan, I., Glickman, O., & Magnini, B. (2006). The PASCAL Recognising Textual Entailment Challenge. *Lecture Notes in Computer Science, 3944*, 177–190. doi:10.1007/11736790_9

Dařena, F., & Žižka, J. (2011). Text Mining-based Formation of Dictionaries Expressing Opinions in Natural Languages. In *Mendel 2011:17th International Conference on Soft Computing.* (pp. 374-381). Brno: University of Technology.

Dařena, F., Žižka, J., & Přichystal, J. (2014). Clients' freely written assessment as the source of automatically mined opinions. *Proceedings of Procedia Economics and Finance (Enterprise and the Competitive Environment 2014 conference, ECE 2014,), 12*(1), 103-110. Brno, Czech Republic.

Dařena, F., Troussov, A., & Žižka, J. (2010). Simulating activation propagation in social networks using the graph theory. *Acta Universitatis Agriculturae et Silviculturae Mendelianae Brunensis, LVIII*(3), 21–28. doi:10.11118/actaun201058030021

Dařena, F., & Žižka, J. (2013). SuDoC: Semi-unsupervised Classification of Text Document Opinions Using a Few Labeled Examples and Clustering. In *Flexible Query Answering Systems.* (pp. 625–636). Heidelberg: Springer. doi:10.1007/978-3-642-40769-7_54

Dave, K., Lawrence, E., & Pennock, D. M. (2003). Mining the peanut gallery: opinion extraction and semantic classification of product reviews. In *Proceedings of the 12th international conference on World Wide Web*. New York, USA. doi:10.1145/775152.775226

Davis, B., Handschuh, S., Troussov, A., Judge, J., & Sogrin, M. (2008, May 26-June 1). Linguistically Light Lexical Extensions for Ontologies. In *Proceedings of the 6th edition of the Language Resources and Evaluation Conference (LREC) in Marrakech, Morocco*.

De Witt Spurgin, S. (1994). The power to persuade: A rhetoric and reader for argumentative writing. NJ: Prentice Hall.

Dean, J. (2014). *Big Data, Data Mining, and Machine Learning: Value Creation for Business Leaders and Practitioners. (Wiley and SAS Business Series)*. Hoboken: Wiley. doi:10.1002/9781118691786

Debole, F., & Sebastiani, F. (2003). Supervised Term Weighting for Automated Text Categorization. In *Proceedings of SAC-03, 18th ACM Symposium on Applied Computing* (pp. 784–788). Melbourne, FL. ACM Press. doi:10.1145/952532.952688

Decker, S., & Frank, M. (2004). The Social Semantic Desktop. *Technical Report DERI-TR-2004-05-02, Digital Enterprise Research Institute (DERI)*. Retrieved from http://www.deri.ie/fileadmin/documents/DERI-TR-2004-05-02.pdf

Delmonte, R., & Pallotta, V. (2011). Opinion Mining and Sentiment Analysis Need Text Understanding. Advances in Distributed Agent-Based Retrieval Tools Studies in Computational Intelligence, 361, 81–95. Berlin: Springer-Verlag.

Demonte, V. (1999). El adjetivo. Clases y usos. La posición del adjetivo en el sintagma nominal. In Bosque, I., & Demonte, V. (Eds.), Gramática descriptiva de la lengua Española. (pp. 129-215). Madrid: Espasa-Calpe.

Demšar, J., Curk, T., & Erjavec, A. (2013). Orange: Data Mining Toolbox in Python. *Journal of Machine Learning Research, 14*, 2349–2353.

Demurova, N. M. (1991). Кэрролл, Л. Приключения Алисы в стране чудес. Moscow: Наука. Retrieved from http://lib.ru/CARROLL/carroll_1.txt

Denecke, K. (2008). Using SentiWordNet for Multilingual Sentiment Analysis. In *Proceeding of the IEEE 24th International Conference Data Eng. Workshop (ICDEW 2008)*. Cancun, Mexico: IEEE Press. doi:10.1109/ICDEW.2008.4498370

Devitt, A., & Ahmad, K. (2007). Sentiment Polarity Identification in Financial News: A cohesion-based Approach. In *Proceeding of the 45th Ann. Meeting Assoc. Computational Linguistics*. Prague, Czech Republic: ACL Press.

Dhillon, I. S., & Modha, D. S. (1999). Concept decompositions for large sparse text data using clustering. *Machine Learning, 42*(1/2), 143–175. doi:10.1023/A:1007612920971

Dietterich, T. (1995). Overfitting and Undercomputing in Machine Learning. *Computing Surveys, 27*(3), 326–327. doi:10.1145/212094.212114

Din, A. (2013). Cliticization and endoclitics generation of Pashto language. In *Proceedings of the 4th Workshop on South and Southeast Asian NLP*. (pp 77-82). Nagoya: Asian Federation of Natural Language Processing.

Ding, C., He, X., Zha, H., Gu, M., & Simon, H. (2001). Spectral min-max cut for graph partitioning and data clustering. In *ICDM '01 Proceedings of the 2001 IEEE International Conference on Data Mining*. (pp. 107-114). Washington: IEEE Computer Society.

Dini, L., & Mazzini, G. (2010). Real Time Customer Opinion Monitoring. In S. Sirmakessis (Ed.), *Text Mining and its Applications: Results of the NEMIS Launch Conference*. (pp. 159–168). Berlin: Springer.

Dolan, W., Vanderwende, L., & Richardson, S. (1993). Automatically deriving structured knowledge bases form online dictionaries. In *Proceedings of the Pacific Association for Computational Linguistic*. (pp. 5-14).

Doms, A., & Schroeder, M. (2005). *GoPubMed: exploring PubMed with the Gene Ontology.* Retrieved from http://nar.oxfordjournals.org/content/33/suppl_2/W783.long

Dorr, B. (1993). *Machine translation. A view from the lexicon.* Cambridge, MA: The MIT Press.

Dorr, B. (1994). Machine translation divergences: A formal description and proposed solution. *Computational Linguistics, 20*(4), 579–633.

Dragas, G. (1980). *Athanasiana: essays in the theology of Saint Athanasius.* London.

Du, J., Roturier, J., & Way, A. (2010). TMX markup: a challenge when adapting SMT to the localisation environment. *In: EAMT 2010 – 14th Annual Conference of the European Association for Machine Translation.*

Duda, R. O., Hart, P. E., & Stork, D. G. (2001). *Pattern Classification.* New York, NY: Wiley.

Dunlap, R. A. (1997). *The Golden Ratio and Fibonacci Numbers.* World Scientific Publishing.

Durant, K. T., & Smith, M. D. (2006). Mining Sentiment Classification from Political Web Logs. In Proceedings of Knowledge Discovery on the Web (WEBKDD'06). Philadelphia, Pennsylvania.

Durran, I. N., Fraser, A., Schmid, H., & Hoang, H. (2013). Can Markov Models Over Minimal Translation Units Help Phrase-Based SMT. In *Proceedings of the 51st Annual Meeting of the Association for Computational Linguistics.* Retrieved from https://www.gala-global.org/what-localization

Ejerhed, E. I. (1996). Finite state segmentation of discourse into clauses. *Natural Language Engineering, 2*(4), 355–364. doi:10.1017/S1351324997001629

Elia, A. (2009). Quantitative Data and Graphics on Lexical Specificity and Index of Readability: The Case of Wikipedia. Revista Electronica de Linguistica aplicada, 8, 248-271.

Engel, D., Whitney, P., Calapristi, A., & Brockman, F. (2009). Mining for emerging technologies within text streams and documents. In *Proceedings of the Ninth SIAM International Conference on Data Mining.*

Estopà, R. (2003). *Extracció de terminologia: elements per a la construcció d'un SEACUSE* [Ph. D. Dissertation]. IULA-UPF, Barcelona.

Esuli, A., & Sebastiani, F. (2005). Determining the semantic orientation of terms through gloss analysis. In *Proceedings of the 14th ACM International Conference on Information and Knowledge Management (CIKM'05).* Bremen, Germany.

Esuli, A., & Sebastiani, F. (2006a). Determining term subjectivity and term orientation for opinion mining. In *Proceedings of the 11rd Conference of the European Chapter of the Association for Computational Linguistics (EACL'06).* Trento, Italy.

Esuli, A., & Sebastiani, F. (2006b). SentiWordNet: A publicy available lexical resource for opinion mining. In *Proceedings of the 5th International Conference on Language Resources and Evaluation.* Genoa, Italy.

Etzioni, O., Cafarella, M. J., Downey, D., Kok, S., Popescu, A.-M., Shaked, T., et al. (2004). Web-scale information extraction. Proceedings of KnowItAll. Retrieved from http://portal.acm.org/ft_gateway.cfm?id=988687&type=pdf&coll=&dl=ACM&CFID=15151515&CFTOKEN=6184618

Etzioni, O., Banko, M., Soderland, S., & Weld, D. S. (2008). Open information extraction from the web. *Communications of the ACM, 51*(12), 68–74. doi:10.1145/1409360.1409378

Evans, V., & Green, M. (2006). *Cognitive Linguistics: An Introduction.* Mahwah, NJ: LEA Publications.

Everett, M. G., & Borgatti, S. P. (2005). Extending centrality. In Carrington, P. J., Scott, J., & Wasserman (Eds.), Models and Methods in Social Network Analysis (pp. 181-201). Cambridge University Press. doi:10.1017/CBO9780511811395.004

Everitt, B. S., Landau, S., Leese, M., & Stahl, S. (2011). *Cluster analysis*. Chichester: Wiley. doi:10.1002/9780470977811

Fairclough, N. (1992). *Discourse and social change*. Cambridge: Polity Press.

Färber, I., Günnemann, S., Kriegel, H., Kröger, P., Müller, E., & Schubert, E. et al. (2010). On Using Class-Labels in Evaluation of Clusterings. In *Proceedings of the 1st International Workshop on Discovering, Summarizing and Using Multiple Clusterings (MultiClust 2010) in conjunction with 16th ACM SIGKDD Conference on Knowledge Discovery and Data Mining (KDD 2010)*. Washington.

Faure, D., & Nedellec, C. (1998). A Corpus-based Conceptual Clustering Method for Verb Frames and Ontologies. In: *Proceedings of the LREC Workshop on adapting lexical and corpus resources to sublanguages and applications*. (pp. 5-12). Granada, Spain.

Faure, D., & Nedellec, C. (1999). Knowledge acquisition of predicate argument structures from technical texts using machine learning. In *The system ASIUM* (pp. 329–334). Knowledge Acquisition, Modeling and Management. doi:10.1007/3-540-48775-1_22

Fayyad, U., Piatetsky-Shapiro, G., & Smyth, P. (Eds.). (1996). *Advances in Knowledge Discovery and Data Mining*. Cambridge, USA: MIT Press.

Feldman, R., & Sanger, J. (2007). *The Text Mining Handbook: Advanced Approaches in Analyzing Unstructured Data*. New York, USA: Cambridge University Press.

Fellbaum, C. (1998). *WordNet: An Electronic Lexical Database*. Cambridge, Mass.: The MIT Press.

Fellbaum, C. (Ed.). (1998). *Wordnet: An Electronic Lexical Database*. Cambridge, MA: MIT Press.

Ferrano, G., & Wanner, L. (2012). Labeling Semantically Motivated Clusters of Verbal Relations. *Procesamiento del Lenguaje Natural*, *49*, 129–138.

Figueiredo, F., Rocha, L., Couto, T., Salles, T., Goncalves, M. A., & Meira, W. Jr. (2011). Word co-occurrence features for text classification. *Information Systems*, *36*(5), 843–858. doi:10.1016/j.is.2011.02.002

Fillmore, C. J., Johnson, C. R., & Petruck, M. R. (2003). Background to framenet. *International journal of lexicography*, *16*(3), 235-250.

Fillmore, C. J. (1976). Frame semantics and the nature of language. *Annals of the New York Academy of Sciences*, *280*(1 Origins and E), 20–32. doi:10.1111/j.1749-6632.1976.tb25467.x

Firth, J. R. (1951/1957). *Papers in Linguistics, 1934-1951*. London: Oxford University Press.

Fonseca, F., & Martin, J. (2009). Beyond Newspeak: Three arguments for the persistence of the informal in the creation and use of computational ontologies. *Knowledge Management Research & Practice*, *7*(3), 196–205. doi:10.1057/kmrp.2009.16

Forcadell, M., & Vallduví, E. (2000). Duplicación clítica: el caso catalán. In J. Ruiz de Mendoza, M. Fornés, J. M. Molina, & L. Pérez (Eds.), *Panorama actual de la lingüística aplicada: conocimiento, procesamiento y uso del lenguaje*. (pp. 679–689). Logroño: Universidad de La Rioja.

Framenet. (2012). Current Project Status. Retrieved from https://framenet.icsi.berkeley.edu/fndrupal/current_status

Frege, G. (1884). *The Foundations of Arithmetic: a logico-mathematical enquiry into the concept of number. English translation by J. L. Austin, B. H* (revised edition 1953). Oxford: Blackwell.

Gabaix, X. (1999). Zipf's Law for Cities: An Explanation. *The Quarterly Journal of Economics*, *114*(3), 739–767. doi:10.1162/003355399556133

Gelbukh, A. F., Alexandrov, M., Bourek, A., & Makagonov, P. (2003). Selection of Representative Documents for Clusters in a Document Collection. In *Proceedings of Natural Language Processing and Information Systems, 8th International Conference on Applications of Natural Language to Information Systems.* (pp.120-126).

GeoNames.org. (n.d.). *GeoNames.* Retrieved from http://www.geonames.org/

Go, A., Huang, L., & Bhayani, R. (2009). Twitter sentiment classification using distant supervision. In CS224N Project Report, Stanford, USA.

Gocci, L. (2009). CAT Tools for Beginners. *Translation Journal, 13*(4), 133–147.

Godbole, N., Srinivasaiah, M., & Skiena, S. (Eds.). (2007). *Large-scale sentiment analysis for news and blogs.* International conference on weblogs and social media (ICWSM'2007). Boulder, Colorado, USA.

Goh, C.-L., Onishi, T., & Sumita, E. (2011). Rule-based reordering constraints for phrase-based SMT. In *proceedings of the 15th conference of the European Association for Machine Translation.* (pp. 113–120).

Gómez-Pérez, A., & Manzano-Macho, D. (Eds.). (2003). *Deliverable 1.5: A Survey of Ontology Learning Methods and Tools, OntoWeb deliverable.* Retrieved from http://www.sti-innsbruck.at/fileadmin/documents/deliverables/Ontoweb/D1.5.pdf

Goodnough, A. (2013). Applicants Find Health Website Is Improving, but Not Fast Enough. *The New York Times.* Retrieved from http://www.nytimes.com/2013/11/21/us/politics/applicants-find-health-website-is-improving-but-not-fast-enough.html?hp&_r=0

Graham, Y., Baldwin, T., Moffat, A., & Zobel, J. (2013). Continuous Measurement Scales in Human Evaluation of Machine Translation. In *Proceedings of the 7th Linguistic Annotation Workshop & Interoperability with Discourse.* (pp. 33–41). Sofia: Association for Computational Linguistics.

Grimm, J., & Grimm, W. (n. d.). *Das tapfere Schneiderlein.* Retrieved from http://www.grimmstories.com/de/grimm_maerchen/das_tapfere_schneiderlein

Grimm, J., & Grimm, W. (n. d.). *El sastrecillo valiente (Siete de un golpe).* Retrieved from http://www.grimmstories.com/es/grimm_cuentos/el_sastrecillo_valiente

Grimm, J., & Grimm, W. (n. d.). *The Valiant Little Tailor.* Retrieved from http://www.grimmstories.com/en/grimm_fairytales/the_gallant_tailor

Grimm, J., & Grimm, W. (n. d.). *Храбрый портняжка.* Retrieved from http://www.grimmstories.com/ru/grimm_skazki/hrabryj_portnjazka

Groza, T., Handschuh, S., Moeller, K., Grimnes, G., Sauermann, L., Minack, E., et al. (2007, September 5-7). The NEPOMUK Project – On the way to the Social Semantic Desktop. In *Proceedings of International Conferences on new Media technology (I-MEDIA-2007) and Semantic Systems (I-SEMANTICS-07)* (pp. 201-210). Graz, Austria..

Gruber, T. R. (1993). A Translation Approach to Portable Ontology Specifications. *Knowledge Acquisition, 5*(2), 199–220. doi:10.1006/knac.1993.1008

Guarino, N. (1998). Formal Ontology in Information Systems. In *Proceedings of FOIS'98* (pp. 3-15). Trento, Italy, 6-8 June 1998. Amsterdam: IOS Press.

Guerra, L., Robles, V., Bielza, C., & Larrañaga, P. (2012). A comparison of clustering quality indices using outliers and noise. *Intelligent Data Analysis, 16*, 703–715.

Guo, Q., & Zhang, M. (2009). Multi-documents Automatic Abstracting based on text clustering and semantic analysis. *Knowledge-Based Systems, 22*(6), 482–485. doi:10.1016/j.knosys.2009.06.010

Gurteen, D. (2007). *KM 2.0: KM goes Social.* Retrieved from http://www.gurteen.com/gurteen/gurteen.nsf/id/km-goes-social

Hahn, U., Romacker, M., & Schulz, S. (2000). MedSynDiKATe – design considerations for an ontology-based medical text understanding system. In *Proceedings of the AMIA Symposium* (p. 330). American Medical Informatics Association.

Halmari, H. C. (2005). In search of "successful" political persuasion. A comparison of the styles of Bill Clinton and Ronald Reagan. In: Hari, H. & T. Virtanen (Eds.), Persuasion across genres. A linguistic approach. (pp. 105-134). Amsterdam / Philadelpia: John Benjamins Publishing Company.

Halpern, A. (1995). *On the placement and morphology of clitics.* Stanford, CA: CSLI Publications.

Han, Z. (2012). *Data and text mining of financial markets using news and social media.* MSc thesis, University of Manchester.

Hand, D., Mannila, H., & Smyth, P. (2001). *Principles of Data Mining.* Cambridge, MA, USA: MIT Press.

Hang, C., Vibhu, M., & Mayur, D. (2006). Comparative Experiments on Sentiment Classification for Online Product Reviews. In *Proceeding of the 21st national conference on Artificial intelligence (AAAI'06).* AAAI Press.

Han, J., & Kamber, M. (2006). *Data Mining: Concepts and Techniques.* San Francisco: Morgan Kaufmann.

Hanneman, R. A., & Riddle, M. (2005). *Introduction to social network methods.* Riverside, CA: University of California. Retrieved from http://faculty.ucr.edu/~hanneman/)

Harris, Z. (1968). *Mathematical Structures of Language.* John Wiley & Sons.

Hastie, T., Tibshirani, R., & Friedman, J. (2013). *The Elements of Statistical Learning: Data Mining, Inference, and Prediction* (2nd Ed.). New York: Springer.

Hearst, M. (1992). Automatic Acquisition of Hyponyms from Large Text Corpora.[Nantes, France.]. *Proceedings of, COLING-92, 539*–545.

Hearst, M. A. (1992). Automatic acquisition of hyponyms from large text corpora. In *Proceedings of the 14th conference on Computational linguistics-Volume 2* (pp. 539-545). doi:10.3115/992133.992154

Heringer, H. J., & Lobin, H. (Eds.), *Dependency and valency. An international handbook of contemporary research* , 1. (pp. 546–570). Berlin, New York: De Gruyter.

Hill, B. M. (1970). Zipf's law and prior distributions for the composition of a population. *Journal of the American Statistical Association, 65*(331), 1220–1232. doi:10.1080/01621459.1970.10481157

Hirst, G. (2009). Ontology and the lexicon. In S. Staab & R. Studer (Eds.), *Handbook on Ontologies.* (pp. 269–292). Berlin: Springer. doi:10.1007/978-3-540-92673-3_12

Hitzler, P., Krotzsch, M., & Rudolph, S. (2009). Knowledge Representation for the Semantic Web. In KI 2009.

Hoang, H. (2007). Factored translation models. In *Proceedings of the 2007 Joint Conference on Empirical Methods in Natural Language Processing and Computational Natural Language Learning.* (pp. 868–876).

Hodge, R., & Kress, G. (1993). ²). *Language as Ideology.* London: Routledge.

Hoffart, J., Suchanek, F. M., Berberich, K., & Weikum, G. (2012). YAGO2: A spatially and temporally enhanced knowledge base from Wikipedia. *Artificial Intelligence, 194*, 28–61. doi:10.1016/j.artint.2012.06.001

Holz, F. (2008). Semantic Structuring of Document Collections and Building of Term Hierarchies – An Unsupervised and Knowledge-free Approach. In *Proceeding of the 8th International Conference on Terminology and Knowledge Engineering (TKE)*.

Holzner, S. (2009). *Facebook Marketing: Leverage Social Media to Grow Your Business*. Indianapolis, Illinois, USA: Que Publishing.

Homestead Act of 1862. (2014). National Park Service. Retrieved from http://www.nps.gov/home/index.htm

Hotho, A., Jaschke, R., Schmitz, C., & Stumme, G. (2006). Information retrieval in folksonomies: Search and ranking. *Lecture Notes in Computer Science*, *4011*, 411–426. doi:10.1007/11762256_31

Hotho, A., Staab, S., & Stumme, G. (2003). *Text Clustering Based on Background Knowledge. Institute of Applied Informatics and Formal Descriptive Methods* (pp. 1–35). Germany: University of Karlsruhe.

Huang, Z., Ng, M. K., & Cheung, D. W.-L. (2001). An empirical study on the visual cluster validation method with fastmap. In *Proceedings of the 7th international conference on database systems for advanced applications (DASFAA 2001)*. (pp. 84-91). Hong-Kong: Springer. doi:10.1109/DASFAA.2001.916368

Huang, A. (2008). Similarity Measures for Text Document Clustering. In *Proceedings of the Sixth New Zealand Computer Science Research Student Conference*. (pp. 49-56).

Hudík, T., & Ruopp, A. (2011). The integration of Moses into localisation industry. *Proceedings of the 15th conference of the European Association for Machine Translation*. (pp. 47–53).

Hunger, H. (1978). *Die hochsprachliche profane Literatur der Byzantiner*. Munchen: Beck.

Hurst, M., & Nigam, K. (2004). Retrieving topical sentiments from online document collections. In *Document Recognition and Retrieval XI Conference*.

Hutchins, W. J. (1986). *Machine translation: past, present, future*. New York: John Wiley & Sons.

Hyland, K. (2008a). As can be seen: Lexical bundles and disciplinary variation. *English for Specific Purposes*, *27*(1), 4–21. doi:10.1016/j.esp.2007.06.001

Hyland, K. (2008b). Academic clusters: Text patterning in published and postgraduate writing. *International Journal of Applied Linguistics*, *18*(1), 41–62. doi:10.1111/j.1473-4192.2008.00178.x

Hymes, D. (1964). Towards Ethnographies of Communication: The Analysis of Communicative Events. *American Anthropologist*, *66*(6), 12–25.

Hymes, D. (1974). *Foundations of Sociolinguistics: An Ethnographic Approach*. Philadelphia: University of Pennsylvania Press.

Intentional. (n. d.). *Dictionary.com Unabridged*. Retrieved from [[REMOVED HYPERLINK FIELD]http://dictionary.reference.com/browse/intentional

Ismail, L., Chang, E., & Karduck, A. P. (2010). In *Proceedings of the IEEE international conference on digital ecosystems and technologies (DEST 2010)*. Dubai, United Arab Emirates: IEEE Press.

Jacob, B., Feldman, R., Kogan, S., & Richardson, M. (2012). *Which News Moves Stock Prices*. Working Paper.

Jain, A. K., & Dubes, R. C. (1988). *Algorithms for Clustering Data*. Engelwood Cliffs, NJ: Prentice Hall.

Jaschke, R., Marinho, L., Hotho, A., Schmidt-Thieme, L., & Stumme, G. (2007). Tag Recommendations in Folksonomies. In *Proceedings of the 11th European Conference on Principles and Practice of Knowledge Discovery in Databases PKDD*, Warsaw, Poland.

Joachims, T. (1998). Text categorization with support vector machines: Learning with many relevant features. In *Proceedings of the Tenth European Conference on Machine Learning*. Berlin, Germany: Springer. doi:10.1007/BFb0026683

Joachims, T. (2002). *Learning to classify text using support vector machines*. Norwell, MA: Kluwer Academic Publishers. doi:10.1007/978-1-4615-0907-3

Jones, G. M., Horning, L. E., & Morrow, J. D. (1922). *A High School English Grammar*. Toronto, London: J. M Dent & Sons.

Judge, J., Nakayama, A., Sogrin, M., & Troussov, A. (2008). *Method and System for Finding a Focus of a Document*. Patent Application US 20080/263038 Kind Code: A1. Filing Date: 02/26/2008.

Judge, J., Sogrin, M., & Troussov, A. (2007, September 26-28, 2007). Galaxy: IBM Ontological Network Miner. In *Proceedings of the 1st Conference on Social Semantic Web (CSSW)*. Leipzig, Germany.

Jurafsky, D., & Martin, J. H. (2009). *Speech and Language Processing: An Introduction to Natural Language Processing, Speech Recognition, and Computational Linguistics* (2nd Ed.). Prentice-Hall.

Kahane, S. (2003). The Meaning-Text Theory. In V. Agel, L.M. Eichinger, H-W. Eroms, P. Hellwig, Kahane, S. (2007). A formalism for machine translation in MTT (including syntactic restructuring). In *Wiener Slawistischer Almanach*, 69, *Proceedings of the 3rd International Conference on Meaning-Text Linguistics*. (pp. 229-238). Munich: Kubon & Sagner.

Kali, R. (2003). The city as a giant component: A random graph approach to Zipf's law. *Applied Economics Letters*, *10*(11), 717–720. doi:10.1080/1350485032000139006

Kang, H., Yoo, S. J., & Han, D. (2012). Senti-lexicon and improved Naive Bayes algorithms for sentiment analysis of restaurant reviews. *Expert Systems with Applications*, *39*(5), 6000–6010. doi:10.1016/j.eswa.2011.11.107

Kannengiesser, C. (1991). *Arius and Athanasius: two Alexandrian theologians*. Hampshire: Gower Publications.

Karypis, G. (2003). *CLUTO: A Clustering Toolkit*. Minneapolis: University of Minnesota, Department of Computer Science.

Kaufman, L., & Rousseeuw, P. J. (2005). *Finding Groups in Data: An Introduction to Cluster Analysis. (Probability and Statistics)*. Hoboken: Wiley.

Kennedy, G. (1992). Preferred ways of putting things. In J. Svartvik (Ed.), *Directions in Corpus Linguistics*. (pp. 335–373). Berlin: Mouton de Gruyter. doi:10.1515/9783110867275.335

Kennedy, G. A. (1994). *New History of Classical Rhetoric*. Princeton, NJ: Princeton, University Press.

Khalilov, M., & Fonollosa, J. A. (2009). N-gram-based Statistical Machine Translation Versus Syntax Augmented Machine Translation: Comparison and System Combination. In *Proceedings of the 12th Conference of the European Chapter of the Association for Computational Linguistics*. (pp. 424–432). Athens, Greece. doi:10.3115/1609067.1609114

Kietz, J. U., Maedche, A., & Volz, R. (2000). A method for semi-automatic ontology acquisition from a corporate intranet. In Workshop Ontologies and text.

Kim, S. M., & Hovy, E. (2006). Identifying and analyzing judgment opinions. In *Proceedings of the Joint Human Language Technology/North American Chapter of the ACL Conference (HLT-NAACL)*. Stroudsburg, PA, USA: ACL. doi:10.3115/1220835.1220861

Kinsella, S., Harth, A., Troussov, A., Sogrin, M., Judge, J., Hayes, C., & Breslin, J. G. (2008). Navigating and Annotating Semantically-Enabled Networks of People and Associated Objects. In T. Friemel (Ed.), *Why Context Matters: Applications of Social Network Analysis* (pp. 79–96). VS Verlag. doi:10.1007/978-3-531-91184-7_5

Kipper Schuler, K. (2005). *VerbNet – a broad-coverage, comprehensive verb lexicon* [PhD thesis]. University of Pennsylvania. Retrieved from http://verbs.colorado.edu/~kipper/Papers/dissertation.pdf

Kis, D. (2003). *Una tomba per a Boris Davidovič* [S. Škrabec Translated] [Original work published 1976]. Manresa: Angle.

Kiš, D. (1979). *Grobnica za Borisa Davidoviča*. Beograd: BIGZ.

Kitchin, R. (2014). *The Data Revolution: Big Data, Open Data, Data Infrastructures and Their Consequences*. London: SAGE Publications.

Klavans, J. (1995). *On clitics and cliticization: The interaction of morphology, phonology and syntax*. New York, London: Garden Publishing Inc.

Kleinberg, J. (2000). The small-world phenomenon: An algorithmic perspective. In *Proceedings of the 32nd ACM Symposium on Theory of Computing*. Portland, OR, USA: ACM.

Klepac, G. (2013). Risk Evaluation in the Insurance Company Using REFII Model. In S. Dehuri, M. Patra, B. M., & A. Jagadev (Eds.) Intelligent Techniques in Recommendation Systems: Contextual Advancements and New Methods (pp. 84–104). Hershey, PA: Information Science Reference. doi:10.4018/978-1-4666-2542-6.ch005

Klepac, G. (2010). Preparing for New Competition in the Retail Industry. In A. Syvajarvi & J. Stenvall (Eds.), *Data Mining in Public and Private Sectors: Organizational and Government Applications* (pp. 245–266). Hershey, PA: Information Science Reference; doi:10.4018/978-1-60566-906-9.ch013

Klepac, G. (2014). Data Mining Models as a Tool for Churn Reduction and Custom Product Development in Telecommunication Industries. In P. Vasant (Ed.), *Handbook of Research on Novel Soft Computing Intelligent Algorithms: Theory and Practical Applications* (pp. 511–537). Hershey, PA: Information Science Reference; doi:10.4018/978-1-4666-4450-2.ch017

Koehn, P. (2010). *Statistical Machine Translation*. Cambridge: Cambridge University Press.

Koteswara Rao, G., & Dey, S. (2011). Decision support for e-governance: A text mining approach. *International Journal of Managing Information Technology*, *3*(3), 73–91. doi:10.5121/ijmit.2011.3307

Kotsiantis, S., Kanellopoulos, D., & Pintelas, P. et al. (2006). Handling imbalanced datasets: A review. *GESTS International Transactions on Computer Science and Engineering*, *30*(1), 25–36.

Kotsiantis, S., & Pintelas, P. (2003). Mixture of expert agents for handling imbalanced data sets. *Annals of Mathematics. Computing & Teleinformatics*, *1*, 46–55.

Kozakov, L., Park, Y., Fin, T., Drissi, Y., Doganata, Y., & Cofino, T. (2004). Glossary extraction and utilization in the information search and delivery system for IBM Technical Support. *IBM Systems Journal*, *43*(3), 546–563. doi:10.1147/sj.433.0546

Kulagina, O., & Mel'čuk, I. (1967). Automatic translation: Some theoretical aspects and the design of a translation system. In A. D. Booth (Ed.), *Machine Translation.* (pp. 139–171). Amsterdam: North-Holland Publishing Company.

Langville, A. N., & Meyer, C. (2006). *Google's PageRank and Beyond: The Science of Search Engine Rankings*. Princeton: Princeton University Press.

Larasati, S. D. (2012). Handling Indonesian clitics: A dataset comparison for an Indonesian-English statistical machine translation system.In *Proceedings of the 26ᵗʰ Pacific Asia Conference on Language, Information and Computation.* (pp. 146-152). Bali: Faculty of Computer Science, Universitas Indonesia.

Lauchert, F. (1911). *Leben des hl.* Köln: Athanasius des Grossen.

Lavie, A., & Agarwal, A. (2005). METEOR: An Automatic Metric for MT Evaluation with Improved Correlation with Human Judgments. In *Proceedings of the ACL Workshop on Intrinsic and Extrinsic Evaluation Measures for Machine Translation.* (pp. 65–72). Association for Computational Linguistics.

Lavoie, B., Kittredge, R., Korelsky, T., & Rambow, O. (2000). A framework for MT and multilingual NLG systems based on uniform lexico-structural processing. In *ANLC 2000.Proceedings of the 6ᵗʰ Conference on Applied Natural Language Processing.* (pp. 60-67). Stroudsburg, PA: Association for Computational Linguistics. doi:10.3115/974147.974156

Leech, G. N. (1980). *Explorations in Semantics and Pragmatics.* Amsterdam: Benjamins B.V. doi:10.1075/pb.i.5

Leech, G., & Fligelstone, S. (1992). Computers and corpus analysis. In C. S. Butler (Ed.), *Computers and Written Texts.* (pp. 115–140). Oxford: Blackwell.

Leong, C. K., Lee, H. Y., & Mak, W. K. (2012). Mining sentiments in SMS texts for teaching evaluation.[Elsevier.]. *Expert Systems with Applications, 39*(3), 2584–2589. doi:10.1016/j.eswa.2011.08.113

Levin, B. (1993). *English Verb Classes and Alternation, A Preliminary Investigation.* The University of Chicago Press.

Lībiete, N., Skadiņš, R., Šarman, J., & Hudík, T. (2012). *Deliverable D6.4 Evaluation of integration in CAT tools.*

Li, C., Wen, J.-R., & Li, H. (2003).Text Classification Using StochasticKeyword Generation. In *Proceedings of ICML-03, 20th International Conference on Machine Learning* (pp. 469–471). Washington, DC, Morgan Kaufmann Publishers, San Francisco.

Li, H. (2002). Word clustering and disambiguation based on co-occurrence data. *Natural Language Engineering, 8*(1), 25–42. doi:10.1017/S1351324902002838

Lin, D., & Pantel, P. (2001). DIRT – Discovery of Inference Rules from Text. In *Proceedings of the ACM SIGKDD Conference on Knowledge Discovery and Data Mining 2001* (pp. 323-328). doi:10.1145/502512.502559

Liu, Q., Xu, K., Zhang, L., Wang, H., Yu, Y., & Pan, Y. (2008). Catriple: Extracting triples from Wikipedia categories. In The Semantic Web (pp. 330-344).

Liu, B. (2010). Sentiment Analysis and Subjectivity. In N. Indurkhya & F. J. Damerau (Eds.), *Handbook of Natural Language* (2nd Ed.). Dublin, Ireland: CRC Press.

Liu, B., & Hu, M. (2004). Mining and Summarizing Customer Reviews. In *Proceeding of ACM SIGKDD International Conference on Knowledge Discovery and Data Mining.* New York: ACM Press.

Liu, Y., Li, Z., Xiong, H., Gao, X., & Wu, J. (2010). Understanding of Internal Clustering Validation Measures. In *Proceedings of ICDM 2010, The 10th IEEE International Conference on Data Mining.* (pp. 911-916). doi:10.1109/ICDM.2010.35

Li, W. (1992). Random Texts Exhibit Zipf's-Law-Like Word Frequency Distribution. *IEEE Transactions on Information Theory, 38*(6), 1842–1845. doi:10.1109/18.165464

Maedche, A., & Staab, S. (2000). Discovering conceptual relations from text. In W. Horn (Ed.), *Proceedings of the 14th European Conference on Artificial Intelligence (ECAI'2000).*

Maedche, A., & Staab, S. (2003). Ontology Learning. In S. Staab & R. Studer (Eds.), *Handbook on Ontologies in Information Systems*. Springer.

Makagonov, P., Sánchez, L. E., & Reyes, C. B. (2013). Based on measuring the human sense of harmony methods and tools for improving the urban image. *моделирование и анализ данных (Modelling and data analysis, 2013*(1), 97-109.

Makagonov, P., Reyes, C. B., & Sidorov, G. (2011). Document Search Images in Text Collections for Restricted Domains on Websites. In R. F. Brena & A. Guzman-Arenas (Eds.), *Quantitative semantics and soft computing methods for the Web: perspectives and applications*. (pp. 183–203). Hershey: IGI Global.

Makagonov, P., Ruiz Figueroa, A., Sboychakov, K., & Gelbukh, A. (2005). Learning a Domain Ontology from Hierarchically Structured Texts. In *Proceedings of Workshop Learning and Extending Lexical Ontologies by using Machine Learning Methods at 22nd International Conference on Machine Learning, ICML 2005. Bonn, Germany*.

Makagonov, P., Sánchez, L. E., & Sboychakov, K. (2009). Criterio de armonia como habilidad inherente del ser humano, aplicada en proyectos arquitectonicos. In E. Köppen (Ed.), *Imagenes en la ciencia. Ciencia en las imagines*. (pp. 83–101).

Malinowski, B. (1923). The problem of meaning in primitive languages. In C. K. Ogden & I. A. Richards (Eds.), The Meaning of Meaning. London: Routledge & Kegan Paul. (pp. 296-336).

Malone, T. W. (1983). How do people organize their desks? Implications for designing office information systems. *ACM Transactions on Office Information Systems*, *1*(1), 99–112. doi:10.1145/357423.357430

Manning, C. D., Raghavan, P., & Schütze, H. (2008). *Introduction to Information Retrieval*. Cambridge: Cambridge University Press. doi:10.1017/CBO9780511809071

Manning, C. D., & Schütze, H. (1999). *Foundations of Statistical Natural Language Processing*. Cambridge, MA, USA: MIT Press.

Mann, W. C., Matthiesen, C. M., & Thompson, S. A. (1992). Rhetorical Structure theory and text analysis. In W. C. Mann & S. A. Thompson (Eds.), *Text description: diverse analyses of a fund raising text*. Amsterdam: John Benjamins. doi:10.1075/pbns.16.04man

Mann, W. C., & Thompson, S. A. (1986). Relational propositions in discourse. *Discourse Processes*, *9*(1), 57–90. doi:10.1080/01638538609544632

Mann, W. C., & Thompson, S. A. (1988). Rhetorical Structure Theory: Towards a functional theory of text organization. *Text—Interdisciplinary Journal for the Study of Discourse*, *8*(3), 243–281. doi:10.1515/text.1.1988.8.3.243

Marconi, D. (1981). Storia della Filosofia del Linguaggio. In G. Vattimo (Ed.), *L'Enciclopedia Garzantina della Filosofia*. Milan: Garzanti Editori.

Marshak, S. (n. d.). Р. Л. Стивенсон. Вересковый мед. Retrieved from http://www.poetry.kostyor.ru/marshak/?n=101

Marsland, S. (2009). *Machine Learning: An Algorithmic Perspective. (Machine Learning & Pattern Recognition)*. Boca Raton: Chapman & Hall/CRC.

Martín, F. J. (2012). *Deconstructing Catalan object clitics*. Ann Arbor, MI: UMI Dissertation Publishing.

Maruev, S., Stefanovsky, D., Frolov, A., Troussov, A., & Curry, J. (2014a). Deep Mining of Custom Declarations for Commercial Goods. *Procedia Economics and Finance*, *12*(1), 397–402.

Masolo, C., Borgo, S., Gangemi, A., Guarino, N., & Oltramari, A. (2003). *WonderWeb Deliverable D18*. Ontology Library.

Massey, L., & Wong, W. (2011). A cognitive-based approach to identify topics in text using the Web as a knowledge source. In *Ontology Learning and Knowledge Discovery Using the Web*. Challenges and Recent Advances. doi:10.4018/978-1-60960-625-1.ch004

Matsuo, Y., & Ishizuka, M. (2004). Keyword extraction from a single document using word co-occurrence statistical information. *International Journal of Artificial Intelligence Tools*, *13*(1), 157–169. doi:10.1142/S0218213004001466

Meijering, E. P. (1968). *Orthodoxy and Platonism in Athanasius*. Leiden.

Mel'čuk, I., & Polguère, A. (Eds.). (2009). Dependency in linguistic description. Amsterdam/Phila-delphia: John Benjamins Publishing Company.

Mel'čuk, I. (1974). *Opyt teorii lingvističeskix modelej Smysl ~ Tekst*. Moskva: Nauka.

Mel'čuk, I. (1988). *Dependency syntax: Theory and practice*. Albany, NY: State University of New York Press.

Mel'čuk, I. (2001). *Communicative organization in natural language*. Amsterdam, Philadelphia: John Benjamins Publishing Company. doi:10.1075/slcs.57

Mel'čuk, I. (2006). *Aspects of the theory of morphology*. Berlin, New York: Mouton De Gruyter.

Mel'čuk, I. (2009). Dependency in natural language. In I. Mel'čuk & A. Polguère (Eds.), *Dependency in Linguistic Description* (pp. 1–110). Amsterdam, Philadelphia: John Benjamins Publishing Company. doi:10.1075/slcs.111.03mel

Mel'čuk, I. (2012). *Semantics: From meaning to text* (Vol. 1). Amsterdam, Philadelphia: John Benjamins Publishing Company. doi:10.1075/slcs.129

Mel'čuk, I., & Wanner, L. (2001). Towards a Lexicographic Approach to Lexical Transfer in Machine Translation (Illustrated by the German ~ Russian Language Pair). *Machine Translation*, *16*(1), 21–87. doi:10.1023/A:1013136005350

Mel'čuk, I., & Wanner, L. (2006). Syntactic Mismatches in Machine Translation. *Machine Translation*, *20*(2), 81–138. doi:10.1007/s10590-006-9013-7

Mel'čuk, I., & Wanner, L. (2008). Morphological mismatches in Machine Translation. *Machine Translation*, *22*(3), 101–152. doi:10.1007/s10590-009-9051-z

Menardi, G., & Torelli, N. (2012). Training and assessing classification rules with imbalanced data. *Data Mining and Knowledge Discovery*, *28*(1), 92–122. doi:10.1007/s10618-012-0295-5

Mendes, A. B., & Cardoso, M. G. M. S. (2006). Clustering supermarkets: The role of experts. *Journal of Retailing and Consumer Services*, *13*(4), 231–247. doi:10.1016/j.jretconser.2004.11.005

Migne, J. P. (1857-1866). *Patrologiae Graecae Cursus Completu*.

Milićević, J. (2007). *La paraphrase. Modélisation de la paraphrase langagière*. Bern: Peter Lang.

Milićević, J. (2009a). Linear placement of Serbian clitics in a syntactic dependency framework. In I. Mel'čuk & A. Polguère (Eds.), *Dependency in Linguistic Description*. (pp. 235–277). Amsterdam: John Benjamins Publishing Company. doi:10.1075/slcs.111.06mil

Milićević, J. (2009b). Serbian auxiliary verbs: Syntactic heads or dependents? In W. Cichocki (Ed.), *Proceedings of the 31st Annual Conference of the Atlantic Provinces Linguistic Association, PAMAPLA*, 31. (pp. 43-53). Brunswick: University of New Brunswick.

Miller, G. A., Beckwith, R., Fellbaum, C., Gross, D., & Miller, K. J. (1990). Introduction to WordNet: An On-line Lexical Database. *International Journal of Lexicography*, *3*(4), 235–244. doi:10.1093/ijl/3.4.235

Miner, G., Elder, J., Hill, T., Nisbet, R., Delen, D., & Fast, A. (2012). *Practical Text Mining and Statistical Analysis for Non-structured Text Data Applications*. Waltham, MA: Academic Press.

Minsky, M. (1974). *A Framework for Representig Knowledge. Department of Artificial Intelligence*. Cambridge, Mass.: MIT.

Mintz, M., Bills, S., Snow, R., & Jurafsky, D. (2009). Distant supervision for relation extraction without labeled data. In *Proceedings of the Joint Conference of the 47th Annual Meeting of the ACL and the 4th International Joint Conference on Natural Language Processing of the AFNLP: Volume 2-Volume 2* (pp. 1003-1011). Association for Computational Linguistics. doi:10.3115/1690219.1690287

Mirchev, U., & Last, M. (2014). Multi-Document Summarization by Extended Graph Text Representation and Importance Refinement. In A. Fiori (Ed.), *Innovative Document Summarization Techniques: Revolutionizing Knowledge Understanding* (pp. 28–53). Hershey, PA: Information Science Reference; doi:10.4018/978-1-4666-5019-0.ch002

Mirhady, D. C. (2007). *Influences on Peripatetic Rhetoric. Essays in honor of W.W. Fortenbaugh*. Brill. doi:10.1163/ej.9789004156685.i-286

Mitchell, T. (1997). *Machine Learning*. Cambridge, MA, USA: McGraw Hill.

Montes, M., Ortega, R., & Villaseñor, L. (2007). Using Lexical Patterns for Extracting Hyponyms from the Web. In MICAI 2007. Advances in Artificial Intelligence, 4827. (pp.904-911). Berlin: Springer.

Morton, K. W., & Mayers, D. F. (2005). *Numerical Solution of Partial Differential Equations, An Introduction*. Cambridge: Cambridge University Press. doi:10.1017/CBO9780511812248

Murphy, G. (2002). *The Big Book of Concepts*. Cambridge, Mass.: MIT Press.

Murphy, L. (2003). *Semantic Relations and the Lexicon: Antonymy, Synonymy and other Paradigms*. Cambridge: Cambridge University Press. doi:10.1017/CBO9780511486494

Murthy, P. R. (2005). *Production And Operations Management*. New Age International.

Myatt, G. J., & Johnson, W. P. (2009). *Making Sense of Data II: A Practical Guide to Data Visualization, Advanced Data Mining Methods, and Applications*. Hoboken, NJ: Wiley. doi:10.1002/9780470417409

Nagar, A., & Hahsler, M. (2012). Using Text and Data Mining Techniques to extract Stock Market Sentiment from Live News Streams. In *International Conference on Computer Technology and Science (ICCTS 2012)*, IACSIT Press, Singapore.

Nasr, A., Rambow, O., Palmer, M., & Rosenzweig, J. (1997). Enriching lexical transfer with cross-linguistic semantic features or how to do interlingua without interlingua. In *Proceedings of the Interlingua Workshop at the MT Summit*. Retrieved from ResearchGate Database.

Nassirtoussi, A. K., Wah, T. Y., Aghabozorgi, S. R., & Ling, D. N. C. (2014). Text mining for market prediction: A systematic review. *Expert Systems with Applications, 41*(16), 7653–7670. doi:10.1016/j.eswa.2014.06.009

Navigli, R., & Velardi, P. (2004). Learning Domain Ontologies from Document Warehouses and Dedicated Websites. *Computational Linguistics, 30*(2), 151–179. doi:10.1162/089120104323093276

Nelson, T. (1974). *Computer Lib/Dream Machines*. sixth printing (May 1978). Nepomuk. Retrieved from http://dev.nepomuk.semanticdesktop.org/wiki/UsingPsewRecommendations

Nesselrath, H. G. (1997). *Einleitung in die Griechische Phillogie*. Leipzig: B. G. Teubner. doi:10.1007/978-3-663-12074-2

Neumann, P. G. (2011). *Statistical metalinguistics and Zipf-Pareto-Mandelbrot*. SRI International Computer Science Laboratory.

Neville, J., Adler, M., & Jensen, D. (2003). Clustering relational data using attribute and link information. In *Proceedings of the Text Mining and Link Analysis Workshop, 18th International Joint Conference on Artificial Intelligence.*

Nietzsche, F. (1873). *On Truth and Lies in an Extra-Moral Sense.*

Niles, I., & Pease, A. (2001). Towards a standard upper ontology. In *Proceedings of the international Conference on Formal ontology in information Systems*-Volume 2001, Ogunquit, Maine, USA, October 17-19, 2001 (pp. 2-9). New York, NY: ACM Press.

NIST. (n. d.). *Automatic Content Extraction*. Retrieved from http://www.itl.nist.gov/iad/894.01/tests/ace/

Orlov, Y. K. (1980). Invisible Harmony. *Mysl´i chislo (Thought and Number), 3*, 70-106.

Ou, W., Elsayed, A., & Hartley, R. (2005). Towards ontology-based semantic processing for multimodal active presentation. In *Games Computing and Creative Technologies*. Conference Papers.

Pak, A., & Paroubek, P. (2010). Twitter as a corpus for sentiment analysis and opinion mining. In *Proceedings of Seventh International Conference on Language Resources and Evaluation (LREC)*. Valletta, Malta.

Pang, B., & Lee, L. (2004). A Sentimental Education: Sentiment Analysis using Subjectivity Summarization based on Minimum Cuts. In *Proceedings of the 42nd Meeting of the association for Computational Linguistics (ACL'04)*. Barcelona, Spain. doi:10.3115/1218955.1218990

Pang, B., & Lee, L. (2008). Opinion Mining and sentiment analysis. In D. W. Oard & M. Sanderson (Eds.), *Foundations and Trends in Information Retrieval*. doi:10.1561/1500000011

Pang, B., Lee, L., & Vaithyanathan, S. (2002). Thumbs up? Sentiment classification using machine learning techniques. In *Proceeding of the International conference on empirical methods in natural language*. Philadelphia, USA: Association for Computational Linguistics.

Pantel, P., & Pennacchiotti, M. (2006): Espresso: Leveraging Generic Patterns for Automatically Harvesting Semantic Relations. In *Proceedings of Conference on Computational Linguistics*. (pp. 113-120). Sydney, Australia: ACL Publications. doi:10.3115/1220175.1220190

Papineni, K., Roukos, S., Ward, T., & Zhu, W.-J. (2002). BLEU: a Method for Automatic Evaluation of Machine Translation. In *Proceedings of the 40th Annual Meeting on Association for Computational Linguistics*. (pp. 311–318). Association for Computational Linguistics.

Parker, W. (2011). *Scientific Models and Adequacy-for-Purpose*. Retrieved from www.lorentzcenter.nl/lc/web/2011/460/presentations/Parker.pdf

Pascal. (n. d.) *About Pascal*. Retrieved from http://www.pascal-network.org/

Patel-Schneider, P. F., & Horrocks, I. (2004). *OWL Web Ontology Language Semantics and Abstract Syntax: Section 2. Abstract Syntax*. Retrieved from http://www.w3.org/TR/2004/REC-owl-semantics-20040210/syntax.html

Pawlowski, J. (2008). Culture Profiles: Facilitating Global Learning and Knowledge Sharing. In *16th International Conference on Computers in Education (ICCE)*. Taipei.

Pei, M., Nakayama, K., Hara, T., & Nishio, S. (2008). Constructing a global ontology by concept mapping using wikipedia thesaurus. In Advanced Information Networking and Applications-Workshops, 2008. AINAW 2008 (pp. 1205-1210). doi:10.1109/WAINA.2008.117

Peirce, C. S. (1893). Extension of the Aristotelian syllogistic. Grand Logic. Princeton University (1997).

Pempek, T. A., Yermolayeva, Y. A., & Calvert, S. L. (2009). College students' social networking experiences on Facebook. *Journal of Applied Developmental Psychology*, *30*(3), 227–238. doi:10.1016/j.appdev.2008.12.010

Pereira, F., Lee, L., & Tishby, N. (1993). Distributional Clustering of English Words. In *Proceedings of the 31st Annual Meeting of the Association for Computational Linguistics*. (pp. 183-190). Columbus, Ohio: Ohio State University. doi:10.3115/981574.981598

Pernot, L. (2000). *La Rhétorique dans l'Antiquité*. Paris: Librairie Générale Française.

Pettersen, A. (1990). *Athanasius and the human body*. Bristol: Bristol Press.

Phan, X. H., Nguyen, L. M., & Horiguchi, S. (2008). Learning to Classify Short and Sparse Text & Web with Hidden Topics from Large-scale Data Collections. In *Proceeding of the 17th international conference on World Wide Web*. (pp. 91-100). New York: ACM. doi:10.1145/1367497.1367510

Pinker, S. (1999). *Words and Rules*. London: Weindefeld & Nicholson.

Poesio, M. (2005). Domain Modelling and NLP: Formal Ontologies? Lexica? Or a Bit of Both? *Applied Ontology*, *1*(1), 27–33.

Popescu, A. M., & Etzioni, O. (2005). Extracting product features and opinion from reviews. In *Proceedings of Human Language Technology Conference and Conference on Empirical Methods in Natural Language Processing*. Vancouver, British Columbia, Canada: Association for Computational Linguistics. doi:10.3115/1220575.1220618

Porter, M. F. (1980). An algorithm for Suffix Stripping. *Program*, *14*(3), 130–137. doi:10.1108/eb046814

Preisler, B. (1997). *A Handbook of English Grammar on Functional Principles*. Aarhus University Press.

Progovac, L. (1996). Clitics in Serbian/Croatian: Comp as the second position. In A. Halpern & A. Zwicky (Eds.), *Approaching second: Second position clitics and related phenomena*. (pp. 411–428). Stanford, CA: CSLI Publications.

Puri, S. (2011). A Fuzzy Similarity Based Concept Mining Model for Text Classification: Text Document Categorization Based on Fuzzy Similarity Analyzer and Support Vector Machine Classifier. *International Journal of Advanced Computer Science and Applications*, *2*(11), 115–121. doi:10.14569/IJACSA.2011.021119

Pushkin, A. C. (1960). *Собрание сочинений в 10 томах*. Moscow: Государственное издательство художественной литературы. Retrieved from http://rvb.ru/pushkin/01text/03fables/01fables/0799.htm

Quinlan, J. R. (1993). *C4.5: Programs for Machine Learning*. San Francisco, CA: Morgan Kaufmann.

Radanović-Kocić, V. (1996). The placement of Serbo-Croatian clitics: A prosodic approach. In A. Halpern & A. Zwicky (Eds.), *Approaching second: Second position clitics and related phenomena*. (pp. 429–446). Stanford, CA: CSLI Publications.

Rambow, O., & Joshi, A. (1997). A formal look at dependency grammars and phrase-structure grammars, with special consideration of word-order phenomena. In L. Wanner (Ed.), *Recent Trends in Meaning-Text Theory*. (pp. 167–190). Amsterdam, Philadelphia: John Benjamins Publishing Company.

Read, J., Bifet, A., Holmes, G., & Pfahringer, B. (2012). Scalable and efficient multi-label classification for evolving data streams. *Machine Learning*, *88*(1-2), 243–272. doi:10.1007/s10994-012-5279-6

Resource Description Framework (RDF) Model and Syntax Specification. (1999). *W3C*. Retrieved from http://www.w3.org/TR/PR-rdf-syntax/

Rinsurongkawong, V., & Eick, C. F. (2010). Correspondence Clustering: An Approach to Cluster Multiple Related Spatial Datasets. In *Proceedings of Asia-Pacific Conference on Knowledge Discovery and Data Mining (PAKDD)*. doi:10.1007/978-3-642-13657-3_25

Rivera-Borroto, O. M., Rabassa-Gutiérrez, M., Grau-Ábalo, R. C., Marrero-Ponce, Y., & García-de la Vega, J. M. (2012). Dunn's index for cluster tendency assessment of pharmacological data sets. *Canadian Journal of Physiology and Pharmacology*, *90*(4), 425–433. doi:10.1139/y2012-002 PMID:22443093

Robertson, A. (1892) *On the Incarnation of the Word*. In K. Knight (Ed.), Nicene and Post-Nicene Fathers, Second Series, Vol. 4. Buffalo, NY: Christian Literature Publishing Co. Retrieved from http://www.newadvent.org/fathers/2802.htm

Roberts, W. R. (1984). *The Rhetoric and the poetics of Aristotle*. New York: The Modern Library.

Rocha, C., Schwabe, D., & Poggi de Aragao, M. (2004). A Hybrid Approach for Searching in the Semantic Web. In *Proceedings of the 13th international conference on World Wide Web* (pp. 374-383). May 17-20, 2004, New York, NY, USA. doi:10.1145/988672.988723

Rodriguez, M. (2011). Knowledge Representation and Reasoning with Graph Databases. Retrieved from http://markorodriguez.com/2011/02/23/knowledge-representation-and-reasoning-with-graph-databases/

Roldanus, J. (1968). *Le Christ et l' home dans la theologie d'Athanase d'Alexandrie*. Leiden.

Romesburg, H. C. (2004). *Cluster analysis for researchers*. Raleigh, NC: Lulu Press.

Rosch, E. (1978). Principles of categorization. In E. Rosh & B. Lloyd (Eds.), *Cognition and Categorization*. (pp. 27–48). Hillsdale, N.J.: LEA Publications.

Rosenfeld, B., & Feldman, R. (2006). URES: an unsupervised web relation extraction system. In *Proceedings of the COLING/ACL on Main conference poster sessions* (pp. 667-674). Association for Computational Linguistics. doi:10.3115/1273073.1273159

Rosh, E., Mervis, C., Gray, W., Johnson, D., & Boyes, P. (1976). Basic objects in natural categories. *Cognitive Psychology*, *8*(3), 382–439. doi:10.1016/0010-0285(76)90013-X

Ross, D. (1974). *Aristotle*. London: Methuen.

Rübenkönig, O. (2006). *The Finite Difference Method (FDM) – An introduction*. Albert Ludwigs University of Freiburg.

Ruiz-Casado, M., Alfonseca, E., & Castells, P. (2005). Automatic Extraction of Semantic Relationships for WordNet by means of Pattern Learning from Wikipedia. In *10th International Conference on Application of Natural Language to Information Systems (NLDB 2005)*. Alicante, Spain, June 2005. Lecture Notes in Computer Science, 3513, 67-79. Springer Verlag. doi:10.1007/11428817_7

Russell, B. (1945). *A History of Western Philosophy*. New York: Simon & Schuster.

Russo, L. (2010). The Automatic Translation of Clitic Pronouns: The ITS-2 System. *Generative Grammar in Geneva*, *6*, 203–220.

Ryu, K., & Choy, P. (2005). An Information-Theoretic Approach to Taxonomy Extraction for Ontology Learning. In P. Buitelaar, P. Cimiano, & B. Magnini (Eds.), *Ontology Learning from Text: Methods, Evaluation and Applications*. (pp. 15–28). Amsterdam: IOS Press.

Sager, J. C. (1990). *A Practical Course in Terminology Processing*. Philadelphia, Amsterdam: John Benjamins Publishing. doi:10.1075/z.44

Salton, G., & McGill, M. J. (1983). *Introduction to Modern Information Retrieval.* New York, NY: McGraw-Hill.

Salton, G., Wong, A., & Yang, C. (1975). A Vector Space Model for Automatic Indexing. *Communications of the ACM, 18*(11), 613–620. doi:10.1145/361219.361220

Sánchez, D., & Moreno, A. (2008). Learning non-taxonomic relationships from web documents for domain ontology construction. *Data & Knowledge Engineering, 64*(3), 600–623. doi:10.1016/j.datak.2007.10.001

Sanderson, M., & Croft, B. (1999). Deriving concept hierarchies from text. In Research and Development in Information Retrieval (pp. 206–213). doi:10.1145/312624.312679

Sankaran, B., Grewal, A., & Sarkar, A. (2010). Incremental Decoding for Phrase-based Statistical Machine Translation. In *Proceedings of the Joint Fifth Workshop on Statistical Machine Translation and MetricsMATR.* (pp. 216–223). Uppsala: Association for Computational Linguistics.

Saratlija, J., Šnajder, J., & Dalbelo Bašić, B. (2011). Unsupervised Topic-Oriented Keyphrase Extraction and its Application to Croatian. In *Lecture Notes in Artificial Intelligence (14th International Conference on Text, Speech and Dialogue).* (pp. 340–347). doi:10.1007/978-3-642-23538-2_43

Sauermann, L. (2005). The semantic desktop – a basis for personal knowledge management. In *Maurer, H., Calude, C., Salomaa, A., &Tochtermann, K.(Eds.), Proceedings of the I-KNOW 05.5th International Conference on Knowledge Management* (pp. 294–301).

Sauermann, L., Bernardi, A., & Dengel, A. (2005). Overview and outlook on the semantic desktop. In S. Decker, J. Park, D. Quan, & L. Sauermann*(Eds.), Proceedings of the First Semantic Desktop Workshop at the ISWC Conference 2005* (pp. 1–18).

Sauermann, L., Kiesel, M., Schumacher, K., & Bernardi, A. (2009). Semantic Desktop. *Social Semantic Web, 2009,* 337–362. doi:10.1007/978-3-540-72216-8_17

Schaeffer, S. E. (2007). Graph clustering. *Computer Science Review, 1*(1), 27–64. doi:10.1016/j.cosrev.2007.05.001

Schiff, J. L. (2008). *Cellular automata; a discrete view of the world.* Hoboken: Wiley-Interscience.

Schmid, H. (1994). Probabilistic Part-of-Speech Tagging Using Decision Trees. In *Proceedings of International Conference on New Methods in Language Processing.* Retrieved from www.cis.uni-muenchen.de/~schmid/tools/TreeTagger/data/tree-tagger1.pdf

Schumacher, K., Sintek, M., & Sauermann, L. (2008, June 1-5). Combining Fact and Document Retrieval with Spreading Activation for Semantic Desktop Search. The Semantic Web: Research and Applications. *Proceedings of5th European Semantic Web Conference, ESWC 2008* (pp. 569-583) *Tenerife, Canary Islands, Spain.*

Sclano, F., & Velardi, P. (2007). TermExtractor: a Web Application to Learn the Shared Terminology of Emergent Web Communities. In *Proc. of the 3rd International Conference on Interoperability for Enterprise Software and Applications (I-ESA 2007).* Funchal (Madeira Island), Portugal, March 28–30th, 2007. doi:10.1007/978-1-84628-858-6_32

Searle, J. (1969). *Speech Acts: An Essay in the Philosophy of language.* Cambridge: Cambridge University Press. doi:10.1017/CBO9781139173438

Searle, J. R. (1979). *Expression and Meaning. Studies in the Theory of Speech Acts.* Cambridge: Cambridge University Press. doi:10.1017/CBO9780511609213

Searle, J. R. (1994). How Performatives Work. In R. M. Harnish (Ed.), *Basic Topics in the Philosophy of Language.* (pp. 75–95). London: Harvester Wheatsheaf.

Searle, J. R. (1996a). What is a Speech Act? In A. P. Martinich (Ed.), *The Philosophy of Language.* (pp. 130–140). Oxford: Oxford University Press.

Searle, J. R. (1996b). Indirect Speech Acts. In A. P. Martinich (Ed.), *The Philosophy of Language.* (pp. 168–182). Oxford: Oxford University Press.

Sebastiani, F. (2002). Machine Learning in automated text categorization. *ACM Computing Surveys, 34*(1), 1–47. doi:10.1145/505282.505283

Seeger, M. (2001). *Learning with labeled and unlabeled data. Technical report.* University of Edinburgh.

Shah, P., Schneider, D., Matuszek, C., Kahlert, R. C., Aldag, B., Baxter, D., et al. (2006). Automatic Population of Cyc: Extracting Information about Named-entities from the Web. In *Proceedings FLAIRS 2006* (pp. 153-158). Melbourne Beach, Florida May 11-13, 2006.

Shalev-Shwartz, S., Singer, Y., & Ng, A. (2004). Online and batch learning of pseudo-metrics. In *Proceedings of the Twenty-First International Conference on Machine Learning.* Banff, Alberta, Canada. doi:10.1145/1015330.1015376

Shannon, C. (1948). A mathematical theory of communication. *The Bell System Technical Journal, 27*(3), 379–423. doi:10.1002/j.1538-7305.1948.tb01338.x

Shapiro, E. Y., & Sterling, L. (1994). *The art of Prolog: advanced programming techniques.* Cambridge, Mass: MIT Press.

Sierra, G., Alarcon, R., Aguilar, C., & Bach, C. (2008). Definitional verbal patterns for semantic relation extraction. *Terminology, 14*(1), 74–98. doi:10.1075/term.14.1.05sie

Sigurd, B., Eeg-Olofsson, M., & Van Weijer, J. (2004). Word length, sentence length and frequency – Zipf revisited. *Studia Linguistica, 58*(1), 37–52. doi:10.1111/j.0039-3193.2004.00109.x

SIL. (n. d.). *SIL.* Retrieved from http://www.sil.org/

Šilić, A., Chauchat, J., Dalbelo Bašić, B., & Morin, A. (2007). N-Grams and Morphological Normalization in Text Classification: A Comparison on a Croatian-English Parallel Corpus. *Progress in Artificial Intelligence –. Lecture Notes in Computer Science, 4874,* 671–682. doi:10.1007/978-3-540-77002-2_56

Skadiņš, R., Skadiņa, I., Pinnis, M., Vasiļjevs, A., & Hudík, T. (2014). Application of Machine Translation in Localization into low-resourced languages. *Proceedings of the 18th conference of the European Association for Machine Translation.*

Smith, B. (2003). Ontology. In L. Floridi (Ed.), *Blackwell Guide to the Philosophy of Computing and Information.* (pp. 155–166). Oxford: Blackwell.

Smith, E., & Medin, D. (1981). *Categories and concepts.* Cambridge, Mass.: Harvard University Press. doi:10.4159/harvard.9780674866270

Snow, R., Jurafsky, D., & Ng, A. (2006). Semantic Taxonomy Induction from Heterogenous Evidence. In *Proceedings of the 21st International Conference on Computational Linguistics and 44th Annual Meeting of the ACL.* (pp. 801–808). Sydney: ACL Publications. doi:10.3115/1220175.1220276

Søgaard, A. (2013). *Semi-Supervised Learning and Domain Adaptation in Natural Language Processing. (Synthesis Lectures on Human Language Technologies).* Morgan & Claypool Publishers.

Solà, J. (2002). Clitic Climbing and Null Subject Languages. *Catalan Journal of Linguistics, 1,* 225–255.

Sombatsrisomboon, R., Matsuo, Y., & Ishizuka, M. (2003). Acquisition of hypernyms and hyponyms from the WWW. In *Proceedings of the 2nd International Workshop on Active Mining.*

Soucy, P., & Mineau, G. W. (2003). Feature Selection Strategies for Text Categorization. In *Proceedings of* Y. Xiang and B. Chaib-Draa (Eds.), *CSCSI-03, 16th Conference of the Canadian Society for Computational Studies of Intelligence* (pp. 505–509). Halifax.

Sowa, J. F., & Majumdar, A. K. (2003). Task-*Oriented Semantic Interpretation*. Retrieved from http://www.jfsowa.com/pubs/tosi.htm

Sowa, J. (2005). Categorization in Cognitive Computer Science. In H. Cohen & C. Lefebvre (Eds.), *Handbook of Categorization and Cognitive Science*. (pp. 141–163). Amsterdam: Elsevier. doi:10.1016/B978-008044612-7/50061-5

Sowa, J. F. (1990). Crystallizing theories out of knowledge soup. In Z. W. Ras & M. Zemankova (Eds.), *Intelligent Systems: State of the Art and Future Directions* (pp. 456–487). London: Ellis Horwood Ltd.

Sowa, J. F. (2000). *Knowledge Representation: Logical, Philosophical, and Computational Foundations*. Pacific Grove, CA: Brooks/Cole Publishing.

Specia, L., & Motta, E. (2006). A hybrid approach for relation extraction aimed at the semantic web. In Flexible Query Answering Systems (564-576). doi:10.1007/11766254_48

Spencer, A., & Louis, A. (2012). *Clitics. An introduction*. Cambridge: Cambridge University Press. doi:10.1017/CBO9781139033763

St Athanasius the Great. (n. d.). Elpenor. Retrieved from http://www.elpenor.org/athanasius/

Staab, S., Domingos, P., Mike, P., Golbeck, J., Li, D., & Finin, T. et al. (2005). Social Networks Applied. *IEEE Intelligent Systems*, 20(1), 80–93. doi:10.1109/MIS.2005.16

Steel, F. A. (n. d.). *Three little pigs*. Retrieved from http://classiclit.about.com/od/threelittlepigs

Stein, B., & zu Eissen, S. M. (2003). Automatic Document Categorization: Interpreting the Performance of Clustering Algorithms. In KI. (pp. 254-266). Springer.

Stein, B., zu Eissen, S. M., & Wißbrock, F. (2003). On Cluster Validity and the Information Need of Users. In *Proceedings of the 3rd International Conference on Artificial Intelligence and Applications (AIA 03)*. (pp. 2165-221).

Steinbach, M., Karypis, G., & Kumar, V. (2000). A Comparison of Document Clustering Techniques. In *Proceedings of the KDD Workshop on Text Mining*.

Stein, D. (2013). Machine Translation – Past, Present, and Future. *Translation: Computation, Corpora. Cognition*, 3(1).

Stevenson, R. L. (2001) Heather Ale: A Galloway Legend. In Edmund Clarence Stedman, ed. (1833–1908). *A Victorian Anthology, 1837–1895*. New York: Bartleby.Com. Retrieved from http://www.bartleby.com/246/961.html

Studer, R., Benjamins, V. R., & Fensel, D. (1998). Knowledge engineering: Principles and methods. *Data & Knowledge Engineering*, 25(1), 161–197. doi:10.1016/S0169-023X(97)00056-6

Su, H., Chen, L., Ye, Y., Sun, Z., & Wu, Q. (2010). A Refinement Approach to Handling Model Misfit in Semi-supervised Learning. In Advanced Data Mining and Applications, Lecture Notes in Computer Science. (pp. 75-86). doi:10.1007/978-3-642-17313-4_8

Suchanek, F. M., Kasneci, G., & Weikum, G. (2007). Yago - A Core of Semantic Knowledge, Unifying WordNet and Wikipedia. In *16th international conference on World Wide Web (WWW 2007)*.

Tadepalli, S., Ramakrishnan, N., & Watson, L. T. (2009). *Clustering constrained by dependencies*. [Technical Report TR-09-12]. Computer Science and Mathematics, Virginia Tech.

Talebook.com. (n. d.) *Сказка про трёх поросят*. Retrieved from http://www.talebook.ru/eng/01/index.htm

Tanaka, J., & Taylor, M. (1991). Object Categories and Expertise: Is the Basic Level in the Eye of the Beholder? *Cognitive Psychology*, *23*(3), 457–482. doi:10.1016/0010-0285(91)90016-H

Thelwall, M., Wilkinson, D., & Uppal, S. (2010). Data mining emotion in social network communication: Gender differences in MySpace. *Journal of the American Society for Information Science and Technology*, *61*(1), 190–199. doi:10.1002/asi.21180

Thompson, G. (1996). Voices in the text: Discourse perspectives on language Reports. *Applied Linguistics*, *17*(4), 501–530. doi:10.1093/applin/17.4.501

Thompson, R. (1971). *Athanasius Contra Gentes and De Incarnatione*. Oxford: Clarendon Press.

Troussov, A., & Nevidomsky, A. (2011). Solving Problems on Graphs with Propagation Algorithms. *An intvited talk at the International Conference on Intelligent Information and Engineering Systems INFOS*. Rzeszów-Polańczyk, Poland.

Troussov, A., Judge, J., Alexandrov, M., & Levner, E. (2011). Social Context as Machine-Processable Knowledge. In *Proceedings of the International Conference on Intelligent Information and Engineering Systems INFOS* (pp. 104-114). Rzeszów - Polańczyk, Poland.

Troussov, A., Dařena, F., Žižka, J., Parra, D., & Brusilovsky, P. (2011). Vectorised Spreading Activation Algorithm for Centrality Measurement. *Acta Universitatis Agriculturae et Silviculturae Mendelianae Brunensis*, *LIX*(7), 469–476. doi:10.11118/actaun201159070469

Troussov, A., Judge, J., Sogrin, M., Akrout, A., Davis, B., & Handschuh, S. (2009a). A Linguistic Light Approach to Multilingualism in Lexical Layers for Ontologies. In G. Demanko, K. Jassem, & S. Szpakowicz (Eds.), *SLT,* 12). Polish Phonetics Association.

Troussov, A., Judge, J., Sogrin, M., Bogdan, C., Edlund, H., & Sundblad, Y. (2008b). Navigating Networked Data using Polycentric Fuzzy Queries and the Pile UI Metaphor Navigation. In *Proceedings of the International SoNet Workshop* (pp. 5-12).

Troussov, A., Levner, E., Bogdan, C., Judge, J., & Botvich, D. (2009). Spreading Activation Methods. In A. Shawkat & Y. Xiang (Eds.), *Dynamic and Advanced Data Mining for Progressing Technological Development*. Hershey: IGI Global.

Troussov, A., Maruev, S., Stefanovsky, D., & Tischenko, S. (2013). *Models and analysis of Techno-Social Environments of Business. RANEPA* [Preprint. In Russian.]. Moscow, Russia.

Troussov, A., & O'Donovan, B. (2003). Morphosyntactic Annotation and Lemmatization Based on the Finite-State Dictionary of Wordformation Elements.*Proceeding of the International Conference Speech and Computer (SPECOM' 2003)*, October 27-29 2003, Moscow, Russia.

Tseng, Y.-H., Lin, C.-J., & Lin, Y. (2007). Text mining techniques for patent analysis. *Information Processing & Management*, *43*(5), 1216–1247. doi:10.1016/j.ipm.2006.11.011

Tulankar, S., Athale, R., & Bhujbal, S. (2013). Sentiment Analysis of Equities using Data Mining Techniques and Visualizing the Trends. *IJCSI International Journal of Computer Science Issues*, *10*(4).

Turney, P. D. (2002). Thumbs up or thumbs down? Semantic orientation applied to unsupervised classification of reviews. In *Proceedings of the 40th annual meeting on association for computational linguistics*. Philadelphia, Pennsylvania.

U.S. Congress. (1862). *Homestead Act of 1862*. Retrieved from http://www.nathankramer.com/settle/article/homestead.htm

Ungerer, F., & Schmid, H. (1996). *An introduction to cognitive linguistics*. New York: Logman.

Uschold, M., & Gruninger, M. (2004). Ontologies and semantics for seamless connectivity. *SIGMOD Record, 33*(4), 58–64. doi:10.1145/1041410.1041420

Van der Galien, J. G. (2003). *Factorial randomness: the Laws of Benford and Zipf with respect to the first digit distribution of the factor sequence from the natural numbers.* Retrieved from http://home.zonnet.nl/galien8/factor/factor.html

van Leeuwen, T. (1996). The representation of social actors. In C. R. Caldas-Coulthard & M. Coulthard (Eds.), *Texts and Practices: Readings in Critical Discourse Analysis.* (pp. 32–70). London: Routledge.

Velic, M., Grzinic, T., & Padavic, I. (2013, June 24-27). Wisdom of Crowds Algorithm for Stock Market Predictions. In *International Conference on Information Technology Interfaces ITI 2013.* Cavtat/Dubrovnik, Croatia.

Vinogradov, V. V. (2011). *The Russian language. Grammatical doctrine of word. Edition Russky yazyk (Russian language)* (G. A. Zolotova, Ed.). Moscow.

Vivaldi, J. (2004). *Extracción de candidatos a términos mediante la combinación de estrategias heterogéneas* [Ph. D. Dissertation]. IULA-UPF, Barcelona.

Vrandecic, D. (2010). *Ontology Evaluation* [PhD thesis]. KIT, Fakult. Wirtschaftswissenschaften, Karlsruhe.

W3C. (2009). *OWL 2 Web Ontology Language: Document Overview.* Retrieved from http://www.w3.org/TR/2009/REC-owl2-overview-20091027/

Wagstaff, K., Cardie, C., Rogers, S., & Schroedl, S. (2001). Constrained K-means Clustering with Background Knowledge. In *Proceedings of the Eighteenth International Conference on Machine Learning.* (pp. 577-584).

Wang, W., & Zhou, Z. (2007). Analyzing co-training style algorithms. Proceedings of Machine Learning: ECML 2007 (pp. 454-465). Springer. doi:10.1007/978-3-540-74958-5_42

Wang, W., Fan, P., Yu, S., & Han, J. (2003). Mining concept-drifting data streams using ensemble classifiers. In *Proceedings of the Ninth ACM SIGKDD International Conference on Knowledge. Discovery and Data Mining.* New York, USA: ACM Press. doi:10.1145/956750.956778

Wanner, L. (Ed.). (1996). *Lexical functions in lexicography and natural language processing.* Amsterdam, Philadelphia: John Benjamins Publishing Company. doi:10.1075/slcs.31

Wasserman, S., & Faust, K. (1994). Social Network Analysis: Methods and Applications. New York: Cambridge University Press. doi:10.1017/CBO9780511815478

Weber, N., & Buitelaar, P. (2006). Web-based ontology learning with isolde. In *Proc. of the Workshop on Web Content Mining with Human Language at the International Semantic Web Conference,* (Vol. 11). Athens GA, USA.

Weerahandi, S. (2003). *Exact Statistical Methods for Data Analysis.* New York, NY: Springer.

Weiss, S. I., & Kulikowski, C. (1991). *Computer Systems That Learn: Classification and Prediction Methods from Statistics.* San Francisco, California, USA: Neural Networks, Machine Learning, and Expert Systems.

Weiss, S. M., Indurkhya, N., Zhang, T., & Damerau, F. J. (2010). *Text Mining: Predictive Methods for Analyzing Unstructured Information.* New York, NY: Springer.

Wermter, J., & Hahn, U. (2005). Finding new terminology in very large corpora. In *Proceedings of the 3rd international conference on Knowledge capture* (pp. 137-144). ACM. doi:10.1145/1088622.1088648

Whitehead, M., & Yaeger, L. (2010). Sentiment Mining Using Ensemble Classification Models. In *Innovations and Advances in Computer Sciences and Engineering* (pp. 509–514). Springer Netherlands. doi:10.1007/978-90-481-3658-2_89

Whitney, P., Engel, D., & Cramer, N. (2009). Mining for surprise events within text streams. In *Proceedings of the Ninth SIAM International Conference on Data Mining* (pp. 617–627). Society for Industrial and Applied Mathematics. doi:10.1137/1.9781611972795.53

Wierzbicka, A. (1996). *Semantics: Primes and Universals*. Oxford: Oxford University Press.

Wikipedia. (2015). Sentence (linguistics). Retrieved from http://en.wikipedia.org/wiki/Sentence_(linguistics)

Wilks, Y., Slator, B., & Guthrie, L. (1996). *Electric Words*. Cambridge, Mass.: MIT Press.

Wilson, T., Wiebe, J., & Hwa, R. (2004). Just how mad are you? Finding strong and weak opinion clauses. In *Proceedings of the 21st Conference of the American Association for Artificial Intelligence (AAAI'04)*. San Jose, USA.

Witten, I. H., Frank, E., & Hall, M. A. (2011). Data Mining: Practical Machine Learning Tools and Techniques. Third Edition. (The Morgan Kaufmann Series in Data Management Systems). Morgan Kaufmann.

Wittgenstein, L. (1953). *Philosophical Investigations*. London: Blackwell.

Wolf, F. (2008). *Aristotle et la politique*. Presses Universitaires de France.

Wong, W. Y. (2009). *Learning lightweight ontologies from text across different domains using the web as background knowledge* (Doctoral dissertation, University of Western Australia).

Wong, W., Liu, W., & Bennamoun, M. (2009). A probabilistic framework for automatic term recognition. *Intelligent Data Analysis*, *13*(4), 499–539.

Wong, W., Liu, W., & Bennamoun, M. (2012). Ontology Learning from Text: A Look back and into the Future.[CSUR]. *ACM Computing Surveys*, *44*(4), 20. doi:10.1145/2333112.2333115

Xu, R., & Wunsch, D. C. (2009). *Clustering*. Hoboken, NJ: Wiley.

Yamada, K., & Knight, K. (2001). A Syntax-based Statistical Translation Model. In *Proceedings of the 39th Annual Meeting on Association for Computational Linguistics*. (pp. 523–530). Toulouse, France.

Yeh, J. H., & Yang, N. (2008). Ontology construction based on latent topic extraction in a digital library. In *Digital Libraries* (pp. 93–103). Universal and Ubiquitous Access to Information. doi:10.1007/978-3-540-89533-6_10

Yuasa, M., Saito, K., & Mukawa, N. (2006). Emoticons convey emotions without cognition of faces: an FMRI study. In *Proceeding of Extended Abstracts on Human Factors in Computing Systems (CHI EA '06)*. ACM. doi:10.1145/1125451.1125737

Yu, H., & Hatzivassiloglou, V. (2003). Towards answering opinion questions: Separating facts from opinions and identifying the polarity of opinion sentences. In *Proceedings of the Conference on Empirical Methods in Natural Language Processing (EMNLP)*. doi:10.3115/1119355.1119372

Zaki, M. J., & Wagner, M. (2014). *Data Mining and Analysis: Fundamental Concepts and Algorithms*. Cambridge: Cambridge University Press.

Zha, H., He, X., Ding, C. H. Q., Gu, M., & Simon, H. D. (2001). Bipartite Graph Partitioning and Data Clustering. In *Proceedings of the 2001 ACM CIKM International Conference on Information and Knowledge Management*. (pp. 25-32). ACM.

Zhang, X., & Zhu, F. (2006). The influence of Online consumer reviews on the demand for experience goods: The case of video games. In *Proceedings of the 27th international conference on information systems (ICIS)*, Milwaukee, USA: AISPress.

Zhang, Z., & Ciravegna, F. (2011). Named entity recognition for ontology population using background knowledge from Wikipedia. In *Ontology Learning and Knowledge Discovery Using the Web: Challenges and Recent Advances*. Hershey: IGI Global. doi:10.4018/978-1-60960-625-1.ch005

Zhao, Y., & Karypis, G. (2001). Criterion Functions for Document Clustering: Experiments and Analysis. [Technical Report #01-40]. University of Minnesota, Department of Computer Science.

Zhao, S., Grasmuck, S., & Martin, J. (2008). Identity construction on Facebook: Digital empowerment in anchored relationships. *Computers in Human Behavior, 24*(5), 1816–1836. doi:10.1016/j.chb.2008.02.012

Zhao, Y., & Karypis, G. (2004). Empirical and Theoretical Comparisons of Selected Criterion Functions for Document Clustering. *Machine Learning, 55*(3), 311–331. doi:10.1023/B:MACH.0000027785.44527.d6

Zheng, R., Li, J., Chen, H., & Huang, Z. (2006). A Framework for Authorship Identification of Online Messages: Writing-Style Features and Classification Techniques. *Journal of the American Society for Information Science and Technology, 57*(3), 378–393. doi:10.1002/asi.20316

Zipf, G. K. (1935). *The Psychobiology of Language*. Houghton-Mifflin.

Zipf, G. K. (1949). *Human Behavior and the Principle of Least Effort*. Cambridge, Massachusetts: Addison-Wesley.

Žižka, J., & Dařena, F. (2012). Parallel Processing of Very Many Textual Customers' Reviews Freely Written Down in Natural Languages. In: *IMMM 2012: The Second International Conference on Advances in Information Mining and Management* (pp. 147-153). IARIA XPS Press.

Žižka, J., Burda, K., & Dařena, F. (2012a). Clustering a very large number of textual unstructured customers' reviews in English. In: Artificial Intelligence: Methodology, Systems, and Applications (pp. 38-47). Springer.

Žižka, J., Burda, K., & Dařena, F. (2012). Clustering a very large number of textual unstructured customers' reviews in English. In *Proceedings of Artificial Intelligence: Methodology, Systems, and Applications*. Heidelberg: Springer. doi:10.1007/978-3-642-33185-5_5

Žižka, J., & Dařena, F. (2011a). Mining Significant Words from Customer Opinions Written in Different Languages. In: *Proceedings of the 14th International Conference on Text, Speech and Dialogue, Lecture Notes in Artificial Intelligence* (pp. 211-218). Springer.

Žižka, J., & Dařena, F. (2011a). Mining Significant Words from Customer Opinions Written in Different Natural Languages. In *Proceedings of the 14th International Conference on Text, Speech and Dialogue, Lecture Notes in Artificial Intelligence.* (pp. 211-218). Heidelberg: Springer.

Žižka, J., & Dařena, F. (2011b). Mining Textual Significant Expressions Reflecting Opinions in Natural Languages. In *Proceedings of the 11th International Conference on Intelligent Systems Design and Applications*. doi:10.1109/ISDA.2011.6121644

Žolkovskij, A., & Mel'čuk, I. (1967). O semantičeskom sinteze. *Problemy Kibernetiki, 19*, 177–238.

Zupan, B., Demšar, J., Petrović, S., Kolar, M, Šarić, F., & Dalbelo Bašić, B. (2008). *orngTxt: Orange data mining tool, Add-On for Text mining* [Computer software].

Zwicky, A. (1977). *On clitics*. Bloomington, IN: Indiana University Linguistics Club.

About the Contributors

Jan Žižka is an Associate Professor at the Department of Informatics, Faculty of Business and Economics, Mendel University Brno, member of SoNet research center, editor-in-chief of International Journal of Information Sciences and Techniques (IJIST), and International Journal of Computer Science & Information Technology (IJCSIT), a member of editorial boards and program committees of several other international scientific journals and conferences. He is also an author and co-author of many journal and conference peer-reviewed articles, and co-editor of several books in the area of informatics. His research areas include artificial intelligence, machine learning, and text/data mining.

František Dařena works as an Associate Professor and head of Information systems working group at the Department of Informatics, Faculty of Business and Economics, Mendel University Brno, he is a member of SoNet research center, author of several publications in international scientific journals, conference proceedings, and monographs, member of editorial board of international journals and editor-in-chief of International Journal in Foundations of Computer Science & Technology (IJFCST). His research areas include artificial intelligence, machine learning, and text/data mining.

***

Jalel Akaichi received his PhD in Computer Science from the University of Sciences and Technologies of Lille (France) in 1996 and then his Habilitation degree from the University of Tunis (Tunisia) in 2008. He is currently an Associate Professor and the Chair of the Master Science in Business Intelligence in the Computer Science Department of Institut Supérieur de Gestion. Jalel Akaichi has published in international journals, book edited chapters and conferences, presented various tutorials, and have served on the program committees of several international conferences and journals. He visited and taught in many institutions such as the State University of New York; Worcester Polytechnic Institute; INSA-Lyon; University of Blaise Pascal; University of Lille 1; University of Toulouse 1; etc.

Pavel Makagonov, Doctor of science, Professor. Between 2003 and 2012 he worked as a professor – researcher at the Division of post graduate education of Technological University of Mixteca (UTM), Mexico. Since 2012, he has been the chief scientific researcher of the Institute of social sciences at the Russian Presidential Academy of National Economy and Public Administration (RANEPA). Research interests include System analysis, Texts processing, Data Mining, and Urban development. He is the author of more than 130 scientific publications, including 9 books and chapters of books and prepared 10 M.Sc. and 12 Ph.D in Russian institutions and in Mexico. Between years 2002 and 2005 worked as scientific consultant and participant in the research project of Mexican National Council on Sciences and Technologies (CONACyT), and in 2010 gave classes as an applicant of master's scholarship of Erasmus Mundus program at Autonomous University of Barcelona.

Olga Acosta López received her Ph.D. in Computer Science from the Autonomous National University of Mexico in 2013. Currently, she carries out a postdoctoral fellowship at the Language and Literature Department of the Pontifical Catholic University of Chile. More recently, she has been hired as adjunct professor by the Engineer School of the Pontificia Universidad Católica de Chile to teach courses on Information Retrieval and Information Extraction.

César Aguilar is an assistant professor of Natural Language Processing in the Department of Language Sciences of Pontificia Universidad Católica de Chile (Santiago, Chile). He has obtained a Ph. D. in Linguistic by the Universidad Nacional Autónoma de México UNAM (Mexico City, México). He was member of the Language Engineering Group ((in Spanish, Grupo de Ingeniería Lingüística, GIL), a research team affiliated to Engineering Institute of UNAM, since 2001 until 2011. He has published several papers on definitional context extraction, recognition of lexical relations and building of specialized text corpora. Currently, he develops a research project focused on the design of an automatic system for extracting terms and definitions in medical texts (both English and Spanish), supported by the Fondo Nacional de Desarrollo Científico y Tecnológico FONDECYT (Project Number: 11130565).

Gerardo Sierra Martíínez is a National Reseacher of Mexico. He leads the Language Engineering Group ((in Spanish, Grupo de Ingeniería Lingüística, GIL) affiliated to Engineering Institute of the Universidad Nacional Autónoma de México (UNAM). He holds a Ph.D. in Computational Linguistics from the University of Manchester, Institute of Science and Technology (UMIST), UK. His research interest is focused on language engineering and includes computational lexicography, concept extraction, corpus linguistics, text mining and forensic linguistics.

Goran Klepac, PhD, University College Professor works as a head of Strategic unit in Sector of credit risk in Raiffeisenbank Austria Inc, Croatia, Europe. In several universities in Croatia, he lectures subjects in domain of data mining, predictive analytics, decision support system, banking risk, risk evaluation models, expert system, database marketing and business intelligence. As a team leader, he successfully finished many data mining projects in different domains like retail, finance, insurance, hospitality, telecommunications, and productions. He is an author/coauthor of several books published in Croatian and English on the subject of data mining.

Marko Velic, PhD, works as a Head of Data Analysis Department at the University Computing Centre, University of Zagreb. He is university college professor and lecturer on several courses from software engineering and data mining domain. Marko is author of several scientific papers and patent applications regarding pattern recognition and computer vision. He is experienced software engineer and entrepreneur and holds several international awards for innovative development. Besides these topics, his interests include artificial intelligence, machine learning and related fields.

Abel Browarnik from Tel Aviv University is at the final stage of his PhD studies. His research interests are in data and text mining and knowledge discovery. He served as the CIO for Academon, the Hebrew University of Jerusalem, and for the Israeli Ministry of Science and the Arts.

Oded Maimon from Tel Aviv University, previously at MIT, is also the Oracle Chair Professor. His research interests are in data and text mining and knowledge discovery and robotics. He has published and presented over two hundreds academic papers (in journals and conferences). Since 1998 he has authored ten research books in the field; and recently one on the nature of consciousness – trying to solve the big picture of knowledge discovery foundation from various perspectives (including philosophy, biology and psychology). Currently he is exploring new concepts and mathematical models of core artificial and biological intelligence. His latest book was published in November 2014, part of the series on Machine Perception and Artificial Intelligence: Data Mining with Decision Trees. He has received awards for best papers and governmental prizes for his academic and industrial work in the knowledge discovery field.

Sergey Maruev: Professor, The Russian Presidential Academy of National Economy and Public Administration. Major Fields of Scientific Research: mathematical modeling, economics of education, business process modeling, social network analysis.

Dmitry Stefanovskyi: Assoc. Prof., Ph.D, The Russian Presidential Academy of national economy and public administration. Major Fields of Scientific Research: mathematical modeling, world economy.

Alexander Troussov: Director of the International Research Laboratory for Mathematical Methods for Social Network Mining, The Russian Presidential Academy of National Economy and Public Administration (RANEPA). Major Fields of Scientific Research: Natural language processing, Information Retrieval, Social and semantic web, social network analysis, graph-based methods.

Jasmina Milićević received her PhD in linguistics from Université de Montréal in 2003; shortly after, she joined the Department of French at Dalhousie University (Halifax, Canada) where she currently holds an appointment as Associate Professor. Her research interests include semantics and lexicology, pedagogical lexicography, paraphrase, and Serbian linguistics, in particular phenomena on the interfaces 'Semantic ~ Syntax' and 'Syntax ~ Morphology', such as grammatical voice and clitics.

Angels Catena received her PhD in Applied linguistics in 2006 from Universitat Autònoma de Barcelona (UAB) where she currently works as Associate Professor. She is the local coordinator of the Eramus Mundus International Masters in Natural Language Processing and Human Language Technology. Her research, carried out at the fLexSem (Phonetics, Lexicology and Semantics) Laboratory of the UAB, includes semantics and French-Spanish contrastive lexicology, in particular building lexical resources for several NLP applications.

Tomáš Hudík graduated from computer science at the Masaryk University, Brno, Czech Republic, where he also obtained his PhD degree in the area of applying machine learning to natural language processing and text mining in 2009. Then, for a year, he worked as a verification engineer at Acision, Brno, Czech Republic. During the three subsequent years, Tomáš Hudík had a position as a machine-translation researcher at Moravia Worldwide, Brno, Czech Republic, where he was engaged intensively in machine translation, machine learning, and the Moses system. Currently, he works as a consultant at Teradata Corporation, Prague, Czech Republic, having a data-science engineer rank. Apart from the natural language processing branch, Tomáš Hudík now deals with Big Data issues using different technologies like MapReduce (Hadoop), Scala, Linux, Pig, including some other data processing tools. He also owns a range of various certificates (Coursera, Hortonworks).

Georgios Alexandropoulos received his PhD in Byzantine Greek Literature and Linguistics from the National and Kapodistrian University of Athens in 2013. He is tutor of Ancient and Modern Greek language and his interests lie in rhetoric, discourse analysis, corpus linguistics. He is author of *The text and context in Julian's political speeches: coherence, intertextuality and communicative goal* (2013), *Christians against the Ethnics* (2014a) and *The epitaphs of Gregory of Nazianzus: a stylistic approach* (2014b).

Index

Printed in the United States
By Bookmasters